EURAC research

EUROPÄISCHE AKADEMIE
ACCADEMIA EUROPEA
EUROPEAN ACADEMY
BOZEN - BOLZANO

Schriftenreihe der Europäischen Akademie Bozen
Bereich
„Minderheiten und Autonomien"

Herausgegeben von
Joseph Marko und Francesco Palermo

Band 30

Alexandra Tomaselli

Indigenous Peoples and their Right to Political Participation

International Law Standards and their Application in Latin America

Nomos

The Deutsche Nationalbibliothek lists this publication in the Deutsche Nationalbibliografie; detailed bibliographic data are available on the Internet at http://dnb.d-nb.de

a.t.: Frankfurt/Main, Univ., Diss., 2015

ISBN 978-3-8487-2663-9 (Print)
978-3-8452-6878-1 (ePDF)

British Library Cataloguing-in-Publication Data
A catalogue record for this book is available from the British Library.

ISBN 978-3-8487-2663-9 (Print)
978-3-8452-6878-1 (ePDF)

Library of Congress Cataloging-in-Publication Data
Tomaselli, Alexandra
Indigenous Peoples and their Right to Political Participation
Alexandra Tomaselli
558 p.
Includes bibliographic references.

ISBN 978-3-8487-2663-9 (Print)
978-3-8452-6878-1 (ePDF)

1. Edition 2016

Acknowledgements

This book is based on my PhD dissertation, which, as with probably any PhD studies, has been a challenging and rich venture during which I had the occasion to meet, work, learn from and, in many cases, to make friends with excellent colleagues and marvellous persons to whom I will always be thankful.

Among them, first and foremost, I owe my most sincere gratitude to my PhD first supervisor "Doktorvater" Prof. Dr. Dr. Rainer Hofmann of the Goethe University of Frankfurt a. M. for having believed in the very first and rough ideas that eventually led me to write the dissertation and for his constant and wise support and his brilliant advice along five dense years. Likewise, I am thankful to my second (external) PhD supervisor, Prof. Dr. Stefan Kadelbach, and to the PhD Commission Chair, Prof. Dr. Thomas Duve, for their insightful comments prior to and during the defence that highly contributed to meliorate the current text.

An equal immense gratitude goes to Prof. Dr. Josef Marko and Dr. Günther Rautz, Dean of the Law School of the University of Graz and Scientific Director (the former) and Coordinator (the latter) of the Institute for Minority Rights at the European Academy of Bolzano (EURAC) for being a constant source of inspiration at both the professional and personal level and for having supported my academic "obsession" with Latin America in all these years during which I had the fortune to work at EURAC. I also owe them my gratitude for giving me the possibility to publish this book within the EURAC series "Minorities and Autonomies". Likewise, I am immensely thankful to EURAC, to all its other "founders" and to all the marvellous colleagues and friends that work both in my Institute and in other departments for creating such a pleasant and productive working environment. I am particularly grateful to Dr. Alice Engl, Ms. Verena Wisthaler and Mr. Sergiu Constantin for having been such good companions during all these years.

I would have never opted for such challenging PhD studies, however, if I would not have the fortune to meet and be inspired by a number of other mentors. Among them, I express my most sincere gratitude to Prof. Dr. Francesco Palermo, Prof. Dr. Jens Woelk, Prof. Bruce Duthu (J.D.), Prof. Fernando Burrows, Prof. Dr. Giovanni Poggeschi, Prof. Dr. Felipe Gomez Isa, Prof. Dr. Salvador Martí i Puig, Prof. Dr. Joshua Castellino, Prof. Dr.

Federico Lenzerini, Prof. Victor Zuluaga, Prof. Dr. Bartolomé Clavero and, last, but certainly not the least, to seven of the most brilliant scholars and colleagues I have ever met: Dr. Elvira Dominguez-Redondo, Prof. Dr. Sia Spiliopoulou-Åkermark, Prof. Dr. Alexandra Xanthaki, Dr. Laura Giraudo, Prof. Dr. Esther Del Campo, Ms. Cristina Boglia, and Prof. Dr. Marzia Rosti.

Among the (young and now expert) colleagues dealing with indigenous issues whom I had the fortune to meet and eventually become very good friends, I owe my whole gratitude to Dr. Silvia Ordoñez Ganoza, Dr. Andrea Ruiz, Dr. Jorge Contesse, Ms. Francisca Del Fierro Veszpremy, Dr. Mayra Feddersen, Dr. Almut Schilling-Vacaflor, Dr. Cathal Doyle, Dr. Jason Tockman, Dr. Rodolfo Cespedes, Ms. Leslie Cloud, Dr. Sara Mabel Villalba, Dr. Isabel Inguanzo, Ms. Amelia Alva, Ms. Chiara Scardozzi and all the other colleagues of the EMPI network (*Encuentros Multidisciplinares sobre Pubelos Indígenas* – Multidisciplinary Network on Indigenous Peoples) for their constant and sincere (mutual) support during our PhD studies, for all the productive and pleasant EMPI annual meetings organized together and for having been a truly remarkable source of inspiration. Among them, my most sincere gratitude goes to Dr. Claire Wright not only for being a marvellous colleague and friend, but also for all her kind and patient work of language revision of this text. Likewise, I am thankful to Mr. Celso Philip Pereira and Ms. Keara Jane Ryder for having corrected some early drafts and final parts of the text, respectively.

I would also like to express my gratitude to all the kind librarians who patiently provided me with the many sources I asked from them and to all the Institutions that I had the fortune to visit during my studies. Apart from EURAC and the Goethe University of Frankfurt a.M., I could collect and consult sources at: The University of Trento, the University of Innsbruck, the Dartmouth College, the University of Deusto, the University of Seville, the *Escuela de Estudios Hispano-Americanos* in Seville, the *Universidad de Chile*, the *Pontificia Universidad Católica de Chile* (PUC), the *Universidad Diego Portales* in Santiago de Chile, the *Universidad Mayor de San Andrés* in La Paz, the *Universidad del Rosario* in Bogotá, and the libraries of the *Agencia Española de Cooperación Internacional para el Desarrollo* in Madrid and of the International Labour Organization in Geneva. I am particularly thankful to Prof. Fernando Burrows, Dr. Laura Giraudo, Prof. Dr. Ana M. Carmona Contreras and Prof. Bruce Duthu (J.D.) for having kindly supported my study visits in the respective universities and centres, and to them and their spouses (in particular, to Lupe and Hilde) for making me feel "at home" during my stays. Likewise, I am immensely grateful to

Cecilia Ängelid, Fredrik Svensson, Daniela Rodriguez Campadello, Erica and Andrea Lavagno and Maria Perez Sanchez-Laulhe for all their crucial help during my fieldwork in Bolivia. Last, but, again, certainly not the least, I owe an immense gratitude to all the indigenous and non-indigenous people and peoples, experts and officials that I had the fortune to meet during my fieldworks and who provided me with priceless information and hints. Apart from those cited in the bibliography, I prefer not to mention them here by name since the majority of them expressed their personal rather than "official" institutional views. This, however, should not be interpreted as a minor thanks, but rather the contrary.

Finally, this study would not have been possible without the love and the constant and patient support of my husband Luca and the affection and the encouragement of our families and of our dearest European and Latin American friends Enrica, Piero, Marina, Alessandro, Mami-Norma, Camila and her family, Silvia O.G., Ilaria and her daughters, Elisa B., Elisa R., Andrea P., Ana María, Isabel-Chabelita, Carola, Elisabeth-la Miss, Giulia and Andrea and their marvellous kids. I dedicate this book to all of them, to whom goes my most heartfelt thanks.

Table of Contents

List of abbreviations

International treaties and bodies

ACHR	American Convention on Human Rights or “Pact of San José, Costa Rica”
CAT	Convention against Torture and Other Cruel, Inhuman or Degrading Treatment or Punishment
CAT-Comm	Committee against Torture
CCPR	Human Rights Committee
CED	Committee on Enforced Disappearance
CEDAW	Convention on the Elimination of All Forms of Discrimination against Women
CEDAW-Comm	Committee on the Elimination of Discrimination against Women
CELAC	Comunidad de Estados Latinoamericanos y Caribeños / Community of Latin American and Caribbean States
CERD	Committee on the Elimination of Racial Discrimination
CESCR	Committee on Economic, Social and Cultural Rights
CMW	Committee on Migrant Workers
CommHR	United Nations Commission on Human Rights (substituted by the Human Rights Council)
CPED	International Convention for the Protection of All Persons from Enforced Disappearance
CRC	Convention on the Rights of the Child
CRC-Comm	Committee on the Rights of the Child
CRPD	Convention on the Rights of Persons with Disabilities
CRPD-Comm	Committee on the Rights of Persons with Disabilities
Draft Declaration	United Nations Draft Declaration on the Rights of Indigenous Peoples (of 1994)
EMRIP	Expert Mechanism on the Rights of Indigenous Peoples

FCNM	Framework Convention for the Protection of National Minorities
GA	United Nations General Assembly
GCG	Global Indigenous Coordination Group for the World Conference
HCNM	High Commissioner on National Minorities of OSCE
HRC	Human Rights Committee
IACommHR	Inter-American Commission on Human Rights
IAtHR	Inter-American Court of Human Rights
ICCPR	International Covenant on Civil and Political Rights
ICCPR-OP1	Optional Protocol to the International Covenant on Civil and Political Rights
ICCPR-OP2	Second Optional Protocol to the International Covenant on Civil and Political Rights, aiming at the abolition of the death penalty
ICERD	International Convention on the Elimination of All Forms of Racial Discrimination
ICESCR	International Covenant on Economic, Social and Cultural Rights
ICESCR-OP	Optional Protocol of the Covenant on Economic, Social and Cultural Rights
ICISS	International Commission on Intervention and State Sovereignty
ICJ	International Court of Justice
ICRMW	International Convention on the Protection of the Rights of All Migrant Workers and Members of Their Families
IFAD	International Fund for Agricultural Development
ILO	International Labour Organization
ILO Convention 107	ILO Convention Concerning the Protection and Integration of indigenous and Other Tribal and Semi-Tribal Populations in Independent Countries, Convention No.107 of 1957
ILO Convention 169	International Labour Organization, Convention Concerning indigenous and Tribal Peoples in Independent Countries, Convention No.169 of 1989

Lund Recommendations	Lund Recommendations on the Effective Participation of National Minorities in Public Life of the High Commissioner on National Minorities (OSCE)
OAS	Organization of the American States
OAS Charter	Charter of the Organization of the American States
OAU	Organization of African Unity
OP-CAT	Optional Protocol to the Convention against Torture and Other Cruel, Inhuman or Degrading Treatment or Punishment
OP-CEDAW	Optional Protocol to the Convention on the Elimination of Discrimination against Women
OP-CRC-AC	Optional protocol to the Convention on the Rights of the Child on the involvement of children in armed conflict
OP-CRC-SC	Optional protocol to the Convention on the Rights of the Child on the sale of children, child prostitution and child pornography
OP-CRPD	Optional Protocol to the Convention on the Rights of Persons with Disabilities
OSCE	Organization for Security and Co-operation in Europe
SPT	Subcommittee on Prevention of Torture
UDHR	Universal Declaration of Human Rights
UN Charter	Charter of the United Nations
UN HR Council	United Nations Human Rights Council
UNDRIP	United Nations Declaration on the Rights of Indigenous Peoples
UPR	United Nations Universal Periodic Review
Vienna Convention	Vienna Convention on the Law of Treaties
WCIP	World Conference on Indigenous Peoples
WGDD	Working Group on the Draft Declaration
WGIP	Working Group on Indigenous Populations
1970 Declaration	Resolution No.2625 "Declaration on Principles of International Law Friendly Relations and Co-operation among States in Accordance with the Charter of the United Nations" adopted on 24 October 1970 by the General Assembly

Domestic laws, bodies or organizations

AIOC	Autonomía Indígena Originaria Campesina / Peasant Native Indigenous Autonomy (Bolivia)
APG	Asemblea del Pueblo Guaraní / Assembly of Guaraní People (Bolivia)
CIDOB	Confederación Indígena del Oriente, Chaco y Amazonía de Bolivia or later Confederación de Pueblos Indígenas de Bolivia / Confederation of (lowlands) indigenous peoples of Bolivia
COICA	Coordinadora de las Organizaciones Indígenas de la Cuenca Amazónica / Coordinating Body of Indigenous Peoples' Organizations of the Amazon Basin
CONAIE	Confederación de Nacionalidades Indígenas del Ecuador / Confederation of Indigenous Nationalities of Ecuador
CONAMAQ	Consejo Nacional de Ayllus y Markas Qullasuyu / National Council of (indigenous) Ayllus and Markas Qullasuyu (Bolivia)
CPE (Bolivia)	Constitución Política del Estado (Bolivia) / Bolivian Constitution
CPIB	Central de Pueblos Indígenas del Beni / Central Organization of Indigenous Peoples of Beni (Bolivia)
CSUTCB	Confederación Sindical Única de Trabajadores Campesinos de Bolivia / Unified Trade Union of Peasant Workers of Bolivia
DMI	Distritos Municipales Indígenas / Indigenous municipal districs (Bolivia)
FENOCIN	Federación Nacional de Organizaciones Campesinas Indígenas y Negras / Federation of Peasant Indigenous and Black Organizations (Ecuador)
INRA	Instituto Nacional de Reforma Agraria / Agrarian Reform National Institute (Bolivia)
ONIC	Organización Nacional Indígena de Colombia / Colombian National Indigenous Organization
OTB	Organizaciones Territoriales de Base / Territorially-based organizations (Bolivia)
SEA	Servicio Estatal de Autonomías / State Autonomy Office (Bolivia)

TCO	Tierra Comunitaria de Origen / Communitarian Native Land (Bolivia)
TIOC	Territorio Indígena Campesino Originario / Peasant Native Indigenous Land (Bolivia)
TIPNIS	Territorio Indígena y Parque Nacional Isiboro-Secure / Indigenous Territory and National Park Isiboro-Secure (Bolivia)

Others

AIP	Andean Indian Programme
CiU	Convergència i Unió / Convergence and Union (Catalan political party)
Cobo-Diaz Study	Study of the Problem of Discrimination against Indigenous Populations
ERC	Esquerra Republicana de Catalunya / Republican Left of Catalonia (Catalan political party)
FARC	Fuerzas Armadas Revolucionarias de Colombia / Revolutionary Armed Forces of Colombia
FPIC	Free, Prior and Informed Consent
FIC	Free and Informed Consent
MAS and MAS-IPSP	Movimiento al Socialismo / Movement for Socialism (Bolivian ruling party of President Morales)
MNR	Movimiento Nacionalista Revolucionario / Revolutionary Nationalist Movement (Bolivian party)
NTA	Non-territorial autonomy
R2P	Responsibility to Protect
SFRY	Socialist Federal Republic of Yugoslavia
SNP	Scottish National Party
TA	Territorial autonomy
UD	Unidad Democratica / Democratic Union (Bolivian party)
URSS	Union of Soviet Socialist Republics
WWI	First World War

Introduction

Over the last few decades, UN bodies have increasingly emphasized the need to improve the political participation of indigenous peoples.[1] However, no international instrument explicitly recognizes this right for indigenous peoples. The ICCPR enshrines the "political rights" (or "political liberties") for all individuals.[2] Article 2.2 of the UN Declaration on the Rights of Persons Belonging to National or Ethnic, Religious and Linguistic Minorities and art.15 of the (binding) Council of Europe's Framework Convention for the Protection of National Minorities recognize the "right to political participation of minorities". There is no "universal formula" for minority participation,[3] but the twofold concept of "political participation" provided by the Lund Recommendations on the Effective Participation of National Minorities in Public Life of the office of the High Commissioner on National Minorities is particularly helpful. Thus, "political participation" implies participation at all levels within the State, especially in decision-making processes. Second, it also includes means of autonomy or self-government.[4]

Minorities and indigenous peoples share many difficulties in having a guaranteed right to political participation in the decision making-processes both at State and local level.[5] Indigenous peoples' claims and rights tend to

---

1 *Inter alia*, the Committee on the Elimination of Racial Discrimination; the Human Rights Committee; the Committee on Economic, Social and Cultural Rights; the General Assembly within the Second International Decade of the World's Indigenous People; the thirteenth UN Permanent Forum on Indigenous Issues of 2014; the first Report of the newly appointed Special Rapporteur on the rights of indigenous peoples, Victoria Tauli Corpuz. For references, see chapter 3, section 3.3.1.2.

2 These rights are enshrined in the ICCPR as follows: Freedom of expression (art.19); freedom of association and assembly (art.21-22); the right to vote and to stand for elections (art.25b); the right to participate in public affairs (art.25a); and the right to equal access to public service (art.25c).

3 Yash Ghai, *Public Participation of Minorities*, Minority Rights Group International, London, 2003, p.3.

4 OSCE HCNM Lund Recommendations on the Effective Participation of National Minorities in Public Life, adopted on 1 September 1999, English version, p.6, at http://www.osce.org/hcnm/30325 [Last access 03.11.2014].

5 On an overview of the difficulties faced by both minorities and indigenous peoples see Prosper Nobirabo Musafiri, "Right to Self-Determination in International Law: Towards Theorization of the Concept of Indigenous Peoples/National Minority?",

overlap substantially with those of minorities.[6] However, indigenous peoples constantly (and fairly) refuse to be treated as minorities,[7] and their situations differ substantially. Moreover, a closer inspection of international human rights law and the international indigenous instruments shows that rights specifically related to the (political) participation of indigenous peoples are enshrined in both the International Labour Organization "Convention Concerning indigenous and Tribal Peoples in Independent Countries", Convention No.169 of 1989 (hereinafter ILO Convention 169), and the UN Declaration on the Rights of Indigenous Peoples (UNDRIP) of 2007. Additionally, such rights have a collective dimension.[8]

The regime of political rights provided for indigenous peoples by the ILO Convention 169, and likewise by the UNDRIP, is known as the "participation-consultation" principle,[9] due to a combined reading of arts.6 and 7 of the former. Both instruments recognize the rights to consultation and the Free, Prior and Informed Consent (FPIC) of indigenous peoples.[10] The UN bodies have stressed the need to also apply these rights properly.

19(4) *International Journal of Minority and Group Rights* 2012, pp.481-532, especially pp.527-531. The author mentions, *inter alia*, the lack of a conducive environment for participation and the lack of consideration of consultations held with minorities. Musafiri, "Right to Self-Determination in International Law ...", pp.527-528.

6 Luis Rodríguez Piñero-Royo, "Political Participation Systems Applicable to Indigenous Peoples", in Marc Weller and Katharine Nobbs (eds.), *Political Participation of Minorities: A Commentary on International Standards and Practice*, Oxford University Press, Oxford, 2010, pp.308-342 , p.309.

7 Gudmundur Alfredsson, "The Right of Self-Determination and Indigenous Peoples", in Christian Tomuschat (ed.), *Modern Law of Self-Determination*, Martinus Nijhoff Publishers, Dordrecht, Boston, London, 1993, pp.41-54, pp.44-45; Wilton Littlechild, "Comment on agenda items at the Oslo Conference on Indigenous Peoples' Rights", in Roxanne Dunbar-Ortiz et al. (eds.), *Indigenous Peoples' Rights in International Law: Emergence and application. Book in Honor of Asbjørn Eide at Eighty*, Gáldu and IWGIA, Kautokeino, Copenhagen, Gáldu Čála serie No.2/2015, 2015, pp.18-23, p.21. For an explicit rejection see the declaration of the Sami Parliament in the Advisory Committee of the Framework Convention for the Protection of National Minorities, First State Report by Norway, 2 March 2001, ACFC/SR(2001)001, p. 4.

8 For other details, see chapter 3, section 3.3.1.2.

9 Rodríguez Piñero-Royo, "Political Participation Systems Applicable to Indigenous Peoples", p.313; Expert Mechanism on the Rights of Indigenous Peoples, "Progress report on the study on indigenous peoples and the right to participate in decision-making", UN Doc. A/HRC/EMRIP/2010/2, 17 May 2010, p.6, para 17.

10 The ILO Convention 169 focuses on the right to consultation and contains only one reference to the "prior and informed consent" (without "free"), whereas the

In the frame of indigenous rights, however, a proposal regarding the political rights of indigenous peoples requires a discussion of indigenous self-determination.[11] Likewise, the right to self-determination of indigenous peoples implies an examination of their right to autonomy/self-government,[12] which has recently been enshrined in the UNDRIP as one of the possible exercises of the former right.

The drafting of a UNDRIP was protracted for many years. It was preceded by a Draft Declaration in 1994 that was substantially revised and finally merged in the UNDRIP, which was adopted in 2007. One of the crucial issue regarded indigenous peoples' right to self-determination. Self-determination in international law, as is widely known, is extremely complex. It has been (and still is) extensively debated both in theoretical terms and in its multiple and potential applications. Many authors have explored the right to self-determination of indigenous peoples. The works on this topic may be broadly divided into two groups.[13] First, a substantial number of scholars described self-determination as mainly expressions of autonomy and, in some cases, political rights and Free, Prior and Informed Consent (FPIC). A second, equally sizeable group of academics have framed the right to self-determination of indigenous peoples as including, in addition to autonomy and political rights, other interlinked aspects such as mutual respect, a remedy to past discrimination and injustices, cultural integrity and identity, land rights, rights to subsistence and natural resources, and to the right to (self-determined) development. This conceptualization also reflects the contents of the UN Declaration on the Right to Development and the Concluding Observations of both the UN Human Rights Committee and the Committee on Economic, Social and Cultural Rights.[14] Therefore, indigenous peoples' right to self-determination is multifaceted. It includes autonomy and political rights as well as their rights to land, natural resources –and thus to consultation and FPIC– identity and cultures, and socio-economic development.

UNDRIP provides a far more specific protection of the FPIC. See further in chapter 3, section 3.3.2.

11 Catherine Iorns, "Dedicated Parliamentary Seats for Indigenous Peoples: Political Representation as an Element of Indigenous Self-Determination", *Murdoch University Electronic Journal of Law*, Volume 10, Number 4 (December 2003), available at http://www.murdoch.edu.au/elaw/issues/v10n4/iorns104nf.html, para.72 [Last access 05.02.2015].

12 In this study, these two terms are considered interchangeable. For details, see chapter 3, sections 3.2.2.2.

13 For references, see chapter 2, section 2.2.4.

14 See chapter 2, section 2.2.2.2.

The demand for political participation by indigenous peoples has increased in the last decades. It is particularly tangible in the context of Latin America. This is mainly due to the rise of indigenous movements, but it also has roots in the last democratic transitions and the current political changes in the countries of Latin America. A new consciousness of indigenous peoples vis-à-vis public affairs and their role in society has been vividly shown throughout the region. Despite many difficulties, indigenous movements in Latin America have a wide outreach and a clear degree of influence at national and regional level. Since the 1990s, autonomy arrangements and political representation have been increasingly claimed and, in some cases, obtained.[15] For instance, during the Bolivian Constituent Assembly in 2007-2008, the indigenous leaders demanded the introduction of a new autonomy system, which they could benefit from, and it was indeed recognized. In Chile, the frustration caused by the limited legislative framework has led to self-declared autonomous indigenous communities, such as the case of the Mapuche Temucuicui community. Currently (July 2015), Chilean authorities are discussing a proposal to create autonomous indigenous municipalities.

Against this background, this study thus addresses the following research questions:

1. May a (composite) right to political participation (including, participation in decision-making bodies, consultation, FPIC and autonomy/self-government) of indigenous peoples descend from their right to self-determination?
2. How is it recognized in international human and indigenous rights law?
3. May this right represent one of the expressions, or better, effective applications of the right to self-determination of indigenous peoples?
4. How is this right recognized and applied at domestic level in Latin America, and more specifically, in the cases of Bolivia and Chile?
5. What considerations may be drawn from its application?

This study thus proposes a *composite right to political participation of indigenous peoples*, identifies its recognition in international human and indigenous rights law, and explores its application in two apparently divergent –but substantially more similar than expected– case studies in Latin America, namely Bolivia and Chile.

The concept of "political participation" used in this study takes inspiration from the abovementioned Lund Recommendations' twofold meaning

15 In Latin America, some autonomy arrangements were established well before (e.g., the the well-known Comarca Kuna Yala in Panama). See chapter 3, section 3.3.3.3.

insofar as the effectiveness of the arrangements endorsed by them may be helpful also for indigenous peoples.[16] Nevertheless, the right of political participation of indigenous peoples framed in this study differs substantially from that of minorities, particularly due to the focus on the preservation of traditional indigenous institutions and their right to consultation and FPIC. Consultations with minorities are much less incisive in comparison to the implications of indigenous peoples' right to consultation and FPIC. Similarities between the theorization of these two rights are, however, inevitable, because they both partly descend from developments of international human rights law. In particular, the prong of participation in decision-making processes, which has been conceived as mainly applicable and relevant for minorities, is also of great importance for indigenous peoples. Thus, since it is widely accepted that indigenous peoples may enjoy minority protection if they freely opt for it,[17] the recognition and theorization of the right to political participation of minorities has served as a reference only when it was also useful for indigenous peoples. In sum, minority protection systems *may* but *do not necessarily have to* be applied to indigenous peoples.

Since there is no assessed method in (legal) human rights research,[18] the method used to address the aforementioned research questions relies on the principles of researching public international law.[19] Therefore, this study analyzes and assesses the core sources of international law in the field: International treaties; customary international law; principles of international law; and judicial decisions (e.g., ICJ, regional human rights courts, particularly the Inter-American Court of Human Rights).[20] It also integrates the analysis with writings of publicists and with non-(strictly)-legally binding outcomes of international organizations (e.g., the Concluding Observations of both the UN Human Rights Committee and the Committee on Economic, Social and Cultural Rights).[21] However, human rights research needs to be

16 Rodríguez Piñero-Royo, "Political Participation Systems Applicable to Indigenous Peoples", p.311.

17 Alexandra Xanthaki and Dominic O'Sullivan, "Indigenous Participation in Elective Bodies: The Maori in New Zealand", 16(2) *International Journal on Minority and Group Rights* 2009, pp.181-207, p.183.

18 See Eva Brems, "Methods in Legal Human Rights Research", in Fons Coomans, Fred Grünfeld and Menno T. Kamminga (eds.), *Methods of Human Rights Research*, Intersetia, Antwerp, Oxford, Portland, 2009, pp.77-90.

19 Kelly Vinopal, *Researching Public International Law*, American Society of International Law, 2013.

20 These are the international law sources also according to art.38 of the Statute of the International Court of Justice (ICJ).

21 Vinopal, *Researching Public International Law*, p.9.

interdisciplinary.[22] Thus, sources from other disciplines (political science, sociology and anthropology) have also been used. This study is then completed by empirical analysis of two case studies (Bolivia and Chile). In fact, international law research also relates to the way in which national legal systems implement or apply international law in their domestic law.[23] The two case studies include analyses of national legislation and its implementation, as well as domestic jurisprudence. Hence, legal sources were critically analyzed, also in light of the relevant literature. In addition to desk research, field research and study-visits were then carried out. They served to consult and collect further materials and references, as well as to contact indigenous organizations and representatives. Other social science research methods (qualitative research, field-based interviews) were used to collect missing data and information. Media sources have been critically analyzed and used to complete the assessment vis-à-vis the legal measures' implementation on the ground. The empirical analyses focus on a period of approximately ten years (2006-2015), and the developments concerning both Bolivia and Chile are updated to July 2015.

Having said this, the two cases of Bolivia and Chile were selected not with the aim of comparing the two legal systems vis-à-vis the protection of indigenous rights, but rather as a contrast. Bolivia is currently the most advanced State in Latin America in terms of the recognition of indigenous rights. Chile provides indigenous peoples with a very limited protection, although it has recently shown very interesting developments.

Thus, the selection of the case studies was based on the following (legal) indicators:

- Ratification/signature of international documents on indigenous peoples' rights (ILO Convention 169 and the UNDRIP);
- constitutional recognition of indigenous peoples;
- constitutional and/or domestic recognition of indigenous rights;
- and, within domestic protection, the recognition of the right to self-determination and political rights, including the right to autonomy.

Thanks to the adoption of the new 2009 Constitution, Bolivia undoubtedly stands at the forefront in terms of the recognition of indigenous rights. As far as this research is concerned, Bolivia matches all the above-mentioned indicators, as follows. Bolivia not only ratified the ILO Convention 169, but

22 David P. Forsythe, "Human Rights Studies: On the Dangers of Legalistic Assumptions", in Fons Coomans, Fred Grünfeld and Menno T. Kamminga (eds.), *Methods of Human Rights Research*, Intersetia, Antwerp, Oxford, Portland, 2009, pp.59-75, p.75.

23 Vinopal, *Researching Public International Law*, p.5.

it is the only State in the world to adopt the (formally, non-binding) UNDRIP as domestic binding legislation with Law No.3760 enacted on 7 November 2007. Art.5 of the Bolivian Constitution lists the official (indigenous) languages thus recognizing the 36 indigenous (native peasant farmer) peoples. Art.2 affirms that the indigenous peoples' right to self-determination consists of their right to autonomy and self-government, since, in the very words of the Constitution, the indigenous ancestors dominated the whole territory and existed before colonization. In addition to this, indigenous institutions, territorial entities, and collective bodies are recognized and promoted, insofar as the Constitution and the national law are respected. Indigenous peoples' rights to self-determination and territoriality are then repeated in art.30, para.4. The specific indigenous right to autonomy is enshrined in the seventh chapter of the Constitution by the establishment of new forms of (territorial) "indigenous native peasant farmer" autonomies, i.e., the *Autonomía Indígena Campesino Originaria* (art.289). Other Latin American States have ratified the ILO Convention 169, constitutionally recognised the indigenous peoples living within their borders, and implemented interesting rights related to indigenous peoples' political participation (e.g., Colombia), but none has implemented the UNDRIP as domestic law. This suggests that –on paper– the Bolivian domestic legal framework is currently the most advanced vis-à-vis indigenous rights' recognition.

In Chile, the constitutional recognition of the indigenous peoples living within its national borders is still pending. Debates on a constitutional reform have been going on since 1991. The first draft was submitted that year to the Senate by the first democratically elected President after Pinochet's dictatorship, Patricio Aylwin. In exchange for support for his future government, in 1989 Aylwin had promised the constitutional recognition of indigenous peoples and of their economic, social, and cultural rights. The concrete outcome of Aylwin's presidency was the enactment of the Indigenous Law (*Ley Indígena*, Law No. 19.253, enacted on 5 October 1993). *Inter alia*, this law recognized the existence of indigenous 'ethnicities' (rather than peoples) (art.1); it constituted a fund for indigenous land and water to fulfill land (re)distribution policies (arts.20-22); and it established the National Corporation of Indigenous Development CONADI (*Corporación Nacional de Desarrollo Indígena*) with the aim of promoting States' policies vis-à-vis indigenous peoples as well as implementing the Indigenous Law (arts.38-40). More recently, President Michelle Bachelet launched a number of policies to expand the recognition of indigenous rights, including their constitutional recognition and political rights, both during her first

(2006-2010) and her second, current mandate (2014-2018). Notwithstanding the (declared) priority given to the implementation of these policies, only one has been achieved so far, i.e., the ratification of the ILO Convention 169. This represented a milestone in indigenous affairs in Chile.

The case of Chile was thus selected for two reasons. First, it is one of the six Latin American countries that have not yet constitutionally recognized the indigenous peoples living within their national borders. The other ones are Cuba, Costa Rica, Dominican Republic, Puerto Rico and Uruguay. However, one of these States recognize the duty of the State to protect indigenous languages (Costa Rica). Second, Chile is the only State out of the other four countries (Cuba, Dominican Republic, Puerto Rico, and Uruguay) to ratify the ILO Convention 169. This aspect had a significant weight in the selection, given the Convention's focus on consultation. In addition, its recent ratification by Chile fuelled the debate on the (limited) implementation of the right to consultation within the country. In the other four countries, the discussion over indigenous political participation is hushed and its implementation rather under-developed. In sum, the case of Chile was selected as one of the less advanced Latin American country in terms of indigenous protection but with an increasingly and interesting debate on indigenous participation within the State.

Hence, this study is structured in two parts. Part 1 illustrates the theoretical debates and Part 2 the empirical analyses. Each part is composed of three chapters each.

In Part 1, Chapter 1 gives an overview of the rights of indigenous peoples at the international level. It tackles the definition issue, the steps taken by both the ILO and the UN to safeguard indigenous rights, and the recent evolutionary human rights jurisprudence that aims to remedy the dispossession of indigenous peoples' lands and thus promote their land rights. Chapter 2 initially introduces the concept (principle and right) of self-determination in international law and its recent developments. This is essential in order to understand the set of problems that arise when approaching indigenous peoples' right to self-determination. This chapter then focuses on the multifaceted concept of the right to self-determination of indigenous peoples and theorizes a *composite right of political participation of indigenous peoples* as one of such facets. The core analysis of chapter 3 regards the recognition of the proposed *composite right of political participation of indigenous people* under international soft and hard law and the elements that fine-tune this concept. International individual political rights and the right to political participation of minorities are also discussed in this chapter.

In Part 2, Chapter 4 offers an overview of the protection of indigenous peoples within the complex Latin American historical context and their recent mobilization. The recognition and the application of the *composite right of political participation* at domestic level and thus whether it may also become one of the expressions, or better, one of the effective applications of the right to self-determination of indigenous peoples, is explored subsequently in the case studies of Bolivia and Chile in chapters 5 and 6, respectively.

1. Indigenous Peoples in International Law

The International Labour Organization (ILO) and the United Nations have contributed to establishing an international *corpus iuris* of indigenous peoples rights, and, along with many non-governmental organizations, have garnered global awareness of their rights. In particular, the adoption of the UN Declaration on the Rights of Indigenous Peoples (UNDRIP) in 2007, although formally non-binding, is considered to be a milestone in the international agenda of indigenous rights (see *infra*). However, since its founding in 1919, the ILO began concerning itself with the working conditions of indigenous peoples,[24] which were often reduced to slavery. Regrettably, this is often still the case today,[25] despite the fact that formal abolitions have long been in place. Thus, this chapter aims to give an overview of the rights of indigenous peoples at the international level by tackling the fundamental question of their (non-)definition (section 1.1),[26] analyzing the steps taken by both the ILO and the UN to safeguard their rights, assessing the current framework of indigenous rights' protection at the international level (section 1.2), and looking –albeit briefly– at the recent evolutionary jurisprudence that aims to remedy the dispossession of their lands and thus promote their land rights (section 1.3).[27] It goes without saying that the question of

24 For an overall analysis of the "ILO regime", see Luis Rodríguez Piñero-Royo, *Indigenous peoples, Postcolonialism, and International Law. The ILO Regime (191-1989)*, Oxford University Press, Oxford, New York, 2005, reprinted in 2010.

25 See, e.g., the case of the Guaraní people in the region of Chaco in Argentina. For a recent reference see Katherine Argote, "Los indígenas guaraníes contra la esclavitud", *El Diario*, 26.09.2013, available at http://www.eldiario.es/ ayudaenaccion/Indigenas-ejercicio-derechos-autonomia-economica_6_17959205 1.html [Last access 07.08.2014].

26 Parts of section 1.1 have appeared in the author's publications Alexandra Tomaselli, "Indios, Indigenous, Native People: not just a question of terminology", Special topic online Indigenous peoples in the Americas, EURAC website, Bolzano/Bozen, 31 January 2008, and Alexandra Tomaselli, "II.5 Indigenous peoples. Should they be defined?", in VV.AA., "Material for specialized media", report of the EURASIA-Net project, EURAC, Bolzano/Bozen, 2008.

27 Parts of section 1.3 will also appear in the author's publication Alexandra Tomaselli, "Indigenous Peoples' Right(s) to Land in Latin America", E-book of the Conference Proceedings, Conference "Land, Water & Resources Rights. Global Governance among the Centrality of Human Life, Environment Sustainability and

establishing legal systems to regulate relations between colonizers and indigenous peoples began with first contact, as will be assessed in chapter 4 in the case of Latin America. This chapter however, focuses on the interplay of international actors dealing with indigenous rights since approximately the 1920s.

1.1 The (Non-)Definition of Indigenous Peoples

According to UN sources, more than 370 million individuals self-identify as indigenous in the present day. It is estimated that there are at least 5,000 different groups, each of which speaks a different language. Indigenous peoples are present in more than 70 countries all over the world, though they are mostly divided between bordering States. In some of these countries (e.g., Bolivia) indigenous peoples represent (at least) 40% of the total population. Examples of indigenous peoples range from the Sami people in Northern Europe to the Torres Strait Aborigines living in Australia, the Shuar people living in the Amazon rainforest, the Maori people in New Zealand, the Inuit in the Arctic and the San people living in different States in the Southern part of Africa.[28]

Taking into consideration this cultural richness and diversity, defining "Indigenous Peoples" is particularly challenging, as is evidenced by the UN's attempts to do so. Looking at a standard dictionary, the word "indigenous" is synonymous to "originating", "innate", or "native". For the word "aborigine", one finds "original", the one "who first inhabited a land/territory". Both these adjectives have similar meanings in English and in Italian, while in French the word for "indigène" is depreciative; consequently, the word "aborigène" is preferred. In Spanish (Castilian), the word "aborigen" is not used when referring to indigenous peoples who are referred to as "indígenas" instead.

Commercial, Extractive & Industrial Production", State University of Milan, University Milano-Bicocca, University Of Gastronomic Sciences, Guest University, IULM, 6-8 July 2015.

28 UN Permanent Forum on Indigenous Issues, "Fact Sheet 1: Indigenous Peoples and Identity", 2006, at http://www.un.org/esa/socdev/unpfii/documents/5session_factsheet1.pdf [Last access 07.08.2014]. For general information on Indigenous peoples see the World Directory of Minorities and Indigenous Peoples of the Minority Rights Group International at http://www.minorityrights.org/directory [Last access 07.08.2014].

The difficulties in defining such a large number of groups scattered around the world first emerged in the report (officially) authored by Mr. Josè R. Martinéz Cobo, appointed Special Rapporteur on the Situation of the Human Rights and Fundamental Freedoms of indigenous Peoples in 1971 by –the then– UN Sub-Commission on Prevention of Discrimination and Protection of Minorities of the Commission on Human Rights (see next section 1.2).

The extensive "Study of the Problem of Discrimination against Indigenous Populations" (hereinafter, Cobo-Diaz Study) was carried out mainly by Augusto Willemsen-Diaz, a staff member of the United Nations Center for Human Rights.[29] It was completed between 1981 and 1984,[30] and contains the following definition, which aimed to be as exhaustive as possible:

> "Indigenous communities, peoples and nations are those which, having a historical continuity with pre-invasion and pre-colonial societies that developed on their territories, consider themselves distinct from other sectors of the societies now prevailing in those territories, or parts of them. They form at present non dominant sectors of society and are determined to preserve, develop and transmit to future generations their ancestral territories, and their ethnic identity, as the basis of their continued existence as peoples, in accordance with their own cultural patterns, social institutions and legal systems".[31]

29 Asbjørn Eide, "Rights of Indigenous Peoples – Achievements in International Law during the Last Quarter of a Century", 26 *Netherlands Yearbook of International Law* 2006, pp.155-212, p.164; Augusto Willemsen-Diaz, "How Indigenous Peoples' Rights Reached the UN", in Claire Charters and Rodolfo Stavenhagen (eds.), *Making the Declaration Work. The United Nations Declaration on the Rights of Indigenous Peoples*, International Work Group for Indigenous Affairs (IWGIA), Doc. No.127, Copenhagen, 2009, pp.16-31, p.23.

30 See all the chapters of the Commission on Human Rights, Sub-Commission on Prevention of Discrimination and Protection of Minorities, "Study of the Problem of Discrimination against Indigenous Populations" on the website of the UN Permanent Forum on Indigenous Issues at http://undesadspd.org/IndigenousPeoples/LibraryDocuments/Mart%C3%ADnez-CoboStudy.aspx [Last access 07.08.2014].

31 Commission on Human Rights, Sub-Commission on Prevention of Discrimination and Protection of Minorities, "Study of the Problem of Discrimination against Indigenous Populations", Chapters XXI-XXII of the Study, "Conclusions, proposals and recommendations", UN Doc. E/CN.4 Sub.2/1983/21/Add.8, 30 September 1983, para. 379.

This definition was used by the Working Group on Indigenous Populations until the early 1990s (see *infra*),[32] and is still used today for "practical purposes".[33] However, as the "Study on treaties, agreements and other constructive arrangements between States and indigenous populations" by Martinez later highlighted, the term "Indigenous Peoples" may be a solid point of reference for those peoples living in the Americas and Australia, but it made little sense in the case of Asia or Africa, where all peoples are considered "indigenous".[34]

Nevertheless, it is relevant to stress here that the Cobo-Diaz Study also contained the principles of "self-identification", and "self-recognition":

> "On an individual basis, an indigenous person is one who belongs to these indigenous populations through self-identification as indigenous (group consciousness) and is recognized and accepted by these populations as one of its members (acceptance by the group)".[35]

In 1989, the ILO Convention 169 was adopted and replaced the previous 1957 Convention. It represents the only binding treaty (for the States that ratify it) on the protection of indigenous rights (see next section 1.2).

The ILO's position was to focus more on the "social situation" of these peoples, rather than on their "descends".[36] The Convention hence acknowledged the principle of "self-identification" and "self-recognition". Its art.1 affirms:

> "1. This Convention applies to: (a) tribal peoples in independent countries whose social, cultural and economic conditions distinguish them from other sections of the national community, and whose status is regulated wholly or partially by their own customs or traditions or by special laws or regulations; (b) peoples in independent

32 Patrick Thornberry, *Indigenous Peoples and Human Rights*, Manchester University Press, Manchester 2002, p.33.

33 See the report of the UN Department of Economic and Social Affairs, *State of the World's Indigenous Peoples*, United Nations, New York, 2009, pp.6-7, available at http://www.un.org/esa/socdev/unpfii/documents/SOWIP_web.pdf [Last access 08.08.2014].

34 Miguel Alfonso Martínez, "Final Report on the Study on treaties, agreements and other constructive arrangements between States and indigenous populations", UN Doc. E/CN.4/Sub.2/1999/20, 22 June 1999, as cited by Thornberry, *Indigenous Peoples and Human Rights*, p.34, note 6.

35 "Study of the Problem of Discrimination against Indigenous Populations", "Conclusions, proposals and recommendations", para. 381.

36 Lee Swepston, "Development of the ILO Conventions", in Roxanne Dunbar-Ortiz et al. (eds.), *Indigenous Peoples' Rights in International Law: Emergence and application. Book in Honor of Asbjørn Eide at Eighty*, Gáldu and IWGIA, Kautokeino, Copenhagen, Gáldu Čála serie No.2/2015, 2015, pp.226-249, p.242.

> countries who are regarded as indigenous on account of their descent from the populations which inhabited the country, or a geographical region to which the country belongs, at the time of conquest or colonisation or the establishment of present state boundaries and who, irrespective of their legal status, retain some or all of their own social, economic, cultural and political institutions.
>
> 2. *Self-identification as indigenous or tribal shall be regarded as a fundamental criterion for determining the groups to which the provisions of this Convention apply.*
>
> 3. The use of the term peoples in this Convention shall not be construed as having any implications as regard the rights which may attach to the term under international law." [Emphasis added].

As stated, until the early 1990s, the Cobo-Diaz definition was used as a "vague gatekeeper".[37] However, while preparing the UN Draft Declaration on the Rights of the Indigenous Peoples (hereinafter, Draft Declaration), even though certain elements were given, the omission of a definition was explained in the report by Erica Irene Daes, Chairperson-Rapporteur of the Working Group on indigenous Populations,[38] on the grounds that:

> "[H]istorically speaking, indigenous peoples have suffered from definitions imposed by others. For example, in the past the criterion for membership of an indigenous population in certain countries was based upon parentage or blood quotient and this is now deemed discriminatory as it denies the right of indigenous people to determine their own membership. For this and other relevant reasons the Working Group would not consider it appropriate to develop a definition of its own without full consultation with indigenous peoples themselves".[39]

As such, Erica Irene Daes envisaged the following elements underlined by the Cobo-Diaz Study as both subjective and objective criteria[40] to define indigenous peoples:[41]

---

37 Thornberry, *Indigenous Peoples and Human Rights*, p.33.

38 The works of the Working Group on Indigenous Populations (WGIP) and the Working Group on the Draft Declaration (WGDD), as well as on the developments of the two texts, are addressed briefly in the next section 1.2 and deepened in chapter 2, sections 2.2.2.3 and 2.2.2.4.

39 Erica-Irene Daes, "Standard-Setting Activities: Evolution of Standards Concerning the Rights of Indigenous People – New Developments and General Discussion of Future Action", on criteria which might be applied when considering the concept of indigenous peoples, UN Doc. E/CN.4/Sub.2/AC.4/1995/3, para.6, p.4.

40 An objective characteristic is, e.g., the culture, while the subjective characteristic is the willingness to preserve it. Thornberry, *Indigenous Peoples and Human Rights*, p.54.

41 Daes, "Standard-Setting Activities", paras.11-17, pp.5-6.

- Traditional lands, as established in art.25 of the Draft Declaration;[42]
- Historical continuity, and being the "First Peoples";[43]
- Distinctive cultural characteristics which distinguish indigenous peoples from the prevailing society in which they live;[44]
- Non-dominance, in the sense that, broadly speaking, indigenous peoples suffer from lower incomes, worse health conditions, less access to education, underrepresentation in political institutions and public life than others in the wider society. Moreover, indigenous peoples often face the absence of a recognized title over the lands on which they live, forced removals, and a consequent pauperization and marginalization.[45]
- Self-identification and Group Consciousness, i.e., "the rightful authority to define and determine whether they are indigenous and how membership is attributed".[46]

However, though art.8 of the Draft Declaration contained a self-identification right for indigenous peoples,[47] the Declaration on the Rights of Indigenous Peoples, adopted by the General Assembly of United Nations on 13 September 2007, does not. Although the criterion contained in art.8 was resisted by many States, curiously, over time the debate became diluted and, in the final session prior to the submission of the text to the Human Rights Council (see chapter 2, section 2.2.2.4), the "attempts to find a definition were succumbing to the complexity of the issue, and precedent indicated that a declaration of this kind was possible without a definition".[48] Indeed,

42 Art.25 of the Draft Declaration stated: "Indigenous peoples have the right to maintain and strengthen their distinctive spiritual and material relationship with the lands, territories, waters and coastal seas and other resources which they have traditionally owned or otherwise occupied or used, and to uphold their responsibilities to future generations in this regard". Daes, "Standard-Setting Activities", para.12, p.5.

43 Daes, "Standard-Setting Activities", para.13, p.5

44 *Ibid.*, paras.14-15, pp.5-6.

45 *Ibid.*, para.16, p.6.

46 *Ibid.*, paras.17, p.6.

47 Art.8 of the Draft Declaration affirmed: "Indigenous peoples have the collective and individual right to maintain and develop their distinct identities and characteristics, including the right to identify themselves as indigenous and to be recognized as such".

48 Luis Enrique Chávez, "The Declaration on the Rights of Indigenous Peoples. Breaking the *Impasse*: the Middle Ground", in Claire Charters and Rodolfo Stavenhagen (eds.), *Making the Declaration Work. The United Nations Declaration on the Rights of Indigenous Peoples*, International Work Group for Indigenous Affairs (IWGIA), Doc. No.127, Copenhagen, 2009, pp.96-106, p.103. Chávez is here referring to the "precedent" of the UN Declaration on the Rights of Persons Belonging to Ethnic, Religious and Linguistic Minorities. Chávez, "The Declaration on

the insertion of a definition may also result in the risk of narrowing the scope of indigenous protection.[49]

Therefore, the UN Permanent Forum on indigenous Issues developed a "modern understanding" of "indigenous peoples" based on the following criteria:

- Self-identification as indigenous peoples at the individual level and acceptation by the community as their member;
- Historical continuity with pre-colonial and/or pre-settler societies;
- Strong links to territories and surrounding natural resources;
- Distinct social, economic or political systems;
- Distinct language, culture and beliefs;
- Form non-dominant groups of society;
- Resolve to maintain and reproduce their ancestral environments and systems as distinctive peoples and communities.[50]

In particular, it is relevant to underline here that the "definition question" of indigenous peoples stems also from the exigency of indigenous peoples to be neither called nor treated as "minorities". As widely known, the definition of minorities elaborated by Francesco Capotorti in 1977 has not been inserted in any international document regarding minority rights. His proposal was the following:

> "A group numerically inferior to the rest of the population of a State, in a non-dominant position, whose members-being nationals of the State-possess ethnic, religious or linguistic characteristics differing from those of the rest of the population and show, if only implicitly, a sense of solidarity, directed towards preserving their culture, traditions, religion or language".[51]

Without going into the pros and cons of this formula, one may note both similarities and differences. As to the former, both indigenous peoples and minorities are defined as non-dominant groups in their societies, they differ or are distinct from the prevailing society, and aim to preserve their cultures. As to the latter, indigenous peoples are called communities, peoples and nations, having an "historical continuity with pre-invasion and pre-colonial

---

the Rights of Indigenous Peoples. Breaking the *Impasse* ...", pp.103 and 106, note 15.

49 Thornberry, *Indigenous Peoples and Human Rights*, pp.57-58.

50 UN Permanent Forum on Indigenous Issues, "Fact Sheet 1: Indigenous Peoples and Identity", p.1.

51 Francesco Capotorti, Special Rapporteur of the Sub-Commission on Prevention of Discrimination and Protection of Minorities, "Study on the Rights of Persons Belonging to Ethnic, Religious, and Linguistic Minorities", UN Doc. E/CN.4/Sub.2/384/Rev.1, New York, 1979, para.568.

societies", and there is a reference to their ancestral territories and their "continued existence". Indeed, minorities are considered a "group, numerically inferior" and "nationals", i.e., citizens, within the State in which they live. However, as highlighted by Thornberry, the Capotorti definition may be applied to many indigenous peoples, as the jurisprudence under art.27 of the International Covenant on Civil and Political Rights (ICCPR) proves (see chapter 2, sections 2.1.4 and chapter 3, section 3.1.2).[52] Paradoxically, it is the indigenous peoples who have made greater progress in the international jurisprudence vis-à-vis this provision and, consequently, minority rights' protection.[53] Nevertheless, indigenous peoples have clearly stated their uneasiness and refusal to be called "minorities" since the first sessions of the Working Group on Indigenous Population.[54] The term "minority" is also often perceived as pejorative and reductive.[55] Additionally, as flagged by Alfredsson, "the definitions are incomplete largely because States are reluctant to deal with the rights of groups or peoples. In part [...] ignorance, lack of tolerance and undoubtedly racism play a role in the lack of codified

52 Thornberry, *Indigenous Peoples and Human Rights*, p.52.

53 *Ibid.*, p.54.

54 See, e.g., Gudmundur Alfredsson, "The Right of Self-Determination and Indigenous Peoples", in Christian Tomuschat (ed.), *Modern Law of Self-Determination*, Martinus Nijhoff Publishers, Dordrecht, Boston, London, 1993, pp.41-54, pp.44-45; Wilton Littlechild, "Comment on agenda items at the Oslo Conference on Indigenous Peoples' Rights", in Roxanne Dunbar-Ortiz et al. (eds.), *Indigenous Peoples' Rights in International Law: Emergence and application. Book in Honor of Asbjørn Eide at Eighty*, Gáldu and IWGIA, Kautokeino, Copenhagen, Gáldu Čála serie No.2/2015, 2015, pp.18-23, p.21. For an explicit rejection see, *inter alia*, the declaration of the Sami Parliament in the Advisory Committee of the Framework Convention for the Protection of National Minorities, First State Report by Norway, 2 March 2001, ACFC/SR(2001)001, p. 4.

55 Especially in terms of rights recognition both at the national and international level. This has also been recognized by the Advisory Committee. Advisory Committee of the Framework Convention for the Protection of National Minorities, First Opinion on the Russian Federation, 13 September 2002, ACFC/INF/OP/I(2003)005, para.26. However, on the need to rethink the common aspects of the *rights* of indigenous peoples and "national minorities", as well as other vulnerable groups, see Will Kymlicka, "Beyond the Indigenous/Minority Dichotomy?", in Stephen Allen and Alexandra Xanthaki (eds.), *Reflections on the UN Declaration on the Rights of Indigenous Peoples*, Hart Publishing, Oxford, Portland, 2011, pp.183-208.

definitions".[56] However, "[t]he absence of complete definitions should not allow a State's government to arbitrarily get away from group protection".[57]

In conclusion, despite the overlap in both their conceptualizations[58] and their claims,[59] the self-identification criterion is to be preferred for both indigenous peoples and minorities, as has been stressed in the case of (European) minorities by art.3 of the Framework Convention for the Protection of National Minorities.[60]

1.2 The international protection of indigenous rights

The first reference in international law to indigenous peoples, albeit at that time referred to as "Indigenous populations", may be found in the Covenant of the League of Nations, which, in art.22, referred to South-West Africa and "certain South Pacific Islands" as territories to be best administered by the Mandatory rules according to the sparseness, small size, and remoteness of their population or the geographical contiguity to the territory of the Mandatory.[61]

---

56 Gudmundur Alfredsson, "Minorities, Indigenous and Tribal Peoples, and Peoples: Definitions of Terms as a Matter of International Law", in Nazila Ghanea and Alexandra Xanthaki (eds.), *Minorities, Peoples and Self-Determination,* Brill, Leiden, 2005, pp.163-172, pp.163-164.

57 Alfredsson, "Minorities, Indigenous and Tribal Peoples, and Peoples ...", p.172. See also the recent analysis of Willem van Genugten, Anna Meijknecht and Bas Rombouts, "Stateless Indigenous People(s). The Right to a Nationality, Including Their Own", 19 *Tilburg Law Review* 2014, pp.98-107.

58 See further in Martin Scheinin, "What are indigenous peoples?", in Nazila Ghanea and Alexandra Xanthaki (eds.), *Minorities, Peoples and Self-Determination,* Brill, Leiden, 2005, pp. 3-13.

59 Rodríguez Piñero-Royo, "Political Participation Systems Applicable to Indigenous Peoples", p.309.

60 Art.3.1 of the Framework Convention for the Protection of National Minorities states: "Every person belonging to a national minority shall have the right freely to choose to be treated or not to be treated as such and no disadvantage shall result from this choice or from the exercise of the rights which are connected to that choice".

61 See the Covenant of the League of Nations at http://avalon.law.yale.edu/20th_century/leagcov.asp [Last access 07.08.2014]. Art.22, para.6 states: "There are territories, such as South-West Africa and certain of the South Pacific Islands, which, owing to the sparseness of their population, or their small size, or their remoteness from the centres of civilization, or their geographical contiguity to the territory of the Mandatory, and other circumstances, can be best administered under the laws of the Mandatory as integral portions of its

The first "official" interaction between indigenous peoples and international bodies were the visits of the Native American Haudenosaunee Chief Deskaheh and the Maori leader T.W. Ratana to Geneva in 1923 and 1925, respectively. They denounced before the League of Nations, albeit unsuccessfully, the incompliance of previous treaties signed by Great Britain and their peoples (see further in chapter 2, section 2.2.1).[62]

During that period, the ILO, founded in 1919 with the Peace Treaty of Versailles and that later became one of the specialized agencies of the UN, was the first organization to start dealing with indigenous peoples by conducting research on indigenous workers in 1921.[63] Five years later, a Committee of Experts on Native Labour was created and a number of conventions were subsequently adopted: the Forced Labour Convention, Convention No.29 of 1930; Recruiting of Indigenous Workers Convention, No.50 of 1936; Contracts of Employment (Indigenous Workers) Convention, No.64 of 1939; and Penal Sanctions (Indigenous Workers) Convention, No.65 of 1939. These Conventions were known as the "Native Labour Code".[64] The American States asked to prioritize the working and living conditions of indigenous peoples starting with the ILO's "First American Regional Labour Conference", which was held in 1936.[65] After the celebration of the "American Regional Conference" of the ILO's Member States in 1948, the Committee of Experts on Social Policy in Non-Metropolitan Territories was established, and, in January 1951, the Committee of Experts on Native Labour held its first session.[66]

The first outcomes of the ILO commitment vis-à-vis indigenous peoples resulted in the launch of the Andean Indian Programme (AIP) in 1952, which lasted until 1972.[67] In 1953, the ILO published an impressive study

territory, subject to the safeguards above mentioned in the interests of the indigenous population."

62 UN Permanent Forum on Indigenous Issues, "History", at http://undesadspd.org/IndigenousPeoples/AboutUsMembers/History.aspx [Last access 07.08.2014].

63 Thornberry, *Indigenous Peoples and Human Rights*, p.320.

64 Swepston, "Development of the ILO Conventions", p.227.

65 *Ibid.*, p.228.

66 Thornberry, *Indigenous Peoples and Human Rights*, p.320.

67 The official sources speak of 250,000 indigenous persons assisted by the programme. International Labour Office, *ILO Convention on indigenous and tribal peoples, 1989 (No.169): A Manual*, International Labour Organization, Ginevra, 2003, p.3.

on the living and working conditions of indigenous peoples.[68] These initiatives certainly garnered international attention for the indigenous peoples and marked the beginning of a regional and supra-national approach on the subject. However, the analysis of the statements of the leaders of AIP suggests a "paternalistic" approach which in any case aimed to "save" indigenous peoples from their cultural backwardness and make them a reliable workforce attitude.[69] Nevertheless, thanks to the ILOs' efforts, the first binding treaty on indigenous rights was adopted in 1957: The ILO "Convention Concerning the Protection and Integration of indigenous and Other Tribal and Semi-Tribal Populations in Independent Countries", Convention No.107 (hereinafter, ILO Convention 107). This convention recognizes, *inter alia*, the indigenous rights to life, education, health and participation,[70] and is still binding for those 17 States that did not ratify the following ILO Convention 169,[71] in accordance with art.36.2 and art.43.2 of the latter. Thus, as highlighted by Xanthaki, ILO Convention 107 proved to be a very

68 International Labour Office, *Indigenous Peoples: Living and Working Conditions of Aboriginal Populations in Independent Countries*, Geneva, 1953.

69 During his mandate within the AIP in 1957-58, the vice-director Jef Rens said that the objective of AIP was a "gigantic campaign of education and enlightenment among the Indian population designed to point the way to a better life [...]; the Indian population forms a reserve of manpower which would prove indispensable in the economic development [...]". Jef Rens, "The Andean Programme," 84 *International Labour Review* (December) 1961, p.441, and Jef Rens, "Mr. Rens' Mission Notes, Andean Indian Project (Spring 1958)," DMCF, Correspondence between the D-G and Mr. Jef Rens, January 1957-December 1958, ILO Doc.Z1/1/1/16(J.6), as cited by Jason Guthrie, "The International Labour Organization, Community Development, and the Roots of the International Technocratic Class, 1944-1966", paper presented at the conference "Transnational Social Policies. Reformist networks and the International Labour Organization (1900-2000)", University of Paris X, 07.05.2009 - 09.05.2009, p.11. In 1953, according to the first regional director of AIP Enrique de Lozada, the success of the Andean program would have to be measured by the actual productivity growth, especially in the agricultural sector. Jason Guthrie, *ibid.*, p.12-13.

70 See the text of the Convention at http://www.ilo.org/indigenous/Conventions/no107/lang--en/index.htm [Last access 08.08.2014].

71 See ratifications at http://www.ilo.org/dyn/normlex/en/f?p=NORMLEX-PUB:11300:0::NO:11300:P11300_INSTRUMENT_ID:312252:NO [Last access 08.08.2014]. The ILO Convention 107 is still in force for Angola, Bangladesh, Belgium, Cuba, Dominican Republic, Egypt, El Salvador, Ghana, Guinea-Bissau, Haiti, India, Iraq, Malawi, Pakistan, Panama, Syrian Arab Republic, and Tunisia.

advanced document in terms of human rights,[72] particularly considering that the two Covenants (International Covenant on Civil and Political Rights (ICCPR) and International Covenant on Economic, Social and Cultural Rights (ICESCR)) were still under discussion, only to be adopted nine years later. Many States expressed their concern and reluctance during the debate for the adoption of ILO Convention 107; for some representatives the convention should have no binding nature; for others, the adoption of such a treaty would have exceeded the ILO's competences.[73] The ILO Convention 107 showed its limitations in the subsequent years. As argued by different experts during the debate on its revision, this Convention had an overall approach aimed to integrate indigenous peoples in an assimilationist way and an inherent paternalistic assumption that indigenous peoples were inferior.[74]

The UN's interest in indigenous peoples began later.[75] Despite an attempt in 1948 by the Bolivian delegation to create a sub-commission dealing with the social problems faced by indigenous peoples in the Americas, which was eventually rejected,[76] no action was taken until a "Special Study on Racial Discrimination in the Political, Economic and Cultural Spheres" was submitted in 1969 to the (then) UN Sub-Commission on Prevention of Discrimination and Protection of Minorities, under the former Commission on

72 Alexandra Xanthaki, *Indigenous Rights and United Nations Standards. Self-deter mination, Culture and Land*, Cambridge University Press, Cambridge, 2007, pp.50-51.

73 Xanthaki, *Indigenous Rights and United Nations Standards*, pp.50-51. Canada and USA were particularly contrasting. However, after the adoption of the Philadelphia Declaration in 1944, during the 26th session of the ILO, the mandate of the organization in the field of social justice was evident.

74 Swepston, "Development of the ILO Conventions", p.226; see also Thornberry, *Indigenous Peoples and Human Rights*, p.338 that cites the comments during the works of revisions. Moreover, the ILO Convention 169 itself in the Preamble states that "… Considering that the developments [since 1957] […] have made it appropriate to adopt new international standards on the subject with a view to removing the *assimilationist* orientation of the earlier standards…" [Emphasis added].

75 For a concise overview on the developments at UN level in the decade of the 1970s, see the recent article of Roxanne Dunbar Ortiz, "The First Ten Years, from Study to Working Group, 1972-1982", in Roxanne Dunbar-Ortiz et al. (eds.), *Indigenous Peoples' Rights in International Law: Emergence and application. Book in Honor of Asbjørn Eide at Eighty*, Gáldu and IWGIA, Kautokeino, Copenhagen, Gáldu Čála serie No.2/2015, 2015, pp.42-87.

76 Augusto Willemsen-Diaz, "How Indigenous Peoples' Rights Reached the UN", p.18.

Human Rights. This study also contained a chapter on indigenous peoples.[77] Following a debate on the subject within the Sub-Commission, it was recommended that the UN Economic and Social Council (ECOSOC) prepare a study on the discrimination suffered by indigenous peoples.[78] This led ECOSOC to adopt Resolution No.1589(L) on 21 May 1971, by which José R. Martínez Cobo was appointed Special Rapporteur on the situation of human rights and fundamental freedoms of indigenous peoples to prepare a "Study on the Problem of Discrimination Against Indigenous Populations".[79] As mentioned in section 1.1,[80] an extensive decennial research was thus initiated by Cobo but eventually carried out mainly by Augusto Willemsen-Diaz. This Study was conducted between 1981 and 1984 and was initially designed to analyze the discrimination against indigenous peoples and to thus find ways to integrate them into mainstream society. However, thanks to the insistence of indigenous organizations, this primary focus was ultimately expanded.[81]

For their part, indigenous peoples started to create their own organizations in the 1950s. In particular, between 27 and 31 October 1975, the first "International Conference of Indigenous Peoples" was held in Port Alberny (Canada), in which indigenous peoples from 18 different countries participated.[82] One of the main products of this conference was the creation of the World Council on Indigenous Peoples, formed by delegates from indigenous organizations across the Americas.[83] In August 1977, Kiruna, in Sweden, hosted the second "International Conference of Indigenous Peoples",

77 Erica-Irene Daes, "The UN Declaration on the Rights of Indigenous Peoples: Background and Appraisal", in Stephen Allen and Alexandra Xanthaki (eds.), *Reflections on the UN Declaration on the Rights of Indigenous Peoples*, Hart Publishing, Oxford, Portland, 2011, pp.11-40, p.11.

78 *Ibid.*, pp.11-12.

79 *Ibid.*, p.12.

80 See notes 29 and 30 on the "Study of the Problem of Discrimination against Indigenous Populations".

81 Eide, "Rights of Indigenous Peoples – Achievements in International Law…", p.165

82 Australia, New Zealand, US, Canada, Denmark (Greenland), Norway, Sweden, Finland, Mexico, Nicaragua, Panama, Venezuela, Colombia, Ecuador, Peru, Paraguay, Bolivia and Argentina. Jens Dahl, *IWGIA. A History*, International Work Group for Indigenous Affairs (IWGIA), Document No.125, Copenhagen, 2009, p.40.

83 Nilo Cayuqueo, "1977 and the Participation of Indigenous peoples in the United Nations and the International Arena", in Roxanne Dunbar-Ortiz et al. (eds.), *Indigenous Peoples' Rights in International Law: Emergence and application. Book in*

in which many delegates participated.[84] This was followed, on 20-23 September 1977, by the "International Conference on Discrimination against the Indigenous Populations in the Americas" which was organized in Geneva under the auspices of the UN Decade for Action to Combat Racism and Racial Discrimination.[85] Other conferences followed, which contributed to promote the creation of the UN Working Group on Indigenous Populations (WGIP) in 1982 by ECOSOC Resolution No.1982/34.[86]

ECOSOC assigned a twofold mandate to the WGIP; to review developments vis-à-vis the human rights of indigenous peoples and to analyze the standards relating to indigenous rights. The WGIP experts had to meet annually prior to the Sub-Commission's sessions.[87] Following this, the Working Group on the Draft Declaration was established by the ECOSOC in 1995 to pursue the preparation of a UN Draft Declaration on the Rights of Indigenous Peoples to be considered and adopted by the General Assembly during the First International Decade of the World's indigenous People (1995-2004). Work was eventually concluded in 2006 and led to the (delayed) adoption of the UN Declaration on the Rights of Indigenous Peoples (UNDRIP) in 2007 (see chapter 2, sections 2.2.2.3 and 2.2.2.4).[88]

However, prior to this, as mentioned, the ILO Convention 107 was revised in the late 1980s and was merged into the ILO Convention 169.[89] During the *travaux preparatoires*, some States were particularly concerned with the use of the word "people" (see also chapter 2, section 2.2.5) and the

Honor of Asbjørn Eide at Eighty, Gáldu and IWGIA, Kautokeino, Copenhagen, Gáldu Čála serie No.2/2015, 2015, pp.38-41, p.39.

84 *Ibid.*

85 Dahl, *IWGIA. A History*, p.40.

86 UN Economic and Social Council, "Establishment of the Working Group on Indigenous Populations", Resolution No.1982/34, UN Doc. E/RES/1982/34, 7 May 1982.

87 UN Economic and Social Council, "Establishment of the Working Group on Indigenous Populations", para. 1.

88 UN Economic and Social Council, "Establishment of a Working group of the Commission on Human Rights to elaborate a draft declaration in accordance with paragraph 5 of General Assembly resolution 49/214", Resolution No. 1995/32, UN Doc. E/RES/1995/32, 25 July 1995.

89 See the text of the Convention concerning Indigenous and Tribal Peoples in Independent Countries at http://www.ilo.org/dyn/normlex/en/f?p=NORMLEX-PUB:12100:0::NO:12100:P12100_ILO_CODE:C169 [Last access 08.08.2014]. See also the webpage of the Working Group on the Draft Declaration at http://www2.ohchr.org/english/issues/indigenous/groups/groups-02.htm [Last access 08.08.2014].

extension of rights to participation and land.[90] The revised text and the adoption of the ILO Convention 169 represented a milestone, especially in the Latin American context, seeing that 15 States ratified it,[91] albeit at different times.[92]

For the purposes of this study, it suffices to note here that the ILO Convention 169 contained, among others, relevant provisions on indigenous peoples' right to participation and consultation (arts.6 and 7), and those relating to land and territory, as well as to natural resources (arts.13-19),[93] although limited in the views of the indigenous delegates participating in the negotiations.[94] Additionally, thanks to the mechanism of Representations under art.24 of the ILO Constitution, indigenous peoples continued to gather in unions to demand the application of these rights.[95] Notwithstand-

---

90 See on participation and the word "people", International Labour Organization, "Partial Revision of the Indigenous and Tribal Populations Convention, 1957 (No.107)", Report IV (2 A), Geneva, 1989, pp.5-7, e 8-12. On land rights, see International Labour Organization, "Partial Revision of the Indigenous and Tribal Populations Convention, 1957 (No.107)", Report IV (1), Geneva 1988, pp.4-5.

91 The first Latin American country to ratify the ILO Convention 169 was Mexico in 1990. Bolivia and Colombia followed in 1991, then Paraguay and Costa Rica in 1993. After, there was a domino effect: Peru in 1994; Honduras in 1995; Guatemala in 1996; Ecuador in 1998; Argentina in 2000; Brazil; the Dominican Republic and Venezuela in 2002; lastly, Chile in 2008 and Nicaragua in 2010. See the ratifications at http://www.ilo.org/dyn/normlex/en/f?p=NORMLEX-PUB:11300:0::NO:11300:P11300_INSTRUMENT_ID:312314:NO [Last access 08.08.2014].

92 The recent ratifications of Chile and Nicaragua are result also of incessant requests by indigenous movements, international organizations and NGOs.

93 As mentioned, for a detailed overview see Rodríguez-Piñero Royo, *Indigenous Peoples, Postcolonialism, and International Law*; see also Xanthaki, *Indigenous Rights and United Nations Standards*, pp.49-101; and Swepston, "Development of the ILO Conventions".

94 On this see the recent article of Dalee Sambo Dorough, "The Revision of International Labour Organization Convention No. 107: A Subjective Assessment", in Roxanne Dunbar-Ortiz et al. (eds.), *Indigenous Peoples' Rights in International Law: Emergence and application. Book in Honor of Asbjørn Eide at Eighty*, Gáldu and IWGIA, Kautokeino, Copenhagen, Gáldu Čála serie No.2/2015, 2015, pp.250-277.

95 The mechanism of representations under article 24 of the ILO Constitution consists in the adoption of recommendations by an ad hoc appointed tripartite committee, which then submits them to the Committee of Experts on the Application of Conventions and Recommendations. Art.24 of the ILO Constitution states: "In the event of any representation being made to the International Labour Office by an industrial association of employers or of workers that any of the Members has

ing their "soft" law nature, the cases of Representations have largely contributed to the interpretation and application of the rights contained in the ILO Convention 169 (see chapter 3, section 3.3.2.2.1). Most importantly, ILO Convention 169 sealed the recognition of collective rights for indigenous peoples,[96] particularly of land rights, also later recognized by the Inter-American Court of Human Rights in the case *Mayagna (Sumo) Awas Tingni Community v. Nicaragua*.[97]

Following the adoption of the ILO Convention 169, a coordination body among UN agencies dealing with indigenous rights was established in 1990.[98] This eventually evolved in the Inter-Agency Support Group on Indigenous Peoples' Issues (see *infra*).[99]

In 1992, the United Nations Conference on Environment and Development held in Rio de Janeiro contained Principle 22 which recognized that indigenous peoples played a vital role in environmental management and development and that States had a duty to recognize and support their identity, culture and interests as well as grant them the possibility to effectively participate in the achievement of sustainable development.[100] Moreover,

failed to secure in any respect the effective observance within its jurisdiction of any Convention to which it is a party, the Governing Body may communicate this representation to the government against which it is made, and may invite that government to make such statement on the subject as it may think fit". See the Representations under art.24 of the ILO Constitution per country at http://www.ilo.org/dyn/normlex/en/f?p=1000:50010:0::NO:50010:P50010_ARTICLE_NO:24 [Last access 23.02.2015].

96 Xanthaki, *Indigenous Rights and United Nations Standards*, p.30. See also the analysis of Dwight G. Newman, "Theorizing Collective Indigenous Rights", 31(2) *American Indian Law Review* 2006-2007, pp.273-289. More broadly on individual and collective rights, see Will Kymlicka, *Multicultural Citizenship: A Liberal Theory of Minority Rights*, Oxford University Press, oxford, New York, 1995, pp.33 ff.

97 Inter-American Court of Human Rights, *Mayagna (Sumo) Awas Tingni Community v. Nicaragua*, Serie C No. 79, Judgment of 31 August 2001. For a recent assessment of this decision after ten years from its adoption, see Felipe Isa Gomez (ed.), *El caso Awas Tigni. Derechos Humanos entre lo local y global*, Universidad de Deusto, Bilbao, 2013. On the Inter-American human rights system and its impact on indigenous rights see below section 1.3, and also chapter 4, section 4.2.

98 Swepston, "Development of the ILO Conventions", p.248.

99 Lee Swepston, an ILO expert and former official who worked directly on the revision of the ILO Convention 107, stated recently that, despite what is declared on the UNPFII website, this Inter-Agency was created before it, i.e., in 1990. Swepston, "Development of the ILO Conventions", p.248.

100 Report of the United Nations Conference on Environment and Development, Rio de Janeiro, 3-14 June 1992, UN Doc. A/CONF.151/26, at http://www.un.org/doc-

Agenda 21 –adopted after the Rio Conference– dedicated chapter No.26 to indigenous peoples.[101]

Among the UN initiatives regarding indigenous rights, the UN General Assembly Resolution No.48/163 proclaimed the first International Decade of Indigenous Peoples beginning in 1995 (1995-2004),[102] followed by the Second Decade from 2005 to 2014 (General Assembly Resolution No.59/174).[103]

During the First Decade, the annual International Day of the World's indigenous Peoples was established as 9th of August, and the Office of the High Commissioner on Human Rights (OHCHR) in Geneva began to organize a fellowship programme for indigenous peoples.[104] Most importantly, the UN Permanent Forum on Indigenous Issues (UNPFII) and the offices of the Special Rapporteur on the Situation of Human Rights and Fundamental Freedoms of Indigenous People or Special Rapporteur on the Rights of Indigenous Peoples were created in 2000 and 2001, respectively. The creation of the former followed a proposal to establish an international Independent Tribunal for indigenous peoples put forward by the Indigenous Initiative for Peace convened by the Nobel Peace Prize Laureate Rigoberta Menchú Tum.[105]

---

uments/ga/conf151/aconf15126-1annex1.htm [Last access 23.02.2015]. In addition, UN Convention on Biological Diversity, also adopted in 1992, affirms in art.8j: "Subject to its national legislation, respect, preserve and maintain knowledge, innovations and practices of indigenous and local communities embodying traditional lifestyles relevant for the conservation and sustainable use of biological diversity and promote their wider application with the approval and involvement of the holders of such knowledge, innovations and practices and encourage the equitable sharing of the benefits arising from the utilization of such knowledge, innovations and practices". See the text of the Convention on Biological Diversity available at http://www.cbd.int/convention/text/default.shtml [Last access 08.08.2014].

101 UN Environment Programme, "Agenda 21", chapter No.26 "Recognising and Strengthening the Role of Indigenous People and their Communities" at http://www.unep.org/Documents.Multilingual/Default.asp?DocumentID=52&ArticleID=74&l=en [Last access 23.02.2015].

102 General Assembly, "International Decade of the World's Indigenous People", Resolution No.48/163, UN Doc. A/RES/48/163 (1993), 21 December 1993.

103 General Assembly, "Second International Decade of the World's Indigenous People", Resolution No.59/174, UN Doc. A/RES/59/174 (2004), 20 December 2004.

104 UN Department of Economic and Social Affairs, *State of the World's Indigenous Peoples*, p.3.

105 Littlechild, "Comment on agenda items at the Oslo Conference ...", p.20.

The UNPFII was then established with ECOSOC Resolution No.2000/22.[106] It is an advisory body to ECOSOC and is composed of sixteen independent experts appointed by both governments and indigenous organizations in each geographical region. The UNPFII is tasked with providing advice and recommendations to the Human Rights Council and the other UN bodies on indigenous issues such as socio-economic development, environment, human rights, culture, education, and indigenous health, as well as raising awareness, coordinating action, and preparing and disseminating information vis-à-vis indigenous issues. A thematic two-week session has been held annually in New York at the seat of the UNPFII since 2002.[107] Several indigenous representatives are actively involved thanks to the UN Voluntary Fund for Indigenous Populations, established in 1985 by General Assembly Resolution No.40/131.[108] In late 2013, the title of this fund was changed to the United Nations Voluntary Fund for Indigenous *Peoples*.[109] Indigenous peoples have contributed substantially to the debates taking place at the UNPFIII sessions.[110]

The Special Rapporteur on the Situation of Human Rights and Fundamental Freedoms of Indigenous People or (since 2010) Special Rapporteur on the Rights of Indigenous Peoples (hereinafter, Special Rapporteur) was

106 Economic and Social Council Resolution No.2000/22, "Establishment of a Permanent Forum on Indigenous Issues", 45th plenary meeting, UN Doc. E/RES/2000/22 (2000), 28 July 2000.

107 UN Permanent Forum on Indigenous Issues, "Permanent Forum: Origin and Development", at http://undesadspd.org/IndigenousPeoples/AboutUsMembers.aspx [Last access 08.08.2014].

108 General Assembly, "United Nations Voluntary Fund for Indigenous Populations", Resolution No.40/131, UN Doc. A/RES/40/131, 13 December 1985. See also the website of the UN Voluntary Fund for Indigenous Peoples, at http://www.ohchr.org/EN/Issues/IPeoples/IPeoplesFund/Pages/IPeoplesFundIndex.aspx [Last access 08.08.2014].

109 Emphasis added. General Assembly, "Rights of indigenous peoples", Resolution No. 68/149, UN Doc. A/RES/68/149, 12 February 2014, para.10, p.5.

110 See, e.g., the lively protest during the 7th Session of the UN Permanent Forum on Indigenous Issues on 2 May 2008 about the UN Collaborative Programme on Reducing Emissions from Deforestation and Forest Degradation in Developing Countries (UN-REDD). The independent production company Sommers Film produced a video of the protest. Sommers Film, "REDD '2nd MAY REVOLT' at the UNPFII", at http://www.youtube.com/watch?v=UtORVi7GybY [Last access 23.02.2015].

appointed by the (then) UN Commission on Human Rights.[111] The Special Rapporteur is an independent expert nominated for a mandate of three years which can be renewed. The duties of the Special Rapporteur includes the analysis of the obstacles to the implementation of indigenous peoples' rights, gathering and exchanging information from and among different parties (governments, indigenous organizations and communities, etc.), and the formulation of recommendations and proposals to remedy violations of indigenous rights. Furthermore, the Special Rapporteur carries out country visits and meets both governmental and indigenous representatives.[112] Finally, the Special Rapporteur has a general duty to cooperate with the other UN bodies dealing with indigenous peoples, particularly with the abovementioned UNPFII and the Expert Mechanism on the Rights of Indigenous Peoples (EMRIP).

The EMRIP was established in 2007 and substituted for the Working Group on Indigenous Populations.[113] It is in charge of providing the Human

111 Commission on Human Rights, "Human rights and indigenous issues", Resolution No.2001/57, UN Doc. E/CN.4/RES/2001/57, 24 April 2001. See following Commission on Human Rights, "Human rights and indigenous issues", Resolution No.2004/62, UN Doc. E/CN.4/RES/2004/62, 21 April 2004; Human Rights Council, "Human rights and indigenous peoples: Mandate of the Special Rapporteur on the situation of human rights and fundamental freedoms of indigenous people", Resolution No.6/12, UN Doc. A/HRC/RES/6/12, 28 September 2007; Human Rights Council, "Human rights and indigenous peoples: Mandate of the Special Rapporteur on the situation of human rights and fundamental freedoms of indigenous people", Resolution No.15/14, UN Doc. A/HRC/RES/15/14, 6 October 2010; Human Rights Council, "Human rights and indigenous peoples: Mandate of the Special Rapporteur on the situation of human rights and fundamental freedoms of indigenous people", Resolution No.29/4, UN Doc. A/HRC/RES/24/9 (2013), 8 October 2013. From 2010 the Special Rapporteur was referred in Human Rights Council, Resolution No.15/14 in the abbreviated title of "Special Rapporteur on the Rights of Indigenous Peoples". So far, three eminent experts have been appointed as Special Rapporteur on the Rights of Indigenous Peoples, namely Rodolfo Stavenhagen (2001-2008), James Anaya (2008-2014), and Victoria Tauli Corpuz (2014-present).

112 Apart from the resolutions mentioned above, see also on the website of the Special Rapporteur on the Situation of Human Rights and Fundamental Freedoms of Indigenous People or Special Rapporteur on the Rights of Indigenous Peoples, at http://www.ohchr.org/en/issues/ipeoples/srindigenouspeoples/pages/sripeoplesindex.aspx [Last access 23.02.2015].

113 Human Rights Council, "Expert mechanism on the rights of indigenous peoples", Resolution No.6/36, UN Doc. A/HRC/RES/6/36, 14 December 2007. See the Working Group on Indigenous Populations website, at http://www2.ohchr.org/english/issues/indigenous/groups/groups-01.htm [Last access 08.08.2014].

Rights Council with thematic reports and advice. Hitherto (July 2015), along with other interim reports, six thematic studies have been submitted to the Human Rights Council on indigenous peoples' right to education (2009); right to participate in decision-making processes (2010-2011); indigenous languages, culture and identity (2012); access to justice for indigenous peoples in general (2013); restorative justice, indigenous juridical systems, and access to justice for indigenous women, children and youth, and persons with disabilities (2014); and on the promotion and protection of indigenous rights in disaster risk reduction, prevention and preparedness initiatives (2014). A seventh study on the promotion and protection of the rights of indigenous peoples with respect to their cultural heritage is under preparation.[114]

As mentioned, in 2007 the UNDRIP was adopted during the sixty-third session of the General Assembly. The difficulties in its adoption are addressed in chapter 2 (sections 2.2.2.3 and 2.2.2.4). Here it suffices to remember that, the *sui generis* character of this Declaration is proved by the fact that, although it cannot be considered a Convention, it represents a "radical novelty" with "a value different from other Declarations",[115] and the rights enshrined in it may be found in other binding international law treaties (e.g., ICCPR, ICESCR, International Convention on the Elimination of All Forms of Racial Discrimination, Convention on the Rights of the Child, Convention Against Torture, International Convention on the Elimination of All Forms of Racial Discrimination against Women, ILO Convention 169, etc.).[116]

114 Expert Mechanism on the Rights of Indigenous Peoples, "Documentation", at http://www.ohchr.org/EN/Issues/IPeoples/EMRIP/Pages/ExpertMechanismDocumentation.aspx [Last access 17.08.2015].

115 Bartolomé Clavero, "Nota sobre el alcance del mandato contenido en el artículo 42 de la Declaración sobre los derechos de los pueblos indígenas y el mejor modo de satisfacerlo por parte del Foro Permanente para las Cuestiones Indígenas, presented by Bartolomé Clavero, Member of the Permanent Forum on Indigenous Issues", UN Doc. E/C.19/2008/CRP.6, 26 March 2008, paras.15 and 16, as cited by Luis Rodríguez Piñero-Royo, "'Where Appropriate': Monitoring/Implementing of Indigenous Peoples' Rights Under the Declaration", in Claire Charters and Rodolfo Stavenhagen (eds.), *Making the Declaration Work. The United Nations Declaration on the Rights of Indigenous Peoples*, International Work Group for Indigenous Affairs (IWGIA), Doc. No.127, Copenhagen, 2009, pp.314-343, p.316.

116 On this, see the extensive and excellent work of Rodríguez Piñero-Royo, "'Where Appropriate': Monitoring/Implementing of Indigenous Peoples' Rights Under the Declaration"; in particular, see the tables comparing the rights enshrined in the UNDRIP and in other treaties at pp.320-322 and pp.324-327.

More recently, the first (United Nations) World Conference on Indigenous Peoples (WCIP) was held in New York between 22 and 23 September 2014, as per Resolution No.65/198 of the General Assembly in 2010.[117] The aims of this high-level plenary meeting of the General Assembly was to share best practices and perspectives on the application of indigenous rights, including the UNDRIP.[118] During its 69th session, the GA adopted the draft resolution discussed during the WCIP held on 22-23 September.[119] In the

---

117 General Assembly, "Indigenous issues", Resolution No. 65/198, UN Doc. A/RES/65/198, 3 March 2011.

118 *Ibid.*, para.8, p.2. Prior to this conference, a preparatory conference was held from 8 to 13 June 2013 in Alta (Norway). As according to the outcome of the 10th Permanent Forum on Indigenous Issues, the conference was hosted by the Sami Parliament of Norway and organized in cooperation with the Global Indigenous Coordination Group for the World Conference (GCG). UN Permanent Forum on Indigenous Issues, "Report on the tenth session", Economic and Social Council Official Records, 2011, Supplement No. 23, UN Docs. E/2011/43 and E/C.19/2011/14, 16-27 May 2011, para.125, p.21. The GCG was established in January 2012 by a resolution of the "Indigenous Peoples' Brainstorming Meeting on the World Conference on Indigenous Peoples 2014" held in Copenhagen. UN World Conference on Indigenous Peoples, "About the Global Coordinating Group", at http://wcip2014.org/background/gcg [Last access 13.10.2014]. The Outcome Document of this preparatory conference was presented to the General Assembly in a Letter signed by the Permanent Missions to the United Nations of Bolivia, Denmark, Finland, Guatemala, Mexico, New Zealand, Nicaragua, Norway and Peru in mid-September 2013. This document was the result of a global consultation process involving representatives of indigenous peoples worldwide and set forth themes and recommendations for the World Conference. General Assembly, "Letter dated 10 September 2013 from the Permanent Representatives of the Plurinational State of Bolivia, Denmark, Finland, Guatemala, Mexico, New Zealand, Nicaragua, Norway and Peru to the United Nations addressed to the Secretary-General", UN Doc. A/67/994, 13 September 2013. The recommendations were organized in the following thematic
subdivisions: Indigenous peoples' lands, territories, resources, oceans and waters; United Nations system action for the implementation of the rights of indigenous peoples; Implementation of the rights of indigenous peoples; and Indigenous peoples' priorities for development with free, prior and informed consent. The General Assembly took note of the Outcome Document in February 2014. General Assembly, "Rights of indigenous peoples", Resolution No.68/149, UN Doc. A/RES/68/149, 12 February 2014, para.2, p.4. Even with a subsequent misunderstanding regarding the organization of the conference, which was blocked by a letter of the GCG requiring more direct participation on the part of indigenous peoples and equal standing with the States, the WCPI was finally held on the scheduled dates (22-23 September 2014).

119 General Assembly, "Outcome document of the high-level plenary meeting of the General Assembly known as the World Conference on Indigenous Peoples", UN Doc. A/RES/69/2, 22 September 2014, based on the General Assembly, "Draft

document, the States, among others, reaffirm their support for the UNDRIP and their commitment to protect, promote and advance the rights of indigenous peoples, in particular to consult indigenous peoples and obtain their Free, Prior and Informed Consent (FPIC; see chapter 3),[120] to encourage other States to ratify the ILO Convention 169,[121] to ensure equal access to high-level education facilities for indigenous children, and in general; to guarantee access to health, housing, water, sanitation, and other economic and social programmes.[122]

The outcome of the WCIP appears particularly promising. Instead of remaining only a statement, concrete actions followed recently. In particular, a report was published in May 2015 on the progress made after the adoption of the resolution.[123] This report contains information that was collected at the last UNPFII of 2015 and from a questionnaire circulated to member States and indigenous organizations.[124] In short, the main goals that should be achieved in the short-term are the following: (1) The implementation of National Actions Plans,[125] and (2) of a "system-wide action plan" to effectively apply the UNDRIP standards;[126] (3) the reform of the EMRIP by

resolution submitted by the President of General Assembly. Outcome document of the high-level plenary meeting of the General Assembly known as the World Conference on Indigenous Peoples", UN Doc. A/69/L.1, 15 September 2014.

120 General Assembly, "Draft resolution submitted by the President of General Assembly ...", paras.3-4.

121 *Ibid.*, para.6.

122 *Ibid.*, para.11.

123 General Assembly and Economic and Social Council, " Progress made in the implementation of the outcome document of the high-level plenary meeting of the General Assembly known as the World Conference on Indigenous Peoples, Report of the Secretary-General", UN Doc. A/70/84-E/2015/76, 15 May 2015.

124 General Assembly and Economic and Social Council, " Progress made in the implementation of the outcome document ...", para.4.

125 General Assembly, "Outcome document of the high-level plenary meeting ...", para.8; General Assembly and Economic and Social Council, " Progress made in the implementation of the outcome document ...", paras.5-12.

126 General Assembly, "Outcome document of the high-level plenary meeting ...", para.31; General Assembly and Economic and Social Council, " Progress made in the implementation of the outcome document ...", paras.13-22, and, in particular para.17 on the working group established within the Inter-Agency Support Group on Indigenous Peoples' Issues (see *infra*) to work on such "system-wide action plan" and that is meeting on a biweekly basis since January 2015.

strengthening its work and impact;[127] an improved participation of indigenous peoples and their organizations in the UN bodies.[128] Finally, the Special Rapporteur on the Rights of Indigenous Peoples Victoria Tauli-Corpuz stressed the necessity to meliorate the coordination of the actions of the UN bodies regarding indigenous rights.[129]

Another recent development, following the eleventh session of the UNPFII of 2012, regards the study on an optional protocol to the UNDRIP "on a potential voluntary mechanism to serve as a complaints body at the international level, in particular for claims and breaches of indigenous peoples' rights to lands, territories and resources at the domestic level".[130] Such study was submitted to the UNPFII during its thirteenth session in 2014.[131] The authors (Dalee Sambo Dorough and Megan Davis, both members of the UNPFII), gathering the outcomes of years of discussion, recommended that a mechanism providing such a complaint procedure should be: Voluntary at the request of the concerned parties (States or indigenous peoples); confined to the provisions of the UNDRIP and to conflicts or contentious issues specifically regarding lands, territories and resources; negotiated through extensive dialogue between the parties on mutually agreed terms; and composed of experienced international lawyers.[132] An expert group meeting on the "Dialogue on an optional protocol to the United Nations Declaration on the Rights of Indigenous Peoples" was held in February 2015.[133] Among

127 General Assembly, "Outcome document of the high-level plenary meeting ...", para.28; General Assembly and Economic and Social Council, " Progress made in the implementation of the outcome document ...", paras.23-33. On these three points, see also the recent statement of the Special Rapporteur on the Rights of Indigenous Peoples Victoria Tauli-Corpuz, "Statement to the 8th session of the EMRIP. Follow up to the World Conference on Indigenous Peoples", 20 July 2015, at http://unsr.vtaulicorpuz.org/site/index.php/en/statements/74-emrip-2015-follow-wcip [Last access 03.08.2015].

128 General Assembly and Economic and Social Council, " Progress made in the implementation of the outcome document ...", paras.34-50.

129 Tauli-Corpuz, "Statement to the 8th session of the EMRIP ...".

130 UN Permanent Forum on Indigenous Issues, "Report on the eleventh session (7-18 May 2012)", Economic and Social Council Official Records, Supplement No. 23, UN Docs . E/2012/43-E/C.19/2012/13, 2012, para 109.

131 UN Permanent Forum on Indigenous Issues, "Study on an optional protocol to the United Nations Declaration on the Rights of Indigenous Peoples focusing on a voluntary mechanism", UN Doc. E/C.19/2014/7, 4 March 2014.

132 UN Permanent Forum on Indigenous Issues, "Study on an optional protocol to the United Nations ...", para.48.

133 UN Permanent Forum on Indigenous Issues, "Expert group meeting on the theme 'Dialogue on an optional protocol to the United Nations Declaration on the Rights of Indigenous Peoples'", UN Doc. E/C.19/2015/8, 17 February 2015.

their conclusions, they also pointed at the EMRIP as a potential oversight body.[134] The outcomes of both the WCIP and this expert meeting were, *inter alia*, objects of further discussion during the 2015 session of the UNPFII.[135]

Among the general human rights treaties, the Convention on the Elimination of All Forms of Racial Discrimination adopted in 1965 has proved to be of particular importance for the protection of indigenous peoples. Besides the monitoring cycle on the implementation of the convention's rights by States parties, the Committee on the Elimination of Racial Discrimination (CERD) may undertake early-warning procedures, and examine interstate complaints as well as individual complaints.[136] On indigenous rights more specifically, General Recommendation No.23 of 18 August 1997 on "Indigenous Peoples" served to ensure the actions of the CERD in cases of discrimination against indigenous peoples.[137]

Also the work of the UN Inter-Agency Support Group on Indigenous Peoples' Issues has been particularly crucial. This is a network of more than 40 UN entities that primarily supports the UNPFII and aims to foster agency cooperation regarding indigenous peoples and their rights.[138]

---

134 UN Permanent Forum on Indigenous Issues, "Expert group meeting on the theme …", paras.50-53.

135 UN Permanent Forum on Indigenous Issues, "Report on the fourteenth session (20 April-1 May 2015)", Economic and Social Council Official Records, Supplement No. 23, UN Docs. E/2015/43-E/C.19/2015/10, 2015.

136 For instance, in the last years, the CERD had sent letters, the first step of the early warning procedure to Brazil, Chile, Colombia, Costa Rica, El Salvador, Panama, Paraguay and Peru all essentially concerning indigenous peoples or afro-descendants. See Committee on the Elimination of Racial Discrimination, "Early-Warning Measures and Urgent Procedures", at http://www.ohchr.org/EN/HRBodies/CERD/Pages/EarlyWarningProcedure.aspx [Last access 23.02.2015].

137 This Recommendation states: "[…] [T]he Committee has consistently affirmed that discrimination against indigenous peoples falls under the scope of the Convention and that all appropriate means must be taken to combat and eliminate such discrimination […]". Committee on the Elimination of Racial Discrimination (CERD), "Indigenous Peoples", General Recommendation No.23, UN Doc. A/52/18, Annex 5, 18 August 1997.

138 For further information, see United Nations Inter-Agency Support Group on Indigenous Peoples' Issues, "Inter-Agency Support Group", at http://undesad-spd.org/IndigenousPeoples/InterAgencySupportGroup.aspx [Last access 24.08.2015]. Among such entities, the Special Rapporteur on the Rights of Indigenous Peoples Victoria Tauli-Corpuz recently praised the work of the International Fund for Agricultural Development (IFAD). Tauli-Corpuz, "Statement to the 8th session of the EMRIP …". See also International Fund for Agricultural Development, "Indigenous peoples", at http://www.ifad.org/english/indigenous/index_full.htm [Last access 24.08.2015].

Finally, among other international organizations, the World Bank has been working with indigenous peoples since the 1970s. After the well-known case of the indigenous protest against the Chico River Dam Project in the Philippines, it adopted, *inter alia*, Operational Directive 4.20 on Indigenous Peoples in 1982, followed by Operational Policy 4.10 in 1991, and the Indigenous Peoples Policy (OP/BP 4.10) in 2005, which was recently revised.[139]

1.3 Indigenous peoples' land dispossession and recent evolutionary jurisprudence

Albeit in different ways and at different times, many indigenous peoples have suffered dispossession of their lands. Two international law doctrines have, among others, played a role in legitimizing these processes. The *terra nullius* principle (in Latin, literally 'nobody's land') derived from Roman law which originally referred to a territory beyond the Roman imperial borders not, or no longer, belonging, to anybody, or not, or no longer, subject to any sovereignty.[140] As for indigenous peoples, in the notorious case of the colonization of Australia, the British settlers took control of the whole island based on the legal fiction provided by this principle.[141] This concept was also assumed in the colonization of Africa after the Berlin Conference

---

139 World Bank, Indigenous Peoples Policy (OP/BP 4.10), revised in April 2013, at http://web.worldbank.org/WBSITE/EXTERNAL/PROJECTS/EXTPOLICIES/EXTOPMANUAL/0,,contentMDK:20553653~menuPK:4564185~pagePK:64709096~piPK:64709108~theSitePK:502184,00.html [Last access 23.02.2015]. On an overview of the World Bank's actions vis-à-vis indigenous peoples see Sia Spiliopoulou Akermark, "The World Bank and Indigenous Peoples", in Nazila Ghanea and Alexandra Xanthaki (eds.), *Minorities, Peoples and Self-Determination,* Brill, Leiden, 2005, pp.93-112; Fergus MacKay, "The Draft World Bank Operational Policy 4.10 on Indigenous Peoples: Progress or More of the Same?", 22(1) *Arizona Journal of International & Comparative Law* 2005, pp.65-98; and the most recent article of Camilo Pérez-Bustillo, "The Counter-Hegemonic Origins and Potential of Human Rights: the Rights of Indigenous Peoples and the World Bank as a Case Study", in Roxanne Dunbar-Ortiz et al. (eds.), *Indigenous Peoples' Rights in International Law: Emergence and application. Book in Honor of Asbjørn Eide at Eighty*, Gáldu and IWGIA, Kautokeino, Copenhagen, Gáldu Čála serie No.2/2015, 2015, pp.470-486.

140 Charles Geisler, "New *Terra Nullius* Narratives and the Gentrification of Africa's 'Empty Lands'", 28(1) *Journal of World Systems Research* 2012, pp. 15-29, p.18.

141 Jérémie Gilbert, *Indigenous Peoples' Land Rights under International Law: From Victims to Actors*, Transnational Publishers, Ardesely, 2006, p.29.

in 1884-1885,[142] as well as that of New England (USA).[143] Although some indigenous peoples had concluded a number of treaties or agreements with the colonizers, territorial rights were generally considered valid solely within a state-run order.[144] Moreover, many indigenous peoples (particularly in the Americas and Australia), did not crop or farm the land, and many were nomads. The following assumption was that indigenous peoples did not have any control over the land and thus no ownership rights, as per the influence of the writings of John Locke, Sir William Blackstone, and even the more indigenous-friendly Jean-Jacques Rousseau.[145] The Creoles' emancipation in Latin America in early 1800 (see also chapter 4) showed a first implicit rejection of this principle. In 1823, the (US President) Monroe Doctrine further claimed that the American continents were no longer to be considered as subjects for future colonization.[146] However, during the decolonization of the Americas, indigenous peoples were never considered capable of any "effective occupation" of the land.[147] Therefore, the territory inhabited by indigenous peoples was often considered *terra nullius*, and they were dispossessed of their lands. Nowadays, the *terra nullius* doctrine has been rejected in both the national and the international spheres. In 1975, the International Court of Justice in the *Western Sahara* case recognized the fictitious nature of this principle,[148] stating that the territory was indeed inhabited by indigenous peoples, and that Spanish colonizers had concluded earlier agreements with a clear social and political organization (the indigenous peoples), thus the land was not *terra nullius*.[149] However, only the

---

142 Gilbert, *Indigenous Peoples' Land Rights under International Law …*, p.27.

143 Colin Samson, "The Rule of *Terra Nullius* and the Impotence of International Human Rights for Indigenous Peoples", *Essex Human Rights Review* Vol. 5 No. 1, July 2008, pp.1-12, p.4.

144 Gilbert, *Indigenous Peoples' Land Rights under International Law…*, p.26.

145 Samson, "The Rule of *Terra Nullius* and …", pp.4-5; Geisler, "New *Terra Nullius* Narratives and …", p.18.

146 Gilbert, *Indigenous Peoples' Land Rights under International Law…*, pp-30-31.

147 *Ibid.*, p.33.

148 International Court of Justice, *Western Sahara*, Advisory Opinion, 16 October 1975, ICJ Reports 1975, p.12, paras.82-83.

149 Xanthaki, *Indigenous Rights and United Nations Standards*, pp.243-244; Gilbert, *Indigenous Peoples' Land Rights under International Law…*, p.28; Siegfried Wiessner, "Indigenous Sovereignty: A Reassessment in Light of the UN Declaration on the Rights of Indigenous Peoples", 41 *Vanderbilt Journal of Transnational Law* 2008, pp.1141-1176, p.1154.

Mabo cases of the early 1990s finally contributed to the authoritative rejection of this principle.[150] In the second case (*Mabo and Others v. Queensland*, No.2, 1992) the indigenous Meriam people claimed the right to their land.[151] By asserting that the Meriam people had been substantially dispossessed of their traditional lands, the Australian High Court granted them a "native title" over the land. Importantly, the Court stated that this title had not expired when the Imperial Crown took control over the country in 1879.[152]

The *uti possidetis* doctrine operated after 1810 in the "decolonization" of Latin America promoted by the Creoles and then during the decolonization period following the Second World War, particularly in Africa.[153] This notion (also derived from Roman law) referred to the ancient litigations on ownership of a real property (*uti possidetis, ita possideatis*, i.e. "as you possess, so you may possess").[154] In the two contexts of decolonization, it essentially meant to "leave the place as one received it".[155] After the Latin American case, this principle was used to secure boundaries at the time of colonies' independence, in accordance with the ICJ in the *Frontier Dispute* case, *Burkina Faso v. Mali*.[156] Indigenous peoples' claims over their homelands were thus denied as per the *uti possidetis* principle and combined with "Blue or Salt Water Thesis" (see also chapter 2, section 2.1.2). As to the former, the national boundaries at the time of independence were to be respected. As to the latter, the term 'colonies' (those territories entitled to independence) was only to be applied to those countries or peoples divided from their colonizers by "salt water".[157]

Recently, an increasing and impressive jurisprudence on indigenous peoples' right to land, particularly that developed by the Inter-American Court

150 Nevertheless, some commentators have argued that the principle is still in use in the case, for instance, of the current rush for land acquisition in Africa. See Geisler, "New *Terra Nullius* Narratives and …", pp.19-24, Samson, "The Rule of *Terra Nullius* and …", pp.6-11, and also Andrew Fitzmaurice, "The genealogy of Terra Nullius", 38(129) *Australian Historical Studies* 2007, pp.1-15.

151 High Court of Australia, *Mabo and Others v. Queensland (No. 2)*, 175 CLR 1 F.C. 92/014, 3 June 1992, at http://www.austlii.edu.au/au/cases/cth/HCA/1992/23.html [Last access 23.02.2015].

152 High Court of Australia, *Mabo and Others v. Queensland (No. 2)*, para.82.

153 Wiessner, "Indigenous Sovereignty: A Reassessment …", p.1150; Gilbert, *Indigenous Peoples' Land Rights under International Law…*, pp.36-37.

154 Gilbert, *Indigenous Peoples' Land Rights under International Law…*, p.36.

155 Wiessner, "Indigenous Sovereignty: A Reassessment …", p.1150.

156 International Court of Justice, *Frontier Dispute* (*Burkina Faso v. Mali*), Judgment, 22 October 1986, ICJ Reports 1986, p.554, para.23.

157 Gilbert, *Indigenous Peoples' Land Rights under International Law…*, pp.35-36.

of Human Rights, has significantly contributed to the promotion and recognition of indigenous peoples' land rights. In particular, the Awas Tigni people of Nicaragua claimed a lawful demarcation of their land based on art.5.3 of the Nicaraguan Constitution (*Mayangna (Sumo) Awas Tingni v. Nicaragua*).[158] The Inter-American Court of Human Rights in 2001 recognized, *inter alia*, their collective right to land within the general property right stated in art.21 of the Inter-American Convention of Human Rights.[159] This decision has been confirmed by the jurisprudence of the Inter-American Court of Human Rights in the following cases: *Comunidad Yakye Axa v. Paraguay* (2005); *Comunidad Indígena Sawhoyamaxa v. Paraguay* (2006); *Comunidad Indígena Xákmok Kásek v. Paraguay* (2010); *Saramaka People v. Suriname* (2007); and *Kichwa Ingenous People of Sarayaku v. Ecuador* (2012).[160]

Additionally, in 2010, the African Commission on Human and Peoples' Rights adopted another landmark decision on indigenous land rights (*Centre for Minority Rights Development (Kenya) and MRG on behalf of Endorois Welfare Council v. Kenya*).[161] The African Commission recognized the right of the Endorois people of Kenya –evicted from their land in the late 1970s– to ownership of their ancestral land and recommended that

158 Inter-American Court of Human Rights, *Comunidad Mayagna (Sumo) Awas Tingni Community v. Nicaragua*, Serie C No. 79, Judgment of 31 August 2001.

159 Inter-American Court of Human Rights, *Comunidad Mayangna (Sumo) Awas Tingni v. Nicaragua*, para.148, which states: "Through an evolutionary interpretation of international instruments for the protection of human rights, taking into account applicable norms of interpretation and pursuant to article 29(b) of the Convention -which precludes a restrictive interpretation of rights-, it is the opinion of this Court that article 21 of the Convention protects the right to property in a sense which includes, among others, the rights of members of the indigenous communities within the framework of communal property, which is also recognized by the Constitution of Nicaragua".

160 Inter-American Court of Human Rights, *Comunidad Yakye Axa v.* Paraguay, Serie C No.125, Judgement of 17 June 2005; Inter-American Court of Human Rights, *Comunidad Indígena Sawhoyamaxa v. Paraguay*, Serie C No.146 Judgement of 29 March 2006; Inter-American Court of Human Rights, case of *Comunidad Indígena Xákmok Kásek v. Paraguay*, Serie C No.214, Judgement of 24 August 2010; Inter-American Court of Human Rights, *Saramaka People v. Suriname*, Serie C No.172, Judgment of 28 November 2007; Inter-American Court of Human Rights, *Kichwa Ingenous People of Sarayaku v. Ecuador*, Serie C No.245, Judgment of 27 June 2012. See also chapter 4, section 4.2.

161 African Commission on Human and Peoples Rights, *Centre for Minority Rights Development ("CEMIRIDE") (Kenya) and Minority Rights Group International on behalf of Endorois Welfare Council v. Kenya (Endorois case)*, Communication No.276/2003, 4 February 2010.

Kenya return their land to them. Moreover, the African Commission found that the rights to religion, property, culture, natural resources, fair compensation, and development enshrined in the African Charter (arts.8, 14, 17, 21 and 22) had also been violated.[162]

This evolutionary jurisprudence thus shows that indigenous peoples' rights to land have recently enjoyed wider recognition that is guaranteed not only by the ILO Convention 169 (arts.13-19)[163] and the UNDRIP (see, e.g., arts.26 and 29),[164] but also by landmark decisions by regional human rights courts. It needs to be finally specified that the right to land of indigenous peoples is a broad concept. Indigenous peoples' traditional vision and attachment to an area of land imply a range of rights far beyond the mere right to property. This concept has been introduced explicitly in ILO Convention 169, art.13, which states that the term "land", in the Convention, "shall include the concept of territories, which covers the total environment of the areas, which the peoples concerned occupy or otherwise use". Nevertheless, as will be discussed below in chapter 2, section 2.2.6, indigenous peoples' land rights, which are of utmost importance, will be considered in this work as a corollary of the concept that will be proposed later as the *composite right to political participation of indigenous peoples*, but not as elements of it. Consequently, they require no further discussion here.

162 African Commission on Human and Peoples Rights, *Endorois case*, Recommendations, p.80, para.1.

163 ILO Convention 169 devoted the second part of the treaty to land rights. The provisions dealing with Indigenous peoples' land rights comprise several aspects: Ownership: Rights to land ownership, possession and/or traditionally occupied, including the obligation of the State to safeguard the lands traditionally accessed by indigenous peoples, especially nomadic and shifting peasants (art.14.1). Demarcation: Duty of the State to demarcate traditionally occupied lands ("steps necessary to identify...") (art.14.2). Natural resources: States' obligation to safeguard indigenous peoples' rights to natural resources, and right to participate in the use, management and conservation of such resources (art.15.1), excluded the sub-surface resources if retained by the State (art.15.2). Relocation and compensation: (although, general) Prohibition of relocation (art.16.1), free and informed consent prior to removal (art.16.2), right to return (art.16.3), and right to compensation (art.16.4 & 5).

164 The UNDRIP, *inter alia*, recognizes the the right to land territories and resources owned, occupied, used or acquired (art.26); and the right to conservation and the protection of the environment; states' obligation to take effective measures to avoid storage of hazardous material without indigenous peoples' free, prior and informed consent (art.29).

2. Self-determination and Indigenous Peoples

2.1 The debated concept of and right to self-determination

Self-determination in international law, as widely known, is extremely complex. It has been (and still is) extensively debated both in theoretical terms and in its multiple and potential applications. Through the different phases of its conceptualization and recognition, self-determination was referred to initially as a sole principle of international law and, later, fully recognized as a right, when it was finally introduced in both article 1 of the International Covenant on Civil and Political Rights (ICCPR) and the International Covenant on Economic, Social and Cultural Rights (ICESCR).[165] As highlighted by Thürer and Burri, self-determination was then given "the characteristic of a fundamental human right, or, more accurately, that of a source or essential prerequisite for the existence of individual human rights, since these rights could not genuinely be exercised without the realization of the–collective–right to self-determination".[166]

Therefore, the concept (principle and right) of self-determination in international law will be briefly introduced here. This introduction to self-determination is essential in order to present the set of problems that arise when approaching indigenous peoples' right to self-determination (see following section 2.2). In particular, despite the clear interconnections, self-determination will be tackled in general terms without referring (too often) to

165 Christian Tomuschat, "Self-Determination in a Post-Colonial World", in Christian Tomuschat (ed.), *Modern Law of Self-Determination*, Dordrecht, Nijhoff, 1993, pp.1-20, p.2; Hurst Hannum, "Rethinking Self-Determination", 34 *Virginia Journal of International Law* 1, 1993-1994, 1994, pp.1-69, p.31; Antonio Cassese, *Self-determination of Peoples. A Legal Reappraisal*, Cambridge University Press, Cambridge, New York, 1995, p.323; Anthony Whelan, "Wilsonian Self-Determination and the Versailles Settlement", 43 *International and Comparative Law Quarterly* 1994, pp.99-115, p.103. The pronouncement of UK during the session of the Security Council on 25 May 1982 is exemplary. Despite their earlier statement regarding self-determination as a sole principle in the 1960s, the UK had, by that time –i.e. the early 1980s– endorsed that self-determination is a right. Cited by Robert McCorquodale, "Self-Determination: A Human Rights Approach", in 43 *International and Comparative Law Quarterly*, 1994, 857-885, p.860, note 19.

166 Daniel Thürer and Thomas Burri, "Self-Determination", in *Max Planck Encyclopedia of Public International Law*, para.10, 2008, Oxford Public International Law, at http://opil.ouplaw.com/home/epil [Last access 27.10.14].

minorities or indigenous peoples. The content and the implications of the right to self-determination of indigenous peoples will be dealt with separately in section 2.2.4. Thus, after briefly exploring the developments of self-determination (sections 2.1.1), particularly after the creation of the UN (section 2.1.2), this section aims to address its legal conceptualization (sections 2.1.3-2.1.4) and to consider the most crucial aspects of self-determination (section 2.1.5). The recent developments in international law regarding the theories of the Responsibility to Protect and the theory of Remedial Secession are also shortly addressed (section 2.1.6). In fact, recent and crucial events (e.g., the secessions of East Timor in 2002, Kosovo in 2008 and of South Sudan in 2010, the recent secessionist movements in Catalonia and in Scotland, the developments in New Caledonia and the annexation of Crimea to the Russian Federation in 2014) have created renewed interest on self-determination among the general public and are challenging traditional principles of international law such as the prohibition of interference/non-intervention and the principle of territorial integrity.[167] Hence, the situations of Scotland, Catalonia and New Caledonia are briefly presented since these are the latest cases in which the population will be or has been called to vote in (very different) referenda to decide upon their "self-determination" (section 2.1.7).

167 As is widely known, the former principle is one of the most significant elements of the Grotian Society, or traditional model of international law and, together with the principle of sovereign equality, implies that States shall respect the fundamental prerogatives of the other members of the international community. In particular, this principle is enshrined in specific customary rules, namely that a State shall refrain from interfering in the internal organization or influencing the internal affairs of another State, or instigating, organizing or officially supporting activities that are prejudicial to other States. Antonio Cassese, *International Law*, Oxford University Press, Oxford, New York, Second Edition, 2005, p.53. With regard to the Grotian Society/traditional vs. Kantian/modern models of international law see Cassese, *International Law*, p.21. The principle of territorial integrity is enshrined in the UN Charter in art.2.4: "All Members shall refrain in their international relations from the threat or use of force against the territorial integrity or political independence of any state, or in any other manner inconsistent with the Purposes of the United Nations". Having concluded that the unilateral Declaration of Independence of Kosovo 17 February 2008 did not violate international law since it was not connected with the unlawful use of force or other egregious violations of *jus cogens*, the International Court of Justice has also recently stated that "[t]he scope of the principle of territorial integrity is confined to the sphere of relations between States". International Court of Justice, *Accordance with International Law of the Unilateral Declaration of Independence in Respect of Kosovo,* Advisory Opinion, 22 July 2010, ICJ Reports 2010, p.403, paras.80-81, and 122.

2.1.1 Brief overview of developments surrounding self-determination

It is broadly accepted that self-determination finds its origins in both the American Declaration of Independence (1776) and the French Revolution (1789).[168] In the former case it referred to the "consent of the governed", and in the latter case to a renunciation of conquest and subsequent annexation to France, in principle, only after holding a plebiscite.[169] Nationalist movements interpreted self-determination in the 19th and beginning of the 20th century as a way of constituting their own States. In accordance with the "principle of nationalities", only "nationally homogenous" States were considered legitimated.[170] Later, as is widely known, the conceptualization of and support for self-determination amongst socialists, including Lenin and Stalin, were based on the pursuit of the socialist political philosophy. For his part, the US President Woodrow Wilson championed the principle of self-determination in 1918.[171]

Wilsonian self-determination derived from the concept of popular sovereignty in the framework of Western democratic theory and was thus equal to the American "consent of the governed", i.e., "the right of peoples freely to choose their government".[172] Wilson, therefore, focused on "[t]he right

---

168 Thürer and Burri, "Self-Determination", para.1; Whelan, "Wilsonian Self-Determination and the Versailles Settlement", p.99; Cassese, *Self-determination of Peoples*, p.11; Joshua Castellino, *International Law and Self-determination*, Martinus Nijhoff Publishers, Leiden, Boston, 2000, p.8. James Crawford, "The Right to Self-Determination in International Law", in Philipp Alston, *Peoples' Rights*, Oxford University Press, 2001, pp.7-67, p.7. See Castellino, *International Law and Self-determination*, note 5, p.8, for references of other works whose authors coincide in tracing the origins of self-determination to the two revolutions. However, Anaya stresses that, apart from the Western thought on self-determination, different Asian and African conceptualizations on self-determination can be observed in the concurring opinion of Judge Ammoun in the *Namibia* case before the International Court of Justice (*Advisory Opinion on the Legal Consequences for States of the Continued Presence of South Africa in Namibia (South West Africa) notwithstanding Security Council Resolution 276 (1970)*, Advisory Opinion, 21 June 1971, ICJ Reports of 1971). Anaya James, *Indigenous Peoples in International Law*, Oxford University Press, New York, Oxford, 1996, p.76 and note 9.

169 Thürer and Burri, "Self-Determination", para.1; Cassese, *Self-determination of Peoples*, pp.11-12.

170 Thürer and Burri, "Self-Determination", para.2. On self-determination and nationalism see note 282.

171 Thürer and Burri, "Self-Determination", paras.3-4; Cassese, *Self-determination of Peoples*, p.19.

172 Cassese, *Self-determination of Peoples*, p.19.

freely to select State authorities and political leaders", i.e., "self-government".[173] This aspect of self-determination has been classified as "internal self-determination" in the later literature.[174]

The peace negotiations of the First World War were formally based on his proposal, but self-determination was far from being fully applied.[175] The concept proposed by Wilson was certainly indeterminate and not thought out for "universal" applications.[176] Wilson was in fact criticized.[177] He himself almost regretted having taken such a strong stance, as expressed in a speech to the Senate Committee of Foreign Relations on 19 August 1919.[178] Thus, although Wilson paid great attention to issues of *Realpolitik*, especially in the 11 February 1918 speech,[179] he was unable to pursue his ideas in the international arena, naively believing that under the League of Nations, the imperialist order would turn into a new, liberal one.[180] He also proposed the inclusion of self-determination in the final text of the Covenant of the League of Nations, but his proposal was eventually rejected.[181]

---

173 *Ibid.*

174 Patrick Thornberry, "The Democratic or Internal Aspect of Self-Determination with some remarks on federalism", in Christian Tomuschat (ed.), *Modern Law of Self-Determination*, Dordrecht, Nijhoff, 1993, pp.101-138, p.101. See section 2.1.4.

175 Thürer and Burri, "Self-Determination", para.4.

176 Wilson himself declared that self-determination, e.g., was not applicable to the USA. Cassese, *Self-determination of Peoples*, note 34 p.23. See also Hannum, "Rethinking Self-Determination", p.3.

177 Secretary of State Robert Lansing criticized Wilson soon after in a note of 20 December 1918 underlining the vagueness of his concept. Cassese, *Self-determination of Peoples*, p.22 and note 31. See also the bitter criticism of Jennings, who stated: "Nearly forty years ago, a Professor of Political Science, who was also President of the United States, President Wilson, enunciated a doctrine which was ridiculous, but which was widely accepted as a sensible proposition, the doctrine of self-determination. On the surface, it seemed reasonable: let the people decide. It was in fact ridiculous, because the people cannot decide until someone decides who are the people". Ivor Jennings, *The Approach to Self-Government*, 1956, pp.55-56, as cited as *incipit* by Whelan, "Wilsonian Self-Determination and the Versailles Settlement", p.99. See *infra*.

178 Cassese, *Self-determination of Peoples*, p.22, note 33.

179 Hannum, "Rethinking Self-Determination", p.4.

180 Cassese, *Self-determination of Peoples*, pp.22-23. Wilson also admitted that he did not expect such a wide echo of his words. Cassese, *Self-determination of Peoples*, p.22, note 33.

181 Hannum, "Rethinking Self-Determination", p.7; Cassese, *Self-determination of Peoples*, pp.23 and 27; Castellino, *International Law and Self-determination*, p.18.

Nevertheless, the rhetoric of self-determination had an effect within the League of Nations.[182] An indirect recognition of the principle of self-determination was embodied by the system of the Mandates according to art.22 of the Covenant of the League of Nations.[183] This system, however, offered paternalistic protection (or territorial control) that had little to do with the "consent of the governed".[184] However, the Aaland Islands case that came before the League of Nations[185] represented a cornerstone in the conceptualization of the principle of self-determination. In particular, three points made by the Commission of Jurists and Commission of Rapporteurs or of Inquiry need to be highlighted here. First, the relationship between self-determination and the protection of minorities was debated by the Commission of Jurists, which found common ground and a shared objective between the two concepts, i.e., to "assure to some national Group the maintenance and free development of its social, ethnical or religious characteristics".[186] Second, despite arguing that the systems of minority protection

182 Thürer and Burri, "Self-Determination", para.4; Cassese, *Self-determination of Peoples*, p.27.

183 Thürer and Burri, "Self-Determination", para.4; Hannum, "Rethinking Self-Determination", p.6.

184 For a critical analysis, see Michael D. Callahan, *Mandates and Empire: The League of Nations and Africa, 1914-1931*, Sussex Academic Press, Eastbourne, 2008, 2nd edition.

185 Located in a strategic position in the Baltic Sea, since 1157 the Aaland Islands remained under Swedish control for centuries before being ceded –together with current Finland– by Sweden to Russia in 1809, according to the Treaty of Frederiksham. After the Russian Revolution, Finland declared its independence in December 1917. The Aaland Islanders rejected the initial offers of autonomy from Finland with the Autonomy Law of 7 May 1920. Finland, in turn, refused to hold a plebiscite, although more than 90% of the population was of Swedish descent. Thus, the question of whether the Aaland Islands should remain with Finland or rejoin Sweden was brought by the United Kingdom before the Council of the League of Nations as a threat to international peace under art.11 of the Covenant. The Commission of Jurists was first appointed to explore whether the matter was of international or purely domestic concern. Afterwards, having adopted the Jurists' view according to which the League of Nations was competent in this case, the Commission of Rapporteurs or of Inquiry was established to recommend how to solve the matter and issued its report in April 1921. This Commission recommended enhancing the guarantees to Aaland Islanders granted by the aforementioned Autonomy Law of 7 May 1920. Hannum, "Rethinking Self-Determination", pp.8-10; Cassese, *Self-determination of Peoples*, pp.28-29; Castellino, *International Law and Self-determination*, p.19.

186 League of Nations, *Report presented to the Council…*, p.6, as cited by Cassese, *Self-determination of Peoples*, p.30 and note 56.

were the sole rational solution for safeguarding both groups and the territorial integrity of the States, both Commissions found that, in some cases, this protection could be considered insufficient, e.g., in cases of oppression and persecution of a group perpetrated by the State.[187] While the Commission of Jurists stated that, in such cases, the matter would acquire an international dimension, the Commission of Rapporteurs or of Inquiry included the possibility of the "separation" of one minority from the State as an exceptional solution ("a last resort").[188] Finally, it is also relevant to underline that the Commission of Jurists clearly identified that the principle of self-determination ("to determine their political fate") could be applied in a number of ways.[189] According to the Commission, the most relevant means were independence ("the formation of an independent State") or annexation ("the right of choice between two existing States").[190]

Nevertheless, no "general right" of self-determination may be said to have arisen in the First World War period,[191] although it was considered to be a relevant political postulate,[192] as confirmed by the Commission of Jurists in the Aaland Islands case.[193] It was invoked on many occasions during the Second World War and proclaimed in the Atlantic Charter in 1941,[194]

187 League of Nations, *Report presented to the Council...*, p.28, as cited by Cassese, *Self-determination of Peoples*, p.31 and note 58.

188 League of Nations, *Report presented to the Council...*, p.28, as cited by Whelan, "Wilsonian Self-Determination and the Versailles Settlement", p.104, Cassese, *Self-determination of Peoples*, note 58 at p.31, and Castellino, *International Law and Self-determination*, p.20. Nevertheless, this was not the case of the Aaland Islands, since they "have never been persecuted nor oppressed by Finland", while Finland was previously occupied by Russia. Thus, it was recognized that the Aalanders were a distinct group from the Finnish population and they deserved fully-fledged protection, which could be provided by Finland. League of Nations, *Report presented to the Council...*, pp.28-29, as cited by Cassese, *Self-determination of Peoples*, p.31-32 in note 58.

189 "Report of the International Committee of Jurists Entrusted by the Council of the League of Nations with the Task of Giving an Advisory Opinion upon the Legal Aspects of the Aaland Islands Question", *Official Journal of the League of Nations*, Special Supplement No.3, October 1920, p.6, as cited by Cassese, *Self-determination of Peoples*, p.30, note 56.

190 *Ibid.*

191 Whelan, "Wilsonian Self-Determination and the Versailles Settlement", p.103; Cassese, *Self-determination of Peoples*, pp.26-27.

192 Tomuschat, "Self-Determination in a Post-Colonial World", p.1; Cassese, *Self-determination of Peoples*, p.27.

193 "Report of the International Committee of Jurists...",, pp.5-6, 21 and ff., as cited by Cassese, *Self-determination of Peoples*, pp.28-29 and notes 48 and 52; Hannum, "Rethinking Self-Determination", p.9.

194 Thürer and Burri, "Self-Determination", para.5.

which in turn had considerable influence over the work on the UN Charter.[195]

2.1.2 United Nations and Self-Determination

After the Second World War, one the main applications of self-determination consisted in the right to decolonization of those peoples living in territories administered by colonial States.[196] However, this was not the initial intention of the drafters of UN Charter.[197] The "principle" of self-determination was specifically inserted twice in the UN Charter, in arts.1.2 and 55.[198] In this way it was with the specific aim of enhancing friendly relations among States and in conjunction with the principle of equal rights.[199] In fact, according to the drafters' intentions the enunciation inserted in the UN Charter was to be narrowed down to mere "self-government",[200] as is also suggested by the insertion of the provisions in Chapters XI and XII of the UN Charter.[201] In addition, the guarantee of territorial integrity, i.e., the prohibition of partial or total interference by a threat of or the actual use of force against the territorial integrity or political independence of any state, is enshrined in art.2.4 of the UN Charter. Thus, its mere incorporation in the Charter, whilst extremely relevant, did not imply per se that the recognition

195 *Ibid.*, para.6.

196 Tomuschat, "Self-Determination in a Post-Colonial World", p.1; Whelan, "Wilsonian Self-Determination and the Versailles Settlement", p.110; Crawford, "The Right to Self-Determination in International Law", p.39; and Cassese, *Self-determination of Peoples*, p.74. There are an impressive number of studies on the UN and the decolonization process. For references, see Cassese, *Self-determination of Peoples*, p.74, note 15.

197 Cassese, *Self-determination of Peoples*, p.44.

198 Art.1.2 of the UN Charter states: "[The Purposes of the United Nations are] [t]o develop friendly relations among nations based on respect for the principle of equal rights and self-determination of peoples, and to take other appropriate measures to strengthen universal peace"; and art.55: "With a view to the creation of conditions of stability and well-being which are necessary for peaceful and friendly relations among nations based on respect for the principle of equal rights and self-determination of peoples […]".

199 Hannum, "Rethinking Self-Determination", p.11; Thürer and Burri, "Self-Determination", para.6.

200 Cassese, *Self-determination of Peoples*, p.42.

201 Chapters XI and XII of the UN Charter deal with the Non-Self-Governing Territories and the International Trusteeship System, respectively. See particularly arts.73 and 76, which, according to Thürer and Burri, contain an implicit reference. Thürer and Burri, "Self-Determination", para.6.

of self-determination was legally binding.[202] The events of the following decades are however evidence of its application.[203]

The anti-colonialist movement gained momentum at the first large-scale Afro-Asian Conference in Bandung (Indonesia) in 1955, where colonialism in all its forms was condemned.[204] Western States were against a postulate of self-determination as decolonization for obvious colonial interests, and, instead, supported the universality of the principle while focusing on its internal dimension of self-determination (i.e., self-government).[205] Moreover, the potential "dangers" of a broader application of this right to non-colonial territories, e.g., to minorities, was stressed.[206] In the early 1950s, Belgium had claimed that several States were administering territories inhabited by culturally and linguistically diverse peoples and not governed by "ordinary law". This is known as the "Belgian Thesis". How territories such as those of the Nagas people in India, or the "tribal" areas in the Philippines, would be excluded from the application of Chapter XI on Non-Self-Governing Territories was indeed unclear.[207] The Belgian Thesis pointed at "underdeveloped groups", which faced similar problems to colonized peoples.[208] The potentiality of this thesis, i.e., of a hypothetical universality of the principle of self-determination, was largely ignored. The aim was rather to "limit the damages" of upcoming decolonization, i.e., limiting the number of "new" States.[209] The General Assembly eventually rejected this thesis and opted to recognize the former colonial borders, in combination with the *uti possidetis* doctrine and the Blue or Salt Water theory (see chapter 1, section 1.3).

202 Thürer and Burri, "Self-Determination", para.8.

203 Tomuschat, "Self-Determination in a Post-Colonial World", p.1.

204 Cassese, *Self-determination of Peoples*, p.44. See also the Final Communiqué of the Asian-African conference of Bandung (24 April 1955) at http://franke.uchicago.edu/Final_Communique_Bandung_1955.pdf [Last access 28.04.2013].

205 Cassese, *Self-determination of Peoples*, pp.46-47. See also Hannum, "Rethinking Self-Determination", p.21 and ff.

206 Hannum, "Rethinking Self-Determination", pp.23-25; Cassese, *Self-determination of Peoples*, p.53.

207 Thornberry, *Indigenous Peoples and Human Rights*, pp.92-93.

208 For the thesis, see the document "Replies of Governments Indicating their Views on the Factors to be Taken into Account in Deciding Whether a Territory is or is not a Territory Whose Peoples have not yet Attained a Full Measure of Self-Government to the Ad Hoc Committee of Factors (Non-Self-Governing Territories), UN Doc. A/AC.67/2, 8 May 1953, pp.3-31 as cited by Thornberry, *Indigenous Peoples and Human Rights*, p.93, note 27.

209 Thornberry, *Indigenous Peoples and Human Rights*, p.93.

Two UN Resolutions –No.1514 ("Declaration on the granting of independence to colonial countries", adopted on 14 December 1960 by the UN General Assembly),[210] and No.1541 ("Principles which should guide Members in determining whether or not an obligation exists to transmit the information called for under Article 73 of the Charter", adopted by the UN General Assembly the day after, on 15 December 1960)[211]– made possible the application of self-determination as a "quasi-legal principle", more widely accepted in the context of decolonization.[212] By that time, events such as the liberation of large countries (e.g., India) from the colonial yoke paved the way for a broader acceptance of the "determination by the peoples of the world".[213]

Importantly, Resolution No.1514 contained the first (official) enunciation of self-determination as a right (of all peoples) that was expressed in the same words in both Covenants (ICCPR and ICESCR), as follows: "All peoples have the right of self-determination; By virtue of that right they freely determine their political status and freely pursue their economic, social and cultural development".[214]

Resolution No.1541 provided the UN members with a list of principles for the application of Chapter XI of the UN Charter (Declaration Regarding Non-Self-Governing Territories).[215] In particular, Principle VI of Resolution 1541 states the three cases in which "self-government" meaning –although not explicitly– "self-determination",[216] can be considered achieved: "(a) Emergence as a sovereign independent State; (b) Free association with an independent State; or (c) Integration with an independent State". The

210 General Assembly Resolution No.1514(XV) adopted on 14 December 1960 during the 947th plenary meeting, XV session. As cited by Castellino, this resolution was passed by 89 votes in favor, 0 abstentions and 9 votes against (in alphabetical order: Australia, Belgium, Dominican Republic, France, Portugal, Spain, South Africa, United Kingdom, United States of America), Castellino, *International Law and Self-determination*, p.22, note 64.

211 General Assembly Resolution No.1541(XV) adopted on 15 December 1960 during the 948th plenary meeting, XV session.

212 Castellino, *International Law and Self-determination*, p.22; Cassese, *Self-determination of Peoples*, p.70.

213 Castellino, *International Law and Self-determination*, p.22 and Resolution No.1514, first paragraph of the Preamble.

214 Resolution No.1514, clause no.2.

215 Thürer and Burri, "Self-Determination", para.9.

216 *Ibid.* and Castellino, *International Law and Self-determination*, p.28.

following Principles VII, VIII and IX explain further what "free association" and "integration with an independent State" imply.[217] Furthermore, Principles IV and V specify the cases in which the obligation to transmit information under art.73.e of the UN Charter exists,[218] i.e., as *prima facie* when the Non-Self-Governing Territory is "geographically separate and is distinct ethnically and/or culturally from the country administering it", but also whenever the territory concerned would be in a position or status of subordination vis-à-vis the administering State due to other elements of administrative, political, juridical, economic or historical nature. This is important to note here in co-relation to the international customary norm of

217 Principles VII, VIII and IX of Resolution No.1541 state: "*Principle VII*: (a) Free association should be the result of a free and voluntary choice by the peoples of the territory concerned expressed through informed and democratic processes. It should be one which respects the individuality and the cultural charac-teristics of the territory and its peoples, and retains for the peoples of the territory which is associated with an independent State the freedom to modify the status of that territory through the expression of their will by democratic means and through constitutional processes. (b) The associated territory should have the right to determine its internal constitution without outside interference, in accordance with due constitutional processes and the freely expressed wishes of the people. This does not preclude consultations as appropriate or necessary under the terms of the free association agreed upon; *Principle VIII*: Integration with an independent State should be on the basis of complete equality between the peoples of the erstwhile Non-Self-Governing Territory and those of the independent country with which it is integrated. The peoples of both territories should have equal status and rights of citizenship and equal guarantees of fundamental rights and freedoms without any distinction or discrimination; both should have equal rights and opportunities for representation and effective participation at all levels in the executive, legislative and judicial organs of government. *Principle IX*: Integration should have come about in the following circumstances: (a) The integrating territory should have attained an advanced stage of self-government with free political institutions, so that its peoples would have the capacity to make a responsible choice through informed and democratic processes; (b) The integration should be the result of the freely expressed wishes of the territory's peoples acting with full knowledge of the change in their status, their wishes having been expressed through informed and democratic processes, impartially conducted and based on universal adult suffrage. The United Nations could, when it deems it necessary, supervise these processes".

218 Art.73.e affirms: "[Members of the United Nations which have or assume responsibilities for the administration of territories [...] [have the] obligation to [...]]: e. to transmit regularly to the Secretary-General for information purposes, subject to such limitation as security and constitutional considerations may require, statistical and other information of a technical nature relating to economic, social, and educational conditions in the territories for which they are respectively responsible other than those territories to which Chapters XII and XIII apply".

Blue or Salt Water and its effects on indigenous peoples (see chapter 1, section 1.3).

Leaving aside for a moment the formulation of the right to self-determination in the two Covenants of 1966, which will be analyzed in section 2.1.3, mention must also be made of Resolution No.2625 "Declaration on Principles of International Law Friendly Relations and Co-operation among States in Accordance with the Charter of the United Nations" adopted on 24 October 1970 by the General Assembly (hereinafter, 1970 Declaration).[219] As is well-known, this resolution is of utmost importance in International Law and was fundamental in crystallizing the consensus over self-determination, beyond its colonial applications.[220] Notably, the 1970 Declaration recognized the codification of seven principles, including the principle of "[...] equal rights and self-determination of peoples",[221] which is developed in detail.[222] In particular, by using the same wording of the two Covenants, the 1970 Declaration poses a duty onto States to enhance the realization of self-determination of peoples, in two ways: a) by promoting friendly relations and cooperation among States; and b) by bringing an end to colonialism with due regard to the will of the peoples concerned. In addition, the 1970 Declaration confirms that, although indirectly, alien subjugation, domination and exploitation constitute a violation of self-determination. Finally, it establishes different ways of implementing the right to self-determination, by (1) the establishment of sovereign and independent States, (2) the free association or integration with existing States, or (3) "the emergence into any other political status freely determined by a people".[223] This last point is of particular importance, since it released the potential for

219 UN General Assembly Resolution No.2625(XXV), "Declaration on Principles of International Law Friendly Relations and Co-operation among States in Accordance with the Charter of the United Nations", adopted on 24 October 1970 by the General Assembly during its 1883rd plenary meeting of the XXV session, UN Doc. A/RES/25/2625.

220 Thürer and Burri, "Self-Determination", para.23; Cassese, *Self-determination of Peoples*, p.70.

221 1970 Declaration, Preamble, letter e) of the second from last paragraph. In the Preamble, at the 14th paragraph, it is also stated that: "[...]Convinced that the principle of equal rights and self-determination of peoples constitutes a significant contribution to contemporary international law, and that its effective application is of paramount importance for the promotion of friendly relations among States, based on respect for the principle of sovereign equality, [...]".

222 1970 Declaration, paragraph "The principle of equal rights and self-determination of peoples".

223 *Ibid.*

other forms of implementation of self-determination.[224] These measures, however, remain subject to the supremacy of the principles of territorial integrity and the national or political unity of the (existing) States, as explicitly recalled by the 1970 Declaration. According to the study by Héctor Gros Espiell, commissioned to analyze the concrete cases of implementation of the UN resolutions,[225] between 1945 and 1979 seventy States gained independence,[226] and between 1979 and the mid-1990s a further seven States followed.[227]

---

224 Cassese, *Self-determination of Peoples*, p.70, Crawford, "The Right to Self-Determination in International Law", p.31 and Castellino, *International Law and Self-determination*, p.36. One may think that the notable division into external and internal self-determination can be traced back to the 1970 Declaration. However, as documented by Cassese, this distinction is to be found already in the works of Wengler in 1957. See section 2.1.4.

225 Héctor Gros Espiell, Special Rapporteur of the Sub-Commission on the Prevention of Discrimination and Protection of Minorities of the Commission on Human Rights, *The Right to Self-Determination. Implementation of the UN Resolutions*, United Nations, New York, 1980, para 23. The other relevant study, previously commissioned but published later, is that carried out by Aureliu Cristescu, Special Rapporteur of the Sub-Commission on the Prevention of Discrimination and Protection of Minorities of the Commission on Human Rights, *The Right to Self-Determination. Historical and Current Development in the basis of the United Nations Instruments*, United Nations, New York, 1981. As Gros Espiell explains in his report, "[Cristescu] analyzed the development of the basic concepts involved in self-determination, whilst [Gros Espiell's] study [deals] mainly with concrete problems and specific situations in relation to the implementation of the United Nations resolutions". Gros Espiell, *The Right to Self-Determination. Implementation of the UN Resolutions*, para 23.

226 Gros Espiell, *The Right to Self-Determination. Implementation of the UN Resolutions*, as cited by Cassese, *Self-determination of Peoples*, p.75.

227 Rhodesia/Zimbabwe, Belize, Brunei, Saint Cristofer and Nevis, Saint Lucia, Saint Vincent and the Grenadines, Namibia. Cassese, *Self-determination of Peoples*, p.75, note 18. Cassese specifies that the cases of South Africa and Israel were not included in the study and he also reports of unsolved situations such as East Timor, Gibraltar, Falklands/Malvinas and Western Sahara. Cassese, *Self-determination of Peoples*, pp.75-76. More recently, as mentioned in the Introduction 2.1, the secessions of East Timor, Kosovo, and South Sudan gave rise to these new States, despite the fact that some are not yet recognized by other States (e.g., Spain has not recognized the independence of Kosovo).

2.1.3 The right to self-determination in the Covenants and the position of the Human Rights Committee

As is widely known, article 1 of both the ICCPR and the ICESCR states as follows:

> "1. All peoples have the right of self-determination. By virtue of that right they freely determine their political status and freely pursue their economic, social and cultural development.
>
> 2. All peoples may, for their own ends, freely dispose of their natural wealth and resources without prejudice to any obligations arising out of international economic co-operation, based upon the principle of mutual benefit, and international law. In no case may a people be deprived of its own means of subsistence.
>
> 3. The States Parties to the present Covenant, including those having responsibility for the administration of Non-Self-Governing and Trust Territories, shall promote the realization of the right of self-determination, and shall respect that right, in conformity with the provisions of the Charter of the United Nations."[228]

This is the result of twenty-six meetings of the Third Committee of the General Assembly.[229] This explains why it took eleven years to conclude the formulation,[230] although it basically did not vary from the version originally adopted in 1955.[231] As stated by the Human Rights Committee (HRC) in its General Comment No.12,[232] the reason why the right to self-determination was set forth in both articles 1 of ICCPR and ICESCR is because of its importance since "its realization is an essential condition for the effective

228 See the text of the International Covenant on Civil and Political Rights (ICCPR) at http://www.ohchr.org/en/professionalinterest/pages/ccpr.aspx, and of the International Covenant on Economic, Social and Cultural Rights (ICESCR) at http://www.ohchr.org/EN/ProfessionalInterest/Pages/CESCR.aspx [Last access 01.07.2014].

229 Hannum, "Rethinking Self-Determination", p.22. Each article of the Covenants was reconsidered one by one during the decade after the initial adoption in 1955. *Ibid.*

230 *Ibid.*, p.19.

231 The very minor differences between the original formulation adopted in 1955 and the one inserted in both the Covenants are the substitution of "the" with "all" at the beginning of the second paragraph and the opening phrase in the third paragraph ("The States Parties to the present Covenant") which was originally "All the States Parties to the Covenant". *Ibid.*, note 89 at p.23.

232 Human Rights Committee, General Comment No.12, "Article 1 (The Right to self-determination of peoples"), adopted during its twenty-first session, 13 March 1984, UN Doc. HRI/GEN/1/Rev.9 (Vol. I). It is relevant to underline here that, as mentioned by the same Human Rights Committee, States were reluctant to report in accordance with art.40 on the application of this right. This also prompted the adoption of this General Comment. See para 3.

guarantee and observance of individual human rights and for the promotion and strengthening of those rights".[233] Furthermore, self-determination is an "inalienable right of all peoples" that "imposes on all States parties corresponding obligations".[234] It is thus fundamental to analyze each paragraph of this article.

2.1.3.1 Article 1.1 and the link with the political rights

The first paragraph refers to those "constitutional and political processes which in practice allow the exercise of this right".[235] Thus, although this paragraph also contains economic (as well as social and cultural) aspects (see further below in section 2.1.3.2), the initial paragraph links self-determination particularly with civil and political rights.[236] Consequently, this provision needs to be read in combination with the civil and political rights recognized in the ICCPR, namely freedom of expression (art.19); the right to peaceful assembly (art.21); the right to freedom of association (art.22); the right to vote (art.25b); and, more broadly, to take part in public affairs (art.25a).[237] This connection, however, also has potential flaws.[238] In other words, the risk of linking self-determination to these (individual)[239] rights may suggest the subordination of self-determination to the derogation contained in art.4.1 of the ICCPR.[240] In addition, the vague formulation of the above-mentioned civil and political rights may leave too much discretion to

233 Human Rights Committee, General Comment No.12, "Article 1 (The Right to self-determination of peoples"), para.1.

234 *Ibid.*, para.2.

235 *Ibid.*, para.4.

236 Cassese, *Self-determination of Peoples*, p.52-53.

237 *Ibid.*, p.53. See also chapter 3, section 3.1.

238 *Ibid.*

239 Cassese refers to civil and political rights as just individual rights, but some of them can be exercised solely in a collective way (e.g., the right to freedom of association). Verstichel Annelie, *Participation, Representation and Identity*, Intersentia, Antwerp, Oxford, Portland, 2009, p.96. See also chapter 3, section 3.2.1.

240 Cassese, *Self-determination of Peoples*, p.53. Art.4.1 of the ICCPR states: "In time of public emergency which threatens the life of the nation and the existence of which is officially proclaimed, the States Parties to the present Covenant may take measures derogating from their obligations under the present Covenant to the extent strictly required by the exigencies of the situation, provided that such measures are not inconsistent with their other obligations under international law and do not involve discrimination solely on the ground of race, colour, sex, language, religion or social origin". Thus, nowadays this should also be balanced with the Responsibility to Protect (see section 2.1.7).

the States which may misapply the right to self-determination.[241] Notwithstanding these loopholes, the correlation between self-determination and civil and political rights implies that these rights are incorporated into the right to self-determination. Consequently, States' decision-making processes need to be examined in order to verify whether the right to self-determination has been rightly implemented.[242] Moreover, "a key right to self-determination is the right to participate democratically in the political system to which you belong, and to participate in decisions as to its future".[243] Likewise, the HRC underlined that the duty to report under art.40 ICCPR also applied to art.1, not only to electoral laws or similar norms.[244]

More broadly, the HRC stated in its General Comment No.12 that "[t]his right and the corresponding obligations concerning its implementation are interrelated with other provisions of the Covenant and rules of international law".[245] Thus, on the one hand, other rights may be considered as expressions of the right to self-determination (e.g., the above-mentioned civil and political rights, or autonomy or FPIC in the case of indigenous peoples, see chapter 3, section 3.3). However, on the other hand, this assumption has also led the HRC to limit the complaint procedure under the Optional Protocol to the International Covenant on Civil and Political Rights (hereinafter, ICCPR-OP1)[246] to the sole rights set forth in the third part of ICCPR (arts.6-27, included), preventing itself from considering any alleged violation of art.1.[247] In the first case in which a violation of art.1 was alleged, *Mikmaq v. Canada* (1984), the HRC avoided making an announcement on the matter. It found that the complaint was inadmissible because of a lack

241 Cassese, *Self-determination of Peoples*, p.54.

242 *Ibid.*

243 Crawford, "The Right to Self-Determination in International Law", p.25.

244 Human Rights Committee, General Comment No.12, "Article 1 (The Right to self-determination of peoples"), para.3.

245 *Ibid.*, para.2.

246 Optional Protocol to the International Covenant on Civil and Political Rights, which was adopted on 16 December 1966 by General Assembly resolution 2200A (XXI) and entered into force on 23 March 1976.

247 Sarah Joseph, Jenny Schultz and Melissa Castan, *The International Covenant on Civil and Political Rights: Cases, Materials, and Commentary*, Oxford University Press, Oxford, New York, 2000, p.100.

of *locus standi* of the representative of the applicant (the Mikmaq tribal society).[248] In the following widely-known case *Lubicon Lake Band v. Canada* (1990), the HRC more explicitly stated:

> "While all peoples have the right of self-determination and the right freely to determine their political status, pursue their economic, social and cultural development and dispose of their natural wealth and resources, as stipulated in article 1 of the Covenant, the question whether the Lubicon Lake Band constitutes a 'people' is not an issue for the Committee to address under the Optional Protocol to the Covenant. *The Optional Protocol provides a procedure under which individuals can claim that their individual rights have been violated. These rights are set out in part III of the Covenant, articles 6 to 27, inclusive.* There is, however, no objection to a group of individuals, who claim to be similarly affected, collectively to submit a communication about alleged breaches of their rights" [emphasis added]. [249]

This self-restraint attitude of the HRC to address alleged collective violations of art.1 is reflected in its later jurisprudence.[250] Thus, despite the duty of States to report on the application of art.1, according to art.40 ICCPR, as mentioned, the HRC has not yet accepted self-determination to be a justifiable right *per se*. However, it underlined that art.1 is relevant for the *interpretation* of other rights proclaimed in the ICCPR, and particularly of arts.25, 26 and 27.[251] Indeed, the position of the HRC in procedural terms does not imply that the right to self-determination is not a legal right under

248 Human Rights Committee, *Mikmaq v. Canada*, Communication No. 78/1980 (30 September 1980), Views adopted on 29 July 1984, UN Doc. Supp. No.40 (A/39/40), 1984.

249 Human Rights Committee, *Lubicon Lake Band v. Canada*, Communication No. 167/1984, Views adopted on 26 March 1990, UN Doc. Supp. No. 40 (A/45/40) 1990, para 32.1.

250 See, e.g., *Ivan Kitok v. Sweden*, Communication No. 197/1985, Views adopted on 27 July 1988, UN Doc. CCPR/C/33/D/197/1985 (1988); *Vid. Marshall et al v. Canada,* Communication No. 205/1986, Views adopted on 4 November 2006, UN Doc. CCPR/C/43/D/205/l986, 1991; *E.P. et al v. Colombia,* Communication No. 318/1988, Views adopted on 25 July 1990, UN Doc. CCPR/C/39/D/318/1988 (1990); and more recently, *Apirana Mahuika et al v. New Zealand,* Communication No. 547/1993, Views adopted on 20 October 2000, UN Doc. CCPR/C/70/D/547/1993 (2000); *J.G.A. Diergaardt (late Captain of the Rehoboth Baster Community) et al. v. Namibia*, Communication No. 760/1997, Views adopted on 25 July 2000, UN Doc. CCPR/C/69/D/760/1997 (2000).

251 Arts. 25, 26 and 27 ICCPR affirm the political rights, the prohibition of any form of discrimination and the rights of minorities to enjoy their own culture, to profess and practice their own religion, or to use their own language. See also chapter 3, section 3.2.1. Among the cases in which the HRC links art.1 and these rights, see the above-mentioned *Apirana Mahuika et al v. New Zealand* and *J.G.A. Diergaardt (late Captain of the Rehoboth Baster Community) et al. v. Namibia*.

the ICCPR,[252] which is confirmed by the requirement of the HCR to report on this right in accordance with its General Comment No.12.[253]

In addition, in the case *Gillot et al v. France* (2002)[254] on alleged violations of arts.25 and 26 ICCPR vis-à-vis the criteria used to identify the electorate to vote for the self-determination referenda in New Caledonia,[255] the HRC affirmed that a self-determination process may justify the application of more restrictive criteria to the right to vote.[256] In this case, the criteria mainly concerned the place of birth and the number of years of residence in New Caledonia (that had to be more than 20), which the applicants did not fulfil and consequently claimed violations of arts.25 and 26. Leaving aside the case itself, it is relevant to underline here that the HRC found the criteria not to be discriminatory but justified in relation to art.1. In particular, the HRC affirmed that:

> "Without expressing a view on the definition of the concept of 'peoples' as referred to in article 1, the Committee considers that, in the present case, it would not be unreasonable to limit participation in local referendums to persons 'concerned' by the future of New Caledonia who have proven sufficiently strong ties to that territory. The Committee notes, in particular, the conclusions of the Senior Advocate-General of the Court of Cassation, to the effect that in *every self-determination process limitations of the electorate are legitimized by the need to ensure a sufficient definition of identity*" [emphasis added].[257]

In other words, in a self-determination process, instrumental measures such as limiting the electorate, may prevail over other rights recognized in the ICCPR. This case thus suggests an application of the right to self-determination by the HRC, at least with regard to, and prevailing over, other political rights. This would ultimately confirm that, according to the HRC, the right to self-determination is broader than political rights.

---

252 Martin Scheinin, "The Right to Self-Determination under the Covenant on Civil and Political Rights", in Pekka Aikio and Martin Scheinin (eds.), *Operationalizing the Rights of Indigenous Peoples to Self-Determination*, Institute for Human Rights, Åbo Akademi University, Saarijärvi, 2000, pp.179-198, p.180.

253 Scheinin, "The Right to Self-Determination under the Covenant on Civil and Political Rights", p.188. See Human Rights Committee, General Comment No.12, "Article 1 (The Right to self-determination of peoples"), para.3.

254 Human Rights Committee, *Ms. Marie-Hélène Gillot et al. v. France*, Communication No. 932/2000, Views adopted on 15 July 2002, UN Doc. A/57/40, 2002.

255 See section 2.1.7.

256 Human Rights Committee, *Ms. Marie-Hélène Gillot v. France*, para 13.16.

257 *Ibid.*

2.1.3.2 Article 1.2 and the right of peoples over natural wealth and resources

This paragraph has often been referred to as "economic self-determination".[258] In its General Comment No.12, the HRC itself stated that "[p]aragraph 2 affirms a particular aspect of the economic content of the right of self-determination".[259] Recently, however, some authors have stressed that economic (and social and cultural) aspects of self-determination are also present in paragraph 1,[260] and that these elements and the political aspect of self-determination are indivisible.[261] Moreover, separating these two elements would imply the denial of each other. The full exercise of "political" self-determination implies taking decisions over economic, social, and cultural matters. Vice versa, a people cannot use its economic resources or decide upon its social and cultural affairs without the possibility of taking decisions over them.[262] The right of peoples over natural wealth and resources follows from the right to choose their own government included in the first paragraph. In fact, a people do not only have the right to choose whom should govern them, but also to demand the chosen government to use the territorial resources for the benefit of all the people.[263]

Another natural consequence is the corresponding duty upon the government to use the resources for the interest of the people concerned.[264] Therefore, ensuring the State's compliance of this right becomes particularly crucial, but it is extremely difficult for peoples to control their States in these matters.[265] States are required by the ICCPR to report on any obstacle that

258 Gudmundur Alfredsson, "Different Forms of and Claims to the Right of Self-Determination", in Donald Clark and Robert Williamson, *Self-Determination. International Perspectives*, MacMillan Press, HoundsMill, Basingstoke and London, 1996 and St. Martin's Press, New York, 1996, pp.58-85, p.74; Alexandra Xanthaki, "The Right to Self-Determination: Meaning and Scope", in Nazila Ghanea and Alexandra Xanthaki (eds.), *Minorities, Peoples and Self-Determination*, Brill, 2005, pp.15-33, p.27.

259 Human Rights Committee, General Comment No.12, "Article 1 (The Right to self-determination of peoples"), para.5.

260 Ben Saul, David Kinley, and Jacqueline Mowbray, *The International Covenant on Economic, Social and Cultural Rights. Commentary, Cases, and Materials*, Oxford University Press, Oxford, 2014, p.56.

261 Saul, Kinley and Mowbray, *The International Covenant on Economic, Social and Cultural Rights*, p.59.

262 *Ibid.*

263 Cassese, *Self-determination of Peoples*, p.55.

264 *Ibid.*, p.56.

265 *Ibid.*

inhibits the free disposal of natural wealth and resources as well as the enjoyment of other rights recognized in the Covenant.[266] However, for instance, a State may concede the control over natural resources to a foreign private company,[267] as often happens,[268] or favor a limited group of beneficiaries.[269] Both these cases would constitute breaches of art.1.2.[270] For instance, the Committee on Economic, Social and Cultural Rights (CESCR)[271] found that the privatization process of Azerbaijan's oil resources in 1997 did not comply with public information, participation, and transparency in accordance with art.1.[272] Notwithstanding the fact that this right implies duties upon both States and the wider International Community,[273] the free disposition of natural wealth and resources presents a major limitation, that is the respect for international treaties or agreements regarding economic cooperation.[274] As abuses may easily occur and pressure from foreign investments takes over, this article needs to be read in conjunction

---

266 Human Rights Committee, General Comment No.12, "Article 1 (The Right to self-determination of peoples"), para.5.

267 Cassese, *Self-determination of Peoples*, p.56.

268 See, e.g., the cases before the Inter-American Court of Human Rights including *Saramaka People v. Suriname* (2007), and *Kichwa Ingenous People of Sarayaku v. Ecuador* (2012) in chapter 3, section 3.3.2.3.

269 Cassese, *Self-determination of Peoples*, p.56. It is worth mentioning here that one may argue that giving land rights to indigenous peoples may infringe art.1.2, but this is irrelevant given the past discrimination and losses suffered by such peoples and should therefore be balanced not only with art.47 of the ICCPR as will be mentioned, but also with the rights contained in the International Covenant on the Elimination of All Forms of Discriminations (ICERD).

270 Cassese, *Self-determination of Peoples*, p.56.

271 The Committee on Economic, Social and Cultural Rights (CESCR), established under United Nations Economic and Social Council (ECOSOC) Resolution No.1985/17 of 28 May 1985, was charged with monitoring functions of ECOSOC of part IV of ICESCR. On 5 May 2013, the Optional Protocol to the International Covenant on Economic, Social and Cultural Rights adopted on 10 December 2008, UN Doc. A/63/435, entered into force three months after the tenth instrument of ratification or accession as according to its art.18. Since then, CESCR may also receive individual complaints in accordance with arts.1 and 2 of the Optional Protocol to the International Covenant on Economic, Social and Cultural Rights.

272 Committee on Economic, Social and Cultural Rights, Concluding Observations on Azerbaijan, UN Doc. E/C.12/1/Add.20, 22 December 1997, as cited by Saul, Kinley and Mowbray, *The International Covenant on Economic, Social and Cultural Rights*, p.67.

273 Human Rights Committee, General Comment No.12, "Article 1 (The Right to self-determination of peoples"), para.5.

274 Cassese, *Self-determination of Peoples*, p.56. This was a particular concern of industrialized States.

with both art.47 of the ICCPR,[275] which guarantees at least a fair compensation to the peoples concerned,[276] and art.25 of the ICESCR,[277] especially after the entry into force of the Optional Protocol to the International Covenant on Economic, Social and Cultural Rights.[278]

2.1.3.3 Article 1.3 and the full exercise of the right to self-determination

The third paragraph imposes a general duty on States to guarantee the full exercise of this right not only vis-à-vis their own peoples, but also to all those peoples that have been deprived of the possibility to exercise it.[279] In other words, "[t]he obligations exist irrespective of whether a people entitled to self-determination depends on a State party to the Covenant or not. It follows that all States parties to the Covenant should take positive action to facilitate realization of and respect for the right of peoples to self-determination".[280] Obviously, such measures must be consistent with other obligations descending from both the UN Charter and international law more broadly, particularly vis-à-vis the prohibition of interference in other States' internal affairs,[281] excluded the cases in which today the Responsibility to Protect (R2P) should prevail (see section 2.1.6).

275 Art.47 of the ICCPR states: "Nothing in the present Covenant shall be interpreted as impairing the inherent right of all peoples to enjoy and utilize fully and freely their natural wealth and resources".

276 Cassese, *Self-determination of Peoples*, p.57.

277 Art.25 of the ICESCR affirms: "Nothing in the present Covenant shall be interpreted as impairing the inherent right of all peoples to enjoy and utilize fully and freely their natural wealth and resources".

278 On the entry into force of the Optional Protocol to the International Covenant on Economic, Social and Cultural Rights see previous note 271.

279 Human Rights Committee, General Comment No.12, "Article 1 (The Right to self-determination of peoples"), para.6. In particular, the HRC also states that "The general nature of this paragraph is confirmed by its drafting history" (para.6).

280 Human Rights Committee, General Comment No.12, "Article 1 (The Right to self-determination of peoples"), para.6.

281 *Ibid.*

2.1.4 Legal conceptualizations of self-determination

This paragraph aims to give an overview of the mainstream legal conceptualization of self-determination, namely the well-known dichotomy of external-internal self-determination, its limits, and other alternative classifications, particularly with regard to indigenous peoples.[282]
The classification that distinguishes between an external and an internal dimension of self-determination is certainly the best known in legal studies. The consensus over this dichotomy is widely accepted, although it is not codified.[283] This distinction has been authoritatively and extensively argued

282 The author is conscious that there have been extensive debates both in legal theory and in political science on self-determination, particularly in reference to the relations between self-determination and nationalism. This section focuses on the legal aspects of the dichotomy between external and internal self-determination and the implications of this dichotomy over the right to self-determination of indigenous peoples. Therefore, suffice it to briefly mention here two of the best-known analyses as well as another recent one. In his book of 1979, Ronen argued that self-determination is essentially an ongoing quest and (until that time) it appeared in (at least) five different manifestations, which also represent five types of quests for self-determination dominant in different periods, as follows: "mid-nineteenth century European national self-determination; late-nineteenth century Marxist class self-determination; post-World War I Wilsonian minorities' self-determination; post-World War II non-European/racial self-determination; and contemporary [in the 1970s] ethnic self-determination". Dov Ronen, *The Quest for Self-Determination*, Yale University Press, New Haven and London, 1979, pp.25-26. Koskenniemi singled out two models of self-determination, namely the classical or Hobbesean one, and the secessionist one. In the former concept, nations are artificial communities, i.e., collections of individuals who are linked mainly by a State decision-procedure. The latter, instead, built upon rousseauian ideas, looks at nationhood as something more fundamental than purely decision-making processes, i.e., something that was lost in the political struggles that led to the formation of a State and that must be referred to in order to escape modern States' legitimation crisis. Martti Koskenniemi, "National Self-Determination Today: Problems of Legal Theory and Practice", 43 *International and Comparative Law Quarterly*, 1994, pp.241-269, pp.249-250. Finally, Summers has recently argued that "the law of self-determination is the product of the interaction between nationalism and international law". Thus, although international law and nationalism are different doctrines, they are connected since the State is fundamental to both of them. Therefore, nationalism occupies a central position in international law and, thus, in self-determination. James Summers, "The Right of Self-Determination and Nationalism in International Law", 12 *International Journal on Minority and Group Rights* 2005, pp.325-354, p.328 and 353.

283 Helen Quane, "The UN Declaration on the Rights of Indigenous Peoples: New Directions for Self-Determination and Participatory Rights?", in Stephen Allen

by Cassese, but can already be found in the works of Wengler in 1957,[284] and, *inter alia*, was also taken up by Lombardi in 1976.[285] Hence, in line with the 1970 Declaration, external self-determination refers to the right to freely determine their international status, i.e., to form a new State or integrate or associate to another,[286] not only in the case of colonial peoples but also other peoples subject to foreign domination or occupation.[287] Internal self-determination, for its part, represents "the right to authentic self-government, that is, the right for a people really and freely to choose its own political and economic regime – which is much more than choosing among what is on offer perhaps from one political or economic position only. It is an ongoing right".[288] Among other scholars, McCorquodale affirmed that external self-determination was mainly applied to colonial situations and the subsequent States' international –thus external– relations. As to the methods for applying external self-determination, he referred to GA Resolution No.1541 (and also the 1970 Declaration), i.e., the emergence of a new independent sovereign State, free association or integration with another State.[289] Moreover, the author specifies that, according to Resolution No.1541, independence or secession are not necessarily implied as the sole means of exercising the right to self-determination and that, in all cases, especially those involving colonial peoples, a consultation with the people concerned should be carried out.[290] Internal self-determination, for its part, is based on the need to have a government that represents the whole population according to the 1970 Declaration and thus regards the "internal" relations of a State, i.e., the right of a people "to choose their political status, the extent of their political participation and the form of government".[291] Danspeckgruber refers to external self-determination as the right of a community or a State to sovereignty and independent external relations while

and Alexandra Xanthaki (eds.), *Reflections on the UN Declaration on the Rights of Indigenous Peoples*, Hart Publishing, Oxford, Portland, 2011, 259-287, p.260.

284 W. Wengler, "Le droit à la libre disposition des peuples comme principe de droit international", 10 *Revue hellénique de droit international*, 1957, p.27, and W. Wengler, *Völkerrecht*, Volume 2, Berlin, 1964, pp.1032-33, as cited by Cassese, *Self-determination of Peoples*, p.70, note 6.

285 A.V. Lombardi, *Bürgerkrieg und Völkerrecht*, Berlin, 1976 as cited by Cassese, *Self-determination of Peoples*, p.70, note 6.

286 Quane, "The UN Declaration on the Rights of Indigenous Peoples ...", p.260 and Cassese, *Self-determination of Peoples*, p.90.

287 Cassese, *Self-determination of Peoples*, p.90.

288 *Ibid.*, p.101.

289 McCorquodale, "Self-Determination: A Human Rights Approach", p.863.

290 *Ibid.*, p.864.

291 *Ibid.*

internal self-determination is "the possibility to democratically elect the leadership and to develop the domestic politics and national institutions of a state".[292]

The first document that recognized this dichotomy explicitly was the Final Act of the Conference on Security and Cooperation in Europe concluded in August 1975 in Helsinki. The Final Act contained the principle of equal rights and self-determination of peoples among the principles guiding the relations between participating States.[293] In particular, after recognising the right to self-determination in conformity with the UN Charter and other norms of international law, including those related to the territorial integrity of States, it stated: "By virtue of the principle of equal rights and self-determination of peoples, all peoples always have the right, in full freedom, to determine, when and as they wish, their *internal and external political status*, without external interference, and to pursue as they wish their political, economic, social and cultural development" [emphasis added].[294]

While the "external" dimension referred particularly to the independence of colonial peoples at that time –as confirmed by the ICJ in the *Namibia* case in 1970[295] and by the yearly resolutions of the UN general Assembly from 1970 onwards–[296] self-determination as "self-administration", i.e. the

292 Wolfgang Danspeckgruber, "Introduction", in Wolfgang Danspeckgruber (ed.), *The Self-Determination of Peoples. Community, Nation and State in an Interdependent World*, Lynne Rienner Publishers, Boulder, London, in association with the Liechtenstein Institute on Self-Determination, Princeton University, 2002, pp.1-9, p.5.

293 Conference on Security and Cooperation in Europe, "Final Act", Helsinki 1975, section "Questions relating to Security in Europe 1. (a) "Declaration on Principles Guiding Relations between Participating States", Principle No.VIII Equal rights and self-determination of peoples.

294 *Ibid.*, second paragraph.

295 International Court of Justice, *Advisory Opinion on the Legal Consequences for States of the Continued Presence of South Africa in Namibia (South West Africa) notwithstanding Security Council Resolution 276 (1970)*, Advisory Opinion, 21 June 1971, ICJ Reports of 1971, History of the Mandate, paras. 42-86.

296 After the adoption of the 1970 Declaration, see UN General Assembly Resolution on "The importance of the universal realization of the right of peoples to self-determination and of the speedy granting of independence to colonial countries and peoples for the effective guarantee and observance of human rights", UN Doc. A/RES/2649(XXV) 1970; "Importance of the universal realization of the right of peoples to self-determination and of the speedy granting of independence to colonial countries and peoples for the effective guarantee and observance of human rights", UN Doc. A/RES/2787(XXVI) 1971; and, with the same title, UN Doc. A/RES/2955(XXVII) 1972, A/RES/3070(XXVIII) in 1973, UN Doc.

"internal" dimension, was put forward by H.S.H. Prince Hans Adam II of Liechtenstein at the Plenary Meeting of the General Assembly on 25 October 1993.[297] Without intending to restrict the right to self-determination to this dimension but rather to suggest an additional realization of self-determination,[298] a proposal for a "Draft Convention on Self-Determination Through Self-Administration" was submitted to the United Nations in April 1994.[299] As underlined by Lapidoth, although in the Declaration the term "self-administration" is used, this document basically described "autonomy", as the speeches at UN prove as well.[300]

A/RES/3246(XXIX) in 1974, UN Doc. A/RES/3382(XXX) in 1975; and so on. See the GA yearly resolutions at http://www.un.org/documents/resga.htm.

297 Plenary Meeting of the General Assembly on 25 October 1993, UN General Assembly Official Records, 48th Session, and 30th Plenary Meeting as cited by Ruth Lapidoth, *Autonomy: Flexible Solutions to Ethnic Conflicts*, United States Institute of Peace, 1997, p.55 and note 25. See also the General Assembly, "Request for the inclusion of an item in the provisional agenda of the forty-eight session. Effective realization of the Right to Self-Determination through Autonomy", UN Doc. A/48/147/Add.1, 29 September 1993; and General Assembly, "Right of Peoples to Self-Determination. Letter dated 28 September 1995 from the Permanent Representative of Liechtenstein to the United Nations addressed to the Secretary General", UN Doc. A/50/492, 2 October 1995.

298 Lapidoth, *Autonomy: Flexible Solutions to Ethnic Conflicts*, p.55.

299 Permanent Representative of Liechtenstein to the United Nations, "Draft Convention on Self-Determination Through Self-Administration", New York, 1994. As a follow up to the commitment of Hans Adam II of Liechtenstein to these issues, the Liechtenstein Institute on Self-Determination at Princeton University (LISD) was founded in 2000 and an overarching work on self-determination based on the Draft Convention on Self-Determination Through Self-Administration was eventually published in 2002, namely Wolfgang Danspeckgruber (ed.), *The Self-Determination of Peoples. Community, Nation and State in an Interdependent World*, Lynne Rienner Publishers, Boulder, London, in association with the Liechtenstein Institute on Self-Determination, Princeton University, 2002. This publication also contains the Draft Convention and a commentary to it by Sir Arthur Watts, "Appendix B. The Liechtenstein Draft Convention on Self-Determination Through Self-Administration", in Wolfgang Danspeckgruber (ed.), *The Self-Determination of Peoples. Community, Nation and State in an Interdependent World*, Lynne Rienner Publishers, Boulder, London, in association with the Liechtenstein Institute on Self-Determination, Princeton University, 2002, pp.365-392.

300 Lapidoth, *Autonomy: Flexible Solutions to Ethnic Conflicts*, p.57. See, e.g, the above-mentioned document in note 297 General Assembly, "Request for the inclusion of an item in the provisional agenda of the forty-eight session. Effective realization of the Right to Self-Determination through Autonomy", UN Doc. A/48/147/Add.1, 29 September 1993. Further on the concept of "autonomy" see chapter 3, section 3.2.2.2.

Afterwards, *inter alia*, the Committee on the Elimination of Racial Discrimination (CERD) embraced this classification in its General Recommendation No.21 on "The right to self-determination" adopted in 1996.[301] In particular, the CERD stated that the external aspect of self-determination consists in the right of all peoples to freely determine their political status and their place in the international community on the basis of the principle of equal rights. It also added that the liberation of peoples from colonialism and the prohibition to subject peoples to alien subjugation, domination, and exploitation are examples of external self-determination. The rights of all peoples to freely pursue their economic, social, and cultural development without outside interference, the (individual) right to take part in the conduct of public affairs at any level –with reference also to article 5.c of the International Convention on the Elimination of All Forms of Racial Discrimination– and, consequently, the conviction that governments should represent the whole population without distinction as to race, color, decent, national, or ethnic origins are, instead, elements of the internal aspect of self-determination.[302]

In its landmark decision *Reference re Secession of Quebec* issued in 1998,[303] the Supreme Court of Canada also adopted the external-internal classification. In particular, the Court stated that internal self-determination consists of "a people's pursuit of its political, economic, social and cultural development within the framework of an existing state",[304] while external self-determination refers to the three dimensions recognized in the 1970 Declaration, namely: independence; free association or integration in an existing state, i.e., annexation; or the emergence into any other freely determined political status.[305] The Court added that, as mentioned, all the international documents that proclaim the right to self-determination also con-

301 Committee on the Elimination of Racial Discrimination, General Recommendation No.21, "The right to self-determination", UN Doc. A/51/18 (1996), 8 March 1996.

302 *Ibid.*, para.4.

303 Supreme Court of Canada, *Reference re Secession of Quebec*, [1998] 2 S.C.R. 217; 16, 17, 18, 19 February and 20 August 1998; Case No.25506, available in the online Canadian Supreme Court Judgments' collection at http://scc-csc.lexum.com/scc-csc/scc-csc/en/item/1643/index.do.

304 *Ibid.*, para.126.

305 *Ibid.* See also the 1970 Declaration sub-heading "The principle of equal rights and self-determination of peoples", which states: "[t]he establishment of a sovereign and independent State, the free association or integration with an independent State or the emergence into any other political status freely determined by a people constitute modes of implementing the right of self-determination by that people".

tain parallel provisions to prevent threats to existing States' territorial integrity or the stability of relations between sovereign States.[306] As widely known, the Court analyzed particularly the question of whether a right to unilateral secession exists, as it dealt with the issue of Quebec. As stated by the same Court, a right to unilateral secession neither exists nor is explicitly denied under international law. However, the Court affirmed that "such a denial is, to some extent, implicit in the exceptional circumstances required for secession to be permitted under the right of a people to self-determination".[307] Thus, the Court turned to the cases in which the right of self-determination can be exercised "externally" and, citing Cassese, it offered a reminder that this right has been recognized solely to two "classes of peoples", namely those under colonial rule and, outside the colonial context, those under alien subjugation, domination, or exploitation.[308] However, the Court also underlined that some commentators identified a third way that would give rise to secession, i.e., when a people is blocked from the meaningful exercise of its right to self-determination internally.[309] In particular, the Court affirmed that, in accordance with the requirement that governments should represent "the whole people belonging to the territory without distinction of any kind", as inserted in the 1993 Vienna Declaration and Programme of Action,[310] it "adds credence to the assertion that such a complete blockage may potentially give rise to a right of secession".[311] It was eventually found that Quebec did not fall into either of the two above-mentioned categories, that is to say colonial people or peoples under alien subjugation, domination, or exploitation, or a people to be denied of meaningful access to government to pursue their political, economic, cultural and social development.[312]

Putting aside its final outcome, this decision remains extremely relevant insofar as it clearly highlighted the subdivision into external and internal self-determination and, most importantly, assessed one of the main under-

---

306 *Ibid.*, para.127.

307 *Ibid.*, para.112.

308 *Ibid.*, para.131. See Cassese, *Self-determination of Peoples*, p.334.

309 Supreme Court of Canada, *Reference re Secession of Quebec*, para.134. This would also be in line with what the Committee of Rapporteurs or of Inquiry of the Aaland Islands had stated, i.e., the possibility of "separation" of one minority from the State although as exceptional solution ("a last resort"). See above section 2.1.1.

310 Vienna Declaration and Programme of Action, UN World Conference on Human Rights, UN Doc. A/CONF.157/24, 25 June 1993.

311 Supreme Court of Canada, *Reference re Secession of Quebec*, para.134.

312 *Ibid.*, para.154.

standings of the right to self-determination, as follows: the right to self-determination under international law "[...] only generates, at best, a right to external self-determination in situations of former colonies; where a people is oppressed, as for example under foreign military occupation; or where a definable group is denied meaningful access to government to pursue their political, economic, social and cultural development. In all three situations, the people in question are entitled to a right to external self-determination because they have been denied the ability to exert internally their right to self-determination".[313]

Hence, the external-internal dichotomy may be summarized as follows. External self-determination refers mainly to the external relations of a State, but also of other actors, and is (mainly) materialized in three forms: independence; free association with or integration into an existing state, i.e., annexation; or the ultimate case of secession in case a people is denied meaningful access to government. Internal self-determination ranges from the recognition and establishment of a self-government or autonomy to a people's right to pursue political, economic, social, and cultural development by choosing its own political and economic regime, and thus to take part in public affairs, within the framework of a State.

Although it is broadly accepted, this dichotomy has also been challenged and criticised. In some cases, potential holders of the right to self-determination such as indigenous peoples have claimed that this dichotomy is unhelpful.[314] Spiry, in particular, proposed abandoning the label "internal self-determination" for a more neutral expression, such as "self-development"

313 *Ibid.*, para.138. This assumption is close to the theory known as the "Voice or Exit". See Albert O. Hirschman, *Exit, Voice and Loyalty. Responses to Decline in Firms, Organizations and States*, Harvard University Press, Cambridge, Massachusetts and London, 1970; and Albert O. Hirschman, "Exit, Voice, and the State", *World Politics*, Vol. 31, No. 1 (Oct., 1978), pp. 90-107.

314 See UN Commission on Human Rights, "Report of the working group established in accordance with Commission on Human Rights resolution 1995/32", E/CN.4/2001/85, 6 February 2001, Fifty-seventh session, p.13, para 78, which reported that: "In a joint statement on behalf of several indigenous organizations from Australia, an indigenous representative said that the distinction between internal and external self-determination suggested by some States was unhelpful. The equating of external self-determination with secession was artificial as it restricted the right and restricted choices. The right of self-determination required States to recognize human rights internally, within their territories, and also at the international level. The participation in United Nations forums was said to be an external expression of self-determination which did not involve secession or independence".

or "self-preservation".[315] According to Anaya, this conceptualization "is premised on the conception [...] of a limited universe of 'peoples' comprising mutually exclusive spheres of community (i.e., states)", thus "ignoring the spectrum of multiple and overlapping spheres of human associations", which are both those organized and those non-ordered as States (see also below).[316] Moreover, Danspeckgruber underlined that "[s]elf-determination's two dimensions [...] are increasingly being challenged by the pressure of greater education and contacts abroad, increased mobility, economic and strategic interdependence, and the globalization of media, but also by an emerging reinsistence upon the traditional national/communal values in decisionmaking, culture, laws and administration".[317]

As an alternative, McCorquodale suggested a "human rights approach" to self-determination.[318] In particular, the author argued that self-determination is a human right, but not an absolute human right. In the author's eyes, this would also be more in line with both State practice and international standards vis-à-vis self-determination.[319] This approach relies on the *corpus iuris* of international human rights law that transcends the "territorial" approach, which is limited to independence and secession. In addition, it would make it possible to avoid the rigidity that the term "peoples" implies, by rather individuating "victims" that may be able to bring a claim for a potential violation of human rights.[320] Thus, the right to self-determination is a human right but is limited in relation to the protection of the rights of others, the general interest of the society, and the need to maintain international peace and security. Such limitations are only applicable in a few cases, e.g., when internal self-determination is already in place and when there is a pressing need of the society concerned to limit it.[321] In sum, McCorquodale's approach is certainly relevant, especially with regard to the attempts to transcend both the "territorial" and "peoples" (limiting) aspects.[322] However, the limitations to the human right of self-determination that the author envisage appear vague (e.g., "the rights of others") and open

315 Emmanuel Spiry, "From 'Self-Determination' to a Right to 'Self-Development' for Indigenous Groups", 38 *German Yearbook of International Law*, 1995, pp.129-286, p.144.

316 Anaya, *Indigenous Peoples in International Law*, p.81.

317 Danspeckgruber, "Introduction", p.5.

318 McCorquodale, "Self-Determination: A Human Rights Approach".

319 *Ibid.*, p.883.

320 *Ibid.*, p.883.

321 *Ibid.*, p.884.

322 See also next section 2.1.6.

to ample discretion on the part of States. Moreover, the "victim" approach has been refused by the Human Rights Committee, as seen above.

By underlining the limits of the internal vs external dichotomy mentioned above, Anaya proposed his conceptualization of self-determination in substantive and remedial forms.[323] The author stated that "the substantive elements of self-determination apply broadly to benefit all segments of humanity", while the remedial aspects (e.g., prescriptions and mechanisms) have a narrower application, i.e., when a group has suffered a violation of substantive self-determination.[324] Thus, the substance of self-determination consists of two normative prongs, namely the "constitutive aspect" and the "ongoing aspect".[325] The former aspect requires that the "governing institutional order" stems from the creation of processes guided by the will of the peoples. For its part, the latter aspect requires that the "governing institutional order", irrespective of its formation or alteration, should allow peoples to live and develop themselves freely on a continuous basis.[326] According to Anaya, this subdivision differs from the internal-external dichotomy since it "identifies two phenomenological aspects of self-determination that apply throughout the spectrum of multiple and overlapping spheres of human association, and that both have implications for the inward- and outward-looking of units of human organization".[327] Therefore, "constitutive self-determination" refers to the formula of arts.1 of both Covenants to the right of peoples to "freely determine their political status", and the "ongoing self-determination" instead "requires a governing order under which individuals and groups are able to make meaningful choices" likely to affect their lives.[328]

Another classification has recently been proposed by Weller.[329] After tackling the most critical aspects vis-à-vis self-determination,[330] which the

323 Anaya, *Indigenous Peoples in International Law*, pp.80-85.

324 *Ibid.*, p.80.

325 *Ibid.*, p.81.

326 *Ibid.*

327 *Ibid.*

328 *Ibid.*, p.82.

329 Marc Weller, *Escaping the Self-Determination Trap*, Martinus Nijhoff Publishers, Leiden, 2008.

330 E.g., the object and scope of self-determination or whether it is a continuing right, etc. *Ibid.*, pp.32-45. See next section 2.1.6 in which these aspects are analyzed more in depth.

author calls "classical" or "colonial",[331] and underlining its disenfranchising power,[332] Weller proposes his "constitutional self-determination" based on constitutional arrangements.[333] Constitutional self-determination may be further subdivided into three types, as follows: "Express self-determination status"; "Effective dissolution of a federal type state"; and "Implied self-determination status".[334] As to the first type, Weller shows evidence of constitutions in which a right to external self-determination is explicitly recognized, e.g., arts.201-204 of the 1947 Constitution of the Federal Republic of the Union of Burma.[335] As to the second type (the "Effective dissolution"), two evident examples are the Union of Soviet Socialist Republics (URSS) and the Socialist Federal Republic of Yugoslavia (SFRY), the dissolutions of which occurred as a matter of fact although they were opposed by the central government.[336] Finally, the "Implied self-determination status" may be envisaged in those cases "where a distinct 'nation' or 'people' inhabit a clearly constitutionally defined territory" and the central government consents to the holding of a referendum on secession.[337] Weller referred, in particular, to the following statement of the Supreme Court of Canada in the above-mentioned decision *Reference re Secession of Quebec*: "a clear majority vote in Quebec on a clear question in favour of secession would confer democratic legitimacy on the secession initiative which all of the other participants in Confederation would have to recognize".[338] In other words, according to the Supreme Court of Canada's decision, a referendum would not automatically mean independence, but (at least) a negotiation should follow.[339] This was also discussed in the current cases of Scotland, Catalonia and New Caledonia (see section 2.1.7).

331 *Ibid.*, p.29.

332 *Ibid.*, p.31. On this point, see also his previous article Marc Weller, "The Self-Determination Trap", 4(1) *Ethnopolitics* 2005, pp.3-28.

333 Weller, *Escaping the Self-Determination Trap*, p.46.

334 *Ibid.*

335 Art.201 of the 1947 Burma Constitution contained the right to secede from the Union following the conditions specified in the following articles, e.g., within ten years from the adoption of the Constitution, by a resolution to be passed by the State Council, etc. *Ibid.*, p.46-47.

336 *Ibid.*, p.55-57.

337 *Ibid.*, p.58.

338 Supreme Court of Canada, *Reference re Secession of Quebec*, para.150.

339 Weller, *Escaping the Self-Determination Trap*, p.58.

In sum, the understandings of self-determination may be recapitulated in the minimalist and the maximalist approaches as categorized by Xanthaki.[340] The former tends to limit self-determination to a principle and not a right; equate it to secession; or to divide it merely into independence on the one hand and democratic government on the other.[341] The latter envisages self-determination with a wider significance, e.g., following more the formulation of both art.1 of ICCPR and ICESCR with regard to economic, cultural and social development.[342] Out of these three dimensions, the right to "economic self-determination", and thus the access to natural resources, appear to be the most accepted.[343] However, as mentioned above (section 2.1.3.2), the four elements (political on the one hand, and economic, social and cultural aspects on the other) are rather indivisible.

To conclude, the external-internal dichotomy of self-determination has deep roots but has also provoked a complex debate on its different meanings. Although some authors have proposed other classifications, some elements that have been classified as belonging either to the external or the internal dimensions seem to remain present in their works. This is the case, for example, of Weller who, despite rejecting the classical understanding, proposes systems of autonomies as an alternative. However, autonomy arrangements have also been identified as part of internal self-determination. Anaya's "constitutive" and "ongoing" self-determination are a good alternative insofar as the author assumes that self-determination may have a starting point and, at the same time, it is also an ongoing process. Moreover, this subdivision does not refer to States solely as beneficiaries of this right. However, the second aspect in particular tends to overlap with "internal-self-determination". The probable added-value of Anaya's proposal lies in conceiving both aspects at a time.

The main problems with this dichotomy concern the content given to each of the two dimensions. As already mentioned, the external dimension regards mainly the external relations of a State and it is thus intimately linked with the concept of sovereignty and Statehood. As widely known, according to art.1 of the 1933 Montevideo Convention on the Rights and Duties of States, "[t]he state as a person of international law should possess the following qualifications: a) a permanent population; b) a defined territory; c) government; and d) capacity to enter into relations with the other

340 Xanthaki, "The Right to Self-Determination: Meaning and Scope", p.20.

341 *Ibid.*

342 *Ibid.*, p.27.

343 *Ibid.*

states". Therefore, according to current international law, only a recognized State may enter into contractual relations with another one. This leads to the conceptualization of external self-determination as the sole way to become a State, i.e., via independence, secession, and annexation. As already pointed out, this is highly problematic since it clashes with the principle of territorial integrity. However, equating the "external dimension" solely to Statehood is limiting, as it has been seen, it may also refer to the political status and a "place" in the international community, as mentioned by CERD in its Recommendation No.21, or to a vast range of "external" relations that differ significantly from, e.g., secession (see also below).

Recently, Summers proposed a reconsideration of the internal and external aspects of self-determination basing his assumptions –similarly to Anaya– on the fact that the "self-determination process involves different units, which have their own internal and external aspects".[344] The author suggests that these four units are the Peoples, the sovereign States, the political units within the State (e.g., self-governments), and the political units distinct from a sovereign State (i.e., non-self-governing territories; freely associated territories; occupied territories; and territories under international administration).[345]

However, the need to reframe self-determination may also lead to a proliferation of different concepts, which, as underlined by Saul, may undermine its normative meaning.[346] The author speaks also of "contradictions" within the different conceptualizations of self-determination,[347] without realizing that he himself is victim of a distorted understanding. He affirms, for example, that according to Harris,[348] self-determination would also require that governments have a democratic base, as Cassese and Crawford also argued, as seen above. Thus, Saul cites the work of Vidmar on self-

344 James Summers, "The Internal and external aspects of self-determination reconsidered", in Duncan French (ed.), *Statehood and Self-Determination. Reconciling Tradition and Modernity in International Law*, Cambridge University Press, Cambridge, New York, 2013, pp.229-249, p.233.

345 *Ibid.*, pp.233-246.

346 Matthew Saul, "The Normative Status of Self-Determination in International Law: A Formula for Uncertainty in the Scope and Content of the Right?", 11(4) *Human Rights Law Review* 2011, pp.609-644, p.614.

347 *Ibid.*

348 Harris, *Cases and Materials on International Law*, Sweet and Maxwell, London, 2010, p.104, as cited by Saul, "The Normative Status of Self-Determination in International Law ...", p.614.

determination and multi-party democracy,[349] and affirms that this author concluded that self-determination does not include a right to democratic government.[350] The argument of Vidmar is built on the presumption that self-determination is a non-absolute human right according to McCorquodale's concept mentioned above. Upon closer inspection, Vidmar however concludes that "a multiparty electoral process by itself cannot guarantee respect for the right of self-determination and does not *per se* mean a fulfilment of this right. Indeed, the electoral process can lead to a situation of a tyranny of the majority".[351] This is immensely different from arguing that self-determination does not include a right to democratic government. Rather, it suggests that a multiparty electoral process does not suffice to guarantee it. This is valid for both the realization of the right to self-determination and to "genuine" political participation (see chapter 3).

Therefore, back to the limits of the classical dichotomy, on the one hand it is certain that, e.g., self-governments nowadays may have also "external" powers,[352] or that in our globalized world a "people" may express their views also in international fora, thus exercising external expressions vastly different from, e.g., a secession. On the other hand, the elements used to describe the external and internal dimensions of self-determination are still (inevitably) present both in international treaties and States' practice. Indeed, the focus needs to detach from the (increasingly misleading) external and internal dichotomy, and to move toward an approach of *multiple expressions of self-determination*, which differ from a right-holder to another, as in the case of indigenous peoples. As stated by Kingsbury, "[s]elf-determination is about the relation between state and community".[353] Thus, a reorientation "from an end-state approach to a *relational* approach of self-

349 Saul, "The Normative Status of Self-Determination in International Law ...", pp.614-615, that cites Jure Vidmar, "The Right of Self-Determination and Multiparty Democracy: Two Sides of the Same Coin?", 10 *Human Rights Law Review* 2010, 239-268 p.268.

350 Saul, "The Normative Status of Self-Determination in International Law ...", pp.614-615.

351 Vidmar, "The Right of Self-Determination and Multiparty Democracy: Two Sides of the Same Coin?", p.267.

352 See Francesco Palermo, "Bridges in Self-Determination Disputes? External Relations of Sub-national Entities and Minority Groups", in Marc Weller and Barbara Metzger (eds.), *Settling Self-Determination Disputes. Complex Power-Sharing in Theory and in Practice*, Martinus Nijhoff, Leiden, Boston, 2008, pp.667-688.

353 Benedict Kingsbury, "Reconstructing Self-Determination: A Relational Approach", in Pekka Aikio and Martin Scheinin (eds.), *Operationalizing the Rights of Indigenous Peoples to Self-Determination*, Institute for Human Rights, Åbo Akademi University, Saarijärvi, 2000, pp.19-38, p.26.

determination" is needed (see also section 2.2.4).[354] This may also be more in line with the principle of territorial integrity, as the threat of or the actual use of force is not necessary to guarantee some of the expressions of self-determination. In addition, there are relatively new exceptions to the principles of non-interference and territorial integrity, such as the "Responsibility to Protect (R2P)" and "Remedial Secession" (see section 2.1.7).

Without going further into this subject-matter, for the aims of this work it suffices to remind that dealing with self-determination becomes problematic as long as States equate it to secession, independence or annexation. Notwithstanding the lively debate in academia, States still perceive self-determination as a threat to their territorial integrity and barely consider alternatives. Thus, in this work, the self-determination dichotomy is used insofar as I mainly refer to what have been classified as belonging to "internal aspects" of self-determination and may become a valid tool for the *composite right to political participation of indigenous peoples* that is proposed later.

Nevertheless, before addressing what self-determination may signify and imply for indigenous peoples in section 2.2, other crucial and highly debated aspects of self-determination shall be discussed in the next section, namely the post-colonial dimension, the legal nature, the alleged singularity, and who are the right-holders to self-determination.

2.1.5 Crucial aspects: Post-colonial self-determination; Self-determination as *jus cogens*; Singularity; and the People referred in Article 1

Since the adoption of the 1970 Declaration and the other GA resolutions from 1970 onwards, as seen above, the main (initial) application of self-determination has been decolonization. This is now widely accepted.[355] Skepticism has been shown to the validity of the right to self-determination beyond the colonial dimension,[356] mainly due to the contested identification and definition of the term "people" in both arts.1 of ICCPR and ICESCR.[357]

354 *Ibid.*, p.22.

355 McCorquodale, "Self-Determination: A Human Rights Approach", p.860; Thomas D. Musgrave, *Self-Determination and National Minorities*, Oxford University Press, Oxford, New York, 2002, p.124.

356 McCorquodale, "Self-Determination: A Human Rights Approach", p.860.

357 Saul, "The Normative Status of Self-Determination in International Law ...", p.614.

However, States' practice and other UN documents support a wider application of self-determination, along with the formulation of the ICCPR and ICESCR.[358] It has been widely accepted, for instance, that self-determination applies to Palestinians, blacks in South Africa and in the former Rhodesia, and to the people of Tibet.[359] In addition, in the "Treaty on the Final Settlement with Respect to Germany" in 1990, it is stated that the "German People" exercised their right to self-determination clearly outside a colonial framework.[360] The same consideration also applies to the dissolution of the former URSS and SFRY.[361] As summarized by Crawford, after 1989, self-determination has been invoked in three types of cases: as justification for intervention in another State; in the form of secession; as a basis for special arrangements, i.e., the recognition of autonomy or special rights, such as "internal" self-determination.[362] In fact, according to the same author, the reference to "a government representing the whole population belonging to the territory" in the 1970 Declaration would have been irrelevant if self-determination was meant to be confined to the decolonization exercise.[363]

358 Tomuschat, "Self-Determination in a Post-Colonial World", pp.2-3; McCorquodale, "Self-Determination: A Human Rights Approach", pp.860-861.

359 McCorquodale cites the following UN Documents: GA Resolution Nos. A/RES/2787(XXVI) of 6 December 1971, A/RES/3089D(XXVIII) of 7 December 1973, and A/RES/3210(XXIX) of 14 October 1974; Commission on Human Rights Resolution No.2(XXXIV) of 14 February 1978 regarding Palestinians; GA Resolution No. A/RES/31/6 of 26 October 1976 and Security Council Resolution Nos.417 and 418 of 4 November 1977 regarding South Africa; Security Council Resolution Nos.216 and 217 of 12 November 1965, and No.232 of 16 December 1966 regarding Rhodesia; and, GA Resolution No. A/RES/1723(XVC) of 20 December 1961 regarding Tibet. McCorquodale, "Self-Determination: A Human Rights Approach", p.861, notes 24, 25, 26, and 27. On Palestina, Thürer and Burri cite the more recent Advisory Opinion of the International Court of Justice, *Legal Consequences of the Construction of a Wall in the Occupied Palestinian Territory*, Advisory Opinion, 9 July 2004, ICJ Reports 2004, p.136. In para.118, the ICJ affirms that whether a "Palestinian people" exist is not an issue and that the right of this people is the right to self-determination. Thürer and Burri, "Self-Determination", para.19.

360 McCorquodale, "Self-Determination: A Human Rights Approach", p.861.

361 *Ibid.*; Tomuschat, "Self-Determination in a Post-Colonial World", p.4; Weller, *Escaping the Self-Determination Trap*, p.152.

362 Crawford, "The Right to Self-Determination in International Law", pp.39-40.

363 *Ibid.*, p.31.

Finally, the requirement of the HRC in its General Comment No.12 to report on the application of the right to self-determination would make no sense if self-determination were limited to decolonization alone.[364]

Having established that self-determination has a post-colonial applicability, the question of its legal nature in international law must be analyzed next. In particular, it is unclear whether the right to self-determination, despite having being recognized in the two Covenants (thus, treaty law), is also international customary law and *jus cogens*. As is widely known, international law has no hierarchy of norms and the two main sources of law are international treaty law and customary law, which stand on equal footing.[365] Within this lack of hierarchy, the relations between these two sources are governed by the following three legal general principles: A later source may derogate an earlier one if it is special in character; however, a later source cannot derogate an earlier one, which is general in character; and a special norm prevails over a general one.[366] *Jus cogens*, however, is a distinct class of general rules with special legal force,[367] i.e., it includes those peremptory norms in accordance with arts.53 and 64 of the Vienna Convention on the Law of Treaties (Vienna Convention).[368] Thus, in principle, *jus cogens* cannot be derogated by any treaty, and any international norm conflicting with it shall be declared null and void.[369] In addition, reservations to *jus cogens* treaty provisions are also prohibited.[370] As stated in arts.53 and 64 of the Vienna Convention:

> "Article 53. […] For the purposes of the present Convention, a peremptory norm of general international law is a norm accepted and recognized by the international community of States as a whole as a norm from which no derogation is permitted

---

364 Human Rights Committee, General Comment No.12, "Article 1 (The Right to self-determination of peoples"), para.3. See also Patrick Thornberry, "Self-Determination and Indigenous Peoples: Objections and Responses", in Pekka Aikio and Martin Scheinin (eds.), *Operationalizing the Rights of Indigenous Peoples to Self-Determination*, Institute for Human Rights, Åbo Akademi University, Saarijärvi, 2000, pp.39-64, p.47.

365 Cassese, *International Law*, p.198.

366 *Ibid.*, p.199.

367 *Ibid.*

368 Stefan Kadelbach, "Jus Cogens, Obligations Erga Omnes and other Rules – The Identification of Fundamental Norms", in Christian Tomuschat and Jean-Marc Thouvenin (eds.), *The Fundamental Rules of the International Legal Order. Jus Cogens and Obligations Erga Omnes*, Martinus Nijhoff Publishers, Leiden, Boston, 2006, pp. 21-40, p.26.

369 Cassese, *International Law*, p.199; see also pp.201 and ff.

370 Kadelbach, "Jus Cogens, Obligations Erga Omnes and other Rules …", p.26.

> and which can be modified only by a subsequent norm of general international law having the same character.
>
> Article 64. [...] If a new peremptory norm of general international law emerges, any existing treaty which is in conflict with that norm becomes void and terminates".

On the one hand, the customary law nature of self-determination seems accepted,[371] but whether self-determination has the status of *jus cogens* is left unsettled. The (second) Special Rapporteur Gros Espiell, in his well-known study briefly mentioned above, argued that self-determination, through its wide application and States' acceptance, has been transformed into a peremptory norm, thus *jus cogens*.[372] However, while citing the Vienna Convention, not yet in force at the time he was writing, the other Special Rapporteur Cristescu concluded that no UN instrument recognized self-determination as having peremptory nature.[373] By analyzing the States' statements at the UN General Assembly during the discussion of both the Draft Articles on the Law of Treaties in 1963 and the 1970 Declaration, Cassese notes that the pronouncements that were favorable to qualify self-determination as *jus cogens* emanated mainly from developing countries and those belonging to the 'socialist' block.[374] Among the Western States, Greece, Spain, and Italy were also favorable.[375] However, during the discussions on the 1970 Declaration, the Netherlands and US expressed contrary views.[376] In 1979, a later US statement vis-à-vis the Soviet invasion of Afghanistan in 1979 also ranked self-determination as *jus cogens*.[377] Thus, although Cassese recognizes that this type of practice by States is rare, he also underlines that Western countries have nevertheless recognized self-determination as fundamental and universal. In other words, a lack of widespread explicit support for the assumption that self-determination is *jus cogens* does not necessary lead to the conclusion that it cannot be considered as such.[378] Exemplary evidence of this reasoning is the recent change of attitude on the

---

371 McCorquodale, "Self-Determination: A Human Rights Approach", p.858.

372 Gros Espiell, *The Right to Self-Determination. Implementation of the UN Resolutions*, p.8 paras.50, 70-88, especially 71, and 74-75.

373 Cristescu, *The Right to Self-Determination. Historical and Current Development in the basis of the United Nations Instruments*, p.24, para.154.

374 Cassese, *Self-determination of Peoples*, pp.136-137.

375 Cassese, *Self-determination of Peoples*, p.137.

376 Saul, "The Normative Status of Self-Determination in International Law ...", p.642.

377 Cassese, *Self-determination of Peoples*, p.138.

378 *Ibid.*, p.140.

part of The Netherlands underlined by Saul.[379] Although this country was against classifying self-determination as *jus cogens* in 1970, in 2009, in the frame of the Kosovo Advisory Opinion,[380] The Netherlands stated that "the obligation to respect and promote the right to self-determination as well as the obligation to refrain from any forcible action which deprives peoples of this right is an obligation arising under a peremptory norm of general international law".[381]

Therefore, suffice it to say here that there is an increasing trend to recognize self-determination as *jus cogens*. The issue regarding its singularity, i.e., whether or not it is a "one-and-for-all right", is now addressed.

As seen above,[382] there is an interconnection between self-determination and other civil and political rights, something also confirmed by the HRC. Furthermore, democracy, as Crawford clearly stated, is a continuing process.[383] Hence, considering the interconnections between democracy and self-determination, the latter cannot be exercised on an occasional basis.[384] This ultimately suggests that the right to self-determination is *a continuing right*.[385] After the Second World War and during the decolonization process, self-determination was equated to independence. Later, with the adoption of the Covenants, the scope broadened and neither option ended with independence nor can it be said to be a "one-and-for-all right". As Cassese pointed out: "The issue of *whether the government of a sovereign State* is in compliance with Article 1 is a *legitimate question*, with reference to any State, *at any point in time*" [emphasis added].[386] The recent (negotiated) referendum in Scotland and the upcoming one in New Caledonia are further evidence of this "ongoing" aspect (see section 2.1.7).

Finally, the disputed issue of who are the "people" referred to in arts.1 of both ICCPR and ICESCR needs to be approached. As mentioned, Wilson was heavily criticized for having proposed the right to self-determination of

379 Saul, "The Normative Status of Self-Determination in International Law ...", p.643.

380 International Court of Justice, *Accordance with International Law of the Unilateral Declaration of Independence in Respect of Kosovo,* Advisory Opinion, 22 July 2010, ICJ Reports 2010, p.403.

381 The Netherlands, Written Statement, 17 April 2009, at para 3.3 as cited by Saul, "The Normative Status of Self-Determination in International Law ...", p.643. For the references, see Saul notes 41 and 179.

382 See section 2.1.4.

383 Crawford, "The Right to Self-Determination in International Law", p.26.

384 *Ibid.*

385 *Ibid.*, pp-25-26 and Cassese, *Self-determination of Peoples*, pp.52 and 54.

386 Cassese, *Self-determination of Peoples*, p.55.

"peoples" without providing any definition of who such peoples were.[387] Many commentators have tried to provide an answer to this question, by proposing alternative approaches. For instance, McCorquodale argued that the "people" approach is misleading and becomes a limiting factor of self-determination,[388] preferring a "victim" approach,[389] as seen above. Cassese, instead, restricted it to the sole "entire populations" living in independent and sovereign States, in territories that have not attained independence, or those living under foreign military occupation.[390] He based his arguments on the *travaux préparatoires* and States' pronouncements of art.1 of the ICCPR.[391] In particular, although he proposed to read art.1 in conjunction with art.27 of the ICCPR, the author explicitly denies that minorities are entitled to the right to self-determination.[392] Conversely, assuming that a minority may also be defined as an "ethnic group", Crawford stated that "a group with historical continuity and consciousness, a group evidently entitled to respect, asserts: 'we are a people'", and appears as such, it should be entitled to the right of self-determination as well, due to the obvious syllogism.[393] Indeed, the relevance of self-identification in defining both minorities and indigenous peoples is underlined both in art.3 of the Framework Convention for the Protection of National Minorities and in art.1.2 of the International Labour Organization (ILO) Convention concerning Indigenous and Tribal Peoples in Independent Countries, Convention No.169 of 1989 (see chapter 3). A broader definition of people is also proposed by Joseph, i.e., a group with a common ethnic or cultural identity, which incorporates political, religious or linguistic aspects, built up over a long period of time.[394] Henrard has also extensively argued that minorities are, at least, entitled to internal self-determination but also to the external self-determination in form of secession in case of threat to their physical and cultural existence.[395] In 1999, New Zealand recognized that there is an

387 See the bitter critic of Jennings reported in note 177.

388 McCorquodale, "Self-Determination: A Human Rights Approach", p.868.

389 *Ibid.*, p.884.

390 Cassese, *Self-determination of Peoples*, p.59.

391 *Ibid.*, pp.60-62.

392 *Ibid.*, p.62.

393 Crawford, "The Right to Self-Determination in International Law", p.39.

394 Sarah Joseph, "Resolving conflicting claims of territorial sovereignty and external self-determination, part 1: A proposed formula", *The International Journal of Human Rights*, Volume 3, Issue 1, 1999, pp. 40-61, pp.42-45.

395 Kristin Henrard, *Devising an Adequate System of Minority Protection. Individual Human Rights, Minority Rights and the Right to Self-Determination*, Martinus Nijhoff Publishers, The Hague, 2000, p.314.

emerging use in international law of applying self-determination to groups within States.[396] This is also in line with the emerging international theory of Remedial Secession (see next section 2.1.6). Marko recently proposed a concept of "political self-determination" for minorities, precisely to escape the trap of (national) self-determination equating to secession.[397] Cassese himself envisages the need to revise the content of self-determination, at least in its internal dimension, to best protect minorities and indigenous peoples.[398]

In conclusion, as asserted by Thornberry, "the meaning of 'people' for purposes of international law is not fixed in stone".[399] Therefore, the most credible option appears to be the logical assumption proposed by the Supreme Court of Canada in the abovementioned case *Reference re Secession of Quebec*, which, without going further into the subject matter, stated that

> "[i]t is clear *that 'a people' may include only a portion of the population of an existing state*. The right to self-determination has developed largely as a human right, and is generally used in documents that simultaneously contain references to 'nation' and 'state'. The juxtaposition of these terms is indicative that the reference to 'people' *does not necessarily mean the entirety of a state's population* [...]"[400] [emphasis added].

As the Courts argues further,[401] if a 'people' were equated to the sole entire population of existing States, as Cassese does, this right would basically have no sense to exist.

396 Statement in general debate during the drafting of the UN Declaration on the Rights of Indigenous Peoples in the Working Group on the Draft Declaration cited by Thornberry, "Self-Determination and Indigenous Peoples: Objections and Responses", p.48 and note 29.

397 Josef Marko, "The Law and Politics of Diversity Management: A Neo-institutional Approach", in 6 *European Yearbook of Minority Issues (EYMI)* 2006/7, 2008, Martinus Nijoff Publishers, Leiden, Boston, pp.251-279, p.266.

398 Cassese, *Self-determination of Peoples*, p.350.

399 Thornberry, "Self-Determination and Indigenous Peoples: Objections and Responses", p.47.

400 Supreme Court of Canada, *Reference re Secession of Quebec*, para.124.

401 *Ibid.*

2.1.6 Recent developments in international law: The Responsibility to Protect and Remedial Secession

The recent shift in international law vis-à-vis the "Responsibility to Protect (R2P)" and the emerging theory of "Remedial Secession" are briefly mentioned here since they touch upon two of the problematic aspects of the application of the right to self-determination: The prohibition of interference/non-intervention and the case of secession.

During the UN Millennium Assembly in September 2000, Secretary General Kofi Annan's spoke of building a new international consensus to respond to massive human rights and humanitarian law violations. Soon after this call, but prior to the reforms of the UN human rights system, an International Commission on Intervention and State Sovereignty (ICISS) was established thanks to the initiative of Canadian Prime Minister Jean Chrétien. The ICISS completed its work on "The responsibility to protect" in 2001. During the 56th session of the United Nations General Assembly, Canada presented its report, which was published in December 2001.[402] In short, the "Responsibility to Protect (R2P)" proposed in the report comprises three sub-responsibilities, i.e., to prevent the root and direct causes that lead to conflicts or crisis and put populations at risk; to react to such situations with proper measures, including military intervention; and, to rebuild, i.e., to provide full assistance to reconstruct and reconcile, especially after a military intervention, addressing the initial causes of the conflict or crisis.[403]

Later, the UN World Summit in 2005 embraced the principle by affirming that "each individual State has the responsibility to protect its populations from genocide, war crimes, ethnic cleansing and crimes against humanity".[404] The Security Council Resolution No.1674, adopted in 2006,[405] also reaffirmed it. In 2008, Secretary General Ban Ki-Moon appointed a

402 Report of the International Commission on Intervention and State Sovereignty-ICISS, "The responsibility to protect", International Development Research Centre, Ottawa, 2001, at http://responsibilitytoprotect.org/ICISS%20Report.pdf. On the establishment of the Commission see ICISS, "The responsibility to protect", p.81 and ff.

403 *Ibid.*, p.XI.

404 General Assembly, "Resolution adopted by the General Assembly on 16 September 2005. 60/1. 2005 World Summit Outcome", UN Doc. A/RES/60/1, 24 October 2005, paras.138-139.

405 Security Council Resolution 1674, adopted 28 April 2006, "On protection of civilians in armed conflict", S/RES/1674 (2006).

"Special Adviser on the Responsibility to Protect" at the Assistant Secretary-General level under the Office of the Special Adviser on the Prevention of Genocide. In 2009 the Secretary-General's "Report on Implementing the Responsibility to Protect"[406] specified three pillars of the R2P, namely (1) "the enduring responsibility of the State to protect its populations, whether nationals or not, from genocide, war crimes, ethnic cleansing and crimes against humanity, and from their incitement";[407] (2) "the commitment of the international community to assist States in meeting those obligations";[408] and (3) "the responsibility of Member States to respond collectively in a timely and decisive manner when a State is manifestly failing to provide such protection" in accordance with the UN Charter.[409]

This shift in international law is particularly relevant insofar as it identifies an exception to the prohibition of interference/non-intervention whenever a State fails to defend its own nationals from serious human rights violations such as genocide, war crimes, ethnic cleansing and other crimes against humanity. The UN Security Council is entitled to adopt measures and prevent States from committing serious human rights violations such as those mentioned above, "in the sense of a responsibility to protect", as according to art.39 of the UN Charter.[410] In principle, the R2P thus entitles States to intervene. Among the (few) cases of the application of R2P, the most notorious and dramatic one, was the case of Libya in 2011.[411]

The theory of "Remedial Secession", as summarized by Vidmar, "suggests that gross and systematic human rights violations can lead a state to lose a part of its territory if oppression is directed against a specific people".[412] In his recent works on self-determination cited above, Weller also

---

406 "Report on Implementing the Responsibility to Protect", UN Doc. A/63/677, 12 January 2009.

407 *Ibid.*, para.11, lett.a.

408 *Ibid.*, para.11, lett.b.

409 *Ibid.*, para.11, lett.c.

410 Rainer Hofmann, "The Use of Force and the Responsibility to Protect", comment prepared for the roundtable discussion on UN reform "Building a New Role for the United Nations: the Responsibility to Protect", Madrid, 2005, *FRIDE Working Paper 12*, pp.1-4, at http://www.fride.org/download/COM_Proteger_ENG_jul05.pdf, p.4.

411 See Security Council, Resolution No.1970 (2011), "Peace and security in Africa", adopted by the Security Council at its 6491st meeting, 26 February 2011, UN Doc. S/RES/1970 (2011); and Security Council, Resolution No.1973 (2011), "The situation in Libya", Adopted by the Security Council at its 6498th meeting, 17 March 2011, UN Doc. S/RES/1973 (2011).

412 Jure Vidmar, "Remedial Secession in International Law: Theory and (Lack of) Practice," *St Antony's International Review* 6, No.1, 2010, pp. 37-56, p.38.

considered the doctrine of remedial secession.[413] The author speaks of "remedial self-determination", and despite the initial academic skepticism, including his own,[414] he argues that the case of Kosovo has accorded wider acceptance of this doctrine.[415] Other authors have expressed skepticism vis-à-vis this theory, arguing that Kosovo in particular would not represent a (or *the*) case in which this doctrine was applied.[416] Del Mar argued that both the conflicting attitudes of States vis-à-vis this case and the reticence of the International Court of Justice in explicitly recognizing Remedial Secession cast doubts over the existence of this theory in practice.[417] Moreover, she added that a State is "a legal entity, not a human rights solution",[418] and that this doctrine shifts the debate away from the real issue of the protection of human rights into a secessionist cause, thus reinforcing the root causes instead of implementing human rights.[419] However, the author forgets to take into account those cases in which a State perpetuates human rights violations against a part or the totality of its populations, a clear example of which could be the current situation of Syria. Thus, putting aside the case of Kosovo, and considering potential applications of this theory in broader terms, whether a population should remain silent and be subject to such violations whenever the international or national human rights system are not applied or executed remains the most crucial issue. Other authors, well before the case of Kosovo, have argued that a secession may be considered a solution in such cases,[420] as also did the Supreme Court of Canada, in case

413 Weller, *Escaping the Self-Determination Trap*, p.59.

414 *Ibid.*, p.59, note 55.

415 *Ibid.*, p.59.

416 Katherine Del Mar, "The Myth of Remedial Secession", in Duncan French (ed.), *Statehood and Self-Determination. Reconciling Tradition and Modernity in International Law*, Cambridge University Press, Cambridge, New York, 2013, pp.79-108.

417 *Ibid.*, p.107.

418 *Ibid.*

419 *Ibid.*, p.108.

420 Tomuschat, "Self-Determination in a Post-Colonial World", p.10; Cassese, *Self-determination of Peoples*, p.120; Franck argued for a right to "decolonization". Thomas Franck, "Postmodern Tribalism and the Right to Secession," in Christine Brölmann, R. Lefeber, and Marjoleine Zieck (eds.), *Peoples and Minorities in International Law*, Dordrecht: Martinus Nijhoff, 1993, pp.3-27, p.14; see also Kristian Myntti, "The Right to Self-Determination and Effective Participation", in Pekka Aikio and Martin Scheinin (eds.), *Operationalizing the Rights of Indigenous Peoples to Self-Determination*, Institute for Human Rights, Åbo Akademi University, Saarijärvi, 2000, pp.85-130, p.128.

a meaningful (internal) self-determination would be denied.[421] Previously, the Committee of Rapporteurs or of Inquiry in charge of the case of the Aaland Islands had also stated that, as an exceptional solution, the "separation" of one minority from the State may be possible.[422] Gross human rights violations have lead the international community to adopt the Responsibility to Protect.

In conclusion, it is sufficient to reiterate here that both the R2P and Remedial Secession are current, fundamental developments in international law. The former undoubtedly envisages an exception to the prohibition of interference/non-intervention and, step by step, is likely to become customary law.[423] The latter is not clearly enshrined in current international law, but an entitlement to it may emerge in the near future.[424] This further suggests that both theories already do or in the future will exert significant influence over the right to self-determination, which is shown once again to be an "ongoing right" in all its dimensions.

2.1.7 Latest quests for self-determination: Scotland, Catalonia, and New Caledonia

Recently, events such as the secessions of East Timor in 2002, Kosovo in 2008, and South Sudan in 2010, the (unlawful) annexation of Crimea to the Russian Federation in 2014,[425] the secessionist movements in Catalonia and Scotland, and the developments in New Caledonia have re-launched the de-

421 Supreme Court of Canada, *Reference re Secession of Quebec*, para.134.

422 See above section 2.1.1.

423 Luke Glanville, "The Responsibility to Protect", in 12(1) *Human Rights Law Review* 2012, pp.1-32, p.32.

424 On this, see also the recent extensive work of Simone van den Driest, *Remedial Secession. A Right to External Self-Determination as a Remedy to Serious Injustices?*, School of Human Rights Research, Volume 61, Intersentia, Cambridge, Mortsel, 2013.

425 Christian Walter, "Postscript: Self-Determination, Secession, and the Crimean Crisis 2014", in Christian Walter, Antje von Ungern-Sternberg, and Kavus Abushov (eds.), *Self-Determination and Secession in International Law*, Oxford University Press, Oxford, New York, 2014, pp.293-311, p.310. Among the recent literature on the Crimean case, see the concise collection of essays included in the special issue edited by Zoran Oklopcic (guest editor), "The Crisis in Ukraine", Special Issue, 16(3) *German Law Journal* 2015, pp.350-712, at https://www.germanlawjournal.com/pdfs/FullIssues/PDF_Vol_16_No_3_full%20issu.pdf [Last access 03.08.2015].

bate on self-determination. There are also (notable) longstanding and pending situations such as Western Sahara.[426] Other cases in which self-determination (and secession) have recently been invoked are Transnistria in Moldova, South Ossetia and Abkhazia in Georgia, and Nagorno Karabakh in Armenia.[427]

The analysis of pending or new quests for self-determination do not fall under the scope of the present work and some of the latest developments are too recent to be carefully assessed. That notwithstanding, it is worth presenting briefly here the situations of Scotland, Catalonia, and New Caledonia since these are the latest cases in which the population will be or has been called to vote in (very different) referenda to decide upon their "self-determination". Although a referendum was also carried out, the annexation of Crimea to Russia is not considered here, since this case involves the violation of the principle of prohibition of the use of force among States in their international relations enshrined in arts.1.1, 2.3, and 2.4 of the UN Charter.[428]

In Scotland, the referendum of the 18 September 2014 was the third one held in the last 40 years.[429] An intergovernmental agreement for a temporary transfer of constitutional authority to the Scottish Parliament was

---

426 For recent analyses, see Anna Khakeea, "The MINURSO Mandate, Human Rights and the Autonomy Solution for Western Sahara", *Mediterranean Politics*, Volume 19, Issue 3, 2014, and Stephen Zunes and Jacob Mundy, *Western Sahara: War, Nationalism and Conflict Irresolution*, Syracuse University Press, Syracuse, 2010.

427 On these cases, see the recent book edited by Christian Walter, Antje von Ungern-Sternberg, and Kavus Abushov (eds.), *Self-Determination and Secession in International Law*, Oxford University Press, Oxford, New York, 2014. See also Stefan Wolff and Annemarie Peen Rodt, "Self-Determination After Kosovo", *Europe-Asia Studies*, Vol.65, No.5, 2013, pp.799-822, and Nina Caspersen, "The South Caucasus after Kosovo: Renewed Independence Hopes?", *Europe-Asia Studies*, Vol.65, No.5, 2013, pp.929-945.

428 As is well known, a system of collective sanctions should apply in case of breaches of the prohibition of the use of violence according to arts.39-51 of the UN Charter. The only exceptions to this principle are foreseen in art.42 (if authorized by the Security Council to maintain or restore international peace and security) and art.51 (cases of self-defense by States until decisions are taken by the Security Council) of the UN Charter. An additional exception may be the emerging, but still contested, principle of the Responsibility to Protect (see above section 2.1.6).

429 The first two were carried out in 1979 and 1997. In the latter, called the "devolution" referendum, 74% of voters supported the devolution of further powers to Scotland. The Economist, "Scottish Nationalism. How did it come to this?", 12 July 2014, at http://www.economist.com/news/britain/21606865-confluence-historical-forces-north-sea-oil-and-absent-minded-politicians-has-put-britains

sealed on 15 October 2012, i.e., the "Edinburgh Agreement".[430] The Yes campaign headed by the Scottish National Party (SNP) leader Alex Salmond was based on the arguments that an "Independent Scotland" would become more democratic, fairer, and richer.[431] The "Better together" campaign had, instead, two main arguments: The fear of losing the pound currency and the uncertain future of entry into the EU.[432] These were two of the main reasons put forward by the "No" voters,[433] who eventually won the referendum with 55.25% votes to 44.65%.[434] A quarter of voters, however, believed that a victory of the "No" vote would, in any case, imply a

[Last access 12.01.2015]. Thus, the Scottish Bill (No. 104 1997-98) was adopted and introduced a Scottish executive body, led by a First Minister, and a new electoral system for the Scottish Parliament, to which those legislative powers not reserved to the UK central parliament were devolved. Oonagh Gay, "The Scotland Bill: Devolution and Scotland's Parliament", 98 *House of Commons Library Research Paper*, 7 January 1998, pp.37-61.

430 Prior to this, the victory of the Scottish National Party (SNP) at the 2007 elections had paved the way for the launch of the "National Conversation" on the future of Scotland and the establishment of the Calman Commission, whose proposals prompted the adoption of the Scotland Act of 2012, which reformed the previous 1998 Act. Nicola McEwen, "The Independence Referendum: Setback or Progress for the National Movement?", *Discover Society, Social Research Publications Policy Press* (University of Bristol), 30.09.2014, at http://www.discoversociety.org/2014/09/30/the-independence-referendum-setback-or-progress-for-the-national-movement. The Memorandum attached to the Agreement regulated in detail how the referendum should be organized, e.g. with regard to the date (before the end of 2014), the franchise, etc. The text of the Edinburgh Agreement (Agreement between the UK Government and the Scottish Government on a referendum on independence for Scotland) of 15 October 2012 is at http://www.scotland.gov.uk/About/Government/concordats/Referendum-on-independence [Last access to all on 12.01.2015].

431 The Economist, "Scottish Nationalism. How did it come to this?".

432 Ian Macwhirter, "The week that put victory firmly within the Yes camp's grasp", *The Herald Scotland*, 30.08.2014, at http://www.heraldscotland.com/comment/columnists/the-week-that-put-victory-firmly-within-the-yes-camps-grasp.25192218 [Last access 12.01.2015].

433 Lord Ashcroft, "How Scotland voted, and why", *Lord Ashcroft Polls*, 19.09.2014, at http://lordashcroftpolls.com/2014/09/scotland-voted [Last access 12.01.2015].

434 Scottish Independence Referendum, "Results", at http://scotlandreferendum.info. The electoral event had the highest turnout rate (84.6%) since the 1959 local elections. Kirsten Rumery, "The Road to a Fairer Scotland? Reflections on the Scottish Referendum, Politics and Society", *Discover Society, Social Research Publications Policy Press* (University of Bristol), 30.09.2014, at http://www.discoversociety.org/2014/09/30/the-road-to-a-fairer-scotland-reflections-on-the-scottish-referendum-politics-and-society [Last access to all 12.01.2015].

further devolution of powers.[435] This was the promise made by Prime Minister David Cameron, the Leader of the Labour Party Ed Miliband, and the Deputy Prime Minister Nick Clegg ten days before the referendum.[436] During his 19 September speech, Cameron announced the preparation of draft legislation by January 2015 and the creation of the Smith Commission.[437] To date (mid-July 2015), there are five draft statutory laws, which should have entered into force on the 1st of April.[438] This system of further devolution would substitute for the Scotland Act of 2012, which has not yet been

435 According to the Ashcroft poll published the day after, 47% of the "No" voters interviewed feared economic issues such as losing the currency, but also an increase in prices and a loss of jobs; 27% based their choice on historical ties to UK; and the last 25% believed that a victory of the "No" vote would anyhow imply a further devolution of powers. Lord Ashcroft, "Post-Referendum Scotland Poll" (Table with a summary of results), 19.09.2014, at http://lordashcroftpolls.com/wp-content/uploads/2014/09/Lord-Ashcroft-Polls-Referendum-day-poll-summary-1409191.pdf [Last access 12.01.2015].

436 Simon Johnson, "David Cameron vows to keep Scottish powers promise", *The Telegraph*, 28.09.2014, at http://www.telegraph.co.uk/news/politics/conservative/11126808/David-Cameron-vows-to-keep-Scottish-powers-promise.html [Last access 12.01.2015].

437 This Commission, headed by Lord Smith of Kelvin, was tasked with taking forward the commitment to further devolution to Scotland and to thus producing pertinent recommendations by 30 November 2014. See the official website of "The Smith Commission", "About", at https://www.smith-commission.scot/about [Last access 12.01.2015]. In short, the proposals were to devolve several powers to Scotland, including: the power to set income tax rates and bands on earned income; the power to concede the right to vote to 16 and 17 year-olds; the power to quantify and disqualify MSPs; and the power to devolve the full income from air passenger duties and aggregate taxes. BBC, "Smith Commission: 'Scotland should set its income tax'", 27.11.2014, at http://www.bbc.com/news/uk-scotland-30225016. The report of the Smith Commission was published on 27 November 2014. The Smith Commission, "Report of the Smith Commission for further devolution of powers to the Scottish Parliament", 27 November 2014, at https://www.smith-com mission.scot/wp-content/uploads/2014/11/The_Smith_Commission_Report-1.pdf [Last access to all 12.01.2015].

438 "The Scotland Act 1998 (River Tweed) Amendment Order 2015", at http://www.legislation.gov.uk/ukdsi/2015/9780111121931/contents;
"The Scotland Act 1998 (Functions Exercisable in or as Regards Scotland) Order 2015", at http://www.legislation.gov.uk/ukdsi/2015/9780111121832/contents; "The Regulatory Reform (Scotland) Act 2014 (Consequential Modifications) Order 2015", at
http://www.legislation.gov.uk/ukdsi/2015/9780111124505/contents;
"The Scotland Act 1998 (Variation of Borrowing Power) Order 2015", at http://www.legislation.gov.uk/ukdsi/2015/9780111125281/introduction; and "The Reservoirs (Scotland) Act 2011 (Restrictions on Disclosure of Information in relation to National Security etc.) Order 2015", at

applied.[439] However, its potential implementation was affected by the UK general elections of May 2015, as expected,[440] in which the three main parties, albeit with differences, developed a devolution agenda for Scotland.[441] Immediately after the referendum, the SNP tripled its membership[442] and started a campaign to abolish the House of Lords.[443] At the elections, after the leadership's handover from Salmond to Nicola Sturgeon, the SNP won 56 seats in the Parliament out of the 59 ones allocated to Scotland: It received 50% of the Scottish votes, i.e., the highest share of votes ever won by a single party in the country.[444] For the first time since 1945, SNP has become the third largest party in the UK House of Commons.[445] After the 2014 referendum, analysts had argued that although the "No" vote had won,

http://www.legislation.gov.uk/ukdsi/2015/9780111123362/contents [Last access 13.07.2015].

439 McEwen, "The Independence Referendum: Setback or Progress for the National Movement?".

440 Thomas Lundberg, "Scottish Politics turned upside down", *Political Insight,* Political Studies Association – PSA, 06.11.2014, at http://www.psa.ac.uk/insight-plus/blog/scottish-politics-turned-upside-down; Paul Carney, "What will be the role of constitutional issues in the UK General Election 2015?", *Centre on Constitutional Change* (University of Edinburgh), 08.01.2015, at http://www.futureukandscotland.ac.uk/blog/what-will-be-role-constitutional-issues-uk-general-election-2015 [Last access to all 12.01.2015].

441 For instance, the Conservative and the Liberal Democrat parties were (officially) in favor of devolving full control over the income taxes, while the Labour party were not. Eve Hepburn, "The Day after the Scottish Referendum", *Political Insight-Political Studies Association* (PSA), 19.09.2014, at http://www.psa.ac.uk/insight-plus/blog/day-after-scottish-referendum [Last access 12.01.2015].

442 McEwen, "The Independence Referendum: Setback or Progress for the National Movement?"; Lundberg, "Scottish Politics turned upside down"; James Mitchell, "Scotland is a different place now", 04.12.14, *Oxford University Press Blog*, at http://blog.oup.com/2014/12/scotland-different-place-post-referendum [Last access 12.01.2015].

443 Tom Gordon, "SNP starts campaign to scrap 'absurd' House of Lords", *The Herald Scotland*, 11.01.2015, at http://www.heraldscotland.com/politics/scottish-politics/snp-starts-campaign-to-scrap-absurd-house-of-lords.26228866 [Last access 12.01.2015].

444 Oliver Hawkins, Richard Keen and Nambassa Nakatudde, "General Elections 2015", *Briefing Paper of the House of Commons Library*, No.CBP7186, 28 July 2015, pp.4 and 9, at http://researchbriefings.files.parliament.uk/documents/CBP-7186/CBP-7186.pdf [Last access 03.08.2015].

445 *Ibid.*

a radical constitutional change for the UK would follow,[446] and that another referendum may be organized sooner than expected.[447] Indeed, the SNP put forward a number of amendments to the devolution reform, but the Conservative Party –that now counts on an overwhelming majority– have backtracked on the promises made before the referendum.[448] Hence, the overall reform remains to be seen.

In Catalonia, independentist thinking has grown exponentially since 2006. Until 2011, in the public opinion polls, the creation of an independent State of Catalonia came second, while the autonomy arrangement was the preferred option.[449] This changed dramatically in 2012, when the independentist preference reached a peak of 44.3%.[450] The interactions of four different factors and the lively political context contributed to propel the independentist cause. These factors were:[451] (1) The change in election results both at national and Catalan level;[452] (2) the constitutional debates, including the notorious decision of Spain's Constitutional Court of June 2010 in

446 Charlie Jeffery, "After the Scottish Referendum: A Constitutional Chain Reaction Unfolds", *Discover Society, Social Research Publications Policy Press* (University of Bristol), 30.09.2014, at http://www.discoversociety.org/2014/09/30/after-the-scottish-referendum-a-constitutional-chain-reaction-unfolds-2.

447 John Curtice, "Evidence and Confusion: More on Recent Scottish Polling", *What Scotland Thinks*, at http://blog.whatscotlandthinks.org/2014/11/evidence-confusion-recent-scottish-polling; Robert Lineira, "A fair and decisive outcome?", *Referendum reflections* (Economic and Social Research Council), at http://www.esrc.ac.uk/news-and-events/features-casestudies/features/32395/carousel-referendum-reflections.aspx [Last access to both 12.01.2015].

448 Craig McAngus, "The UK Government has backtracked on welfare devolution-but not on the Smith Commission", *Centre on Constitutional Change* (University of Edinburgh), 01.07.2015, at http://www.centreonconstitutionalchange.ac.uk/blog/uk-government-has-backtracked-welfare-devolution-not-smith-commission [Last access 03.08.2015].

449 In 2006, the former collected 13.9% of the preferences, while the latter 38.2%; in 2011, the former had 28.2% and the latter 30.3% of preferences. Jordi Argelaguet, "From Autonomism to Independentism: The Growth of Secessionism in Catalonia (2010-2013)", in Jaime Lluch (ed.), *Constitutionalism and the Politics of Accommodation in Multinational Democracies*, Palgrave Macmillan, 2014, pp.108-131, p.111 and table 5.1, Palgrave e-book at http://www.palgraveconnect.com/pc/doifinder/10.1057/9781137288998.0001 [Last access 29.01.2015]. The author analyzed the surveys of the Catalan *Centre d'Estudis d'Opinió* (CEO) from 2006 to 2013.

450 Argelaguet, "From Autonomism to Independentism …", p.111.

451 *Ibid.*, p.114.

452 The antagonism between the Popular Party and the Catalan pro-independence parties may fall under this first aspect: After the referendum on the Catalan Statute in

which it declared the unconstitutionality of 14 articles and reinterpreted a further 27 of the (new) 2006 Catalan Statute of Autonomy;[453] (3) the economic and other financial crisis-related problems;[454] and (4) the unofficial referendum of 2009,[455] with the (partially) consequent structuring of a mass social movement favoring independence.[456]

The probable last straw was the central government's refusal of the Catalan Parliament's proposal for a new fiscal agreement ("fiscal pact") similar to the one enjoyed by the regions of Basque Country or Navarre.[457] After-

June 2006, it was the former that filed the constitutional appeal against it. Additionally, at the Catalan regional elections held in November 2010, Artur Mas of the moderate rightwing nationalist coalition *Convergència i Unió* – CiU (Convergence and Union) was elected the new President. His party gained further support in the Catalan local elections held in May 2011. Later that year, the Popular Party won the national elections. Argelaguet, "From Autonomism to Independentism ...", pp.116-117.

453 Decision No.31 of 28 June 2010 of the Spanish Constitutional Court (*Tribunal Constitucional*), Spanish Offical Bulletin No.172 of 16 July 2010 (*Tribunal Constitucional, Sentencia 31/2010, de 28 de junio de 2010, Boletín Oficial del Estado núm. 172, de 16 de julio de 2010*).

454 In particular, in 2005, the data surrounding the fiscal deficit were made public and Catalonia's deficit amounted to -8.7%. This figure referred to the amount of investments and payments from the central government to Catalonia that was largely inferior in comparison to the tax revenues collected in this region. This also fuelled the massive protest that took place in Barcelona against the public investment policy in 2007. Argelaguet, "From Autonomism to Independentism ...", p.115.

455 In September 2009, cultural associations based in the village Arenys de Munt near to Barcelona organized an unofficial referendum for independence, which had a spillover effect in other areas of Catalonia. On 11 April 2011, the last of this type of referenda was held in Barcelona, which had a turnout of 23%, and 93.3% of votes resulted in favor of "independence". Argelaguet, "From Autonomism to Independentism ...", p.116. On this occasion, it is likely that only those who were already pro-independence went to vote.

456 Pro-independence sectors at the institutional level (*Associació de Municipis per la Independència*/Association of Municipalities for Independence) and from civil society (*Assemblea Nacional Catalana*/National Assembly of Catalonia) that started to organize conferences and debates on "the right to self-determination" since early 2012. Argelaguet, "From Autonomism to Independentism ...", p.117. They also organized a massive march for the *Diada*, the Catalan day, on 11 September 2012, demanding the independence of Catalonia as a "European State" Iñaki Pardo Torregrosa, "La Diada de Catalunya 2012, minuto a minuto", 11.09.2012, *La Vanguardia*, at http://endirecto.lavanguardia.com/politica/20120911/54348914 325/diada-de-catalunya-2012.html [Last access 29.01.2015].

457 This occurred one week after this march (20 September 2012). Montserrat Guibernau, "Calls for independence in Catalonia are part of an evolution of Spain's democracy that the country's constitution may have to come to accommodate",

wards, the events escalated. Catalan regional elections were brought forward to November 2012 and based on a sort of plebiscite on the right to self-determination.[458] Those political parties campaigning for "the right to decide" won.[459] On 18 December 2012, the CiU and the leftist *Esquerra Republicana de Catalunya* – ERC (Republican Left of Catalonia) signed an agreement that also included a "consultation on the future of Catalonia" to be carried out during the following legislature.[460] On 22 January 2013, the Catalan Parliament adopted Resolution No.5/X that contained the "Declaration of sovereignty and right to decide of the people of Catalonia".[461] In December 2013, the Catalan government agreed to hold a referendum on 9 November 2014 with two questions instead of just one, differently from Scotland.[462] The following January 2014, the Catalan government approved a law asking the central government to devolve the competence to invoke a

08.10.2012, *EUROPP – European Politics and Policy*, Blog of the London School of Economics, at http://blogs.lse.ac.uk/europpblog/2012/10/08/catalonia-independence-spain-constitution [Last access 29.01.2015].

458 Miquel Noguer Bau, "Mas pone rumbo a la autodeterminación", 26.09.2012, *El País Cataluña*, at http://ccaa.elpais.com/ccaa/2012/09/25/catalunya/1348575206_207361.html [Last access 29.01.2015].

459 As well as CiU, the leftist *Esquerra Republicana de Catalunya* – ERC (Republican Left of Catalonia), the green-leftist *Iniciativa per Catalunya Verds – Esquerra Unida i Alternativa* ICV-EUiA (Initiative for Catalonia Greens – Alternative and United Left), and the extreme left and pro-independence party Candidatura d'Unitat Popular – CUP (Popular Unity Candidature). Argelaguet, "From Autonomism to Independentism …", p.119.

460 Argelaguet, "From Autonomism to Independentism …", p.119.

461 This document stated that the Catalan people are "a sovereign political and legal subject" for reasons of democratic legitimacy. See the Resolution No.5/X of 2013 at http://www.parlament.cat/actualitat/R5_X_sobirania.pdf [Last access 29.01.2015].

462 The first question was: "Do you want Catalonia to become a State?" *(¿Quiere que Cataluña se convierta en un Estado?)*; possible answers: yes or no. Second question, only if the reply to the first one was yes: "Do you want this State to be independent?" *(¿Quiere que este Estado sea independiente?)*; possible answers: yes or no. Miquel Noguer Bau, "'¿Quiere que Cataluña sea un Estado? Y ¿que sea un Estado independiente?'", 12.12.2013, *El País Cataluña*, at http://ccaa.elpais.com/ccaa/2013/12/12/catalunya/1386848019314345.html [Last access 29.01.2015].

referendum,[463] which was denied on 8 April 2014.[464] However, a consultation law was prepared and approved in September 2014 by the Catalan government.[465] The central government filed this law for unconstitutionality[466] and the Spanish Constitutional Court suspended it as a precautionary measure.[467] For its part, the Catalan government tried in vain to appeal against this suspension.[468] Finally, in mid-October 2014, Artur Mas declared that

463 Roger Mateos, "El Parlament aprova amb 87 vots a favor demanar al Congrés la competència del referéndum", 16.01.2014, *Revista Ara.Cat*, at http://www.ara.cat/politica/arrenca-ple-parlament-referendum01067293447.html [Last access 29.01.2015].

464 Fernando Garea, "La Constitución frena la consulta", *El País*, 08.04.2014, at http://politica.elpais.com/politica/2014/04/08/actualidad/1396986575_704072.html [Last access 29.01.2015]. The arguments against the consultation are based on arts.2 and 8 of the Spanish Constitution that affirm, respectively, the "indissoluble unity of the Spanish nation", and the duty of the Army to guarantee Spain's sovereignty, independence, territorial integrity, and constitutional framework.

465 Law No.10 of 26 September 2014, *Ley 10/2014, de 26 de septiembre, de consultas populares no referendarias y otras formas de participación ciudadana*, at http://portaldogc.gencat.cat/utilsEADOP/PDF/6715/1373015.pdf [Last access 29.01.2015].

466 Spanish State Council, "Recurso de inconstitucionalidad contra determinados preceptos de la Ley de Cataluña 10/2014, de 26 de septiembre, de consultas populares no referendarias y otras formas de participación ciudadana", *Boletín Oficial del Estado*, Doc. No.964/2014, and "Impugnación de disposiciones sin fuerza de ley y resoluciones de las Comunidades Autónomas previstas en el artículo 161.2 de la Constitución contra el Decreto 129/2014, de 27 de septiembre, de convocatoria de la consulta popular no referendaria sobre el futuro político de Cataluña", Doc. No.965/2014, both of 28 September 2014, at https://www.boe.es/buscar/doc.php?id=CE-D-2014-964, and at https://www.boe.es/buscar/doc.php?id=CE-D-2014-965, respectively [Last access to both on 29.01.2015].

467 Spanish Constitutional Court, "Impugnación de disposiciones autonómicas (título V LOTC) n.º 5830-2014, contra el Decreto del Presidente de la Generalitat de Cataluña 129/2014, de 27 de septiembre, de convocatoria de consulta popular no referendaria sobre el futuro político de Cataluña, y sus anexos", *Boletín Oficial del Estado* No.237 of 30 September 2014, at https://www.boe.es/boe/dias/2014/09/30/pdfs/BOE-A-2014-9864.pdf [Last access 29.01.2015].

468 Miquel Noguer Bau, "La Generalitat invoca ante el TC la "legitimidad del derecho a decidir", 01.10.2014, *El País Cataluña*, at http://ccaa.elpais.com/ccaa/2014/10/01/catalunya/1412165338_056081.html [Last access 29.01.2015]. Eventually, in February 2015, the Spanish Constitutional Court ruled a partial unconstitutionality of the law regulating the consultation (Law No.10 of 26 September 2014). Constitutional Court (*Tribunal Constitucional*), decision No.31 of 25 February 2015, Spanish Offical Bulletin No.64 of 16 March

the consultation would become a process of citizen participation (*participación ciudadana*) to assess the will of Catalans towards "their political future".[469] The results published on the Catalan government's ad hoc website "Participa2014" registered a participation of 2,344,828 individuals, of which 80.9% voted "yes" to both questions; another 10% voted "yes" to the first question, but "no" to the second (independent state).[470]

This vote was most probably an act of protest and cannot but be defined as "symbolic" since, *inter alia*, there was no official control over the census of voters, there were fewer polling stations than during elections, and the stations were run by volunteers.[471] Indeed, this vote may have channeled other social and economic frustrations.[472] Additionally, the formulation of the two questions was misleading. The first question asked if the voter would be in favor of Catalonia becoming a "State"; and only in the second question was the independence of Catalonia under discussion. In fact, it is interesting that 10% voted "no" to the latter question: This may mean that this section of the Catalan population, together with another part that did not vote, would also be satisfied with a more substantial devolution of powers, as requested by the Catalan government during 2012. Other authors have also proposed a federal solution for Catalonia and Spain to avoid the secession of the former from the latter.[473] Spanish national elections are now

2015 (*Sentencia 31/2015, de 25 de febrero de 2015, Boletín Oficial del Estado núm.64, de 16 de marzo de 2015*).

469 Miquel Noguer Bau, "Mas propone diluir la consulta en un proceso de participación ciudadana", 14.10.2014, *El País Cataluña*, at http://ccaa.elpais.com/ccaa/2014/10/13/catalunya/1413228751_388842.html [Last access 29.01.2015].

470 See http://www.participa2014.cat. Recently, the Supreme Court of Justice of Catalonia (*Tribunal Superior de Justicia de Cataluña*), following a lawsuit of the Spanish state public prosecutor, started an investigation procedure against Artur Mas and twelve of his councilors for crimes of civil disobedience, perversion of justice, usurpation and misappropriation of public funds. Jesús García, "El TSJC investigará a Mas por desobediencia en la consulta del 9-N", El País, 22.12.2014, http://politica.elpais.com/politica/2014/12/22/actualidad/1419242895_942303.html [Last access to both 29.01.2015].

471 Dani Cetra, "A symbolic and non-binding vote on independence in Catalonia", Centre on Constitutional Change, 10.11.2014, at http://www.futureukandscotland.ac.uk/blog/symbolic-and-non-binding-vote-inde pendence-catalonia [Last access 29.01.2014].

472 Camil Ungureanu, "Las dos caras del nacionalismo independentista", El País, 31.10.2014, at http://elpais.com/elpais/2014/10/22/opinion/1414004304_177203.html [Last access 29.01.2014].

473 Francesc Trillas, "The Spanish government should offer Catalonia a referendum on federalism, not independence", *EUROPP – European Politics and Policy*, Blog

planned for November 2015 and a defeat of the Popular Party may create a new "window of opportunity" for the Catalan demands.[474] Indeed, although it is symbolic, the vote of more than 2.3 million of citizens cannot be underestimated.[475] Regional elections are also scheduled on 27 September 2015 and based, similarly to 2012, on a sort of "plebiscitary" vote on the potential independence.[476] After the municipal elections of 25 may 2015, in which the CiU lost the city of Barcelona (although it was confirmed as the most voted-for party in Catalonia),[477] the CiU coalition was dissolved in mid-June 2015.[478] In sum, the Catalan case is still under development and much will depend on the results of both the regional and national elections.

Since its colonization by France in 1853, New Caledonia has undergone many institutional changes. It became a French overseas territory under the 1946 French Constitution. In the early 1980s, pro- and anti-independence movements started to clash and its status was still undefined (autonomy vs. a State trusteeship). After a local referendum on self-determination in 1987, a "dialogue mission" carried out in 1988 and the Matignon Accords of 26 June 1988, the question of New Caledonian self-determination was put to a referendum of universal suffrage ordered by the French Government with Referendum Act (No. 88-1028) of 9 November 1988. This Act also contained statutory provisions in preparation for New Caledonia's self-determination. The referendum was approved with 57% votes in favor and was to be planned in December 1998. In 1998, a new agreement, the Noumea Accord, was reached and the transition period was extended. According to the Noumea Accord, a significant number of State competences were transferred to New Caledonia, with the exception of the justice system, public

of the London School of Economics, at http://blogs.lse.ac.uk/europpblog/2014/11/25/the-spanish-government-should-offer-catalonia-a-referendum-on-federalism-not-independence [Last access 29.01.2015].

474 Cetra, "A symbolic and non-binding vote on independence in Catalonia".

475 *Ibid.*

476 Javier Oms, "CiU se desintegra: 'El proyecto político de la federación se ha acabado'", *El Mundo*, 18.06.2015, at http://www.elmundo.es/cataluna/2015/06/18/55829b7a22601d1a5c8b457f.html [Last access 13.07.2015].

477 La Vanguardia, "Elecciones municipales: CiU se mantiene como primera fuerza municipal en Catalunya pero pierde la capital", *La Vanguardia*, 25.05.2015, at http://www.lavanguardia.com/politica/20150524/54431816635/resultados-elecciones-catalunya.html [Last access 13.07.2015].

478 It dissolved after 37 years. Official data assured that such a separation was a "friendly divorce", and both parties continued with their political independentist agenda. Oms, "CiU se desintegra: 'El proyecto político de la federación se ha acabado'".

order, defense, finance, and foreign affairs. These powers were to be transferred to New Caledonia after a referendum, after which either New Caledonia would become independent or autonomy would be maintained. Three referendums were planned for 2014 onwards.[479] The three Provincial Assemblies of New Caledonia were elected on 11 May 2014. By casting a majority vote of three-fifths, these Assemblies have the power to call for the first of these referendums.[480] In November 2014, on the first official visit of a French President to the territory, President Hollande declared that the date for the referendum should be decided by the New Caledonian Congress. However, if this body failed to set a date before 2017, the plebiscite would be organized by France in order to comply with the amendments to arts.76-77 of the French Constitution regarding this territory.[481] Other recent debates regarded who should be entitled to vote in this upcoming referendum. The new Caledonian government asked to amend the Noumea Accord in order to enlarge the electorate beyond the voters registered in

479 Human Rights Committee, *Ms. Marie-Hélène Gillot et al. v. France*, Communication No. 932/2000, Views of the 15 July 2002, UN Doc. A/57/40 at 270 (2002); Delphine Roucaute, "Nouvelle-Calédonie: après les élections, le référendum en ligne de mire", Le Monde, 12 May 2014, at http://www.lemonde.fr/les-decodeurs/article/2014/05/12/nouvelle-caledonie-apres-les-elections-le-referendum-en-lig ne-de-mire44154704355770.html; BBC, "New Caledonia profile", 02.10. 2014, at http://www.bbc.com/news/wor ld-asia-pacific-16740838 [Last access 12.01.2015].

480 Roucaute, "Nouvelle-Calédonie: après les élections, le référendum en ligne de mire"; Rowena Dickins Morrison, "Preparing self-determination: crucial elections in New Caledonia", 11 May 2014, SOGIP project, at http://sogip.wordpress.com/2014/05/11/preparing-self-determination-crucial-elec tions-in-new-caledonia-11-may-2014-part-1-en; ABC/AFP, "New Caledonia elections: French loyalists win, independence supporters gain ground", *Australian Broadcasting Corporation ABC*, 12 May 2014, at http://www.abc.net.au/news/2014-05-12/an-new-caledonia-elections/5445380 [Last access to all 12.01.2015]. Denice Fisher, "Elections for the future of New Caledonia", *The Interpreter*, Lowy Institute for International Policy, 20 May 2014, at http://www.lowyinterpreter.org/post/2014/05/20/Elections-for-the-future-of-New-Caledonia.aspx?COLLCC=1622397185&COLLCC=1700024601&.

481 Nicolas Chapuis, "A Nouméa, Hollande choisit la prudence", Le Monde, 17 November 2014, at http://www.lemonde.fr/politique/article/2014/11/17/a-noume a-hollande-choisit-la-prudence_4524591_823448.html; in English see Radio New Zealand International, "New Caledonia referendum a must", 18 November 2014, at http://www.radionz.co.nz/international/pacific-new s/259 613/new-caledonia-referendum-a-must. See the text of the French Constitution at http://www.assemblee-nationale.fr/connaissance/constitution.asp [Last access to all 12.01.2015]

1998, whom should be the sole ones entitled to vote.[482] The amendment was approved soon after the meeting of the Accord's signatories held in early June 2015.[483] A commission may hence be established to revise the list of voters in view of the upcoming referendum.[484]

In sum, the three cases of Scotland, Catalonia, and New Caledonia share the existence of influential independentist movements but are extremely different from each other in terms of the referenda's status, timeframe, and modalities. The former two are regions of two established states (Spain and UK respectively) and enjoy diverse degrees of autonomy,[485] the latter is an ex French colony and currently an overseas territory. Again, in the former two, the referenda were carried out in extremely different modalities in September (Scotland) and November (Catalonia) 2014, while in the latter the referendum will probably be held before or during 2018.[486] However, in Scotland and New Caledonia the referenda were and are negotiated with their central governments and regulated by different Acts. Additionally, in Scotland, in the latest polls, the majority of interviewees agree that both the referendum and the campaigns were held in a fair way.[487] In Catalonia, the plebiscite has been repeatedly denied by the Spanish authorities. Finally, in

---

482 Laura Philippon, «Nouvelle-Calédonie: un Comité des signataires exceptionnel ce vendredi à Matignon», 04.06.2015, *Outre-mer 1ère/France*, at http://www.la1ere.fr/2015/06/04/nouvelle-caledonie-un-comite-des-signataires-e xceptionnel-ce-vendredi-matignon-261673.html [Last access 13.07.2015].

483 Outre-mer 1ère/France, "Le Sénat adopte à la quasi unanimité le projet de loi organique sur le corps électoral de Nouvelle-Calédonie », *Outre-mer 1ère/France*, 30.06.2015, at http://www.la1ere.fr/2015/06/29/le-senat-adopte-la-quasi-unanimite-le-projet-de-loi-organique-sur-le-corps-electoral-de-nouvelle-caledonie-267908.html [Last access 13.07.2015].

484 See art.3 of the (French) Organic law No.2015-987 of 5 August 2015 on the consultation about the access to sovereignty of New Caledonia (*Loi organique n° 2015-987 du 5 août 2015 relative à la consultation sur l'accession de la Nouvelle-Calédonie à la pleine souveraineté*), which modified arts.218-1 and 218-2 of the (French) Organic law No.99-209 of 19 March 1999 on New Caledonia (*Loi organique n° 99-209 du 19 mars 1999 relative à la Nouvelle-Calédonie*), at http://www.legifrance.gouv.fr/eli/loi/2015/8/5/2015-987/jo/texte [Last access 17.08.2015].

485 The author is obviously aware of the contested annexations in the past of both Scotland and Catalonia to UK and Spain respectively, and of the persecution and acts of discrimination, e.g., against the Catalans under Franco's dictatorship. However, since this study focuses on the right to self-determination of indigenous peoples, the cases here are only briefly presented to complete the framework of recent debates on self-determination.

486 BBC, "New Caledonia profile".

487 Lineira, "A fair and decisive outcome?".

both Catalonia and Scotland, the secessionist movements also appeared to channel other types of popular frustration,[488] particularly vis-à-vis the economic crisis in connection with the potential loss of autonomy (Catalonia) or a lost opportunity to further enhance it (Scotland). Indeed, the results of the referendum in Scotland may suggest popular support for a wider devolution of powers, albeit effective and not solely promised. This same assumption may also apply to Catalonia: The increase in secessionist supporters in the polls from 2011 onwards may be read as an expression of dissatisfaction with the current –and potentially reduced– autonomy arrangement. The constant refusal of the Spanish central government to the so-called "Catalan autonomy project" have fuelled these feelings.

In conclusion, while the situation in New Caledonia is still pending, the other two cases may suggest that effective autonomy arrangements and further devolution of powers may meet popular demands and needs within the self-determination discourse without opting for an extreme solution such as secession. This would also be in line with the theory of Remedial Secession: Catalonia and Scotland cannot be framed as cases in which the population is violently repressed. However, their aspirations to be more autonomous are or have indeed been repressed. Thus, an effective and, as said, not only promised devolution of powers, perhaps in the form of a federation, may potentially be the optimal solution in similar cases.

Finally, for the aims of this study, it is important to highlight that self-determination continues to show multiple expressions and that autonomy may be one of the most effective ways of exercising it, but by no means the only one.

2.1.8 Concluding remarks

The debates on the right to self-determination briefly described in this section show that the right to self-determination is (necessarily) evolving.[489] In

488 See Ungureanu, "Las dos caras del nacionalismo independentista" for Catalonia, and, for Scotland, Norman Bonney, "What happens if Scotland votes 'Yes' in the independence referendum?", *British Politics and Policy at LSE*, at http://blogs.lse.ac.uk/politicsandpolicy/what-happens-if-scotland-votes-yes, or at http://bit.ly/1l9sUM1 [Last access to all 12.01.2015].

489 Cassese, *Self-determination of Peoples*, p.52 and 55; Crawford, "The Right to Self-Determination in International Law", p.25 and 26; Alfredsson, "Different Forms of and Claims to the Right of Self-Determination", p.79; Hurst Hannum, "Self-Determination in the Post-Colonial Era", in D. Clark and R. Williamson (eds.), *Self-*

particular, the classical dichotomy of external and internal self-determination has shown its limits. Undoubtedly, some aspects such as independence, secession, and annexation on the one hand and self-government on the other tend to meet resistance in mainstream academic understandings, as well as in States' practices. Nevertheless, it is certain that, e.g., self-governments, nowadays may have also "external" powers, or that in our globalized world a "people" may express their views also in international fora, thus exercising external expressions vastly different from, e.g., a secession. Recent and current events such as the independence of Kosovo, as well as the debates on the Responsibility to Protect and Remedial Secession challenge the prohibition of interference/non-intervention and the principle of territorial integrity, suggesting that these principles of international law may soon be revised. Likewise, those scholars who are skeptical on the Kosovo precedent acknowledge that a "Kosovo argument" is or will be used by various subjects in international diplomacy.[490] Therefore, as affirmed by Weller, "[t]here is […] emerging a sense that it is necessary to escape from the current self-determination trap, either by engineering new forms of co-governance within States, or by accepting that secession cannot in the end ruled out if other options do not suffice".[491] Indeed, a crucial issue that remains very controversial is the recognition of a right to secession within the right to self-determination. Hence, the focus needs to detach from the (increasingly misleading) external-internal dichotomy, and to move toward an approach of *multiple expressions of self-determination*, which differ from a right-holder to another, as in the case of indigenous peoples. This may also be more in line with the principle of territorial integrity, as the threat of or the actual use of force is not necessary to guarantee some of the expressions of self-determination.

In sum, there is a considerable need to understand self-determination as a flexible principle that underlines the whole international order,[492] "rethinking the concept […] and suggesting possible avenues for the future

Determination: International Perspectives, MacMillan Press, Houndmills, 1996, pp.12-40, pp.26 and 37.

490 Snežana Trifunovska, "The Impact of the 'Kosovo Precedent' on Self-Determination Struggles", in James Summers (ed.), *Kosovo: A Precedent?*, Martinus Nijhoff, Leiden, Boston, 2011, pp. 375-393, p.393.

491 Marc Weller, "Why the Legal Rules on Self-Determination Do Not Resolve Self-Determination Disputes", in Marc Weller and Barbara Metzger (eds.), *Settling Self-Determination Disputes. Complex Power-Sharing in Theory and in Practice*, Martinus Nijhoff, Leiden, Boston, 2008, pp.17-45, p.45.

492 Thürer and Burri, "Self-Determination", para.26.

development of the law in this area".[493] In this context, indigenous peoples' right to self-determination, as will be analyzed in the next section 2.2, represents one of these further developments. It differs from the general right to self-determination since it has many (more) facets and is probably undergoing even greater development, particularly vis-à-vis the recent adoption of the United Nations Declaration on the Rights of Indigenous Peoples.

2.2 The right to self-determination of Indigenous Peoples

2.2.1. Introduction

Claims to self-determination by indigenous peoples started soon after the end of First World War (WWI). Wilson's speech also inspired indigenous chiefs, who in the early 1920s traveled to Geneva to put their claims before the League of Nations. As mentioned in chapter 1, both the Native American General Levi, also known as Haudenosaunee Chief Deskaheh, and the Maori leader T.W. Ratana sought to complain about the non-compliance of previous treaties signed by Great Britain in 1923 and 1925, respectively. They were eventually denied access to the new international organization.[494] In particular, Deskaheh, chief of one of the six Iriquos Confederacy, the Younger Bear Clan, tried to claim a violation of Iriquos sovereignty as guaranteed in the Jay Treaty of 1794 and the Treaty of Ghent of 1814 between Great Britain and United States. After WWI, the Iriquos had fallen under Canadian rule.[495] After vain attempts before the Governor of Canada and even King George V of Great Britain, General Levi had put his trust in the newly established League of Nations in Geneva, where he waited for a year to be heard. Thanks to his linguistic and diplomatic capacities, he had gained the support of States such as Estonia, Ireland, Panama and (at that time) Persia. However, despite these allies, Great Britain was able to deny him access to the League of Nations.[496]

493 Cassese, *Self-determination of Peoples*, p.341.

494 United Nations Permanent Forum on Indigenous Issues, "History", at http://undesadspd.org/IndigenousPeoples/AboutUsMembers/History.aspx [Last access 07.08.2014].

495 Joshua Castellino, "Conceptual Difficulties and the Right to Indigenous Self-Determination", in Nazila Ghanea and Alexandra Xanthaki (eds.), *Minorities, Peoples and Self-Determination*, Brill, Leiden, 2005 pp.55-74, p.56.

496 Castellino, "Conceptual Difficulties and the Right to Indigenous Self-Determination" p.56; Littlechild, "Comment on agenda items at the Oslo Conference ...", p.20. For a history of indigenous movements see Les Malezer, "Permanent Forum

The relationship between these supranational organizations and indigenous peoples has profoundly changed over the years. As stated by the UN Secretary General Kofi Anan at the end of the session of the United Nations Permanent Forum on Indigenous Issues in 2002, indigenous peoples (should) have a "home" at the UN.[497] However, despite all the developments at international level, the recognition of the right to self-determination of indigenous peoples, and more importantly, *which implication and application* of the right to self-determination, is still a thorny issue. As mentioned in the previous section, States still tend to equate self-determination to Statehood and thus independence or secession. Nevertheless, indigenous peoples are among those groups that do not necessarily ask for their own State, at least not all of them.[498] Only in case of persistent repressive acts

---

on Indigenous Issues: 'Welcome to the Family of the UN'", in Joshua Castellino and Niamh Walsh (eds.), *Indigenous peoples and International Law*, Leiden, Boston, Martinus Nijhoff Publishers, Raoul Wallenberg Institute Human Rights Library, Volume 20, 2005, pp.67-85.

497 The UN Secretary General Kofi Anan stated "You have a home at the United Nations [...] you will make an immense contribution to the Organization's mission of peace and governance", reported by Castellino, "Conceptual Difficulties and the Right to Indigenous Self-Determination" p.57.

498 There is a wide consensus on this both in the reports of the UN Working Group on Indigenous Populations (see section 2.2.2.3) and among academics dealing with indigenous rights. The authors also cite statements by indigenous spokespersons during the works of both the UN Draft Declaration and the UNDRIP. See Erica-Irene Daes, "The Right of Indigenous Peoples to 'Self-Determination' in the Contemporary World Order", in Donald Clark and Robert Williamson, *Self-Determination. International Perspectives*, MacMillan Press, HoundsMill, Basingstoke and London, 1996 and St. Martin's Press, New York, 1996, pp.47-57, p.54; Snežana Trifunovska, "One Theme in Two Variations – Self Determination for Minorities And Indigenous Peoples", 5 *International Journal on Minority and Group Rights*, 1997, pp.175-197, p.194; Patrick Thornberry, "Self-Determination and Indigenous Peoples: Objections and Responses", in Pekka Aikio and Martin Scheinin (eds.), *Operationalizing the Rights of Indigenous Peoples to Self-Determination*, Institute for Human Rights, Åbo Akademi University, Saarijärvi, 2000, pp.39-64, pp.53, 55 and 64; Kingsbury, "Reconstructing Self-Deter mination: A Relational Approach", pp.24-25; John B. Henriksen, "The Right of Self-Determination: Indigenous Peoples versus States", in Pekka Aikio and Martin Scheinin (eds.), *Operationalizing the Rights of Indigenous Peoples to Self-Determination*, Institute for Human Rights, Åbo Akademi University, Saarijärvi, 2000, pp.131-142, pp.137 and 141; Kristian Myntti, "The Right to Self-Determination and Effective Participation", in Pekka Aikio and Martin Scheinin (eds.), *Operationalizing the Rights of Indigenous Peoples to Self-Determination*, Institute for Human Rights, Åbo Akademi University, Saarijärvi, 2000, pp.85-130, p.88; James Anaya, "The Right of Indigenous Peoples to Self-Determination in the Post-Declaration Era", in Claire Charters and Rodolfo Stavenhagen (eds.), *Making the Declaration*

by governments, the theory of Remedial Secession may find an application in the case of indigenous peoples.[499] Probably, to affirm that no indigenous people across the world aspire to Statehood would be reductive. However, apart from the aforementioned attempts during the 1920s and of the Belgian thesis mentioned earlier (see section 2.1.2), the majority of statements made by indigenous spokespersons over the last thirty years suggest that Statehood would be a desired option for very few indigenous peoples.[500] Rather, there is a pressing necessity to rethink the right of self-determination of indigenous peoples since the adoption of the Draft Declaration on the Rights of Indigenous Peoples of 1993.[501] Nowadays, after the adoption of the new formula contained in the United Nations Declaration on the Rights of Indigenous Peoples of 2007, other forms of expressions of this right need to be taken seriously into account.

Thus, this section aims to unravel the multifaceted right to self-determination of indigenous peoples. There is no intention to reduce the content of this right to one or more of these different facets. Rather, there are three main objectives. First, to analyze how the right to self-determination of indigenous peoples has developed at the UN level (section 2.2.2). Also a brief reference to the two American and African regional human rights systems is included (section 2.2.3). Second, to assess the manifold expressions of this multi-faceted right of indigenous peoples (sections 2.2.2 and 2.2.4), by briefly addressing the implications of the use of the term "people" in the case of indigenous peoples (section 2.2.5). The third and final main objective is to introduce the overall goal of this work, i.e., to ascertain whether a *composite right to political participation of indigenous peoples* may represent one of the expressions of the multi-faceted right to self-determination of indigenous peoples (sections 2.2.4 and 2.2.6).

Work. The United Nations Declaration on the Rights of Indigenous Peoples, International Work Group for Indigenous Affairs (IWGIA), Doc. No.127, Copenhagen, 2009, pp.184-198, p.185; Mauro Barelli, "Shaping Indigenous Self-Determination: Promising or Unsatisfactory Solutions?", in 13(3) *International Community Law Review* 2011, pp.413-436, p.418.

499 Barelli, "Shaping Indigenous Self-Determination: Promising or Unsatisfactory Solutions?", p. 426.

500 Thornberry, "Self-Determination and Indigenous Peoples: Objections and Responses", p.63 and Daes, "The Right of Indigenous Peoples to 'Self-Deter mination' in the Contemporary World Order", p.54.

501 Craig Scott, "Indigenous Self-Determination and Decolonization of the International Imagination: A Plea", 18 *Human Rights Quarterly* 1996, pp.814-820, p.819.

2.2.2 The right to self-determination of indigenous peoples in the UN standards

An increasing number of UN bodies have been dealing with indigenous peoples' rights. In this section, primary attention will be given to the Cobo-Diaz Study and the works of the UN Human Rights Committee, the Committee on Economic, Social and Cultural Rights, the Working Group on Indigenous Populations (WGIP), and the Working Group on the Draft Declaration (WGDD), including the texts of the 1994 United Nations Draft Declaration on the Rights of Indigenous Peoples (Draft Declaration) and of the 2007 United Nations Declaration on the Rights of Indigenous Peoples (UNDRIP). The aim is to assess the elements that these bodies considered to be part of the right to self-determination. In particular, the Cobo-Diaz Study has been often overlooked by the literature despite the fact that some core elements of self-determination, which have been recognized in the UNDRIP, were already considered in this study.

Since the creation of the UN Permanent Forum on Indigenous Issues in 2000, the appointment of the Special Rapporteur on the Situation of Human Rights and Fundamental Freedoms of Indigenous People (hereinafter, Special Rapporteur) in 2001, and the establishment of the Expert Mechanism on the Rights of Indigenous Peoples in 2007, the landscape vis-à-vis the international arena of actors that deal with the protection of indigenous rights has unquestionably changed. In addition, the direct participation of indigenous representatives during the sessions of these bodies has considerably increased. However, these bodies are not directly in charge of addressing the right to self-determination of indigenous peoples, although they inevitably –but indirectly– touched upon this fundamental right in their work. The same situation applies to the relevant sessions of the Committee on the Elimination of Racial Discrimination (CERD). Since the aim of this study is rather to focus on what I call one expression of the multi-faceted right to self-determination of indigenous peoples, i.e., their *composite right to political participation*, the outputs of the UN Permanent Forum on Indigenous Issues and the Expert Mechanism on the Rights of Indigenous Peoples will be analyzed in the next chapter (section 3.3). This is also due to the recent interest shown by these two bodies on the topic of indigenous participation.[502] Finally, the reports of the Special Rapporteur, together with

502 The second thematic study of the Expert Mechanism on the Rights of Indigenous Peoples precisely addressed the right of Indigenous peoples to participate in decision-making bodies. See the Reports of the Expert Mechanism on the Rights of

the documents of the UN Universal Periodic Review,[503] will mainly serve in the analysis of the two case studies (Bolivia and Chile, chapters 5 and 6, respectively).

2.2.2.1 References to the right of self-determination of indigenous peoples in the "Study of the Problem of Discrimination against Indigenous Populations"

As seen in chapter 1, in 1971 José Ricardo Martínez Cobo was appointed "Special Rapporteur on the situation of human rights and fundamental freedoms of indigenous peoples" by the (then) UN Sub-Commission on Prevention of Discrimination and Protection of Minorities. After more than a decade of extensive research, carried out mainly by Augusto Willemsen Diaz, a staff member of the United Nations Center for Human Rights,[504] the comprehensive "Study of the Problem of Discrimination against Indigenous Populations" (Cobo-Diaz Study) was completed between 1981 and 1984.[505]

Indigenous Peoples, "Progress report on the study on indigenous peoples and the right to participate in decision-making", UN Doc. A/HRC/EMRIP/2010/2, 17 May 2010, and "Final study on indigenous peoples and the right to participate in decision-making", UN Doc. A/HRC/EMRIP/2011/2, 26 May 2011. In addition, the thirteenth session of the UN Permanent Forum on Indigenous Issues in New York on 12-23 May 2014 focused on the special theme: "Principles of good governance consistent with the United Nations Declaration on the Rights of Indigenous Peoples: articles 3 to 6 and 46". See at http://undesads pd.org/IndigenousPeoples/UNPFIISessions/Thirteenth.aspx
[Last access 19.07.2014].

503 Despite the initial skepticism of human rights activists, the first cycle of UPR, which has seen the 100% engagement of States, has been rather successful and had three positive results: the human rights system of every State has been examined; an extensive database on human rights information for each country has been created; and, most importantly, the engagement of States has shown evidence of *opinio juris*, thus consolidating human rights standards. Finally, the UPR has had a considerable impact on States: A non-collaborating State within the UPR system would lose its prestige before the international community. Elvira Dominguez-Redondo, "The Universal Periodic Review. Is there life beyond naming and shaming in human rights implementation?", 4 *New Zealand Law Review* 2012, pp.673-706, pp.705-706.

504 Eide, "Rights of Indigenous Peoples – Achievements in International Law ...", p.164; Augusto Willemsen-Diaz, "How Indigenous Peoples' Rights Reached the UN", p.23.

505 See all the chapters of the "Study of the Problem of Discrimination against Indigenous Populations" on the website of the UN Permanent Forum on Indigenous Issues at

The initial aim of the Cobo-Diaz Study was to outline discrimination vis-à-vis Indigenous peoples and the obstacles for their "full integration" into the wider society.[506] However, this initial focus changed as a result of the insistence of indigenous organizations,[507] which had gained greater influence at the UN level especially after the "International Conference on Discrimination against the Indigenous Populations in the Americas" held in 1977 in Geneva. Thus, the Cobo-Diaz Study extensively covered a variety of indigenous issues, including the definition question and self-determination.

References to self-determination were first included in Chapter XVIII of the Cobo-Diaz Study, which dealt with "Political rights".[508] The authors reported that, at that time (in the early 1980s), indigenous communities and organizations were constantly referring to self-determination, which "they consider[ed] the only form that would enable them to take over the reins of their destiny and which they claim as an inalienable right to determine for themselves the future course of their existence".[509] However, they added that, upon closer inspection, indigenous peoples' claims to self-determination varied significantly, ranging from the establishment of autonomy arrangements with specific competences to the recognition of Statehood. In fact, regarding the latter claim, they highlighted the set of problems linked to the treaties signed between some indigenous communities and the former colonial State, which were disregarded by the successor independent State.[510]

In Chapters XXI-XXII of the Cobo-Diaz Study, "Conclusions, proposals and recommendations",[511] it is finally stated that "[s]elf-determination, in

---

http://undesadspd.org/IndigenousPeoples/LibraryDocuments/Mart%C3%ADnez-CoboStudy.aspx [Last access 08.08.2014].

506 Eide, "Rights of Indigenous Peoples – Achievements in International Law ...", p.165.

507 *Ibid.*

508 UN Commission on Human Rights, Sub-Commission on Prevention of Discrimination and Protection of Minorities, "Study of the Problem of Discrimination against Indigenous Populations", Chapter 18, "Political Rights", UN Doc. E/CN.4 Sub.2 /1983/21/Add.6, adopted during the Thirty-seventh session, 24 May 1984.

509 Chapter 18, "Political Rights", UN Doc. E/CN.4 Sub.2 /1983/21/Add.6, para.148.

510 *Ibid.*

511 UN Commission on Human Rights, Sub-Commission on Prevention of Discrimination and Protection of Minorities, "Study of the Problem of Discrimination against Indigenous Populations", Chapters XXI-XXII of the Study, "Conclusions, proposals and recommendations", UN Doc. E/CN.4 Sub.2/1983/21/Add.8 adopted during the Thirty-sixth session, on 30 September 1983.

its many forms, must be recognized as the basic precondition for the enjoyment by indigenous peoples of their fundamental rights and the determination of their future".[512] Moreover, the authors specified that the "right to self-determination exists at various levels and includes economic, social, cultural and political factors".[513]

The Cobo-Diaz Study's Conclusions, prior to the concluding announcement on self-determination and under the same heading of "Political Rights", affirm that indigenous peoples' representation in public offices and in elective or other posts should not be subject to special requirements, such as the ability to read and write, or manipulative practices such as gerrymandering,[514] and that it should be effective rather than symbolic, and thus ensured by appropriate measures, e.g., by guaranteeing reserved seats in parliaments or local assemblies, as well as in other State bodies.[515] The right to live freely on their lands "by virtue of their very existence" was also stressed, especially taking into consideration the historical factors, as well as issues of discrimination and exploitation, surrounding indigenous peoples.[516] Finally, the authors underlined that all the instruments aimed to achieve a "proper participation" of indigenous peoples in the matters affecting them, with the necessity to respect and support their internal organizational structures, given that they are part of their culture.[517]

In sum, according to the Cobo-Diaz Study, self-determination constitutes an "exercise of free choice" by indigenous peoples, and it may have "internal and external expressions". Consequently, forms of autonomy within a State included the collective right "to be different", but not necessarily the right to secede from the State in which an indigenous people lives.[518] In addition, vis-à-vis indigenous autonomy, the authors affirmed that "[g]overnments must abandon their policies of intervening in the organization and development of indigenous peoples and *must grant them autonomy*, together with the capacity for managing the relevant economic processes in the manner which they themselves deem appropriate to their interests and needs" [emphasis added].[519]

---

512 *Ibid.*, para.581.
513 *Ibid.*, para.582.
514 *Ibid.*, para.575.
515 *Ibid.*, para.576.
516 *Ibid.*, para.577.
517 *Ibid.*, para.579
518 *Ibid.*, para.582.
519 *Ibid.*, para.579.

For the aim of this section, suffice it to underline here that even in the Cobo-Diaz Study, the multi-faceted nature of the right of self-determination of indigenous peoples was outlined. This right thus implies: Economic, social, cultural, and political aspects; land rights and political participation in public and State affairs as well as respect for internal organizations; and autonomy. Moreover, self-determination is the basic "precondition" for the enjoyment of all indigenous peoples' rights.

2.2.2.2 The UN Human Rights Committee, the Committee on Economic, Social and Cultural Rights and the right to self-determination of indigenous peoples

Both the Human Rights Committee (HRC) and the Committee on Economic, Social and Cultural Rights (CESCR) have inevitably dealt with the right to self-determination of indigenous peoples. The former has approached self-determination, although not directly, both in cases of individual complaints according to ICCPR-OP1 and in the reporting procedure of States according to art.40 of the ICCPR. Since May 2013, the latter may scrutinize individual complaints but, as of today (July 2015), there are six pending cases but no views of any communication have yet been published.[520] Thus, CESCR has analyzed the application of art.1 solely in the reporting procedure according to art.16 of the ICESCR.

As seen in section 2.1.3, since the first cases involving indigenous claimants, the HRC refused to consider alleged violations of art.1, that is to say of the right to self-determination.[521] Moreover, in recent cases, such as *Ángela Poma Poma v. Peru* (2009), the HRC reaffirmed that individuals can claim violations of the rights set forth in the ICCPR according to the procedure provided by the ICCPR-OP1, but that these rights do not include those contained in art.1.[522] In fact, in all cases regarding indigenous issues, the HRC has considered violations of the rights recognized in art.27 of ICCPR, which is considered the *grundnorm* of minority protection. Although

520 Committee on Economic, Social and Cultural Rights, "Table of Pending Cases", at http://www.ohchr.org/EN/HRBodies/CESCR/Pages/PendingCases.aspx [Last access 03.08.2015].

521 As seen in section 2.1.4, since the widely known decision in the *Lubicon Lake Band v. Canada* (1984), the HRC consolidated this position in all of its later jurisprudence.

522 HRC, *Ángela Poma Poma v. Peru*, Communication No. 1457/2006, Views adopted on 27 March 2009, UN Doc. CCPR/C/95/D/1457/2006, para.6.3.

indigenous peoples have repeatedly affirmed their rejection of being treated as "minorities", as the current well-defined *corpus iuris* on the protection of the two groups confirms (see also chapter 1), in many cases indigenous peoples have benefitted from the protection provided by art.27. Despite the non-recognition of violations of their right to self-determination, for instance, in the notorious cases *Lovelace v. Canada* (1981), the HRC found that Canada had violated art.27. Ms Lovelace, registered since her birth as "Maliseet Indian" under Canadian Law, had lost her right to live on the reserve for having married a non-indigenous man in 1970 and from whom she eventually divorced. At that time, the ICCPR was not in force. Thus, the HRC analyzed the situation from 19 August 1976 onwards, when Canada was bound to comply with the ICCPR. Due to the continued denial for Ms Lovelace to reside in the Tobique Reserve even after 1976 (and her subsequent divorce), the HRC found that Ms Lovelace was denied her right to enjoy her culture in community with other members and that art.27 had thus been infringed.[523] In the aforementioned case *Ominayak and the Lake Lubicon Band v. Canada* (1990), apart from inaugurating the jurisprudence against a recognition of the justifiability of the right to self-determination, the HRC recognized a violation of art.27 in favor of the Lubicon band, also recognizing that possession of land is part of their culture.[524] The environmental degradation caused by the exploitation of natural resources and the construction of a pulp mill in the Lubicon Cree territories in the province of Alberta had affected the health conditions but also the traditional and subsistence activities of this indigenous people. According to the HRC "the rights protected by article 27, include the right of persons, in community with others, to engage in economic and social activities which are part of the culture of the community to which they belong".[525] Thus, "[h]istorical inequities, to which the State party refers, and certain more recent developments threaten the way of life and culture of the Lubicon Lake Band, and constitute a violation of article 27 so long as they continue".[526]

523 HRC, *Sandra Lovelace v. Canada*, Communication No. R.6/24, Views adopted on 30 July 1981, UN Doc. Supp. No. 40 (A/36/40), paras. 17 and 19.

524 Martin Scheinin, "The Right to Self-Determination under the Covenant on Civil and Political Rights", in Pekka Aikio and Martin Scheinin (eds.), *Operationalizing the Rights of Indigenous Peoples to Self-Determination*, Institute for Human Rights, Åbo Akademi University, Saarijärvi, 2000, pp.179-198, p.195.

525 HRC, *Lubicon Lake Band v. Canada*, Communication No. 167/1984 (26 March 1990), Views adopted on 26 March 1990, UN Doc. Supp. No. 40 (A/45/40) at 1 (1990), para 32.2.

526 *Lubicon Lake Band v. Canada*, para.33. For an overview on the HRC jurisprudence and more generally of the UN Treaty bodies jurisprudence involving indigenous

Notwithstanding the self-restraint attitude of the HRC vis-à-vis the justifiability of the right to self-determination, and the limited (practical) impact of its jurisprudence upon indigenous peoples' rights,[527] three further aspects of the works of both the HRC and the CESCR are worth mentioning in this section, as follows.

First, since 1999, in their Concluding Observations in the reporting procedure vis-à-vis an increasing number of States, the Committees have rec-

peoples until early 2000, see Fergus MacKay, "A Briefing on Indigenous Peoples' Rights and the United Nations Human Rights Committee", Forest Peoples Programme, 2001, at http://www.forestpeoples.org/sites/fpp/files/publication/2010/10/unhrcfppbriefdec01eng.pdf [Last access 14.07.2014]. For a collection of the UN Human Rights Treaty Bodies jurisprudence pertinent to indigenous peoples' rights, see Fergus MacKay, "Indigenous Peoples and United Nations Human Rights Treaty Bodies: A Compilation of Treaty Body Jurisprudence 1993-2004", Vol. I, Forest Peoples Programme, 2005, at http://www.forestpeoples.org/sites/fpp/files/publication/2010/09/unjurisprudencecompsept05eng.pdf [Last access 14.07.2014]; Fergus MacKay, "Indigenous Peoples and United Nations Human Rights Treaty Bodies. A Compilation of UN Treaty Body Jurisprudence. Volume II, 2005-2006", Forest Peoples Programme, 2007, at http://www.forestpeoples.org/sites/fpp/files/publication/2010/09/unjurisprudencecompvol206eng.pdf [Last access 14.07.2014]; Fergus MacKay, "Indigenous Peoples and United Nations Human Rights Bodies. A Compilation of UN Treaty Body Jurisprudence and the Recommendations of the Human Rights Council. Volume III, 2007-2008", Forest Peoples Programme, 2009, at http://www.forestpeoples.org/sites/fpp/files/publication/2010/08/unjurisprudencecompvol30708eng.pdf [Last access 14.07.2014]; Fergus MacKay, "Indigenous Peoples and United Nations Human Rights Bodies. A Compilation of UN Treaty Body Jurisprudence and the Recommendations of the Human Rights Council. Volume IV, 2009-2010", Forest Peoples Programme, 2011, at http://www.forestpeoples.org/sites/fpp/fil es/publication/2011/02/indigenouspeoples-and-human-rights-bodies-jurispruden ce-2009-2010.pdf [Last access 14.07.2014]; Fergus MacKay, "Indigenous Peoples and United Nations Human Rights Bodies. A Compilation of UN Treaty Body Jurisprudence, the Recommendations of the Human Rights Council and its Special Procedures, and the Advice of the Expert Mechanism on the Rights of Indigenous Peoples. Volume V, 2011-2012", Forest Peoples Programme, 2013, at http://www.forestpeoples.org/sites/fpp/files/publication/2013/01/cos-2011-12.pdf. More generally, on both Covenants and the works of both Committees, see Joseph, Schultz and Castan, *The International Covenant on Civil and Political Rights* (and following editions); and Saul, Kinley and Mowbray, *The International Covenant on Economic, Social and Cultural Rights*.

527 On the use of the "minority clause" as a "double-edged sword" and the limits of the HRC avenue to tackle indigenous rights, and, particularly, their right to self-determination, see Castellino, "Conceptual Difficulties and the Right to Indigenous Self-Determination", pp.62-63.

ognized indigenous peoples as "peoples" entitled to the right of self-determination,[528] or at least, some rights or expressions included within this right.[529] In addition, despite the fact that the Concluding Observations of both the HRC and the CESCR are not binding, Committees establish and clarify the content of States' obligations under the Covenants.

Thus, in the Concluding Observations on Canada's Fourth Periodic report of 1999, in addition to urging the State to report adequately on the implementation of art.1,[530] the HRC made, for the first time, a clear connection between indigenous peoples and the right to self-determination:

> "The Committee notes that, as the State party acknowledged, the situation of the aboriginal peoples remains 'the most pressing human rights issue facing Canadians'. In this connection, the Committee is particularly concerned that the State party has not yet implemented the recommendations of the Royal Commission on Aboriginal Peoples (RCAP). With reference to the conclusion by RCAP that without a greater share of lands and resources institutions of aboriginal self-government will fail, the Committee emphasizes that the right to self-determination requires, inter alia, that all peoples must be able to freely dispose of their natural wealth and resources and that they may not be deprived of their own means of subsistence (art.1, para. 2). The Committee recommends that decisive and urgent action be taken towards the full implementation of the RCAP recommendations on land and resource allocation. *The Committee also recommends that the practice of extinguishing inherent aboriginal rights be abandoned as incompatible with article 1 of the Covenant*" [emphasis added]. [531]

As noted by MacKay, the HRC adopted similar Concluding Observations on Mexico and Norway in 1999 and Australia in 2000.[532]

In general, numerous references to positive or (mostly) worrying developments vis-à-vis indigenous rights –and thus the Committee's concern to enhance their protection under art.27 or other articles of ICCPR (e.g., arts.2 and 25)– may be found in almost all of their Concluding Observations. The

528 Henriksen, "The Right of Self-Determination: Indigenous Peoples versus States", p.136; MacKay, "A Briefing on Indigenous Peoples' Rights and the United Nations Human Rights Committee", p.10.

529 Myntti, "The Right to Self-Determination and Effective Participation", p.101.

530 HRC, "Concluding observations of the Human Rights Committee: Canada", 7 April 1999, UN Doc. CCPR/C/79/Add.105, para. 7.

531 *Ibid.*, para. 8.

532 MacKay, "A Briefing on Indigenous Peoples' Rights and the United Nations Human Rights Committee", p.11. See HRC, "Concluding observations of the Human Rights Committee: Mexico", 27 July 1999, UN Doc. CCPR/C/79/Add.109, para. 19; HRC, "Concluding observations of the Human Rights Committee: Norway", 1 November 1999, UN Doc. CCPR/C/79/Add.112, para. 17; and HRC, "Concluding observations of the Human Rights Committee: Australia", 28 July 2000, UN Doc. CCPR/CO/69/AUS, para. 506.

HRC reports examples that range from issues of forced sterilizations of indigenous women in the Concluding Observations on Peru in 2000 considered under art.27,[533] to a lack of an appropriate investigation into crimes allegedly committed by State security forces and agents (also) against indigenous leaders in the Concluding Observations on the Philippines in 2003 vis-à-vis arts.2, 6 and 9 of the ICCPR.[534]

More specifically on the right to self-determination, the HRC expressed its concern on the lack of compliance of art.1 in the ICCPR, often in combination with art.27, in the case of indigenous peoples in its Concluding Observations, *inter alia*, on Sweden (2002),[535] Brazil (2005),[536] the United States (2006),[537] Canada (2006),[538] Chile (2007,[539] and 2014[540]), Panama (2008),[541] Mexico (2010),[542] and Finland (2013).[543]

The CESCR referred to indigenous peoples and misapplications of art.1 of ICESCR, often in combination with art.15 on the right to take part in cultural life, in its Concluding Observations in the case, e.g., of the Russian Federation (2003),[544] and increasingly after on the Philippines (2008),[545]

533 HRC, "Concluding observations of the Human Rights Committee: Peru", 15 November 2000, UN Doc. CCPR/CO/70/PE, para.21.

534 HRC, "Concluding observations of the Human Rights Committee: Philippines", 1 December 2003, UN Doc. CCPR/CO/79/PHL, para. 8.

535 HRC, "Concluding observations of the Human Rights Committee: Sweden", 24 April 2002, UN Doc. CCPR/CO/74/SWE, para.15.

536 HRC, "Concluding observations of the Human Rights Committee: Brazil", 1 December 2005, UN Doc. CCPR/C/BRA/CO/2, para.6.

537 HRC, "Concluding observations of the Human Rights Committee: United States", 25 September 2006, UN Doc. CCPR/C/USA/CO/3, para.37.

538 HRC, "Concluding observations of the Human Rights Committee: Canada", 20 April 2006, UN Doc. CCPR/C/CAN/CO/5, paras. 8-9.

539 HRC, "Concluding observations of the Human Rights Committee: Chile", 18 May 2007, UN Doc. CCPR/C/CHL/CO/5, para 19.

540 HRC, "Concluding observations of the Human Rights Committee: Chile", 13 August 2014, UN Doc. CCPR/C/CHL/CO/6, para 10.

541 HRC, "Concluding observations of the Human Rights Committee: Panama", 17 April 2008, UN Doc. CCPR/C/PAN/CO/3, para 21.

542 HRC, "Concluding observations of the Human Rights Committee: Mexico", 17 May 2010, UN Doc. CCPR/C/MEX/CO/5, para 22.

543 HRC, "Concluding observations of the Human Rights Committee: Finland", 22 August 2013, UN Doc. CCPR/C/FIN/CO/6, para 16.

544 CESCR, "Concluding observations of the Committee on Economic, Social and Cultural Rights: Russian Federation", 12 December 2003, UN Doc. E/C.12/1/Add.94, paras.11 and 39.

545 CESCR, "Concluding observations of the Committee on Economic, Social and Cultural Rights: Philippines", 1 December 2008, UN Doc. E/C.12/PHL/CO/4, para. 16.

Sweden (2008),[546] Brazil (2009),[547] Cambodia (2009),[548] the Democratic Republic of Congo (2009),[549] Argentina (2011)[550], New Zealand (2012),[551] El Salvador (2014),[552] Guatemala (2014),[553] Nepal (2014),[554] and Paraguay (2015).[555]

The second relevant aspect of the works of both the HRC and the CESCR, for the aims of this section, is to explore how the right to self-determination of indigenous peoples has been shaped by both Committees in their Concluding Observations. Both Committees mainly referred to para.2 of art.1 when dealing with indigenous peoples, thus on the free disposal of natural wealth and resources and the guarantee of means of subsistence, with particular reference to indigenous land rights. This attitude was most probably triggered by the changes in the international arena vis-à-vis economic self-determination (see section 2.1.3.2). However, the Committees also referred to participation in decision-making, consultation, and Free, Prior and Informed Consent (FPIC).

In particular, the HRC urged the following actions by the State Party to comply with art.1 vis-à-vis indigenous peoples:

546 CESCR, "Concluding observations of the Committee on Economic, Social and Cultural Rights: Sweden", 1 December 2008, UN Doc. E/C.12/SWE/CO/5, para. 15.

547 CESCR, "Concluding observations of the Committee on Economic, Social and Cultural Rights: Brazil", 12 June 2009, UN Doc. E/C.12/BRA/CO/2, para. 9.

548 CESCR, "Concluding observations of the Committee on Economic, Social and Cultural Rights: Cambodia", 12 June 2009, UN Doc. E/C.12/KHM/CO/1, paras.15-16.

549 CESCR, "Concluding observations of the Committee on Economic, Social and Cultural Rights: Democratic Republic of Congo", 16 December 2009, UN Doc. E/C.12/COD/CO/4, paras 13-15.

550 CESCR, "Concluding observations of the Committee on Economic, Social and Cultural Rights: Argentina", 14 December 2011, UN Doc. E/C.12/ARG/CO/3, paras.8-10.

551 CESCR, "Concluding observations of the Committee on Economic, Social and Cultural Rights: New Zealand", 31 May 2012, UN Doc. E/C.12/NZL/CO/3, para.11.

552 CESCR, "Concluding observations on the combined third, fourth and fifth periodic reports of El Salvador", 19 June 2014, UN Doc. E/C.12/SLV/CO/3-5, para.27.

553 CESCR, "Concluding observations on the third periodic report of Guatemala", 9 December 2014, UN Doc. E/C.12/GTM/CO/3, para.6.

554 CESCR, "Concluding observations on the third periodic report of Nepal", 12 December 2014, UN Doc. E/C.12/NPL/CO/3, para.9.

555 CESCR, "Concluding observations on the fourth periodic report of Paraguay", 20 March 2015, UN Doc. E/C.12/PRY/CO/4, para.6.

- To enhance the participation of indigenous peoples in State institutions,[556] and to secure their participation in decision-making processes affecting their traditional lands and natural resources;[557]
- To (effectively) consult indigenous communities before granting licenses for the economic exploitation of disputed lands,[558] and for decision-making in those areas that are likely to affect their rights;[559]
- To seek the FPIC of indigenous peoples likely to be affected by economic activities related to natural resource exploitation;[560]
- To ensure the access of all indigenous people to adequate education and health services;[561]
- To guarantee the access to their ancestral lands,[562] and to demarcate them;[563]
- To recognize the collective use of indigenous ancestral lands;[564]
- To decrease land and natural resource exploitation and the granting of licenses, since they may result in the wiping out of indigenous peoples,[565] or the violation of the rights recognized in the ICCPR.[566]

The CESCR raised its concern vis-à-vis the application of art.1 with respect to indigenous peoples and recommended that State parties undertake the following necessary measures:

- To ensure that indigenous peoples are not deprived of their means of subsistence;[567]

556 HRC, Concluding Observations on Mexico, 1999, para.19.

557 HRC, Concluding Observations on Australia, 2000, para.506; on Sweden, 2002, para.15; on United States, 2006, para.37; on Finland 2013, para.16.

558 HRC, Concluding Observations on Chile, 2007, para.19; on Panama, 2008, para.21.

559 HRC, Concluding Observations on Mexico, 2010, para 22; on Chile, 2014, para 10.

560 HRC, Concluding Observations on Panama, 2008, para.21; on Chile, 2014, para 10.

561 HRC, Concluding Observations on Panama, 2008, para.21.

562 HRC, Concluding Observations on Chile, 2014, para 10.

563 HRC, Concluding Observations on Brazil, 2005, para.6; on Chile, 2007, para.19.

564 HRC, Concluding Observations on Panama, 2008, para.21.

565 HRC, Concluding Observations on Canada, 2006, para.8.

566 HRC, Concluding Observations on Chile 2007, para.19; on Panama 2008, para.21.

567 CESCR, Concluding Observations on Russian Federation 2003, para.39; on Argentina 2011, para.10.

- To secure the recognition of land rights to indigenous peoples,[568] including a legal mechanism to enable indigenous peoples to claim them;[569]
- To demarcate indigenous lands;[570]
- To ensure the effective enjoyment of indigenous peoples' rights over ancestral domains, lands and natural resources;[571]
- To receive proper compensation and enjoy tangible benefits from the exploitation of their resources;[572]
- To ensure the effective participation of indigenous peoples in decision-making on issues that affect them;[573]
- To consult indigenous peoples with due regard for their right to participate in informed decisions that affect their lives;[574]
- To seek the FPIC of indigenous peoples likely to be affected by economic activities related to natural resource exploitation,[575] or any development project;[576]
- To ensure that indigenous peoples' FPIC has truly been obtained for those decisions that may directly affect the exercise of their economic, social and cultural rights.[577]

Thus, the two Committees envisaged that a proper application of the right to self-determination would also include indigenous land rights, the duty to consult indigenous peoples and to obtain their FPIC, to guarantee their

568 CESCR, Concluding Observations on Russian Federation 2003, para.11; on Sweden 2008, para.15; on Cambodia 2009, para.16; on El Salvador 2014, para.27; on Guatemala 2014, para.6; on Nepal 2014, para.9; and on Paraguay 2015, para.6.

569 CESCR, Concluding Observations on Paraguay 2015, para.6.

570 CESCR, Concluding Observations on Brazil 2009, para.9; on Argentina 2011, para.8.

571 CESCR, Concluding Observations on Philippines 2008, para.16; on Democratic Republic of Congo 2009, para.13; on Guatemala 2014, paras.6-7.

572 CESCR, Concluding Observations on Democratic Republic of Congo 2009, para.13; on Argentina 2011, para.9; on New Zealand 2012, para.11; on El Salvador 2014, para.27.

573 CESCR, Concluding Observations on Argentina 2011, para.10; on Nepal 2014, para.9.

574 CESCR, Concluding Observations on Cambodia 2009, para.16; Democratic Republic of Congo 2009, para.15; Argentina 2011, para.9; on Guatemala 2014, para.7.

575 CESCR, Concluding Observations on Argentina 2011, para.9; on Guatemala 2014, para.7.

576 CESCR, Concluding Observations on Nepal 2014, para.9.

577 CESCR, Concluding Observations on Paraguay 2015, para.6.

means of subsistence, and fair compensation in case of natural resource exploitations likely to affect them. This shows how the right to self-determination of indigenous peoples has broadened over the years, in part thanks to the work of other UN agencies and the indigenous organizations themselves.

Finally, the third aspect that is worth mentioning in this section is the HRC's –albeit timid– application of Free, Prior and Informed Consent (FPIC) in the aforementioned case *Ángela Poma Poma v. Peru*. In this case, the claimant, an indigenous Aymara woman leaving in the Andean highland and raising alpacas, llamas, and other smaller animals, alleged a violation of art.1.2 by the Peruvian State. According to the author, the works to divert groundwater since the 1950s first caused the degradation and drought of their land and, second, the death of thousands of heads of livestock. Thus, the traditional means of subsistence had collapsed and her family (and the entire community) were deprived of their livelihoods. The HRC eventually admitted the case and found a violation of art.27 and art.2.3 read in conjunction with art.27. More interestingly, however, the HRC stated:

> "In the Committee's view, the admissibility of measures which substantially compromise or interfere with the culturally significant economic activities of a minority or indigenous community depends on whether the members of the community in question have had the opportunity to participate in the decision-making process in relation to these measures and whether they will continue to benefit from their traditional economy. *The Committee considers that participation in the decision-making process must be effective, which requires not mere consultation but the free, prior and informed consent of the members of the community.* In addition, the measures must respect the principle of proportionality so as not to endanger the very survival of the community and its members" [emphasis added].[578]

In addition, the HRC observed that neither the claimant nor her community were consulted at any time by the Peruvian State concerning the construction of the wells. Moreover, no studies were undertaken in order to determine the impact of diverting groundwater, nor were the negative consequences minimized or the damages repaired. Since the author was unable to continue benefiting from her traditional economic activity, the HRC considered that the measures adopted by the Peruvian State have substantively compromised her way of life and culture.[579] Thus, although this case was eventually decided in the light of art.27, the recognition of the necessity of

---

578 HRC, *Ángela Poma Poma v. Peru*, para.7.6.

579 *Ibid.*, para.7.7.

indigenous FPIC by the HRC is a major achievement in the international protection of indigenous rights.[580]

2.2.2.3 Self-determination of indigenous peoples in the Draft Declaration on the Rights of Indigenous Peoples

The Working Group on Indigenous Populations (WGIP) was established in 1982. This body, as one of the workings groups of the (then) Sub-Commission on Prevention of Discrimination and Protection of Minorities under the UN Commission on Human Rights, was tasked by the UN Economic and Social Council (ECOSOC) with a twofold mandate to review developments vis-à-vis the human rights of indigenous peoples and to analyze the standards relating to indigenous rights. The experts involved in the WGIP met annually for 5 working days prior to the Sub-Commission's sessions.[581]

Since their fourth session held in 1985, the WGIP decided to focus on the second task and thus to devote more attention to setting standards vis-à-vis indigenous rights.[582] Their efforts resulted in the "United Nations Draft Declaration on the Rights of Indigenous Peoples" adopted by the Sub-Commission on Prevention of Discrimination and Protection of Minorities in 1994 (see following section 2.2.2.4).[583]

580 On the pros and cons of this case, see Katja Göcke, "The Case of *Ángela Poma Poma v. Peru* before the Human Rights Committee. The Concept of Free, Prior ad Informed Consent and the Application of the International Covenant on Civil and Political Rights to the Protection and the Promotion of Indigenous Peoples' Rights", in A. von Bogdandy and R. Wolfrum (eds.), *Max Planck Yearbook of United Nations Law*, Volume 14, Brill, Leiden, 2010, pp.337-370.

581 UN Economic and Social Council, "Establishment of the Working Group on Indigenous Populations", Resolution No.1982/34, UN Doc. E/RES/1982/34, twenty-eighth plenary meeting of the UN Economic and Social Council, 7 May 1982.

582 UN Economic and Social Council, Sub-Commission on Prevention of Discrimination and Protection of Minorities, "Report of the Working Group on Indigenous Populations on its fourth session", 27 August 1985, thirty-eighth session, UN Doc. E/CN.4/Sub.2/1985/22, Annex I. See also Erica-Irene Daes, "The UN Declaration on the Rights of Indigenous Peoples: Background and Appraisal", in Stephen Allen and Alexandra Xanthaki (eds.), *Reflections on the Un Declaration on the Rights of Indigenous Peoples*, Hart Publishing, Oxford, Portland, 2011, pp.11-40, p.17; and Willemsen-Diaz, "How Indigenous Peoples' Rights Reached the UN", p.28.

583 The Sub-Commission on Prevention of Discrimination and Protection of Minorities, "Draft United Nations Declaration on the Rights of Indigenous Peoples", Resolution No.1994/45 of 26 August 1994, thirty-sixth meeting. The text is widely available online. *Inter alia*, see at http://www.un-documents.net/c4s29445.htm [Last access 28.07.2014]. See also "Report of the Sub-Commission on Prevention

The WGIP paid particular attention to the right of self-determination, also thanks to the extensive indigenous participation in its sessions.[584] In addition, during the World Council of Indigenous Peoples held in Panama in 1984, the newly appointed Chairperson-Rapporteur of WGIP, Erica Irene A. Daes,[585] met (literally) hundreds of indigenous persons, who insisted that the UN should protect Indigenous peoples' rights and fundamental freedoms, in the form of a declaration or even a convention.[586] After what Daes calls "painful consultations", 17 principles were adopted at the World Council of Indigenous Peoples to serve as the basis for a potential Declaration.[587] The first of these principles included the right to self-determination of indigenous peoples in the identical form of the ICCPR and ICESCR and the addition of the adjectives "indigenous" before peoples and "religious" before development.[588] In 1985, a group of indigenous organizations[589] submitted another relevant declaration of principles to the WGIP.[590] In this

of Discrimination and Protection of Minorities on its Forty-Sixth Session (Geneva, 1-26 August, 1994)", 28 October 1994, UN Doc. E/CN.4/Sub.2/1994/56, pp.103-117.

584 Thanks to the openness of the WGIP members, the mobilization of indigenous leaders, and the work of Augusto Willemsen-Diaz, the number of participants during the WPIG sessions –including indigenous, States' and other NGOs representatives– grew to an extraordinarily total of 1,000. Willemsen-Diaz, "How Indigenous Peoples' Rights Reached the UN", pp.27-28; Littlechild, "Comment on agenda items at the Oslo Conference ...", p.19.

585 The first two WGIP working sessions in 1982 and 1983 were held under the chairmanship of Asbjørn Eide.

586 Daes, "The UN Declaration on the Rights of Indigenous Peoples: Background and Appraisal", p.12.

587 Daes, "The UN Declaration on the Rights of Indigenous Peoples: Background and Appraisal", p.12. The 17 principles are reproduced in this article of Daes, but are also available in the above-mentioned report by the UN Economic and Social Council, Sub-Commission on Prevention of Discrimination and Protection of Minorities, "Report of the Working Group on Indigenous Populations on its fourth session" (hereinafter cited by its UN Doc. E/CN.4/Sub.2/1985/22), Annex III as specified by Daes, "The UN Declaration on the Rights of Indigenous Peoples: Background and Appraisal", p.13, note 7.

588 "All indigenous peoples have the right of self-determination. By virtue of this right they freely determine their political status and freely pursue their economic, social, religious and cultural development". Also the pronoun "that" was substituted by "this".

589 The Indian Law Resource Center, Four Directions Council, National Aboriginal and Islander Legal Service, National Indian Youth Council, Inuit Circumpolar Conference, and the International Indian Treaty Council. Daes, "The UN Declaration on the Rights of Indigenous Peoples: Background and Appraisal", p.14.

590 Also this declaration of principles is reproduced in Daes, "The UN Declaration on the Rights of Indigenous Peoples: Background and Appraisal", pp.14-16, but it

case, the right to self-determination was inserted as a second principle, as follows: "All indigenous nations and peoples have the right to self-determination, by virtue of which they have the right to whatever degree of autonomy or self-government they choose. This includes the right to freely determine their political status, freely pursue their own economic, social and cultural development, and determine their own membership and/or citizenship, without external interference".[591] Daes, as Chairperson of the WGIP, insisted that both these documents should be taken into due account for the drafting of a declaration.[592]

During the above-mentioned fourth session of the WGIP in 1985, many indigenous representatives gave statements on the right to self-determination.[593] Some addressed it specifically in terms of autonomy or self-government, or control over the land and their economic, social, and cultural systems. Others spoke in the context of self-determination requesting the revision of the concepts of discovery, conquest, and *terra nullius* or respect for the treaties signed by indigenous peoples and the previous colonial Power according to the international law principle of *pacta sunt servanda*.[594] Seven draft principles were then proposed during this session of the WGIP,[595] which were extended to 14 in the fifth WGIP session,[596] but none of these contained the right to self-determination. Neither was the right to self-determination inserted in the Working Paper prepared by Daes for the sixth

may also be found in the abovementioned UN Doc. E/CN.4/Sub.2/1985/22, Annex IV as specified by Daes, "The UN Declaration on the Rights of Indigenous Peoples: Background and Appraisal", p.14, note 8.

591 Daes, "The UN Declaration on the Rights of Indigenous Peoples: Background and Appraisal", p.14 by referring to UN Doc. E/CN.4/Sub.2/1985/22, Annex IV.

592 Daes, "The UN Declaration on the Rights of Indigenous Peoples: Background and Appraisal", p.17.

593 *Ibid.*, p.20.

594 *Ibid.*, p.21, that cites the UN Doc. E/CN.4/Sub.2/1985/22, para.79.

595 UN Doc. E/CN.4/Sub.2/1985/22, Annex II.

596 See UN Economic and Social Council, Sub-Commission on Prevention of Discrimination and Protection of Minorities, "Report of the Working Group on Indigenous Populations on its fourth session", 24 August 1987, thirty-ninth session, UN Doc. E/CN.4/Sub.2/1987/22, Annex II. See also Erica-Irene Daes, "The Spirit and Letter of the Right to Self-Determination of Indigenous Peoples: Reflections on the Making of the United Nations Draft Declaration", in Pekka Aikio and Martin Scheinin (eds.), *Operationalizing the Rights of Indigenous Peoples to Self-Determination*, Institute for Human Rights, Åbo Akademi University, Saarijärvi, 2000, pp.67-84, p.67.

session in 1988,[597] most probably due to the resistance of States, but a number of "paragraphs and principles" pointed towards political participation and autonomy.[598]

After the next meeting and careful revisions, in which both the concerns of States and those of indigenous organizations were taken into consideration,[599] the draft discussed in 1991 at the ninth session included an "operative paragraph 1"[600] which provided that: "Indigenous peoples have the right to self-determination, in accordance with international law. By virtue of this right, they freely determine their relationship with the States in which they live, in a spirit of coexistence with other citizens, and freely pursue their economic, social, cultural and spiritual development in conditions of

597 UN Economic and Social Council, Sub-Commission on Prevention of Discrimination and Protection of Minorities, Sub-Commission on Prevention of Discrimination and Protection of Minorities, "A working paper by Ms. Erica-Irene A. Daes containing a set of draft preambular paragraphs and principles for insertion into a universal declaration of indigenous rights", fortieth session, 21 June 1988, UN Doc. E/CN.4/Sub.2/1988/25.

598 Daes, "The UN Declaration on the Rights of Indigenous Peoples: Background and Appraisal", p.27. These paragraphs and principles read as follows: "21. The right to participate fully in the political, economic and social life of their State and to have their specific character duly reflected in the legal system and in political institutions, including proper regard to and recognition of indigenous laws and customs. 22. The right to participate fully at the State level, through representatives chosen by themselves, in decision-making about and implementation of all national and international matters which may affect their life and destiny. 23. The collective right to autonomy in matters relating to their own internal and local affairs, including education, information, culture, religion, health, housing, social welfare, traditional and other economic activities, land and resources administration and the environment, as well as internal taxation for financing these autonomous functions. 24. The right to decide upon the structures of their autonomous institutions, to select the membership of such institutions, and to determine the membership of the indigenous people concerned for these purposes". UN Doc. E/CN.4/Sub.2/1988/25.

599 See Daes, "The UN Declaration on the Rights of Indigenous Peoples: Background and Appraisal", pp.26-29.

600 The word "operative paragraphs" was finally substituted with "articles" during the eleventh session of the WGIP in 1993. Daes, "The UN Declaration on the Rights of Indigenous Peoples: Background and Appraisal", p.29.

freedom and dignity".[601] Self-determination was also mentioned in the preambular paragraphs 12 and 14, while operative paragraphs 23 and 24 dealt with elements of autonomy.[602]

The following year, a new formula of the same operative paragraph 1 was proposed, as follows, "Indigenous peoples have the right to self-determination, in accordance with international law by virtue of which they may freely determine their political status and institutions and freely pursue their economic, social and cultural development. An integral part of this is the right to autonomy and self-government".[603] Paragraph 27 then previewed autonomy as follows: "Indigenous peoples have the right to autonomy in matters relating to their own internal and local affairs, including education, information, mass media, culture religion, health, housing, employment, social welfare in general, traditional and other economic and management activities, land and resources administration, environment and entry of non-members [...] as well as internal taxation for financing these autonomous functions". In addition, operative paragraph 28 stated that: "Indigenous peoples have the right to decide upon the structures of their autonomous institutions, to select the membership of such institutions according to their own procedures, and to determine the membership of the indigenous peoples concerned for these purposes; States have the duty to recognize and respect the integrity of such institutions and their memberships".[604]

Among the other proposals raised by indigenous organizations that year, it is worth mentioning the one made by the International Organization of Indigenous Resource Development, which held its summit in Denver in 1992. They submitted a written proposal as follows: "Indigenous peoples have the right to self-determination, in accordance with international law. By virtue of this right, they freely determine their relationships with States, in spirit of coexistence, and freely pursue their cultural, spiritual, economic

601 Thornberry, "Self-Determination and Indigenous Peoples: Objections and Responses", p.43; UN Economic and Social Council, Sub-Commission on Prevention of Discrimination and Protection of Minorities, "Report of the Working Group on Indigenous Populations on its ninth session", 15 August 1991, UN Doc. E/CN.4/Sub.2/1991/40, p.32.

602 *Ibid.*

603 Thornberry, "Self-Determination and Indigenous Peoples: Objections and Responses", p.43. See UN Economic and Social Council, Sub-Commission on Prevention of Discrimination and Protection of Minorities, "Report of the Working Group on Indigenous Populations on its tenth session", 20 August 1992, UN Doc. E/CN.4/Sub.2/1992/33, p.46.

604 *Ibid.*

and social development in conditions of freedom and dignity".[605] In addition, they proposed to frame the right to autonomy according to the following formula: "Indigenous peoples have the right to self -government or autonomy within the State, if they so desire, as one element of the exercise of their right to self -determination. This includes the right to determine their own membership, and the nature, structure, procedure and membership of their own autonomous institutions, as well as the right to establish autonomous institutions for the maintenance of public order and resolution of disputes".[606]

Later, Daes prepared a revised working paper, which was submitted at the forty-fifth session of the Sub-Commission on Prevention of Discrimination and Protection of Minorities in June 1993.[607] It contained another formulation of the operative paragraph relating to self-determination, as follows: "Indigenous peoples have the right of self-determination, in accordance with international law, subject to the same criteria and limitations as apply to other peoples in accordance with the Charter of the United Nations. By virtue of this, they have the right, inter alia, to negotiate and agree upon their role in the conduct of public affairs, their distinct responsibilities and the means by which they manage their own interests. An integral part of this is the right to autonomy and self-government".[608] The operative paragraphs 29 and 30 contained further references to autonomy: "Operative paragraph 29. Indigenous peoples have the right to autonomy and self-government in

605 Commission on Human Rights, Sub-Commission on Prevention of Discrimination and Protection of Minorities, Working Group on Indigenous Populations, "Standard-Setting Activities: Evolution of Standards Concerning the Rights of Indigenous Populations. Note by the Secretary-General. Information received from non-governmental organizations", "Report of the Tribal Summit on the Draft Declaration on the Rights of Indigenous Peoples, Denver, 16-18 June 1992 organized by the International Organization of Indigenous Resource Development", UN Doc. E/CN.4/Sub.2/AC.4/1992/3/Add.1, Annex I, 1 July 1992, p.5, cited by Gudmundur Alfredsson, "The Right of Self-Determination and Indigenous Peoples", p.42, note 3.

606 "Report of the Tribal Summit on the Draft Declaration on the Rights of Indigenous Peoples, UN Doc. E/CN.4/Sub.2/AC.4/1992/3/Add.1), p.9, paragraphs 23-24 of Annex I. See also Alfredsson 1993, p.43.

607 Commission on Human Rights, Sub-Commission on Prevention of Discrimination and Protection of Minorities, "Draft declaration on the rights of indigenous peoples. Revised working paper submitted by the Chairperson-Rapporteur, Ms. Erica-Irene Daes, pursuant to Sub-Commission resolution 1992/33 and Commission on Human Rights resolution", forty-fifth session, 8 June 1993, UN Doc. 1993/31E/CN.4/Sub.2/1993/26.

608 *Ibid.*, p.4.

matters relating to their internal and local affairs, including culture, religion, education, information, media, health, housing, employment, social welfare, economic activities, land and resources management, environment and entry by non-members, as well as internal taxation for financing these autonomous functions; Operative paragraph 30. Indigenous peoples have the right to determine the structures and to select the membership of their autonomous or self-governing institutions in accordance with their own procedures".[609]

At the eleventh session of the WGIP held in July 1993, indigenous representatives insisted on maintaining the right of self-determination and the solution of spelling it the same way as in the ICCPR and ICESCR was put forward.[610] The majority of the indigenous representatives supported the idea since they sought for their right to self-determination to be equivalent to that of all peoples.[611] As Daes put it in the "Explanatory note concerning the draft declaration on the rights of indigenous peoples", "[i]t would be inadmissible and discriminatory to argue that these peoples do not have the right to self-determination merely because they are indigenous".[612] Thus, it was a matter of both non-discrimination but also of dignity. Moreover, the indigenous representatives were serving the needs and expectations of their communities.[613] This also explains why indigenous peoples spent ten long years at the WGIP insisting that the right to self-determination should be inserted in the declaration with the wording of both Covenants.[614] Some indigenous representatives did not want to reduce the right to self-determination to a specific conceptualization and thus decide for all indigenous

609 *Ibid.*, p.9

610 Daes, "The UN Declaration on the Rights of Indigenous Peoples: Background and Appraisal", p.32. See the debates during the eleventh session reported by the UN Economic and Social Council, Sub-Commission on Prevention of Discrimination and Protection of Minorities, "Report of the Working Group on Indigenous Populations on its fourth session", 23 August 1993, forty-fifth session, UN Doc. E/CN.4/Sub.2/1993/29.

611 Myntti, "The Right to Self-Determination and Effective Participation", p.88.

612 Commission on Human Rights, Sub-Commission on Prevention of Discrimination and Protection of Minorities, "Explanatory note concerning the draft declaration on the rights of indigenous peoples", by Erica-Irene A. Daes, forty-fifth session, 19 July 1993, UN Doc. E/CN.4/Sub.2/1993/26/Add.1, para.25.

613 Maivân Clech Lâm, *At the Edge of the State: Indigenous Peoples and Self-Determination*, Transnational Publishers, Ardsley, New York, 2000, p.58.

614 *Ibid.*, p.60.

peoples throughout the world.[615] Many other indigenous representatives expressed their preference for constitutional reforms within existing States,[616] in order to avoid the secessionist discourse. Notwithstanding the wave of vigorous reservations made by many governments, some States joined in considering self-determination as not (solely) equivalent to secession, but rather (also) as constitutional reforms (e.g., the Australian delegate).[617]

Finally, the United Nations Draft Declaration on the Rights of Indigenous Peoples (hereinafter, Draft Declaration) was adopted by the Sub-Commission on the Prevention of Discrimination and Protection of Minorities in 1994, which recognized the right to self-determination in art.3. It received the identical formulation of ICCPR and ICESCR with the substitution of the opening word "All" into "Indigenous", as follows: "Indigenous peoples have the right of self-determination. By virtue of that right they freely determine their political status and freely pursue their economic, social and cultural development". In addition, self-determination was inserted in the preambular paragraphs 14 and 15,[618] and references to colonization and dispossession of indigenous peoples' lands were also added.[619] The right to autonomy was inserted in art.31, as follows: "Indigenous peoples, as a specific form of exercising their right to self-determination, have the right to autonomy or self-government in matters relating to their internal and local affairs, including culture, religion, education, information, media, health,

615 *Ibid.*, pp.62-63.

616 Commission on Human Rights, Sub-Commission on Prevention of Discrimination and Protection of Minorities, "Explanatory note concerning the draft declaration on the rights of indigenous peoples", by Erica-Irene A. Daes, forty-fifth session, 19 July 1993, UN Doc. E/CN.4/Sub.2/1993/26/Add.1, para.28.

617 Daes, "The Spirit and Letter of the Right to Self-Determination of Indigenous Peoples ...", pp.71-72.

618 Preambular paragraphs 14 and 15 of the Draft Declaration affirm: "*Acknowledging* that the Charter of the United Nations, the international Covenant on Economic, Social and Cultural Rights and the International Covenant on Civil and Political Rights affirm the fundamental importance of the right of self-determination of all peoples, by virtue of which they freely determine their political status and freely pursue their economic, social and cultural development, *Bearing in mind* that nothing in this Declaration may be used to deny any peoples their right of self-determination".

619 Thornberry, "Self-Determination and Indigenous Peoples: Objections and Responses", p.44. See preambular paragraph 5 of the Draft Declaration, which states: "*Concerned* that indigenous peoples have been deprived of their human rights and fundamental freedoms, resulting, inter alia, in *their colonization and dispossession of their lands, territories and resources*, thus preventing them from exercising, in particular, their right to development in accordance with their own needs and interests" [apart the incipit, emphasis added].

housing, employment, social welfare, economic activities, land and resources management, environment and entry by non-members, as well as ways and means for financing these autonomous functions".

In conclusion, the link between the right to self-determination and autonomy was evident since the Draft Declaration, and it has been "sealed" in the text of the UNDRIP. In addition, the rights to political participation occupied a relevant place (arts.4,[620] arts. 19-22),[621] while a duty to consult indigenous peoples was inserted in the sixteenth preambular paragraph and in arts.16 and 37.[622] These elements are particularly relevant in the light of the

620 Article 4 states: "Indigenous peoples have the right to maintain and strengthen their distinct political, economic, social and cultural characteristics, as well as their legal systems, while retaining their rights to participate fully, if they so choose, in the political, economic, social and cultural life of the State".

621 "Article 19. Indigenous peoples have the right to participate fully, if they so choose, at all levels of decision-making in matters which may affect their rights, lives and destinies through representatives chosen by themselves in accordance with their own procedures, as well as to maintain and develop their own indigenous decision-making institutions; Article 20. Indigenous peoples have the right to participate fully, if they so choose, through procedures determined by them, in devising legislative or administrative measures that may affect them; States shall obtain the free and informed consent of the peoples concerned before adopting and implementing such measures; Article 21. Indigenous peoples have the right to maintain and develop their political, economic and social systems, to be secure in the enjoyment of their own means of subsistence and development, and to engage freely in all their traditional and other economic activities. Indigenous peoples who have been deprived of their means of subsistence and development are entitled to just and fair compensation. Article 22. Indigenous peoples have the right to special measures for the immediate, effective and continuing improvement of their economic and social conditions, including in the areas of employment, vocational training and retraining, housing, sanitation, health and social security. Particular attention shall be paid to the rights and special needs of indigenous elders, women, youth, children and disabled persons [emphasis added]".

622 The sixteenth preambular paragraph reads as follows: "Encouraging States to comply with and effectively implement all international instruments, in particular those related to human rights, as they apply to indigenous peoples, *in consultation and cooperation with the peoples concerned*"; as to the articles mentioned, "Article 16. Indigenous peoples have the right to have the dignity and diversity of their cultures, traditions, histories and aspirations appropriately reflected in all forms of education and public information. States shall take effective measures, *in consultation with the indigenous peoples concerned*, to eliminate prejudice and discrimination and to promote tolerance, understanding and good relations among indigenous peoples and all segments of society; Article 37. *States shall take effective and appropriate measures, in consultation with the indigenous peoples concerned, to give full effect to the provisions of this Declaration*. The rights recognized herein shall be adopted and included in national legislation in such a manner that indigenous peoples can avail themselves of such rights in practice [emphasis added]".

present work. Nevertheless, the expression "[...] they freely determine their political status and freely pursue their economic, social and cultural development" in the right of self-determination of indigenous peoples implies many more aspects, as will be discussed below (section 2.2.4).

2.2.2.4 The shaping of the right to self-determination of indigenous peoples from the Draft Declaration to the UNDRIP's formula

Following the adoption of the Draft Declaration by the Sub-Commission on the Prevention of Discrimination and Protection of Minorities in 1994, the UN Commission on Human Rights established an open-ended inter-sessional subsidiary body, the Working Group on the Draft Declaration (WGDD), with the sole purpose of elaborating a Declaration on the basis of the Draft Declaration.[623] The reason behind the creation of this additional body is most probably linked to the concerns of the States on the Draft Declaration,[624] which had already been expressed in the fifty-first session of the Commission on Human Rights held in 1995.[625] Conversely, the indigenous representatives admitted at this session as observers were in favour of immediately adopting the text, but the States' reluctance prompted the need for further negotiations and, therefore, the creation of the WGDD.[626] Given the open-ended character of this working group, ECOSOC consultative status was requested for indigenous organizations to attend the WGDD session.[627] Notwithstanding a lesser degree of openness in comparison with the WGIP, no indigenous organization was denied the request of this status and thus indigenous peoples' participation remained high.[628]

As mentioned in chapter 1, it took more than a decade for the WGDD to finally submit a text to the (reformed) UN Human Rights Council. The right to self-determination was one of the most controversial issues, although not

623 UN Economic and Social Council, "Establishment of a working group of the Commission on Human Rights to elaborate a draft declaration in accordance with paragraph 5 of General Assembly resolution 49/214", Resolution No. 1995/32, UN Doc. E/RES/1995/32, fifty-second plenary meeting of the UN Economic and Social Council, 25 July 1995.

624 Barelli, "Shaping Indigenous Self-Determination: Promising or Unsatisfactory Solutions?", p.419.

625 Chávez, "The Declaration on the Rights of Indigenous Peoples. Breaking the *Impasse* ...", p.96.

626 *Ibid.*, p.97.

627 *Ibid.*

628 Willemsen-Diaz, "How Indigenous Peoples' Rights Reached the UN", p.28.

the only one.[629] Indigenous representatives were keen to keep the text of the Draft Declaration without any changes.[630] However, since the third session of the WGDD, proposals to revise the text were advanced and discussed.[631]

As to art.3 and the right to self-determination, States often changed their views. For instance, at the first session of the WGDD in 1996, a group of States fiercely opposed the recognition of this right.[632] At the following session, Bolivia, Colombia, and Fiji agreed to include the right to self-determination, as did Switzerland, Pakistan, and Finland in 2000, Norway and Cuba in 2001, and Guatemala and Mexico in 2002.[633] Another evidence of the changing attitudes of States are the cases of Canada and the Russian Federation, which were in favor of inserting this article in 2000,[634] but, at the final adoption of the UNDRIP in 2007, voted against it and abstained, respectively (see *infra*). During the 2004 session, other States proposed inserting a reference to political unity and territorial integrity in art.3, which prompted further discussions and counterproposals from both parties.[635] In addition, Australia and USA insisted on including a direct reference to self-

629 Barelli, "Shaping Indigenous Self-Determination: Promising or Unsatisfactory Solutions?", p.419. E.g., indigenous peoples' rights to land and natural resources were part of the last consultations to States held in July 2007 on the text of the Declaration. Daes, "The UN Declaration on the Rights of Indigenous Peoples: Background and Appraisal", p. 35.

630 Chávez, "The Declaration on the Rights of Indigenous Peoples. Breaking the *Impasse* ...", p.99.

631 Chávez, "The Declaration on the Rights of Indigenous Peoples. Breaking the *Impasse* ...", p.100.

632 Commission on Human Rights, "Report of the Working Group established in accordance with Commission on Human Rights resolution 1995/32 of 3 March 1995", fifty-second session, 4 January 1996, UN Doc. E/CN.4/1996/84 paras.42-46.

633 This reconstruction is of Xanthaki, *Indigenous Rights and United Nations Standards*, p.110. The views of the States may be found in the following UN Documents, in order: E/CN.4/1997/102 (1996), paras. 332, 317 and 330; E/CN.4/2000/84 (1999), paras.64, 67 and 70; E/CN.4/2001/85 (2001), paras.82 and 70; and E/CN.4/2004/85 (2004), paras. 16 and 17.

634 Xanthaki, *Indigenous Rights and United Nations Standards*, p.110, by referring at the UN Doc. E/CN.4/2000/84 (1999) paras.50 and 61.

635 Xanthaki, *Indigenous Rights and United Nations Standards*, pp.110-111; Barelli pp.419-420.

government and autonomy in art.3.[636] Although some indigenous representatives were in favor of reconsidering some aspects, an agreement could not be reached.[637]

After the eleventh session of the WGDD in 2006, chairperson Luis-Enrique Chávez proposed to reconcile the parties by introducing two amendments, namely an additional preambular paragraph that referred to the respect of the principle of territorial integrity, albeit indirectly,[638] and moving art.31 on the right to autonomy to art.4, thus suggesting a combined reading of the two articles.[639] *Inter alia*, in their writings of 2000 and 1993, respectively, both Thornberry and Sanders foresaw that this would become an acceptable compromise. Evaluating what could be the best and worst solutions for both parties (indigenous peoples and States), Thornberry affirmed that the option to move art.31 of the Draft Declaration to general Part I would have been considered as an acceptable, but not the preferred, alternative for indigenous peoples.[640] Highlighting the unsettled character of self-determination both in general terms and for Indigenous peoples, Sanders stated that if "'self-determination' survives in a declaration on the rights of indigenous peoples, it will have a particular meaning. It will be descriptive of rights of

636 Xanthaki, *Indigenous Rights and United Nations Standards*, p.111.

637 Barelli, "Shaping Indigenous Self-Determination: Promising or Unsatisfactory Solutions?", p.420.

638 Preambular paragraph 15 before the eleventh session stated: "*Bearing in mind* that nothing in this Declaration may be used to deny any peoples their right of self-determination". The proposal was to change it into the following: "*Bearing in mind* that nothing in this Declaration may be used to deny any peoples their right of self-determination, exercised in conformity with international law". The phrase "exercised in conformity with international law" according to the chairperson could refer and thus respect the principle of territorial integrity. Barelli, "Shaping Indigenous Self-Determination: Promising or Unsatisfactory Solutions?", p.420. See Commission on Human Rights, "Report of the working group established in accordance with Commission on Human Rights resolution 1995/32 of 3 March 1995 on its eleventh session", sixty-second session, 22 March 2006, UN Doc. E/CN.4/2006/79, Annex I, "Revised Chairman's summary and proposal on the draft Declaration", p.16.

639 Barelli, "Shaping Indigenous Self-Determination: Promising or Unsatisfactory Solutions?", p.420; Commission on Human Rights, "Report of the working group established in accordance with Commission on Human Rights resolution 1995/32 of 3 March 1995 on its eleventh session", sixty-second session, 22 March 2006, UN Doc. E/CN.4/2006/79, Annex I, "Revised Chairman's summary and proposal on the draft Declaration", pp.21-23. See also Chávez, "The Declaration on the Rights of Indigenous Peoples. Breaking the *Impasse* ...", p.102.

640 Thornberry, "Self-Determination and Indigenous Peoples: Objections and Responses", pp.60-61.

self-government or autonomy for territorially based indigenous peoples within States".[641]

Despite disagreements, especially on the part of the States regarding the coexistence of the right to self-determination on one hand and the right to autonomy as an expression of the right to self-determination on the other, the chairperson finally submitted the text to the Human Rights Council, which adopted it on 29 June 2006, albeit without consensus.[642] Therefore, the Council submitted its Resolution to the General Assembly, annexing the text of the Declaration.

Afterwards, during its fifty-third session held in late November 2006, the Third Committee of the General Assembly had before it a draft resolution submitted by a considerable number of States that were in favor of the adoption of the text of the Declaration approved by the Human Rights Council.[643] However, on behalf of the group of African States, Namibia requested that the text of the draft resolution should be amended and to "allow time

---

641 Douglas Sanders, "Self-Determination and Indigenous Peoples", in Christian Tomuschat (ed.), *Modern Law of Self-Determination*, Martinus Nijhoff Publishers, Dordrecht, Boston, London, 1993, pp.55-81, p.81.

642 Human Rights Council Resolution No. 2006/2, "Working group of the Commission on Human Rights to elaborate a draft declaration in accordance with paragraph 5 of the General Assembly resolution 49/214 of 23 December 1994", 29 June 2006. The resolution was adopted by a recorded vote of 30 in favor (Azerbaijan, Brazil, Cameroon, China, Cuba, Czech Republic, Ecuador, Finland, France, Germany, Guatemala, India, Indonesia, Japan, Malaysia, Mauritius, Mexico, Netherlands, Pakistan, Peru, Poland, Republic of Korea, Romania, Saudi Arabia, South Africa, Sri Lanka, Switzerland, United Kingdom of Great Britain and Northern Ireland, Uruguay, Zambia), 2 against (Canada and the Russian Federation) and 12 abstentions (Algeria, Argentina, Bahrain, Bangladesh, Ghana, Jordan, Morocco, Nigeria, Philippines, Senegal, Tunisia, Ukraine); other States were not represented. Barelli, "Shaping Indigenous Self-Determination: Promising or Unsatisfactory Solutions?", p.421.

643 Daes, "The UN Declaration on the Rights of Indigenous Peoples: Background and Appraisal", p.34. See General Assembly, Report of the Human Rights Council, "Working group of the Commission on Human Rights to elaborate a draft declaration in accordance with paragraph 5 of General Assembly resolution 49/214 of 23 December 1994", sixty-first session, 20 November 2006, UN Doc. A/C.3/61/L.18/Rev.1, Revised draft resolution submitted by Armenia, Bolivia, Bosnia and Herzegovina, Cameroon, Congo, Costa Rica, Croatia, Cuba, Cyprus, Denmark, Dominican Republic, Ecuador, Estonia, Fiji, Finland, France, Germany, Greece, Guatemala, Haiti, Hungary, Latvia, Liechtenstein, Lithuania, Mexico, Panama, Paraguay, Peru, Portugal, Slovenia, Spain, Switzerland and the former Yugoslav Republic of Macedonia.

for further consultations thereon", while aiming "to conclude its consideration of the Declaration before the end of its sixty-first session".[644] The Third Committee of the General Assembly adopted these amendments with 84 votes in favor, 67 against and 25 abstentions.[645] The concern over the need for further consultations on the issues of the definition of indigenous peoples, self-determination, ownership of land and resources, establishment of distinct political and economic institutions, and national and territorial integrity was reiterated during the eighth ordinary session of the Assembly of the African Union held in January 2007.[646]

Subsequently, in May 2007, 67 Member States submitted a Letter to the President of the General Assembly, Sheika Haya Rashed Al Kalifa, flagging the negative aspects that reopening the text of the declaration may cause. The President, therefore, appointed an Ambassador, Hilario G. Davide Jr., to undertake further consultations and to report to her by mid-July 2007, which he did. Seven States (Australia, Canada, Colombia, Guyana, New Zealand, Russian Federation and Suriname) replied to Ambassador Davide that, *inter alia*, they would consider supporting the Declaration if the most pressing concerns were approached again by a thematic approach. Thus, amendments were discussed in relation to eight topics, i.e., self-determination, self-government, and indigenous institutions (current UNDRIP arts.3, 4, 5 and 33); lands, territories and natural resources (arts.26 and 29); means of redress (arts. 11 and 28); FPIC (arts. 10, 19, 32.2); rights of third parties (art.46); intellectual property rights (arts.11 and 31); military issues (art.30);

---

644 General Assembly, Report of the Human Rights Council, "Working group of the Commission on Human Rights to elaborate a draft declaration in accordance with paragraph 5 of General Assembly resolution 49/214 of 23 December 1994 – Namibia (on behalf of States Members of the United Nations that are members of the Group of African States): amendments to draft resolution A/C.3/61/L.18/Rev.1", sixty-first session, 20 November 2006, UN Doc. A/C.3/61/L.57/Rev.1, , para.2-3. See also Barelli, "Shaping Indigenous Self-Determination: Promising or Unsatisfactory Solutions?", p.421; Stefania Errico, "The UN Declaration on the Rights of Indigenous Peoples is Adopted: An Overview", *Human Rights Law Review*, Vol.7, No.4, 2007, 756-759, p.757.

645 General Assembly, "Report of the Third Committee", sixty-first session, 6 December 2006, UN Doc. A/61/448. See the votes at para.17.

646 Assembly of the African Union, "Decision on the United Nations Declaration on the Rights of Indigenous Peoples", Doc. ASSEMBLY/AU/9 (VIII) ADD.6, eighth ordinary session, 30 January 2007, at http://www.ohchr.org/en/Issues/IPeoples/Pages/Declaration.aspx [Last access 18.07.2014].

and education (art.14).[647] These consultations did not lead to amendments of the wording and the position of arts.3 and 4, but a strong reference to the principle of "territorial integrity" was inserted into the final wording of art.46.1.[648] Finally, at the end of July, the President sent a letter to all the Permanent Representatives with the last reports of Ambassador Davide, including the results of the consultations, and her hope of adopting the Declaration in September 2007 within the sixty-first session, as was the case.[649]

Thus, the United Nations Declaration on the Rights of Indigenous Peoples was adopted on 13 September 2007 with 143 votes in favor, 4 against and 11 abstentions.[650]

However, all the States that voted against eventually endorsed the UNDRIP as follows: Australia on 3 April 2009,[651] New Zealand on 20 April

647 Daes, "The UN Declaration on the Rights of Indigenous Peoples: Background and Appraisal", pp.35-36.

648 Barelli, "Shaping Indigenous Self-Determination: Promising or Unsatisfactory Solutions?", p.422. Art.46.1 of the UNDRIP reads as follows: "Nothing in this Declaration may be interpreted as implying for any State, people, group or person any right to engage in any activity or to perform any act contrary to the Charter of the United Nations or construed *as authorizing or encouraging any action which would dismember or impair, totally or in part, the territorial integrity or political unity of sovereign and independent States*" [emphasis added].

649 Daes, "The UN Declaration on the Rights of Indigenous Peoples: Background and Appraisal", p.36.

650 General Assembly, "Resolution 61/295. United Nations Declaration on the Rights of Indigenous Peoples", Resolution adopted by the General Assembly on 13 September 2007, UN Doc. A/RES/61/295. See also the webpage of United Nations Human Rights, "Declaration on the rights of indigenous peoples", at http://www.ohchr.org/en/Issues/IPeoples/Pages/Declaration.aspx [Last access 18.07.2014].

651 Jenny Macklin MP, Minister for Families, Housing, Community Services and Indigenous Affairs, "Statement on the United Nations Declaration on the Rights of Indigenous Peoples", Parliament House Canberra, 3 April 2009, at http://www.un.org/esa/socdev/unpfii/documents/Australia_official_statement_endorsement_UNDRIP.pdf [Last access 18.07.2014].

2010,[652] Canada on 12 November 2010,[653] and USA on 9 December 2010.[654]

Hence, the right to self-determination of indigenous peoples is spelled out in art.3 of the UNDRIP in the wording of arts.1 of the two Covenants ICCPR and ICESCR with the substitution of the adjective "all" with "indigenous" as follows: "Indigenous peoples have the right to self-determination. By virtue of that right they freely determine their political status and freely pursue their economic, social and cultural development". Art.4 states that: "Indigenous peoples, in exercising their right to self-determination, have the right to autonomy or self-government in matters relating to their internal and local affairs, as well as ways and means for financing their autonomous functions". Finally, self-determination is also mentioned in the preambular paragraphs 15 and 16, with the reference to international law,[655] while territorial integrity and political unity, as mentioned, were secured by art.46.1.

652 New Zealand Ministerial Statements, "UN Declaration on the Rights of Indigenous Peoples–Government Support", Ministerial Statements, 20 April 2010, at http://www.parliament.nz/en-nz/pb/debates/debates/49HansD_20100420_00000071/ministerial-statements-%E2%80%94-un-declaration-on-the-rights-of [Last access 18.07.2014].

653 Government of Canada, Aboriginal Affairs and Northern Development Canada, "Canada's Statement of Support on the United Nations Declaration on the Rights of Indigenous Peoples", 12 November 2010, at http://www.aadnc-aandc.gc.ca/eng/1309374239861/1309374546142 [last access 18.07.2014].

654 US Department of State, "UN Declaration on the Rights of Indigenous Peoples Review", 9 December 2010, at http://www.state.gov/s/tribalconsultation/declaration [Last access 18.07.2014]; US Department of State, "Announcement of U.S. Support for the United Nations Declaration on the Rights of Indigenous Peoples. Initiatives to Promote the Government-to-Government Relationship & Improve the Lives of Indigenous Peoples", 9 December 2010, at http://www.state.gov/documents/organization/184099.pdf [Last access 18.07.2014].

655 They affirm: "*Acknowledging* that the Charter of the United Nations, the International Covenant on Economic, Social and Cultural Rights and the International Covenant on Civil and Political Rights, as well as the Vienna Declaration and Programme of Action, affirm the fundamental importance of the right to self-determination of all peoples, by virtue of which they freely determine their political status and freely pursue their economic, social and cultural development, *Bearing* in mind that nothing in this Declaration may be used to deny any peoples their right to self-determination, exercised in conformity with international law".

2.2.2.5 The UNDRIP regime of self-determination and the right to autonomy of indigenous peoples

The adoption of the UNDRIP certainly represents a major achievement for the indigenous rights' agenda. Despite its non-binding nature in *stricto sensu*, it is the most wide-ranging and cutting-edge international instrument on indigenous peoples' rights.[656] However, vis-à-vis the right to self-determination, as seen in the previous section 2.2.2.4, the final compromise to move the article on indigenous peoples' right to autonomy after the right to self-determination may suggest an attempt by States to limit the application of the latter to the scope of the former, which in turn is doubtfully recognized in international law. Although Anaya suggested interpreting the right to self-determination of indigenous peoples inserted in the UNDRIP as a vehicle for (re)conciliation and for "reversing the legacies of empire, discrimination, and cultural suffocation",[657] how this conciliation should start remains unclear. In fact, a number of authors expressed their scepticism (and indigenous peoples' disappointment) particularly vis-à-vis this potentially reductive recognition of the right to self-determination.[658]

Nevertheless, the combination of these two rights may also have positive effects, especially taking into consideration the increasingly widespread State practice in recognizing autonomous arrangements at the domestic (mainly, constitutional) level (see chapter 3, section 3.3.3). This section thus addresses the pros rather than the cons by highlighting how the UNDRIP may serve as a starting point for the codification of a right to autonomy of indigenous peoples in international law within their right to self-determination, albeit without reducing the scope of the latter.

As seen, the right to autonomy of indigenous peoples was clearly spelled out as a part, form, evolution or exercise of the right to self-determination

---

656 Claire Charters and Rodolfo Stavenhagen, "The UN Declaration on the Rights of Indigenous Peoples: how it came to be and what it heralds", in Claire Charters and Rodolfo Stavenhagen (eds.), *Making the Declaration Work. The United Nations Declaration on the Rights of Indigenous Peoples*, International Work Group for Indigenous Affairs (IWGIA), Doc. No.127, Copenhagen, 2009, pp.10-14, p.10.

657 Anaya, "The Right of Indigenous Peoples to Self-Determination in the Post-Declaration Era", p.196.

658 See, e.g., Timo Koivurova, "From High Hopes to Disillusionment: Indigenous Peoples' Struggle to (re)Gain Their Right to Self-determination", in 15(1) *International Journal on Minority and Group Rights* 2008, pp-1-26; Irene Watson and Sharon Venne, "Talking up Indigenous Peoples' original intent in a space dominated by state interventions", in Elvira Pulitano (ed.), *Indigenous Rights in the Age of the UN Declaration*, Cambridge University Press, Cambridge, 2012, pp.87-109.

in the Draft Declaration (art.31) as well as in the 2007 UNDRIP (art.4). According to Rodríguez Piñero-Royo, the emphasis on self-government by the two declarations derives also from the fact that "despite centuries of colonial rule and assimilation policies, most indigenous peoples have preserved some sort of self-governing structures in managing their own affairs".[659] The wording of indigenous peoples' right to autonomy changed substantially from the Draft Declaration to the UNDRIP. The States were not generally in favour of having a list of potential competences of indigenous autonomies, especially vis-à-vis the management of natural resources,[660] as the formulation of art.31 of the Draft Declaration. This article recognized the right to autonomy or self-government of indigenous peoples as follows: "Indigenous peoples, as a specific form of exercising their right to self-determination, have the right to autonomy or self-government in matters relating to their internal and local affairs, including culture, religion, education, information, media, health, housing, employment, social welfare, economic activities, land and resources management, environment and entry by non-members, as well as ways and means for financing these autonomous functions". Thus, the current art.4 of the UNDRIP may be seen as a reduced version of the former art.31 of the Draft Declaration. Art 4 states: "Indigenous peoples, in exercising their right to self-determination, have the right to autonomy or self-government in matters relating to their internal and local affairs, as well as ways and means for financing their autonomous functions". An indigenous scholar has argued that this text is "very limiting and dangerous to the self-determination of Indigenous Nations because the words *internal and local affairs* [...] are not explained or elaborated from an Indigenous perspective. [...] States can impose their own meanings [...] [and they] could be constructed to mean exercising autonomy only over the affairs in our villages, reservations, or other local areas" [emphasis in the original].[661] In fact, art.4 of the UNDRIP may be subject to a different interpretation than the Draft Declaration vis-à-vis the realization of the right to self-determination through autonomy. The Draft

659 Rodríguez Piñero-Royo, "Political Participation Systems Applicable to Indigenous Peoples", p. 328.

660 Helen Quane, "The UN Declaration on the Rights of Indigenous Peoples: New Directions for Self-Determination and Participatory Rights?", in Stephen Allen and Alexandra Xanthaki (eds.), *Reflections on the UN Declaration on the Rights of Indigenous Peoples*, Hart Publishing, Oxford, Portland, 2011, 259-287, p.270.

661 Chairmane White Face Zumila Wobaga, *Indigenous Nations' Rights in the Balance. An Analysis of the Declaration on the Rights of Indigenous Peoples*, Living Justice Press, Saint Paul (MN, USA), 2013, p.41.

Declaration recognizes the right to autonomy as *one of the ways* to exercise it ("[i]ndigenous peoples, as a specific form of exercising their right to self-determination [...]"). Therefore, the "shortened" art.4 of the UNDRIP may imply that the right to autonomy is the primary way for indigenous peoples to exercise their right to self-determination. Nevertheless, upon closer inspection, art.4 affirms that "[i]ndigenous peoples, in exercising their right to self-determination, have the right to autonomy or self-government [...]", but not that this is the *only way* to exercise their right to self-determination. Therefore, art.4 suggests as well that the right to autonomy exists for indigenous peoples but just as one of the exercises or expressions of their (wider) right to self-determination. Hence, according to the UNDRIP, indigenous peoples do have the right to autonomy, which *derives* from their right to self-determination, but *it does not limit* the scope of it. This conclusion should also lead States to seriously comply with indigenous peoples' right to autonomy and not to reduce it, as the above-cited indigenous scholar highlighted.

However, one may wonder whether autonomy would suffice for indigenous peoples. As seen, many indigenous peoples are uninterested in secession, but affirming that none of them aspire to Statehood may be reductive.[662] Thornberry noted that autonomy may be '[t]oo little for indigenous peoples. Suggestions that they should adopt the concept of autonomy as a general focus for their claims do not appeal. Autonomy is seen as a grant, not as a right; it is viewed as static, not dynamic'.[663] Nevertheless, since the late 1980s, the quest for autonomy has been a growing trend, also fostered by flourishing States' practice. During this period, many indigenous organizations' agendas in Latin America have included claims for autonomy, albeit with much confusion.[664] Rosa de la Fuente interestingly reported that indigenous movements and organizations in Mexico shared this feeling. She interviewed Margarito Ruiz Hernández, a member of the Maya-Tojolab people, who is also a former deputy, expert, and active promoter and member of various indigenous and non-indigenous organizations in the Central

---

662 See section 2.2.1.

663 Patrick Thornberry, "Images of Autonomy and Individual and Collective Rights in International Instruments on the Rights of Minorities", in Markko Suksi (ed.), *Autonomy: Applications and Implications*, The Hague, Cambridge, Dordrecht, Martinus Nijhoff Publishers, 1998, pp.97-124, p.123

664 Héctor Díaz-Polanco, *Autonomía regional. La autodeterminación de los pueblos indios*, D.F. Mexico, Siglo Veintiuno Editores, 1991, p.150.

American country. He affirmed that 'notwithstanding the wide use of the term autonomy, everybody understands it in different ways'.[665]

Examples of legally-established or recognised indigenous (territorial) autonomies or self-governments may be found in (at least) the following countries: Bangladesh, Bolivia, Canada, Colombia, Ecuador, Greenland (Denmark), India, Indonesia, Mexico, Nicaragua, Nunavut, Panama, Venezuela, Taiwan and USA (see chapter 3, section 3.3.3).

In sum, the right to autonomy may be seen as one of the facets of the right to self-determination, conceiving self-determination in a broader sense (see sections 2.2.4 and 2.2.6). Within this conceptualisation, Díaz-Polanco had already argued that "the autonomy is [just] *one of the systems* through which socio-cultural groups exercise their right to self-determination" [emphasis added].[666] Thus, although a right to autonomy does not yet exist under international law,[667] the Declarations, and particularly the UNDRIP, may be the pioneering, necessary, and decisive steps towards the recognition that that this right is emerging in international law, at least for indigenous peoples.

2.2.3 The right to self-determination of indigenous peoples in the two American and African regional human rights systems

Albeit very briefly, it is also relevant to report in this chapter the developments vis-à-vis the right to self-determination of indigenous peoples in the two American and African regional human rights systems.

Despite the lack of any specific norm addressing indigenous peoples' rights in the American Convention on Human Rights adopted in 1969 in San José (Costa Rica), from which the name of Pact of San José derives, the Inter-American Commission on Human Rights and Inter-American Court of Human Rights have developed an extensive jurisprudence on indigenous rights, which is analyzed in more detail vis-à-vis indigenous political rights in chapters 3 (section 3.3.2) and 4. They started in 1989 the

665 Rosa De la Fuente, *La Autonomía en Chiapas. Un Nuevo imaginario Socio-Espacial*, Madrid, Catarata, 2008, p.70.

666 Díaz-Polanco, *Autonomía regional. La autodeterminación de los pueblos indios*, p.157.

667 Hurst Hannum, "The Road to Autonomy in Aceh", in Panel "State Sovereignty and Regional Autonomy: The Asian Experience", *Proceedings of the Annual Meeting of the American Society of International Law*, Vol. 102, 2008, 116-118, p.118.

work on the "Proposed American Declaration on the Rights of Indigenous Peoples", and established a Working Group of the OAS Permanent Council in 1999 –with an increasing indigenous participation since 2001. However, after the adoption of a Draft Declaration on 26 February 1997,[668] the works were suspended due to a lack of funding in 2012. The process resumed recently (December 2014), but in May 2015 the Indigenous Caucus withdrew from the negotiations alleging lack of good-will from the States.[669]

Regarding self-determination, there is no mention of this right of indigenous peoples in the "Proposed American Declaration on the Rights of Indigenous Peoples",[670] but a right to self-government is enshrined in art.15, which contains the wording of arts.1 of the both Covenants but states:

> "1. Indigenous peoples have the right to freely determine their political status and freely pursue their economic, social, spiritual and cultural development, and accordingly, they have the right to autonomy or self-government with regard to inter alia culture, religion, education, information, media, health, housing, employment, social welfare, economic activities, land and resource management, the environment and entry by nonmembers; and to determine ways and means for financing these autonomous functions.
>
> 2. Indigenous peoples have the right to participate without discrimination, if they so decide, in all decision-making, at all levels, with regard to matters that might affect their rights, lives and destiny. They may do so directly or through representatives chosen by them in accordance with their own procedures. They shall also have the right to maintain and develop their own indigenous decision-making institutions, as well as equal opportunities to access and participate in all state institutions and fora".

668 For general information see the OAS website, "Draft Declaration on the Rights of Indigenous Peoples", at http://www.oas.org/en/iachr/indigenous/activities/declaration.asp [Last access 28.07.2014].

669 The text of the American Declaration should have been finally discussed during the OAS General Assembly in June 2015. During one of the most recent negotiations held in Washington in May 2015, the Indigenous Caucus alleged a lack of good will by the governments of Colombia, Brazil, Belize, Ecuador, Argentina, Chile, and Venezuela. Apparently, at the last moment, these States tried to introduce some changes to the text that would undermine the standards for the protection of indigenous rights, particularly in comparison with those contained in the UNDRIP. Cultural Survival. "Indigenous Caucus Withdraws from Negotiations on the Draft American Declaration on the Rights of Indigenous Peoples", 19 May 2015, at http://www.culturalsurvival.org/news/indigenous-caucus-withdraws-negotiations-draft-american-declaration-rights-indigeno us -peoples [Last access 21.08.2015].

670 See the text at http://www.cidh.oas.org/Indigenas/Indigenas.en.01/Preamble.htm [Last access 28.07.2014].

Thus, the first paragraph offers reminders of the text of the (UN) Draft Declaration of 1994 vis-à-vis the right to autonomy (then art.31), while the second paragraph refers to a variety of political rights at different levels.

More interestingly, the "African (Banjul) Charter on Human and Peoples' Rights", which was adopted on 27 June 1981 and entered into force on 21 October 1986,[671] recognizes in art.20 that:

> "1. All peoples shall have the right to existence. They shall have the unquestionable and inalienable right to self-determination. They shall freely determine their political status and shall pursue their economic and social development according to the policy they have freely chosen.
>
> 2. Colonized or oppressed peoples shall have the right to free themselves from the bonds of domination by resorting to any means recognized by the international community.
>
> 3. All peoples shall have the right to the assistance of the States parties to the present Charter in their liberation struggle against foreign domination, be it political, economic or cultural".

Thanks to this broad conceptualization, the African Commission on Human and Peoples' Rights adopted decisions on the right to self-determination involving indigenous peoples including, *inter alia*, the notorious case of *Katangese Peoples' Congress v. Zaire* (1995),[672] in which a violation of art.20.1 was alleged. Although the African Commission did not recognize any infringement of any right contained in the African Charter and did not address the issue of whether the claimant –the Katanga people– were a people thus entitled to self-determination, for the aims of this study two aspects of this decision are particularly relevant. First, the African Commission stated that "self-determination may be exercised in any of the following ways independence, selfgovernment, local government, federalism, confederalism, unitarism or any other form of relations that accords with the wishes of the people but fully cognisant of other recognised principles such as sovereignty and territorial integrity".[673] Second, the African Commission declared that, in absence of violations of human rights, the Katanga people should exercise "a variant of self-determination that is compatible with the

671 Organization of African Unity (OAU), Doc. No.CAB/LEG/67/3 rev. 5, 21 I.L.M. 58 (1982), at http://www.achpr.org/files/instruments/achpr/banjul_charter.pdf [Last access 28.07.2014].

672 African Commission on Human and Peoples' Rights, *Katangese Peoples' Congress v. Zaire*, Communication No.75/92 (1995).

673 *Ibid.*, para.4.

sovereignty and territorial integrity of Zaire".[674] Thus, the African Commission not only recognized a variety of ways of exercising self-determination albeit respecting sovereignty and territorial integrity, but, by doing so, it essentially concluded that such variants of self-determination are possible, and, therefore, self-determination may not be equated solely to secession or independence.

2.2.4 The multifaceted right to self-determination of indigenous peoples

As a further consequence of the protracted works on the UNDRIP, many authors explored what the right to self-determination of indigenous peoples may imply. The works on this topic may be broadly divided into two groups, as follows. First,[675] a substantial number of scholars described self-determination as mainly expressions of autonomy and, in some cases, political

674 *Ibid.*, para.6.

675 See, in chronological order: Gudmundur Alfredsson, "Different Forms of and Claims to the Right of Self-Determination", in Donald Clark and Robert Williamson, *Self-Determination. International Perspectives*, MacMillan Press, HoundsMill, Basingstoke and London, 1996 and St. Martin's Press, New York, 1996, pp.58-85; Asbjørn Eide, "Peaceful Group Accommodation as an Alternative to Secession in Sovereign States", in Donald Clark and Robert Williamson, *Self-Determination. International Perspectives*, MacMillan Press, HoundsMill, Basingstoke and London, 1996 and St. Martin's Press, New York, 1996, pp.87-109; Daes, "The Right of Indigenous Peoples to 'Self-Determination' in the Contemporary World Order"; Trifunovska, "One Theme in Two Variations ..."; Lauri Hannikainen, "Self-Determination and Autonomy in International Law", in Markku Suksi (ed.), *Autonomy: Applications and Implications*, Kluwer Law International, The Hague, Cambridge MA, Dordrecht, 1998, pp.79-95; Myntti, "The Right to Self-Determination and Effective Participation"; Carolina E. Foster, "Articulating Self-determination in the Draft Declaration on the Rights of Indigenous Peoples", *European Journal of International Law* 2001, Vol.12, No.1, pp.141-157; Paul J. Magnarella, "The Evolving Right of Self-Determination of Indigenous Peoples", 14 *Saint Thomas Law Review* 2001-2002, pp.452-447; Federico Lenzerini, "Sovereignty Revisited: International Law and Parallel Sovereignty of Indigenous Peoples", 42 *Texas International Law Journal* 2006, pp.155-189; Jungwon Park, "Integration of Peoples and Minorities: An Approach to the Conceptual Problem of Peoples and Minorities with Reference Self-determination under International Law", 13 *International Journal of Minority and Group Rights* 2006, pp.69-93; Xanthaki, *Indigenous Rights and United Nations Standards*; Barelli, "Shaping Indigenous Self-Determination: Promising or Unsatisfactory Solutions?"; Quane, "The UN Declaration on the Rights of Indigenous Peoples ..."; Prosper Nobirabo Musafiri, "Right to Self-Determination in International Law: Towards Theorization of the Concept of Indigenous Peoples/National Minority?", 19 *International*

rights and the FPIC, thus following the language of both Declarations more closely. Second, [676] an equally sizeable group of academics envisaged a more multi-faceted concept that, in addition to autonomy and political rights, includes other interlinked aspects such as mutual respect, a remedy to past discrimination and injustices, cultural integrity and identity, land rights, rights to subsistence and natural resources, and to the right to (self-determined) development, in line with the UN Declaration on the Right to

Journal of Minority and Group Rights 2012, pp.481-532; Malgosia Fitzmaurice, "The question of indigenous peoples' rights: a time for reappraisal?", in Duncan French (ed.), *Statehood and Self-Determination. Reconciling Tradition and Modernity in International Law*, Cambridge University Press, Cambridge, New York, 2013, pp.349-376.

676 See, in chronological order: James Anaya, *Indigenous Peoples in International Law*, Oxford University Press, New York, Oxford, 1996; James Anaya, "Self-Determination as a Collective Human Rights under Contemporary International Law", in Pekka Aikio and Martin Scheinin (eds.), *Operationalizing the Rights of Indigenous Peoples to Self-Determination*, Institute for Human Rights, Åbo Akademi University, Saarijärvi, 2000, pp.3-18; Daes, "The Spirit and Letter of the Right to Self-Determination of Indigenous Peoples ..."; Henriksen, "The Right of Self-Determination: Indigenous Peoples versus States"; Ted Moses, "The Right to Self-Determination and Its Significance to the Survival of Indigenous Peoples", in Pekka Aikio and Martin Scheinin (eds.), *Operationalizing the Rights of Indigenous Peoples to Self-Determination*, Institute for Human Rights, Åbo Akademi University, Saarijärvi, 2000, pp.155-177; Scheinin, "The Right to Self-Deter mination under the Covenant on Civil and Political Rights"; Taiaiake Alfred, "From Sovereignty to Freedom: Towards An Indigenous Political Discourse", 3 *Indigenous Affairs* 2001, pp.22-34; Lorie M. Graham, "Resolving Indigenous Claims to Self-Determination", 10 *ILSA Journal of International and Comparative Law* 2003-2004, pp.385-420; Peter Manus, "Sovereignty, Self-Determination and Environment-Based Cultures: The Emerging Voice of Indigenous Peoples in International Law", 23 *Wisconsin International Law Journal* 2005, pp.553-642; Jerémié Gilbert, *Indigenous Peoples' Land Rights under International Law. From Victims to Actors*, Transnational Publisher, Ardesley NY, 2006; Marco Aparicio-Wilhelmi, "El Derecho de los Pueblos Indígenas a la Libre Determinación", in Mikel Berraondo (ed.), *Pueblos Indígenas y Derechos Humanos*, Serie Derechos Humanos, Vol.14, Universidad de Deusto, Bilbao, 2006, pp.399-421; Siegfried Wiessner", Indigenous Sovereignty: A Reassessment in Light of the UN Declaration on the Rights of Indigenous Peoples", 41 *Vanderbilt Journal of Transnational Law* 2008, pp.1141-1176; Joshua Castellino, "Territorial Integrity and the 'Right' to Self-Determination: An examination of the Conceptual Tools", 33(2) *Brooklyn Journal of International Law* 2008, pp.503-568; Cathal Doyle and Jerémié Gilbert, "Indigenous Peoples and Globalisation: From 'Development Agression' to 'Self-Determinted Development'", *European Yearbook of Minority Issues*, Vol.8, 2009, Martinus Nijhoff Publishers, Leiden, Boston, 2011, pp.219-267.

Development,[677] and the recent Concluding Observations of both the HRC and the CESCR. This subdivision may be observed irrespective of whether the authors wrote before or after the adoption of the Draft Declaration or the UNDRIP, although, after the adoption of the latter, the debates on indigenous political rights, and not just autonomy, increased.[678] However, it is relevant to underline here that the authors writing in the late 1990s were very concerned about recognizing both the external and internal dimensions of self-determination to indigenous peoples, a concern expressed specifically by States until the very adoption of the UNDRIP. Thus, those authors opted for an "internal dimension", mainly through the exercise of the right to autonomy. Yet, as seen in section 2.1.4, the internal-external self-determination dichotomy may support a tendency on the part of States to equate self-determination solely to secession or independence. Additionally, as seen, many indigenous peoples are uninterested in secession or independence, except when the theory of remedial secession may find an application. The dichotomy tends to limit the scope of the right to self-determination, which, particularly for indigenous peoples, as seen also in the Concluding Observations of the HCR and CESCR, remains complex and multifaceted. As stated by Fitzmaurice, the dichotomy is unhelpful,[679] especially vis-à-

677 General Assembly, Declaration on the Right to Development, UN Doc. A/RES/41/128, 4 December 1986. Art. 1.2 states: "The human right to development also implies the full realization of the right of peoples to self-determination, which includes, subject to the relevant provisions of both International Covenants on Human Rights, the exercise of their inalienable right to full sovereignty over all their natural wealth and resources".

678 See, e.g., Barelli, "Shaping Indigenous Self-Determination: Promising or Unsatisfactory Solutions?"; Quane, "The UN Declaration on the Rights of Indigenous Peoples ..."; Marco Aparicio Wilhelmi, "Los derechos políticos de los pueblos indígenas en la Declaración de Naciones Unidas", in Mikel Berraondo (ed.), *La Declaración sobre los Derechos de los Pueblos Indígenas. Punto y seguido*, AlterNativa, Barcelona, 2008, pp.35-56; and Diego Blázquez Martín, "Algunas Reflexiones Acerca delos Derechos de Representación Política de los Pueblos Indígenas al Hilo de la Declaración", in Natalia Álvarez Molinero, J. Daniel Oliva Martínez, Nieves Zúñiga García-Falces (eds.), *Declaración sobre los Derechos de los Pueblos Indígenas. Hacia un Mundo Intercultural y Sostenible*, Catarata, Madrid, 2009, pp.267-282. The aspects of participation, FPIC and autonomy were relevant also in the Draft Declaration, but they gained a clearer shape in the UNDRIP. In particular, although mainly in the formulation of "free and informed consent" (without "prior", apart art.30) –as in the case of art.16.2 of the ILO Convention 169– FPIC was inserted also into the Draft Declaration in five articles (arts. 10, 12, 20, 27, 30).

679 Fitzmaurice, "The question of indigenous peoples' rights: a time for reappraisal?", p.374

vis the right to self-determination of indigenous peoples. In sum, the broadening of the scope of the right to self-determination and the recognition of its multi-faceted nature reflects a development along the years as well as the continued attempts of many authors –both before and after the adoption of the UNDRIP– to focus on autonomy and political rights. These attempts appear to be aimed somehow –by paraphrasing Weller–[680] at escaping the "trap" of external self-determination in the case of indigenous peoples.

In more detail, after the adoption of the Draft Declarations, eminent scholars such as Eide underlined that, by underlining that self-determination cannot be discussed in general or abstract terms[681] and that it varies substantially from one context to another,[682] a right to "some form of autonomy within sovereign states" to enable indigenous peoples to preserve their identity and ensure their effective political participation, including consultation,[683] was finding some support in the relevant international practice until then.[684] Therefore, according to Eide, "[t]erritorial integrity and basic political stability should be ensured through a process of inclusion and adaptation by which all groups are given the possibility to be equally at home in the common state, and yet to be able to assert and to safeguard their separate identity and to control the resources required for it".[685] In particular, he stressed the potentialities of autonomy and power-sharing within the dimension of self-determination of indigenous peoples to provide them with instruments to secure their equality, preserve their own identity, and to control natural and/or other resources. Daes also affirmed that a more pragmatic approach would lead to the assumption that the right to self-determination of indigenous peoples implies a duty onto States to accommodate their aspirations trough constitutional reforms aimed at establishing power-sharing arrangements.[686] Similarly, Alfredsson, concerned about finding an acceptable proposal for both indigenous peoples and States, argued that "meaningful self-government, political representation in national affairs,

680 Weller, *Escaping the self-determination trap*.

681 Eide, "Peaceful Group Accommodation as an Alternative to Secession in Sovereign States", p.87.

682 *Ibid.*, p.88.

683 *Ibid.*, p.107.

684 *Ibid.*, p.89.

685 *Ibid.*, p.107.

686 Daes, "The Right of Indigenous Peoples to 'Self-Determination' in the Contemporary World Order", p.53.

and an economic foundation in rights to land and resources, would contribute to the satisfaction and better life of indigenous peoples within states".[687] Although Alfredsson underlines that the right to (external) self-determination may be a satisfactory measure for (some) indigenous peoples,[688] he concludes that nevertheless indigenous peoples may obtain greater benefits from aspirations to autonomy, self-government, political participation and national representation, especially if these aspirations are not presented as self-determination as such.[689] Agreeing with Alfredsson on abandoning the language of self-determination to avoid the equation with secession or independence,[690] Trifunovska suggested that a number of arrangements adopted by States may (also) correspond to indigenous peoples' claims, although not always.[691] Among these arrangements of "pluralistic democratic" States, the author envisaged constitutional and legislative measures, effective economic and political participation, conciliation instruments, "interethnic" governmental and non-governmental bodies, and administrative agencies dealing with indigenous peoples' issues of concern, such as education, health, employment, housing, etc.[692]

More specifically on autonomy, Hannikainen underlined that "an autonomous arrangement can realize internal self-determination in quite a meaningful way and can be a good model of decentralization".[693] In fact, according to the author, until then, "[i]ndigenous peoples have weighty international legal arguments to demand autonomy as the principal form of their right to internal self-determination; their right to autonomy may well become a rule of general international law".[694] Along similar lines, Magnarella proposed "two structural alternatives" for pluralistic States, applicable also to indigenous peoples, to create autonomous cantons according to the Swiss model or regions with a number of competences following the

687 Alfredsson, "Different Forms of and Claims to the Right of Self-Determination", p.68.

688 *Ibid.*

689 *Ibid.*, p.70.

690 Trifunovska, "One Theme in Two Variations ...", p.196.

691 *Ibid.*, p.193.

692 *Ibid.*, p.192.

693 Hannikainen, "Self-Determination and Autonomy in International Law", p.90.

694 *Ibid.*, p.89.

Italian model.[695] As he noted, some States had already established autonomous arrangements for indigenous peoples worldwide,[696] and, by underlining that "[s]elf-determination consists of those processes and structures trough which a people gain and maintain control over their own destinies",[697] he concluded that many ways of accommodating indigenous peoples' and States' claims may be found, although fairness and peace should be guaranteed.[698] Moreover, Lenzerini argues for a just and fair pluralistic legal system and proposes the recognition of indigenous autonomy, considering it as parallel to States' sovereignty and an emerging provision of international customary law, in other words as a degree of indigenous sovereignty.[699] In concrete terms, Park affirmed that a "[p]eople within a State, [thus, also indigenous peoples] as the holders of the right to self-determination under international law, should have the right to choose their form of government, and their economic, social, and cultural systems, based on their entitlement to democratic representative government".[700] Lastly, in the light of the adoption of the UNDRIP, Fitzmaurice recently underlined that "the discussion on the right to self-determination of peoples [thus, also indigenous peoples], has to be more practical, [...] and take into account new developments", among which one of the most relevant according to the author is the right to autonomy of indigenous peoples as recognized in art.4 of UNDRIP.[701]

In addition to the autonomy dimension, authors such as Myntti, Foster, Xanthaki, Barelli, Quane and Musafiri also highlighted the dimension of political rights (see chapter 3, section 3.3.1) within the right to self-determination of indigenous peoples. Thus, analyzing the work on the Draft Declaration, the ILO Convention 169, and the observations of both the CERD and the HRC until the late 1990s, Myntti stated that "self-determination should, in first place, be interpreted as the right of indigenous peoples to freely negotiate their political status and representation in the states in which they live".[702] In addition, Foster argued that "when self-determination is understood to refer to representative government this can include

695 Magnarella, "The Evolving Right of Self-Determination of Indigenous Peoples", p.439.

696 *Ibid.*, p.447.

697 *Ibid.*, p.433.

698 *Ibid.*, p.447.

699 Lenzerini, "Sovereignty Revisited ...", p.189.

700 Park, "Integration of Peoples and Minorities ...", p.93.

701 Fitzmaurice, "The question of indigenous peoples' rights: a time for reappraisal?", p.375.

702 Myntti, "The Right to Self-Determination and Effective Participation", p.128.

different levels of autonomy",[703] which may have positive effects in terms of identity-building for indigenous peoples, since they would have a formal place in the public arena of States.[704] Thus, she concludes that "the clearest requirement of self-determination is representative government", which "requires avenues for genuine political participation".[705] However "[s]elf-determination must enable not only the free determination of [indigenous peoples'] political status, but also the free pursuit of their economic, social and cultural development".[706] Analyzing States' attitudes in the reports of the WGIP and WGDD and the Draft Declaration, Xanthaki underlined that an interpretation of self-determination as autonomy and participation at State level, albeit reductive in her view and more focused on the former aspect than the latter,[707] would probably be the most widely accepted solution by States for the final adoption of the Declaration.[708] After the UNDRIP was adopted, Barelli argued that "there are reasons to believe that indigenous participatory rights, as understood in the UNDRIP in the context of self-determination, can produce some positive results",[709] since this "participatory rights" focus does not necessarily restrict the scope of self-determination and may take the form of autonomy.[710] Additionally, the political rights enshrined in the UNDRIP, including the FPIC, are broader than those recognized in human rights law, enjoying a collective dimension.[711] Quane further affirmed that the UNDRIP paved the way for new developments of the right to self-determination of indigenous peoples, including the right to autonomy and self-government as stated in art.4 of UNDRIP as well as the recognition of extensive participatory rights, in both their individual and collective dimensions.[712] Finally, approaching the difficulties in recognizing the right to self-determination as well as political rights for indigenous peoples (and minorities), Musafiri recently argued that, to accommodate their claims, the –what he calls "heterogeneous" States–[713] should

703 Foster, "Articulating Self-determination in the Draft Declaration …", p.153.
704 *Ibid.*
705 *Ibid.*, p.156.
706 *Ibid.*
707 Xanthaki, *Indigenous Rights and United Nations Standards*, p.112.
708 *Ibid.*, pp.282-283.
709 Barelli, "Shaping Indigenous Self-Determination: Promising or Unsatisfactory Solutions?", p.435.
710 *Ibid.*
711 *Ibid.*
712 Quane, "The UN Declaration on the Rights of Indigenous Peoples ...", p.286.
713 Musafiri, "Right to Self-Determination in International Law …", p.531.

acknowledge that indigenous peoples have "a right to be included in the decision-making process, [and] a right to self-governance".[714]

As mentioned, many other authors have considered other facets of the right to self-determination, often taking into consideration the visions of indigenous peoples themselves. As Thornberry put it, "self-determination described by indigenous representatives is already very specific, with elements of respect for traditions, histories and world view, and protection of lands and territories".[715] Anaya, proposing his "ongoing and constitutive self-determination" (see section 2.1 in this chapter) for indigenous peoples, albeit as a "principle" and not a right to self-determination, envisaged particularized norms by mapping international law in place at the time that may represent the requirements of the self-determination of indigenous peoples in remedial terms vis-à-vis past wrongs, i.e., non-discrimination, cultural integrity, lands and resources, social welfare and development, and self-government.[716] Explaining the spirit of the Draft Declaration in a later publication, Daes reported how this right was translated into indigenous languages, i.e., as freedom, integrity and respect. Thus, she argued that "self-determination means the freedom for indigenous peoples to live well, to live according to their own values and beliefs, and to be respected by their non-indigenous neighbors".[717] In addition, two further "true spirits of self-determination" of indigenous peoples are "land and mutual respect".[718] Alfred also agreed that an indigenous perspective on self-determination includes first and foremost a "regime of respect".[719] Adding another aspect, Henriksen highlighted that, according to the understanding of indigenous peoples themselves, self-determination is mainly conceived as "the right to be in control of their lives and their own destiny".[720] Manus agreed with this

714 *Ibid.*, p.532.

715 Thornberry, "Self-Determination and Indigenous Peoples: Objections and Responses", p.63

716 Anaya, *Indigenous Peoples in International Law*, p.97 and ff. See also pp.183-184. On reparations to Indigenous peoples under international and comparative law, see also the recent work of Federico Lenzerini (ed.), *Reparations for Indigenous Peoples. International and Comparative Perspectives*, Oxford University Press, Oxford, New York, 2008.

717 Daes, "The Spirit and Letter of the Right to Self-Determination of Indigenous Peoples ...", p.79.

718 *Ibid.*

719 Alfred 2001, p.30

720 Henriksen, "The Right of Self-Determination: Indigenous Peoples versus States", p.137.

broad definition and added that this type of delineation of self-determination may also include "the protection of indigenous peoples' relationships with the environment".[721] Scheinin suggested that "[i]ndigenous peoples [...] should put more emphasis on the economic or resource dimension of the right to self-determination as justification for their more general claims on self-determination and in their everyday struggle for a stronger say in decision-making that affects their lives",[722] thus combining both political and economic self-determination (see section 2.1 in this chapter). However, Moses argued that self-determination has not only these two latter dimensions, but also implies a variety of interdependent rights,[723] including the very important right to subsistence.[724] Graham spoke of a broad indigenous self-determination which includes "norms that surround" it, i.e., "control of lands and resources, protection of culture, social and economic development, and some form of autonomy and self-governance", which were all based on indigenous peoples' right to self-determination, although many times this right was not directly spelled out in their claims.[725] More specifically, in his extensive work, Gilbert showed how self-determination has broadened to include "a right for indigenous peoples to freely determine the use of their territories and to enter territorial negotiations",[726] therefore, FPIC,[727] and land rights connected to (territorial) autonomies.[728] Furthermore, at the "Workshop on Methodologies regarding Free, Prior and Informed Consent and Indigenous Peoples" organized in 2005 by the UN Permanent Forum on Indigenous Issues, it was argued that FPIC is "integral to the exercise of the right of self-determination by indigenous peoples and

721 Manus, "Sovereignty, Self-Determination and Environment-Based Cultures ...", p.570.

722 Scheinin, "The Right to Self-Determination under the Covenant on Civil and Political Rights", p.198.

723 Moses, "The Right to Self-Determination and Its Significance to the Survival of Indigenous Peoples", p.157. On the interdependence of human rights and indigenous rights, see the recent work of Helen Quane, "A Further Dimension to the Interdependence and Indivisibility of Human Rights?: Recent Developments concerning the Rights of Indigenous Peoples", 25 *Harvard Human Rights Journal* 2012, pp.49-83.

724 Moses, "The Right to Self-Determination and Its Significance to the Survival of Indigenous Peoples", p.164.

725 Graham, "Resolving Indigenous Claims to Self-Determination", p.418.

726 Gilbert, *Indigenous Peoples' Land Rights under International Law*, p.215.

727 *Ibid.*, p.219.

728 *Ibid.*, p.229.

[…] an integral component of their rights to lands, territories and resources".[729] Similarly, the Expert Mechanism on the Rights of Indigenous Peoples has recently reiterated that FPIC is an integral part of the right to self-determination of indigenous peoples,[730] as several other authors have also done.[731] While criticizing the uncertainties surrounding the meaning of self-determination, Castellino noted that "self-determination, especially in its territorial dimension, […] remains the only vehicle through which indigenous rights to territory can be expressed".[732] After the adoption of the UNDRIP, Wiessner envisaged a set of measures necessary to maintain indigenous "sovereignty" –conceived more in the sense of indigenous cultural integrity and identity, as highlighted by indigenous leaders–[733] by guaranteeing the recognition of indigenous peoples' land rights, local and internal self-government, the respect of their FPIC, the protection of their cultural identity and languages, and their participation at international level and in international decision-making bodies such as the UN.[734] Indeed, more broadly, the right to self-determination of indigenous peoples may be conceived as to the right to control one's own destiny and to preserve one's own culture,[735] or "the right to decide their political status and to determine what their future will be, in compliance with relevant rules of international law and the principle of equality and non-discrimination".[736] Turning to development, art.1.2 of the abovementioned UN Declaration on the Right to

---

729 Permanent Forum on Indigenous Issues, "Report of the International Workshop on Methodologies regarding Free, Prior and Informed Consent and Indigenous Peoples", 17 February 2005, UN Doc. E/C.19/2005/3, para.41.

730 Expert Mechanism on the Rights of Indigenous Peoples, "Final study on indigenous peoples and the right to participate in decision-making", 26 May 2011, UN Doc. A/HRC/EMRIP/2011/2, para.21, p.20.

731 Cathal Doyle and Jill Cariño "Making Free, Prior & Informed Consent a Reality, Indigenous Peoples and the Extractive Sector" (2013), at http://www.piplinks.org/system/files/Consortium+FPIC+report+-+May+2103.+-+web+version.pdf [Last access 01.08.2014], p.3; and Andrea Carmen, "The Right to Free, Prior and Informed Consent. A Framework for Harmonious Relations and New Processes of Redress", in Jackie Hartley, Paul Joffe and Jennifer Preston (eds.), *Realizing the UN Declaration on the Rights of Indigenous Peoples: Triumph, Hope and Action*, Purich Publishing, Saskatoon, 2010, pp.120-134, p.120.

732 Castellino, "Territorial Integrity and the 'Right' to Self-Determination …", p.565

733 Wiessner", Indigenous Sovereignty: A Reassessment …", pp.1170-1174.

734 *Ibid.*, pp.1174-1175.

735 Quane, "The UN Declaration on the Rights of Indigenous Peoples ...", p.262.

736 International Law Association, "Final Report on the Rights of Indigenous Peoples", Sofia Conference, 2012, p.30, para.5, at http://www.ila-hq.org/down

Development (1986) foresees that this right also implies the full realization of the right to self-determination and, in particular, of the exercise of the inalienable right to full sovereignty over all their natural wealth and resources. Aparicio-Wilhelmi stressed that self-determination and "ethnically-based development" (in Spanish: *etnodesarrollo*) of indigenous peoples are interlinked, since the latter implies the effective control over their land, natural resources and the socio-economic organization, which automatically leads to the former,[737] particularly in the form of self-governments.[738] Finally, Doyle and Gilbert have recently argued that, in addition to being an expression of indigenous peoples' right to self-determination, the rights to self-government and autonomy, participation in decision-making, and the preservation and development of their institutions are also "enablers" to exercise their right to development, which in turn, is interlinked with the right to self-determination and may lead to what the authors call "self-determined development".[739]

In conclusion, the conceptualization of the right to self-determination of indigenous peoples has undergone substantial developments both in the practice of international law, as seen above, and in academia, as seen in this section. This reflects the evolving nature of this right in the case of indigenous peoples as well.[740] Starting from the concepts of autonomy and political rights, which remain essential parts of indigenous peoples' right to self-

---

load.cfm/docid/227B560E-F0F5-4773-BECC974CFC6A11B8 [Last access 28.07.2014]

737 Aparicio-Wilhelmi, "El Derecho de los Pueblos Indígenas a la Libre Determinación", pp.407-408.

738 *Ibid.*, p.412.

739 Doyle and Gilbert, "Indigenous Peoples and Globalisation: From 'Development Agression' to 'Self-Determinted Development'", p.246. On the right to development of Indigenous peoples, see also Rainer Hofmann and Juri Alistair Gauthier, "Indigenous Peoples and the Right to Development", in A. Eide, J. Möller, I. Ziemele (eds.), *Making Peoples Heard. Essays on Human Rights in Honour of Gudmundur Alfredsson* (Martinus Nijhoff Publishers, Leiden 2011), pp. 439-461; Joshua Castellino, "Indigenous Rights and the Right to Development: Emerging Synergies or Collusion?", in Stephen Allen and Alexandra Xanthaki (eds.), *Reflections on the Un Declaration on the Rights of Indigenous Peoples*, Hart Publishing, Oxford, Portland, 2011, pp.367-386; and Felipe Gómez Isa, "El derecho al desarrollo de los Pueblos Indígenas", in Felipe Gómez Isa and Mikel Berraondo (eds.), *Los derechos indígenas tras la Declaración. El desafío dela implementación*, Vol.20, Universidad de Deusto, Bilbao, 2013, pp.175-190.

740 On the evolving nature of the right to self-determination of indigenous peoples, see, e.g., Myntti, "The Right to Self-Determination and Effective Participation", p.108; Henriksen, "The Right of Self-Determination: Indigenous Peoples versus

determination, other facets such as indigenous peoples' rights to land, natural resources –and thus to consultation and FPIC–, identity and cultures, and socio-economic development may also be included in indigenous peoples' right to self-determination. As seen above, this has also been clarified by both the HRC and the CESCR. In fact, the interdependence of all these facets appears clear. Indigenous autonomy arrangements, as will be explained in chapter 3, section 3.3.3, tend to be established in relation to specific territories, which thus suggests that, within the framework of the right to self-determination, control over and the use of lands and natural resources should be recognized. This may also lead to the socio-economic development of indigenous peoples and the potential preservation of indigenous cultures and languages. These last three aspects may be part of the competences of the autonomy/self-government. Additionally, to guarantee all this, political rights may make it possible to have a say both in the national political arena and in local governments, together with the rights to consultation and FPIC, which play a key role in guaranteeing indigenous peoples a fair use of lands and natural resources (see chapter 3, section 3.3.2).

Hence, a *composite right of political participation of indigenous peoples* that refers to the combination of (1) (a) *ad hoc* political rights (indigenous peoples' representation in State bodies or in other public posts, including in decision-making processes and in the judiciary, both at national and local level) and their (b) rights to consultation and (c) free, prior and informed consent (FPIC) on the one hand, and (2) autonomy/self-government arrangements (including the preservation of indigenous traditional institutions) on the other, may be seen as one of the expression of the multi-faceted right to self-determination of indigenous peoples (see chapter 3, section 3.3). In fact, as mentioned, only a shift "from an end-state approach to a relational approach to self-determination",[741] i.e., self-determination as the relation between a State and a community[742] may offer one the most effective ways to realize the right to self-determination, particularly for indigenous peoples. As affirmed by Gilbert, "the mix of democratic rights and territorial issues entrenched in self-determination would certainly play an increasingly important role in the future. Of course, such an approach needs

States", p.139; Daes, "The Spirit and Letter of the Right to Self-Determination of Indigenous Peoples ...", p.79.

741 Kingsbury, "Reconstructing Self-Determination: A Relational Approach", p.22.

742 *Ibid.*, p.26.

flexibility from both States on the issue of territorial sovereignty, and indigenous peoples on their view to self-determination".[743] This type of "language" of self-determination, furthermore, suggests to States that the risk of secession is limited. Secession could thus become a viable option solely in those cases of a potential application of Remedial Secession, that is to say, when a State is brutally repressing the human rights of their citizens or of a part of them.

2.2.5 The implications of the use of the term "people"

This section aims to conclude the overview on the multi-faceted right to self-determination of indigenous peoples by briefly addressing the implications of the use of the term "people" in relation to this right in the case of indigenous peoples.

As seen in section 2.1.5, the right to self-determination enshrined in the two Covenants has been applied beyond colonialism, is an "ongoing" right, and it cannot be equated to the sole entire population of existing States, otherwise there would be no sense to have it exist. Thanks to the adoption of the UNDRIP, the right to self-determination in the same wording of the Covenants has been recognized specifically for indigenous peoples as well.

States' uneasiness with the recognition of the right to self-determination for indigenous peoples due to the use of the term "peoples" is widely known and has deep roots. This has been highly debated in the *travaux préparatoires* regarding the wording of art.1 of the ILO Convention 169 and in the prolonged process of adopting both the Draft Declaration and the UNDRIP. The use of the word "people" in the ILO Convention 169 –versus the term "population" employed in the former ILO Convention 107 adopted in 1957– represented a contentious issue for the majority of States.[744] The final compromise was found in the formulation of art.1.3 of the ILO Convention 169 as follows: "[t]he use of the term peoples in this Convention shall not be construed as having any implications as regards the rights which may attach to the term under international law". As to the work on the Draft Declaration, the use of the word "people" proved to be problematic since

743 Gilbert, *Indigenous Peoples' Land Rights under International Law*, p.225.

744 International Labour Organization, "Partial Revision of the Indigenous and Tribal Populations Convention, 1957 (No.107). Report IV (1), 76th Session 1989", Geneva, 1988, pp.4-5; International Labour Organization, "Partial Revision of the Indigenous and Tribal Populations Convention, 1957 (No.107). Report IV (2 A), 76th Session 1989", Geneva, 1989, pp.5-7, and 8-12.

the very first sessions of the WGIP.[745] The debates regarding the right to self-determination mentioned above (sections 2.2.2.3 and 2.2.2.4) were also fuelled by the use of the word "people" and its potential implications in terms of secession or independence.[746] Later, since its establishment, the WGDD had to face problems vis-à-vis the use of the word "peoples" given that it could not be used in the denomination of the working group itself,[747] nor was it easily accepted in the following working sessions.[748]

However, the (potential) refusal to recognize indigenous peoples as a "people" would be discriminatory; it would also represent an issue of continued suppression of sovereignty since the first colonisations: Indigenous peoples existed (well) before the (creation of the) States. International law shall reply to this following its precedents according to inter-temporal law.[749] Finally, it would also be a denial of reality and current international law practice. Indigenous peoples are undoubtedly a "people" in social, cultural, and "ethnological" terms.[750] One may still counter-argue whether they are a "people" under international law and in the terms of the right to self-determination included in both arts.1 of the ICCPR and ICESCR. And the answer would be that yes, they are, otherwise neither the HRC nor the CESCR would have considered and increasingly cited in their Concluding Observations the duty to report on the application of art.1 of both Covenants

745 E.g., some members of WGIP expressed their hesitation to use the word "people". Daes, "The UN Declaration on the Rights of Indigenous Peoples: Background and Appraisal", p.18, that cites the UN Economic and Social Council, Sub-Commission on Prevention of Discrimination and Protection of Minorities, "Report of the Working Group on Indigenous Populations on its fourth session", 27 August 1985, Thirty-eighth session, UN Doc. E/CN.4/Sub.2/1985/22, p..15, para.63.

746 See also Myntti, "The Right to Self-Determination and Effective Participation", p.87.

747 Chávez, "The Declaration on the Rights of Indigenous Peoples. Breaking the *Impasse …*", p.97.

748 Xanthaki, *Indigenous Rights and United Nations Standards*, p.109, that cites the report of the Working Group on the Draft Declaration of 2000, in which it was decided to use the term "indigenous peoples" in brackets. See Commission on Human Rights, "Report of the Working Group established in accordance with Commission on Human Rights Resolution 1995/32", UN Doc. E/CN.4/2001/85, Annex I, 6 February 2001, p.29.

749 Castellino, "Conceptual Difficulties and the Right to Indigenous Self-Deter mination", pp.68-74, who convincingly argues that the inter-temporal rule was followed in case of serious crimes against humanity by the establishment *a posteriori* of the criminal courts. See also Patrick Thornberry, *Indigenous Peoples and Human Rights*, pp.87-88.

750 Myntti, "The Right to Self-Determination and Effective Participation", p.113.

vis-à-vis indigenous peoples (section 2.2.2.2). In addition, indigenous peoples are certainly a matter of concern to customary international law, since the two required elements of State practice and *opinio juris* are contemporarily met. In other words, there is sufficient States' practice in recognizing both indigenous peoples and their rights, which in turn leads to a satisfactory *opinio juris* to recognize those. The contemporary existence of these two elements of customary international law leads to the conclusion that indigenous peoples are a matter of customary international law.[751]

Indigenous peoples may thus be considered as a "specific people".[752] As stated by Molinero, the peculiarity of indigenous peoples' international legal status relates to the fact that they somehow stand in between the recognition that States grant to other States as a full subject of international law and the recognition that States grant to non-State actors with no sovereign aim.[753] Indeed, indigenous peoples stand as States or non-State actors in the international arena.[754] However, they demand more rights than a non-State actor,[755] but not necessarily a Statehood. As mentioned, the majority of indigenous peoples rather aspire to a (recognized and effective) right to self-determination which implies more facets, as confirmed by both the HRC and the CESCR, by the African Commission on Human and Peoples' Rights in the case *Katangese Peoples' Congress v. Zaire*, and the academia (see previous sections 2.2.2.2, 2.2.3 and 2.2.4).

In conclusion, questioning whether indigenous peoples are a "people" (and therefore have a right to self-determination) is put in incorrect terms. Indigenous peoples do have the right to self-determination. Furthermore,

---

751 Federico Lenzerini, "The Trail of Broken Dreams: The Status of Indigenous Peoples in International Law", in Federico Lenzerini (ed.), *Reparations for Indigenous Peoples. International and Comparative Perspectives*, Oxford University Press, Oxford, New York, 2008, pp.73-116, p.97.

752 See, e.g., Thornberry, "Self-Determination and Indigenous Peoples: Objections and Responses", p.55.

753 Natalia Álvarez Molinero, "El Sujeto Indígena y el Derecho de Autodeterminación en la Declaración de Naciones Unidas sobre Derechos de los Pueblos Indígenas: ¿Tienen los Pueblos Indígenas Personalidad Jurídica Internacional?", in Natalia Álvarez Molinero, J. Daniel Oliva Martínez, Nieves Zúñiga García-Falces (eds.), *Declaración sobre los Derechos de los Pueblos Indígenas. Hacia un Mundo Intercultural y Sostenible*, Catarata, Madrid, 2009, pp.233-265, p.222.

754 Claire Charters, "A Self-Determination Approach to Justifying Indigenous Peoples' Participation in International Law and Policy Making", 17(2) *International Journal on Minority and Group Rights* 2010, pp.215-240, p.229

755 Álvarez Molinero, "El Sujeto Indígena y el Derecho de Autodeterminación ...", p.222.

the right to self-determination of indigenous peoples is multifaceted, as discussed above. Both UN practice, especially of the two Committees, and the attitude of certain States, as seen during the *travaux préparatoire* of the Draft Declaration and the UNDRIP, suggests that the recognition of this right, and therefore the recognition of indigenous peoples as a "people", should no longer be an issue. Rather, the core problem concerns *which expression of the multi-faceted right to self-determination indigenous peoples may effectively exercise as right-holders*. Against this background, this study focuses on one of the expressions of the multi-faceted right to self-determination of indigenous peoples, i.e., the proposed *composite right to political participation of indigenous peoples*.

2.2.6 Concluding remarks

The second part of this chapter aimed to unravel the multifaceted right to self-determination of indigenous peoples and to ascertain whether a *composite right to political participation of indigenous peoples* may represent one of the expressions of such multi-faceted right.

The multi-faceted nature of the right to self-determination of indigenous peoples was already outlined in the Cobo-Diaz Study, and it included: Economic, social, cultural, and political aspects; land rights and political participation in public and State affairs as well as respect for internal organizations; and autonomy. Moreover, self-determination was conceived as the basic "precondition" for the enjoyment of all indigenous peoples' rights.

Since 1999, in their Concluding Observations, both the HRC and the CESCR, have recognized indigenous peoples as "peoples" entitled to the right of self-determination in the reporting procedure vis-à-vis an increasing number of States. The two Committees envisaged that a proper application of the right to self-determination would also include indigenous land rights, the duty to consult indigenous peoples and to obtain their FPIC, to guarantee their means of subsistence, and fair compensation in case of natural resource exploitations likely to affect them. This shows how the right to self-determination of indigenous peoples has broadened over the years, also thanks to the work of other UN agencies and the indigenous organizations themselves. Finally, the HRC recognized the right to Free, Prior and Informed Consent (FPIC) of indigenous peoples in the aforementioned case *Ángela Poma Poma v. Peru*.

The right to self-determination of indigenous peoples has finally been specifically recognized in art.3 of the UNDRIP in the wording of arts.1 of the two Covenants ICCPR and ICESCR.

In short, the conceptualization of the right to self-determination of indigenous peoples has undergone substantial developments both in the practice of international law and in academia. Starting from the concepts of autonomy and political rights, which remain essential parts of indigenous peoples' right to self-determination, other facets such as indigenous peoples' rights to land, natural resources –and thus to consultation and FPIC–, identity and cultures, and socio-economic development may also be included in indigenous peoples' right to self-determination. Furthermore, such facets may find interdependent applications, *inter alia*, in their rights to autonomy, participation, land, consultation, and FPIC. Finally, these facets are recognized in the UNDRIP and also in international law, in treaties such as the ICCPR and ICESR, as seen in this chapter, and the ILO Convention 169, as will be discussed in the next chapter.

Against this background, this study thus proposes a *composite right to political participation of indigenous peoples* as one expression of the multifaceted right to self-determination of indigenous peoples. This proposal refers to the combination of (1) (a) *ad hoc* political rights (indigenous peoples' representation in State bodies or in other public posts, including in decision-making processes and in the judiciary, both at national and local level) and their (b) rights to consultation and (c) free, prior and informed consent (FPIC) on the one hand, and (2) autonomy/self-government arrangements (including the preservation of indigenous traditional institutions) on the other.

There is no intention to reduce the content of this right to one or more of these different facets. This proposal aims to focus on the rights of indigenous peoples to "have a say" in national and local political arenas and in all matters likely to affect them, which implies much more than the mere political participation in elections enjoyed by every citizen (see further chapter 3, section 3.3.1). In particular, although autonomy has been seen as the other side of the coin of land rights,[756] indigenous peoples' land rights and right to development are not considered here as elements of this proposed *composite right to political participation*, but rather as corollaries of it. As mentioned, these rights of indigenous peoples are intimately linked and mutually interdependent with each other and may be seen as (other) facets of indigenous peoples' right to self-determination. In other words, these rights

756 Gilbert, *Indigenous Peoples' Land Rights under International Law*, pp.226-231.

go hand in hand since one cannot be exercised without the other. Therefore, they are considered here as distinct rights, although interdependent with the other group of rights included in the *composite right to political participation of indigenous peoples*.

The conceptualization of this *composite right* under international law will be explored in chapter 3. How this *composite right* is recognized and applied at domestic level and thus whether it may also become one of the expressions, or better, effective applications of the right to self-determination of indigenous peoples will be explored subsequently in two case studies (chapters 5 and 6). Therefore, the right of indigenous peoples to participate in international decision-making is not addressed in this study.[757]

757 On the increasing legitimacy of indigenous participation at international level, Charters has recently explored the increasing importance of the participation of Non-State Actors and the right of indigenous peoples to participate in international law-making. In particular, this author argued that indigenous peoples should not participate in all decisions as States, but certainly when the adoption of certain measures is likely to affect them. Charters, "A Self-Determination Approach to Justifying Indigenous Peoples' Participation ...", pp.215-240, in particular pp.222 and 240.

3. One expression of the multi-faceted Right to Self-Determination of Indigenous Peoples: The Composite Right to Political Participation

3.1 "Political rights" in human rights law

3.1.1 Introduction

A common and comprehensive "right to political participation" *per se* is not explicitly recognized by any instrument of human rights protection, except the Council of Europe's Framework Convention on National Minorities, art.15.

Nevertheless, a number of human rights are often referred to as "political rights" and/or "political liberties", i.e., freedom of expression, freedom of association and assembly, and the right to vote and to stand for elections.[758] Indeed, the aforementioned rights belong to what is widely accepted as the "first generation" of human rights, which started to be formally recognized as of the eighteenth century.[759] Clauses dealing with regular and free elections were inserted in the 1776 Virginia Declaration of Rights,[760] (paras.5 and 6).[761] The 1789 Declaration of the Rights of Man and the Citizen art.6 affirms that "[l]aw is the expression of the general will. All citizens have the right to take part personally, or by their representatives, [in] its formation", i.e., a prototype of the right to participate in the overall decision-

758 Bollen proposed the following two 'working definitions' for these categories: "Political rights exist to the extent that the national government is accountable to the general population and each individual is entitled to participate in the government directly or through representatives". Likewise, "[p]olitical liberties exist to the extent that the people of a country have the freedom to express any political opinions in any media and the freedom to form or to participate in any political group". Bollen Kenneth A., "Political Rights and Political Liberties in Nations: An Evaluation of Human Rights Measures, 1950 to 1984", 8 *Human Rights Quarterly* 567 (1986), 567-591, p.568.

759 Christian Tomuschat, *Human Rights. Between Idealism and Realism*, Oxford University Press, Oxford, New York, 2003, p.26.

760 Tomuschat, *Human Rights. Between Idealism and Realism*, p.26.

761 See the the 1776 Virginia Declaration of Rights at http://www.consti tution.org/bcp/virg_dor.htm [Last access 03.11.2014].

making process. In addition, art.11 aimed to guarantee an archetype of freedom of expression.[762] The American and French experiences influenced the early constitutions of the 1800s, especially vis-à-vis the guarantee of holding elections to vote for representatives in the separate organs of the State (e.g., the "Provisional Constitutional Ruling" of Chile in 1812, the Constitutions of Norway in 1814 and of Belgium in 1831). Needless to say, the contexts in which these rights were exercised were highly influenced by the societal division into socio-economic classes, racist theories, etc. For instance, in the USA the right to vote was to be exercised solely by "white" men.[763] One has to wait for the universal suffrages of the early/mid-1900s to see the fair and equal application of the right to vote, although this is not yet guaranteed in all States.

Leaving aside the constitutional evolution of the recognition of these rights –which does not fall under the scope of this study– the turning point at international level clearly was the adoption of the Universal Declaration of Human Rights (UDHR) in 1948 and especially of the ICCPR and ICESCR in 1966 (the so called "Bill of Human Rights"),[764] which will be analyzed in the sections below.

3.1.2 The "political rights"

Despite its non-binding nature, the UDHR states the right to freedom of opinion and expression (art.19); the right to freedom of peaceful assembly and association (art.20); and the "right to take part in the government of his country, directly or through freely chosen representatives" (art. 21, para.1). In addition, art.21, para.3, declares that the authority of the government shall be based on the will of the people, which is to express "in periodic and genuine elections which shall be by universal and equal suffrage and shall

762 Art.11 stated: "The free communication of ideas and opinions is one of the most precious of the rights of man; every citizen can then freely speak, write, and print, subject to responsibility for the abuse of this freedom in the cases is determined by law". English citations are taken from the 1789 Declaration of the Rights of Man and the Citizen at http://www.historyguide.org/intellect/declaration.html [Last access 03.11.2014].

763 Palermo Francesco, Woelk Jens, *Diritto Costituzionale Comparato dei Gruppi e delle Minoranze*, CEDAM, Padova, 2008, p.216.

764 Manfred Novak, "The International Covenant on Civil and Political Rights", in Raija Hanski and Marku Sukksi (eds.), *An Introduction to the International protection of Human Rights. A Textbook*, Abo Academy University of Turku, Abo, 1997, pp.79-98, p.82.

be held by secret vote or by equivalent free voting procedures". All these rights are recognized to "everyone".

The (binding) ICCPR is the treaty that eventually enshrined "political rights" at the international level. The following political rights were recognized: Freedom of expression (art.19); freedom of association and assembly (art.21-22); the right to vote and to stand for elections (art.25b); the right to participate in public affairs (art.25a); and the right to equal access to public service (art.25c).[765] They are intimately interlinked and mutually dependent on one another.[766] In addition, the participation and representation of women have been further guaranteed in art.7-8 of the Convention on the Elimination of All Forms of Discrimination against Women, adopted in 1979.[767]

In particular, art.25 of the ICCPR contains what are referred to as "political rights" or the "rights of political participation".[768] Notably, this provision addresses State parties' citizens, in contrast to the universal principles

765 Verstichel, *Participation, Representation and Identity*, pp.96-97.

766 Human Rights Committee, General Comment No.25 states: "Freedom of expression, assembly and association are essential conditions for the effective exercise of the right to vote […]". Human Rights Committee, General Comment No. 25 "The right to participate in public affairs, voting rights and the right of equal access to public service (Art. 25)", UN Doc. CCPR/C/21/Rev.1/Add.7, 12 July 1996, para.12, at http://ccprcentre.org/doc/ICCPR/General%20Comments/CCPR.C.21.Rev1.Add7_%28GC25%29_En.pdf [Last access 03.11.2014].

767 These articles state: "Article 7. States Parties shall take all appropriate measures to eliminate discrimination against women in the political and public life of the country and, in particular, shall ensure to women, on equal terms with men, the right: (a) To vote in all elections and public referenda and to be eligible for election to all publicly elected bodies; (b) To participate in the formulation of government policy and the implementation thereof and to hold public office and perform all public functions at all levels of government; (c) To participate in non-governmental organizations and associations concerned with the public and political life of the country.
Article 8. States Parties shall take all appropriate measures to ensure to women, on equal terms with men and without any discrimination, the opportunity to represent their Governments at the international level and to participate in the work of international organizations."

768 Novak, "The International Covenant on Civil and Political Rights", p.84; Joseph, Schultz and Castan, *The International Covenant on Civil and Political* Rights, p.495. Art.25 states: "Every citizen shall have the right and the opportunity, without any of the distinctions mentioned in article 2 and without unreasonable restrictions: (a) To take part in the conduct of public affairs, directly or through freely chosen representatives; (b) To vote and to be elected at genuine periodic elections which shall be by universal and equal suffrage and shall be held by secret ballot,

of the other ICCPR rights.[769] General Comment No.25 of the Human Rights Committee (HRC), however, points out the principle of non-discrimination among citizens stating that "[n]o distinctions are permitted between citizens in the enjoyment of these rights on the grounds of race, colour, sex, language, religion, political or other opinion, national or social origin, property, birth or other status".[770]

General Comment No.25 specifies further the peculiarities of this complex article. First, "[art.]25 lies at the core of democratic government based on the consent of the people and in conformity with the principles of the Covenant".[771] Thus, no particular system of government is required as long as it functions as a democracy.[772] This is rather tautological if one presumes that a democratic State requires free and regular elections established by law in order to be called as such. However, what follows is that various political systems appear compatible with this article, including "presidential", bicameral, unicameral, unitary and federal systems.[773]

Second, the conduct of public affairs may be indirect or direct (art.25a). The former is basically exercised through elected representatives, who should be freely chosen by citizens by secret ballot among a free choice of candidates (art.25b).[774] The latter may be exercised by voting at general elections, standing as a candidate, and acting as an elected representative or an appointed public official (art.25c),[775] by "exercis[ing] [public] power as members of legislative bodies or by holding executive office".[776] This is in line with the perspective contained in art.21, para.3 of the UDHR according to which this "power" has been delegated by the "sovereign" population to

guaranteeing the free expression of the will of the electors; (c) To have access, on general terms of equality, to public service in his country."

769 Joseph, Schultz and Castan, *The International Covenant on Civil and Political* Rights, p. 496 and, HRC, General Comment No.25, para.3.

770 Human Rights Committee, General Comment No.25, para.3.

771 Human Rights Committee, General Comment No. 25, para.1.

772 Joseph, Schultz and Castan, *The International Covenant on Civil and Political* Rights, p.497.

773 *Ibid.*

774 Human Rights Committee, General Comment No.25, para.15 on the free choice of candidates, and para.20 on the secret ballot.

775 Although neither the ICCPR nor the HRC defines the term 'public service', it certainly refers to all positions within the executive, judiciary, legislature and other areas in the public administration. Joseph, Schultz and Castan, *The International Covenant on Civil and Political* Rights, p.511.

776 Human Rights Committee, General Comment No.25, para.6.

manage the *res publica*. In other words, art.25 requires governmental accountability.[777]

In addition, citizens exercise other forms of direct participation in public affairs when participating in processes to choose constitutional adoptions and reforms; in referendums; in other electoral processes; in popular assemblies which take decisions over local issues or the affairs of particular communities; and in bodies which have been created to represent citizens in consultation with the government.[778] In particular, this last form of direct participation may be interpreted with a twofold meaning: On the one hand, representative bodies may be established after consultation with the government; on the other hand, such bodies may be created to allow citizens to enter into consultations with the government. In fact, "[c]itizens also take part in the conduct of public affairs by exerting influence through public debate and dialogue with their representatives or through their capacity to organize themselves. This participation is supported by ensuring freedom of expression, assembly and association".[779]

Further, the "opportunity to vote" and the "quality of vote" are essential elements of the right to vote:[780] "States must take effective measures to ensure that all persons entitled to vote are able to exercise that right".[781] Thus, registration shall be generally facilitated and residence requirements should be reasonable.[782] Other obstacles such as illiteracy, language barriers, poverty or impediments to freedom of movement that may affect the exercise of the right to vote should be removed.[783] As to the "quality of vote", the General Comment No.25 specifies that, although art.25 does not (and cannot) impose any electoral system on State parties, the system adopted by them must "guarantee and give effect to the free expression of the will of electors" respecting the principles of "one person-one vote" and the equal standing and value of each vote.[784] It follows that a number of systems may comply with art.25b, comprising those based on proportional representation, constituency voting, preferential voting, electoral colleges, and other

777 Human Rights Committee, General Comment No.25, para.7. See also Manfred Nowak, *U.N. Covenant on Civil and Political Rights: CCPR Commentary*, N.P. Engel Publishers, Kehl am Rhein, 1993, p.441.

778 Human Rights Committee, General Comment No.25, para.6.

779 *Ibid.*, para.8.

780 Joseph, Schultz and Castan, *The International Covenant on Civil and Political* Rights, pp.502-505.

781 Human Rights Committee, General Comment No.25, para.11.

782 *Ibid.*

783 *Ibid.*, para.12.

784 *Ibid.*, para.21.

combinations.[785] In addition, practices of drawing electoral boundaries, such as the (discriminatory) 'gerrymandering', must be avoided.[786]

In relation to elections, the concept of "genuine periodic elections" in letter b of art.25 is particularly relevant, as underlined also by the HRC in paras.19-20 of its General Comment No.25. First, the genuineness of elections may be ensured by establishing an independent electoral authority which supervises the electoral process,[787] e.g., international observers.[788] Second, as mentioned above with regard to indirect participation, citizens entitled to vote must be free to choose any candidate, to vote against any of the options or proposals in case of referenda or plebiscites, and to freely support or oppose the government "without undue influence or coercion of any kind which may distort or inhibit the free expression of the elector's will. Voters should be able to form opinions independently, free of violence or threat of violence, compulsion, inducement or manipulative interference of any kind".[789] In this perspective, the HRC underlined the importance of free press and media and the full respect of the abovementioned freedoms of arts.19, 21 and 22 of the ICCPR to guarantee the "free expression of the will of the electors" of art.25b.[790] The General Comment, however, does not mention the private and/or monopolized media that may adversely affect elections,[791] especially in the contemporary digital area.

Additionally, the HCR flags the role of political parties in conducting public affairs and their obligation to respect art.25 in guaranteeing citizens the rights contained in this norm.[792] It is silent, however, on those cases in which general elections take place with a limited number of parties and, consequently, a limited political agenda,[793] which is particularly relevant in

785 Joseph, Schultz and Castan, *The International Covenant on Civil and Political* Rights, p.504.

786 *Ibid.*

787 Joseph, Schultz and Castan, *The International Covenant on Civil and Political* Rights, p.508.

788 Human Rights Committee, "Consideration of Reports submitted by States Parties under article 40 of the Covenant. International Covenant on Civil and Political Rights. Comments of the Human Rights Committee. Mexico", UN Doc. CCPR/C/79/Add.50, 18 April 1994, para.16 of the English version or para.15 of the Spanish version.

789 Human Rights Committee, General Comment No.25, para.19.

790 *Ibid.*, para.25.

791 Joseph, Schultz and Castan, *The International Covenant on Civil and Political* Rights, p.510.

792 Human Rights Committee, General Comment No.25, para.26.

793 Joseph, Schultz and Castan, *The International Covenant on Civil and Political* Rights, p.510.

the case of bipartisan systems. The question which arises is whether citizens may really freely choose when confronted with a rather simple dichotomy. Another relevant factor on which the General Comment No.25 is silent about is corruption, which systematically denies the fair and equal exercise of the right to participate in public affairs.[794] Measures to prevent and avoid corruption and bribery should be seriously adopted by States.[795]

Finally, a pre-condition for the exercise of both direct and indirect participation in public affairs is the respect of the right to equality and the principle of non-discrimination (art.2 ICCPR),[796] which is specifically mentioned in art.25 itself and further clarified by the HRC in paras.4, 6, 10, 14, 15 and 23 of its General Comment No.25. First, the HRC recalls that the conditions to which the exercise of (all) the rights contained in art.25 may be subject to should be reasonable and objective.[797] Second, it declares that no unreasonable restrictions should be imposed where a mode of direct participation is established by citizens.[798] Third, restrictions and the deprivation of the right to vote should be reasonable, for instance, "[i]t is unreasonable to restrict the right to vote on the ground of physical disability or to impose literacy, educational or property requirements",[799] and "[i]f conviction for an offence is a basis for suspending the right to vote, the period of such suspension should be proportionate to the offence and the sentence".[800] Fourth, on the right to stand for elections, restrictions on the eligibility of

794 *Ibid.*, p.501.
795 *Ibid.*, p.501.
796 The author is aware of the conceptual dichotomy between substantive and formal equality as well as of the overlaps between the right to equality and of (direct and indirect) non-discrimination and of the ongoing debates. This kind of conceptual debate does not fall under the scope of this writing. Thus, to the aims of this study, the following (working) definition are assumed. The concept of "formal equality" refers to the Aristotelian equality formula according to which all who are the same must be treated equally (before the law). The "substantive equality", also called equality of results, *de facto*, material or relative equality, is referred to as that which remove the material or immaterial obstacles that impede to specific persons or groups to stand equally with others (e.g., disabled people). Also Verstichel says that it "is not clear to what extent this equality refers to [...] formal equality or to substantive equality". However, the HRC uses the terms "effective opportunity" in para.23 of the General Comment No.25 to refer to the obligation of States to guarantee to their citizens the enjoyment of the rights contained in art.25. The use of these words may refer to substantive equality. Verstichel, *Participation, Representation and Identity*, p.133.
797 Human Rights Committee, General Comment No.25, para.4.
798 *Ibid.*, para.6.
799 *Ibid.*, para.10.
800 *Ibid.*, para.14.

candidates must follow objective and reasonable criteria, and the application of discriminatory requirements such as education, residence, descent, or political affiliation must be avoided.[801] Lastly, other logistical aspects such as nomination dates, fees or deposits should be reasonable,[802] i.e., not becoming a material obstacle to the exercise of this right. This last aspect is particularly relevant in the case of conditions required in public competitions to appoint civil servants (the equal access to public service guaranteed by letter c of art.25).[803] However, a high burden of financial costs may also adversely affect political candidacy, as in the case of the USA.[804]

3.1.3 Concluding remarks

"Political rights" in the existing human rights standards under international law may be summarized in the dichotomy of "direct and indirect participation" included in art.25a and completed by a number of preconditions, as summarized in the framework established below.

As seen, the preconditions to exercise the "political rights" are the respect of the freedom of expression and the freedom of association and assembly. These freedoms, especially the former, guarantee the right to (freely) vote. The right to vote is relevant in both the dimensions of direct and indirect participation. On the one hand, this right is the primary instrument to participate directly in general elections and in all the other expressions of direct participation. On the other hand, without this right there would be no indirect participation through elected representatives. In exercising this right,

801 *Ibid.*, para.15. See also para.17 on the unreasonable requirement to be affiliated to specific parties or minimum numbers of supporters which *de facto* denies candidacy. See also the HRC case of *Bwalya v. Zambia* (314/88), which confirmed that the one-party system does not comply with art.25. Human Rights Committee, *Chiiko Bwalya v. Zambia*, Communication No. 314/1988, UN Doc. CCPR/C/48/D/314/1988, 27 July 1993; Joseph, Schultz and Castan, *The International Covenant on Civil and Political* Rights, p.506.

802 Human Rights Committee, General Comment No.25, para.16.

803 For further elaboration on what requirements may be considered reasonable or not, see also the Human Rights Committee, *Debreczeny v. The Netherlands*, Communication No. 500/1992, UN Doc. CCPR/C/53/D/500/1992, 4 April 1995. Joseph, Schultz and Castan, *The International Covenant on Civil and Political* Rights, p.506.

804 Human Rights Committee, "Consideration of Reports submitted by States Parties under article 40 of the Covenant. International Covenant on Civil and Political Rights. Comments of the Human Rights Committee. United States of America", UN Doc. CCPR/C/79/Add.50, 7 April 1995, para.24.

particular attention should be paid to the aforementioned aspects concerning the "opportunity to vote"; the "quality of vote"; the guarantee of "genuine" elections (secret ballot, periodic elections, and supervision); and of the respect of the free will of electors. Finally, as previously argued, the right to equality and the principle of non-discrimination play a key role in many forms of implementation of both direct and indirect participation (e.g., the one person-one vote principle; equal access to public service; etc.). In addition, the other three elements are also interlinked since freedom of expression is a pre-condition to exercise the right to vote and is a *condicio sine qua non* to guarantee freedom of association and assembly which, in turn, is needed to create parties and/or open debates to allow electors to gather information, and thus support their right to vote freely.

Under "direct participation" fall all those forms of expression of the citizenry's political will such as general elections, referendums, constitutional adoptions and reforms, other electoral processes, popular assemblies to decide on local issues or particular communities, bodies representing citizens, as well as the right to stand as a candidate and as an elected representative, the right to access public service and serve as public official (public administration, judiciary, executive, legislative). "Indirect participation" is realized through elected representatives, who must be freely chosen and accountable.

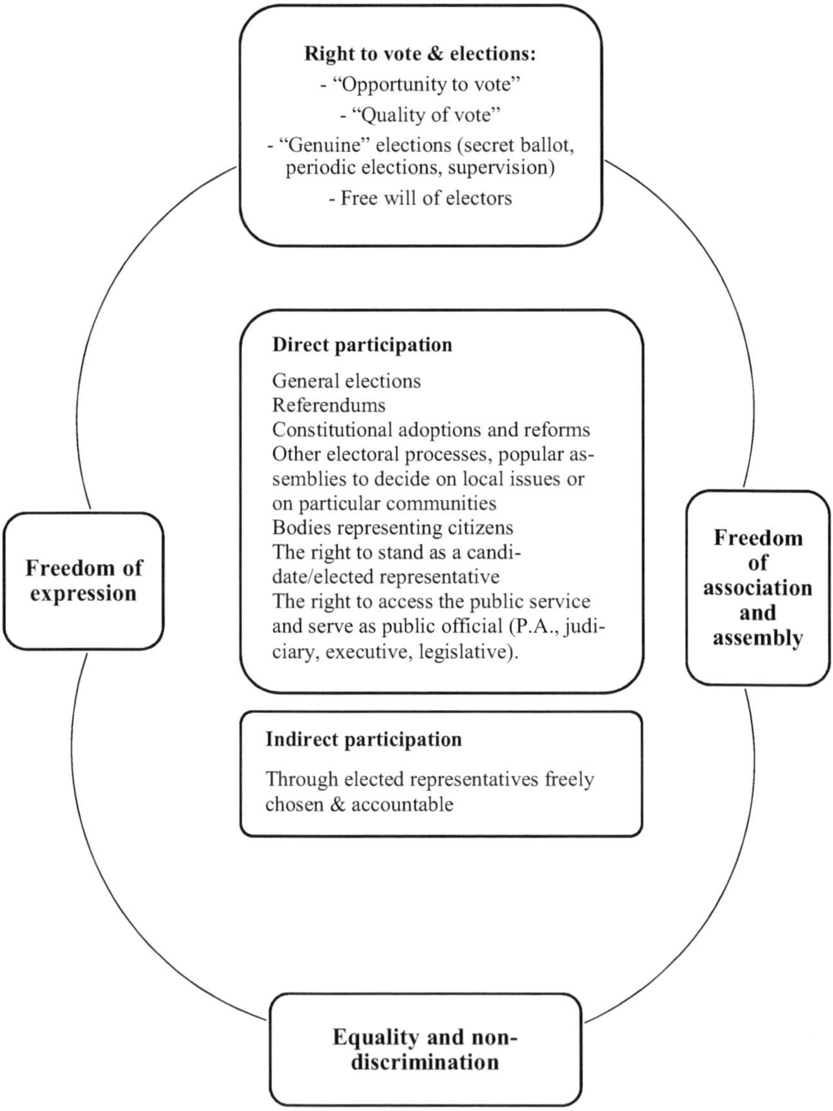

Fig. 3.1: Political rights in Human Rights Law

Source: Own elaboration

3.2 The right to political participation of (national) minorities[805]

This section aims to analyze the right to political participation expressively recognized to (national) minorities in the Framework Convention for the Protection of National Minorities (FCNM) of 1995 as well as the theoretical debate on its conceptualization, which has been extensively and increasingly considered over the last decades. The aim is to look at the debate vis-à-vis this right to find potential cross-fertilization regarding the proposed *composite right to political participation of indigenous peoples*, although without intending to apply a minority protection system to indigenous peoples (see further in section 3.3).

The soft and hard law provisions that will be mentioned below –together with many others that will not be approached here–[806] show the urgency and the emphasis placed at the international (and regional) level on the right to political participation of (national) minorities. The importance of this issue has been underlined more or less explicitly by a variety of treaties and documents, not only as a general human right provision aimed at guaranteeing the political participation of groups that would otherwise be excluded, but also as a way to foster the "stability and peaceful majority-minority relations".[807]

3.2.1 Legal standards

3.2.1.1 Political rights of minorities in art.27 of the ICCPR

Art.27 of the ICCPR is considered as the *grundnorm* of minority protection, according to its broad conception.[808] Neither this provision, nor the *travaux*

---

805 Hereinafter the term "minority" and "person(s) who belong to a minority" will be used interchangeably and in their broader conceptualization. See chapter 1.

806 There are many documents on electoral processes, *inter alia*, the OSCE "Guidelines to Assist National Minority Participation in the Electoral Process" of 2001. See also arts.15 and 20 of the "Central European Initiative Instrument for the Protection of National Minorities", opened for signature in 1994.

807 Rainer Hofmann, "Political Participation of Minorities", 6 *European Yearbook of Minority Issues (EYMI)* 2006/7, 2008, pp.5-17, p.6; Marc Weller, "Article 15", in Marc Weller (ed.), *The Rights of Minorities. A Commentary on the European Framework Convention for the Protection of National Minorities*, Oxford, New York, Oxford University Press, 2005, pp.429-461, p.456.

808 Art.27 of the ICCPR states: "In those States in which ethnic, religious or linguistic minorities exist, persons belonging to such minorities shall not be denied the right,

préparatoires of the Covenant, directly address participation or forms of representation of minorities.[809] However, General Comment No.23 of the HRC on art.27 contains a paragraph on cultural rights, which affirms that:

> "With regard to the exercise of the cultural rights protected under article 27, the Committee observes that culture manifests itself in many forms [...]. The enjoyment of those rights may [thus] require positive legal measures of protection and measures *to ensure the effective participation of members of minority communities in decisions which affect them*" [emphasis added].[810]

Therefore, the cultural rights of minorities may imply the adoption of measures to ensure the effective participation of their members in decisions likely to affect them.[811] However, the HRC has always kept a fairly cautious approach vis-à-vis the recognition of a "collective dimension" of political rights.[812] Thus, the right to participate of minorities recognized by the HRC in its General Comment No.23 as part of their cultural rights of art.27 shall refer, in principle, solely to their individual rights.

This excessively individual dimension has been criticized by a member of the HRC itself, namely Martin Scheinin, who wrote an individual concurring opinion in the communication *J.G.A. Diergaardt et al. v. Namibia*

---

in community with the other members of their group, to enjoy their own culture, to profess and practise their own religion, or to use their own language".

809 Annelies Verstichel, "Recent Developments in the UN Human Rights Committee's approach to Minorities, with a Focus on Effective Participation", 12 *International Journal on Minority and Group Rights* 2005, pp.25-41, p.40.

810 Human Rights Committee, General Comment No.23, "The rights of minorities (Art. 27)", UN Doc. CCPR/C/21/Rev.1/Add.5, 8 April 1994, para.7.

811 Verstichel, "Recent Developments in the UN Human Rights Committee's approach to Minorities ...", p.40. See also Human Rights Committee, *Länsman et al. v. Finland*, Communication No. 511/1992, UN Doc. CCPR/C/52/D/511/1992, 8 November 1994, paras.9.5 and 9.6, which recalls paragraph 7 of the General Comment No.23. In this communication, the claimants, who belong to the Sami people, alleged that art.27 had been violated since Finland had given the company *Arktinen Kivi Oy* (Arctic Stone Company) a permit to quarry stones in an area used also for reindeer herding (Mount *Riutusvaara*). The HRC motivated its decision stating that the petitioners were consulted during the proceedings of the delivery of this permit and that reindeer herding in the area was not yet adversely affected (paras.9.5 and 9.6). If the permit was to be approved on a larger scale, it would constitute a violation of art.27 (para.9.8).

812 Verstichel, "Recent Developments in the UN Human Rights Committee's approach to Minorities ...", pp.27 and 40.

(2000).[813] This case involved the descendants of indigenous Khoi and Afrikaans settlers, who in 1872 moved from Cape to a territory then included within Namibia's frontiers and founded a self-ruled community called "Rehoboth Baster Community". As Namibia became independent on 21 March 1990 and by the adoption of a regional law in 1996, the territory corresponding to the Rehoboth Baster Community was divided into two regions, thus preventing them from preserving control over their community as they had done for more than 120 years. Therefore, they claimed a violation of art.25 ICCPR, alleging that they were eventually reduced to two minorities within the regional territories.[814] The HRC stressed that the rights enshrined in art.25 are rather individual rights, thus, the political rights of the Rehoboth Baster Community's members were not violated, as their political rights in the regional and national contexts were guaranteed.[815] However, Scheinin highlighted that the individual dimension of the political rights contained in art.25 was stressed excessively.[816] He argued that in similar situations, as well as the individual right to vote, "some forms of local, regional or cultural autonomy may be called for in order to comply with the requirement of effective rights of participation".[817] Moreover, as reminded by Verstichel, most of the political rights recognized at international level, such as the right to freedom of association and assembly, "make sense when exercised in group".[818]

In sum, with regard to the rights enshrined in the ICCPR, members of minorities certainly enjoy the individual political rights recognized in arts.25 and 26. Additionally, based on art.27, their cultural rights may also

813 *Ibid.*, p.35. See Human Rights Committee, *J.G.A. Diergaardt (late Captain of the Rehoboth Baster Community) et al. v. Namibia*, Communication No. 760/1997, UN Doc. CCPR/C/69/D/760/1997, 6 September 2000.

814 The Rehoboth Baster Community also claimed the violation of art.1 of the ICCPR on the right to self-determination. On the interrelation between art.1 and arts.25 and 26, see chapter 2, section 2.1.3.1.

815 Verstichel, "Recent Developments in the UN Human Rights Committee's approach to Minorities ...", pp.34-35. As Verstichel recalls, however, this is a particularly delicate case as privileges were granted to the white minority according to the apartheid system present at that time. In addition, the claimants might have had more chances if they had alleged the violations more clearly. Verstichel, "Recent Developments in the UN Human Rights Committee's approach to Minorities ...", p.35.

816 *Ibid.*, p.35.

817 Human Rights Committee, *J.G.A. Diergaardt et al. v. Namibia*, Individual opinion by Martin Scheinin (concurring), also cited by Verstichel, "Recent Developments in the UN Human Rights Committee's approach to Minorities ...", p.35.

818 Verstichel, *Participation, Representation and Identity*, p.96.

imply the adoption of measures to ensure their effective participation in decisions likely to affect them. Although such participation has been conceived by the HRC as part of minorities' individual rights, Scheinin and Verstichel, *inter alia*, have highlighted that the right to political participation of minorities under art.27, as well in arts.25 and 26 of the ICCPR, may imply further dimensions, as will be discussed below.

3.2.1.2 *Ad hoc* political rights of minorities

The right to "effective participation" for persons belonging to (national) minorities has been articulated in a number of international and regional documents since 1990, especially within the European context.

The Document of the Copenhagen Meeting (Conference on the Human Dimension) of the then Conference on Security and Cooperation in Europe (later Organization for Security and Cooperation in Europe – OSCE) and the Charter of Paris for a New Europe –both of 1990– imposed a duty on member States to respect the right to participation in public affairs of minorities.[819] Effective participation in cultural, religious, social, economic, and public life was then recognized by art.2.2 of the 1992 UN Declaration on the Rights of Persons Belonging to National or Ethnic, Religious, and Linguistic Minorities.[820]

A direct reference to the right of political participation of national minorities can be found in art.15 of the later Framework Convention for the Protection of National Minorities (FCNM) of 1995,[821] which states:

> "The Parties shall create the conditions necessary for the effective participation of persons belonging to national minorities in cultural, social and economic life and in public affairs, in particular those affecting them."

---

819 See para.35 of the Copenhagen Document of the Conference on Security and Co-operation in Europe (CSCE), which imposes a duty on States to respect this right of (persons belonging to) minorities with regard to public affairs. See also Krzysztof Drzewicki, "The Lund Recommendations on the Effective Participation of National Minorities in Public Life – Five Years After and More Years Ahead", 12 *International Journal on Minority and Group Rights* 2005, pp.123-131, p.124.

820 Art. 2.2 of the UN Declaration on Minorities states: "Persons belonging to minorities have the right to participate effectively in cultural, religious, social, economic and public life."

821 Even though, according to Weller, "a number of overlapping provisions [affect] full and effective participation", *inter alia*, article 4.2, 5.1, 7, and 12.1. Weller, "Article 15", p.434. See the text of the FCNM at http://conventions.coe.int/Treaty/en/Treaties/html/157.htm [Last access 03.11.2014].

The Advisory Committee on the FCNM[822] has also highlighted a number of practices and recommendations based on the monitoring procedure of the FCNM. Indeed, the text of art.15 of the FCNM "provides only limited guidance",[823] whereas the FCNM Explanatory Report and the later FCNM Advisory Committee's Commentary on the Effective Participation of Persons Belonging to National Minorities in Cultural, Social and Economic Life and in Public Affairs of 2008 provide more details. The former suggests, *inter alia*, the promotion of consultation, involvement in national and regional development plans and in the decision-making process, and decentralized or local forms of government. The latter "set out the Advisory Committee's interpretation of the provisions within the Framework Convention relating to the effective participation of persons belonging to national minorities",[824] providing a fundamental overview of and guidance for all the stakeholders involved in minority protection (e.g., States, officials, minorities, NGOs, academics, etc.).[825]

At the conference on "Governance and Participation: Integrating Diversity" –organized by the OSCE High Commissioner on National Minorities (HCNM)[826] and the Office of the Democratic Institutions and Human Rights of the OSCE in October 1998 and attended by all the OSCE States– the Chairman remarked that "concrete follow-up activities, including the further elaboration of the various concepts and mechanisms of good gov-

---

822 The Advisory Committee on the Framework Convention for the Protection of National Minorities is in charge of providing the analysis of legislation and practice regarding minorities in the signatory countries of the FCNM, in order to fulfil the monitoring system of the FCNM. See http://www.coe.int/en/web/minorities/ad visory-committee [Last access 03.11.2014].

823 Hofmann, "Political Participation of Minorities", p. 9.

824 Advisory Committee on the Framework Convention for the Protection of National Minorities, "Commentary on the Effective Participation of Persons Belonging to National Minorities in Cultural, Social and Economic Life and in Public affairs", Council of Europe Doc. No. ACFC/31DOC(2008)001, 5 May 2008, p.4, at http://www.coe.int/t/dghl/monitoring/minorities/3_fcnmdocs/PDF_Commentary-Participation_en.pdf [Last access 03.11.2014].

825 The commentary inserted in the Explanatory Report of the FCNM (pp.22-23, para.80), in particular, mentions means of consultation through representative institutions, involvement in national and regional development plans that may affect minorities, effective participation in the decision-making processes and elected bodies at national and local levels, and decentralized or local forms of government.

826 "The post of the OSCE High Commissioner on National Minorities was established in 1992 to identify and seek early resolution of ethnic tensions that might endanger peace, stability or friendly relations between OSCE participating States". OSCE HCNM website at http://www.osce.org/hcnm [Last access 03.11.2014].

ernance with the effective participation of minorities" should be implemented.[827] Afterwards, the HCNM "Lund Recommendations on the Effective Participation of National Minorities in Public Life" (hereinafter, Lund Recommendations) were adopted in September 1999.[828] This is an instrument of "soft" law, but provides "a wide range of forms of effective participation with potential applicability to national minorities",[829] and gives a detailed and accurate list of specific measures which may serve as guidelines for the States in order to ensure the effective participation of national minorities.[830]

Finally, in May 1999, a set of recommendations with regard to national minorities and their participation in public life was adopted by the United Nations Working Group on Minorities.[831] In particular, the concepts of autonomy, self-governance, and self-determination have been repeatedly addressed by the Working group since its establishment.[832]

3.2.2 Theoretical debate

The right to political participation has been extensively elaborated with regard to (national) minorities in Europe as an effect also of the adoption of the FCNM and the Lund Recommendations.[833]

Basic and common denominators of the right to political participation of minorities are certainly the recognition and the application of human rights

827 Drzewicki, "The Lund Recommendations on the Effective Participation of National Minorities in Public Life ...", p.124.

828 OSCE High Commissioner on National Minorities, Lund Recommendations on the Effective Participation of National Minorities in Public Life, September 1999.

829 Drzewicki, "The Lund Recommendations on the Effective Participation of National Minorities in Public Life ...", p.127.

830 For further analysis of the Lund recommendations, see, *inter alia*, Kristin Henrard, "'Participation', 'Representation' and 'Autonomy' in the Lund Recommendations and their Reflections in the Supervision of the FCNM and Several Human Rights Conventions", 12 *International Journal on Minority and Group Rights* 2005, pp.133-168; John Packer, "The Origin and Nature of the Lund Recommendations on the Effective Participation of National Minorities in Public Life", 11(4) *Helsinki Monitor* 2000, pp.29-61.

831 See European Centre for Minority Issues, "Towards Effective Participation of Minorities", UN Doc. E/CN.4/Sub.2/AC.5/1999/WP.4, 1999.

832 See Marc Weller, "Working Paper Towards a General Comment on Self-Determination and Autonomy", UN Doc. E/CN.4/Sub.2/AC.5/2005/WP.5, 25 May 2005.

833 Weller, "Article 15", p.460.

standards as seen in the previous section (3.1). As mentioned, these "political rights" are framed as individual rights, but some of them are materialized when exercised by a group, such as the freedom of association and assembly.[834] This is extremely relevant in the application of these human rights standards to minorities and beyond. In addition, special mechanisms to avoid discrimination against vulnerable groups should be taken into account, e.g., in the case of a "minority within minorities".[835]

Although there is no "universal formula" for minority participation,[836] in this study, the concept of "political participation" follows the Lund Recommendations twofold meaning in view of the effectiveness of the arrangements endorsed by them also for indigenous peoples.[837] Therefore, first, "political participation" implies participation at all levels within the State, especially in decision-making processes. Second, it also includes means of autonomy or self-government.[838]

3.2.2.1 Participation within the State

The first dimension of the right to political participation for minorities involves a number of aspects. Weller speaks of granting minorities "a voice in governance of the state as a whole", [839] which would imply the guarantee of equal opportunities in electoral process, such as the registration of minority parties and the ensured representation of persons belonging to minorities in decision-making processes.[840] Marko addresses art.15 of the FCNM, recalling: (1) the link with art.4 of the FCNM which aims to achieve "full and effective equality"; (2) the discretion left to States parties of the FCNM

834 Verstichel, *Participation, Representation and Identity*, p.96.

835 Henrard, "'Participation', 'Representation' and 'Autonomy' in the Lund Recommendations ...", p.142.

836 Ghai, *Public Participation of Minorities*, p.3.

837 Rodríguez Piñero-Royo, "Political Participation Systems Applicable to Indigenous Peoples", p.311.

838 OSCE High Commissioner on National Minorities, Lund Recommendations on the Effective Participation of National Minorities in Public Life, p.6.

839 Weller, "Article 15", pp.430-431.

840 *Ibid.*, p.434. Weller analyses extensively the States' practice, the Advisory Committee's Opinions and the State Reports under the FCNM, and highlights: (1) "issues of state construction", (2) representation of minorities in executive agencies and judiciary", (3) cultural, social and economic participation". In the first 'category', in particular, aspects of "constitutional design of the state, electoral processes and procedures, and mechanism designed to enhance a minority voice in decision making" are addressed. See Weller, "Article 15", pp.434-455.

to implement art.15 and the minimum standards of "consultative mechanisms and some form of representation in decision-making and elected bodies" that should be respected;[841] (3) the need to specify the terms "effective" and "participation", by underlining the aim of the FCNM to integrate minorities "in the sense of inclusion in public affairs, cultural, social and economic life" and by meaning a "voice" to minorities that should be heard seriously and taken into account by the mainstream society.[842] In particular, Marko proposes his legal instrument to realize the right to political participation, namely the "integration through representation and participation". As to "representation", the author singles out freedom of association, electoral mechanisms (e.g., exemption of threshold requirement), reserved seats, proportional representations, or "ethnic quotas". Instead, consultative bodies, and instruments of "effective" influence, such as the veto-powers in affairs concerning or affecting the minorities are instruments of "participation".[843]

Analyzing Weller and Marko, Hofmann identifies two issues related to the dimension of participation of minorities within the State: "effective participation and electoral representation", and "effective political participation and consultative mechanisms".[844]

Illustrating "effective participation and electoral representation", Hofmann underlines on the one hand the importance of (1) freedom of association, the right to form political parties representing a specific group or a minority, the right to vote, and the right to stand as a candidate; and, on the other hand, of (2) electoral systems, thresholds in proportional representation systems, reserved seats, and veto systems.[845]

Following, the author deals with forms of consultation ("effective political participation and consultative mechanisms") and distinguishes three mechanisms in States' practices: (1) "mechanism of co-decision", (2)

841 Joseph Marko, "Effective Participation of National Minorities. A Comment on Conceptual, Legal and Empirical Problems", Council of Europe Document DH-MIN(2006)014, 20 October 2006, p.3.

842 *Ibid.*

843 *Ibid.*, pp.4-5.

844 Hofmann, "Political Participation of Minorities", pp.9-15.

845 *Ibid.* In particular, Hofmann recalls the importance of reviewing the "proportional representation systems", which, in the case of veto powers, for example, may even block the adoption of legislative measures. See also Advisory Committee on the Framework Convention for the Protection of National Minorities, First Opinion on Bosnia and Herzegovina, ACFC/INF/OP/I(2005)003, 11 May 2005, paras.100-101.

"mechanism of consultation *stricto sensu*", and (3) "mechanism of coordination".[846] The former may include "original decision-making powers" of minority consultative councils or an obligation for the State to hear these councils before adopting a legislative measure.[847] The second mechanism may consist in three types of minority representative councils at regional or local level, as follows: (a) bodies organized and composed of minority representatives dealing with and presenting minority issues at parliament or government level; (b) bodies attached to or part of high-ranking governmental offices; or (c) governmental bodies comprising representatives from both the government and the minority. The third "mechanism of coordination" is formed by experts or representatives of minorities but with limited tasks, e.g., to comment on legislative measures. Thus, this mechanism tends to be the less genuine one.[848]

Henrard argues that "participation in decision-making" for minorities is related with the issue of "representation", including participation in different levels of public life (parliament, courts, etc.) and in elections. Additionally, such participation also implies consultations, which means "having a say", for instance, in a non-binding consultation process or enjoying a full veto power.[849] Similar views were also expressed in the document prepared by the European Centre for Minority Issues for the UN in 1999, according to which decision-makers need to consult minorities on those measures likely to affect them and create chances for involving them in the decision-making processes.[850]

De Varennes also identifies the importance of "advisory bodies" in enhancing the participation of minorities and especially to consult them in matters likely to affect them.[851] In addition, the author recalls a number of instruments to enhance the participation of minorities at State level. These are, for instance, reserved seats in the parliament, a proportional electoral system rather than the majoritarian one, a reduced vote threshold, a minority

---

846 Hofmann, "Political Participation of Minorities", p.14; Weller "Article 15", pp.447-451.

847 *Ibid.*

848 Hofmann, "Political Participation of Minorities", p.14.

849 Henrard, "'Participation', 'Representation' and 'Autonomy' in the Lund Recommendations …", p.134.

850 European Centre for Minority Issues, "Towards Effective Participation of Minorities", UN Doc. E/CN.4/Sub.2/AC.5/1999/WP.4, 1999.

851 Fernand De Varennes, "Towards Effective Political Participation and Representation of Minorities", UN Doc. E/CN.4/Sub.2/AC.5/1998/WP.4, 1 May 1998, subparagraph titled "3. Possible Mechanisms for Increasing Effective Participation and Representation of Minorities".

legislative veto, or reserved powers. Although the author is conscious that few seats in parliament may not prevent the "tyranny of the majority", they may nevertheless contribute to giving minorities both a voice and visibility.[852] In fact, as underlined by the European Court of Human Rights, to ensure a fair and proper treatment vis-à-vis minorities, particular attention should be paid to avoid the abuse of dominant positions.[853]

Ghai affirms that the right to "participation" of minorities includes taking part in political parties, standing for elections, and voting, but also "forms of enacting legislation, [...] [,] [...] mechanisms for consultation and negotiations [,] [...] bring[ing] relevant facts to decision-makers, argu[ing] their position before decision-makers, propos[ing] reform, be[ing] co-decision makers, veto[ing] legislative or administrative proposals, and establish[ing] and manag[ing] [...] own institutions in specified areas".[854]

Finally, Musafiri recently identified the following mechanisms to facilitate minority representation: lowered thresholds for minority political parties to enter the Parliament; the reduction of the quorum required for the registration of minority political parties; a favourable delimitation of electorates, particularly in the case of a majoritarian electoral system; and extra funding for minority political parties.[855]

In conclusion, many of the aspects vis-à-vis the participation of minorities within the State underlined by the aforementioned experts partly overlap and may be summarized as follows:

a) Means of "representation" at all institutional levels (national and local parliaments, judiciary, administrative national and local organs, and other State and local bodies), including those mechanisms that allow such representation (e.g., reserved seats) and fair electoral rights and processes (e.g., the right for groups to form their own political parties, the right to stand as a candidate, proportional vs. majoritarian system, lower thresholds for minority political parties, a favorable delimitation of electorates, and systems allowing a genuine representation of the minority);
b) Effective and genuine forms of consultation, including mechanisms to facilitate co-decisions or joint decisions and/or binding consultations with minority organizations, institutions and/or movements (e.g., the double entrenchment of acts or various degrees of veto powers), and

852 *Ibid.*

853 European Court of Human Rights, *Chassagnou and others v. France*, Applications Nos.25088/94, 28331/95 and 28443/95, Judgement, 29 April 1999, para.112.

854 Ghai, *Public Participation of Minorities*, p.4.

855 Musafiri, "Right to Self-Determination in International Law …", p.516.

spaces for direct dialogue and interaction with the State (e.g., negotiations).

Aspects that fall under "representation" may also be essential in "consultation", for instance, in the case of a consultative body composed of minority representatives.

3.2.2.2 Participation in the form of autonomy/self-government

The second aspect of the political participation of minorities relates to forms of autonomy or self-government. Some scholars envisage a substantial difference between the two concepts. As cited by Welhengama,[856] among others, Crawford affirms that "autonomy [is] a preliminary stage of the development of self-government".[857] Lapidoth, instead, recognizes similarities between the two concepts but argues that "self-government implies a considerable degree of self-rule, whereas autonomy is a flexible concept, its substance rang[es] from limited powers to very broad ones. In addition, self-government usually applies to a specific region, whereas autonomy can be personal".[858]

Legally speaking, the concept of autonomy/self-government has no clear boundaries.[859] In particular, "autonomy" was initially utilized by sociologists[860] to indicate the personal right to govern one's own affairs, i.e., the "authority to govern, to administer, and to judge".[861] Some authors have stated that the right to autonomy is a principle under international law "at least [for] territorial minorities".[862] However, no right to autonomy is found

856 Gnanapala Welhengama, *Minorities' Claims: From Autonomy to Secession. International Law and State Practice*, Aldershot, Burlington, 2000, p.101.

857 James Crawford, *The Creation of States in International Law*, Clarendon Press, Oxford, 1979, pp.211-212.

858 Ruth Lapidoth, *Autonomy: Flexible Solutions to Ethnic Conflicts,* United States Institute of Peace Press, Washington, 1997, pp.53-54.

859 Frederick Harhoff, "Institutions of Autonomy", 55 *Nordic Journal of International Law* 1986, pp.31-40, p.31, as cited by Welhengama, *Minorities' Claims: From Autonomy to Secession*, p.98.

860 Welhengama, *Minorities' Claims: From Autonomy to Secession*, p.98.

861 Georg Jellinek, *Allgemeine Staatslehre,* H. Gentner, Bad Hamburg vor der Höhe, 3rd edition, 1960, as cited by Welhengama, *Minorities' Claims: From Autonomy to Secession*, p. 98.

862 Douglas Sanders, "Is Autonomy a Principle of International Law?", 55 *Nordic Journal of International Law* 1986, pp.17-21, p.17, as cited by Hans Joachim

in any binding international treaty.[863] Indeed, to date, autonomy arrangements have been provided only at the constitutional level.[864] In other countries, the interplay of international bilateral or multilateral treaties secured such autonomy arrangements.[865]

If one assumes the correspondence, or at least the many similarities, between autonomy and self-government –although distinct when applied to municipalities, entire regions, or in forms of quasi-federal arrangements–[866] the Council of Europe's (CoE) European Charter of Local Self-Government, which was adopted in 1985 and entered into force in 1988, should be mentioned. Ratified by almost all CoE member States, this charter states that: "Local self-government denotes the right and the ability of local authorities, within the limits of the law, to regulate and manage a substantial share of public affairs under their own responsibility and in the interests of the local population" (art.3.1).

The literature has shed considerable light on the concept of autonomy. Hannum and Lillich asserted that "[a]utonomy is understood to refer to independence of action on the internal or domestic level, as foreign affairs and defence normally are in the hands of the central or national government".[867] In particular, they argue that "autonomy is a relative term that describes the extent or degree of independence of a particular entity rather than defining a particular minimum level of independence that can be designated as the status of 'autonomy'".[868] Moreover, equating autonomy and

---

Heintze, "On the Legal Understanding of Autonomy", in Markku Suksi (ed.), *Autonomy: Applications and Implications*, Kluwer Law International, The Hague, Cambridge MA, Dordrecht, 1998, pp.7-32, p.13.

863 Heintze, "On the Legal Understanding …", p.13; see also Zelin A. Skurbaty, "Introduction", in Zelin A. Skurbaty (ed.), *Beyond a One-Dimensional State: An Emerging Right to Autonomy?,* Martinus Nijhoff Publishers, Leiden, Boston, 2005, pp.xxxi–lviii, p.xxxvii.

864 Francesco Palermo, "When the Lund Recommendations are Ignored: Effective Participation of National Minorities through Territorial Arrangements", 16(4) *International Journal on Minority and Group Rights* 2009, pp.653-663, p.657.

865 See the examples provided by Yoram Dinstein, "Autonomy (International Guarantees of Autonomy)", in Zelin A. Skurbaty (ed.), *Beyond a One-Dimensional State: An Emerging Right to Autonomy?,* Martinus Nijhoff Publishers, Leiden, Boston, 2005, pp.243-254, pp.248 ff.

866 Palermo, "When the Lund Recommendations …", p.654, note 6.

867 Hurst Hannum and Richard B. Lillich, "The Concept of Autonomy in International Law", in Yoram Dinstein (ed.), *Models of Autonomy*, Transaction Books, Rutgers, New Brunswick, 1981, pp.215-254, p.218.

868 Hurst Hannum and Richard B. Lillich, "The Concept of Autonomy in International Law", 74(4) *American Journal of International Law (AJIL)*, pp.858-889, p.885.

self-government, they state: "Autonomy and self-government are determined primarily by the degree of actual as well as formal independence enjoyed by the autonomous entity in its political decision-making process."[869] However, "[a]utonomy and self-government [...] do not necessarily imply that a territory must be wholly independent and comparable to a sovereign state".[870] Finally, "autonomy and self-government refer essentially to the internal government of a territory".[871]

Exploring authors' works from the early twentieth century to the late 1990s, Lapidoth finds four main approaches vis-à-vis autonomy: "a right to act upon one's own discretion in certain matters; [...] synonymous for independence; [...] synonymous with decentralization; [...] [one entity] that has exclusive powers of legislation, administration, and adjudication in specific areas". In particular, Lapidoth notes that, in the literature on minorities, autonomy signifies "limited self-rule".[872] Moreover, she suggests her own (self-defined) "eclectic" definition: "A territorial political autonomy is an arrangement aimed at granting to a group that differs from the majority of the population in the state, but that constitutes the majority in a specific region, a means by which it can express its distinct identity."[873] Along the same lines, Hannum affirmed that autonomy is the balance between the State and the legitimate expressions of identity of smaller groups.[874] However, the case of Hong Kong illustrates that autonomy arrangements can be established even if not based on ethnic criteria.[875] In the same years, Héctor Díaz-Polanco proposed a definition of autonomy that took into account the conceptual dichotomy between a general *laissez-faire* and a proper political-legal regime.[876] According to Díaz-Polanco, the latter could be seen as a special regime of self-government given to communities that, in this way,

869 Hannum and Lillich, "The Concept of Autonomy ...", in Dinstein, *Models of Autonomy*, p.218.

870 Hannum and Lillich, "The Concept of Autonomy ...", *AJIL*, p.886.

871 *Ibid.*

872 Lapidoth, *Autonomy: Flexible Solutions to Ethnic Conflicts*, pp.29-33.

873 *Ibid.*, p.30. This conceptualization is very much focused on a territorial autonomy, see *infra*.

874 Hurst Hannum, *Autonomy, Sovereignty, and Self-Determination: The Accommodation of Conflicting Rights*, University of Pennsylvania Press, 1996, p.475, as cited by Heintze, "On the Legal Understanding ...", p.17.

875 Heintze, "On the Legal Understanding ...", p.16; Lapidoth, *Autonomy: Flexible Solutions to Ethnic Conflicts*, p.25.

876 Díaz-Polanco, *Autonomía regional: La autodeterminación de los pueblos indios*, pp.151-153.

exercise their authority as well as some decentralized legal and administrative powers.[877] Díaz-Polanco is, however, very cautious in advancing a definition that could embrace the considerable amount of diversity present in autonomy arrangements worldwide. He instead proposes some "basic borders" (*contornos elementales*).[878] To this end, Díaz-Polanco strongly suggests that due consideration of the historical and socio-political aspects of each community or group be taken into account because it is not possible to advance a catch-all definition *a priori*.

More specifically on minorities, autonomy may be conceptualized as both non-territorial autonomies (NTAs) and territorial autonomies (TAs). As mentioned, Marko defined them as one of the legal instruments which may realize the right to political participation.[879]

A NTA constitutes supra-regional/national organizations for minorities over certain issues, e.g., cultural bodies in charge of bilingual education for dispersed communities.[880] In the words of Heintze: "Cultural autonomy is the autonomous self-government of cultural affairs by the group or minority."[881] Thus, according to Henrard "the common denominator [...] [of an NTA] is that the competences are transferred […] in relation to a certain community irrespective of size and place of residence in the State".[882] A typical example of "cultural autonomy" is the Estonian experience between the two World Wars. The Estonian 1925 Cultural Autonomy Law allowed minorities with over 3,000 members (in this case, Germans, Russians, and Swedes) to elect a body in charge of limited powers in the fields of education, culture, youth affairs, etc., wherever there was a substantial consensus within the group.[883]

Analyzing the writings of Weller and Marko, Hofmann identifies a third dimension in addition to the two aforementioned ones, namely "effective

877 *Ibid.*, pp.151 and 168.

878 *Ibid.*

879 Marko, "Effective Participation of National Minorities. A Comment on Conceptual, Legal and Empirical Problems", pp.4-5.

880 Close to this definition is Heintze's "personal autonomy", i.e., based on the personality principle; Heintze 2005, p.22. Among the NTAs, the author mentions also the category of 'functional autonomy', which occurs when selected State functions and rights are transferred to private minority organizations. Heintze 2005, p.23.

881 Heintze, "On the Legal Understanding …", p.21. For an in-depth analysis of cultural autonomy, see also Steven C. Roach, *Cultural Autonomy, Minority Rights, and Globalization*, Ashgate, Aldershot, Hampshire, Burlington VT, 2006.

882 Henrard, "'Participation', 'Representation' and 'Autonomy' in the Lund Recommendations …", p.141.

883 Heintze, "On the Legal Understanding …", p.21.

participation and state construction" in which he analyses the concepts of "cultural autonomy" elaborated on by Marko and Weller. [884] In broad terms, a "cultural autonomy" may be applied to those minorities with formal legal status, which represent a consistent part of the population, but are dispersed throughout the territory of a State, or do not constitute a "majority" in a given area.[885] For instance, in Hungary, minority institutions established under public law had a rather successful "say" in the regulation of a number of "cultural affairs" (e.g., public education and cultural institutions, management of media, etc.).[886] According to these models, the minorities should exercise a sort of "self-government" through representative bodies.[887]

Lapidoth has particularly underlined the advantages of the NTAs, although recognizing the added value of the more expanded powers normally enjoyed by TAs. The author argued that the former may be applied to all persons belonging to a minority/group irrespective of their place of residence within the country. The latter, instead, involves the whole population of a territory and its composition may change rapidly.[888] Also, Lijphart agrees on the functionality of the NTAs as a means of power-sharing for a divided society.[889]

Hannum and Lillich also took into account the concept of cultural autonomy, but subdivided the means of autonomy for "social or ethnic groups" into personal and territorial autonomies. Cultural autonomy, instead, was transversal to both of them. In other words, according to these authors, cultural autonomy is applicable on a personal/individual base or within one territory.[890]

---

884 Hofmann, "Political Participation of Minorities", pp.11-15.

885 *Ibid.*, p.11; Weller, "Article 15", pp.434-440; Marko, "Effective Participation of National Minorities. A Comment on Conceptual, Legal and Empirical Problems", pp.3-5.

886 Hofmann, "Political Participation of Minorities", p.11.

887 *Ibid.* See Hungarian Law No. 77 of 1993 on the Rights of National and Ethnic Minorities as amended by Law No. 114/2005 and, reformed by the most recent Law No. 179/2011. For a thorough analysis of the previous Hungarian system, see Niamh Walsh, "Minority Self-Government in Hungary: Legislation and Practice", 2 *Journal on Ethnopolitics and Minority Issues in Europe* 2000, at http://www.ecmi.de/fileadmin/doc/JEMIE04Walsh30-07-01.pdf [Last access 03.11.2014]. For a more recent analysis, see Emma Lantschner, Sergiu Constantin and Joseph Marko (eds.), *Practice of Minority Protection in Central Europe*, Nomos, Baden-Baden, 2012.

888 Lapidoth, *Autonomy: Flexible Solutions to Ethnic Conflicts*, p.40.

889 Arend Lijphart, "Constitutional Design for Divided Societies", 15(2) *Journal of Democracy* 2004, pp.96-109, p.105.

890 Hannum and Lillich, "The Concept of Autonomy ...", *AJIL*, pp.883-884.

Weller also takes into consideration the NTAs arguing for (1) "the entitlement of minorities to [their] auto-determination", and the (2) "internal democracy of minority communities".[891] These two layers imply: (1) the right to arrange issues of direct importance for minorities as expression of their identity in form of "cultural autonomy" and the right to organize political processes such as "territorial autonomy" in areas where a "local majority" live; (2) the possibility to form a "minority governance" and the duty for it to be as transparent as possible vis-à-vis the State in which the minority live.[892]

However, in the most recent debates on autonomies and minorities, some authors (Palermo, Suksi) have questioned whether this form of autonomy is just a "lighter" or "easier" form of autonomy, i.e., the solution to be adopted when a TA cannot be established due to the State's attitude, the given political or economic context, or for other reasons.[893] Moreover, the success of these models apparently rely on the actual degree of representation of the minorities concerned, as well as on the availability of financial resources.[894]

As an alternative mean to protect a given group, a territorial autonomy (TA) may be found in a specific territory where the group represents the "majority" or a "sizeable" minority.[895] In particular, the TA provides a group with self-ruling bodies and may also be granted independent executive powers, representative bodies elected by the residents in the territory, and, according to each case, a number of legislative competences although not just decentralized powers.[896] Hofmann further underlines that these models depend as well on the genuine representation of minorities and an

891 Weller, "Article 15", pp.430-431.

892 *Ibid.*, p.434. Analysing the States' practice, the Advisory Committee's Opinions and the State Reports under the FCNM, Weller highlights: (1) "issues of state construction", (2) "representation of minorities in executive agencies and judiciary", (3) "cultural, social and economic participation". In the first 'category', in particular, aspects of "constitutional design of the state, electoral processes and procedures, and mechanism designed to enhance a minority voice in decision making" are addressed. See Weller, "Article 15", pp.434-455.

893 Statements made during the EURAC-ECMI Expert Meeting "Territorial and Non-territorial Autonomy. Minorities and Territory", Bolzano/Bozen, 16-17 November 2011 by Francesco Palermo ("The Territorial Logic: Its Value and Limits"), and Markku Suksi ("Non-Territorial Autonomy: The Meaning of '(Non-)Territoriality'").

894 Hofmann, "Political Participation of Minorities", p.11.

895 Heintze, "On the Legal Understanding …", pp.18 and 21; Hofmann, "Political Participation of Minorities", p.11; Weller, "Article 15", p.439.

896 Hofmann, "Political Participation of Minorities", p.11.

adequate financial/fiscal autonomy.[897] In fact, problematic issues regarding representation at State level are relevant at regional or local level as well. Henrard additionally flags, *inter alia*, the difficulty of finding "a complete identity of ethnicity and territory",[898] recalling the risk, for instance, of "minorities within minorities" being further excluded.

The constitutional framework and the political situation of the concerned State are particularly relevant for the establishment of a TA. In some cases, federal systems or regional structures have been established[899] in order to give the "power to regulate and run regional and local affairs [...][including culture] education, language policies and media".[900] In his recent work, Suksi suggested that "[a]n arrangement with a territorial autonomy normally involves a singular entity in what otherwise would be a unitary state, introducing thereby an asymmetrical feature in the state through transfer of exclusive law-making powers on the basis of provisions that often are of special nature".[901] De Varennes underlined how federal systems and non-federal territorial autonomy arrangements may be useful mechanisms to increase the participation and representation of minorities. As mentioned, minorities would form a *de facto* majority in given territories (in the case that settlements are concentrated), thus enhancing their chances to access and govern at local level. The creation of sub-units within a State and the general decentralization of powers go in the same direction. However, the author also states that more effective participation and representation of minorities is also possible without –or in combination with– territorial (political) autonomy, recalling the above-mentioned concept of NTA.[902] Indeed, as stated by Lapidoth as well, the establishment of either a TA or a NTA does not exclude the other, since a group could in principle enjoy a TA in a specific territory and a NTA, e.g., outside that territory but within the state borders.[903]

897 *Ibid.*

898 Henrard 2005, p.142.

899 Examples can be the Åland Islands, South Tyrol or the Eastern Cantons of Belgium. Hofmann, "Political Participation of Minorities", p.11, and Weller "Article 15", p.439.

900 Hofmann, "Political Participation of Minorities", p.11.

901 Markku Suksi, *Sub-State Governance through Territorial Autonomy*, Springer, Heidelberg, Dordrecht, 2011, p.139.

902 De Varennes, "Towards Effective Political Participation and Representation of Minorities", sub-paragraph titled "3. Possible Mechanisms for Increasing Effective Participation and Representation of Minorities".

903 Lapidoth, *Autonomy: Flexible Solutions to Ethnic Conflicts*, p.39.

Finally, by analyzing and summarizing other works, Weller and Nobbs have identified the following characteristics which are necessary for a TA: Demographic distinctiveness; devolution, not decentralization, that is the exercise of the public power not on behalf of the State but as the result of a full devolution of public authority; legal entrenchment, which implies the autonomy's legal anchorage to the State order (e.g., constitutional recognition); legal supremacy, but no secession unless if so provided; statute-making powers; significant competences; parallel action, meaning parallel exercise of powers with the State; limited external relations powers; legislative, adjudicative and executive institutions; and integrative mechanisms of the autonomous unit within the national system.[904] However, all these definitions do not take into account the economic complexities, which are of utmost importance and may affect the creation (and the functionality) of autonomous units, especially during times of financial constraint, such as the present one.

In conclusion, if adequately developed, both TA and NTA arrangements may realize and meet minorities' expectations of governing their own issues, at least to some extent. At the same time, the States' dominance (and anxiety) over territorial sovereignty may be mitigated. Moreover, autonomy arrangements may potentially avoid (new or the prolongation of) conflicts and/or secessions. As confirmed by Skurbaty, "[a]utonomy can effectively be used as a means to preserve and promote the identities of the groups, to foster economic development and to either prevent or mitigate the state-group or inter-group conflicts".[905]

3.2.3 Concluding remarks

The right to political participation of minorities has been specifically recognized in art.15 of the (binding) Council of Europe's Framework Convention for the Protection of National Minorities. Moreover, art.2.2 of the UN Declaration on the Rights of Persons Belonging to National or Ethnic, Religious, and Linguistic Minorities, affirms that: "Persons belonging to minorities have the right to participate effectively in cultural, religious, social, economic and public life". The need to ensure this right to minorities has

904 Marc Weller, "Introduction", in Marc Weller and Katherine Nobbs (eds.), *Asymmetric Autonomy and the Settlement of Ethnic Conflicts*, University of Pennsylvania Press, Philadelphia, 2010, pp.1-13, pp.4-5.

905 Skurbaty, "Introduction", p.xliv.

been particularly stressed in the works of the OSCE and the HCNM Lund Recommendations which were adopted in September 1999. During the same year, a set of recommendations with regard to (national) minorities and their participation in public life was adopted by the United Nations Working Group on Minorities. Therefore, it may be argued that the right to political participation of minorities is widely recognized in international law as of the 1990s, especially in the European context.

Basic and common denominators of this right are the recognition and the application of human rights standards as seen in section 3.1. As mentioned, these "political rights" are framed as individual rights, but some of them are materialized when exercised by a group, such as the freedom of association and assembly.[906] Special mechanisms to avoid discrimination against vulnerable groups should be taken into account, e.g., to protect the "minority within minorities".[907] As seen, there is no "universal formula" for minority participation,[908] but the twofold concept of "political participation" provided by the Lund Recommendations is particularly helpful, also for indigenous peoples.[909] Therefore, the "political participation" of minorities implies first participation at all levels within the State, especially in the decision-making processes. Second, it also includes means of autonomy or self-government in both forms of non-territorial (NTAs) and territorial autonomies (TAs).

3.3 The Composite Right to Political Participation of Indigenous Peoples

After having analyzed how a *composite right to political participation of indigenous peoples* descends and represents one of the facets of their right to self-determination in chapter 2, section 2.2, and having seen the key components of the right to political participation in human rights law and in the case of minorities in the previous sections, this section aims to explore how this proposed *composite right* is recognized in international law and could thus be applied within domestic law.

This proposed *composite right* refers to a combination of (1) (a) *ad hoc* political rights (indigenous peoples' representation in State bodies or in

906 Verstichel, *Participation, Representation and Identity*, p.96.

907 Henrard, "'Participation', 'Representation' and 'Autonomy' in the Lund Recommendations …", p.142.

908 Ghai, *Public Participation of Minorities*, p.3.

909 Rodríguez Piñero-Royo, "Political Participation Systems Applicable to Indigenous Peoples", p.311.

other public posts, including in decision-making processes and in the judiciary, both at national and local level) and their (b) rights to consultation and (c) free, prior and informed consent (FPIC) on the one hand, and (2) autonomy/self-government arrangements (including the preservation of indigenous traditional institutions) on the other. These sub-rights are recognized not only in international law and international human rights law as seen in the previous sections, but also in international indigenous instruments such as the ILO Convention 169, "Convention concerning Indigenous and Tribal Peoples in Independent Countries" adopted in 1989 and the UN Declaration on the Rights of Indigenous Peoples (henceforth, ILO Convention 169 and UNDRIP, respectively). In addition, given the focus of this study on Latin America, the jurisprudence on the subject matter of the Inter-American Court of Human Rights also needs to be taken into account.

In the conceptualization of this composite right for indigenous peoples, there are certain similarities with the theoretical debate regarding the right to political participation of minorities. Both groups face difficulties in having a guaranteed right to political participation in the decision making-processes both at State and local level[910] and therefore both groups need *ad hoc* rights. Thus, the *composite right to political participation of indigenous peoples* here proposed may also be conceived as composed by two prongs, as follows:

1. Participation through representation in State bodies or in other public posts, including in decision-making processes and in the judiciary, both at national and local level, as well as their rights to consultation and free, prior and informed consent (FPIC); and
2. Participation through autonomy/self-government arrangements and the preservation of indigenous institutions.

It is relevant to stress here that there is no intention of applying a system designed for minority protection to indigenous peoples. Although indigenous peoples' claims and rights tend to overlap substantially with those of minorities,[911] indigenous peoples constantly refused to be treated as minorities as seen in chapter 1. Moreover, as will be shown in this section, the right of political participation of indigenous peoples differs substantially

910 On an overview of the difficulties faced by both minorities and indigenous peoples see Musafiri, "Right to Self-Determination in International Law ...", pp.527-531. The author mentions, *inter alia*, the lack of a conducive environment for participation and the lack of consideration of consultations held with minorities. Musafiri, "Right to Self-Determination in International Law ...", pp.527-528.

911 Rodríguez Piñero-Royo, "Political Participation Systems Applicable to Indigenous Peoples", p.309.

from that of minorities, particularly due to the focus on the preservation of traditional indigenous institutions and their right to consultation and FPIC. Consultations with minorities are much less incisive in comparison to the implications of indigenous peoples' right to consultation and FPIC, as will be discussed below. Similarities between the theorization of these two rights are, however, inevitable, because they both partly descend from developments of international human rights law. In particular, the prong of participation in decision-making processes, which has been conceived as mainly applicable and relevant for minorities, is also of great importance for indigenous peoples (see section 3.3.1.1). Thus, since it is widely accepted that indigenous peoples may enjoy minority protection if they freely opt for it,[912] the recognition and theorization of the right to political participation of minorities will serve as a reference here only when it is also useful for indigenous peoples. In sum, minority protection systems *may* but *do not necessarily have to* be applied to indigenous peoples.

Thus, this section aims to explore how this *composite right to political participation of indigenous peoples* is recognized in the international *corpus iuris* regarding indigenous peoples, by looking at their sub-rights of participation in State bodies or other public posts, including decision-making processes and in the judiciary, both at national and local level (section 3.3.1.2), to consultation and FPIC (section 3.3.2.1), to autonomy/self-government and to preserve indigenous traditional institutions (section 3.3.3.1). To do so, an analysis is offered of the decisions of the Inter-American Courts of Human Rights vis-à-vis the rights to participation of indigenous peoples in domestic decision-making processes and to consultation and FPIC (sections 3.3.1.3 and 3.3.2.3); and, ultimately, a summary is given of how this composite right may be conceptualized (section 3.3.4). How this *composite right* is recognized and applied at domestic level and whether it may thus become one of the expressions, or better, effective applications of the right to self-determination of indigenous peoples will be explored subsequently in concrete case studies (chapters 5 and 6).

912 Alexandra Xanthaki and Dominic O'Sullivan, "Indigenous Participation in Elective Bodies: The Maori in New Zealand", 16 *International Journal on Minority and Group Rights* 2009, pp.181-207, p.183.

3.3.1 Participation of indigenous peoples in domestic decision-making processes

3.3.1.1 Introduction

In the UN "Working Paper on the Relationship & Distinction between the Rights of Persons Belonging to Minorities & Those of Indigenous Peoples'", published in 2000, Eide proposed a difference between minorities and indigenous peoples based on the right to political participation. He wrote: "[W]hereas the Minority Declaration [Declaration on the Rights of Persons Belonging to National or Ethnic, Religious, and Linguistic Minorities of 1992] and other instruments concerning persons belonging to minorities aim at ensuring a space for pluralism in togetherness, the instruments concerning indigenous peoples are intended to allow for a high degree of autonomous development".[913] In particular, it was argued that "[t]he right to participation [for indigenous peoples] in the larger society is in the Draft [Declaration on the Rights of Indigenous Peoples of 1994] given a secondary significance and expressed as an optional right". In fact, arts.19 and 20 of the Draft Declaration and art.5 of the UNDRIP state that indigenous peoples have the right to participate fully in the political, economic, social, and cultural life of the State, *if they so choose*. The underlying assumption for Eide was that –if indigenous peoples "have full authority of their own to make the relevant decisions"–[914] their participation in the larger society would not be required.[915] However, even in the optimistic case in which indigenous peoples would enjoy full authority and effective decision-making powers over their territories and/or their communities, other national provisions or policies may in any case affect them, at least indirectly (e.g., in the case of an environmental policy regarding a region bordering the "indigenous territory"). Therefore, the cited articles of both the Draft Declaration and the UNDRIP rather aim to prevent a forced participation of indigenous peoples than giving them an "optional right".

The importance of the participation of indigenous peoples in domestic decision-making processes have been increasingly stressed by UN bodies. In its General Recommendation No.23 adopted in 1997, the Committee on

913 Asbjørn Eide and Irene-Erica Daes, "Working Paper on the Relationship & Distinction between the Rights of Persons Belonging to Minorities & Those of Indigenous Peoples'", UN Doc. E/CN.4/Sub.2/2000/10, 2000, para.8.

914 *Ibid.*

915 *Ibid.*

the Elimination of Racial Discrimination (CERD) urged States to "[e]nsure that members of indigenous peoples have equal rights in respect of effective participation in public life and that no decisions directly relating to their rights and interests are taken without their informed consent".[916] More recently, the CESCR recognized among the core obligations of States under art.15.1 of the ICESCR to "allow and encourage the participation of persons belonging to minority groups, indigenous peoples or to other communities in the design and implementation of laws and policies that affect them" in its General Comment No.21 of 2009 on the right of everyone to take part in cultural life.[917] In the case *Ángela Poma Poma v. Peru* (2009), the HRC also stated that the participation of indigenous peoples in the decision-making process must be effective and not mere consultation is required, but rather the FPIC of all members of the community (see also chapter 2, section 2.2).[918]

As for the UN bodies dealing directly with indigenous rights, the aim to "[p]romot[e] full and effective participation of indigenous peoples in decisions which directly or indirectly affect them (incl., Free, Prior and Informed Consent – FPIC)" was the second of the five objectives included in the Draft (then adopted) Programme of Action for the UN Second International Decade of the World's Indigenous Peoples (2005-2014).[919] Later, the Expert Mechanism on the Rights of Indigenous Peoples decided to address the right of indigenous peoples to participate in decision-making bodies in

916 Committee on the Elimination of Racial Discrimination (CERD), General Recommendation XXIII, "Indigenous Peoples", 18.08.1997, fifty-first session, UN Doc. A/52/18, annex V, 1997, para.4d.

917 Committee on Economic, Social and Cultural Rights, General comment No. 21, "Right of everyone to take part in cultural life (art. 15, para. 1 (a), of the International Covenant on Economic, Social and Cultural Rights)", 21 December 2009, UN Doc. E/C.12/GC/21, para.55.

918 Human Rights Committee, *Ángela Poma Poma v. Peru*, Communication No. 1457/2006, Views adopted on 27 March 2009, UN Doc. CCPR/C/95/D/1457/2006, para.7.6.

919 General Assembly, "Draft Programme of Action for the Second International Decade of the World's Indigenous People", Sixtieth session, 18 August 2005, UN Doc. A/60/270, para.9; See also the brochure of the Second International Decade of the World's Indigenous People at http://www.un.org/esa/soc dev/unpfii/documents/brochure_2nd_decade.pdf [Last access 30.07.2014]. The Second International Decade of the World's Indigenous People was established by adopted by the General Assembly on 20 December 2004, UN Doc. A/RES/59/174. See also the webpage of the Second International Decade of the World's Indigenous People at http://www.un.org/en/events/indigenousday/second.shtml [Last access 30.07. 2014].

its second thematic study finalized in 2011.[920] During 2014, the thirteenth session of the UN Permanent Forum on Indigenous Issues focused on the special theme of "Principles of good governance consistent with the United Nations Declaration on the Rights of Indigenous Peoples: articles 3 to 6 and 46".[921] *Inter alia*, during this session, full participation of indigenous peoples in decision-making and their "participatory governance" at national level was proposed by the Indigenous Peoples' Major Group as one of the first goals to achieve in the post-2015 agenda.[922] The newly appointed Special Rapporteur on the rights of indigenous peoples, Victoria Tauli Corpuz, also stressed the relevance of Indigenous peoples' participation in decision-making processes to combat prejudice and discrimination and to promote good relations among Indigenous peoples and all other segments of society in her first report before the Human Rights Council in 2014.[923] Finally, after the first UN World Conference on Indigenous Peoples (WCIP), held in New York in September 2014, the GA adopted a draft resolution during its sixty-

920 Expert Mechanism on the Rights of Indigenous Peoples, "Progress report on the study on indigenous peoples and the right to participate in decision-making", 17 May 2010, UN Doc. A/HRC/EMRIP/2010/2, and "Final study on indigenous peoples and the right to participate in decision-making", 26 May 2011, UN Doc. A/HRC/EMRIP/2011/2. See at http://www.ohchr.org/en/issues/ipeoples/emrip/pages/emripindex.aspx [Last access 30.07.2014].

921 UN Permanent Forum on Indigenous Issues, thirteenth session on "Principles of good governance consistent with the United Nations Declaration on the Rights of Indigenous Peoples: articles 3 to 6 and 46", New York, 12-23 May 2014, see at http://undesadspd.org/IndigenousPeoples/UNPFIISessions/Thirteenth.aspx [Last access 30.07.2014].

922 UN Permanent Forum on Indigenous Issues, "Item 7 (continued), Ongoing priorities and themes and follow-up: (d) Post-2015 development agenda", thirteenth session, 12-23 May 2014, UN Doc. E/CN.19/2014/CRP.3, pp.3-4. The Indigenous Peoples' Major Group is one of the Major Groups of the UN Division for Sustainable Development (DSD), which is in charge of leading the promotion and coordination works regarding the implementation of the UN sustainable development agenda since the United Nations Conference on Environment and Development (UNCED), held in Rio de Janeiro on 3-14 June 1992. See "About the Division for Sustainable Development", at http://sustainable development.un.org/about.html. See also the list of Major Groups at http://sustainabledevelopment.un.org/major-groups.html, and the webpage of Indigenous Peoples' Major Group at http://sustainabledevelop ment.un.org/index.php?menu=165 [Last access to all 30.07.2014].

923 Human Rights Council, Report of the Special Rapporteur on the rights of indigenous peoples, Victoria Tauli Corpuz, UN Doc. A/HRC/27/52, 11 August 2014, para.41.

ninth session in which States reaffirmed their commitment to protect, promote and advance the rights of indigenous peoples, and in particular to consult indigenous peoples and to obtain their FPIC.[924]

Therefore, the participation of indigenous peoples in the decision-making bodies of the State remains essential. This section will analyze how the rights of indigenous peoples to participate in (national) decision-making bodies (part of the first aspect of the proposed *composite right*) are safeguarded by the international documents dealing specifically with their rights (ILO Convention 169 and the UNDRIP). It is relevant to underline here that the regime of political rights provided for indigenous peoples by the ILO Convention 169, and likewise by the UNDRIP, is also known as the "participation-consultation" principle,[925] due to a combined reading of arts.6 and 7 of the former.[926] However, for the reasons argued above, and in consideration of the increasing importance of both the right to consultation and the FPIC, the right of indigenous peoples to participation in domestic decision-making bodies will be analyzed here separately.

3.3.1.2 The *ad hoc* rights of indigenous peoples to participation in domestic decision-making processes

Both the binding International Labour Organization (ILO) Conventions on indigenous rights, i.e., ILO Convention 107 ("Convention concerning the Protection and Integration of Indigenous and Other Tribal and Semi-Tribal Populations in Independent Countries" adopted in 1957) and the ILO Convention 169 ("Convention concerning Indigenous and Tribal Peoples in Independent Countries" adopted in 1989),[927] as well as the UNDRIP, contain

924 General Assembly, "Outcome document of the high-level plenary meeting of the General Assembly known as the World Conference on Indigenous Peoples", sixty-ninth session, 22 September 2014, UN Doc. A/RES/69/2 based on the "Draft resolution submitted by the President of General Assembly", sixty-ninth session, 15 September 2014, UN Doc. A/69/L.1, paras.3-4.

925 Rodríguez Piñero-Royo, "Political Participation Systems Applicable to Indigenous Peoples", p.313; Expert Mechanism on the Rights of Indigenous Peoples, "Progress report on the study on indigenous peoples and the right to participate in decision-making", p.6, para 17.

926 See *infra* the text of the two articles.

927 As seen in chapter 1, the ILO Conventions No. 107 and 169 are the only binding documents with regard to indigenous issues to date. In fact, the former, even though it is closed to ratification, remains in force for those States which have not ratified the latter (art.43.2). Both conventions have been signed and ratified by a

a number of provisions vis-à-vis the rights of indigenous peoples to participate in domestic decision-making bodies.

The ILO Convention 107, which may be defined as a brave attempt to advance indigenous protection and working conditions after the end of the Second World War, although paternalistic in its content,[928] contains a timid provision in art.5a on the a duty of the governments to

> "seek the collaboration of these populations and of their representatives [...] [in] applying the provisions of this Convention relating to the protection and integration of the populations concerned".

The ILO Convention 169 uses a different approach and is far more incisive than the previous convention. In addition, the regime of political rights provided for indigenous peoples by this convention recognizes indigenous peoples as a group, therefore going beyond the individual nature of the political rights provided by the ICCPR.[929]

Key provisions of the ILO Convention 169 regarding the right of indigenous peoples to participate in decision-making bodies are arts.2.1, 6.1b and 7.

In particular, art.2.1 states a general obligation for the State to develop actions with the participation of indigenous peoples for the protection of their rights, as follows:

> "1. Governments shall have the responsibility for developing, *with the participation of the peoples concerned*, co-ordinated and systematic action to protect the rights of these peoples and to guarantee respect for their integrity." [Emphasis added].

Moreover, art.6.1b establishes that:

> "1. In applying the provisions of this Convention, governments shall: [...] (b) establish means by which *these peoples can freely participate, to at least the same extent as other sectors of the population, at all levels of decision-making in elective institutions and administrative and other bodies responsible for policies and programmes which concern them*". [Emphasis added].

And art.7.1 affirms:

> "1. The peoples concerned shall have *the right to decide their own priorities for the process of development as it affects* their lives, beliefs, institutions and spiritual well-being and the lands they occupy or otherwise use, and to exercise control, to the extent possible, over their own economic, social and cultural development. In

---

number of States. See http://www.ilo.org/indigenous/Conventions/no107/lang--en/index.htm.

928 Comment of Sweden in the "Partial Revision", Report VI(2), 1998, 4 as reported by Thornberry 2002, p.338.

929 Xanthaki and O'Sullivan, "Indigenous Participation in Elective Bodies: The Maori in New Zealand", p.185.

> addition, they *shall participate in the formulation, implementation and evaluation of plans and programmes for national and regional development which may affect them directly.*" [Emphasis added].

Furthermore, paras.2, 3 and 4 of the same article assert the duty of governments to cooperate with indigenous peoples on the improvement of their conditions of life, work, health and education; in the assessment studies on social, cultural and environmental plans that may affect them; and on the national environmental policies involving their territories.

Notably, art.15.1 also provides that:

> "1. The rights of the peoples concerned to the natural resources pertaining to their lands shall be specially safeguarded. These rights include *the right of these peoples to participate in the use, management and conservation of these resources*." [Emphasis added].

Furthermore, the participation of indigenous peoples is foreseen in the elaboration of policies aimed at mitigating the difficulties faced by indigenous peoples vis-à-vis new conditions of life and work (art.5c); the preparation of vocational training programmes of general application (art.22.1); in the promotion of traditional economic activities, such as hunting, fishing, trapping and gathering (art.23.1); and in the developments and implementation of education programmes and services (art.27, paras.1-2).

Finally, art.33 states that:

> "1. The governmental authority responsible for the matters covered in this Convention shall ensure that agencies or other appropriate mechanisms exist to administer the programmes affecting the peoples concerned, and shall ensure that they have the means necessary for the proper fulfilment of the functions assigned to them.
>
> 2. These programmes shall include:
>
> (a) the planning, co-ordination, execution and evaluation, *in co-operation with the peoples concerned*, of the measures provided for in this Convention;
>
> (b) the proposing of legislative and other measures to the competent authorities and supervision of the application of the measures taken, *in co-operation with the peoples concerned*." [Emphasis added].

Therefore, the ILO Convention 169 provides an extensive set of norms vis-à-vis the right of indigenous peoples to participate in decision-making processes, which, as highlighted in the "Study on indigenous peoples and the right to participate in decision-making" of the Expert Mechanism on the Rights of Indigenous Peoples, may be summarized as follows:

> "The right to participation (art. 2, 5–7, 15, 22, 23); […]
>
> The State's obligation to cooperate with indigenous peoples (art. 7, 20, 22, 25, 27, 33);

Indigenous peoples' right to decide their own priorities (art. 7);

The obligation to refrain from taking measures contrary to the freely-expressed wishes of indigenous peoples (art. 4); [...]

Indigenous peoples' right to exercise control over their own development (art. 7);

Indigenous peoples' right to effective representation (art. 6 and 16)."[930]

The UNDRIP articulates the right of indigenous peoples to participate in the domestic decision-making process in arts.5, 18 and 27:

"Article 5. Indigenous peoples have the right to maintain and strengthen their distinct political, legal, economic, social and cultural institutions, while *retaining their right to participate fully, if they so choose, in the political, economic, social and cultural life of the State.*"

"Article 18. Indigenous peoples have the right *to participate in decision-making in matters which would affect their rights, through representatives chosen by themselves* in accordance with their own procedures, as well as to maintain and develop their own indigenous decisionmaking institutions."

"Article 27. States shall establish and implement, in conjunction with indigenous peoples concerned, a fair, independent, impartial, open and transparent *process, giving due recognition to indigenous peoples' laws, traditions, customs and land tenure systems, to recognize and adjudicate the rights of indigenous peoples pertaining to their lands, territories and resources*, including those which were traditionally owned or otherwise occupied or used. *Indigenous peoples shall have the right to participate in this process.*" [Emphasis added]

Furthermore, participation of indigenous peoples should be ensured in matters involving indigenous interests such as the right to the preservation and the manifestation of their culture and their traditions (12.2 and 31.2); indigenous peoples' access to education (art.14.3); and the cross-border cooperation of one indigenous people divided by states' frontiers (art.36.2).

In sum, according to the ILO Convention 169, indigenous peoples have the right to participate in domestic decision-making processes in both elective and administrative institutions and in other bodies responsible for policies and programmes which concern them (art.6.1b); in the formulation, implementation and evaluation of plans and programmes for national and regional development which may affect them directly (art.7.1); in the use, management and conservation of these resources (art.15); and to decide their own priorities for the process of development that may affect them (art.7.1). Governments have to develop, together with indigenous peoples,

930 Expert Mechanism on the Rights of Indigenous Peoples, "Progress report on the study on indigenous peoples and the right to participate in decision-making", pp.7-8, para.26. Other references were made to arts.6 and 16 on the rights to consultation and FPIC, which will be dealt with in the next subsection.

coordinated and systematic actions to protect their rights and to guarantee respect for their integrity (art.2.1). Additionally, the participation of indigenous peoples is required in the elaboration of mitigating policies vis-à-vis indigenous peoples' new conditions of life and work (art.5c) and vocational training programmes (art.22.1); in the promotion of traditional economic activities, (art.23.1); and in the developments and implementation of education programmes and services (art.27, paras.1-2). Finally, the domestic programmes affecting indigenous peoples administered by the agencies or other appropriate mechanisms established by States shall include the planning, co-ordination, execution, and evaluation of the measures provided by the Convention, the proposing of legislative and other measures and the supervision of the implementation of the adopted measures with the cooperation of indigenous peoples (art.33).

According to the UNDRIP, indigenous peoples have the right to participate freely and fully in the political, economic, social, and cultural life of the State (art.5); in decision-making in matters which would affect their rights, through representatives chosen by themselves (art.18); in the process to recognize indigenous peoples' laws, traditions, customs and land tenure systems (art.27); and when matters involve their interests such as the preservation and the manifestation of their culture and their traditions (arts.12.2 and 31.2), access to education (art.14.3), and cross-border cooperation amongst indigenous peoples (art.36.2).

3.3.1.3 Ways to implement the right participation of indigenous peoples in domestic decision-making processes

Having assessed the recognition of the right of Indigenous peoples to participate in domestic decision-making processes in both the ILO Convention 169 and the UNDRIP, the mechanisms that may ensure this participation needs to be specified here.

As recently highlighted by Xanthaki and O'Sullivan, indigenous peoples worldwide tend to be poorly represented in parliaments, and other national political parties hardly enhance indigenous agendas. This occurs particularly when they constitute a numeric minority of the population,[931] as will also be shown in the case of Chile (chapter 6). Thus, indigenous represent-

931 Xanthaki and O'Sullivan, "Indigenous Participation in Elective Bodies: The Maori in New Zealand", p.181.

atives are often outvoted. Moreover, the widespread discriminatory practices vis-à-vis indigenous peoples affect their participation, which is also aggravated by their poor access to information and economic capacity.[932] This supports the assumption that mere political rights recognized in human rights law cannot ensure indigenous participation in domestic decision-making bodies and thus additional political rights need to be recognized, which in turn fulfil their right to equality as well. Therefore, similarly to minorities, this type of participation of Indigenous peoples within the State structure may be guaranteed by means of "representation" at all institutional levels. However, indigenous representativeness should be not be conceived as isolated but rather as *one* of the interconnected actors of the wider national society.[933] In addition, the participation and representation of indigenous women should also be enhanced in accordance with art.7-8 of the Convention on the Elimination of All Forms of Discrimination against Women, as seen in section 3.1. Finally, this participation shall not be manipulated or distorted by using sexist language, as has recently occurred in the case of Chiapas (Mexico).[934]

Therefore, indigenous peoples should be enabled to access national and local parliaments, judiciary, other governmental bodies, such as ministries, and other public offices, particularly those that may adopt measures likely to affect them.

In addition to the guarantee of basic political rights, the following mechanisms may ensure, or at least promote, the "representation" of indigenous peoples and enable them to have a say at national level:

- Reservation of seats or "quotas" in the abovementioned bodies;
- Recognition of the right for indigenous peoples to form their own political parties;

932 Secretariat of the UN Permanent Forum of Indigenous Issues, "Examination of the situation of indigenous peoples and their participation in democracies and electoral processes in Latin America under the United Nationas Declaration on the Rights of Indigenous Peoples", UN Doc. E/C.19/2014/6, 26 February 2014, para.44, p.11.

933 Ampam Karakras, "¿Quién habla por quién? Reflexiones sobre la representatividad y legitimidad de organizaciones y la institucionalidad indígena, estatal y de la cooperación internacional", in Sabine Speiser (ed.), *¿Quién habla por quién? Representatividad y legitimidad de organizaciones y representantes indígenas. Un debate abierto*, Unidad Coordinadora de Pueblos Indígenas en América Latina y el Caribe (KIVLAK) and Deutsche Gesellschaft für Internationale Zusammenarbeiten (GIZ), Quito, 2013, pp.19-38, p.20.

934 Secretariat of the UN Permanent Forum of Indigenous Issues, "Examination of the situation of indigenous peoples and their participation in democracies ...", p.13, para.54.

- Lower thresholds for indigenous parties;
- The possibility for indigenous peoples to engage in other political parties to bring forward their agenda;
- A proportional electoral system, that may more easily grant the access of indigenous peoples to elective bodies in comparison to a majoritarian one, provided that indigenous peoples constitute a sufficient numerical portion of the whole population and are able to reach the necessary threshold of votes to be admitted in the elective bodies;
- *Ad hoc* parliamentary/local assemblies' procedures, including the right to veto or, at least, a reinforced enactment procedure, e.g., as a twofold approval of an act (to avoid the consequent blocking or paralysis of enactment procedures) whenever measures likely to affect indigenous peoples have to be adopted;
- Use of indigenous languages in States' acts;
- Educational training on indigenous peoples' cultures of other parliamentary or public staff;
- The creation of specialized governmental bodies with the direct participation of members of indigenous peoples or consultative bodies composed of indigenous representatives with negotiating powers on the decisions likely to affect indigenous peoples.

Lastly, similar considerations made on the "genuineness" of representatives of minorities also applies to indigenous peoples. In other words, a potential indigenous "representative" may pursue individual aims rather than effectively represent her/his community. A way suggested by an indigenous Shuar scholar to verify the legitimacy of a representative is to verify at community level whether s/he has a mandate[935] and speaks for personal interests or of a limited group.[936] In fact, the legitimacy of indigenous representatives may be solely assessed by whom s/he is representing.[937] Additionally, Ströbele-Gregor recently reported that the forced adaptation of indigenous peoples to Western liberal models of representativeness on the one hand, and the preservation of traditional decision-making processes on the other hand may generate a tension that adversely affects indigenous representatives, who eventually risk opting for populist arguments rather than arguing for the real needs of the community.[938] Nevertheless, the author also notes

935 Karakras, "¿Quién habla por quién? Reflexiones sobre la representatividad ...", p.25.

936 *Ibid.*, p.29.

937 *Ibid.*, p.37.

938 Juliana Ströbele-Gregor, "Autoridad, poder y liderazgo: Observaciones conceptuales acerca de la práctica de representación de los pueblos indígenas", in Sabine

that today a new generation of very committed indigenous representatives who are also able to combine both elements (Western liberal democratic and traditional values) is gaining prominence.[939]

In conclusion, the abovementioned list and these last considerations are most probably far from being exhaustive. However, they reflect some of the States' practice[940] and provide for some mechanisms that may enable indigenous peoples to exercise this sub-right of participation in domestic decision-making processes, which forms part of the proposed *composite right of political participation of indigenous peoples*.

3.3.1.4 The Yatama case before the Inter-American Court of Human Rights and Indigenous peoples' electoral rights

As will be seen in chapter 4, the Inter-American Court of Human Rights (Inter-American Court of Human Rights) has developed an extensive jurisprudence vis-à-vis indigenous rights despite the lack of any direct recognition of indigenous peoples' protection in the American Convention on Human Rights (Pact of San José, 1969).

Regarding the right of indigenous peoples to participate in decision-making processes, the *Yatama v. Nicaragua* case (2005)[941] needs to be mentioned. This decision follows a recent trend of Latin American countries to involve indigenous peoples and their organizations in national elections by admitting electoral subscription groups, which started with the adoption of the Participation Popular Law in Bolivia in 1994 (see further in chapter 5).[942] However, this decision stems to have denounced a violation of the

Speiser (ed.), *¿Quién habla por quién? Representatividad y legitimidad de organizaciones y representantes indígenas. Un debate abierto*, Unidad Coordinadora de Pueblos Indígenas en América Latina y el Caribe (KIVLAK) and Deutsche Gesellschaft für Internationale Zusammenarbeiten (GIZ), Quito, 2013, pp.73-89, p.87.

939 *Ibid.*

940 See the results of the extensive survey realized by the Inter-Parliamentary Union (IPU) and the United Nations Development Programme (UNDP) in 2009 in the report prepared by Oleh Protsyk, "The representation of minorities and indigenous peoples in parliament", published by IPU and UNDP, Mexico, 2010, and at http://www.ipu.org/splz-e/chiapas10/overview.pdf [Last access 30.07.2014].

941 Inter-American Court of Human Rights, *YATAMA v. Nicaragua*, Serie C. No.127, Judgment of 23 June 2005.

942 Rodríguez Piñero-Royo, "Political Participation Systems Applicable to Indigenous Peoples", p.319.

right of indigenous peoples to participate in elections due to a sort of gerrymandering.

As will be explained in section 3.3.3.3, in Nicaragua two autonomous regions have been established by art.5.3 of the 1987 Constitution, i.e., the North Atlantic and the South Atlantic Autonomous Regions. The local indigenous organization YATAMA (in indigenous *Miskitu* language: *Yapti Tasba Masraka Nanih Asla Takanka*, which means "Organization of the sons of Mother Earth") aimed to run for the municipal elections in October 2000, but was eventually excluded due to the lack of a formal requirement in accordance with art.82 of Electoral Law No.331 of 2000.[943] The new law required that all political parties willing to run for such elections had to provide candidates in at least 80% of the municipalities in each autonomous region. However, the Miskito indigenous people, the main supporter of YATAMA, live predominantly in the North Atlantic Autonomous Region and were thus unable to provide the required number of delegates in the southern region.[944] Therefore, YATAMA was excluded from the electoral roll as a result of a decision issued on 15 August 2000 by the Nicaraguan Supreme Electoral Council,[945] arguing that YATAMA has neither received the legal status that would enable it to run for elections, as other political parties, nor has it reached the abovementioned sufficient number of candidates. Although the latter aspect was correct, the former was not since YATAMA had received its legal status earlier that year. However, the Nicaraguan Supreme Court of Justice confirmed the decision of the Supreme Electoral Council and eventually the Miskitu indigenous people could not vote for their party, which resulted in very low levels of participation in the elections. An additional concern was that the YATAMA candidates for the 2000 elections had been selected following the indigenous community's procedures. The community rules meant that a candidate could stand for elections only once. Therefore, these candidates could not stand for elections for the following term in 2004.[946]

The Court thus found violations of arts.8.1 (right to a fair trial), 25.1 (right to judicial protection), 23 (right to participate in government) and 24 (right to equal protection) of the American Convention on Human Rights.[947] In particular, the Inter-American Court of Human Rights underlined that the condition required by the State to allow YATAMA to run for elections as a

943 *Ibid.*, p.320.

944 *Ibid.*

945 Inter-American Court of Human Rights, *YATAMA v. Nicaragua*, p.2, para.2.

946 *Ibid.*, p.25, para.110.

947 *Ibid.*, p.104, paras.2-4.

political party –which did not take into consideration indigenous customs and rules– was

> "an undue limitation of the exercise of a political right, entailing an unnecessary restriction of the right to be elected, taking into account the circumstances of the instant case, which are not necessarily comparable to the circumstances of all political groups that may be present in other national societies or sectors of a national society".[948]

Moreover, the Court added that:

> "[the] requirement of Electoral Act No.331 of 2000 constitutes a disproportionate restriction that unduly limited the political participation of the candidates proposed by YATAMA for the municipal elections of November 2000. It did not take into account that the indigenous and ethnic population is a minority in the SAAR [South Atlantic Autonomous Region], or that there were municipalities in which they did not have the support to present candidates or where they were not interested in seeking this support".[949]

Thus, the Miskitu indigenous people "were affected by legal and real discrimination, which prevented them from participating, in equal conditions, in the municipal elections of November 2000".[950] Lastly, the Court urged Nicaragua to

> "adopt all necessary measures to ensure that [indigenous peoples] [...] *can participate, in equal conditions, in decision-making on matters and policies that affect or could affect their rights and the development of these communities, so that they can incorporate State institutions and bodies and participate directly and proportionately to their population in the conduct of public affairs, and also do this from within their own institutions and according to their values, practices, customs and forms of organization*, provided these are compatible with the human rights embodied in the Convention".[951] [Emphasis added].

3.3.2 Consultation and Free, Prior and Informed Consent (FPIC)

3.3.2.1 The recognition of the rights to Consultation and Free, Prior and Informed Consent (FPIC)

Both the ILO Convention 169 and the UNDRIP recognize the rights to consultation and to Free, Prior and Informed Consent (FPIC). However, the

948 *Ibid.*, p.89, para.219.
949 *Ibid.*, p.90, para.223.
950 *Ibid.*, p.90, para.224.
951 *Ibid.*, p.90, para.225.

former focuses on the right to consultation and contains only one reference to the "free and informed consent" (without "prior"), whereas the latter provides a far more specific protection of the FPIC, as will be assessed here. Needless to say, this is also due to developments vis-à-vis indigenous protection over the almost twenty years that separates the two documents, as well as the direct contributions of indigenous peoples to the work on the UNDRIP.

The key provision of the ILO Convention 169 regarding the right to consultation is art.6, paras.1a and 2, which states:

> "1. In applying the provisions of this Convention, governments shall:
>
> (a) *consult the peoples concerned*, through appropriate procedures and in particular through their representative institutions, whenever consideration is being given to legislative or administrative measures which may affect them directly; [...]
>
> 2. The *consultations* carried out in application of this Convention shall be *undertaken*, in *good faith and in a form appropriate to the circumstances, with the objective of achieving agreement or consent to the proposed measures*." [Emphasis added].

In addition, art.15.2 on the exploitation of natural resources by the State, establishes:

> "[...] 2. In cases in which the State retains the ownership of mineral or sub-surface resources or rights to other resources pertaining to lands, *governments shall establish or maintain procedures through which they shall consult these peoples, with a view to ascertaining whether and to what degree their interests would be prejudiced, before undertaking or permitting any programmes for the exploration or exploitation of such resources pertaining to their lands*. The peoples concerned shall wherever possible participate in the benefits of such activities, and shall receive fair compensation for any damages which they may sustain as a result of such activities." [Emphasis added].

And art.17.2 that:

> "[...] 2. The peoples concerned shall be consulted whenever consideration is being given to their capacity to alienate their lands or otherwise transmit their rights outside their own community."

Together with the right of indigenous peoples to participate in decision-making processes, indigenous peoples shall be consulted on the organisation and operation of special training programmes based on the economic environment, social and cultural conditions and practical needs of indigenous peoples (art.22.3), and in the establishment of indigenous educational institutions and facilities (art.27.3). In addition, art.28.1 foresees that, whenever children could not be taught to read and write in their own indigenous language or in the language most commonly used by their community, indigenous peoples shall be consulted on the adoption of measures aimed to ensure teaching in these languages.

Finally, art.16.2 provides that "free and informed consent" is required when a relocation of indigenous peoples is (exceptionally) necessary. When their consent cannot be obtained, appropriate procedures should be adopted by States and guaranteed to indigenous peoples, including public inquiries. Moreover, a fair compensation, including the return to their lands or, if that is not possible, the granting of other comparable lands, should be ensured (art.16, paras.3-5).

Regarding the protection provided by the UNDRIP, the rights of indigenous peoples to both consultation and FPIC are recognized in nine different provisions. In particular, arts. 19 and 32, which foresee both duties upon States. In addition, the nineteenth preambular paragraph reads:

> "*Encouraging* States to comply with and effectively implement all their obligations as they apply to indigenous peoples under international instruments, in particular those related to human rights, in consultation and cooperation with the peoples concerned".

Therefore, Indigenous peoples shall be consulted on effective measures that: Combat prejudices and discrimination toward indigenous cultures and promote tolerance, understanding and good relations among Indigenous peoples and other sectors of the society (art.15.2); and protect indigenous children from economic exploitation or carrying out any hazardous or harmful work (art.17.2).

More broadly, art.19 provides that:

> "Article 19. States shall consult and cooperate in good faith with the indigenous peoples concerned through their own representative institutions in order to obtain their free, prior and informed consent before adopting and implementing legislative or administrative measures that may affect them."

Subsequently, the duty to consult indigenous peoples, and thus their right to be consulted through appropriate procedures and in particular through their representative institutions, is foreseen prior to using their lands or territories for military activities (art.30.2), and –in good faith, i.e., with the aim of obtaining their FPIC– prior to the approval of any project affecting their lands or territories and other resources, particularly in connection with the development, utilization or exploitation of mineral, water, or other resources (art.32.2).

Finally, indigenous peoples shall be consulted by States on the effective measures to be taken to: facilitate the exercise and ensure the implementation of their right to maintain and develop cross-border contacts, relations and cooperation (art.36.2); and achieve the objectives of the Declaration (art.38).

With regard to FPIC, the UNDRIP also foresees the duty of States to obtain it with regard to the exceptional, forced removal of Indigenous peoples from their lands, which also implies a just and fair compensation (art.10); before the adoption or implementation of any legislative or administrative measure likely to affect them, as mentioned above (art.19); and on exceptional storage or disposal of dangerous materials on indigenous peoples' lands or territories (art.29).

Also, the UNDRIP states that effective mechanisms of redress, including restitution, should be provided by States whenever indigenous peoples' cultural, intellectual, religious, and spiritual property is taken without their FPIC (art.11). Moreover, indigenous peoples have a right to redress in those cases in which the lands, territories and resources traditionally owned or otherwise occupied or used by indigenous peoples have been confiscated, taken, occupied, used, or damaged without their FPIC (art.28). These provisions may be seen as an application *a posteriori* and with remedial aims of their right to FPIC.

Finally, art.32, as seen above, requires the FPIC of indigenous peoples prior to the approval of any project likely to affect indigenous peoples' lands or territories and other resources, particularly in connection with the development, utilization or exploitation of mineral, water, or other resources.

Therefore, the rights to consultation and FPIC of indigenous peoples may be summarized in the following table:

	ILO Convention 169	*UNDRIP*
Right to consultation (and UNDRIP, also to FPIC) on legislative or administrative measures likely to affect indigenous peoples	Art.6	Art.19
Right to consultation before undertaking or permitting any programmes for the exploration or exploitation of such resources pertaining to indigenous peoples' lands	Art.15.2	
Right to consultation when indigenous peoples' lands may be alienated	Art.17.2	
Right to consultation and FPIC prior to the approval of any project affecting their lands or territories and other resources, particularly in connection with the development, utilization or exploitation of mineral, water or other resources		Art.32.2
Right to consultation on the organization and operation of special training programmes based on the economic environment, social and cultural conditions and practical needs of indigenous peoples	Art.22.3	
Right to consultation on the establishment of indigenous educational institutions and facilities	Art.27.3	
Right to consultation on the adoption of measures aimed to ensure teaching to read and write in their own indigenous language or in the language most commonly used by the indigenous community	Art.28.1	
Right to consultation prior to using indigenous peoples' lands or territories for military activities		Art.30.2
Right to consultation on implementing the right to maintain and develop cross-border contacts, relations and cooperation		Art.36.2
Right to consultation to achieve the objectives of the Declaration		Art.38
No relocation without F(P)IC	Art.16.2 (only FIC)	Art.10 (full FPIC)
Right to redress if without FPIC (cultural, intellectual, religious, and spiritual property)		Art.11
Right to redress if without FPIC (land)		Art.28
No storage or disposal of hazardous material without FPIC		Art.29

Table 3.1: The rights to consultation and FPIC of indigenous peoples

Although the UNDRIP certainly provides a broader recognition of the right of indigenous peoples to obtain their FPIC as well as the duty to consult indigenous peoples in key cases such as prior to using indigenous lands or territories for military activities, the ILO Convention 169 also foresees a rather incisive right to consultation of indigenous peoples, which is of particular relevance in the Latin American context. In fact, 15 out of 20 Latin

American countries ratified the ILO Convention 169,[952] and, despite the initial misapplication of this right, the debate on the right to consultation of indigenous peoples has been relaunched recently in the subcontinent particularly due to terrible accidents such as those that occurred in Bagua in 2009 (see chapter 4) but also thanks to the adoption of the ILO Convention 169 by Chile in 2008 and the consultations of indigenous peoples carried out since 2009 (see chapter 6), and the adoption by Peru of the Law No. 29785 on the Right to the Prior Consultation of Indigenous peoples in 2011.[953] Additionally, as will be analyzed in chapter 4, the two new Constitutions of both Bolivia and Ecuador have also paved the way for a broader recognition of indigenous peoples' rights and, in particular, to their rights to consultation and FPIC.

To conclude this overview, the other international treaties that recognize the relevance of FPIC for indigenous peoples need to be mentioned.[954]

---

952 In alphabetical order: Argentina (2000), Bolivia (1991), Brazil (2002), Chile (2008), Colombia (1991), Costa Rica (1993), Dominica (2002), Ecuador (1998), Guatemala (1996), Honduras (1995), Mexico (1990), Nicaragua (2010), Paraguay (1993), Peru 1994), and Venezuela (2002). See ratifications at http://www.il o.org/dyn/normlex/en/f?p=1000:11300:0::NO:11300:P11300_INSTRUMENT_ID:312314 [Last access 01.08.2014].

953 In Spanish, "Ley N°29785, Ley del derecho a la consulta previa a los pueblos indígenas u originarios, reconocido en el Convenio 169 de la Organización Internacional del Trabajo (OIT)", at http://www.congreso.gob.pe/ntley/Imagene s/Leyes/29785.pdf [Last access 01.08.2014], followed by the executive regulation with Decree No.001-2012 ("Reglamento de la Ley N° 29785, Decreto Supremo N° 001-2012-MC"), at http://www.trabajo.gob.pe/archivos/file/SNIL/normas/20 12-04-03_001-2012-MC_2221.pdf [Last access 01.08.2014]. For an overview on the Latin American debates on the right to consultation of indigenous peoples, see, Luis Gonzalo Uscátegui Gómez (ed.) *El derecho a la consulta previa en América Latina. Del reconocimiento formal a la exigibilidad de los derechos de los pueblos indígenas*, ILSA-Instituto Latinoamericano de Servicios Legales Alternativos, Bogotà, 2009; for a general analysis of the right to consultation of indigenous peoples of Perù, see Amelia Isabel Alva Arévalo, "Algunas reflexiones sobre los alcances del derecho a la consulta previa post movilización social indígena en la selva peruana", 10(2) *Revista de Investigaciones Políticas y Sociológicas* 2011, pp. 97-116; finally, on the perspectives of the Amazonian indigenous peoples living in Perù, see Silvia Ordoñez Ganoza, "La Relación entre los Pueblos Indígenas de la Amazonía con el Estado Peruano desde la Perspectiva de los Indígenas Awajún de Huampami", 43 *Iberoamericana. Nordic Journal of Latin American and Caribbean Studies* 2013, pp.67-90.

954 Cathal Doyle and Jill Cariño "Making Free, Prior & Informed Consent a Reality. Indigenous Peoples and the Extractive Sector" (2013), at http://www.pip links.org/system/files/Consortium+FPIC+report+-+May+2103+-+web+version.p df [Last access 01.08.2014], pp.7-10. See also Parshuram Tamang, "An Overview

In the Leticia Declaration International Meeting of Indigenous Peoples and Other Forest-dependent Peoples adopted in 1996, it was stated that no activities could be carried out in forests without indigenous peoples' "full and informed consent"[955] and moreover that no traditional knowledge should be used without their "prior informed consent".[956]

In the General Recommendation No.23 of CERD on "Indigenous Peoples" adopted in 1997, it was specified that no decision should be taken without the indigenous peoples' "informed consent".[957]

In the "Akwé: Kon guidelines" of 2004 on the interpretation of benefit-sharing (art.8j) of the Convention on Biological Diversity of 1992, the FPIC of indigenous peoples was considered a required condition for the protection of indigenous peoples' cultures.[958] Additionally, the "Nagoya Protocol on Access to Genetic Resources and the Fair and Equitable Sharing of indigenous Arising from their Utilization to the Convention on Biological Diversity" states that the FPIC of indigenous peoples shall be sought to access both genetic resources (art.6) and traditional knowledge associated with such genetic resources (art.7).[959]

Given the increasing importance of FPIC, in January 2005 the Secretariat of the UN Permanent Forum on Indigenous Issues carried out an "International Workshop on Methodologies regarding Free, Prior and Informed

---

of the Principle of Free, Prior and Informed Consent and Indigenous Peoples in International and Domestic Law and Practices", paper presented at the "International Workshop on Methodologies regarding Free, Prior and Informed Consent and Indigenous Peoples" organized by the Secretariat of the UN Permanent Forum on Indigenous Issue, New York, UN Doc. PFII/2004/WS.2/8, 17-19 January 2005, at www.un.org/esa/socdev/unpfii/documents/workshop_F PIC_tamang.doc [Last access 01.08.2014].

955 Leticia Declaration International Meeting of Indigenous Peoples and Other Forest-dependent Peoples, under the heading of General Principles, 1996, Proposals for Action, para.2, clause No.3.

956 Leticia Declaration, para.6.

957 Committee on the Elimination of Racial Discrimination (CERD), General Recommendation No.23, "Indigenous Peoples", UN Doc. A/52/18, annex V, 18 August 1997, para.4d.

958 Doyle and Cariño, "Making Free, Prior & Informed Consent a Reality …", p.9. See the Convention on Biological Diversity, "Akwé: Kon guidelines", at http://www.cbd.int/doc/publications/akwe-brochure-en.pdf [Last access 01.08.2014].

959 Nagoya Protocol on Access to Genetic Resources and the Fair and Equitable Sharing of Benefits Arising from their Utilization to the Convention on Biological Diversity, 29 October 2010, at http://www.cbd.int/abs/doc/protocol/nagoya-pro tocol-en.pdf [Last access 01.08.2014].

Consent and Indigenous Peoples" convened by Economic and Social Council decision No.2004/287 of 22 July 2004.[960]

Later, the General Comment No.21 of the CESCR of 2009 on the right of everyone to take part in cultural life foresaw respect for FPIC in matters concerning indigenous peoples.[961]

As mentioned in chapter 2, section 2.2, and shown above, in the *Ángela Poma Poma v. Peru* case (2009), the HRC stated that not mere consultation is required, but also the FPIC of all members of the community, in order to ensure the effective participation of indigenous peoples in decision-making processes.[962]

On the side of international enterprises, the FPIC has been recognized, *inter alia*, in the recent report of the International Finance Corporation (IFC), of the World Bank Group, "IFC Performance Standards on Environmental and Social Sustainability", effective as of 1 January 2012, and which requires clients to seek indigenous peoples' FPIC for projects that may have adverse impacts on indigenous communities.[963]

Regarding regional human rights jurisprudence, in addition to the decisions of the Inter-American Court of Human Rights that will be analyzed in the subsequent section 3.2.2.3, the *Endorois v. Kenya* case of 2010 is worth mentioning here, since the African Commission on Human and Peoples' Rights concluded that:

> "[...] [in relation to] any development or investment projects that would have a major impact within the Endorois territory, *the State has a duty not only to consult*

960 Permanent Forum on Indigenous Issues, "Report of the International Workshop on Methodologies regarding Free, Prior and Informed Consent and Indigenous Peoples", UN Doc. E/C.19/2005/3, 17 February 2005. See the other documents of the Workshop at http://undesadspd.org/IndigenousPeoples/MeetingsandWorkshops/InternationalWorkshoponFPIC.aspx [Last access 01.08.2014].

961 Committee on Economic, Social and Cultural Rights, General Comment No. 21, "Right of everyone to take part in cultural life (art. 15, para. 1 (a), of the International Covenant on Economic, Social and Cultural Rights)", UN Doc. E/C.12/GC/21, 21 December 2009, paras.36, 37, and 55.

962 Human Rights Committee, *Ángela Poma Poma v. Peru*, Communication No. 1457/2006, UN Doc. CCPR/C/95/D/1457/2006, 27 March 2009, para.7.6.

963 International Finance Corporation, World Bank Group, "IFC Performance Standards on Environmental and Social Sustainability", 1 January 2012, p.14 and pp.47-52, at http://www.ifc.org/wps/wcm/connect/c8f524004a73daeca09afdf998895a12/IFC_Performance_Standards.pdf?MOD=AJPERES [Last access 01.08.2014]. On the respect of the FPIC of Indigenous peoples in business see Jeremie Gilbert, Helen Tugendhat, Valérie Couillard and Cathal Doyle, "Business, Human Rights and Indigenous Peoples: The Right to Free, Prior and Informed Consent", Forest Peoples Programme, Working Paper Series, April 2009.

> *with the community, but also to obtain their free, prior, and informed consent*, according to their customs and traditions."[964] [Emphasis added]

Finally, it is relevant to stress here that in 2011 John Ruggie, the UN Special Rapporteur on Business and Human Rights, flagged the high financial burdens (up to $30 million per week) due to the disruptions and lawsuits caused by missed opportunities for dialogue between extractive industries and Indigenous peoples in various parts of the world.[965] In the recent report of First Peoples Worldwide, in fact, these financial losses have been further assessed in a number of cases and it has been proved that investors, shareholders, and corporations will minimize their financial risk and maximize their investments if they respected Indigenous peoples rights, in particular FPIC, and work proactively with indigenous communities.[966]

3.3.2.2 The content and implications of the indigenous peoples' rights to Consultation and Free, Prior and Informed Consent (FPIC)

The recent debates on the differences between the right to consultation and to FPIC, particularly at the UN level, tend to focus on three issues, namely that the content and result of the latter is binding whereas the former is not;[967] that FPIC may be considered as an additional element of the right to consultation;[968] and that FPIC is more widely recognised in other international treaties. While the latter two assumptions are widely accepted, the

---

964 African Commission on Human and Peoples Rights, *Centre for Minority Rights Development ("CEMIRIDE") (Kenya) and Minority Rights Group International on behalf of Endorois Welfare Council v. Kenya (Endorois case)*, Communication No.276/2003, 4 February 2010, para.291.

965 Michel Connor, "Business and Human Rights: Interview with John Ruggie", *Business Ethics. The Magazine of Corporate Responsibility*, 30 October 2011, at http://business-ethics.com/2011/10/30/8127-un-principles-on-business-and-human-rights-interview-with-john-ruggie [Last access 03.11.2014].

966 First Peoples Worldwide, "Indigenous Rights Risk Report", 2013, p.3, at http://www.firstpeoples.org/images/uploads/R1KReport2.pdf [Last access 03.11.2014].

967 See, e.g., Raquel Z. Yrigoyen Fajardo, "El Derecho a la Libre Determinación del Desarrollo. Participación, Consulta y Consentimiento", in Marco Aparicio Wilhelmi (ed.), *Los Derechos de los Pueblos Indígenas a los Recursos Naturales y al Territorio. Conflicto y Desafíos en América Latina*, Icaria Editorial, Barcelona, 2011, pp.103-146, p.123.

968 See *infra*, but particularly according to the Inter-American Court of Human Rights in the case *Saramaka People v. Suriname*, Serie C No.172, Judgment of 28 November 2007.

first one seems rather to be the result of a narrow interpretation of the ILO Convention 169, as will be assessed in this section. It is nevertheless true that States tend to grant Indigenous peoples the right to consultation, since they perceive it as a "softer" obligation.[969] However, suffice it to stress here that, according to ILO sources, the (undoubtedly binding) right to consultation is highly relevant and *must* always be carried out for any legislative measures likely to affect Indigenous peoples, including amendments, *inter alia*, to the national constitution, new land laws, property law or land ownership, education, or health.[970]

3.3.2.2.1 The core elements of the right to consultation

According to James Anaya –the (second) Special Rapporteur of the United Nations on the Situation of the Human Rights and Fundamental Freedoms of Indigenous Peoples (abbreviated, since 2010, as Special Rapporteur on the Rights of Indigenous Peoples)– the right to consultation is one of the pillars that safeguards the right of Indigenous peoples to participate in the adoption of measures likely to affect them.[971] In fact, according to the Inter-American Court of Human Rights in the *Saramaka v. Suriname* case of 2007 (see below), the right to participate of indigenous peoples is not embodied by consultation alone, and, together with the FPIC, constitutes the base for exercising the fundamental rights of indigenous peoples.[972]

As for the content of both rights, as seen in the previous subsection, art.6 of the ILO Convention 169 and arts.19, 30.2 and 32.2 of the UNDRIP give

---

969 Amelia Isabel Alva Arévalo, *El Derecho a la Consulta previa de los Pueblos Indígenas en Derecho Internacional*, Cuadernos Deusto de Derechos Humanos, No.76, Universidad de Deusto, Bilbao, 2014, p.97.

970 International Labour Organization, "ILO Convention on Indigenous and Tribal Peoples, 1989 (No 169): A Manual", at http://pro169.org/res/materials/en/ge neral_resources/Manual%20on%20ILO%20Convention%20No.%20169.pdf, p.15.

971 James Anaya, "Comentarios del Relator Especial sobre los derechos de los pueblos indígenas en relación al documento titulado 'Propuesta de gobierno para una nueva normativa de consulta y participación indígena de conformidad a los artículos 6° y 7° del Convenio 169 de la organización Internacional del Trabajo', Chile", November 2012, at http://unsr.jamesanaya.org/docs/special/2012-11-29-unsr-comentarios-a-propuesta-reglamento-consulta-chile.pdf [Last access 01.08.2014], p.9, para.29.

972 Anaya, "Comentarios del Relator Especial ...", para.33, and James Anaya "Annual Report of the Special Rapporteur on the rights of indigenous peoples", UN Doc. A/HRC/21/47, 6 July 2012, para.49.

substantial indications on how the consultations shall be executed. Therefore, core elements for the exercise of this right are as follows:

- Through appropriate procedures (art.6.1a ILO Convention 169; art.30.2 UNDRIP);
- Through their representative institutions (art.6.1a ILO Convention 169; arts.19, 30.2 and 32.2 UNDRIP);
- In good faith (art.6.2 ILO Convention 169; arts.19 and 32.2 UNDRIP);
- In a form appropriate to the circumstances (art.6.2 ILO Convention 169);
- With the aim of achieving agreement or consent (art.6.2 ILO Convention 169) and FPIC (art.16.2 of ILO Convention 169 –although without "prior", and arts.19 and 32.2 of UNDRIP).

In addition, both the Inter-American Court of Human Rights and the ILO Committee of Experts on the Application of Conventions and Recommendations (hereinafter CEACR or ILO Committee) have contributed to shaping further the content of the right to consultation contained in the ILO Convention 169, as has been summarized by Anaya in five crucial elements,[973] as follows:

1. *Prior*, which, as remembered by the Inter-American Court of Human Rights in the Case of the *Saramaka People v. Suriname*, implies that the consultation must be carried out before the realization of a development plan or work/construction affecting Indigenous peoples and more specifically "at the early stages of a development or investment plan, not only when the need arises to obtain approval from the community";[974]
2. *Not reduced to mere information*, as confirmed by the CEACR in a case of Representation under art.24 of the ILO Constitution for incompliance of the ILO Convention 169 by Colombia. In particular, the ILO Committee stated that consultation with indigenous communities involves the establishment of a genuine dialogue between the two parties characterized by transparent mutual communication, understanding, respect and good faith, and the sincere desire to reach an agreement. Therefore,

973 James Anaya, "Principios Internacionales aplicables a la Consulta en relación con la reforma constitucional en Chile", 24 April 2009, pp.5-10, at http://www.ohchr.org/Documents/Issues/IPeoples/SR/InformeConsulta Chile.pdf [Last access 01.08.2014].

974 Inter-American Court of Human Rights, *Saramaka People v. Suriname*, Serie C No.172, Judgment of 28 November 2007, para.133, as cited by Anaya, "Principios Internacionales aplicables…", pp.5-6, paras.21-22.

a meeting of mere information cannot be considered in accordance with the provisions of the ILO Convention 169.[975]

3. *In good faith and at a level of mutual trust*, which means, as stated by the CEACR in a case of Representation under art.24 of the ILO Constitution for incompliance of the ILO Convention 169 by Guatemala, the need to deploy efforts to try to achieve consensus on procedures, to facilitate access through broad information, and to create a climate of mutual trust that is conducive to productive dialogue between the parties.[976]
4. *Adequate*, in the following threefold meaning:
   a. *Realized through indigenous representative institutions*, as described by the ILO in two cases of Representation under Art.24 of the ILO Constitution for incompliance of the ILO Convention 169 by Brazil and Mexico. In the first case, the ILO Committee asserted that the opinions of the different indigenous peoples involved in the consultation should be taken into account.[977] In the case of Mexico, by recognizing the diversity of indigenous peoples, the CEACR clarified that the ILO Convention 169 does not impose a model of representative institution, but requires that it reflects the indigenous peoples' own internal process. However, the ILO Committee also offers a reminder that it is essential to ensure that consultation takes place with truly representative institutions of the peoples concerned. In fact, the principle of representation

975 International Labour Organization/Organización Internacional del Trabajo, *Informe del Comité establecido para examinar la reclamación en la que se alega el incumplimiento por Colombia del Convenio sobre pueblos indígenas y tribales, 1989 (núm. 169), presentada en virtud del artículo 24 de la Constitución de la OIT por la Central Unitaria de Trabadores (CUT)*, GB.276/17/1, GB.282/14/3 (2001) para.90, as cited by Anaya, "Principios Internacionales aplicables…", para.21, p.5.

976 International Labour Organization/Organización Internacional del Trabajo, *Informe del Comité encargado de examinar la reclamación en la que se alega el incumplimiento por Guatemala del Convenio sobre pueblos indígenas y tribales, 1989 (núm. 169), presentada en virtud del artículo 24 de la Constitución de la OIT por la Federación de Trabajadores del Campo y la Ciudad (FTCC)*, GB.294/17/1, GB.299/6/1 (2007), para.53, as cited by Anaya, "Principios Internacionales aplicables…", para.23, p.6.

977 International Labour Organization/Organización Internacional del Trabajo, *Informe del Comité encargado de examinar la reclamación en la que se alega el incumplimiento por Brasil del Convenio sobre pueblos indígenas y tribales, 1989 (núm. 169), presentada en virtud del artículo 24 de la Constitución de la OIT por el Sindicato de Ingenieros del Distrito Federal (SENGE/DF)*, GB.295/17, GB.304/14/7 (2009), para.42, as cited by Anaya, "Principios Internacionales aplicables…", para.28, pp.7-8.

is an essential component of the right to consultation, but it is difficult to determine who represents a particular community, as also seen above in section 3.3.1.3. Thus, the CEACR concludes that a consultation process can only be considered appropriate if it has been realized through indigenous institutions or the true representatives of the affected communities, something that shall be verified or verifiable;[978]
b. *Held in a comprehensible language*, so that the consulted indigenous peoples are able to understand what is being asked, in accordance with art.12 of the ILO Convention 169;[979]
c. *And carried out with a proper allocation of time*, which means that the consultation may be considered adequate when it is executed in a reasonable temporal dimension that allows a high participation of indigenous peoples by taking into account material and institutional obstacles,[980] as well as by pondering the socio-cultural patterns and decisional timeframes of the indigenous peoples concerned.[981]

5. *Systematic and transparent*, as recently specified by the ILO Committee: The regime provided by the ILO Convention 169 does not imply the application of the right to consultation solely in specific cases, but rather a systematic implementation of the Convention in coordination and cooperation with Indigenous peoples through the gradual establishment of specific consultative mechanisms and bodies.[982]

---

978 International Labour Organization/Organización Internacional del Trabajo, *Informe del Comité encargado de examinar la reclamación en la que se alega el incumplimiento por México del Convenio sobre pueblos indígenas y tribales, 1989 (núm. 169), presentada en virtud del artículo 24 de la Constitución de la OIT por el Frente Auténtico del Trabajo (FAT)*, GB.283/17/1, GB.289/17/3 (2004), para.102, as cited by Anaya, "Principios Internacionales aplicables…", p.8, para.29.

979 Anaya, "Principios Internacionales aplicables…", pp.8-9, para.32.

980 *Ibid.*

981 International Labour Organization/Organización Internacional del Trabajo *Informe del Comité establecido para examinar la reclamación en la que se alega el incumplimiento por Colombia…*, para.79, as cited by Anaya, "Principios Internacionales aplicables…", p.9, para.33.

982 International Labour Organization/Organización Internacional del Trabajo *Informe de la Comisión de Expertos en Aplicación de Convenios y Recomendaciones*, Informe III (Parte 1A), Conferencia Internacional del Trabajo, 96th meeting, Geneva, 2007, p.600, as mentioned by Anaya, "Principios Internacionales aplicables…", pp.9-10, para.37.

In the above-mentioned "Report of the International Workshop on Methodologies regarding Free, Prior and Informed Consent and Indigenous Peoples", consultation is described as one of the key components of the consent procedure, and that it should be as follows:

- Undertaken in good faith;
- By establishing a genuine dialogue between the parties that would allow them to find proper solutions;
- In an environment of mutual respect;
- With sufficient time and an effective system of inter-communication among the parties;
- Through indigenous peoples' own freely-chosen representatives and customary or other institutions.[983]

Regarding the content of the consultation, Anaya declared that the outcome of the consultation is not legally binding in *stricto sensu*, as affirmed by the ILO Committee in the above mentioned case of Representation under Art.24 of the ILO Constitution for incompliance of the ILO Convention 169 by Mexico in 2004.[984] However, although the CEACR concluded that "both the National Congress and the state legislatures were not unaware of the opinions of the indigenous peoples with respect to the reforms, but were not obliged to accept them", it also added that "[i]t would have been helpful if they [the National Congress and the state legislatures] had established a mechanism to try to a*chieve agreement or consent concerning the measures proposed*" [emphasis added].[985] The same applies to the above-mentioned case of Representation under art.24 of the ILO Constitution for incompliance of the ILO Convention 169 by Colombia, in which the ILO Committee stressed that consultation with indigenous communities involves the sincere desire to reach an agreement.[986] In fact, art.6.2 of the ILO Convention 169 requires that an agreement or consent should be reached in good faith.

983 UN Permanent Forum on Indigenous Issues, "Report of the International Workshop on Methodologies regarding Free, Prior and Informed Consent and Indigenous Peoples", 17 February 2005, UN Doc. E/C.19/2005/3, para.47.

984 Anaya, "Principios Internacionales aplicables…", p.10, para.38, by citing International Labour Organization/Organización Internacional del Trabajo, *Informe del Comité encargado de examinar la reclamación en la que se alega el incumplimiento por México…*, para.105.

985 International Labour Organization/Organización Internacional del Trabajo, *Informe del Comité encargado de examinar la reclamación en la que se alega el incumplimiento por México…*, para.74.

986 International Labour Organization/Organización Internacional del Trabajo, *Informe del Comité encargado de examinar la reclamación en la que se alega el incumplimiento por Colombia…*, para.77.

Moreover, as will be explained in the case of Chile in chapter 6, some consultations have taken place where the outcome had legally-binding effects.

3.3.2.2.2 Free, Prior and Informed Consent (FPIC)

On the content of FPIC, the abovementioned "Report of the International Workshop on Methodologies regarding Free, Prior and Informed Consent and Indigenous Peoples", highlighted that the three components (free, prior and informed) imply respectively:

- That no coercion, intimidation or manipulation is exercised upon indigenous peoples;[987]
- That consent is sought sufficiently in advance before the granting of any authorization or start of the activities, by respecting the time required by indigenous peoples for their "consultation/consensus",[988] and own decision-making processes; this also implies that the FPIC should be sought in phases of assessment, planning, implementation, monitoring, evaluation, and closure of a project;[989]
- That full information is provided and

> "covers (at least) the following aspects:
>
> a. The nature, size, pace, reversibility and scope of any proposed project or activity;
>
> b. The reason(s) for or purpose(s) of the project and/or activity;
>
> c. The duration of the above;
>
> d. The locality of areas that will be affected;
>
> e. A preliminary assessment of the likely economic, social, cultural, and environmental impact, including potential risks and fair and equitable benefit-sharing in a context that respects the precautionary principle;
>
> f. Personnel likely to be involved in the execution of the proposed project (including indigenous peoples, private sector staff, research institutions, government employees and others);
>
> g. Procedures that the project may entail".[990]

Moreover, after assessing that consultation (and participation) are core elements of the consent process, the "Report of the International Workshop on

---

987 UN Permanent Forum on Indigenous Issues, "Report of the International Workshop on Methodologies regarding Free, Prior and Informed Consent and Indigenous Peoples", para.46.

988 *Ibid.*

989 *Ibid.*, para.48.

990 *Ibid.*, para.46.

Methodologies regarding Free, Prior and Informed Consent and Indigenous Peoples" adds also that:

- Indigenous peoples should indicate which representative institutions or representatives are entitled to express consent on behalf of the affected peoples or communities;
- Accurate information should be given to indigenous peoples in a form and language that are accessible and comprehensible, as well as by taking into account indigenous oral traditions and languages.[991]

Finally, verifications of a fair respect and application of FPIC as described above should be ensured by specific procedures and that consent could be withdrawn whenever the elements of the FPIC have not been respected.[992]

This would lead to the assumption that FPIC is a right "to say no", as also concluded –in the case of proposed development projects of extractive industries– by the UN Workshop on Indigenous Peoples, Private Sector Natural Resource, Energy and Mining Companies and Human Rights held in 2001.[993] More recently, the Guidelines of the UN Collaborative Programme on Reducing Emissions from Deforestation and Forest Degradation in Developing Countries (UN-REDD programme) of 2013 foresee that "consent" is a freely given decision that may be "yes" or "no" and given and withheld in any phase of the project. Therefore, it is not a one-off-process.[994]

3.3.2.2.3 Consultation and FPIC

It is clear that the right to consultation and FPIC share many common elements and, more correctly, the former is essential to achieve the latter. FPIC has been referred to both as a "principle" and a "right". In one of his latest reports, the second Special Rapporteur on the Rights of Indigenous Peoples

---

991 *Ibid.*, para.48.

992 *Ibid.*.

993 Commission on Human Rights, Sub-Commission on Prevention of Discrimination and Protection of Minorities, Working Group on Indigenous Populations, "Report of the Workshop on Indigenous Peoples, Private Sector Natural Resource, Energy and Mining Companies and Human Rights", UN Doc. E/CN.4/Sub.2/AC.4/2002 /3, 17 June 2002, para. 52.

994 UN-REDD programme, "Guidelines on Free, prior and Informed Consent", January 2013, at http://www.un-redd.org/Launch_of_FPIC_Guidlines/ta bid/10597 6/Default.aspx or directly at www.unredd.net/index.php?option=com_docman &task=doc_download&gid=8717&Itemid=53 [Last access 01.08.2014].

James Anaya referred to the FPIC as "principle",[995] while other authors argue that it is a "right" and deal with it as such.[996] This is probably due to the formulation contained in the UNDRIP, which does not consider the FPIC as a right. However, it is a duty upon the States, which implies the individuation of a right-holder, in this case the Indigenous peoples. In addition, in the case of doubts about the legally-binding status of the UNDRIP, FPIC is considered by both the HRC and the CESCR, as well as academics, under the right to self-determination, as seen in the previous chapter (section 2.2). Moreover, the right to consultation is enshrined in the undoubtedly binding ILO Convention 169 and it is also considered an expression of the right to self-determination. Therefore, to assert that the outcome of a consultation would not be binding, whereas the FPIC would be, is a contradiction in terms. Given that the realization of a consultation with no effects would have little sense, suffice it to say here that, particularly in the formulation of the (binding) ILO Convention 169, especially in the Latin American context, the right to consultation must provide effects, at least to some extent, which are to achieve the agreement or consent of the concerned indigenous peoples (art.6.2, ILO Convention 169). In fact, similarly to the debates on participatory democracy,[997] which see consultations as a means to further legitimize public authorities' decisions over issues of public interest and prevent acts of protest by the citizens –and thus ameliorate the relations between the national/local government and the citizenry– the realization of proper and fair consultations not only would entitle indigenous peoples to a more equal treatment but would also decrease their discontent and frustration and thus enhance social security, which is what, in general, political participation aims to achieve. Hence, as recently pointed out by the CEACR, consultation should become a mean of genuine dialogue, social

995 James Anaya, "Report of the Special Rapporteur on the rights of indigenous peoples. Extractive industries and indigenous peoples", UN Doc. A/HRC/24/41, 1 July 2013, paras.26-36.

996 E.g., Jeremie Gilbert, Helen Tugendhat, Valérie Couillard and Cathal Doyle, "Business, Human Rights and Indigenous Peoples ..."; Raquel Z. Yrigoyen Fajardo, "El Derecho a la Libre Determinacion del Desarrollo ..."; and Andrea Carmen, "The Right to Free, Prior and Informed Consent. A Framework for Harmonious Relations and New Processes of Redress", in Jackie Hartley, Paul Joffe and Jennifer Preston (eds.), *Realizing the UN Declaration on the Rights of Indigenous Peoples: Triumph, Hope and Action*, Purich Publishing, Saskatoon, 2010, pp.120-134.

997 See, *inter alia*, Diana C. Mutz, *Hearing the Other Side. Deliberative versus Participatory Democracy*, Cambridge University Press, Cambridge, New York, 2006.

cohesion, and a tool for the prevention and resolution of conflicts.[998] However, as stated above, the right to consultation must provide effects, at least to some extent, which are to achieve the agreement or consent of the affected indigenous peoples (art.6.2, ILO Convention 169).

3.3.2.3 Jurisprudence vis-à-vis the right to consultation and FPIC of Indigenous peoples

As well as the *Endorois case* cited above (section 3.3.2.1), the Inter-American Court of Human Rights has recently adopted two pivotal decisions vis-à-vis the right to consultation and FPIC of indigenous peoples, namely in the cases of *Saramaka People v. Suriname* (2007)[999] and *Kichwa Ingenous People of Sarayaku v. Ecuador* (2012).[1000]

The first case, brought before the Court by the Association of Saramaka Authorities and twelve Saramaka captains, concerned the alleged violations committed by the State of Suriname in conceding logging and mining concessions in the Upper River region, where the Saramaka people live. In particular, the applicants claimed their rights to use and enjoy the territory that they have traditionally occupied and used, to judicial protection, to own property according to their communal traditions, and to adopt domestic legal provisions to ensure and guarantee these rights had been violated by the State.[1001] The claimants also sought consideration over the ongoing adverse effects related to the flooding of Saramaka territory in the 1960s, which the Court did not consider admissible given the timeframe and that some controversies related to the dam were still pending before the Suriname domestic courts.[1002] Therefore, the Court considered the facts alleged between 1997 and 2004, a period during which Suriname had conceded at least four logging concessions and several mining concessions to both Saramaka and non-Saramaka members and foreign companies on the territory traditionally

---

998 ILO Committee of Experts on the Application of Conventions and Recommendations, "General Observation on Convention No. 169, 79th Session, 2008", 2009, p.60.

999 Inter-American Court of Human Rights, *Saramaka People v. Suriname*, Serie C No.172, Judgment of 28 November 2007.

1000 Inter-American Court of Human Rights, *Kichwa Ingenous People of Sarayaku v. Ecuador*, Serie C. No.245Judgment of 27 June 2012.

1001 Inter-American Court of Human Rights, *Saramaka People v. Suriname*, p.2, para.2.

1002 *Ibid.*, pp.4-5, paras.11-17.

owned by the Saramaka.[1003] Thanks to a systemic interpretation technique of both arts.1 of the two Covenants and art.27 of the ICCPR and since Suriname had not ratified the ILO Convention 169 as in other cases before the Inter-American Court of Human Rights,[1004] the Court considered violations of the right to property under art.21 of the American Convention on Human Rights.[1005] Therefore, the Court concluded that the Saramaka people were protected under international human rights law that "secures the right to the communal territory they have traditionally used and occupied".[1006] Eventually, the Court found that Suriname did violate arts.21.1 and 25 of the American Convention on Human Rights.[1007] For the aims of this study, the following points are of particular interest.

First, the Court pointed out three safeguards for the Saramaka people's right to property aimed at preserving, protecting and guaranteeing the special relationship of the Saramakas with their territory and against the issuance of concessions within their territory that may put at risk their survival as a tribal people, namely:

> "First, the State must ensure the *effective participation* of the members of the Saramaka people, in conformity with their customs and traditions, regarding any development, investment, exploration or extraction plan [...] within Saramaka territory. Second, the State must guarantee that the Saramakas will receive a *reasonable benefit* from any such plan within their territory. Thirdly, the State must ensure that *no concession* will be issued within Saramaka territory *unless and until* independent and technically capable entities, with the State's supervision, perform *a prior environmental and social impact assessment*."[1008] [Emphasis added].

In addition, the Court affirmed that

> "the State has a duty to actively consult with said community according to their customs and traditions [...]. This duty requires the State to both accept and disseminate information, and entails constant communication between the parties. These consultations must be in good faith, through culturally appropriate procedures and

1003 *Ibid.*, p.42, para.142.

1004 Marcos A. Orellana, "Saramaka People v. Suriname. Judgement (Preliminary Objections, Merits, Reparations, and Costs), Serie C, No.172. Inter-American Court of Human Rights, November 28, 2007", 102 *American Journal of International Law* 2008, pp.841-847, p.843. The first case in recognizing indigenous peoples' collective right to land is Inter-American Court of Human Rights, *Mayagna (Sumo) Awas Tingni Community v. Nicaragua*, Serie C No. 79, Judgment of 31 August 2001 (see chapter 1).

1005 Inter-American Court of Human Rights, *Saramaka People v. Suriname*, p.28, para.95.

1006 *Ibid.*, p.28, para.96.

1007 *Ibid.*, p.54, para.185.

1008 *Ibid.*, p.38, para.129.

with the objective of reaching an agreement. Furthermore, the Saramakas must be consulted, in accordance with their own traditions, at the early stages of a development or investment plan, not only when the need arises to obtain approval from the community, if such is the case. Early notice provides time for internal discussion within communities and for proper feedback to the State. The State must also ensure that members of the Saramaka people are aware of possible risks, including environmental and health risks, in order that the proposed development or investment plan is accepted knowingly and voluntarily. Finally, consultation should take account of the Saramaka people's traditional methods of decision-making";[1009]

and that

> "regarding large-scale development or investment projects that would have a major impact within Saramaka territory, the State has a duty, not only to consult with the Saramakas, but also to obtain their free, prior, and informed consent, according to their customs and traditions."[1010]

Also, the Court considered that there is a difference between consultation and FPIC, and therefore that

> "the safeguard of effective participation that is necessary when dealing with major development or investment plans that may have a profound impact on the property rights of the members of the Saramaka people to a large part of their territory must be understood to additionally require the free, prior, and informed consent of the Saramakas, in accordance with their traditions and customs."[1011]

The very recent case of *Kichwa Ingenous People of Sarayaku v. Ecuador* (hereinafter abbreviated as *Sarayaku v. Ecuador*) regarded a petition against Ecuador brought before the Inter-American Court of Human Rights by the Association of the Kichwa People of Sarayaku, the Center for Economic and Social Rights, and the Center for Justice and International Law. Violations of the rights of the Sarayaku Kichwa people to: Property (art.21 of the American Convention on Human Rights); life, judicial guarantees and judicial protection (arts. 4, 8, and 25, respectively); freedom of movement and residence (art.22); and personal integrity (art.5) were alleged by the plaintiffs. The claims concerned the granting of concessions of oil exploration and exploitation activities and the consequent use of explosives in the Sarayaku Kichwa territory without having consulted them or obtaining their consent.[1012] The Sarayaku Kichwa live in different parts of the province of Pastaza, along the banks of the Bobonaza River in the Amazonian region of Ecuador,[1013] in one undivided parcel of land (Block 9), which was granted

1009 *Ibid.*, p.40, para.133.
1010 *Ibid.*, p.40, para.134.
1011 *Ibid.*, p.41, para.137.
1012 Inter-American Court of Human Rights, *Sarayaku v. Ecuador*, pp.4-5, paras.1-3.
1013 *Ibid.*, p.16, para.52.

to all the communities of the Bobonaza River –thus including them– by Ecuador in 1992.[1014] The Sarayaku Kichwa people have approximately 1,200 members, which are further subdivided into five different groups.[1015] Their subsistence is based on traditional activities such as collective family-based farming, hunting, fishing and gathering.[1016] In 2004, the Sarayaku registered their Statute before a governmental body, which included indications on the dimension of their territory, which may be increased later.[1017]

In 1995, after a call for proposals, the State granted a concession to the State Oil Company of Ecuador (PETROECUADOR), consociated with the *Compañía General de Combustibles S.A.* and *Petrolera Argentina San Jorge S.A.*, for the exploration and exploitation of hydrocarbons in Block No.23 of the Amazonian basin.[1018] These companies therefore had two obligations, namely to prepare an Environmental Impact Assessment and to make every effort to preserve the existing ecological balance also in the surrounding area of the block granted.[1019] However, the former was completed in 1997 but was never executed.[1020] The latter was not taken seriously into account: The companies' lawyers tried to obtain Sarayaku consent by offering them different types of doubtful monetary compensations,[1021] and ignored the Ecuadorian Constitution and domestic legislation which, in addition to the ILO Convention 169, requires consultations with indigenous peoples and compensations according to official tables provided by the State.[1022] Afterwards, the Sarayaku fell under the protection of the national Ombudsman,[1023] and an *Amparo* constitutional protection claim was put be-

1014 *Ibid.*, p.18, para.61.
1015 *Ibid.*, p.16, para.52.
1016 *Ibid.*, p.17, para.54.
1017 *Ibid.*, pp.18-19, para.61.
1018 *Ibid.*, pp.19-20, paras.63-64.
1019 *Ibid.*, p.19, para.67.
1020 *Ibid.*, p.19, para.69.
1021 *Ibid.*, p.21, para.73.
1022 *Ibid.*, p.22, paras.76-77. Apart art.84.5 of the Ecuadorian Constitution of 1998, which requires the consultation of Indigenous peoples on all natural resources exploitations projects likely to affect them, the Ecuadorian laws to which the Court refers are the following: "Promotion of Investment and Citizen Participation Act", adopted by Decree Law 2000-1, Registration number 144 of August 18, 2000; and art.9 of the "Regulations to substitute the Environmental Regulations for Hydrocarbon Operations", adopted by Executive Decree 1215, Official Record 265 of February 13, 2001.
1023 Inter-American Court of Human Rights, *Sarayaku v. Ecuador*, p.23, para.86.

fore the First Civil Judge of Pastaza against the oil companies in 2002. However, the hearing never took place.[1024] After a report of the Ecuadorian Human Rights Committee, which underlined serious damages perpetrated by the companies to the indigenous peoples, their sacred sites and their surrounding environment,[1025] and other serious facts, such as alleged threats to the community by the companies in question,[1026] in 2009 the activities were blocked.[1027] Notwithstanding this and the new protection of indigenous peoples' rights provided for in the Ecuadorian Constitution that entered into force in 2008, another agreement was signed between the State and the companies in 2010.[1028]

Eventually, the Court found that Ecuador violated the rights to consultation, to indigenous communal property, and to cultural identity, in accordance with art.21 of the American Convention on Human Rights on the right to property; the rights to life and to personal integrity (arts.4 and 5), which according to the Court had been severely jeopardized; and the right to judicial guarantees and judicial protection (arts.8 and 25).[1029]

For the aims of this study, is of utmost importance to stress that, by showing how the right to consultation of indigenous peoples is increasingly enshrined in both international and domestic legislations and jurisprudence,[1030] the Court concluded that

> "*the obligation to consult*, in addition to being a treaty-based provision, *is also a general principle of international law*"[1031] [emphasis added].

In addition, the Court stated that:

> "Given that the State must guarantee these rights to consultation and participation at *all stages of the planning and implementation of a project* that may affect the territory on which an indigenous or tribal community is settled, or other rights essential to their survival as a people, *these dialogue and consensus-building processes must be conducted from the first stages of the planning or preparation of the proposed measure, so that the indigenous peoples can truly participate in and influence the decision-making process*, in accordance with the relevant international standards. In this regard, the State must ensure that *the rights of indigenous peoples are not ignored in any other activity or agreement reached with private individuals,*

1024 *Ibid.*, p.24, paras.87-91.
1025 *Ibid.*, pp.27-28, paras.105-106.
1026 *Ibid.*, pp.28-29, paras.107-113.
1027 *Ibid.*, p.30, para.117.
1028 *Ibid.*, p.31, para.123.
1029 *Ibid.*, p.39, para.341.
1030 *Ibid.*, pp.41-45, para.164.
1031 *Ibid.*, p.45, para.164.

> *or in the context of decisions of the public authorities that would affect their rights and interests.*"[1032] [Emphasis added].

Moreover, by recalling the precedent case of *Saramaka People v. Suriname*, the Court set some parameters to assess whether the actions of the Ecuadorian State vis-à-vis the Sarayaku community respected those

> "minimum standards and essential requirements of a valid consultation process with indigenous communities [...] [which are]: (a) the prior nature of the consultation; (b) good faith and the aim of reaching an agreement; (c) appropriate and accessible consultation; (d) the environmental impact assessment, and (e) informed consultation".[1033]

Inter alia, the Court notably stressed that the consultation is an obligation of the State, which cannot be avoided by delegating it to a company[1034] and that

> "the State's failure to conduct a serious and responsible consultation [...] encouraged, by omission, a climate of conflict [...]. Although it is true that numerous meetings took place, [...] it is also evident that there was a disconnect between these efforts and a clear determination to seek consensus, which encouraged situations of tension and dispute".[1035]

Thus, in conclusion:

> "The State, by failing to consult the Sarayaku People on the execution of a project that would have a direct impact on their territory, *failed* to comply with its obligations, under the principles of international law and its own domestic law, *to adopt all necessary measures to guarantee the participation of the Sarayaku People, through their own institutions and mechanisms and in accordance with their values, practices, customs and forms of organization, in the decisions made regarding matters and policies that had or could have an impact on their territory, their life and their cultural and social identity, affecting their rights to communal property and to cultural identity.*"[1036] [Emphasis added].

In sum, in these two aforementioned decisions the Inter-American Court of Human Rights recognized the following points:

- In case of large scale projects, three safeguards shall be respected, namely, (1) the effective participation of indigenous peoples in the plans, (2) a reasonable benefit for indigenous peoples deriving from such plans, and (3) that no concession shall be given until an independent body carries out an environmental and social impact assessment;

1032 *Ibid.*, p.46, para.167.
1033 *Ibid.*, p.50, para.178.
1034 *Ibid.*, p.53, para.187.
1035 *Ibid.*, p.56, para.198.
1036 *Ibid.*, p.66, para.232.

- The duty of States to actively consult the indigenous peoples requires: Accepting and disseminating information, including raising awareness on all possible environmental and health risks; constant communication between the parties; good faith; and culturally appropriate procedures and with the objective of reaching an agreement;
- The consultation must be carried out at the early stages of a development or investment plan, not when the need to obtain the consent from the community arises; this implies internal discussion within the communities according to traditional methods of decision-making and proper feedback to the State;
- The right to consultation is a general principle of international law, increasingly recognized by States and domestic courts;
- Consultation is an obligation of the State, which cannot be avoided by delegating it to a company;
- An improper consultation may lead to internal conflicts;
- And, by failing to comply with the right to consultation, a State does not respect the right of Indigenous peoples to participate in decision-making processes in the adoption of measures likely to affect them.

3.3.3 Indigenous peoples' rights to autonomy/self-government and to preserve their traditional institutions

In this section, the second part of the proposed *composite right to political participation of indigenous peoples* is addressed. Therefore, indigenous peoples' rights to autonomy/self-government and to preserve their traditional institutions will be tackled here. The relevant international provisions contained in both the ILO Convention 169 and the UNDRIP will be first analyzed (section 3.3.3.1). The focus of the UNDRIP on the right to autonomy has already been discussed in chapter 2, section 2.2.2.5, while the general debate on the concept of autonomy/self-government, particularly vis-à-vis minorities, has been considered in section 3.2 of this chapter. However, the debate on the right to autonomy of indigenous peoples needs to be introduced here (section 3.3.3.2). Finally, legally established or recognized experiences of indigenous autonomies at domestic level will be discussed (section 3.3.3.3). In many of these forms of self-government, indigenous traditional institutions are not only preserved but also serve as the main bodies that run these autonomies. This explains the interdependence of these sub-rights.[1037]

3.3.3.1 International provisions recognizing the right to autonomy/self-government of indigenous peoples and to preserve and/or establish their traditional institutions

Although the ILO Convention 169 does not recognize the right to autonomy of indigenous peoples as the UNDRIP does in its art.4 (see chapter 2, section 2.2.2.5) –due to the timeframe and the developments in indigenous peoples rights occurred between the adoption of the two documents– the fifth preambular paragraph of the former affirms:

> "*Recognizing* the aspirations of these peoples to exercise control over their own institutions, ways of life and economic development and to maintain and develop their identities, languages and religions, within the framework of the States in which they live".

In addition, art.1.1b declares that, *inter alia*, the "peoples" to which the ILO Convention 169 applies to are those that "retain some or all of their own social, economic, cultural and political institutions".

Furthermore, a number of provisions relate to the promotion, respect, safeguard, development of and the right to retain indigenous institutions, as follows:

- Art.2.2b, according to which governments shall include measures to protect the rights of indigenous peoples with regard to indigenous customs, traditions, and institutions;
- Art.4.1., which provides that indigenous "persons", institutions, property, labor, cultures and environment shall be safeguarded by appropriate measures;
- Art.5.b, which foresees that the integrity of indigenous values, practices, and institutions shall be respected;
- Art.6.1c, which affirms that the means, including the necessary resources, for the full development of indigenous peoples' own institutions and initiatives should be established;

1037 The sections 3.3.3.2, 3.3.3.3 and 3.3.3.4 are based on parts of the author's previous article Alexandra Tomaselli, "*Autonomía Indígena Originaria Campesina* in Bolivia: Realizing the indigenous autonomy?", 1 *European Diversity and Autonomy Papers* (EDAP) 2012, pp.1-56, at http://www.eurac.edu/edap [Last access 26.02.2015].

- Art.7.1.1, which, as seen, recognizes the right of indigenous peoples to decide their own priorities for the process of development as it also affects their institutions;
- Art.27, which enshrines the right of indigenous peoples to establish their own educational institutions and facilities;
- And, finally, art.8, paras.1-2, which importantly states:

> "1. In applying national laws and regulations to the peoples concerned, due regard shall be had to their customs or customary laws.
>
> 2. These peoples *shall have the right to retain their own customs and institutions*, where these are not incompatible with fundamental rights defined by the national legal system and with internationally recognised human rights. Procedures shall be established, whenever necessary, to resolve conflicts which may arise in the application of this principle." [Emphasis added]

As to the UNDRIP, apart from the aforementioned and analyzed art.4 (chapter 2, section 2.2.2.5), arts.5 and 20.1 on indigenous institutions are also particularly important, as follows:

> "Article 5. Indigenous peoples *have the right to maintain and strengthen their distinct political, legal, economic, social and cultural institutions*, while retaining their right to participate fully, if they so choose, in the political, economic, social and cultural life of the State."
>
> "Article 20. 1. Indigenous peoples *have the right to maintain and develop their political, economic and social systems or institutions*, to be secure in the enjoyment of their own means of subsistence and development, and to engage freely in all their traditional and other economic activities." [Emphasis added].

3.3.3.2 The debate on the right to autonomy of indigenous peoples

The claim for autonomy has been on the indigenous organizations' agendas in Latin America since the late 1980s, although much confusion surrounded this concept.[1038] The indigenous right to autonomy was included in proposals for a declaration approved by indigenous representatives and organizations in Geneva on 26 July 1985 in preparation for the fourth session of the UN Working Group on Indigenous Populations (WGIP), i.e., the 1985 Declaration of Principles on the Rights of Indigenous Peoples. In this Declaration, which was redrafted and resubmitted for the fifth session of the WGIP the following year, among the proposed indigenous peoples' rights,

1038 Díaz-Polanco, *Autonomía regional: La autodeterminación de los pueblos indios*, p.150; Rosa de la Fuente, *La autonomía indígena en Chiapas: Un nuevo imaginario socio-espacial,* Catarata, Madrid, 2008, p.70.

principle No.2 included the right to autonomy or self-government whereas the full independence was not achievable.[1039] In the Quito Declaration in 1990 –at the first continental meeting of indigenous peoples– autonomy, in terms of self-government and control over territory, was also claimed as a way to realize the right to self-determination but within the frame of the "nation-State".[1040] Thanks to the following wave of constitutional reforms in Latin America (see chapter 4), the autonomy discourse gained momentum especially in this region.[1041]

At international level, the debate on indigenous autonomies was then (re)launched in 1991, when a group of experts met in Greenland under the auspices of the United Nations Human Rights Commission.[1042] In particular, they emphasized the potential of autonomy and self-government for indigenous peoples as a means of realizing their right to self-determination and to foster national unity, thus securing, rather than threatening, the respect of the principle of territorial integrity.[1043] In particular, in para.2 of section 5 ("Conclusions and Recommendations"), it is clearly stated that:

> "Indigenous Peoples have the right to self-determination as provided for in the International Covenants on Human Rights and public international law and as a consequence of their continued existence as distinct peoples. [...] An integral part of this [right] is the inherent and fundamental right to autonomy and self-government."

According to this report, the core elements of an indigenous autonomy are: The political will (and openness) on the part of governments to establish it (para.25); a legal anchorage via constitutional reforms, treaties, statutory provisions or other legal arrangements (para.27); a clear subdivision of powers given to indigenous peoples' autonomies in order to avoid conflicts

1039 Díaz-Polanco, *Autonomía regional: La autodeterminación de los pueblos indios*, p.163; see also James Anaya, *Indigenous Peoples in International Law*, Oxford, New York, Oxford University Press, 2nd edition, 2004, pp.298-299.

1040 Díaz-Polanco, *Autonomía regional: La autodeterminación de los pueblos indios*, p.163. See the Declaration of Quito (Ecuador) by the Indigenous Alliance of the Americas on 500 Years of Resistance, July 1990, at http://www.native web.org/papers/statements/quincentennial/quito.php#declaration

1041 Francisco López Bárcenas, "Autonomías indígenas en América: de la demanda de reconocimiento a su construcción", in Mikel Berraondo (ed.), *Pueblos Indígenas y Derechos Humanos*, Universidad de Deusto, Bilbao, 2006, pp.423-450, p.435.

1042 Lapidoth, *Autonomy: Flexible Solutions to Ethnic Conflicts*, p.18. See the Commission on Human Rights, "Report of the Meeting of Experts to Review the Experience of Countries in the Operation of Schemes of Internal Self-Government for Indigenous Peoples", Nuuk (Greenland), 24-28 September 1991, UN Doc. E/CN.4/1992/42, 25 November 1991.

1043 Commission on Human Rights, "Report of the Meeting ...", paras. 16, 21, 24, 35, 52 and 54 and section 5, "Conclusions and Recommendations".

of competences with the State (para.30); indigenous jurisdiction over lands, resources, economic matters, cultural, and other affairs (para.28); mechanisms for cross-border cooperation for those indigenous peoples living in bordering States (para.29); and fiscal autonomy, i.e., financial powers (e.g., to levy taxes, forms of revenue, secured funding; para.40). Needless to say, rights over land, as well as control over renewable and non-renewable resources, are the prerequisite for indigenous autonomy (para.35).[1044] In this sense, much attention is paid to the more environmentally-sustainable indigenous practices of land management (paras.35-39), which were also recognized one year later during the United Nations Conference on Environment and Development.[1045] The use of "personal autonomy", although mainly referring to cultural autonomy, is very briefly mentioned in the case of the Sami in Norway, whose parliament, at that time, had just started to work (para.47).[1046] Last, but not least, the direct participation of indigenous peoples in (national) planning and development projects shall be fostered (para.41).

Recently, Henriksen has classified indigenous peoples autonomies into four types: "(1) territorial autonomy, (2) institutional autonomy without clear territorial affiliation, implemented through traditional or modern indigenous peoples' institutions, (3) objectively limited autonomy, e.g. limited to language and culture, (4) autonomy relative to legislative regulations and the administration of justice, e.g., by virtue of accepting indigenous peoples' application of customary law in the regulation of certain matters

1044 All these elements are then also inserted in Commission on Human Rights, "Report of the Meeting ...", section 5, "Conclusions and Recommendations". In particular, para.3 of section 5 states: "Self-government, self-administration and self-management of indigenous peoples constitute elements of political autonomy."

1045 Principle 22 in "Annex I – Rio Declaration on Environment and Development" of the Report of the United Nations Conference on Environment and Development, Rio de Janeiro, 3-14 June 1992, UN Doc. A/CONF.151/26, at http://www.un.org/documents/ga/conf151/aconf15126-1annex1.htm [Last access 23.02.2015]; UN Environment Programme, "Agenda 21", chapter No.26 "Recognising and Strengthening the Role of Indigenous People and their Communities" at http://www.unep.org/Documents.Multilingual/Default.asp?DocumentID=52&ArticleID=74&l=en [Last access 23.02.2015].

1046 On the Sami parliaments, see Eva Josefsen, "The Saami and the National Parliaments – Channels for Political Influence", 2 *Gáldu Čála Journal of Indigenous Peoples Rights* 2007, pp.5-28, at http://www.galdu.org/go vat/doc/national_parlaments.pdf [Last access 05.08.2014]; Alexandra Tomaselli and Petra Granholm, "The Frustrations of the Right to Political Participation of Minorities: Practical Limitations in the Case of the Nordic Sámi and the Roma", 8 *European Yearbook of Minority Issues* 2009, 2011, pp.149-185.

in indigenous communities."[1047] Thus, apart from the first type, the last three types may be grouped under the concept of NTA (and, mainly, cultural autonomy) mentioned above in section 3.2.2.2.

In her work on indigenous (territorial) autonomies, Loukacheva has identified the following characteristics:[1048]

- strong, voluntary will of the population to achieve autonomy;
- existence of particular geographical, demographic, or historical factors;
- cultural, linguistic, and ethnic distinctiveness;
- creation of a legislative body elected by local residents in a democratic way and capable of enacting its own legislation, as well as the establishment of an executive body;
- provision of conditions for economic sustainability, a financial base versus fiscal dependency on central/federal authorities, and pragmatic expectations of future financial independence and liability for managing its own affairs;
- the desire and ability of all residents of the autonomous entity to be a part of existing, or developing, structures and institutions, making them more amenable to peoples' aspirations and needs.[1049]

3.3.3.3 Forms of indigenous autonomies

Apart *de facto* autonomy arrangements of indigenous peoples living in remote areas, formally recognized (territorially-based) indigenous autonomies may be found (at least) in the Americas (Bolivia,[1050] Canada, Colombia, Ecuador, Mexico, Nicaragua, Panamá, the USA, and Venezuela); in Asia (Bangladesh and Indonesia); and in Europe with the case of Greenland.

In the Central American countries, the autonomy arrangements resulted from post-conflict negotiations, although in very different contexts and timeframes.[1051] In particular, the well-known Comarca Kuna Yala, the indigenous territorial autonomy established on the Panama coast, was firstly

1047 John B. Henriksen, "Sami Self-Determination. Autonomy and Self-Government: Education, Research and Culture", 2 *Gáldu Čála Journal of Indigenous Peoples Rights* 2009, pp.7-40, p.14.

1048 Natalia Loukacheva, "On Autonomy and Law", *Globalization and Autonomy Online Compendium Research Articles*, 19 July 2005, at http://globalautonomy.ca/global 1/article.jsp?index=RA_Loukacheva_AutonomyLaw.xml [Last access 05.08.2014], "Introduction".

1049 *Ibid.*, "Concluding Remarks".

1050 See chapter 5.

1051 Loukacheva, "On Autonomy and Law", "Concluding Remarks".

(legally) recognized by the 1928 constitutional reform (art.4)[1052] and by Law No.59 enacted in 1930, after the 1925 Tule Revolution. Following this, Law No.2, enacted in 1938, recognized the *Comarca* (known as San Blas until the adoption of Law No.99 in 1998) and Law No.16, enacted in 1953, regulated and recognized the general Kuna Congress and its local congresses. However, there are a total of five *Comarcas* in Panama. Pursuant to art.5 of the 1972 Panama Constitution and subsequent amendments, special territorial arrangements may be created by law. Thus, the Kuna Yala and the other *Comarcas* have been established by domestic legislation, as follows: Comarca Embera Wounaan by Law No.22/1983; Comarca Madugandi by Law No.24/1996; Comarca Ngobe-Bugle by Law No.10/1997; Comarca Wargandi by Law No.34/2000.[1053]

In Nicaragua, the 1987 Constitution (art.5.3) recognized autonomy arrangements for the indigenous communities of the Atlantic Coast. The Autonomy Statute was adopted by Law No.28 adopted the same year.[1054] The autonomy discourse followed the Nicaraguan Revolution (*Revolución Popular Sandinista*), which reached its peak in 1979. An Autonomy National Commission was formed on 6 December 1985 and worked on the aforementioned statute.[1055] Nevertheless, the Nicaraguan arrangements that divide the coast into two autonomous units (North and South), also mentioned above in the case of *YATAMA v. Nicaragua*, cannot be described as an indigenous autonomy as such. Indeed, a proportional system regulates the election of the autonomous bodies, which govern a territory where the non-indigenous population (Afro-descendants and mainly *Mestizos*) represent the majority.[1056]

1052 Panama Constitution of 1894 and subsequent amendments in 1925 and 1928.

1053 For an overview of the *Comarca* system, see Artinelio Hernandez, Atilio Martínez, Bernal Castillo and Irik Limnio, "Informe Nacional de Panama", LATAUTONOMY Project Report, 2003; see also James Howe, "The Kuna of Panama: Continuing Threats to Land and Autonomy", in David Maybury-Lewis (ed.), *The Politics of Ethnicity: Indigenous Peoples in Latin American States*, Harvard University Press, Cambridge MA, 2002.

1054 Josefina Hidalgo Blandón et al., "Informe Nacional: Regiones Autónomas del Atlántico de Nicaragua", LATAUTONOMY Project report, 2004, p.7.

1055 Manuel Ortega Hegg, "La Autonomia Regional en Nicaragua", LATAUTONOMY Project Report, 2003, pp.17-20; for in-depth analyses on the Nicaraguan case, see Luciano Baracco (ed.), *National Integration and Contested Autonomy: The Caribbean Coast of Nicaragua*, Algora Publications, New York, 2011.

1056 Rodríguez Piñero-Royo, "Political Participation Systems Applicable to Indigenous Peoples", pp.322 and 332. The only guarantee for indigenous peoples is the at-least-one 'indigenous seat' pursuant to art. 19 of the Nicaraguan Autonomy Statute.

In Mexico, the 2001 constitutional reform explicitly recognized indigenous peoples' rights to self-determination and, through its exercise, to autonomy (art.2.5a).[1057] However, the implementation of this right is left to each federal unit (art.2.5). Chiapas is well known for the implementation of indigenous autonomies. In particular, in the late 1980s, the formation of the Tojolabal indigenous autonomy through the establishment in Chiapas of a Permanent Assembly composed of approximately 300 indigenous leaders was a pioneering experience. Inspired by the developments in Nicaragua, this experience was promoted to re-establish the traditional indigenous authorities that had stepped down, especially with the introduction of the State and church institutions. After 1994, however, the Zapatista Movement also played an undeniable role in the "autonomic" discourse.[1058] Additionally, in the State of Oaxaca, approximately 75% of the municipalities vote for their councilors according to their own regulatory systems,[1059] as guaranteed by the Oaxaca Constitution in arts.16 and 25 and by art.113 of Decree 185 of 1992.[1060]

In South America, the Colombian constitutional reforms of 1991 also included forms of indigenous autonomy, drawing upon the Hispanic institution of the *resguardos* system recognized by Law No. 89 in 1890.[1061] Arts.286 and 287 of the reformed constitution define the territorial units (departments, districts, municipalities and indigenous territories) that are autonomous (also according to art.1), thus introducing the notion of Indigenous Territorial Unit (*Entitad Territorial Indígena*), which are also known as *resguardos indígenas* (art.329) and subsequently regulated by Law No. 160 enacted in 1994.[1062]

1057 Laura Giraudo and Juan Martín Sánchez, "Neoindigenismo y movimientos indígenas en América Latina", in Carlos Malamud, Paul Isbell and Concha Tejedor (eds.), *Anuario Iberoamericano* 2008, Ediciones Pirámide, Madrid, 2008, pp.63-76, p.66.

1058 De la Fuente, *La autonomía indígena en Chiapas: Un nuevo imaginario socio-espacial*, pp.67-69. On Chiapas and the complex Mexican case, see also Araceli Burguete Cal y Mayor (ed.), *Indigenous Autonomy in Mexico,* IWGIA Document No. 94, IWGIA, Copenhagen, 2000.

1059 Secretariat of the UN Permanent Forum of Indigenous Issues, "Examination of the situation of indigenous peoples and their participation in democracies ...", para.64, p.14.

1060 *Decreto 185, Código de Instituciones Políticas y Procedimientos Electorales de Oaxaca* (CIPPEO), 12 February 1992 and following amendments.

1061 Rodríguez Piñero-Royo, "Political Participation Systems Applicable to Indigenous Peoples", pp.329-330.

1062 See Law No.160/1994 at http://www.secretariasenado.gov.co/senado/basedoc/ley_0160_1994.html, and chapter XIV on the *resguardos indígenas* at

In the case of Ecuador, the 1998 Constitution recognized, *inter alia*, the (collective) right to develop and maintain indigenous peoples' traditional forms of creating and exercising authority (art.84.7), as well as indigenous peoples' territories (*circunscripciones*) (art.224), which were to be ruled by autonomous bodies (arts.228 and 241).[1063] The existing and new indigenous peoples territories (*circunscripciones*) are recognized in the new constitution adopted in 2008 (art.60). They may become 'special arrangements' (art.242) and, after a referendum, autonomous units (art.257; see also art.238).

In Venezuela, the 1999 Constitution also mentions indigenous municipalities (art.169), but refers primarily to the Indigenous Law enacted in late 2005 (*Ley Orgánica de Pueblos y Comunidades Indígenas*, Law No.38,344/2005).

Analyzing the Latin-American experiences, Rodríguez Piñero-Royo has advanced a subdivision of the existing indigenous autonomies in the subcontinent into three categories, namely: The "multi-ethnic" regional system, i.e., autonomy arrangements for a given territory with a "mixed" (indigenous and non-indigenous) population (e.g., Nicaragua and Mexico);[1064] demarked indigenous territories with formal recognition (e.g., Colombia and Panama); and, finally, the "communitarian autonomy" at village level through the "indigenization of the municipal space", as in, according to the author, the cases of Mexico, Ecuador and Bolivia.[1065] However, Bolivia is probably a variant of the second and third categories, since the new system

---

http://www.secretariasenado.gov.co/senado/basedoc/ley_0160_1994_pr001.html [Last access 05.08.2014]. On the Colombian case, see Astrid Ulloa, "Colombia: Autonomías indígenas en ejercicio. Los retos de su consolidación", in Miguel González, Araceli Burguete Cal y Mayor and Pablo Ortiz-T. (eds.), *La autonomía a debate: Autogobierno indígena y Estado plurinacional en América Latina*, FLACSO, GTZ, Ministerio Federal de Cooperación Económica y Desarrollo, IWGIA, CIESAS, Universidad Intercultural de Chiapas, Quito, 2010, pp.149-176, at http://www.iwgia.org/iwgia_files_publications_files/0468_Libro_autonomia_a_debate_eb.pdf [Last access 05.08.2014].

1063 On the Ecuadorian case, see Pablo Ospina Peralta, "Estado plurinacional y autogobierno territorial: Demandas indígenas en Ecuador", in Miguel González, Araceli Burguete Cal y Mayor and Pablo Ortiz-T. (eds.), *La autonomía a debate: Autogobierno indígena y Estado plurinacional en América Latina*, FLACSO, GTZ, Ministerio Federal de Cooperación Económica y Desarrollo, IWGIA, CIESAS, Universidad Intercultural de Chiapas, Quito, 2010, pp.201-218.

1064 This could also be the case of Greenland, except for the fact that the indigenous population is more than 85% of the total (see below).

1065 Rodríguez Piñero-Royo, "Political Participation Systems Applicable to Indigenous Peoples", pp.333-334.

of indigenous autonomies also includes territorial arrangements wider than a municipality, despite demarcation problems (see chapter 5, section 5.4).

Indigenous peoples' territorial arrangements established in Asia, namely the Chittagong Hill Tracts (CHT) in Bangladesh and the special autonomy regimes in Indonesia, had been created mainly to settle conflicts. As to the former, the Chittagong Hill Tracts Peace Accord was signed on 2 December 1997 between the indigenous rebel forces and the government. It contained, *inter alia*, many amendments of the Hill District Local Government Council Acts enacted in 1989,[1066] thus devolving powers to the Hill District Councils –now to be elected and not appointed (art.B.6)– over land, "tribal law" and social justice, and education (art.B.34). In addition, a regional council with 22 members –of which two-thirds are to be indigenous (art.C.3)– and with administrative and consultation powers within the CHT was created (section C). Although this agreement is quite advanced, it has remained basically unimplemented due to on-going militarization, immigration, and land-taking in the area.[1067] As to Indonesia, special arrangements for autonomy in Papua and Aceh were established in 2001 and 2005, respectively.[1068] Indigenous local authorities, self-government and legislation over, *inter alia*, land management, social services and local development were recognized in both laws.[1069] However, human rights violations vis-à-vis indigenous peoples in Papua persist nowadays, and in Aceh –where the prior conflict was more intense– the lowering of expectations in relation to the peace accord is fuelling new violent actions.[1070]

1066 Rangamati Hill District Local Government Council Act, 1989; Bandarban Hill District, Local Government Council Act, 1989; and Khagrachari Hill District Local Government Council Act, 1989.

1067 Rodríguez Piñero-Royo, "Political Participation Systems Applicable to Indigenous Peoples", p.336. On the Bangladeshi case, see Asian Indigenous and Tribal Peoples Network (AITPN), "Implementation of CHT Peace Accord: Will they, Won't they?", 4(1-2) *Indigenous Rights Quarterly* 2009, at http://www.aitpn.org/IRQ/Vol-IV/issue_1-2/story04.html [Last access 05.08.2014].

1068 Special Autonomy Law for the Papua province, Law No. 21/2001 of 23 October 2001; and Law No. 11/2006 on the Governing of Aceh of 11 June 2005, both cited by Rodríguez Piñero-Royo, "Political Participation Systems Applicable to Indigenous Peoples", p.337, notes 144 and 146, respectively.

1069 See arts.1d, f, l and p; 19; 43; 49; 51; 56-66 of the Special Autonomy Law for the Papua province; and arts.1.7; 1.10; 1.16; 16-17; 96 and 98 of the Law on the Governing of Aceh as cited by Rodríguez Piñero-Royo, "Political Participation Systems Applicable to Indigenous Peoples", p.337, notes 146-151.

1070 Rodríguez Piñero-Royo, "Political Participation Systems Applicable to Indigenous Peoples", pp.337-338. On the Indonesian cases, see Esther Heidbüchel, *The West*

The reservations system in US was born as a form of subjugation of Native Americans, but, according to the Indian Reorganization Act (or "Indian New Deal") adopted on 18 June 1934, they became quasi forms of self-government with powers over internal affairs and formalized judicial systems. The adoption of the "Tribal Self-Governance Demonstration Project" by the US Congress on 22 December 1987 led to bilateral negotiations and the signing of the "Self-Governance Compacts and Annual Funding Agreements", formally allowed access to the management and planning of programmes of tribal governments.[1071] However, the real and effective functionality of the reservations in general and the Tribal Councils, in particular, as apparently just "toy parliaments",[1072] is highly contested[1073] and the overall system is "much discredited".[1074]

Canada and Greenland also have forms of, or potential, indigenous autonomies.[1075] In the former, the Nunavut territory and self-government were established by the "Nunavut Land Claims Agreement" of 1993. However, recent research highlighted that this is still far from being called a success, as many socio-economic challenges have not yet been resolved.[1076] In Greenland, the "Act on Greenland Self-Government" entered into force on 21 June 2009, after the successful referendum held the previous November and replacing the home rule granted in 1979.[1077] Denmark retained foreign affairs and defence powers, while Greenland finally obtained powers of self-rule over, *inter alia*, judicial affairs and natural resources. In a territory

---

Papua Conflict in Indonesia: Actors, Issues and Approaches, Johannes Herrmann J&J-Verlag, Wettenberg, 2007.

1071 Rodríguez Piñero-Royo, "Political Participation Systems Applicable to Indigenous Peoples", p.330.

1072 Ronald West, "The American Companion Report", in Mark D. Dole and Ronald West, *The Right of Self-Determination of Peoples and its Application to Indigenous Peoples in the USA*, Nomos, Baden-Baden, 2000, pp.67-111, p.79.

1073 For a recent and complete analysis of the complex US case, see Bruce Duthu, *American Indians and the Law*, Viking, New York, 2008.

1074 Rodríguez Piñero-Royo, "Political Participation Systems Applicable to Indigenous Peoples", p.330.

1075 On both cases, see Natalia Loukacheva, *The Arctic Promise: Legal and Political Autonomy of Greenland and Nunavut,* University of Toronto Press, Toronto, Buffalo, London, 2007.

1076 See André Légaré, "Canada's Experiment with Aboriginal Self-Determination in Nunavut: From Vision to Illusion", in 15(2-3) *International Journal on Minority and Group Rights* 2008, pp.335-367.

1077 On Greenland (old) home rule, see Lise Lyck, "Greenland: Ten Years of Home Rule", in 25(155) *Polar Record* 1989, pp.343-346.

where over 85 per cent of the population is Inuit,[1078] it is suggested that indigenous peoples have, in principle, a great potential to rule Greenland's self-government.[1079]

3.3.3.4 Final considerations on indigenous peoples and autonomy

To conclude, having examined both theory and practice, some common features of indigenous autonomies may be suggested. It goes without saying that what follows is not an exhaustive list. Rather, on the contrary, the aim is to stimulate further reflection and debate.

Territory: Given the indigenous peoples' (generally) strong connection with the land, a TA seems preferable to NTA arrangements. Nevertheless, NTAs (e.g., an indigenous education board) shall not be excluded *a priori*, especially either for those territories inhabited by both indigenous and non-indigenous populations or where the members of indigenous peoples are dispersed within the country. Additionally, the ILO Convention 169 foresees the participation of the traditional authorities with regard to indigenous customs, traditions, and institutions, property, labor, cultures and environment, own educational institutions and facilities, and to decide their own priorities. This, in sum, may form part of NTA systems for indigenous peoples. Finally, as mentioned in the case of minorities, both TA and NTA arrangements may coexist and work.[1080]

Rights over the land and over renewable and non-renewable natural resources: The respect and full application of these rights are strictly connected with the previous element (territory). States shall avoid land relocation, as this would imply a loss of livelihoods and culture and, ultimately, would pose a threat to indigenous peoples' survival. If indigenous peoples

---

1078 Sara Olsvig, "Greenland", *in* International Work Group for Indigenous Affairs, *The Indigenous World 2011*, Copenhagen, 2011, pp.22-28, p.22, at http://www.IWGIA.org/IWGIA_files_publications_files/0454_THE_INDIGE-NOUS_ORLD-2011_eb.pdf [Last access 05.08.2014].

1079 On these recent developments, see Mark Nuttall, "Self-Rule in Greenland: Towards the World's First Independent Inuit State?", 3-4 *Indigenous Affairs* 2008, at http://www.IWGIA.org/IWGIA_files_publications_files/IA_3-08_Greenland.p df [Last access 05.08.2014].

1080 The NTA arrangements were present, e.g., in the Mexican debate with regard to solely migrant and/or urbanized Indigenous peoples, or those living abroad. De la Fuente, *La autonomía indígena en Chiapas: Un nuevo imaginario socio-espacial,* p.79.

(legitimately) agreed to the transferred,[1081] land restoration and distribution of benefits derived from natural resources' exploitation should be guaranteed to them. Additionally, fair environmental policies shall be pursued.

Customary law and their own institutions: The respect for and the application of traditional indigenous peoples' political organizations, as seen above, their own institutions and justice systems, within or outside the state system (e.g., as a form of municipality as in Bolivia or their own institutions recognized by law as in Panama's *Comarcas*) are other key elements. In some cases, this may almost be a *condicio sine qua non* to preserve indigenous cultures. However, one of the most problematic aspects linked to the application of indigenous peoples' customary law is where their law is contrary to human rights standards. In addition, other problems arise with regard to their laws' interaction and coordination with the State justice system. As in the case of Bolivia, the limit to the respect of human rights standards and a law defining what falls under the courts' or the indigenous peoples' justice systems' competences may be a solution.[1082] However, each case should be seriously analyzed before advancing any legal arrangement.

Financial aspects: As underlined by the theories examined, the financial burden of indigenous peoples' autonomies shall be guaranteed, also via special powers (e.g., to levy taxes) as suggested by the 1991 Nuuk experts' meeting.

Education and culture: It goes without saying that these aspects are of the utmost importance to preserve indigenous peoples' language, religion, customs, and other cultural features, and thus should be part of an indigenous autonomy's powers.

However, the precondition for territorial and non-territorial indigenous autonomy, as stated by the 1991 Nuuk experts' meeting, is the political will and openness on the part of governments to create and to fully and transparently implement an autonomy arrangement for the Indigenous peoples living within their countries.

1081 The term 'legitimately' here is used in the sense of obtaining their free, prior and informed consent via a fair consultation.

1082 The Bolivian Constitution states clearly the supremacy of human rights standards over the constitutional provisions and the need to interpret the latter according to the former (see arts.13, para. IV; 14, para. III; 256; and 410, para. II). The Jurisdictional Law (Law No.073/2010) *Ley de Deslinde Jurisdiccional*, enacted on 29 December 2010, contains respect for fundamental rights (art. 5) and, in particular, the absolute prohibition of lynching and the death penalty. See chapter 5.

3.3.4 Final considerations on the recognition of the *composite right of political participation of indigenous peoples*

This section explored how the sub-rights that compose the proposed *composite right of political participation of indigenous peoples* are recognized in specific international instruments of protection of indigenous rights such as the ILO Convention 169 and the UNDRIP. The decisions of the Inter-American Court of Human Rights in the cases *YATAMA v. Nicaragua* (2005), *Saramaka People v. Suriname* (2007), and *Sarayaku v. Ecuador* (2012) have also been analyzed since they recognized judicially the need to ensure Indigenous peoples' rights to participation in elections and decision-making processes, as well as their right to consultation. Besides the participation through Indigenous peoples' representation in State bodies or in other public posts –including in decision-making processes and in the judiciary, both at national and local level –the CEACR of the ILO and other UN Bodies have substantially framed the content of both the rights to consultation and FPIC. Furthermore, the latter also finds recognition in other international treaties, such as the 1996 Leticia Declaration, the CERD General Recommendation No.23, in the 2004 "Akwé: Kon guidelines" on the interpretation of benefit-sharing (art.8j) of the Convention on Biological Diversity of 1992, and the "Nagoya Protocol on Access to Genetic Resources and the Fair and Equitable Sharing of Benefits Arising from their Utilization to the Convention on Biological Diversity" (arts.6-7). Finally, in addition to the conceptual debates presented in chapter 2 (section 2.2.2.5) and section 3.2 of this chapter, this section discussed further indigenous peoples' rights to autonomy/self-government arrangements and the preservation of indigenous institutions and gave a brief overview of several formally-recognized indigenous autonomies (Canada, Colombia, Ecuador, Mexico, Nicaragua, Panamá, USA, and Venezuela in the Americas; Bangladesh and Indonesia in Asia; and Greenland in Europe).

3.4 Concluding remarks

This chapter focused on the recognition under international soft and hard law of a *composite right of political participation of indigenous peoples* and identified elements that could fine-tune this concept. As seen in chapter 2, sections 2.2.4 and 2.2.5, the *composite right* proposed here descends from the right to self-determination and, without limiting the scope of the latter, refers to a combination of (1) (a) ad hoc indigenous political rights, thus indigenous peoples' representation in State's bodies or in other public posts, including in decision-making processes and in the judiciary, both at national and local level, but also their (b) right to consultation and to (c) FPIC on the one hand, and (2) to indigenous autonomy/self-government, as well as the preservation of their own traditional institutions on the other hand.

This chapter demonstrated that these sub-rights are fully recognized not only in international human rights law, but also in minority protection and, more specifically and importantly, in indigenous international instruments such as the ILO Convention 169 and the UNDRIP. Furthermore, the recent jurisprudence of the Inter-American Court of Human Rights (*YATAMA v. Nicaragua* (2005), *Saramaka People v. Suriname* (2007), *Sarayaku v. Ecuador* (2012)) have contributed to hardening the three components of (a) their participation in decision-making in decisions likely to affect them, with particular attention to access to elections of indigenous peoples and formation of indigenous political parties, and thus their representation; (b) their right to consultation; and to (c) their FPIC. Likewise, both the CESCR in its General Comment No.21 of 2009 and the HRC in the case of *Ángela Poma Poma v. Peru* (2009)[1083] have flagged their importance by requiring (a) the participation of indigenous peoples in the design and implementation of laws and policies likely to affect them, (b) that participation of indigenous peoples in the decision-making process must be effective, and (c) that not mere consultation is carried out, but (d) the FPIC of all members of the community is finally obtained. In particular, the reasoning by both the Inter-American Court of Human Rights and the HRC in the abovementioned decisions demonstrated the interdependence of these rights. This has also been pointed out by the Programme of Action of the UN Second International Decade of the World's Indigenous Peoples (2005-2014) and, more recently, by the Expert Mechanism on the Rights of Indigenous Peoples and the UN Permanent Forum on Indigenous Issues. Additionally, despite the debates on whether the outcome of the consultation is binding –which, as seen above, would be a contradiction in terms– the practice of providing consultation *and* FPIC in megaprojects affecting indigenous peoples is increasingly required by both UN bodies and multinational companies worldwide. Similarly, both the right to consultation and FPIC have been sufficiently defined by both UN and ILO bodies, as well as the Inter-American Court of Human Rights, as requiring full and not merely superficial information, including a preliminary assessment of all potential risks; a proper allocation of time; a language understandable to indigenous peoples; and taking into

1083 For further details, see chapter 2, section 2.2.2.2 and chapter 3, section 3.3.2.1.

account the cultural and social patterns of the indigenous peoples concerned. Lastly, both the right to consultation and FPIC must be: Systematic and transparent and exercised prior to the commencement of and during any project likely to affect indigenous community; in good faith and at a level of mutual trust; realized through indigenous representative institutions; with no use of coercion, intimidation or manipulation; and aimed at reaching an agreement or a consent, including the right "to say no".

Regarding the second aspect of the composite right proposed here, as seen in chapter 2, section 2.2, the right to autonomy has been gradually recognized and may become an international standard, at least for indigenous peoples (and minorities), as the extensive State practice in different parts of the world clearly illustrate. As seen above, the peculiarity of indigenous autonomies, then, is the combination of preserving and applying both national/constitutional arrangements together with traditional institutions and customary law.

Hence, the aforementioned international soft and hard law touching upon the elements of the *composite right* proposed here show an increasing international interest and concern vis-à-vis the participation rights of indigenous peoples. This is due to the difficulties faced by indigenous peoples in having an effective say in their domestic political arena. However, as seen in this chapter, a number of mechanisms may be applied to ensure this participation and the effective application of these rights. These range from those designed to ensure indigenous peoples' representation, e.g., by the allocation of reserved seats in parliamentary assemblies to *ad hoc* parliamentary/local assemblies' procedures, including (various degrees of) the right to veto or, at least, a reinforced enactment procedure. In addition, fair and transparent consultations and the requirement of FPIC, as described above, enhance the chances of indigenous peoples of having a say on projects likely to affect them. Finally, indigenous autonomies and the preservation of indigenous institutions epitomize indigenous peoples' local spaces for control and management over their lands and natural resources, their socio-cultural and economic development, and, thus, of their lives.

Therefore, by grouping these sub-rights and enhancing indigenous peoples' participation at all levels, the *composite right of indigenous political participation* presented here is primarily proposed as a tool to answer indigenous peoples' claims and to embody one expression of the multi-faceted right to self-determination of indigenous peoples. However, considering the growing international and national interest in the subject and the empowerment of indigenous peoples' movements, particularly in Latin America (see chapter 4), this *composite right* may also become a solution of compromise acceptable for States to thus promote peaceful relations and mutual understanding between indigenous peoples and other sectors of the society. This, in principle, should also enhance stability and security. How this *composite right* is recognized and applied at domestic level and whether it may also become one of the expressions, or better, as mentioned, one of the effective applications of the right to self-determination of indigenous peoples will be explored subsequently in concrete case studies (chapters 5 and 6).[1084]

Thus, the proposed *composite right to political participation of Indigenous peoples*, as mentioned, may be subdivided into the twofold concept of

1. Participation through indigenous peoples' representation in State bodies or in other public posts, including in decision-making processes and in the judiciary, both at national and local level, as well as their rights to consultation and free, prior and informed consent (FPIC); and
2. Participation through autonomy/self-government arrangements and the preservation of indigenous institutions.

Basic human political rights, including direct and indirect electoral rights, and the fundamental freedoms of expression, assembly, and association are relevant for both levels and constitute the basis of the exercise of the *composite right to political participation of indigenous peoples*. Questions of representation are raised at both levels but are of primary importance especially in terms of the participation in decision-making processes. However, this type of participation needs to be conceived more broadly, as seen in the previous sections, and thus also includes the allocation of public posts to indigenous peoples in the judiciary as well as in other public bodies. Consultations and FPIC are considered instruments of participation in decision-making processes since they embody a way to guarantee that indigenous peoples have a say in projects and national policies that are likely to affect them. Finally, systems of (mainly, territorial rather than non-territorial) indigenous autonomies/forms of self-government, as mentioned, are of particular importance since they likely become local spaces that are controlled and managed by indigenous peoples, who may enjoy powers over their

1084 As mentioned in the chapter 2, the right of indigenous peoples to participate at the decision-making level at international level is not addressed in this work. However, the legitimacy of indigenous peoples' participation at international level has recently been explored by Charters, who, inter alia, argued that indigenous peoples should participate not in all decisions as States, but certainly when the adoption of certain measures is likely to affect them. Charters, "A Self-Determination Approach to Justifying Indigenous Peoples' Participation ...", pp.222 and 240.

lands and natural resources and socio-cultural and economic development, thus determining their future and their lives.

Ultimately, the proposed *composite right* certainly embodies a collective right. This is clear regarding the case of the sub-rights to consultation and FPIC on one hand and the rights to autonomy/self-government and the preservation of indigenous institutions on the other. However, the *ad hoc* indigenous political rights (such as participation in State bodies) are also considered here as a collective expression of indigenous peoples. Hence, the individual rights of members of indigenous peoples to participate in public life are considered as parallel but not part of this proposed *composite right to political participation of indigenous peoples*.

It is important to stress that the author is conscious that the *composite right to political participation of indigenous peoples* proposed here certainly belongs to a Western liberal human rights matrix. Nevertheless, where some of the political rights proposed here have been applied, the level of social exclusion of indigenous peoples has decreased, at least in the Latin American context.[1085] Therefore, as mentioned, this *composite right* is proposed with the aim of enhancing the application of indigenous rights through the promotion of their political participation more specifically, as well as finding a solution of compromise with States.

Hence, the proposed *composite right to political participation of indigenous peoples* may be summarized graphically in the following scheme, which will be used to assess the case studies (chapters 5-6).

1085 Ströbele-Gregor, "Autoridad, poder y liderazgo …", p.86.

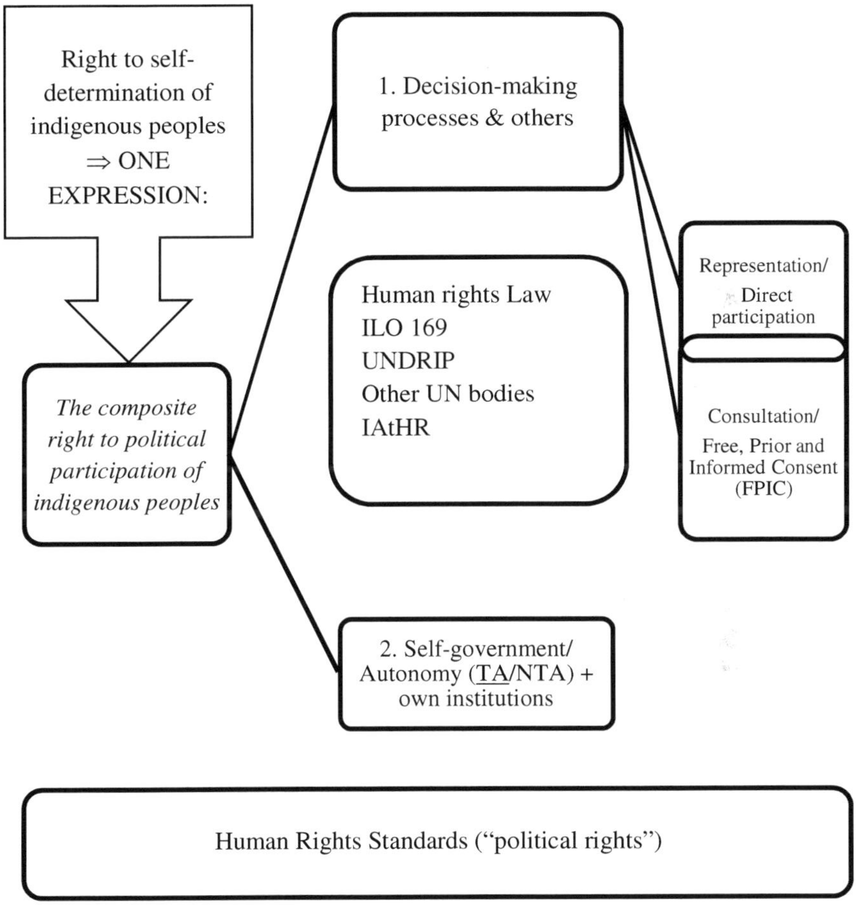

Fig. 3.2: The Composite Right to Political Participation of Indigenous Peoples

Source: Own elaboration

4. The peculiar Latin American context: Regional protection of indigenous rights and indigenous movements

At the dawn of the first "*grito de independencia*" (call for independence) on 10 August 1809 in Quito (Ecuador), indigenous peoples in Latin America likely did not imagine that their conditions would worsen following the independence wars with the Spanish Crown's *Virreinatos* (viceroyalties).[1086] After suffering massive losses in both human and territorial terms, systems of special legislations, such as local parliaments and bilateral agreements, had regulated the relations among colonizers and the natives until then.[1087] Notwithstanding the acquisition of citizenship and of (formal) equality before the law as per a Decree enacted by the Spanish Parliament (*Cortes*) in 1810,[1088] the aspirations of the then-called Creoles[1089] to establish "new nations", however, included a recognition of the "*Indios*"[1090] for

1086 The viceroyalties were established around 1550 and lasted until the wars of independence in the early 1800s. There were four of them: The Viceroyalty of New Spain, which included present-day Mexico, the southern-west territories of United States, and all of Central America; the Viceroyalty of New Granada, which roughly comprised present-day Panama, Colombia, and parts of Venezuela and Ecuador; the Viceroyalty of Peru, in the current territories of Peru, part of Ecuador and the Brazilian Amazon rainforest, and the northern part of Chile (the other part of the territory was not "conquered" yet); and finally, the Viceroyalty of the Río de la Plata, which included present-day Argentina, Bolivia, Paraguay, and Uruguay. See Patricio Hidalgo Nuchera, "Expansión, gobierno y defensa de las Indias", in Juan Bosco Amores Carredano (ed.), *Historia de América*, Editorial Ariel, Barcelona, 2006, pp.287-325, pp.313-320.

1087 Hidalgo Nuchera, "Expansión, gobierno y defensa de las Indias", p.317 and ff.

1088 Laura Giraudo, *La questione indigena in America Latina*, Carocci, Roma, 2009, p.25.

1089 The term "Creole" is here used in its historical connotation, i.e., to refer to the descendants of Spaniards that were born in the Americas. Giraudo, *La questione indigena in America Latina*, p.16.

1090 Rodolfo Stavenhagen, "Indigenous Peoples and the State in Latin America: An Ongoing Debate", in Rachel Sieder, *Multiculturalism in Latin America. Indigenous Rights, Diversity and Democracy*, Palgrave Macmillan, New York 2002, pp.24-43, pp28-29. The term *indio* in this text is used in its historical context and without any intention to attribute to it a pejorative meaning as is described , e.g., in the first dictionary of the Castellan language (1726-1739), in which this term was associated to "barbarian, primitive" or "easy to convince". Giraudo, *La questione indigena in America Latina*, p.15

instrumental purposes only. For instance, during the negotiations of the Cadiz Constitution between 1810 and 1812, the Creoles based their arguments on the existence of indigenous peoples and *mestizos* with the sole aim of obtaining more deputies in the *Cortes*.[1091] This tendency was confirmed in the paternalistic treatment of indigenous peoples in the first Latin American Constitutions or in the "benevolent assimilation" of the *indigenismo* expressed during the 1940s. In the 200 years after the wars of independence, the protection of indigenous peoples passed through different phases, as will be outlined in section 4.1. In spite of their announced "extinction" during the 1960s and the brutal repression during the dictatorships,[1092] indigenous peoples have increasingly raised their voices and mobilized, as will be analyzed in section 4.3.[1093] However, notwithstanding the international echo of indigenous peoples rights seen in the previous chapters and the aforementioned active role of other international bodies such as the Inter-American Court of Human Rights (section 4.2), indigenous peoples, as well as other vulnerable groups (e.g., the afro-descendants), still remain at the fringes of Latin American society. This chapter thus aims to give a brief overview of the protection of indigenous peoples within the complex Latin American historical context and of their recent mobilization.

1091 Gloria de los Ángeles Zarza Rondón, "El largo camino hacia la ciudadanía: la población indígena en la Constitución de 1812", in AA.VV., *Actas XIV Encuentro de los Latinoamericanistas de España, Congreso Internacional, 1810-2010: 200 años de Iberoamérica*, Santiago de Compostela 15-18 September 2010, pp.2639-2650, p.2643.

1092 E.g., the 36 years of civil war in Guatemala. Some sociologists announced indigenous peoples' impending extinction during the 1960s. Stavenhagen, "Indigenous Peoples and the State in Latin America: An Ongoing Debate", p.29

1093 Parts of sections 4.1.1 and of 4.2 will also appear in the author's publication Alexandra Tomaselli, "Indigenous Peoples' Right(s) to Land in Latin America", E-book of the Proceedings of the Conference "Land, Water & Resources Rights. Global Governance among the Centrality of Human Life, Environment Sustainability and Commercial, Extractive & Industrial Production", State University of Milan, University Milano-Bicocca, University Of Gastronomic Sciences, Guest University IULM, 6-8 July 2015.

4.1 The protection of indigenous peoples in the Latin American Constitutions

4.1.1 Introduction

The term Latin America refers to the extensive territory from the *Tierra del Fuego* in the South to Mexico in the North, subdivided into 20 States (apart from those not speaking a "Latin" language, i.e., Belize, French Guyana, Guyana, and Suriname). Needless to say, the subcontinent represents a complex context in geographical, demographic, and cultural terms. The total population is estimated to amount to little less than 600 million (not including the Caribbean islands),[1094] out of which between 30 and 50 million are indigenous,[1095] that is to say 5-9% of the total population. Indigenous peoples live in very different environments in Latin America: coastal areas, the

1094 Data for 2012 provided by the *Comisión Económica para América Latina* – CEPAL, *Centro Latinoamericano y Caribeño Demografico* – CELADE, "Observatorio demográfico 2012. Proyecciones de población = Demographic observatory 2012. Population projections", August 2013, table 1, p.33, at http://www.cepal.org/publicaciones/xml/1/50561/ObservatorioDemografico2012.pdf.pdf [Last access 11.08.2014]. The total population of Latin America is estimated to be 593,637,000.

1095 Fabiana Del Popolo, Ana María Oyarce, Susana Schkolnik and Fernanda Velasco of *Comisión Económica para América Latina*, "Censos 2010 y la inclusión del enfoque étnico: hacia una construcción participativa con pueblos indígenas y afrodescendientes de América Latina", Santiago de Chile, 2010, pp.68-69, and p.71, at http://www.eclac.cl/publicaciones/xml/3/37453/S57SyC-L3095e-P.pdf [Last access 11.08.2014]. These are, and cannot be anything but, estimates for three main reasons. First, in the list of questions within a census, a query on self-identification as an indigenous person is not always included. Second, although much has changed recently, indigenous peoples are more likely to self-identify as such, compared to in the past, though this is also due to the merging of the social sectors of "peasants" during the agrarian reforms from the 1960s onwards. Finally, some areas are extremely remote, both in the Andes and in the Amazon rainforest, and not all indigenous peoples may or may have (ever) been reached. On these issues, see Laura Giraudo and Juan Martín Sánchez, "Neoindigenismo y movimientos indígenas en América Latina", in Carlos Malamud, Paul Isbell and Concha Tejedor (eds.), *Anuario Iberoamericano* 2008, Ediciones Pirámide, Madrid, 2008, pp. 63-76. On an overview and comparison of methodologies of censuses and their respective outcomes, see Susana Schkolink and Fabiana del Popolo, "Los censos y los pueblos indígenas en América Latina: Una metodología Regional", paper presented at the conference "Pueblos Indígenas y afrodescendientes de América Latina y Caribe: relevancia y pertinencia de la información sociodemográfica para políticas y programas", *Comisión Económica para América Latina* – CEPAL, Santiago de Chile, 27-29 April 2005, at http://www.cepal.org/celade/noti cias/paginas/7/21237/fdelpopolo-sscholnick.pdf [Last access 13.08.2014].

Andes, the Amazon, etc., but increasingly in urban areas.[1096] The richness of their cultures is inestimable: At least 400 different linguistic varieties are spoken among indigenous peoples in the subcontinent.[1097] However, these data do not reflect the degree of heterogeneity within these peoples: For instance, in Colombia alone, where indigenous peoples make up 1.61% of the total population, (approximately 500,000 people), there are no less than 80 different indigenous peoples.[1098]

Broadly speaking, indigenous peoples are among the poorest, if not the poorest, sectors of the society. As is widely known, there are immense inequalities in terms of wealth within Latin American societies, although in recent years the situation has improved slightly.[1099] The same is also the case in countries which have a higher GDP, such as Chile, where the highest poverty rates are registered in areas primarily inhabited by indigenous peoples.[1100] Additionally, indigenous peoples are at the mercy of internal conflicts due to the drug trade or paramilitary groups, as is the case with the FARC (*Fuerzas Armadas Revolucionarias de Colombia*/Revolutionary Armed Forces of Colombia).[1101]

1096 Fabiana Del Popolo, Ana María Oyarce, Susana Schkolnik and Fernanda Velasco of *Comisión Económica para América Latina*, "Censos 2010 y la inclusión del enfoque étnico …", pp.54-59.

1097 Other sources indicate the 8%. Álvaro Bello, *Etnicidad y ciudadanía en América Latina. La acción colectiva de los pueblos indígenas*, United Nations, Santiago de Chile, 2004, p.51.

1098 Bello, *Etnicidad y ciudadanía en América Latina*, pp.52-53.

1099 Alicia Bárcena, "Distribuir la Riqueza. La pobreza y la desigualdad han disminuido en América Latina en los últimos años, pero aún queda mucho por hacer", *Finanzas & Desarrollo*, March 2011, pp.20-21.

1100 See the Chilean surveys (Chilean) Ministry of Social Development/Ministerio de Desarrollo Social, "CASEN 2011. Encuesta de Caracterización Socioeconómica Nacional. Indicadores de Pobreza" at http://observatorio.ministeriodesarrollo social.gob.cl/layout/doc/casen/pobreza_casen_2011.pdf [Last access 11.08.2014], 2011, p.14, and (Chilean) Ministry of Social Development/Ministerio de Desarrollo Social, "MIDEPLAN, División Social, Encuesta CASEN 2009" at http://www.mideplan.cl/casen/Estadisti cas/pobreza.html [Last access 11.08.2014]. As to the latter, by selecting the year 2009, in table "3. Situación de Pobreza a nivel de personas, por Región y zona", the poverty rates are reported per region. The regions with the highest poverty rates (adding together the percentages related to the "indigent" and the "poor-non indigent" people) are Atacama, Maule, Bío Bío, La Araucanía and Los Rios, all areas densely inhabited by indigenous peoples.

1101 Bello, *Etnicidad y ciudadanía en América Latina*, p.66. As widely known, since September 2012 a "Peace Process" has started between the Colombian government guided by Santos and the FARC, initially held in Norway and then moved to La Habana (Cuba). The re-election of Juan Manuel Santos on 15 June 2014 suggests

As for politics, the Latin American political context is characterized as particularly lively. Far from offering an exhaustive analysis of Latin American political arenas, it suffices here to stress two recent and opposing phenomena. On the one hand, following the "third wave of democratization"[1102], extended presidencies suggest a new tendency to centralize and monopolize political power in the hands of a few, very charismatic leaders. This is valid in both the apparently "indigenous-friendly" cases, such as Rafael Correa in Ecuador, Evo Morales in Bolivia, and the departed Hugo Chavez in Venezuela, and the less (or not at all) "indigenous-friendly" cases such as the Luís Inácio Lula da Silva-Dilma Vana Rousseff Linhares governments of the Workers' Party (*Partido dos Trabalhadores*) in Brazil and the Kirchner family in Argentina. Paradoxically, many of these leaders have been largely elected by the population due to their anti-neoliberal agendas.[1103] Neoliberalism, along with macroeconomic growth, implies great costs for the majority of the population (e.g., the reduction in workers' wages, job losses, higher unemployment rates, reductions in social services, etc.).[1104] This globalization-driven economic process has therefore aggra-

---

that the "Peace Process" is likely to continue. For consistently updated information in English on the peace process, see the website of the Washington Office on Latin America, "Monitoring Progress in Colombia's Peace Dialogues", at http://colombiapeace.org [Last access 26.02.2015]. According to the Colombian National Indigenous Organization ONIC (*Organización Nacional Indígena de Colombia*), as reported by Survival International, it is estimated that 35 indigenous people are displaced every day and one indigenous person is murdered every 40 hours. Survival International, "Colombia's most recently contacted tribe violently forced from homes", 25 April 2014, at http://www.survivalinternational.org/ne ws/10207 [Last access 11.08.2014].

1102 Huntington identified three global "waves of democratization": 1828-1926, 1943-1962, and 1974-1991 (date in which his book was published). Hagopian and Mainwaring, and the authors of the chapters of the book edited by them, have further analyzed this "third wave" in Latin America (post-1978), after which date only Peru experienced a democratic crisis. See Samuel P. Huntington, *The Third Wave: Democratization in the Late Twentieth Century*, University of Oklahoma Press, Norman OK, 1991; and Frances Hagopian and Scott P. Mainwaring (eds.), *The Third Wave of Democratization in Latin America. Advances and Setbacks*, Cambridge University Press, Cambridge, New York, 2005.

1103 Richard H. Harris, "Dependency, Underdevelopment, and Neoliberalism", in Richard H. Harris and Jorge Nef (eds.), *Capital, Power, and Inequality in Latin America and the Caribbean*, Rowman & Littlefield Publishers, Lanham MD, 2008, pp.49-95, p.90.

1104 *Ibid.*, p.89.

vated existing inequalities by widening the socio-economic gap among different sectors of society.[1105] Neoliberalism has lost its legitimacy among many Latin Americans, fuelling social protests, particularly from 1990s onwards.[1106] This led, as mentioned, to the election of anti-neoliberal political leaders, who nevertheless continue to build clientelist networks and centralize power, thus ignoring both the rules and the citizenry's demands.[1107]

On the other hand, among the many protest movements in the subcontinent, six of them have recently had a major impact and therefore need to be briefly mentioned here.[1108] First, the 2011 students' protest in Chile led to the election of the most notorious leader of the movement (Camila Vallejo) as a representative in the coalition with Michelet Bachelet's party "New Majority" (*Nueva Mayoría*; see further in chapter 6).[1109] Second, the increasing indigenous protests regarding their rights (see section 4.3), the

1105 Menno Vellinga, "Globalization and Neoliberalism: Economy and Society in Latin America", 32(2) *Iberoamericana. Nordic Journal of Latin American and Caribbean Studies* 2002, pp.25-43, p.38.

1106 Harris, "Dependency, Underdevelopment, and Neoliberalism", p.90, Vellinga, "Globalization and Neoliberalism …", p.38

1107 Laura Tedesco and Rut Diamint, "Latin America Democracy. What to do with the Leaders?", 33(1) *Bulletin of Latin American Research* 2014, pp.31-45, p.43. See also the recent and frequent use by Andean leaders of the so called "Regimes of Exception" (i.e., the concentration of powers in the executive branch and the concomitant suspension of human rights to overcome suspected "exceptional threats" outside military dictators indigenous peoples) flagged by Claire Wright, "Executives and Emergencies: Presidential Decrees of Exception in Bolivia, Ecuador, and Peru", 60 *Documentos de Trabajo Instituto de Estudios Latinoamericanos IELAT* 2014, pp.1-34, at http://www.ielat.es/inicio/repositorio/DT_60_Claire_Wright_Web.pdf [Last access 19.08.14].

1108 They may also be considered part of the number of social protests that recently erupted in many parts of the world. Such manifestations have also been fuelled by the financial crisis and have mainly been led by a "new" and rising socio-economic middle class. Among these protests, see, e.g., Occupy Wall Street in November 2011, in Istanbul against Erdogan since May 2013, despite his recent (official) reelection, or the protests in India regarding violence against women since late 2012. For an overview on these protests see Slavoj Žižek, "Trouble in Paradise", 35(14) *London Review of Books* 2013, pp.11-12; for an analysis on the diversity of the movements' requests and the role of the "new" and rising middle class, see Francis Fukuyama, "The Middle-Class Revolution", The Wall Street Journal, 28.06.2013, at http://online.wsj.com/news/articles/SB10001424127887323873904578571472700348086 [Last access 19.08.2014].

1109 Another three student-favored leaders have been elected with a remarkable majority, although with different parties, namely Giorgio Jackson (*Revolución Democratica*), Gabriel Boric (Indipendent), and Karol Cariola (*Juventudes Comunistas*). See Redacción BBC Mundo, "Los exlíderes estudiantiles que arrasaron en las elecciones en Chile", 18.11.2013, *BBC*, at http://www.bbc.co.uk/mundo/noticias/20

most notorious of which are the marches that began in 2011 in Bolivia, targeting the construction of a highway on TIPNIS (*Territorio Indígena y Parque Nacional Isiboro-Secure*). Third, the Mexican movement for Peace with Justice and Dignity (*Movimiento por la Paz con Justicia y Dignidad*) against the impunity of the Mexican government due to the disappearance or murder of 60.000 people since 2002. Fourth, the protests against corruption in Brazil that started in 2011 and swelled in 2013 with the increase of the ticket prices and public expenditure for the 2014 World Cup. Fifth, the constant movement of the "Ladies in White" (*Damas de Blanco*) that have protested in support of political prisoners in Cuba since 2003.[1110] Finally, the recent social protests started by students' movements in February 2014 and soon sustained and spread among the population against social inequalities fuelled by the opponents of the successor of Hugo Chavez, Nicolas Maduro.[1111]

4.1.2 An excursus on indigenous peoples' recognition in the Latin American constitutions and recent developments

The recognition of indigenous peoples in the Latin American constitutional orders may be subdivided into four distinct phases which followed the main historical periods of the subcontinent. First, colonization, during which time indigenous peoples were essentially segregated. Second, independence, which aimed to assimilate them. Third, the *indigenismo* period, that started in the 1940s with an "integrationist" approach that aimed to nullify cultural diversities. Lastly, the present-day recognition,[1112] which, starting with the

13/11/131118_chile_elecciones_exlideres_estudiantiles_arrasan_para_diiputados_ch.shtml [Last access 19.08.2014]; Redacción Semana, "Camila Vallejo: de líder estudiantil a diputada", 18.11.2013, *Semana*, at http://www.semana.com/mundo/articulo/lider-estudiantil-camila-vallejo-diputada-en-chile/365018-3 [Last access 19.08.2014].

1110 On these first five movements, see Salvador Martí i Puig, "Protesta Política en América Latina", *Foreign Policy en Espanol/Esglobal*, 23.04.2012.

1111 These events are too recent to be properly assessed, but see the brief and concise analysis by Juan Carlos Triviño, "Venezuela en crisis: la revolución chavista a prueba", Opinión CIDOB, No.232, 7 April 2014, at http://www.cidob.org/es/publicaciones/opinion/america_latina/venezuela_en_crisis_la_revolucion_chavista_a_prueba [Last access 11.08.2014].

1112 Vicente Cabedo Mallol, *Constitucionalismo y Derecho Indígena en América Latina*, Universidad Politécnica de Valencia, Amadis, 2004, p.82; and Giraudo, *La questione indigena in America Latina*, pp.10-11.

1988 Brazilian Constitution, has also been called "multicultural constitutionalism".[1113] However, in six of these 20 States, indigenous peoples are yet to be constitutionally recognized (Chile, Costa Rica, Cuba, Dominican Republic, Puerto Rico and Uruguay).

Needless to say, the Constitutions, which will be subsequently cited,[1114] are the outcome of political processes that were once imposed and recently have become more participatory. The critical and fundamental political milestones of each of the Latin American States cannot be discussed here. Thus, this paragraph seeks to draw a *fil rouge* on the current or missed opportunities of constitutional recognition of indigenous peoples.[1115] In addition, three main issues vis-à-vis indigenous rights need to be considered as they partially intersect the abovementioned historical phases: The recognition of indigenous peoples as a "people", although frustrated by "civilizing" policies; indigenous collective property and land rights that were acknowledged or tolerated during colonization, but subsequently subject to significant direct or indirect reductions; and indigenous peoples' cultural and autonomy rights, which, as seen in the previous chapters, are vociferously claimed in the present day.[1116]

During colonization –a political dominion of the Christian matrix–[1117] the first legislation vis-à-vis the *indios* was a combination of (the then) Spanish law, which included Roman, Canonic, Castilian, and indigenous customary laws and varied according to whether an indigenous people had

1113 Donna Van Lee Cott, *The Friendly Liquidation of the Past: the politics of diversity in Latin America*, University of Pittsburgh Press, Pittsburgh, 2000, p.17; see also *infra*.

1114 The texts for the Constitutions that will be subsequently cited, if not specified otherwise, have been accessed on the Miguel de Cervantes Virtual Library, at http://www.cervantesvirtual.com/portales/constituciones_hispanoamericanas/catalogo_paises [Last access 11.08.2014].

1115 For a recent and concise analysis of the latest Latin American constitutional trends, see Anna Barrera, Detlef Nolte and Almut Schilling-Vacaflor, *New Constitutionalism in Latin America from a Comparative Perspective: A Step Towards Good Governance?*, Proceedings of the homonymous conference organized by the German Institute of Global and Area Studies (GIGA) of Hamburg (Germany), 25-26 November 2010, Hamburg, 2011, at http://www.giga-ham burg.de/sites/default/files/md_pdf/conference_paper_schilling_nolte_barrera.pdf [Last access 12.08.2014].

1116 This subdivision has been drawn by Bartolomé Clavero, "Derechos Indígenas y Constituciones Latinoamericanas", in Mikel Berraondo (ed.), *Pueblos Indígenas y Derechos Humanos*, Universidad de Deusto, Bilbao, 2006, pp.313-338; see also Giraudo, *La questione indigena in America Latina*, pp.10-11.

1117 Giraudo, *La questione indigena in America Latina*, p.18.

been subjugated by the Spaniards or not. The *ad hoc* legislation of the Spanish American territories mirrored such an amalgamation of laws due to the emergence of new legal situations and geographical and social conditions, which contributed to the creation of an "Indian law" *in stricto sensu*.[1118] These rules included, for instance, the Valladolid New Laws (*Leyes Nuevas*) of 1542. These laws, *inter alia*, abolished (solely, officially) the practice of indigenous slavery and of *encomiendas*.[1119] Other examples were the jurisdictional regulations of the Viceroyalties' Audiences (*Audiencias virreinales*), founded approximately in the late 1520s;[1120] the Council of the Indies (*Consejo de Indias*) of 1524;[1121] and the *Recopilación de Leyes de Indias* of 1680.[1122] Additionally, the indigenous *Cabildos* (similar to municipalities), were ruled by indigenous chiefs, i.e., the *Caciques*, or, in the Andean zones, the *Curacas*,[1123] and some were completely out of the Spaniards' control.[1124] Frontier agreements among the colonizers and indigenous peoples were also frequent, such as that which prompted the creation of the *Parliamento de Quillín* in 1644 between the Spaniards and the Mapuche people. This act ruled that the customary law of the latter should have been respected by the former and, in exchange, the latter became subject to the Spanish Crown but as "free vassals" of the King.[1125]

Nevertheless, the establishment of the Bourbon dynasty in Spain and that of Braganza in Portugal, as well as the tendency towards the creation of absolutist monarchies in the 1700s, marked a radical change with respect to assimilationist policies that followed during the independence movements. These dynasties aimed to gain more control over the overseas territories through, *inter alia*, the abrogation of the aforementioned *ad hoc* legislation.[1126] Among the most notorious reforms, those enacted by the Portuguese Marquis of Pombal abolished all those forms of self-government and

1118 *Ibid.*, p.19.

1119 Hidalgo Nuchera, "Expansión, gobierno y defensa de las Indias", p.313. The practices of *encomiendas* consisted of presenting a group of indigenous youngsters to a colonizer who then had to work on his lands in exchange for their "evangelization".

1120 Miguel Molina Martínez, "La organización administrativa de las Indias", in Juan Bosco Amores Carredano (ed.), *Historia de América*, Editorial Ariel, Barcelona, 2006, pp. 215-285, pp.275-278.

1121 Giraudo, *La questione indigena in America Latina*, p.19.

1122 *Ibid.*, p.20.

1123 *Ibid.*, p.21.

1124 Molina Martínez, "La organización administrativa de las Indias", p.275.

1125 Giraudo, *La questione indigena in America Latina*, p.23.

1126 *Ibid.*, p.24.

autonomy in the present-day Brazilian territory run by the Creoles.[1127] These acts fuelled the discontent that subsequently burst out in indigenous protests such as the one lead by the notorious Tupac Amaru,[1128] the negotiations of the Cadiz Constitution of 1812, and, eventually, the wars of independence.[1129]

As mentioned above, the core characteristics of the first Latin-American constitutions vis-à-vis indigenous peoples were, on the one hand, the proclamation of their formal equality in relation to the Creoles before the law (although with indirectly discriminating implications, such as the right to vote but only for those who were literate), and on the other hand, the paternalistic and civilizing approach, which materialized in religious conversions or in "corrective" education and protection aimed at achieving national integration.[1130] A glaring example of this approach was the Venezuelan Constitution of 1811, in which articles 200 and 201 revoked any special regulations for indigenous peoples in the name of "formal equality" and the failed previous system, which had damaged Indigenous peoples by allowing their isolation and non-integration. In addition, local governments had the responsibility to save indigenous peoples from their rusticity, and the lands

1127 More specifically, see Julio Sanchéz Goméz, "El Brasil portugués", in Juan Bosco Amores Carredano (ed.), *Historía de América*, Editorial Ariel, Barcelona, 2006, pp.877-960, pp.897-903. Among the economic, religious, and other reforms, there was one that prohibited the use of the *Nheengatu* language, which was a mixture of Portuguese and indigenous languages, and thus a *lingua franca*.

1128 Scarlett O'Phelan Godoy, "Algunas reflexiones sobre las Reformas Borbónicas y las rebeliones del siglo XVIII", in Charles F. Walker (ed.), *Entre la retórica y la insurgencia: las ideas y los movimientos sociales en los Andes, siglo XVIII*, Centro de Estudios Regionales Andinos "Bartolomé de las Casas", Cusco, 1995, pp.309-317, p.309. As to Tupac Amaru (II), for a very short time, he was a *Cacique* who led a major indigenous revolt against the Spaniards in the Viceroyalty of Peru in the late 1700s. His real name was José Gabriel Condorcanqui, but he adopted the name of the last Inca monarch executed by the Spaniards in 1572. See the recent work of Charles F. Walker, *The Tupac Amaru Rebellion*, Harvard University Press, Cambridge MA, London, 2014.

1129 Giraudo, *La questione indigena in America Latina*, p.24. See also Fernando Mires, *La rebelión permanente: las revoluciones sociales en América Latina*, Siglo XXI, Mexico, 1988, pp.59-79.

1130 For the subsequent historical reconstructions, see Clavero, "Derechos Indígenas y Constituciones Latinoamericanas"; Giraudo, *La questione indigena in America Latina*, pp.24-27; Cabedo Mallol, *Constitucionalismo y Derecho Indígena en América Latina*; Stavenhagen, "Indigenous Peoples and the State in Latin America: An Ongoing Debate"; Bello, *Etnicidad y ciudadanía en América Latina*.

occupied and used by indigenous peoples had to be taken away from them to be given to "real Lords" (*verdaderos señores*).[1131]

Notwithstanding these attempts, Giraudo has underlined the change in legal status of the *indio* and the fact that the deprivation of collective lands was discontinued.[1132] For instance, an "Indigenous Republic" was re-established in Guatemala between 1839 and 1871, albeit without recognizing the citizenship of indigenous peoples; and the practice of the tax levy on indigenous communities was reintroduced in the Andean countries (Peru, Bolivia, and Ecuador) following independence in the 1820s and continued for thirty years.[1133] However, these practices were completely abolished around 1850 and the indigenous lands were forcibly privatized by law, as in Mexico in 1857, or declared public property, as in Chile in 1866.[1134]

Throughout the 19th century, Latin America was characterized by a sequence of constitutions and institutional instability. Thus, the second constitutional phase vis-à-vis indigenous rights started in early 1900. *indigenismo* also had a considerable influence on constitutionalism.[1135] The new

1131 Similar provisions were inserted, e.g., art.128 of the 1819 and art.64.15 of the 1853 Argentinean Constitutions; art.87.10 of the 1823 and art.75.10 of the 1828 Peruvian Constitutions; art.47.6 of the 1822 Chilean Constitution; art.68 of the 1830 Ecuadorian Constitution; and art.72.15 of the 1870 Paraguayan Constitution. The only exceptions to such an approach were the 1824 Mexican and 1835 Guatemalan Constitutions, which, similar to the American one of 1787, foresaw in arts.50.11 and 83.32, respectively, the possibility for the parliamentary assemblies to trade with foreign nations and indigenous "tribes", thus recognizing indigenous peoples as legal persons able to enter into contractual relations.

1132 Giraudo, *La questione indigena in America Latina*, p.27.

1133 *Ibid.*

1134 Bello, *Etnicidad y ciudadanía en América Latina*, p.49.

1135 The term *indigenismo* is used to define different concepts, historical periods, and even political initiatives. In this chapter, this term is used to refer to those Latin American national and continental policies pursued in the 20th century. However, for the sake of clarity, it needs to be specified here that the First *Indigenista* Congress was held in Pátzcuaro, Michoacán (Mexico) in 1940, and, based on the homonymous document (*Tratado de Pátzcuaro*, art.16), the Interamerican Indigenist Institute was created. This Institute later became an agency of the Organization of American States in the 1960s. In 1948 the National Indigenous Institute of Mexico was also created and later reformed in 2003 and transformed into the *Comisión Nacional para el Desarrollo de los Pueblos Indígenas* (CONADEPI). See Giraudo, *La questione indigena in America Latina*, p.31 and ff.; Bello, *Etnicidad y ciudadanía en América Latina*, pp.62-63 and 68. For a detailed analysis of *indigenismo* and the indigenous participation in the works of the Interamerican Indigenist Institute, see Laura Giraudo, "El Instituto Indigenista Interamericano y la participación indígena (1940-1998)", 62(3) *América Indígena* 2006, pp.6-34.

approach consisted of a kind of "friendly assimilation",[1136] aiming to absorb indigenous peoples in the "nation-State"[1137] and with a very limited recognition of collective land rights.[1138]

It is noteworthy that, in 1945, the Ecuadorian and Guatemalan Constitutions provided for the duty of the State to (also) protect indigenous collective lands (art.146.10 Ecuador Const. of 1945) and declared that communitarian lands were inalienable, imprescriptible, indivisible, and not subject to dispossession (art.96 Guatemala Const. of 1945),[1139] respectively. In particular, the Guatemalan Constitution of 1945 is defined as the Latin American *Magna Carta* of indigenous rights.[1140] For instance, the possibility to enact laws taking into due account indigenous necessities, conditions, practices, uses, and customs was foreseen in art.83.

Parallel to the *indigenismo* apex between the 1940s and 1970s, the agrarian reforms introduced by the Mexican revolution of 1917 had the twofold effect of prompting large public works in remote lands and including indigenous peoples in the category of peasants/*campesinos*, particularly in Bolivia, Chile, Guatemala, Mexico and Peru.[1141] Therefore, the first movements of farmers and workers also involved indigenous peoples.[1142]

1136 Bello, *Etnicidad y ciudadanía en América Latina*, p.191.

1137 Stavenhagen, "Indigenous Peoples and the State in Latin America: An Ongoing Debate", p.27.

1138 Clavero, "Derechos Indígenas y Constituciones Latinoamericanas", p.320. For instance, arts.27, paras.7-8 of the 1917 Mexican Constitution allowed indigenous "tribes" to enjoy collective lands as other sectors of the population after the *Zapatista* revolution. The two Peruvian Constitutions of early 1900 recognized the imprescriptible right to indigenous communal property of specific lands (art.41 of 1920 Const.), then guaranteed by the State (arts.193.10 and 209 of 1933 Const.). A unique case was Panama, which, after having gained independence from Colombia in 1903 and following the Tule Revolution, in 1928 reformed the 1904 Constitution (art.4) and recognized the indigenous *Comarcas*, as seen in chapter 3, section 3.3.3.

1139 The text of the 1945 Guatemalan Constitution is not available in the Virtual Library of Miguel de Cervantes, but at http://www.bibliojuridica.org/libros/5/2210/24.pdf [Last access 12.08.2014].

1140 Cabedo Mallol, *Constitucionalismo y Derecho Indígena en América Latina*, p.211.

1141 Bello, *Etnicidad y ciudadanía en América Latina*, p.63. Deborah J. Yashar, *Contesting Citizenship in Latin America. The Rise of Indigenous Movements and the Postliberal Challenge*, Cambridge University Press, Cambridge, New York, 2005, p.61.

1142 Bello, *Etnicidad y ciudadanía en América Latina*, pp.63-64; Nieves Zúñiga García-Falces, "Emergencia del Movimiento indígena en América Latina: de 'objeto' a 'sujeto'", in Salvador Martí i Puig and Josep Maria Sanahuja (eds.), *Etnicidad, autonomía y gobernabilidad en América Latina*, Universidad de Salamanca, Salamanca, 2004, pp.35-52, pp.36-37 and 48.

Subsequently, the dictatorships and the crisis of the Latin American democracies in the second half of the century obviously marked another disruption of the relationship between States and indigenous peoples. The democratic transitions, starting in the 1980s, became the time to introduce the constitutional recognition and protection of indigenous peoples, who progressively organized themselves into social movements of increasing political impact.[1143] For instance, albeit still in the days of the civil war, the Guatemalan Constitution of 1985 recognized the existence of indigenous peoples and their right to collective lands (arts.66-67), as well as their right to cultural identity and bilingual education (arts.58 and 76).

That being said, the 1988 Brazilian Constitution represented a real cornerstone. Although indigenous peoples amount to approximately 0.5% of the total population, arts.231-232 recognized indigenous social organizations, customs, languages, and traditions, as well as "original" rights over their lands and the future federal protection of them. Regrettably, a reform of these articles is currently under debate: According to the draft reform, the level of protection of indigenous lands will be lowered.[1144] This casts a shadow on the preservation of indigenous lands, which are also constantly subject to abuses by the logging companies.[1145]

Subsequently, the Colombian Constitution of 1991 and the reforms to the Bolivian Constitution of 1967 in 1994 mark the beginning of what has been defined as the Latin American "multicultural constitutionalism".[1146] Accordingly, from the 1990s onward, a number of other Latin America Constitutions (Nicaragua in 1987, Paraguay in 1992, Peru in 1993, Ecuador in 1998, the reforms in Guatemala in 1998, and in Mexico in 1994 and 1995)[1147] included at least three of the five elements that compose this model:

1143 Bello, *Etnicidad y ciudadanía en América Latina*, p.64; Stavenhagen, "Indigenous Peoples and the State in Latin America: An Ongoing Debate", pp.31-32. See also Salvador Martí i Puig, "Después de la 'década de los pueblos indígenas', ¿Qué?", 227 *Nueva Sociedad* 2010, pp.68-82.

1144 See Gregory Morton and Manuela Carniero da Cunha, "Indigenous Rights and Brazilian democracy: An Interview Manuela Carneiro da Cunha", *Cultural Anthropology*, Serie "Protesting Democracy in Brazil", at http://www.culanth.org/fieldsights/460-indigenous-rights-and-brazilian-democracy-an-interview-manuela-carneiro-da-cunha [Last access 12.08.2014].

1145 See, e.g., the reports of Survival International at http://www.survivalinternational.org/tribes/brazilian [Last access 12.08.2014].

1146 Van Lee Cott, *The Friendly Liquidation of the Past*, p.17.

1147 See also Martí i Puig, "Después de la 'década de los pueblos indígenas', ¿Qué?", p.74.

- Recognition of the rhetorical multicultural nature of indigenous societies and the existence of indigenous peoples as distinct sub-state social collectivities;
- Recognition of indigenous customary law as part of the ordinary law;
- Indigenous property rights protected from collective sale, dismemberment, or confiscation;
- Status or official recognition of indigenous languages;
- Guarantee of bilingual education.[1148]

In particular, the 1994 constitutional reform in Bolivia established that it is a multi-ethnic and pluri-cultural State (art.1), while the Colombian Constitution of 1991 recognized indigenous territories as administrative territorial units equal to others (e.g., the provinces/*departamentos*, art.286), the use of customary law in these territories (art.246) and two reserved seats for indigenous peoples in the Senate (art.171).

Other constitutional recognitions followed in a domino effect. The recognition of the existence of indigenous peoples, the right to their cultural identity and also to the ownership or use of lands or territories, together with, in many cases, the collective nature of their rights and the use of customary law were introduced in the Constitutions of the following countries: Paraguay in 1992 (arts.62-64, 66-77, 140 and 268); Nicaragua in 1993 and 2000 (arts.5,8,11, 89-91, 180-181); Peru in 1993 (arts.2, 17, 48, 89, 149); Argentina in 1994 (art.75); Ecuador in 1998 (arts.3,24,62,83-84, 97, 161, 224, 228 and 241); and Mexico (art.2), as reformed in 2001.[1149] The reform of the Honduran Constitution of 1999 foresaw, however, only a general duty to protect indigenous peoples (art.346).

Lastly, the recent Venezuelan and Ecuadorian constitutions are worth mentioning in greater detail here, while the new 2009 Bolivian Magna Carta

---

1148 Van Lee Cott, *The Friendly Liquidation of the Past*, pp.265-278. See, in particular, table 4 at pp.266-267.

1149 For an overview, see Giraudo, *La questione indigena in America Latina*, pp.131-133, and, for a thematic analysis, see Gonzalo Aguilar, Sandra LaFosse, Hugo Rojas and Rebecca Steward, "South/North Exchange of 2009. The Constitutional Recognition of Indigenous Peoples in Latin America", 2(2) *Pace International Law Review Online Companion* 2010, pp.44-104, at http://digitalcommons.pace.edu/cgi/viewcontent.cgi?article=1017&context=pilronline [Last access 26.02.2015]. Apart from the case of Panama mentioned above on the indigenous *Comarcas*, since the adoption of the Constitution of 1928, other forms of recognition followed in the Constitution of 1946 (arts.5, 94 and 208) and of 1973 (arts.5, 86, 104, 120, 123). Regarding the Mexican constitutional reform in particular, the right to self-determination within an autonomy was inserted in art.2 (see also chapter 3, section 3.3.3).

will be analyzed in chapter 5. It suffices to highlight here that the Bolivian Constitution was also adopted by way of a referendum in February 2009 and contains similar provisions aimed at extending the powers of the President, albeit much less incisively in comparison with the Ecuadorian Constitution (see below).[1150]

Introduced in 1999 during the first term of Hugo Chavez, the Venezuelan Constitution devotes Chapter 8 to the rights of indigenous peoples (*De los derechos de los pueblos indígenas*). This chapter, *inter alia*, guarantees their cultural rights, the rights to land, to benefit from natural resources, to intellectual property rights, and to political participation. Additionally, art.9 recognizes all indigenous languages as official throughout the State.

The 20th Ecuadorian constitution was adopted by a national referendum on 28 September 2008.[1151] Apart from the provisions that secure an extension of the powers of the President,[1152] it is sufficient to stress the considerable participation of indigenous organizations such as *Confederación de Nacionalidades Indígenas del Ecuador* (CONAIE) [1153] and *Federación Nacional de Organizaciones Campesinas Indígenas y Negras* (FENOCIN)[1154] as members of the Constituent Assembly.[1155] In addition, art.1 of the Constitution states that Ecuador is an "intercultural and plurinational" State, replacing the aforementioned qualifications of "multi-cultural and

1150 For instance, the legislative initiative is in the hands of the executive body chaired by the President (art.162); the possibility to present law drafts, but not fully-fledged decrees as is the case of Ecuador, in economic matters (art.172.24); and the possibility to be reelected (art.168).

1151 See The Economist, "Ecuador's new constitution. In good faith", 02.10.2008, at http://www.economist.com/node/12342501?story_id=12 342501 [Last access 12.08.2014].

1152 See for example, the general power of legislative initiative (art.134); the exclusive legislative competence in the case of changes with regard to taxes, public expenditure, or the political-administrative division of the country (art.135), as well as in monetary policy and finance, previously in the hands of the Central Bank of Ecuador (art.261); the possibility of issuing emergency decrees on economic matters or to dissolve parliament if this blocks the "National Development Plan"(art.148); or the possibility of being re-elected (art.144).

1153 See the *Confederación de Nacionalidades Indígenas del Ecuador* (CONAIE) website at http://www.conaie.org [Last access 12.08.2014].

1154 See the *Federación Nacional de Organizaciones Campesinas Indígenas y Negras* (FENOCIN) website at http://www.fenocin.org [Last access 12.08.2014].

1155 Pablo Ortiz-T. "Ecuador", in International Work Group for Indigenous Affairs, *The Indigenous World 2009*, IWGIA, Copenhagen, 2009, at http://www.iwgia.org/publications/search-pubs?publication_id=212, or directly at http://www.iwgia.org/iwgia_files_publications_files/0212_I_09.pdf, pp.148-160, p.150 [Last access 13.08.2014].

multi-ethnic" of the 1998 Constitution and also giving greater recognition to indigenous peoples, at least on paper. The Kichwa (or Quechua) and Shuar indigenous languages gained the status of official languages of "intercultural communication" at the State level and the other indigenous languages may be used officially in the areas where they are spoken (art.2.2). Additionally, other key indigenous rights were constitutionally guaranteed (e.g., the right to free, prior, and informed "consultation", collective land, culture, and their own institutions, etc. in arts.56-60), partly recognized already in the 1998 Constitution (arts.83-85). Art.171 includes a more incisive right than the one recognized in art.191 of the 1998 Constitution in relation to the use of indigenous customary law within their own territory (so-called "indigenous justice"). Another important change is the introduction of the concept of *buen vivir*, the indigenous Kichwa concept of *Sumak Kawsay*, which, broadly speaking, includes the right to water, food, a healthy environment, cultural identity, etc., reflecting also some universal human rights (arts.12-34).

In sum, the majority of the present-day Latin-American Constitutions officially recognize indigenous peoples; at the least, their existence and/or the duty to protect them. As mentioned, this recognition is still lacking in Chile, Cuba, Costa Rica, Puerto Rico, Dominican Republic and Uruguay. However, Costa Rica, as per the respective reforms of 1999, foresees the duty of the State to protect indigenous languages.[1156]

To conclude this overview of the constitutional recognition of indigenous peoples, it is relevant to emphasize that, in addition to these provisions, a number of Latin American States have adopted domestic legislations either aimed at implementing constitutional norms or, in their absence, providing Indigenous peoples with a minimum protection of their rights. Many countries also established national commissions and tasked them with primary implementation powers on matters involving indigenous interests.[1157] Notwithstanding these extensive constitutional and domestic provisions, their

1156 Law No.7878/1999 that reformed art.76 of the 1949 Costa Rican Constitution.

1157 *Inter alia*, in chronological order, see: *Lei 6.001/73 "Estatuto das Sociedades Indígenas"* in Brazil (still in force); *Ley N.904/81 "Estatuto de las Comunidades Indígenas"* in Paraguay (reformed in 1991 by *Ley N.125/91,* in 1996 by *Ley N. 919/96,* and in 2003 by *Ley N.199/03); Ley N.23.302/85 "Protección de Comunidades Aborígenes"* in Argentina; *Ley N.19.253/93 "Protección, Fomento y Desarrollo de los Indígenas"* in Chile; *Ley N.38344/2005, "Ley Orgánica de Pueblos y Comunidades Indígenas"* in Venezuela. Regarding the national commissions, apart from the abovementioned case of Mexico and of the Interamerican Indigenist Institute transformed in 2003 into the *Comisión Nacional para el Desarrollo de los Pueblos Indígenas* (CONADEPI), other bodies are: *Comisión Nacional de*

application remains uncertain and far from guaranteed. In general, a lack of rule of law in many Latin American societies plays a negative role vis-à-vis the protection of indigenous rights.[1158] The so called *Recurso de Amparo* (or *Recurso de Protección*) –those proceedings before the domestic Courts to claim a violation of a constitutional fundamental right– is one of the most successful mechanisms at enhancing the respect of indigenous rights in many Latin American countries.[1159] Since 2009, this has been the case in Chile, where a number of Courts of Appeal (*Cortes de Apelaciones*) competent for such proceedings –in accordance with art.20 of the Chilean Constitution– have recognized the violation of the constitutional rights of indigenous peoples, in conjunction with the rights recognized in the UNDRIP and the ILO Convention 169 (see chapter 6)

4.2 The role of the Inter-American human rights bodies in protecting indigenous rights

As mentioned in chapters 1 and 3, the Inter-American Commission of Human Rights and the Inter-American Court of Human Rights (hereinafter, IACommHR or "Commission", and IAtHR or "Court", respectively) have increasingly played a relevant role in the protection of indigenous rights. These bodies have adopted landmark decisions notwithstanding the absence

---

Asuntos Indígenas in Costa Rica since 1992; *Corporación Nacional de Desarrollo Indígena* (CONADI) in Chile since 1993 (see also chapter 6); *Consejo Nacional de Planificación y Desarrollo de los Pueblos Indígenas y Negros* (CONPLADEIN) in Ecuador since 1997, and the *Consejo de Desarrollo de las Nacionalidades y Pueblos del Ecuador* (CODENPE) since 1998; *Consejo Nacional de Desarrollo Indígena* (CNDI) and the *Comisión Permanente de Asuntos Indígenas de la Asamblea Legislativa* in Panama since 2000; the *Comisión Permanente de Pueblos Indígenas de la Asamblea Nacional* and the *Comisión Nacional de Demarcación y Garantía del Hábitat y Tierras de los Pueblos Indígenas* in Venezuela, also since 2000. This list has been compiled by Bello, *Etnicidad y ciudadanía en América Latina*, p.68.

1158 Gonzalo Aguilar, Sandra LaFosse, Hugo Rojas and Rebecca Steward, "South/North Exchange of 2009. The Constitutional Recognition …", p.104.

1159 See Allan R. Brewer-Carías, *Constitutional Protection of Human Rights in Latin America. A Comparative Study of Amparo Proceedings*, Cambridge University Press, Cambridge, 2009. The *Recurso de Amparo* originates from the Mexican Constitution of 1857, which was influenced by the American one. Since approximately 1850, nearly all of the Latin American constitutions have introduced such a mechanism, although with minor differences in each State as per the domestic procedure. Allan R. Brewer-Carías, *Constitutional Protection of Human Rights in Latin America*, pp.81 and 89.

of any type of provision on indigenous peoples in the Charter of the Organization of American States (OAS) of 1948, the American Declaration on the Rights and Duties of Man also of 1948, or in the binding American Convention on Human Rights – Pact of San José (ACHR) of 1969.[1160]

The ACHR was initially signed by 12 States and, according to its art.74.2, came into force in 1978 thanks to its ratification by 11 State Parties.[1161] In addition to listing the rights to be protected, the ACHR also regulates the competences and procedures before the IACommHR and the IAtHR. The former has been operational since 1959,[1162] when the Inter-American Council of Jurists started working on the draft of the ACHR.[1163] The latter started working once the Convention came into force in 1978, although its first decision was adopted in 1988.[1164] Both these entities are formed by seven members, but the IACommHR is located in Washington D.C. –where there is also the headquarters of the OAS– while the IAtHR has been established in San José, Costa Rica.[1165] Almost all Latin American countries (19 out of

---

1160 The Inter-American Democratic Charter was the sole OAS treaty that explicitly mentioned indigenous peoples until the adoption of the 2013 Inter-American Convention Against Racism, Racial Discrimination, and Related Forms of Intolerance. The former stated in its art.9 that "[…] the promotion and protection of human rights of indigenous peoples and migrants, and respect for ethnic, cultural and religious diversity in the Americas contribute to strengthening democracy and citizen participation". See art.9 of the Inter-American Democratic Charter, at http://www.oas.org/charter/docs/resolution1_en_p4.htm. The 2013 Inter-American Convention Against Racism, Racial Discrimination, and Related Forms of Intolerance mentions indigenous peoples in the 6th preambular paragraph, which affirms: "*Taking into account* that the victims of racism, racial discrimination, and other related forms of intolerance in the Americas are, inter alia, people of African descent, indigenous peoples, and other racial and ethnic groups or minorities, or groups that by reason of their lineage or national or ethnic origin are affected by such manifestations […]". See the Inter-American Convention Against Racism, Racial Discrimination, and Related Forms of Intolerance at http://www.oas.org/en/sla/dil/inter_american_treaties_A-68_racism.asp [Last access 04.02.2015].

1161 See ACHR ratifications at www.oas.org/en/iachr/mandate/Basics/conven tion-rat.asp [Last access 12.08.2014].

1162 Declaration of the Fifth Meeting of Consultation of Ministries of Foreign Affairs, Santiago de Chile, 12-18 August 1959, Final Act, OAS Doc. OEA/Ser.C/II.5, p. 11, para.2.

1163 Declaration of the Fifth Meeting of Consultation of Ministries of Foreign Affairs, para.1 of section "Human Rights", p. 11.

1164 Inter-American Court of Human Rights, *Velásquez Rodríguez* v. *Honduras*, Series C No.4, Judgement of 29 July 1988.

1165 For further details, see Organization of American States, "Human Rights", at www.oas.org/en/topics/human_rights.asp [Last access 12.08.2014].

20) have accepted the jurisdiction of the IAtHR in accordance with art.62 of the ACHR.[1166] Finally, in addition to the ACHR and the two operative bodies, a number of other thematic conventions complete the inter-American system of human rights.[1167]

The evolution of the jurisprudence vis-à-vis indigenous rights provided by the Inter-American human rights system may be divided into three temporal phases: the late-indigenist period (*tardo-indigenista*) during the 1970s; the growing interest during the 1980s and 1990s; and the present-day evolutionary phase beginning in the late 1990s, promoted also by the

1166 Other American States recognize a jurisdictional procedure before the Commission and according to the ACHR (1), or, in absence of ratification of the Convention, according to the Declaration (2). Among the first groups are Dominica, Granada (independent State of Antilles), and Jamaica. In the second group: Antigua and Barbuda, Bahamas, Belize, Canada, Cuba (excluded by OAS since 1962), the United States, Trinidad and Tobago, and other islands (San Cristobál y Nieve, Santa Lucia, San Vicente and the Grenadines). Luis Rodríguez-Piñero Royo, "El sistema interamericano de los derechos humanos y los pueblos indígenas", Mikel Berraondo (ed.), *Pueblos Indígenas y Derechos Humanos*, Universidad de Deusto, Bilbao, 2006, pp.153-203, pp.158 and 165. See also Enzamaria Tramontana, "The Contribution of the Inter-American Human Rights Bodies to Evolving International Law on Indigenous Rights over Land and Natural Resourses", 17 *International Journal on Minority and Group Rights* 2010, pp.241-263.

1167 The Inter-American Convention to Prevent and Punish Torture, which was adopted in 1985 and entered into force in 1987; the Additional Protocol to the American Convention on Human Rights in the area of Economic, Social and Cultural Rights ("Protocol of San Salvador"), which was adopted in 1988 and entered into force in 1999; the Protocol to the American Convention on Human Rights to Abolish the Death Penalty, which was adopted in 1990 and entered into force in 1991; the Inter-American Convention on the Prevention, Punishment and Eradication of Violence against Women ("Convention of Belém do Pará"), which was adopted in 1994 and entered into force in 1995; the Inter-American Convention on Forced Disappearance of Persons, which was adopted in 1994 and entered into force in 1996; the Inter-American Convention on the Elimination of All Forms of Discrimination against Persons with Disabilities, which was adopted in 1999 and entered into force in 2001; the previously mentioned Inter-American Democratic Charter, adopted in 2001; the Declaration of Principles on Freedom of Expression adopted by the IACHR at its 108th Regular Period of Sessions, held on 2-20 October 2000; and the Principles and Best Practices on the Protection of Persons Deprived of Liberty in the Americas, adopted by the IACHR at its 131th Regular Period of Sessions, held on 3-14 March 2008. For details see "Basic Documents in the Inter-American System", at www.oas.org/en/iachr/mandate/Basics/intro.asp [Last access 12.08.2014].

debates on an Inter-American Convention on the Rights of Indigenous Peoples (see chapter 1).[1168]

In 1973, during the second UN decade against racial discrimination, the Commission adopted a resolution on indigenous peoples (*Protección Especial para las Poblaciones Indígenas. Lucha contra el Racismo y la Discriminación Racial*),[1169] affirming that, due to historical reasons and moral and humanitarian principles, the States had a "sacred" duty to protect them.[1170]

However, the Commission maintained a prudent attitude vis-à-vis the first case involving indigenous rights. In 1972, case No. 1690 *Comunidades Guahibos (Colombia)* dealt with acts of torture occurring in August 1970 against the indigenous community of the Panas region (Meta, Colombia) and which were allegedly committed by the national administrative security force (*Departamento Administrativo de Seguridad*). The IACommHR dismissed the case on 15 June of the same year by ruling that the supplementary evidence requested by the Commission and provided by the Colombian government were sufficient. The latter was even praised by the former for having been frank and loyal.[1171]

Two years later, in 1975, case No.1802 involved the Aché people of Paraguay denouncing acts of persecution against their communities. Serious violations such as the murder of an Aché member, the selling of indigenous children, the denial of medical assistance during epidemics, inhuman labor conditions, and other acts aimed at destroying the Aché culture were charged by this indigenous people against the State of Paraguay.[1172] Initially, since the alleged violations were particularly grave, the IACommHR

1168 Rodríguez-Piñero Royo, "El sistema interamericano de los derechos humanos y los pueblos indígenas", p.160.

1169 OAS Doc. No. OEA/Ser.P.AG/doc. 305/73, rev.1, 14 March 1973, as cited by Rodríguez-Piñero Royo, "El sistema interamericano de los derechos humanos y los pueblos indígenas", p.160.

1170 OAS Doc. No. OEA/Ser.P.AG/doc. 305/73, rev.1, p.89. Rodríguez-Piñero Royo, "El sistema interamericano de los derechos humanos y los pueblos indígenas", p.160.

1171 Inter-American Commission on Human Rights, *Informe anual de la Comisión Interamericana de Derechos Humanos 1973,* OAS Document No. OEA/Ser.L/V /II.32, doc.3 rev.2, 14 February 1974, Section 2, Title 2 "Comunicaciones Dirigidas a la Comisión", as cited by Rodríguez-Piñero Royo, "El sistema interamericano de los derechos humanos y los pueblos indígenas", p.161. See the text of this *Informe* at http://www.cidh.oas.org/annualrep/73 sp/indice.htm [Last access 12.08.2014].

1172 Inter-American Commission on Human Rights, Case Tribu Aché (Paraguay), No.1802, 27 May 1977, First "Considerando", at http://www.cidh.org/indi

adopted a strong stance and sternly suggested to the Paraguayan government that it adopt effective measures to protect the Aché community.[1173] Subsequently, the Commission appointed a Rapporteur, Dr. Robert F. Woodward, who traveled to Paraguay and concluded that, on the contrary, the policies of Paraguay aimed to promote "assimilation and the protection" of indigenous peoples, according to the limited sources. Therefore, the Commission dismissed this case on the basis of the Rapporteur's conclusions.[1174]

As highlighted by Rodríguez-Piñero Royo,[1175] the attitude of the Commission in these first years of activity was unquestionably subject to the influence of *indigenismo*'s ideas of "friendly assimilation" mentioned above. Furthermore, the Commission's members may have adopted a reluctant and prudent attitude to avoid jeopardizing the legitimacy of the Convention vis-à-vis the other States, many of which were still run by military dictatorships.

In the 1980s, the Commission played a more decisive role in indigenous rights, although it was still hesitant. Case no.7615 in 1985 *(Resolución Nº12/85, Brasil)* concerned the realization of a trans-Amazonian highway in the indigenous Yanomami territory, on which the foundation of a natural park was to be built. Serious damages to the Yanomami people in terms of both health and environment were alleged. Although it did not rule on the construction of the highway, the IACommHR adopted a friendly binding resolution and ordered the Brazilian government to adopt preventive measures of healthcare for the Yanomami people and to demarcate the homonymous park, which was eventually established in 1992.[1176] In the subsequent case No.7964 in 1984, serious rights violations were alleged by the

genas/jurisprudencia/casos%20cidh/2.caso.1802.paraguay.doc [Last access 12.08.2014].

1173 *Ibid.*, paras.2-3.

1174 Inter-American Commission on Human Rights, *Informe anual de la Comisión Interamericana de Derechos Humanos 1975,* OAS Document No.OEA/Ser.L/V/II.37, doc.20 corr.1, 28 June 1976, Section 3, Title 3 "Comunicaciones Dirigidas a la Comisión", No.13 "Paraguay", at http://www.cidh.oas.org/annualrep/75sp/indice.htm [Last access 12.08.2014]. See also Rodríguez-Piñero Royo, "El sistema interamericano de los derechos humanos y los pueblos indígenas", p.161.

1175 Rodríguez-Piñero Royo 2006, p.161.

1176 See Fergus MacKay, *Guía para los derechos de los pueblos indígenas en el sistema interamericano*, International Work Group for Indigenous Affairs (IWGIA), Copenhagen, 2002, p.55-59. See also the Commission's resolution, Inter-American Commission on Human Rights/Comisión Interamericana de Derechos Humanos, Resolution No.12/85 (in Spanish), case No.7615 (Brazil), 5 March 1985, at

indigenous Miskito communities during the forced relocations to which they were subjected. These communities were initially in favor of the Sandinist regime, but soon after opposed it due to their assimilationist policies. Despite attempts to find a friendly solution, the lack of cooperation by the Nicaraguan government forced the Commission to eventually dismiss the case and publish a report containing proposals and recommendations (e.g., to promote the participation of indigenous peoples, to study the issue of ancestral lands, etc.).[1177]

In 1990, the creation of the Rapporteurship on the Rights of Indigenous Peoples marked a crucial development. This body is (still) in charge of promoting and coordinating the Commission's authority vis-à-vis indigenous rights,[1178] and to collaborate with a Working Group tasked with preparing an American Declaration on the Rights of Indigenous Peoples, a draft of which was approved in 1997 (its adoption is still pending).[1179]

---

http://www.cidh.org/indigenas/Brasil7615.htm [Last access 12.08.2014]; Rodríguez-Piñero Royo, "El sistema interamericano de los derechos humanos y los pueblos indígenas", pp.161-162.

1177 See Inter-American Commission on Human Rights/Comisión Interamericana de Derechos Humanos, *Resolución sobre el Procedimiento de Solución Amistosa sobre la Situación de los Derechos Humanos de un Sector de la Población Nicaragüense de Origen Miskito c. Nicaragua* and *Informe sobre la situación de los derechos humanos de un sector de la población nicaragüense de origen miskito*, OAS Doc. No. OEA/Ser.L/V/II.62, 29 November 1983, at http://www.ci dh.org/countryrep/Miskitosesp/Indice.htm. See also MacKay, *Guía para los derechos de los pueblos indígenas en el sistema interamericano*, pp.59.64.

1178 See the website of the Rapporteurship on the Rights of Indigenous Peoples at http://www.oas.org/en/iachr/indigenous/default.asp [Last access 12.08.2014].

1179 See the website of the Working Group (*Grupo de Trabajo Encargado de Elaborar el Proyecto de Declaración Americana sobre los Derechos de los Pueblos Indígenas*) at http://www.oas.org/consejo/sp/CAJP/Indigenas.asp [Last access 12.08.2014]. During the meeting of the Working Group to prepare the "Draft American Declaration on the Rights of Indigenous Peoples" in November 2009, a classification on the provisions that could facilitate consensus on the Declaration text was adopted. Among the "difficult texts", there were also provisions on the "Right to [autonomy] or [and] self-government" and on "Traditional forms of property and cultural survival. Right to land, territory, and resources", which would become arts.20 and 24, respectively, of a developed text. Organization of American States, Committee on Juridical and Political Affairs, Working Group to Prepare the Draft American Declaration on the Rights of Indigenous Peoples, "Classification of provisions that could facilitate consensus - Updated upon the conclusion of the Eleventh Meeting of Negotiations", OAS Doc. Nos. OEA/Ser.K/XVI, GT/DADIN/doc.329/08 rev. 3, 19 November 2009, p.16, at http://www.oas.org/dil/GT-DADIN-doc_329-08_rev3_eng.pdf [Last access 12.08.2014]. As mentioned in chapter 2, section 2.2.3, the works on the "Draft

The decision of the Inter-American Court of Human Rights on the case of *Comunidad Mayagna (Sumo) Awas Tingni v. Nicaragua* finally marked a pivotal change.[1180] As seen in chapter 1, section 1.3, in 2001, the Awas Tigni indigenous people of Nicaragua claimed the demarcation or their land according to art.5.3 of the Nicaraguan Constitution. *Inter alia*, the Court recognized that the indigenous community had a collective right to land within the general property right enshrined in art.21 of the Inter-American Convention of Human Rights.[1181] The IAtHR confirmed its precedent in subsequent cases, including *Comunidad Yakye Axa v. Paraguay* (2005), *Comunidad Indígena Sawhoyamaxa v. Paraguay* (2006), *Comunidad Indígena Xákmok Kásek v. Paraguay* (2010).[1182] Additonally, in the cases of *Mary & Carrie Dann v. Stati Uniti* (2002) and *Comunidades Mayas v. Belize* (2004), the Commission recalled the *Awas Tingni* case on the right to collective

---

American Declaration on the Rights of Indigenous Peoples" were then suspended due to a lack of funding in 2012. The process resumed recently (December 2014), and the text of the American Declaration should have been finally discussed during the OAS General Assembly in June 2015. However, in May 2015 the Indigenous Caucus withdrew from the negotiations. It alleged a lack of good will by the governments of Colombia, Brazil, Belize, Ecuador, Argentina, Chile, and Venezuela. Apparently, at the last moment, these States tried to introduce some changes in the text that would undermine the standards for the protection of indigenous rights, particularly in comparison with those contained in the UNDRIP. Cultural Survival. "Indigenous Caucus Withdraws from Negotiations on the Draft American Declaration ...".

1180 Inter-American Court of Human Rights, *Comunidad Mayangna (Sumo) Awas Tingni v. Nicaragua*, Serie C No.79, Judgment of 31 August 2001. For an analysis, see James Anaya and Claudio Grossman, "The Case of Awas Tingni v. Nicaragua: A New Step in the International Law of Indigenous Peoples", 19(1) *Arizona Journal of International and Comparative Law* 2002, pp.1-15.

1181 Inter-American Court of Human Rights, *Comunidad Mayangna (Sumo) Awas Tingni v. Nicaragua*, para.148, which states: "Through an evolutionary interpretation of international instruments for the protection of human rights, taking into account applicable norms of interpretation and pursuant to article 29(b) of the Convention –which precludes a restrictive interpretation of rights–, it is the opinion of this Court that article 21 of the Convention protects the right to property in a sense which includes, among others, the rights of members of the indigenous communities within the framework of communal property, which is also recognized by the Constitution of Nicaragua".

1182 Inter-American Court of Human Rights, *Comunidad Yakye Axa v. Paraguay*, Series C No.125, Judgement of 17 June 2005; Inter-American Court of Human Rights, case of *Comunidad Indígena Sawhoyamaxa v. Paraguay*, Series C No.146, Judgement of 29 March 2006; Inter-American Court of Human Rights, case of *Comunidad Indígena Xákmok Kásek v. Paraguay*, Series C No.214, Judgement of 24 August 2010.

land.[1183] Additionally, the Court continued to adopt landmark decisions vis-à-vis other indigenous rights. As seen in chapter 3, among these, the following cases are worth mentioning: *Yatama v. Nicaragua* (2005), on the right to participation in elections of Indigenous peoples;[1184] and *Saramaka People v. Suriname* (2007)[1185] and *Kichwa Ingenous People of Sarayaku v. Ecuador* (2012)[1186] on indigenous peoples' rights to consultation and to free, prior, and informed consent (FPIC).

4.3 *The increasing negotiating power of indigenous movements in Latin America*

Over the last decades, indigenous movements in Latin America have increased their negotiating powers. As mentioned (section 4.1.2), agrarian reforms prompted the creation of peasants' (*campesinos*) and workers' trade unions, which inevitably also included indigenous peoples. States that controlled and subsidized trade unions[1187] granted rights previously denied to indigenous peoples as a result of being relabeled "peasants".[1188] Therefore, peasant federations became the primary institutional avenue for indigenous peoples to interact with the State,[1189] although this essentially occurred exclusively in the Andean highlands.[1190] The considerable number of indigenous peoples organized within corporatist forms lasts until this very day (e.g., the *Confederación Sindical Única de Trabajadores Campesinos de*

1183 Inter-American Commission on Human Rights, *Mary and Carrie Dann v. United States*, Report No.75/02, Case No.11,140, 27 December 2002, at http://www.cidh.org/annualrep/2002eng/USA.11140.htm, http://www.cidh.org/annualrep/2002eng/USA.11140a.htm, and http://www.cidh.org/annualrep/2002eng/USA.11140b.htm [Last access 12.08.2014]; Inter-American Commission on Human Rights, *Fondo Comunidades Indígenas Mayas del Distrito de Toledo Belice*, Report No.40/04, Case No.12,053, 12 October 2004, para.114, at http://www.cidh.org/annualrep/2004sp/belize.12053.htm, and http://www.cidh.org/annualrep/2004sp/Belize.12053a.htm [Last access 12.08.2014].

1184 Inter-American Court of Human Rights, *YATAMA v. Nicaragua*, Series C No.127, Judgment of 23 June 2005.

1185 Inter-American Court of Human Rights, *Saramaka People v. Suriname*, Serie C No.172, Judgment of 28 November 2007.

1186 Inter-American Court of Human Rights, *Kichwa Ingenous People of Sarayaku v. Ecuador*, Serie C. No.245, Judgment of 27 June 2012.

1187 Yashar, *Contesting Citizenship in Latin America*, p.57.

1188 *Ibid.*, p.61.

1189 *Ibid.*, p.60.

1190 *Ibid.*, p.62.

Bolivia – CSUTCB in Bolivia), albeit with the erosion of what Yashar calls the corporatist citizenship regime caused by the neoliberal one which culminated in the 1980s and 1990s.[1191] This change of citizenship regime, according to Yashar, challenged the spaces of local autonomy that indigenous peoples had secured thanks to the granting of lands and labor laws in the highlands and the essential absence of the state in the lowlands (Amazonian region).[1192] This factor, as well as the construction of "transcommunity networks" and the availability of a "political associational space" represent the three elements that propelled the emergence of indigenous movements.[1193] Additionally, neoliberal policies had promoted free markets in labor and lands,[1194] thus undermining land security and social resources for indigenous peoples in the highlands[1195] and threatening indigenous peoples in the lowlands due to plans of expansion and exploitation of the Amazonian resources.[1196] Such consequences prompted the anti-neoliberal, or post-liberal, agenda of indigenous peoples.[1197] During the same time frame, indigenous peoples had also achieved the organizational capacity to organize and sustain a movement[1198] based on the previous networks supported by the State itself, as well as unions, churches, and NGOs.[1199] Finally, in both the highlands and lowlands, indigenous peoples had reached the sufficient "political associational space" to begin to mobilize.[1200]

The "ethnicization" of movements, which then promoted the "indigenous emergency/urgency" (*emergencia indígena*) in the early 1990s, according

1191 *Ibid.*, p.65. According to Yashar, the corporatist citizenship regime was pursued by Latin American states by extending social rights (e.g., labor rights, healthcare, and education), privileging corporatist modes of interest, thus collective units, addressing collective concerns, while the neoliberal citizenship regime favored the individual as the primary political subject. Yashar, *Contesting Citizenship in Latin America*, pp.48-49.
1192 *Ibid.*, p.63.
1193 *Ibid.*, p.55.
1194 *Ibid.*, p.66.
1195 *Ibid.*, p.67.
1196 *Ibid.*, p.70.
1197 *Ibid.*, p.66.
1198 *Ibid.*, p.71.
1199 *Ibid.*, p.73.
1200 *Ibid.*, p.76.

to Bengoa,[1201] have also been underlined by other authors.[1202] Other academics, however, have shown that these mobilizations were not a sort of "resurgence" but rather a question of visibility,[1203] and, I would add, of opportunity. As Yashar put it, "[o]ne must therefore ask not only why indigenous peoples would want to organize along indigenous lines, but also when they confronted the opportunity to do so, and where they had the capacity to mobilize accordingly".[1204] The numerous past indigenous rebellions, defined as "everyday forms of resistance",[1205] certainly cannot be overlooked. However, Yashar's variables convincingly explain why indigenous movements erupted in the 1990s rather than earlier.

In any case, for the aims of this work, it is sufficient to flag the empowerment of indigenous movements starting from the impressive indigenous marches which occurred in the two capital cities of La Paz and Quito in 1990.

The march for "Territory and Dignity", the first of nine marches organized (so far) in Bolivia, involved a dozen different indigenous peoples from the lowlands. Beginning in the city of Trinidad and ending in La Paz, the march covered a distance of approximately 400 miles/650 kilometres and lasted 35 days.[1206] The march was supported by the *Central de Pueblos Indígenas del Beni* (CPIB), an indigenous regional organization affiliated with the larger *Confederación Indígena del Oriente, Chaco y Amazonía de Bolivia* – CIDOB.[1207] This march also emblematically aimed to challenge the invisibility and "savage" stereotype of the Amazonian indigenous peoples.[1208] Their core demand was the official recognition of indigenous territories in the lowlands,[1209] which the State eventually granted (see chapter 5). Later, in May of the same year, undoubtedly pressured by the march to

1201 José Bengoa, *La emergencia indígena en América Latina*, Mexico City, Fondo de Cultura Economica, 2nd edition, 2007.

1202 Bello, *Etnicidad y ciudadanía en América Latina*, pp.63-64; Zúñiga García-Falces, "Emergencia del Movimiento indígena en América Latina …", pp.36-37 and 48;

1203 Giraudo and Martín Sánchez, "Neoindigenismo y movimientos indígenas en América Latina", pp.63-76, in particular p.70

1204 Yashar, *Contesting Citizenship in Latin America*, p.55.

1205 James C. Scott, *Weapons of the Weak: Everyday Forms of Peasant Resistance*, Yale University Press, New Haven CT, 1985.

1206 Xavier Albó, "Making the Leap from Local Mobilization to National Politics", 29(5) *NACLA Report in the Americas* 1996, pp.15-22, p.15.

1207 Recently renamed *Confederación de Pueblos Indígenas de Bolivia*. See their website at http://www.cidob-bo.org [Last access 13.08.2014].

1208 Yashar, *Contesting Citizenship in Latin America*, p.204.

1209 *Ibid.*, p.204.

La Paz, given that some activists had seen footage of it,[1210] the *Confederación de Nacionalidades Indígenas del Ecuador* (CONAIE) organized a ten-day mobilization that blocked roads, impeded commercial transport, and occupied churches.[1211] Many other indigenous communities and organizations joined the protest and, apart from land rights, their common demands regarded access to services and autonomy.[1212]

Both marches represented a milestone in (re)affirming the existence of indigenous peoples as another social player within the State. This was particularly relevant for the numerically smaller indigenous peoples of the lowlands,[1213] although they had started to organize in the 1960s and more decisively with the creation of COICA (Coordinating Body of Indigenous Peoples' Organizations of the Amazon Basin)[1214] in 1984. Moreover, the echo of the 1990 marches increased after the 1992 celebrations of the Quincentenary of Columbus' arrival.[1215] These marches embodied what has now become one of the main instruments in the hands of indigenous peoples to enter into real and proper negotiations with the government.[1216] In other words, thanks to these marches and their mobilization, indigenous movements became "new interlocutors" of the State[1217] and a key political factor,[1218] which explains their fundamental relevance in the context of Latin America.

Massive indigenous marches continue to be organized and prove to be significant tools of political negotiations. In general, indigenous peoples

---

1210 *Ibid.*, p.81.

1211 *Ibid.*, p.144.

1212 *Ibid.*, p.147.

1213 Kitula Libermann and Armando Godínez (eds.), *Territorio y dignidad: Pueblos indígenas y medio ambiente en Bolivia*, Nueva Sociedad, Caracas, 1992, p.59.

1214 The Federation of Shuar Centers (*Federacion Interprovincial de Centros Shuar*) was created in Ecuador in 1964, and in 1984 indigenous organizations from Bolivia, Colombia, Ecuador, and Peru met in Lima and founded the abovementioned COICA – *Coordinadora de las Organizaciones Indígenas de la Cuenca Amazónica* (Coordinating Body of Indigenous Peoples' Organizations of the Basin). Michael Kearney and Stefano Varese, "Indigenous Peoples: Changing Identities and Forms of Resistance", in Richard H. Harris and Jorge Nef (eds.), *Capital, Power, and Inequality in Latin America and the Caribbean*, Rowman & Littlefield Publishers, Lanham MD, 2008, pp.196-224, pp.214-215.

1215 Erick D. Langer, "Introduction", in Eric D. Langer and Elena Munoz, *Contemporary Indigenous Movements in Latina America*, Scholarly Resources Inc., Wilmington DE, 2003, pp.xi-xxix, p.xv.

1216 Zúñiga García-Falces, "Emergencia del Movimiento indígena en América Latina …", pp. 35-52, at 35.

1217 Yashar, *Contesting Citizenship in Latin America*, p.80.

1218 Langer, "Introduction", p.xi.

tend to claim their rights to autonomy and self-government, as well as to land, territories, and natural resources.[1219] Whereas the outcomes of the marches in Bolivia will be mentioned in chapter 5, the achievements (and failures) of all the indigenous movements throughout Latin American cannot be discussed further here, because they have already been extensively analyzed elsewhere.[1220] Suffice it to mention here a few of the massive marches which have occurred recently, the majority of which reiterated the aforementioned claims.

- In 2008, approx. 10,000 indigenous individuals marched from the Colombian Cauca to Bogotá to demand the end of the internal conflict-induced violence;[1221]
- In 2009, in Bagua (Peru), approx. 5,000 indigenous individuals protested against forest exploitation, and, after violent clashes with the police, some were killed.[1222]
- In 2010, there was a march in "Qhapaq Ñan" (Argentina) which was fuelled by the celebrations of the bicentenary of independence and involved approx. 20-25,000 indigenous individuals who marched from Salta to Buenos Aires. These indigenous peoples demanded recognition

---

1219 Kearney and Varese, "Indigenous Peoples: Changing Identities and Forms of Resistance", p.220.

1220 In chronological order, see Alison Brysk, *From Tribal Village to Global Village: Indian Rights and International Relations in Latin America*, Stanford University Press, Stanford CA, 2000; Kay B. Warren and Jean E. Jackson, *Indigenous Movements, Self-Representation and the State in Latin America*, University of Texas Press, Austin, 2002; Yashar, *Contesting Citizenship in Latin America*; Donna Van Lee Cott, *From Movements to Parties in Latin America. The Evolution of Ethnic Politics*, Cambridge University Press, Cambridge, New York, 2005; Salvador Martí i Puig (ed.), *Pueblos Indígenas y Política en América Latina. El Reconocimiento de sus Derechos y el Impacto de sus Demandas a inicio del Siglo XXI*, Fundació CIDOB, Barcelona, 2007.

1221 Myrna Cunningham Kain, "La participación política de los pueblos indígenas. Escenarios, estrategias, modalidades y resultados", in Felipe Gomez Isa and Mikel Berraondo (eds.), *Los derechos indígenas tras la Declaración. El desafío de la implementación*, Universidad de Deusto, Bilbao, 2013, pp.247-285, p.254.

1222 *Ibid.*, pp.258-259. The incidents of Bagua had echoed internationally, not only because this was the first recent uprising of indigenous peoples in the country since many years, but also due to the violent repression by the Peruvian police. See the report by the Peruvian ombudsman: Defensoría del Pueblo, "Informe sobre la actuación de la Defensoría del Pueblo en los sucesos acontecidos en las ciudades de Bagua y Utcubamba", 2009, at http://www.defensoria.gob.pe/module s/Downloads/documentos/INFORME-ACTUACIONES-BAGUA.pdf
[Last access 13.08.2014].

of their land rights and of the right to their free, prior, and informed consent (FPIC);[1223]

- In Bolivia, between 2011 and 2012, between 5-10,000 indigenous individuals participated in the two marches against the aforementioned construction of the highway in TIPNIS (*Territorio Indígena y Parque Nacional Isiboro-Secure*);1224
- In 2012, approx. 20,000 indigenous individuals from across Ecuador marched to Quito demanding respect for their right to water, life, and dignity (*Marcha plurinacional por el agua, la vida y la dignidad*) and against large-scale mining and hydroelectric projects, as well as the enlargement of the oil exploration territories into the Amazon rainforest. They also advocated a fast enactment of the "Water Law",[1225] which was eventually adopted on 24 June 2014 and which abrogates the privatization of water resources that are now in the hands of a national authority,[1226] while indigenous peoples can manage it at local level;[1227]
- From 2011 to 2014, hundreds of indigenous individuals participated in various protests in Brazil against the World Cup and to demand demarcations of their lands.[1228]

1223 Cunningham Kain, "La participación política de los pueblos indígenas …", p.252.

1224 *Ibid.*, pp.252-253.

1225 *Ibid.*, pp.255-255.

1226 For an overview, see El Telégrafo, "Asamblea aprobó la Ley de Aguas", *El Telégrafo*, 24.06.2014, at http://www.telegrafo.com.ec/politica/item/concluyo-de bate-sobre-ley-de-aguas-documento.html [Last access 14.08.2014].

1227 According to local newspapers, indigenous peoples organized a march against the adoption of this law the day before its adoption. They considered that, although they eventually declared that its adoption was a fundamental step forward, they would have preferred to have more direct control of the water resources. See Redacción Cuenca, "La marcha en contra de la Ley de Aguas seguirá pese a la aprobación de norma", *El Comercio*, 24.06.2014, at http://www.elcomer cio.com/actualidad/marcha-ley-aguas-ecuador-indigenas.html; Redacción EFE verde, "La nueva ley de Agua de Ecuador preocupa a los colectivos indígenas", *EFE verde*, 25.06.2014, at http://www.efeverde.com/noticias/el-parlamen to-de-ecuador-aprueba-una-ley-de-agua-que-preocupa-los-colectivos-indigenas; Redacción El Universo, "Caminata indígena contra Ley de Aguas llega hoy a Loja", *El Universo*, at http://www.eluniverso.com/noticias/2014/06/23/no ta/3140796/caminata-indigena-llega-hoy-loja [Last access to all articles 14.08.2014].

1228 See, e.g., Survival International, "The Dark Side of Brazil: Police teargas Indians at anti-World Cup protest", 30 May 2014, at http://www.survival international.org/news/10258 [Last access 13.08.2014].

Lastly, three more aspects regarding the increasing –albeit still limited– influence of indigenous movements in the subcontinent needs to be mentioned here: The evolution of indigenous movements into political parties; their participation in both Constituent Assemblies of Ecuador and Bolivia; and their support of indigenous candidates at the presidential elections.

As to the first point, the most glaring example is the indigenous peoples' movement-based party *Movimiento de Unidad Plurinacional Pachakutik*, formed by the influential CONAIE movement. *Pachakutik* has played a relevant role since the 1996 elections, gaining the support of 80% of the indigenous peoples in the country at the time.[1229] However, since 2002 the party has lost strength due, primarily, to internal divisions among its members and its expulsion from the government of Lucio Gutiérrez in 2003.[1230] This negative trend has continued until recently. In the 2013 elections, *Pachakutik* received only 20% of the vote from the electorate in areas where the majority of indigenous peoples live.[1231] Apparently, this collapse of votes is due to structural factors within the indigenous peoples' movement, such as the weakening of CONAIE and its inability to satisfy the demands of different indigenous sectors, as well as contextual factors, such as recent dubious alliances or the divisions among local candidates.[1232] Therefore, although the evolution of *Pachakutik* was impressive during the 1990s, its recent failures cast a shadow over indigenous peoples' effective participation within the Ecuadorian parliamentary assembly.[1233] In comparison with other situations (see, e.g., Chile, chapter 6) however, the achievement of founding and organizing a rather successful indigenous political party is surely noteworthy. Additonally, as mentioned, the *Confederación de Nacionalidades Indígenas del Ecuador* (CONAIE) and *Federación Nacional*

1229 Van Lee Cott, *From Movements to Parties in Latin America*, p.99.

1230 Donna Van Lee Cott, "De los movimientos a los partidos: retos para los movimientos de los pueblos indígenas", in Salvador Martí i Puig (ed.), *Pueblos Indígenas y Política en América Latina: El reconocimiento de sus derechos y el impacto de sus demandas a inicios del siglo XXI*, Fundació CIDOB, Barcelona, 2007, pp.103-125, p.106.

1231 Secretariat of the UN Permanent Forum of Indigenous Issues, "Examination of the situation of indigenous peoples and their participation in democracies and electoral processes in Latin America under the United Nationas Declaration on the Rights of Indigenous Peoples", UN Doc. E/C.19/2014/6, 26 February 2014, para.24, p.7.

1232 *Ibid.*

1233 For a recent analysis of the Ecuadorian case, see Philipp Altmann, *Die Indigenenbewegung in Ecuador. Diskurs und Dekolonialität*, Reihe Global Studies, Transcript Verlag, Bielefeld, 2013.

de Organizaciones Campesinas Indígenas y Negras (FENOCIN) actively participated as members of the Constituent Assembly.[1234]

Finally, indigenous movements also supported indigenous candidates during presidential elections. This is the case, for example, of the Nobel prize-winning Rigoberta Menchú Tum in Guatemala in 2007. As the first indigenous woman to stand as a candidate in these elections, she only obtained 2.42% of the popular vote,[1235] although indigenous peoples in Guatemala constitute at least 40% of the total population, according to the official data of the 2002 census.[1236] In 2011, Rigoberta Menchú Tum ran for President once again, although this time she was supported by the leading indigenous Winaq party and another indigenous woman, Laura Reyes, stood for Vice-President within the *Partido Renovación Democrática*.[1237] They eventually lost, but one minister and two governors of indigenous origin were appointed.[1238] These are certainly impressive achievements for Guatemala. That being said however, indigenous peoples are still widely underrepresented, considering that, as mentioned, they represent approximately 40% of the total population.[1239]

Finally, the Presidency of Juan Evo Morales Ayma of the *Movimiento al Socialismo* (MAS) party in Bolivia needs to be briefly mentioned here. Prior to his election in 2005, the Aymara politician Victor Hugo Cardenas Conde was appointed vice-president in the cabinet of Gonzalo Sanchez de Lozada in the 1993-1997 legislature and greatly contributed to the adoption of many

---

1234 Pablo Ortiz-T., "Ecuador", p.150.

1235 See Inés Benítez, "Rigoberta Menchú llego para quedarse", 28 August 2007, *Inter Press Service*, http://indigenous peoplesnoticias.net/nota.asp?idnews=41977 [Last access 13.08.2014].

1236 Schkolink and del Popolo, "Los censos y los pueblos indígenas en América Latina: Una metodología Regional", p.19, table 9. However, other sources indicated that indigenous peoples constitute at least the 60% of the total population of Guatemala. See Silvel Elías, "Guatemala", in International Work Group for Indigenous Affairs, *The Indigenous World 2014*, IWGIA, Copenhagen 2014, pp.76-84, p.76 at http://www.iwgia.org/publications/search-pubs?publication_id=671, or directly at http://www.iwgia.org/iwgia_files_publications_files/0671_I2014eb.pdf [Last access 13.08.2014].

1237 Secretariat of the UN Permanent Forum of Indigenous Issues, "Examination of the situation of indigenous peoples and their participation in democracies ...", p.10, para.40.

1238 *Ibid.*

1239 Schkolink and del Popolo "Los censos y los pueblos indígenas en América Latina: Una metodología Regional", p.10, para.41.

decisive legislative measures,[1240] such as the Popular Participation Law (Law No. 1551/1994), the Forest Law (Law No. 1700/1996) and the *Instituto Nacional de Reforma Agraria* (INRA) Law (Law No. 1715/1996; see chapter 5). During the Presidential elections of 2002, Morales garnered 21% of the vote.[1241] The neoliberal crisis, the well-renowned 2000 Cochabamba Water Wars, and the 2003 Gas War also contributed to support his presidential bid.[1242] Morales won the presidential elections on 18 December 2005 with 53.7% of the vote, the highest percentage ever reached by a candidate since the re-establishment of democracy in 1982.[1243] However, despite his wide indigenous support, shortly thereafter he refused to propose a number of indigenous organizations to organize special constituencies in order to increase indigenous participation in the Constituent Assembly.[1244] Recently, opposition to the abovementioned construction of the highway in the TIPNIS Park also displays a growing discontent of indigenous peoples vis-à-vis his conduct. Thus, although his election in 2005, 2009 and 2014 had marked an unquestionable milestone for both Bolivian history and indigenous peoples worldwide, critical indigenous voices are internally increasing (see further in chapter 5).

4.4 Concluding remarks

This chapter has offered an overview of the phases of indigenous peoples' constitutional protection in the complex Latin American context until the recent adoption of the innovative Constitutions of Ecuador and Bolivia. As

1240 Willem Assies, "Pueblos Indígenas y Reforma del Estado en América Latina", in Willem Assies, Gemma van der Haar and André Hoekema (eds.), *El reto de la diversidad: Pueblos indígenas y reforma del Estado en América Latina*, El Colegio de Michoacán, Zamora-Michoacán, 1999, pp.21-55, p.35.

1241 Langer, "Introduction", p.xi.

1242 Xavier Albó, "Bolivia: Avances y tropezones hacia un nuevo país plurinacional e Intercultural", in Salvador Martí i Puig (ed.), *Pueblos Indígenas y Política en América Latina: El reconocimiento de sus derechos y el impacto de sus demandas a inicios del siglo XXI*, Fundació CIDOB, Barcelona, 2007, pp.335-359, pp.344-349.

1243 International Work Group for Indigenous Affairs, *The Indigenous World 2007*, IWGIA, Copenhagen 2009, p.186, at http://www.iwgia.org/publications/search-pubs?publication_id=83, or directly at http://www.iwgia.org/iwgia_files_publications_files/00 83_NY-THE_INDIGENOUS_ORLD-2007.pdf [Last access 14.08.2014].

1244 International Work Group for Indigenous Affairs, *The Indigenous World 2007*, p.188.

seen, and as is painfully obvious, constitutional protection *per se*, albeit extremely advanced, does not guarantee a fair application of its provisions. The *Amparo* proceedings may be a useful tool to safeguard indigenous constitutional rights and some indigenous claimants have been increasingly successful as a result (see chapter 6). The evolving and groundbreaking jurisprudence of the Inter-American Court of Human Rights show a growing recognition and protection of indigenous peoples in the region. The Court has also become the leading avenue to litigate indigenous rights. Likewise, indigenous movements from the 1960s and particularly after the 1990s have become influential actors in Latin American political arenas. Similarly, their participation in electoral processes has progressed. Nevertheless, although the present decade should be "the" Latin American decade,[1245] further enhanced by the creation of CELAC in late 2011,[1246] the region is still home to huge socio-economic differences, which are acute in the case of indigenous peoples.[1247] Thus, even in the lively context of Latin America, indigenous peoples still face substantial obstacles and their participation needs to be further enhanced.[1248] Hence, the recognition and application of the *composite right to political participation of indigenous peoples* proposed in chapter 3 at domestic level will be explored subsequently in two opposing case studies; Bolivia and Chile (chapters 5 and 6). The overall aim

1245 See Fabíola Ortiz, "América Latina confía en que ésta será su década", *IPs Noticias*, 30.04.2011, http://www.indigenouspeoplesnoticias.net/nota.asp?idnews=98088 [Last access 19.08.2014].

1246 The Community of Latin American and Caribbean States (*Comunidad de Estados Latinoamericanos y Caribeños* – CELAC) is a regional organization that aims to foster political collaboration, integration, and cooperation among Latin American and Caribbean countries. See para.31 of the Caracas Declaration, 3 December 2011, at http://www.sela.org/attach/258/default/Declaracion_de_Caracas.pdf [Last access 19.08.2014]. Also indigenous peoples are considered in the CELAC in para.17, which states that their (and afro-descendants') struggles and moral, political, economic, spiritual, and cultural contributions have been decisive in the construction of Latin American and Caribbean identities, nations, and democracies. So far, a further other two CELAC summits have both been held in Cuba, in January, in 2013 and 2014. For an overview of the creation of CELAC, see Sistema Económico Latinoamericano y del Caribe, "El proceso de creación de la CELAC", http://www.sela.org/view/index.asp?ms=258&pageM s=97495 [Last access 19.08.2014].

1247 See Raúl Pierri, "Desigualdad, el talón de Aquiles", *IPS Noticias*, 19.03.2012, http://www.indigenous peoplesnoticias.net/nota.asp?idnews=100374 [Last access 19.08.2014].

1248 Secretariat of the UN Permanent Forum of Indigenous Issues, "Examination of the situation of indigenous peoples and their participation in democracies …", p.11, para.76.

is to assess whether this *composite right* may also become one of the expressions, or better, effective applications of the right to self-determination of indigenous peoples.

5. The Bolivian case

This chapter analyses the recognition and application of the composite right to political participation of indigenous peoples proposed in chapter 3 at the domestic level in the case of Bolivia. As is widely known, in the last decade, far-reaching legal and institutional changes have been adopted in Bolivia. As mentioned in the Introduction, indigenous peoples in Bolivia are (theoretically) provided with the highest existing standards of legal protection in Latin America, and, likely, in the world. However, as is painfully obvious, theory is far from practice, and the same is true for Bolivia. Therefore, after briefly introducing the Bolivian context, the first relevant reforms from the 1990s onwards (section 5.1), and the international and current domestic legal framework that protect indigenous rights (section 5.2), primary attention will be given to the implementation of the rights that enable indigenous peoples to exercise the proposed composite right to political participation, which follows a twofold approach (see chapter 3, and, particularly, section 3.4). As such, indigenous peoples' representation in State's bodies or in other public posts, including in decision-making processes and in the judiciary, both at national and local level, as well as their rights to consultation and free, prior and informed consent (FPIC) will be addressed first (section 5.3). Indigenous autonomy/self-government arrangements and the preservation of indigenous institutions will be then explored (section 5.4). The latter aspect is of particular importance since a new complex system of autonomies, including the Peasant Native Indigenous Autonomy (*Autonomía Indígena Originaria Campesina* – AIOC), was introduced in the 2009 Bolivian constitutional order.[1249]

1249 Previous versions of sections 5.1.2, 5.4.2, 5.4.3, 5.4.4.2 and 5.4.4.6 of this chapter have appeared in Alexandra Tomaselli, "*Autonomía Indígena Originaria Campesina* in Bolivia: Realizing the indigenous autonomy?", in *European Diversity and Autonomy Papers* (EDAP), no.1/2012, pp.1-56, http://www.eurac.edu/edap.

5.1 Introduction to the Bolivian context

5.1.1 Socio-economic data

A vast majority of the Bolivian population are indigenous, or of indigenous origin. It is very arduous to evaluate the almost unavoidable *mestizaje* along family lines since the Conquista. However, a system of "Indian registers" was kept until early 1900, for utilitarian purposes (payment of tolls) rather than statistical ones. For instance, the *mestizos* were exempted from such payment in early 1900 only if they were able to demonstrate that they were not indigenous.[1250] Nevertheless, the 1900 census only included four categories (white, *mestizo*, indigenous, and black), and 46% of the total population self-identified as indigenous under the heading of "race and *castas*".[1251] In the 1950 census in Bolivia, that number grew to 63% of the population.[1252] This increase was likely due to the registration of indigenous individuals by the census' officials on the basis of the language they spoke or whether they were wearing traditional clothing.[1253] After the Agrarian reform, as seen in chapter 4 and will be discussed briefly below, the categories of indigenous peoples and peasants were merged. However, the censuses of 1976, 1992, and 2001 registered similarly high percentages of indigenous peoples.[1254]

1250 See Ramiro Molina Barrios, Milenka Figueroa and Isabel Quisbert, "Los pueblos indígenas de Bolivia: diagnóstico sociodemográfico a partir del censo del 2001", Comisión Económica para América Latina y el Caribe (CEPAL), Santiago de Chile, 2005, pp.12-14 and, in particular, p.15.

1251 Molina Barrios, Figueroa and Quisbert, "Los pueblos indígenas de Bolivia: diagnóstico sociodemográfico a partir del censo del 2001", pp.15-16. The system of "castas" (castes) was used to categorize the population according to their origins and the various processes of *mestizaje* that inevitably followed. Molina Barrios, Figueroa and Quisbert, "Los pueblos indígenas de Bolivia: diagnóstico sociodemográfico a partir del censo del 2001", p.14.

1252 Molina Barrios, Figueroa and Quisbert, "Los pueblos indígenas de Bolivia: diagnóstico sociodemográfico a partir del censo del 2001", p.16. See also Giraudo and Sánchez, "Neoindigenismo y movimientos indígenas en América Latina", 70.

1253 Molina Barrios, Figueroa and Quisbert, "Los pueblos indígenas de Bolivia: diagnóstico sociodemográfico a partir del censo del 2001", p.16.

1254 Molina Barrios, Figueroa and Quisbert, "Los pueblos indígenas de Bolivia: diagnóstico sociodemográfico a partir del censo del 2001", p.16. See also José Luis López Fuentes, *El derecho a la libre determinación de los pueblos indígenas en Bolivia*, Centro de Ecología y Pueblos Andinos (CEPA), Latinas Editores, Oruro, 2007, pp.105-111.

The 2001 census included three specific questions to more accurately nuance the vast indigenous portion of the Bolivian population. These questions regarded the language of use; a self-declaration; and mother tongue.[1255] Combining these criteria and giving more relevance to self-identification and one data or other concerning the language, it is estimated that 65.8% of Bolivians above 15 years (3,229,239 out of 4,904,161) was indigenous according to the 2001 census.[1256] Out of these, the majority of indigenous peoples self-identified as Quechua (50%), followed by: Aymara (41.2%), Chiquitano (Besiro, Napeca, Paunaca and Moncoca: 3.6%), Guaraní (Ava, Izoceño and Simba: 2.5%) and Mojeño (Trinitario, Javeriano, Loretano and Ignaciano: 1.5%). The numerous other indigenous peoples did not exceed 0.2%.[1257] The indigenous peoples represent a large majority of the population (up to 90% in Potosí) particularly in the Western-Andean departments/*departamentos* (La Paz, Cochabamba, Oruro, Potosí and Chuquisaca), whereas in the Eastern ones (Santa Cruz, Tarija, Beni, and Pando) the highest proportion they reach is 40%, in Santa Cruz.[1258] However, it needs to be stressed here that many indigenous peoples migrated internally from their original communities to the departments of Santa Cruz, Cochabamba, and La Paz in search of job opportunities.[1259] As for literacy rates, the 2001 data registered 82% of indigenous peoples as having the ability to read and write, approximately 12.5% less in comparison to the non-indigenous population.[1260] However, as to the rates of school attendance of young indigenous peoples, the percentages were

1255 Molina Barrios, Figueroa and Quisbert, "Los pueblos indígenas de Bolivia: diagnóstico sociodemográfico a partir del censo del 2001", pp.25-29.

1256 *Ibid.*, p.32. The total Bolivian population according to 2001 was of 8,274,325 persons, out of which 8,261,554 replied to the question "Which language do you speak?". The replies to this questions were native language, bilingual (native language and Spanish/Castilian), Spanish/Castilian and/or other foreign languages, or none. By combining the data of both native and bilingual speakers, also of children aged between 0-14 years, the indigenous population appear to reach 66.4% in 2001. *Ibid.*, pp.41-42.

1257 *Ibid.*, p.39. Among the other indigenous peoples, in alphabetical order, they self-identified as Araona, Ayoreo, Baure, Canichana, Cavineño, Cayubaba, Chácobo Chimán-Tsimane, Ese-ejja/Chama, Guarasugwe, Guarayo, Itonama, Joaquiniano, Leco, Machineri Yine, Moré, Mosetén, Movima, Pacahuara, Reyesano-Maropa, Sirionó, Tacana, Tapieté, Urus (Uru-chipaya, Murato, Uruito), Weenhayek-Mataco, Yaminawa, Yuki, and Yurakaré, plus approx. 32,000 unspecified indigenous people. *Ibid.*, p.40, table IV.2.

1258 *Ibid.*, p.44.

1259 *Ibid.*, p.55 and ff.

1260 *Ibid.*, p.71.

quite low, reaching worrisome thresholds in rural areas, particularly regarding girls and women.[1261] Finally, with regard to employment rates, the indigenous peoples registered higher percentages than the non-indigenous population,[1262] which is also generally richer (see next section 5.1.2).

The official data of the 2012 census, published in 2013, registered an oddly sharp decrease in people above 15 years old self-identifying as indigenous (or Afro-Bolivian) to 40.6%.[1263] The total population of Bolivia at the time was 10,027,254,[1264] of whom only 6,916,732 (69%) replied to the question of whether or not they belong to an "indigenous nation or people".[1265] Indeed, faced with the option of selecting neither an indigenous people nor Bolivian[1266], 31% of the population did not provide any answer as many indigenous peoples were probably migrating or not in a stable situation during the time of the census. In any case, it suffices to underline here that, out of these 2.8 million of self-declared indigenous peoples, 2.4 million live in the highlands and around 178,000 in the lowlands.[1267] The five larger indigenous peoples (Quechua, Aymara, Chiquitano, Guaraní and Mojeño) registered the greatest decline in numbers, with almost 18% in the case of Quechuas and 25% of the three latter groups. However, other

1261 Among the youngsters between 13-20 years, only 65% attended school, but in rural areas that number drops to 57.3%, where only 51% of girls attend school. Molina Barrios, Figueroa and Quisbert, "Los pueblos indígenas de Bolivia: diagnóstico sociodemográfico a partir del censo del 2001", p.76.

1262 61.7% of indigenous peoples compared to 57% non-indigenous. Molina Barrios, Figueroa and Quisbert, "Los pueblos indígenas de Bolivia: diagnóstico sociodemográfico a partir del censo del 2001", p.112.

1263 I.e., 2,806,592 of 6,916,732 provided an answer to this question. Instituto Nacional de Estadística (INE), "BOLIVIA. Características de población y vivienda Censo Nacional de Población y Vivienda 2012", 31 July 2013, p.31, at http://www.ine.gob.bo:8081/censo2012 or directly at http://www.ine.gob.bo:8081/censo2012/PDF/resultadosCPV2012.pdf [Last access 20.08.2014]. Interestingly, here, as well as with regard to reserved seats (see below section 5.3.1), the afro-descendants (Afro-boliviano) in Bolivia are included as indigenous peoples.

1264 *Ibid.*, p.4.

1265 *Ibid.*, p.31.

1266 *Ibid.*, p.31. 4.032.014 replied that they do not belong to an indigenous people (or Afro-Bolivian) and 73.707 declared themselves to not be indigenous.

1267 Leonardo Tamburini, "Bolivia (2014)", in International Work Group for Indigenous Affairs (IWGIA), The Indigenous World 2014, IWGIA, Copenhagen, 2014, pp.167-175, p.170.

lowlands peoples expanded their numbers; the Araona, for example, increased from 90 to 910 people.[1268]

5.1.2 Marginalization of indigenous peoples, the 1990 reforms, and the new Constitution

Although indigenous peoples have always represented a large part of the Bolivian population, they have also long been marginalized in the country. The most notorious uprising before independence was the 184-days siege of La Paz led by Túpac Katari (Júlian Apasa Nina) and his wife Bartolina Sisa.[1269] Bolivia gained independence and became a Republic in 1825. As mentioned in chapter 4, the foundation of the new State by the Creoles did not include the end of the exploitation and the exclusion of indigenous peoples in Bolivia.[1270] This does not mean that the indigenous peoples were simply subjugated. Rather, the relation among the new Bolivian political elites and the various indigenous leaders remained ambiguous and utilitarian according to the different phases of Bolivian history. The colonial regime of tolls' payment, work, and services imposed on indigenous peoples was maintained until the late 1870s to ensure sufficient revenue for the newly established state.[1271] Indigenous peoples also participated in the construction of the Bolivian "national project".[1272]

Far from analyzing Bolivian history in detail, it is sufficient to demonstrate the complexity of the relationship by underlining the elucidatory role of Aymara indigenous peoples in the auxiliary armies of the rebel forces in the Bolivian civil wars of 1870 and 1899. The involvement of indigenous peoples in the first war, according to the same rebels, could have generated at least two positive developments for the –at

1268 Tamburini, "Bolivia (2014)", p.170.

1269 See Beatriz Rossells, "Los cementerios, los héroes y la memoria patriótica en Bolivia", *Revista Domínios Da Imagem*, Vol. 7, No.13, 2013, pp.8-23.

1270 Rodolfo Stavenhagen, "Promotion and protection of all human rights, civil, political, economic, social and cultural rights, including the right to development. Report of the Special Rapporteur on the situation of human rights and fundamental freedoms of indigenous people. Mission to Bolivia", Human Rights Council, eleventh session, 18 February 2009, UN Doc.A/HRC/11/11, para.12, p.5.

1271 Molina Barrios, Figueroa and Quisbert, "Los pueblos indígenas de Bolivia: diagnóstico sociodemográfico a partir del censo del 2001", p.14.

1272 On this, see Marta Irurozqui Victoriano, "The Sound of the *Pututos*. Politicisation and Indigenous Rebellions in Bolivia, 1826-1921", *Journal of Latin American Studies*, Vol. 32, No. 1, Andean Issue (Feb., 2000), pp. 85-114.

that time (still) officially called– *indios*:[1273] First, the recuperation of their land; and second, their "public reincorporation [...] [into the] national [Bolivian] people". [1274] During the First Independence War and the following decades after the creation of the republic in 1825, the *indios* had been, in fact, recognized as *vecinos* or citizens.[1275] However, in the 1870s they were renamed *la indiada*.[1276] The more *la indiada* was considered a threat to the Bolivian state, especially regarding its territorial control and autonomous political and justice systems, the more frequently its members were found guilty of attempting to harm national unity.[1277] Thus, their participation in the rebels' forces would have meant their "final liberation" from what was impeding them from enjoying the full status of "members of Bolivia".[1278] In this way, acting as "patriots", the indigenous population regained a presence in the public sphere.[1279] Notwithstanding their participation in the forces, a couple of decades later, the Mohoza massacre in Pando in 1899 during the Federal War marked a change in perception in the form of the 'criminalization' of *la indiada*.[1280] A proper justification of (re)classifying these people(s) as enemies and uncivilized peoples in need of education was hence established with the massacre.[1281] This implied a negation of the legitimacy of their political and social claims.[1282] However, it is most likely that their role in the revolution was limited because of their

1273 Marta Irurozqui Victoriano, "Conversos a la patria boliviana: Identidad y participación política indígenas en las revoluciones de 1870 y 1899", in VV.AA., *Relaciones sociales e identidades en América: IX Encuentro-Debate América latina ayer y hoy*, Barcelona, 2004, pp.385–400, p.392. Marta Irurozqui Victoriano is a leading expert on Bolivian nineteenth-century history, which explains why only her works have been cited.

1274 *Ibid.*, p.392.

1275 *Ibid.*

1276 *Ibid.*

1277 *Ibid.*, pp.392-393.

1278 *Ibid.*, p.393.

1279 *Ibid.*, p.394.

1280 Between 28 February and 1 March 1899, 120 people were killed in Pando by the indigenous auxiliary forces. However, they had simply obeyed a military order. Marta Irurozqui Victoriano, "Los hombre Chacales en armas: Militarización y criminalización indígenas en la revolución federal boliviana de 1899", in Marta Irurozqui Victoriano (ed.), *La mirada esquiva: Reflexiones históricas sobre la interacción del Estado y la ciudadanía en los Andes, (Bolivia, Ecuador y Perú), siglo XIX*, Consejo Superior de Investigaciones Científicas, Madrid, 2005, pp.285-320, p.310.

1281 Irurozqui Victoriano, "Conversos a la patria boliviana ...", pp.398-399.

1282 *Ibid.*, p.399.

status as menaces and thus the possibility that they could have changed the political scenario.[1283]

Without going into further details, suffice it here to flag that in early 1900 a number of indigenous protests took place, such as an insurrection in 1921 in the village of Jesús de Machaca, when the local Aymara people demanded the recognition of their own authorities and organizational structure, albeit without much success.

In 1952, massive popular mobilizations in both urban and rural areas brought the leaders of the revolution to power: the *Movimiento Nacionalista Revolucionario* (MNR) political party.[1284] However, protests in rural areas escalated and the MNR organized society into class-based groups, thus equating indigenous peoples to peasants (*campesinos*). Among the populist measures adopted, citizenship rights were finally extended, universal suffrage was recognized, and rural education meliorated. Additionally, the MNR started a land reform in 1953. Prior to this reform, it is estimated that 95% of the cultivable lands were in the hands of solely 8% of landholders, who used only 0.8% of these lands.[1285] Considerable territory was thus distributed to *campesinos*,[1286] but today large landowners still retain 90% of the total land, while the remaining 10% is owned by family farms, many of whom are indigenous.[1287] Additionally, the agrarian reform had a few detrimental effects. In the highlands, the creation of small land holdings was frustrated by the increasing fragmentation of these tiny lands through inheritance. In the lowlands, farming and forestry industries were favoured at the expense of indigenous peoples by the discretionary distribution of successive *de facto* governments,[1288] especially during the dictatorship between 1964 and 1982.

In these years, indigenous peoples started to mobilize within trade unions, as seen in chapter 4, section 4.3, among these, the *Confederación Sindical Única de Trabajadores Campesinos de Bolivia* – CSUTCB in the highlands, and, later, the *Confederación Indígena del Oriente, Chaco y Amazonía de Bolivia* – CIDOB (recently renamed *Confederación de Pueblos Indígenas de Bolivia*) in the lowlands. Another landmark event was the 1973 Tiahuanacu manifesto, in which self-determination and autonomy

---

1283 *Ibid.*

1284 Yashar, *Contesting Citizenship in Latin America*, p.155

1285 *Ibid.*, p.156.

1286 *Ibid.*, p.158.

1287 Stavenhagen, "Promotion and protection of all human rights ... Mission to Bolivia", para.28, p.9.

1288 *Ibid.*

were claimed by Aymara intellectuals.[1289] For the aims of this study, the focus is limited to the developments in the legal framework after the 1990 march for "Territory and Dignity",[1290] which represented a milestone in (re)affirming the existence of indigenous peoples and their movements as another social player within the Bolivian state.[1291]

Thanks to this march and to a second wave of reforms promoted by the Aymara vice-president Victor Hugo Cardenas in the cabinet of Sanchez de Lozada in 1993-1997, many legislative measures were adopted.[1292] These included (in chronological order): the Environmental Law (Law No. 1333/1992); the constitutional reform of 1994; the Popular Participation Law (Law No. 1551/1994); the Forest Law (Law No. 1700/1996); the Law on the National Institute of Land Reform (*Instituto Nacional de Reforma Agraria* – INRA; Law No. 1715/1996); and the (second) Municipality Law (Law No. 2028/1999). As Postero has pointed out, these "reforms were the result of strategic articulations between the ruling *Movimiento Nacional Revolucionario* (MNR) party and indigenous groups".[1293]

Regarding the 1994 reform of the 1967 Constitution, the main achievements vis-à-vis indigenous peoples claims were the constitutional definition of Bolivia as a "multi-ethnic and pluricultural state" (art.1); the recognition of socio-economic and cultural rights to indigenous peoples; and the introduction of forms of collective properties, namely the *Tierras Comunitarias de Origen* (TCO) in art.171.1. The adoption of this provision was the result of an arduous negotiation within the government of Sanchez de Lozada since many deputies were against the use of the word

1289 Edward L. Cleary, *Mobilizing for Human Rights in Latin America*, Kumarian Press, Sterling VA, 2007, pp.59-60.

1290 Another six marches followed between 1994 and 2009. The seventh march took place in June 2010. Its core claim was to revise the draft Autonomy Law. Leonardo Tamburini, "Bolivia (2011)", in International Work Group for Indigenous Affairs, *El mundo indígena 2011*, IWGIA, Copenhagen, 2011, pp.174-182, p.177. The eighth and ninth marches, instead, regarded the indigenous territory *Territorio Indígena y Parque Nacional Isiboro-Secure* (TIPNIS).

1291 For an overview on the evolution of Bolivian indigenous movements since the 1950s see Yashar, *Contesting Citizenship in Latin America*, pp.152-223, and Van Lee Cott, *From Movements to Parties in Latin America*, pp.49-98.

1292 Willem Assies, "Pueblos Indígenas y Reforma del Estado en América Latina", in Willem Assies, Gemma van der Haar and André Hoekema (eds.), *El reto de la diversidad: Pueblos indígenas y reforma del Estado en América Latina*, El Colegio de Michoacán, Zamora-Michoacán, 1999, pp.21-55, at 35. Prior to this, on 11 December 1991, Bolivia also ratified ILO Convention 169. See also section 5.2.

1293 Nancy Grey Postero, *Now We Are Citizens*, Stanford University Press, Stanford, 2007, pp.124-25.

"indigenous territories". Eventually, the term "collective lands" was preferred, also to accommodate the demands of the lowland indigenous peoples. [1294] Moreover, the indigenous communities, associations, and unions were granted legal personality (art.171.2), and the indigenous authorities were authorized to apply indigenous customary law as alternative forms of conflict resolution within the limits of the Constitution and the other national laws (art.171.3).[1295] Another relevant constitutional revision regarded the election of the 130 deputies of the Lower Chamber (Chamber of Deputies), half of which had to be elected in uninominal circumscriptions (art.68). This allowed direct elections of candidates by simple majority for the first time. Prior to this reform, Bolivians could vote for the Presidential candidate only and thus for his/her party.[1296]

The INRA Law regulated access to the recognition and establishment of these TCOs (arts.3.3 and 41.1.5) under the supervision of the Agrarian Reform National Institute (*Instituto Nacional de Reforma Agraria* – INRA), arts.13-18). According to art.41.1.5 of the INRA Law, the TCOs are "geographical areas which constitute the habitat of indigenous and native peoples and communities, which have traditionally been accessed and where they maintain and develop their own forms of economic, social and cultural organization in order to ensure their survival and development. They are *inalienable, indivisible, irreversible*, *collective*, composed of communities or associations, *non-forfeitable* and *imprescriptible*" [emphasis added].[1297] In addition, art.3.3 of the INRA Law declared that entitlement to a TCO "*cannot be reversed, alienated, burdened, seized or acquired by prescription*. The distribution and redistribution for individual and family use within the [TCOs] shall be governed by the community rules, according to their rules and customs" [emphasis added].[1298]

1294 Fundación Konrad Adenauer Stiftung (KAS), *Participación Política Indígena. Mitos y Realidades*, Fundación Konrad Adenauer Stiftung, La Paz, 2006, p.74.

1295 Although a proposal for a Community Justice Law was advanced, it was never adopted. Xavier Albó, "Bolivia: From Indian and Campesino Leaders to Councillors and Parliamentary Deputies", in Rachel Sieder (ed.), *Multiculturalism in Latin America. Indigenous Rights, Diversity and Democracy*, Palgrave Macmillan, New York, 2002, pp.74-102, p.80.

1296 Alcides Vadillo, "Constitución Política del Estado y pueblos indígenas: Bolivia, país de mayoría indígena", in Magdalena Gomez (ed.), *Derecho Indígena. Seminario Internacional*, Instituto Nacional Indigenista, Mexico City, 1997, pp.331-355, p.335.

1297 My translation of art.41.1.5 of the INRA Law at http://www.ine.gob.bo/indicadoresddhh/archivos/viole/nal/Ley%20N%201715.pdf [Last access 20.08.2014].

1298 My translation of art.3.3 of the INRA Law. For a recent and thorough analysis of the TCOs, see Gonzalo Colque and Juan Pablo Chumacero, *Informe 2010:*

The new 2009 constitution converted the TCO into TIOC *Territorio Indígena Campesino Originario* (see Transitory Disposition 7; and arts.269.1 and 394). [1299] Notwithstanding this important achievement, 58.2% of the TCOs/TIOCs in the Amazon region are still affected by territorial discontinuity today, which undermines the exercise of indigenous peoples' land rights within these territories.[1300]

Finally, the Popular Participation Law increased the number of municipalities to more than 300. Prior to this law, barely 20 municipalities effectively existed.[1301] The first municipal elections were held in 1985 as per the (first) Municipality Law of 1985 (Law No.696/1985),[1302] and since 1987 they were organized separately from the general elections every two years until 1995. [1303] Thanks to the Popular Participation Law, the municipalities were given 20% of the government's yearly revenues and a wider range of responsibilities (arts.14 and 20 of the Popular Participation Law). [1304] Most importantly, however, was the creation of the *Organizaciones Territoriales de Base* (OTB), defined as a "social player for popular participation" (art.3). They are composed of indigenous communities and peoples (or neighbouring committees) according to their rules and procedures and represented by their authorities (art.3). This provision essentially allowed for the recognition of traditional indigenous

---

Territorios Indígena Originario Campesinos en Bolivia Entre la Loma Santa y la Pachamama, Fundación Tierra, La Paz, 2011; for a map of the TCOs, see CIDOB, "Mapas de Bolivia con las TCO's", at http://www.cidob-bo.org/cpti/mapa.htm [Last access 20.08.2014].

1299 The *Decreto Supremo* (Supreme Decree) No. 727, adopted on 6 December 2010, ruled the conversion process from TCO to TIOC, of which the Agrarian Reform National Institute is in charge (art. 1). Nevertheless, this switching process is long and controversial due to some administrative requirements of the Agrarian Reform National Institute (INRA) that need to be complied with. Erbol, "El cambio de nombre de TCO a TIOC significará otro trámite", *Erbol Comunicaciones Periódico Digital*, 12.04.2011, at http://erbol.com.bo/noticia.php?identificador=2147483943178 [Last access 20.08.2014].

1300 Colque and Chumacero, *Informe 2010: Territorios Indígena Originario Campe sinos en Bolivia*, p.108.

1301 Assies, "Pueblos Indígenas y Reforma del Estado en América Latina", p.35.

1302 *Ley Orgánica de Municipalidades*, adopted on 10 January 1985, Law No.696 of 1985.

1303 Esther Del Campo, "Participación Política y Democracia Local en Bolivia", in Esther Del Campo (ed.), *Democratización y Descentralización en Bolivia*, Catarata, Madrid, 2007, pp.15-42, pp.15 and 37, note 1.

1304 See also *ibid.*, pp.16 and 18.

organizations in rural areas (unions, *ayllus*,[1305] etc.) and neighbouring committees in the cities.[1306] The limit was one OTB for one territorial unit (art.6) and more than 15,000 OTBs were registered in three years (1994-1997).[1307] The OTBs were recognized as legal personalities (art.4) as well as having a number of rights and obligations that allowed an effective improvement in indigenous participation within the municipalities.[1308] Thus, on the one hand, thanks to this law, 464 indigenous (and *campesino*) authorities (i.e., 29% of the total number of councillors of the country) were voted at the 1997 municipal elections and therefore designated as councillors in the local municipal offices for the first time ever.[1309] On the other hand, the recognition of 300 municipalities subdivided indigenous territories and put the TCOs under different administrations.[1310] This risk was then partially overcome by using art.17.3 of the Popular Participation Law that allowed the creation of a *Distrito Municipal* in territories characterized by geographic, sociocultural, productive, or economic continuity in order to provide common public services (art.18). On this legal basis, indigenous peoples started to create their own *Distritos Municipales Indígenas* (DMI). The first DMI was Isoso, located in the Santa Cruz

1305 Broadly speaking, an *ayllu* is an Andean (nowadays, mainly *aymara* and *quechua*) complex social hierarchical and territorial structure and organization, which implies more levels of *ayllus* interlinked by symbolism and internal self-management. Luis Jesús Jilamita Murillo and Veimar Gastón Soto Quiroz, *Los ayllus en el actual departamento de Potosí: Una aproximación a la comprensión de su historia y situación contemporánea*, Soluciones Prácticas, Potosí, 2005, pp.17-19.

1306 Albó, "Bolivia: From Indian and Campesino Leaders to Councillors and Parliamentary Deputies", p.79.

1307 Benjamin Kohl, "Democratizing Decentralization in Bolivia: The Law of Popular Participation", 23 *Journal of Planning Education and Research* 2003, pp.153-164, p.156.

1308 See arts.7-8, and also art.10 on the *Comité de Vigilancia* (a kind of Security Committee) composed by one OTB representative with the aim of supervising the good administration of the municipality. These committees essentially acted as a bridge between the OTBs and the municipal authorities. Albó, "Bolivia: From Indian and Campesino Leaders to Councillors and Parliamentary Deputies", p.79.

1309 Albó, "Bolivia: From Indian and Campesino Leaders to Councillors and Parliamentary Deputies", pp.81-82.

1310 René Orellana Halkyer, "Municipalización de Pueblos Indígenas en Bolivia: Impactos y perspectivas", in Willem Assies, Gemma van der Haar, and André Hoekema (eds.), *El reto de la diversidad: Pueblos indígenas y reforma del Estado en América Latina*, El Colegio de Michoacán, Zamora-Michoacán, 1999, pp.315-340, pp.317 and 337.

department.[1311] The number of DMIs increased quickly. In 2004 the news agency Enlared declared the existence of 140 DMIs.[1312] Later, according to Galindo Soza (cited by Colque), in 2008 there were at least 73 DMIs.[1313] Nevertheless, the DMIs were eventually deprived of any competence and their administrative autonomy remained very low.[1314]

In 1999, the Municipalities Law and Supreme Decree No. 26142/2001 went further. The former formally recognized the DMIs (arts.166-167) and established the possibility of forming a grouping of municipalities (*mancomunidad*) to return "ethnic or cultural unity" to indigenous peoples (art.158.3). The latter gave priority to the creation of *mancomunidades* of DMIs to avoid the fragmentation of sociocultural units across the municipalities' borders (art.23). Despite this favorable legal framework, in practice many problems regarding inefficient financial management and widespread corruption arose within the municipalities and gave room for further discontent.[1315] Postero also pointed out that this wave of reforms led to a "neoliberal multiculturalism" that promoted clientelism and corruption.[1316]

Between January and April 2000, large protests were organized in Cochabamba against the privatizations of water resources and the increase of the prices of water supplies approved by Law No.2029/2000. These protests are also known as the Cochabamba Water Wars that expanded to other cities. Law No.2029/2000 was finally abrogated in April. The demonstrators were indigenous, *campesinos,* and also *cocaleros* (coca leaf growers).[1317] Since the 1970s, in fact, influential military officers had

---

1311 Gonzalo Colque, "Rediseño de gobiernos locales indígenas en Bolivia", Fundación Tierra, La Paz, 2010, at http://justgovernancegroup.org/es/Assets/PDFs/Gobiernos%20Locales%20Indigenas%20Bolivia%20COLQUE%20Abril%202010.pdf, p.1.

1312 Enlared Municipal, "Bolivia tiene 140 distritos municipales indígenas", *Agencia de Noticias Enlared-BolPress*, 22.11.2005, at http://www.bolpress.com/art.php?Cod=2005004635 [Last access 20.08.2014]. Official data were not found.

1313 Colque, "Rediseño de gobiernos locales indígenas en Bolivia, p. 1.

1314 Orellana Halkyer, "Municipalización de Pueblos Indígenas en Bolivia: Impactos y perspectivas", pp.321 and 337.

1315 Kohl, "Democratizing Decentralization in Bolivia: The Law of Popular Participation", p.161 and Orellana Halkyer, "Municipalización de Pueblos Indígenas en Bolivia: Impactos y perspectivas", p.337.

1316 Postero, *Now We Are Citizens*, p.125 and ff.

1317 López Fuentes, *El derecho a la libre determinación de los pueblos indígenas en Bolivia*, p.123 and Amy Goodman, "Cochabamba, la guerra del agua y el cambio climático", Democracy Now, 22.04.2010, at http://www.democracynow.org/e

diverted economic resources meant to develop the Eastern areas from subsistence programs to the production of the more lucrative coca leaf, which is part of the Andean diet and is innocuous.[1318] Due to the increase in demand for cocaine in Western countries and the economic crisis, the coca-cocaine economy grew considerably. Drug-traffickers left the production of the coca leaf to small producers and soon this route became the sole viable option for many peasants who remained trapped in this kind of economy.[1319] The coca leaf growers gained particular strength and prominence within the *Confederación Sindical Única de Trabajadores Campesinos de Bolivia* – CSUTCB in the 1990s.[1320] The aforementioned constitutional change regarding the uninominal circumscriptions encouraged many other parties to stand for elections in 1997.[1321] Leaders of the *Asemblea por la Soberanía de los Pueblos* (ASP) party came from the *cocaleros* movement. Among them were Evo Morales, Félix Sánchez, Néstor Guzman, and the CSUTCB President Román Loayza, who served as national deputy for the 1997-2002 term. Morales was expelled from the legislature in January 2002 and began his campaign for Presidency with the *Movimiento al Socialismo* (MAS) party.[1322] During the 2002 Presidential elections, after a failed attempt to ally with the MAS, Aymara Felipe Quispe, founder of the *Movimiento Indígena Tupac Katari* (MIKTA) in 1978, former secretary of the CSUTCB, and founder and leader of the party *Movimiento Indígena Pachakuti* (MIP), stood as candidate.[1323] None of them won, but Morales came second in a field of eleven candidates.[1324]

In 2003, from El Alto, the satellite city above of La Paz, indigenous peoples (mainly the Aymara) began a massive protest against President Sanchez de Lozada's proposal to allow foreign companies to export gas from the gas-rich *Oriente* region. After six weeks of violent clashes and a heavy toll of 80 deaths, the president resigned and fled to Miami. The

s/blog/2010/4/22/cochabamba_la_guerra_del_agua_y_el_cambio_climtico [Last access on 20.08.2014].

1318 Albó, "Bolivia: From Indian and Campesino Leaders to Councillors and Parliamentary Deputies", p.78.

1319 *Ibid.*

1320 Yashar, *Contesting Citizenship in Latin America*, p.186 and Van Lee Cott, *From Movements to Parties in Latin America*, p.67.

1321 Van Lee Cott, *From Movements to Parties in Latin America*, p.71.

1322 Yashar, *Contesting Citizenship in Latin America*, p.186. For a detailed analysis on Evo Morales' politics, see Sven Harten, *The Rise of Evo Morales and the MAS*, Zed Books, London, New York, 2011.

1323 Van Lee Cott, *From Movements to Parties in Latin America*, pp.77-78.

1324 Yashar, *Contesting Citizenship in Latin America*, p.186.

former vice President Carlos Mesa replaced him and promised to call a constituent assembly and referendum on gas export policies.[1325] The latter was eventually held in July 2004[1326] but the former, however, could not be set before another two-month strike that obliged Mesa to resign as well.[1327] It needs to be stressed here that a constituent assembly had already been demanded by indigenous peoples in their fourth march in 2002.[1328]

The crisis of the neoliberal system, in place since 1985,[1329] the Water and Gas Wars, and subsequent events contributed to the institutional revolution that followed in Bolivia.[1330] Morales won the presidential elections on 18 December 2005 with 53.7% of the vote, the highest percentage ever reached by a candidate since the re-establishment of democracy in 1982 (see also chapter 4, section 4.3).[1331] Since early 2006, the call for a Constituent Assembly was a priority within the political agenda of Morales.[1332] However, despite his wide indigenous electorate, he refused to accept the proposal of a number of indigenous organizations to organize special constituencies in order to increase indigenous participation in the Constituent Assembly.[1333] Hence, the MAS decided to elect the members

1325 Postero, *Now We Are Citizens*, p.2.

1326 *Ibid.*

1327 *Ibid.*, p.3.

1328 Xavier Albó, "Bolivia: Avances y tropezones hacia un nuevo país plurinacional e Intercultural", in Salvador Martí i Puig (ed.*), Pueblos Indígenas y Política en América Latina: El reconocimiento de sus derechos y el impacto de sus demandas a inicios del siglo XXI*, Fundació CIDOB, Barcelona, 2007, pp.335-359, p.353. For more detail on the fourth march, see Carlos Romero Bonifaz, *El Proceso constituyente boliviano: el hito de la cuarta marcha de tierras bajas*, Centro de Estudios Jurídicos e Investigación Social-CEJIS, Santa Cruz de la Sierra, 2005.

1329 Yashar, *Contesting Citizenship in Latin America*, p.182.

1330 Albó, "Bolivia: Avances y tropezones hacia un nuevo país plurinacional e Intercultural", pp.344-349.

1331 International Work Group for Indigenous Affairs, *The Indigenous World 2007*, IWGIA, Copenhagen 2009, at http://www.iwgia.org/publications/search-pubs?publication_id=83, or directly at http://www.iwgia.org/iwgia_files_publi cations_files/0083_NY-THE_INDIGENOUS_ORLD-2007.pdf, p.186 [Last access 14.08.2014].

1332 Claire Wright, "Estado, Justicia y ciudadanía en el constitucionalismo boliviano", 3(2) *Cuestiones Jurídicas* 2009, pp.55-72, p.62.

1333 International Work Group for Indigenous Affairs, *The Indigenous World 2007*, p.188.

of the Constituent Assembly through party lists and eventually obtained the majority of the seats, albeit not the absolute majority.[1334]

The Constituent Assembly was set in Sucre in 2006. The MAS party aimed to put forward three proposals regarding indigenous peoples, namely: a new territorial organization; political control; and a system of indigenous justice.[1335] Among the indigenous organizations, the CSUTCB and the Consejo Nacional de Ayllus y Markas del Qullasuyu (CONAMAQ) – founded in 1997– focused their requests on: the identification of Bolivia as a plurinational State; the recognition of indigenous languages as well as other indigenous rights such as rights to education, food, housing and health; and the recognition of indigenous territories and autonomy.[1336] Regarding the last point, in the same period, nine major indigenous peoples organizations, both from the highlands and the lowlands, proposed and conceptualized indigenous autonomy in the joint project called *Pacto de Unidad*.[1337] This shows, in particular, why the autonomy flag did not belong solely to the Bolivian Amazonian *Oriente*. Prior to and during the Constituent Assembly, indigenous peoples have been vociferous in claiming their autonomy.[1338] During the same year (2006) however, as

1334 Stéphanie Rousseau, "Indigenous and Feminist Movements at the Constituent Assembly in Bolivia", 46(2) *Latin American Research Review* (LARR) 2011, pp.5-28, p.12.

1335 Wright, "Estado, Justicia y ciudadanía en el constitucionalismo boliviano", p.62.

1336 Almut Schilling-Vacaflor, "Identidades indígenas y demandas político-jurídicas de la CSUTCB y el CONAMAQ en la Constituyente boliviana", 23-24 *T`inkazos Revista de Ciencias Sociales* 2008, pp.149-166, p.151.

1337 Confederación Sindical Única de Trabajadores Campesinos de Bolivia-CSUTCB; Confederación de Pueblos Indígenas de Bolivia-CIDOB; Confederación Sindical de Colonizadores de Bolivia-CSCB; Federación Nacional de Mujeres Campesinas de Bolivia, 'Bartolina Sisa'-FNMCB-BS; Consejo Nacional de Ayllus y Markas del Qullasuyu-CONAMAQ; Coordinadora de Pueblos Étnicos de Santa Cruz-CPESC; Movimiento Sin Tierra de Bolivia-MST; Asamblea del Pueblo Guaraní-APG; Confederación de Pueblos Étnicos Moxeños de Beni-CPEMB. Asamblea Nacional de Organizaciones Indígenas, Originarias, Campesinas y de Colonizadores de Bolivia, "Propuesta para la Nueva Constitución Política del Estado: Por un Estado plurinacional y la autodeterminación de los pueblos y naciones indígenas, originarias y campesinas", Sucre, 5 August 2006, 22(166) *Revista OSAL – Observatorio Social de América Latina* 2007, at http://biblioteca.clacso.edu.ar/ar/libros/osal/osal22/AC22Documento.pdf [Last access 20.08.2014].

1338 Chuvirú, Marcela, "Bolivia", in Málaga Montoya (ed.), *Seminario Regional Andino. Pueblos indígenas y democracia intercultural: un debate desde los países andinos; Bolivia, Ecuador, Colombia, Venezuela, Chile, Perú*, Centro de Estudios Regionales Bartolomé de las Casas, Cuzco, 2008, pp.51-54, p.53; Marxa Nadia Chávez León, "'Autonomías indígenas' y 'Estado Plurinacional'. Proyectos

instructed by Morales, in the notorious autonomy referendum, 57.5% of the national electorate voted against the decentralization process.[1339] In the four eastern departments (Beni, Pando, Santa Cruz, and Tarija) the majority of the votes were in favour.[1340]

Subsequently, the text approved by the Constituent Assembly at the end of 2007 was denied legitimacy by the *Oriente* political forces, especially by the civic movements, which prepared self-made autonomy statutes and self-organized elections in July 2008.[1341] In light of this, one month later, on 10 August, a national referendum was called to reconfirm or to revoke the presidential mandate. Morales obtained more than 67% of the votes in favour.[1342] Violence and civil disturbances took place in the *Oriente* between August and September, until the tragedy in Pando, where 20 indigenous people were killed and more than 100 were wounded. Another march into the city of Santa Cruz of approximately 20,000 indigenous people, who were also unhappy with portions of the constitution, resulted in the beginning of negotiations between the eastern departments and the central government. Finally, after debates in Cochabamba and at the Congress of the Republic, as well as another march, this time headed by Morales himself, negotiations ended on 21 October 2008. The changes in the text of the constitution also affected the new system of the Peasant Native Indigenous Autonomy (AIOC), which acquired a clearer form due to the amendments.[1343] The final text of the constitution was at last

políticos de los movimientos indígenas y campesinos en Bolivia", 24 *Revista OSAL* 2008, pp.51-71, p.59; El Diario, "Autonomías indígenas y departamentales inician un amplio debate en la Asamblea", *El Diario*, 1 July 2007, at http://www.el diario.net/noticias/2007/2007_07/nt070701/2_04plt.php [Last access 20.08.2014].

1339 Leonardo Tamburini, "Bolivia (2010)", in International Work Group for Indigenous Affairs, *The Indigenous World 2010*, IWGIA, Copenhagen, 2010, 195–206, at 200.

1340 Fernando Mayorga, "Referéndum y Asamblea Constituyente: Autonomías Departamentales en Bolivia", 37 *Reforma y Democracia-Revista del CLAD* 2007, pp.1–2, at http://www.clad.org/portal/publicaciones-del-clad/revista-clad-refor ma-democracia/articulos/037-febrero-2007/0055707 [Last access 20.08.2014].

1341 Leonardo Tamburini, "Bolivia (2009)", in International Work Group for Indigenous Affairs, *The Indigenous World 2009*, IWGIA, Copenhagen, 2009, pp.174-183, at 175.

1342 *Ibid.*, pp.178-179.

1343 *Ibid.*, p.181.

approved via another national referendum on 25 January 2009, with 61.43% of votes in favour.[1344]

5.2. *The legal framework vis-à-vis indigenous peoples in Bolivia*

5.2.1 International human rights law applicable to indigenous peoples in Bolivia

Bolivia is one of the 51 original members of the United Nations.[1342] It has acceded to or ratified all core human rights treaties and has been reviewed twice by the HRC for the Universal Periodic Review (UPR) in 2010 and 2014.[1343]

Bolivia signed the ICERD on 7 June 1966 and ratified it on 22 September 1970. However, only recently (on 14 February 2006)[1344] has it accepted the competence of the treaty's monitoring body (the Committee on the Elimination of Racial Discrimination, CERD) to receive and consider communications from individuals or groups of individuals.[1345] Moreover, it did not sign the Amendment to art.8 of the ICERD on the financing of the CERD, which is not yet in force.[1346]

1344 Bolpress, "Evo promulga el sábado la primera Constitución aprobada en referéndum popular", 02.02.2009, *Bolpress*, at http://www.bolpress.com/art.php?Cod=2009020206 [Last access 24.08.2014].

1342 Bolivia officially accessed the UN and signed the UN Charter on 14 November 1945. See the United Nations membership at http://www.un.org/en/members/growth.shtml and http://www.un.org/en/members [Last access 21.08.2014].

1343 The first UPR conducted on Bolivia was during the 7th session (8-19 February 2010) on 10 February 2010, see http://www.ohchr.org/EN/HR Bodies/UPR/Pages/BOSession7.aspx. The second one was held during the 20th (27 October-7 November 2014) on 28 October 2014, see at http://www.ohchr.org/EN/HR Bodies/UPR/Pages/BOSession20.aspx [Last access to both 04.02.2015].

1344 See the United Nations Treaty Collection, Status of Treaties, ICERD, at http://treaties.un.org/Pages/ViewDetails.aspx?src=TREATY&mtdsg_no=IV-2& chapter=4&lang=en, and http://treaties.un.org/Pages/ViewDetails.aspx?src=TREATY&mtdsg_no=IV-2& chapter=4&lang=en#EndDec [Last access 21.08.2014].

1345 Art.14.1 ICERD states "A State Party may at any time declare that it recognizes the competence of the Committee to receive and consider communications from individuals or groups of individuals within its jurisdiction claiming to be victims of a violation by that State Party of any of the rights set forth in this Convention. No communication shall be received by the Committee if it concerns a State Party which has not made such a declaration".

1346 UN Doc. CERD/SP/45. See the United Nations Treaty Collection, Status of Treaties, Amendment to art.8 of the ICERD, at

Bolivia acceded to the ICCPR and its ICCPR-OP1, as well as the ICESCR, on 12 Aug 1982.[1347] Regarding the ICESCR-OP, which entered into force in May 2013 and enabled the CESCR to receive and consider communications for individual complaints, Bolivia signed it on 12 February 2010 and ratified it on 13 January 2012, without any declarations or reservations.[1348] In 2013, Bolivia also finally acceded to the ICCPR-OP2 on the abolition of the death penalty.[1349] This was one of the recommendations of the 2010 UPR.[1350]

As for the Convention on the Elimination of All Forms of Discrimination against Women, Bolivia signed it in 1980 and ratified it ten years after, with no declarations or reservations.[1351] In 2000, Bolivia also ratified the Optional Protocol to this Convention (OP-CEDAW), which entered into force that year and allows the Committee on the Elimination of Discrimination against Women (CEDAW) to receive communications from individuals or group of individuals (art.2 OP-CEDAW).[1352]

The Convention against Torture and Other Cruel, Inhuman or Degrading Treatment or Punishment (CAT) was signed by Bolivia in 1985 and ratified

http://treaties.un.org/Pages/ViewDetails.aspx?src=TREATY&mtdsg_no=IV-2-a &chapter=4&lang=en [Last access 20.08.2014].

1347 See the United Nations Treaty Collection, Status of Treaties, ICCPR, ICESCR and ICCPR-OP1, respectively, at http://treaties.un.org/Pages/ViewDetails.aspx?src=TREATY&mtdsg_no=IV-4&chapter=4&lang=en, http://treaties.un.org/Pages/ViewDetails.aspx?src=TREATY&mtdsg_no=IV-3&chapter=4&lang=en, and http://treaties.un.org/Pages/ViewDetails.aspx?src=TREATY&mtdsg_no=IV-5&chapter=4&lang=en [Last access 21.08.2014].

1348 See the United Nations Treaty Collection, Status of Treaties, ICESCR-OP, at http://treaties.un.org/Pages/ViewDetails.aspx?src=TREATY&mtdsg_no=IV-3-a &chapter=4&lang=en [Last access 21.08.2014].

1349 Bolivia acceded to this on 12 July 2013 with no declarations or reservations. See the United Nations Treaty Collection, Status of Treaties, ICCPR-OP2, at http://treaties.un.org/Pages/ViewDetails.aspx?src=TREATY&mtdsg_no=IV-12 &chapter=4&lang=en [Last access 21.08.2014].

1350 Report of the Working Group on the Universal Periodic Review, Bolivia (Plurinational State of), Human Rights Council, fourteenth session, Universal Periodic Review, UN Doc. A/HRC/14/7, 15 March 2010, para.98.1.

1351 See the United Nations Treaty Collection, Status of Treaties, CEDAW, at http://treaties.un.org/Pages/ViewDetails.aspx?src=TREATY&mtdsg_no=IV-8& chapter=4&lang=en [Last access 21.08.2014].

1352 See the United Nations Treaty Collection, Status of Treaties, OP-CEDAW, at http://treaties.un.org/Pages/ViewDetails.aspx?src=TREATY&mtdsg_no=IV-8-b &chapter=4&lang=en [Last access 21.08.2014].

in 1999.[1353] In 2006, Bolivia also deposited the declarations under arts.21 and 22 of CAT to recognize the Competence of the Committee against Torture.[1354]

Bolivia signed and ratified the Convention on the Rights of the Child (CRC) in 1990;[1355] accepted the amendment to art.43.2 of the CRC on the increase of the number of experts in the Committee from ten to eighteen;[1356] acceded to the Optional Protocol to the Convention on the Rights of the Child on the Involvement of Children in Armed Conflict in 2004;[1357] and ratified the Optional Protocol to the Convention on the Rights of the Child on the Sale of Children, Child Prostitution and Child Pornography in 2003.[1358]

In 2000, Bolivia also acceded to the International Convention on the Protection of the Rights of All Migrant Workers and Members of their Families (ICRMW), which has not been signed, acceded to or ratified by the majority of Western countries; [1359] and in 2008 it ratified the International Convention for the Protection of All Persons from Enforced

1353 See the United Nations Treaty Collection, Status of Treaties, CAT, at http://treaties.un.org/Pages/ViewDetails.aspx?src=TREATY&mtdsg_no=IV-9 &chapter=4&lang=en [Last access 21.08.2014].

1354 See the United Nations Treaty Collection, Status of Treaties, CAT, at http://treaties.un.org/Pages/ViewDetails.aspx?src=TREATY&mtdsg_no=IV-9 &chapter=4&lang=en by clicking on "Bolivia (Plurinational State of)" [Last access 21.08.2014].

1355 See the United Nations Treaty Collection, Status of Treaties, CRC, at http://treaties.un.org/Pages/ViewDetails.aspx?src=TREATY&mtdsg_no=IV-11 &chapter=4&lang=en [Last access 21.08.2014].

1356 See the United Nations Treaty Collection, Status of Treaties, Amendment to art.43 (2) of the Convention on the Rights of the Child, at http://treaties.un.org/Pages/ViewDetails.aspx?src=TREATY&mtdsg_no=IV-11-a&chapter=4&lang=en [Last access 21.08.2014].

1357 See the United Nations Treaty Collection, Status of Treaties, CRC-OP1, at https://treaties.un.org/Pages/ViewDetails.aspx?src=TREATY&mtdsg_no=IV-11-b&chapter=4&lang=en; Bolivia declared that the minimum age for compulsory military service is 18 and for the voluntary one 17, see Declarations and Reservations to CRC-OP1 at http://treaties.un.org/Pages/ViewDetails.aspx?src=TREATY&mtdsg_no=IV-11-b&chapter=4&lang=en#EndDec [Last access 21.08.2014].

1358 See the United Nations Treaty Collection, Status of Treaties, CRC-OP2, at http://treaties.un.org/Pages/ViewDetails.aspx?src=TREATY&mtdsg_no=IV-11-c &chapter=4&lang=en [Last access 21.08.2014].

1359 See the United Nations Treaty Collection, Status of Treaties, ICRMW, at http://treaties.un.org/Pages/ViewDetails.aspx?src=TREATY&mtdsg_no=IV-13&chapter=4&lang=en [Last access 21.08.2014].

Disappearance (CPED),[1360] which entered into force in 2010. However, Bolivia has not yet recognized the competence of the Committee to receive and consider communications from or on behalf of individuals in accordance with arts.31-21 of CPED.[1361]

Finally, the Convention on the Rights of Persons with Disabilities (CRPD), adopted in 2006 and entered into force in 2008, and its Optional Protocol (OP-CRPD) to recognize the competence of the Committee on the Rights of Persons with Disabilities to receive and consider communications from or on behalf of individuals or groups of individuals (art.1, OP-CRPD) were both ratified by Bolivia in November 2009.[1362]

Regarding the 2010 and 2014 UPRs, many recommendations to Bolivia concerned the improvement of children's and women's treatment, education and labor conditions,[1363] and the prevention of violence against them.[1364] More specifically on indigenous peoples, it was recommended that for Bolivia to combat discrimination against indigenous peoples[1365], it must guarantee the full enjoyment of indigenous peoples' rights;[1366] secure

1360 See the United Nations Treaty Collection, Status of Treaties, CPED, at http://treaties.un.org/Pages/ViewDetails.aspx?src=TREATY&mtdsg_no=IV-16&chapter=4&lang=en [Last access 21.08.2014].

1361 See the Declarations recognizing the competence of the Committee under arts.31 and 32 of CPED at http://treaties.un.org/Pages/ViewDetails.aspx?src=TREATY&mtdsg_no=IV-16&chapter=4&lang=en#EndDec [Last access 04.02.2015].

1362 See the United Nations Treaty Collection, Status of Treaties, CRPD, at http://treaties.un.org/Pages/ViewDetails.aspx?src=TREATY&mtdsg_no=IV-15&chapter=4&lang=en, and CRPD Optional Protocol Signatures and Ratifications at http://www.un.org/disabilities/countries.asp?id=166 [Last access 21.08.2014].

1363 Report of the Working Group on the Universal Periodic Review, Bolivia (Plurinational State of), Human Rights Council, fourteenth session, Universal Periodic Review, UN Doc. A/HRC/14/7, 15 March 2010, para.98; Report of the Working Group on the Universal Periodic Review, Bolivia (Plurinational State of), Human Rights Council, twentieth session, Universal Periodic Review, UN Doc. A/HRC/28/7, 17 December 2014, paras. 79-80, 113.31-113.45, 114.9, 114.21, 114. 114.84-87, 114.115-122, 115.1, 115.5-10. During the 2010 UPR, the then-debated adoption of a law pertaining to discrimination of children and women was also addressed (Report UPR Bolivia 2010, para.98), while in 2014 Bolivia was recommended to implement it (Report UPR Bolivia 2014, paras.114.31-114.41; see also next section 5.2.2). In 2014, it was recommended that for Bolivia to ratify the UNESCO Convention against Discrimination in Education. Report UPR Bolivia 2014, paras.113.2 and 113.3.

1364 Report UPR Bolivia 2014, paras.114.88-111.

1365 Report UPR Bolivia 2010, para.98, nos.4, 21 and 22; Report UPR Bolivia 2014, paras.114.35, 114.67 and 114.126.

1366 Report UPR Bolivia 2010, para.98, no.45.

the conformity of the indigenous justice systems to human rights standards;[1367] combat the mortality and meliorate the health conditions of indigenous women; [1368] guarantee a life of dignity for indigenous peoples;[1369] implement indigenous peoples' rights, in particular, their rights to participation and consultation;[1370] to address the precarious situation of the Guaraní peoples.[1371]

Within the Organization of American States (OAS), Bolivia signed the Charter of the Organization of American States (OAS Charter) on the day of its adoption on 30 April 1948 and ratified it towards the end of 1950, in accordance with art.139 of the OAS Charter.[1372] Bolivia did not sign the American Convention on Human Rights-Pact of San José (ACHR), upon its adoption on 22 November 1969 but ratified it later on in June 1979, by depositing its ratification the following month (ex art.74.2 of the ACHR).[1373] In 1993, Bolivia also recognized the competence of the Inter-American Commission on Human Rights and the Inter-American Court of Human Rights, under art.45 and 62 of the Convention, respectively.[1374] As for the other OAS Conventions, Bolivia ratified, in chronological order: the Inter-American Convention on the Prevention, Punishment and Eradication of Violence against Women "Convention of Belem do Pará" in 1994;[1375] the Inter-American Convention on Forced Disappearance of Persons in 1999;[1376] the Inter-American Convention on the Elimination of All Forms

1367 *Ibid.*, para.98, nos.45, 46 and 74; Report UPR Bolivia 2014, para.114.127.

1368 Report UPR Bolivia 2010, para.98, no.69.

1369 *Ibid.*, para.98, no.75.

1370 *Ibid.*, para.98, no.76; Report UPR Bolivia 2014, paras.113.46 and 114.131.

1371 Report UPR Bolivia 2010, para.98, no.77.

1372 See Charter of the Organization of American States, Signatories and Ratifications, at http://www.oas.org/dil/treaties_A-41_Charter_of_the_Organization_of_American_States_sign.htm [Last access 21.08.2014].

1373 See American Convention on Human Rights-Pact of San José, Signature, Ratifications and Accessions, at http://www.cidh.oas.org/basicos/english/Basic4.Amer.Conv.Ratif.htm [Last access 21.08.2014].

1374 See Declarations/Reservations/Denunciations/Withdrawals to the ACHR, 3.Bolivia, at http://www.cidh.oas.org/basicos/english/Basic4.Amer.Conv.Ratif.htm#3. [Last access 21.08.2014].

1375 See Signatures and Current Status of the Inter-American Convention on the Prevention, Punishment and Eradication of Violence against Women "Convention of Belem do Pará", at http://www.oas.org/juridico/english/sigs/a-61.html [Last access 21.08.2014].

1376 See Signatures and Current Status of the Inter-American Convention on Forced Disappearance of Persons, at http://www.oas.org/juridico/english/sigs/a-60.html [Last access 21.08.2014].

of Discrimination against Person with Disabilities in 2003;[1377] and, in 2006, the Inter-American Convention to Prevent and Punish Torture[1378] and the Additional Protocol to the American Convention on Human Rights in the Area of Economic Social and Cultural Rights "Protocol of San Salvador".[1379] Bolivia has not yet signed the Protocol to the American Convention on Human Rights to Abolish the Death Penalty, blocked since 1990 and not yet in force.[1380] Regarding the recent Inter-American Convention Against All Forms of Discrimination and Intolerance and Inter-American Convention Against Racism, Racial Discrimination and Related Forms of Intolerance adopted by OAS in June 2013, Bolivia has not yet signed it either.[1381] Finally, the Inter-American Democratic Charter, which was the sole OAS-adopted document citing indigenous peoples in its art.9,[1382] –prior to the adoption of the 2013 Inter-American Convention Against Racism, Racial Discrimination, and Related Forms of Intolerance– was supported by Bolivia, along with the majority of the American States, which voted for the adoption of the Charter on 11 September 2001[1383].

More specifically on the rights of indigenous peoples, Bolivia promptly ratified the ILO Convention No.169, "Convention concerning Indigenous

1377 See Signatures and Current Status of the Inter-American Convention on the Elimination of All Forms of Discrimination against Person with Disabilities, at http://www.oas.org/juridico/english/sigs/a-65.html [Last access 21.08.2014].

1378 See Signatures and Current Status of Ratifications of the Inter-American Convention to Prevent and Punish Torture, at http://www.oas.org/juridico/english/sigs/a-51.html [Last access 21.08.2014].

1379 See Signatures and Current Status of Ratifications of the Additional Protocol to the American Convention on Human Rights in the Area of Economic Social and Cultural Rights "Protocol of San Salvador", at http://www.oas.org/juridico/english/sigs/a-52.html [Last access 21.08.2014].

1380 See Signatures and Current Status of Ratifications of the Protocol to the American Convention on Human Rights to Abolish the Death Penalty, at http://www.oas.org/juridico/english/sigs/a-53.html [Last access 04.02.2015].

1381 See Signatures and Current Status of Ratifications of the Inter-American Convention Against All Forms of Discrimination and Intolerance and of the Inter-American Convention Against Racism, Racial Discrimination, and Related Forms of Intolerance at http://www.oas.org/en/sla/dil/inter_american_treaties_A-69_discrimination_intolerance_signatories.asp, and http://www.oas.org/en/sla/dil/inter_american_treaties_A-68_racism_signatories.asp, respectively [Last access 04.02.2015].

1382 See art.9 of the Inter-American Democratic Charter, at http://www.oas.org/charter/docs/resolution1_en_p4.htm [Last access 04.02.2015].

1383 See the Inter-American Democratic Charter "Actas de las sesiones", at http://scm.oas.org/doc_public/SPANISH/HIST_01/AC00535T06.doc [Last access 21.08.2014].

and Tribal Peoples in Independent Countries" (ILO Convention 169) in 1991 with Law No.1257.[1384] This ratification also contributed to the adoption of the constitutional reform and other domestic legislation during the 1990s, as discussed above (section 5.1.2).[1385] In 1999, the Bolivian Central of Workers (COB) claimed a violation of the ILO Convention 169 with the special complaint procedure of Representations under art.24 of the ILO Constitution, on behalf of the indigenous organizations Confederation of Indigenous Peoples of Bolivia (CIDOB) and affiliates: the Coordinating Body of Ethnic Peoples of Santa Cruz (CPESC), the Central of Indigenous Peoples of Beni (CPIB), and the Indigenous Central of the Amazon Region of Bolivia (CIRABO).[1386] The COB alleged that the Government had conceded 86 forestry concessions, 27 of which were on indigenous territories (TCOs) that had received a provisional title by the order (*Resolución de inmovilización*) of the National Institute of Land Reform (INRA) and that thus no new settlements, grants, adjudications, or forestry concessions could be granted.[1387] The tripartite Committee eventually concluded that environmental and socio-cultural impact studies should be carried out jointly with the indigenous peoples concerned before authorizing natural resource exploration and exploitation in areas traditionally occupied by them, particularly in the case of large-scale exploitation projects.[1388] Moreover, it added that, despite the extensive domestic protection provided to indigenous lands thanks to the INRA Law, no consultation under art.6.1.a or art.15 of the ILO Convention 169 was

1384 See Ratifications of C169 - Indigenous and Tribal Peoples Convention, 1989 (No.169), at http://www.ilo.org/dyn/normlex/en/f?p=1000:11300:0::NO:11300:P11300_INSTRUMENT_ID:312314 [Last access 21.08.2014].

1385 Carlos Villarroel Sandoval, "La Aplicación en Bolivia del Convenio 169 sobre los Pueblos Indígenas y Tribales en Países Independientes de la OIT", in José Emilio Rolando Ordóñez Cifuentes (ed.), *Análisis Interdisciplinario del Convenio 169 de la OIT. IX Jornadas Lascasianas*, Mexico City, 2000, pp.189-207, p.195.

1386 International Labour Organization, "Report of the Committee set up to examine the representation alleging non-observance by Bolivia of the Indigenous and Tribal Peoples Convention, 1989 (No. 169), made under art.24 of the ILO Constitution by the Bolivian Central of Workers (COB)", case of Representation under art.24 of the ILO Constitution against Bolivia, ILO Doc. Nos.GB.272/8/1 and GB.274/16/7, 1999, at http://www.ilo.org/dyn/normlex/en/f?p=1000:50012:0::NO:50012:P50012_COMPLAINT_PROCEDURE_ID,P50012_LANG_CODE:2507170,en:NO [Last access 21.08.2014].

1387 International Labour Organization, "Report of the Committee set up to examine the representation alleging non-observance by Bolivia …", para.10.

1388 International Labour Organization, "Report of the Committee set up to examine the representation alleging non-observance by Bolivia …", para.39.

carried out.[1389] Finally, the tripartite Committee stated that the Government should apply art.15 of the ILO Convention 169, especially when large tracts of indigenous land are likely to be affected.[1390]

Lastly, it needs to be pointed out that Bolivia has been the first and only state that has "ratified" and implemented the UNDRIP as domestic, binding legislation. As it was a binding treaty, Law No.3760 issued on 7 November 2007 (less than two months after its adoption by UN General Assembly) gave binding effect to the UNDRIP's provisions.[1391]

5.2.2 Domestic protection of indigenous peoples' rights

After the violent clashes in the *Oriente* and the various debates, as discussed above in section 5.1.2, the new Bolivian Constitution (*Constitución Política del Estado* – CPE) was finally adopted by referendum in February 2009.[1392] The text is extremely long and articulate. Art.1 states that Bolivia is a social unitary state based on plurinational and collective law; it is free, independent, sovereign, democratic, intercultural, decentralized, and with autonomies (see section 5.4) and is founded on political, economic, legal, cultural, and linguistic pluralism within the "integrative process" of the country. [1393] In particular, "plurinational" character, also adopted by Ecuador as seen in chapter 4, section 4.2, is given to all the organs of the

1389 International Labour Organization, "Report of the Committee set up to examine the representation alleging non-observance by Bolivia …", para.40.

1390 International Labour Organization, "Report of the Committee set up to examine the representation alleging non-observance by Bolivia …", para.44.b.

1391 See on the official Bolivian gazette "Ley No 3760 del 07 Noviembre 2007, Gaceta N° 3039 del 08 Noviembre 2007", at http://www.derechoteca.com/gacetabolivia/ley-3760-del-07-noviembre-2007.htm [Last access 12.08.2014].

1392 The Constitution was approved with 61.43% of votes in favor. See La Jornada, "CNE: 61.43% de los bolivianos aprobaron la nueva Constitución", 03.02.2009, at http://www.jornadanet.com/Hemeroteca/n.php?a=27395-1&f=20090203 [Last access on 12.08.2014]. On the previous drafts and clashes, see Taylor Matthew, "Evo Morales hails 'new Bolivia' as constitution is approved", The Guardian, 26.01.2009, at http://www.guardian.co.uk/world/2009/jan/26/bolivia [Last access on 12.08.2014]; and Crabtree John, "Bolivia's controversial constitution", Open Democracy, 10.12.2007, at http://www.opendemocracy.net/article/democracy_power/politics_protest/bolivia_constitution [Last access 12.08.2014].

1393 My translation of art.1, which in the original reads as follows: "Bolivia se constituye en un Estado Unitario Social de Derecho Plurinacional Comunitario, libre, independiente, soberano, democrático, intercultural, descentralizado y con autonomías. Bolivia se funda en la pluralidad y el pluralismo político, económico, jurídico, cultural y lingüístico, dentro del proceso integrador del país."

State such as: the Parliamentary Assembly (art.145 and ff.; hereinafter Plurinational Assembly or Parliament), the Constitutional Court (arts.178-179), etc.

Regarding indigenous peoples, their right to self-determination was inserted in art.2 and may be expressed in forms of autonomy, self-government, their own culture, and recognition of their own institutions in conformity with the Constitution and other domestic laws. In addition, this same provision recognizes the pre-existence and pre-colonial territorial dominion of indigenous peoples, thus highlighting their unjust subjugation. Art.5.1 grants official status to 36 indigenous languages,[1394] and thus recognizes those indigenous peoples, 2 of which live in the highlands (Quechua and Aymara) and the other 34 in the lowlands. Moreover, the central and autonomous regional governments must use at least two different languages, therefore one or more native languages in addition to Castilian (art.5.2). Notably, all Bolivians have the right to cultural self-identification (art.21.1).

In addition to a long list of human rights (chapters 3, 5 and 6 of the Constitution), chapter four (title II, part I [arts.30-32]) includes the specific fundamental rights of indigenous peoples, who are called "Peasant Native Indigenous Nations and Peoples (*Naciones y Pueblos Indígena Originario Campesinos*).[1395] They are defined as those "human collectives that share a cultural identity, language, historical tradition, institutions, territoriality and world-vision (*cosmovisión*) and whose existence is prior to the Spanish colonizing invasion" (art.30.1, author's own translation).

Art.30.2 contains a list of indigenous peoples' fundamental rights. Among these, the following are particularly relevant: the indigenous rights to their cultural identity, religious beliefs, spirituality, practices and

1394 Aymara, Araona, Baure, Bésiro, Canichana, Cavineño, Cayubaba, Chácobo, Chimán, Ese Ejja, Guaraní, Guarasu?We, Guarayu, Itonama, Leco, Machajuyaikallawaya, Machineri, Maropa, Mojeño-Trinitario, Mojeño-Ignaciano, Moré, Mosetén, Movima, Pacawara, Puquina, Quechua, Sirionó, Tacana, Tapiete, Toromona, Uru-Chipaya, Weenhayek, Yaminawa, Yuki, Yuracaré and Zamuco.

1395 The choice of using the three words was adopted during the Constituent Assembly to meet the request of the members claiming that part of the population self-identified with one or more of these adjectives. Gonzalo Colque and Carlos Sotomayor, "Nuestros Derechos en la Constitución", Fundación Tierra, La Paz, 2010, p.13. However, as recently underlined by Fontana, this is rather a narrative of the "plurinational 'imagined community'" contingent strategy of the last years. Lorenza Fontana, "The 'indigenous native peasant' trinity: imagining a plurinational community in Evo Morales' Bolivia", 32(3) *Environment and Planning D: Society and Space* 2014, pp.518-534, p.530.

customs, and world-vision (*cosmovisión*; art.30.2 no.2); again, to self-determination (art.30.2 no.4); to collective ownership of lands and territories (art.30.2, no.6); to collective intellectual property rights (art.30.2, no.11); to intercultural and bilingual education (art.30. no.12); to exercise their own political, legal, and economic systems (art.30.2, no.14); to consultation whenever an administrative or legislative measure is likely to affect them (art.30.2, no.15); to benefit-sharing from the exploitation of natural resources (art.30.2, no.16); and to participation within the state organs (art.30.2, no.18).

In the second part, title III, chapter four, the system of peasant native indigenous jurisdiction is recognized (arts.190-192). In particular, art.190.1, recognizes the right of indigenous peoples to exercise their own jurisdictional functions and competences through their authorities and by applying their own principles, cultural values, norms and procedures, to be coordinated with the ordinary justice system, with a law on jurisdictional separation (*Deslinde Jurisdiccional*; art.192.3) which was adopted soon after (see below).

The right to autonomy of indigenous peoples is to be found in the third part, title I, chapter seven of the Constitution, in which the new forms of indigenous (territorial) autonomies are given constitutional shape (arts.289-296, and 303-304). The legal ground of the (Bolivian) indigenous right to autonomy is once more the right to self-determination to be exercised via the right to self-government, i.e., the Peasant Native Indigenous Autonomy (*Autonomía Indígena Campesino Originaria* – AIOC; art.289; see below section 5.4).

As mentioned, the Constitution also converted the TCO into TIOC *Territorio Indígena Campesino Originario* (arts.269.1, 394 and 403; and Transitory Disposition No.7). In particular, in principle, art.403.1 provides the TIOC with substantial protection recognizing the integrity of the TIOC, which includes indigenous peoples' rights to: Land; the exclusive use and exploitation of renewable natural resources in accordance with national law; informed and prior consultation and to benefit-sharing from the exploitation of non-renewable natural resources; the application of their own customary law to be managed by their own representative structures according to their own development purposes and cultural principles.

A number of relevant norms were prepared and enacted in a domino effect by the Plurinational Assembly between 2009 and 2010 to give execution to the constitutional provisions, for instance, the Law on the Plurinational Electoral Organ No.18/2010 (*Ley del Órgano Electoral Plurinacional*); the Law on Judicial Body No.25/2010 (*Ley del Órgano*

Judicial); the Electoral Law No.26/2010 (*Ley del Régimen Electoral*) preceded by the Transitory Electoral Law No. 4021/2009 (*Ley de Regimen Electoral Transitorio*) to allow administrative elections in April 2010; the Law on the Plurinational Constitutional Court No.27/2010 (*Ley del Tribunal Constitucional Plurinacional*); the Autonomy Law No.31/2010 (*Ley Marco de Autonomías y Descentralización*); the Law Against Racism and All Forms of Discrimination No.45/2010; (*Ley Contra el Racismo y Toda Forma de Discriminación*); the Law on the Rights of Mother Earth No.71/2010 (*Ley de Derechos de la Madre Tierra*); and the Law on Jurisdictional Separation No.73/2010 (*Ley de Deslinde Jurisdiccional*). Some of these laws will be discussed below insofar as they regard the implementation of the *composite right* to political participation of indigenous peoples in Bolivia (sections 5.3 and 5.4). Other norms, e.g., those adopted after the marches to defend indigenous territory *Territorio Indígena y Parque Nacional Isiboro-Secure* (TIPNIS) will also be explored. Suffice it to add here that the abolition of the Ministry for Indigenous and Native Peoples' Affairs (MAIPO) two years after its creation was one of the first decisions of the first Morales administration since it was considered discriminatory to have such a ministry in a country where a large part of the population is indigenous. Since then, indigenous affairs were mainstreamed into the political agenda.[1396]

Nevertheless, after the legislative boom during 2010 and the clashes and contested consultation on the TIPNIS between 2011 and 2013 (see section 5.3.2.3), no progress has been made regarding laws affecting indigenous rights [1397] apart from the Law on Linguistic Rights and Policies No.269/2012 (*Ley General de Derechos y Políticas Lingüísticas*).[1398] In

1396 Stavenhagen, "Promotion and protection of all human rights ... Mission to Bolivia", para.28, p.19.

1397 Leonardo Tamburini, "Bolivia (2014)", in International Work Group for Indigenous Affairs, *The Indigenous World 2014*, IWGIA, Copenhagen, 2014, 167-175, p.173.

1398 Art.6 of this Law notably recognized "collective linguistic rights", which include education in the mother tongue; use of the official languages with public authorities (therefore, in Spanish plus an indigenous language spoken by the majority of people living in a region as according to art.5.2 Const. and art.8 of this law); to retake indigenous toponymies; intellectual property rights over works in indigenous languages; and develop their own education institutions. Finally, art.13.2 affirms that universities shall establish programs to teach all official languages, therefore also the indigenous ones. It remains to be seen how this promising law will be implemented.

general, the legislative initiative has rather been driven by the Government.[1399]

Lately, the adoption of new laws on consultation, land, forest, mining, hydrocarbons, as well as the Statutes of Santa Cruz, Beni and Chuquisaca that are not yet approved, were part of the announced political agenda for 2014.[1400] Out of these, the Law on Mining and Metallurgy (Law No.535/14) was adopted in May 2014 (see section 5.3.2.1).[1401] The draft law on consultation (*Anteproyecto de Ley de consulta previa, libre e informada*), which was long discussed and elaborated together with indigenous organizations during 2013 but also very contested by the main indigenous organizations CIDOB and CONAMAQ, was officially presented by the Ministry of the Government and "submitted" to President Morales in May 2014.[1402] However, the work on this law has probably come to a halt due to the general elections of 12 October 2014.

5.3 Indigenous peoples' participation in decision-making processes

This paragraph will tackle the first component of the implementation of the *composite right* to political participation of indigenous peoples in Bolivia. This aspect, as discussed in chapter 3 and, particularly, in section 3.4, concerns (a) indigenous peoples' representation in State bodies or in other public posts, including decision-making processes and in the judiciary, both at the national and local level, as well as their rights to (b) consultation and (c) free, prior and informed consent (FPIC). Therefore, in this section, the inclusion of indigenous representatives in the Bolivian national and local Parliaments and in other public posts, such as in the judiciary, will be considered first (section 5.3.1). The implementation of their rights to consultation and FPIC will then be explored (section 5.3.2). The analysis of the legal frameworks vis-à-vis these two aspects will be conducted

1399 Grace I. Deheza, "Bolivia 2011: Gobernando con el Conflicto", 32(1) *Revista de Ciencia Política (Santiago SciELO)* 2012, pp.31-48, p.45.

1400 Tamburini, "Bolivia (2014)", p.167 and p.174, note 1.

1401 Ley de Minería y Metalúrgia, Law No.535 enacted on 28 May 2014.

1402 Los Tiempos, "Ley de Consulta Previa va a Congreso", *Los Tiempos*, 13.05.2014, at http://www.lostiempos.com/diario/actualidad/nacional/20140513/ley-de-consulta-previa-va-a-congreso_254741_557403.html [Last access 04.12.2014]. On the pros and cons of this draft law see next section 5.3.2.1, and also Ruben Pinto Vargas, "Análisis del anteproyecto de Ley de Consulta Previa, Libre e Informada", *Foro Boliviano sobre Medio Ambiente y Desarrollo*, 12.11.2013, at http://www.fobomade.org.bo/art-2253 [Last access 04.12.2014].

separately on each of them and will be completed by an assessment of their application.

5.3.1 Indigenous peoples' representation at national and local level

Before approaching indigenous peoples' participation within the State, it needs to be specified that the new Bolivian electoral system is framed by the Constitution, the Electoral Law No.26/2010 and the later Law No.421/2013 (Law on the distribution of seats), *Ley de Distribución de Escaños entre Departamentos*, enacted on 7 October 2013, which slightly modified Law No.26/2010. As mentioned, prior to the adoption of the latter laws, the precedent Transitory Electoral Law No. 4021/2009 was the framework for both the Presidential elections of 2009 and the Departmental and Municipal elections of April 2010 (arts.25-26 of Law 4021/2009).[1403]

The 2009 Constitution followed the model of the 1994 reforms mentioned above (section 5.1.2); it foresees a bicameral Parliament composed of two Chambers of Deputies and Senators (art.145 Const.; hereinafter Lower and Upper Chambers, respectively). The former is composed of 130 deputies, half of which are elected within each department[1404] in uninominal circumscriptions by simple majority[1405] and the remaining half in pluri-nominal circumscriptions according to a proportional system. The number of deputies for each department must proportionally reflect the population according to the national census (art.146 Const.).

The Transitory Electoral Law No. 4021/2009 (art.32), which was reported in the later Electoral Law No.26/2010 (art.57), assigned a pre-determined number of seats according to the results of the 2001 census. The number of seats should have been revised by law according to the new census mentioned above for the upcoming 2014 general elections and 2015 departmental and municipal elections (art.146.6 Const.). However, despite the increase of 1.75 million of inhabitants from the census of 2001 (8,274,325) to that of 2012 (10,027,254), for the 2014 general elections the

1403 According to art.269 of the Constitution, Bolivia is subdivided into four types of territorial units, i.e., departments, provinces, municipalities, and TIOCs.

1404 There are 9 departments of Bolivia, namely La Paz, Cochabamba, Oruro, Potosí and Chuquisaca in the West/highlands, and Santa Cruz, Tarija, Beni and Pando in the East/lowlands.

1405 See the maps of the uninominal circumscriptions at http://politicadebolivia.blogspot.it on the left menu [Last access 22.08.2014].

number of both deputies and senators remained the same.[1406] The Chamber of Senators (or Senate) is composed of 36 members, four for each department, who are elected with a proportional system (art.148 Const.). The Transitory Electoral Law No. 4021/2009 (art.39) and the Electoral Law No.26/2010 (art.54) do not specify anything further, although the latter clarifies that Senators are voted for within the presidential and vice-presidential lists.[1407] Legislative bills may be submitted by both Chambers, the citizens, the executive body/government, the Supreme Court, and the autonomous governments of each territorial entity (art.162 Const.; on the autonomous system, see section 5.4). Nevertheless, in 2011 alone, President Morales adopted 356 Supreme Decrees, while Vice-President Álvaro García Lineras directed and presented the draft laws of the government to the Parliament.[1408]

Art.30.2 of the 2009 Constitution contains a list of indigenous rights, including the right to exercise their own political, legal, and economic systems (art.30.2, no.14) and to participate within the State organs (art.30.2, no.18). More in detail, art.147.2 states that indigenous peoples should be proportionally represented within the Plurinational Assembly (the Parliament). Moreover, art.146.7 and art.147.3 introduce the concept of special circumscriptions to elect (peasant native) indigenous representatives (*circunscripciones especiales indígena originario campesinas*). The former article states that the special circumscriptions will be established only in rural areas in those departments where indigenous peoples constitute a numerical minority. The latter provision affirms that other special circumscriptions will be established by law irrespective of the criteria set forth in the former norm.

However, the Transitory Electoral Law No. 4021/2009 only established 7 special circumscriptions to elect the same number of deputies in the Lower Chamber (arts.32 and 35), thus solely implementing art.147.3 of the Constitution but not the other abovementioned norm. This indeed fuelled

1406 Supreme Electoral Court/Tribunal Supremo Electoral, "Resultados de las Elecciones General 2014", La Paz, 2014, p.10, at http://www.oep.org.bo [Last access 01.12.2014]. Art.1 of No.421/2013 modifies art.56 of Law No.26/2010 but confirms the total number of deputies to 130.

1407 According to art.166 of the Constitution, both the President and the Vice-President are directly elected by the population. The combined candidate for these two mandates will result elected if he/she obtains the simple majority of the valid votes or if he/she takes at least 40% of the total valid votes and the following candidate attains 10% fewer votes (i.e., there is a difference of 10% of the votes between the first and second candidate).

1408 Deheza, "Bolivia 2011: Gobernando con el Conflicto", p.45.

indigenous malcontent when the Transitory Electoral Law No.4021 was adopted in April 2009.

The indigenous organizations had repeatedly requested 36 reserved seats for indigenous representatives (one for each constitutionally recognized indigenous people) or at least 14.[1409] Indeed, the seven reserved seats were assigned to each of the following departments: La Paz, Cochabamba, Oruro, Santa Cruz, Tarija, Beni and Pando, thus excluding Potosí and Chuquisaca (art.32 Transitory Electoral Law No. 4021/2009). The same provision also outlined which specific indigenous peoples could vote in each of these special circumscriptions to elect the one indigenous representative within the department they lived in. For instance, for the special circumscription of La Paz, the Afrobolivian, Mosetén, Leco, Kallawaya, Tacana and Araona peoples could vote in addition to voting the other deputies in the other uninominal and plurinominal circumscriptions. The Aymara and Quechua peoples, indeed constituting a wide numerical majority within the country, as seen above, could not vote for the special circumscriptions. This somehow justified the partial implementation of the Constitution, since the seats were assigned only to the numerically inferior indigenous peoples. However, as seen above, the constitutional text required not only a proportional representation of indigenous peoples, but also more special circumscriptions, namely those where the indigenous peoples are a minority and those irrespective of this criterion. Despite the aforementioned protest, both the Electoral Law No.26/2010 and the later Law No.421/2013 –that (slightly) modified Law No.26/2010– confirmed the legal setting of the Transitory Electoral Law No.4021/2009 in their art.57 and art.1 respectively regarding the 7 special circumscriptions corresponding to the 7 reserved seats.

Needless to say, 7 deputies out of 130 may be easily outvoted. Many other of the 123 deputies may also be indigenous given the high percentage of Indigenous peoples in the country. In a recent analysis, the former vice-president Víctor Hugo Cárdenas argues that from the 1979 to the 2009 elections, the percentage of indigenous congress persons in the Lower Chamber increased from 1.38% to 22.89% [1410] and that the current

1409 Leonardo Tamburini, "Bolivia (2010)", in International Work Group for Indigenous Affairs, *The Indigenous World 2010*, IWGIA, Copenhagen, 2010, 195-206, p.196.

1410 Víctor Hugo Cárdenas, "Participación Política Indígena y Políticas Públicas para Pueblos Indígenas en Bolivia", in Víctor Hugo Cárdenas et al. (eds.), *Participación Política Indígena y Políticas Públicas para Pueblos Indígenas en América Latina*, Konrad Adenauer Stiftung, LA Paz, 2011, pp.17-64, p.28.

Parliament includes at least 38 deputies and 6 (16.66%) senators of indigenous descent. Nonetheless, this data cannot be confirmed by any official source. The electoral bodies, in fact, do not register details regarding the origins of members. [1411] Additionally, even if this data was incontrovertibly proved, the percentage flagged by Cárdenas will be significant (one-third of the Parliament) [1412] but still potentially outvoted. Other sources state that until 1993 the number of indigenous members within the Parliament had barely reached 2%.[1413] Therefore, there is no guarantee that indigenous voices are fully taken into account. Moreover, the relationship between President Morales' government and indigenous peoples is increasingly deteriorating and fuelling new protests (see section 5.3.2).

After the 2009 elections, the MAS controlled two-thirds of both Chambers of the Parliament and the other parties at the opposition (*Plan Progreso para Bolivia-Convergencia Nacional – PPB-CN; Unidad Nacional – UN-CP; Alianza Social – AS*) had essentially no power to modify the draft laws be it during the discussion or in the commissions.[1414] According to the results of the recent 2014 elections, in which 87.90% of voters participated, Morales was reelected President with an overwhelming majority of votes (61.36%) gained by his party MAS-IPSP (*Movimiento al Socialismo* IPSP). According to the Bolivian political scientist Diego Ayo Saucedo, Morales won not only thanks to an improved electoral strategy, especially in comparison with the other candidates, but mostly because these elections were highly symbolical. In essence, in the Bolivian social imaginary, Morales still embodies *the* change: A national rebirth; the distribution of wealth to the poor; the participation of indigenous peoples and peasants in the decision-making bodies; a legitimized political system;

1411 This detail is flagged by Albó, "Bolivia: From Indian and Campesino Leaders to Councillors and Parliamentary Deputies", p.83, regarding the 1997 and 1999 elections, but is also valid in the most recent elections, as according to both the Transitory Electoral Law No.4021/2009 (arts.19-24) and the Electoral Law No.26/2010 (arts.98-99), the details regarding origins are not required to be listed in the electoral register (*Padrón Electoral*).

1412 38 indigenous congresspersons plus the 7 reserved seats account for 34.6% of votes.

1413 Departament de la Presidència (ed.), *Bolivia: la refundación de un país/Bolívia: la refundació d'un país*, Casa América Catalunya, Barcelona, 2006, p.15.

1414 Deheza, "Bolivia 2011: Gobernando con el Conflicto", p.46. E.g., out of the ten commissions at the Senate, MAS controls 8. Deheza, "Bolivia 2011: Gobernando con el Conflicto", p.46.

and a new role for Bolivia in the international arena.[1415] The other parties gained approximately 25% of the votes (*Unidad Democratica* – UD, 24.23%) or less (*Partido Demócrata Cristiano* – PDC, 9.04%; *Movimiento Sin Miedo* – MSM, 2.71%; *Partido Verde de Bolivia-Instrumento de la Ecología Política* – PVB-IEP 2.65%).[1416] Therefore, MAS-IPSP gained 121 seats (25 in the Upper Chamber, and 88 in the Lower Chamber) and can essentially disregard the other parties.[1417] Furthermore, they recently announced a new constitutional reform to guarantee the reelection of Morales until 2025.[1418]

At local level, the Departmental Assemblies/Parliaments should also include indigenous representatives to be voted by indigenous peoples according to their customary rules and procedures (art.277 Const.). Each Department shall decide in its Statute the criteria to elect the members of their parliaments (art.278.2 Const.). Thus, its implementation is yet to be seen since only few of nine departments (e.g., Pando, La Paz, and Potosí) received the constitutional approval of their Statutes by the Plurinational Constitutional Court, other departmental Statutes are under review by the Plurinational Constitutional Court (e.g., Oruro) or under revision by the Departmental Assemblies (e.g., Cochabamba) since they were not completely approved by the Constitutional Court. [1419] However, the

1415 Diego Ayo Saucedo, "Evo ganó antes de las elecciones", *Página Siete*, 09.11.2014, at http://www.paginasiete.bo/ideas/2014/11/9/gano-antes-elecciones-37557.html [Last access 15.12.2014].

1416 Supreme Electoral Court/Tribunal Supremo Electoral, "Resultados de las Elecciones General 2014", p.2. The presidential candidate of the PVB-IEP party was Fernando Vargas, President of the TIPNIS' coordination body and leader of the two marches against the construction of the highway in this Park (see below section 5.3.2.3).

1417 In the Upper Chamber, the *Unidad Democratica*-UD gained 9 seats and the *Partido Demócrata Cristiano*-PDC only two; in the Lower Chamber, the former party gained 32 seats, and the latter only 10. The other two parties did not reach the minimum threshold of 3% and therefore gained no seats. The MAS-IPSP also gained 8 out of the 9 "supra-national" representatives for the Bolivian external relations that, in accordance with arts.265-266 of the 2009 Constitution, are also voted by universal suffrage. The ninth of these representatives instead belongs to the *Unidad Democratica*-UD party. Supreme Electoral Court/Tribunal Supremo Electoral, "Resultados de las Elecciones General 2014", pp.18-19.

1418 Infobae Ámerica/AFP, "Evo Morales quiere reformar la Constitución para ir por su cuarto mandato presidencial", 19.05.2015, *Infobae Ámerica*, at http://www.infobae.com/2015/05/19/1729749-evo-morales-quiere-reformar-la-constitucion-ir-su-cuarto-mandato-presidencial [Last access 28.08.2015].

1419 C. Corz and Y. Donoso, "TCP declara constitucional y viabiliza vigencia Estatuto Autonómico de Pando", *La Razón*, 09.04.2014, at http://www.la-razon.com/in

Transitory Electoral Law No.4021/2009, which regulated the 2010 administrative elections for departmental and municipal authorities, specified the number of reserved seats for indigenous peoples for the parliamentary assembly of each department in the following manner: Beni, 2 reserved seats for indigenous peoples and another two for peasants out of 30 (art.66.1);[1420] Tarija, 3 reserved seats out of 30 for each indigenous people (Guaraní, Weenhayek and Tapiete; art.66.2); Pando, 1 reserved seat for indigenous peoples out of 16 (art.66.3); Santa Cruz 5 reserved seats for indigenous peoples out of 28 (art.66.4); Chuquisaca 2 reserved seats for indigenous peoples out of 21 (art.67.1); La Paz 5 reserved seats for indigenous peoples out of 45 (art.67.1); Cochabamba 2 for indigenous peoples reserved seats out of 34 (art.67.1); Oruro, 1 reserved seat for indigenous peoples out of 33 (art.67.1); and none in Potosí (out of 32 parliamentary members; art.67.1). In general, all of these indigenous representatives were voted by simple majority and according to their own customary rules and procedures (apart from Pando, where the Departmental assemblies comprise one representative for each municipality of the Department, art.66.2).

These criteria were not included in the later Electoral Law No.26/2010 that specified that the members of the Departmental assemblies shall be voted by simple majority in the uninominal circumscriptions. Indigenous representatives were to be voted according to their own customary rules and procedures. The seats of the pluri-nominal circumscriptions were to be distributed following a proportional system of those political organizations (*organizaciones políticas*, therefore not only parties that call them as such but also registered organizations) that reach at least the minimum threshold of 3% of the total valid votes (art.66). This last rule should also be applied to the municipal parliaments (arts.72-73 Electoral Law No.26/2010), while the mayors were to be voted by simple majority (art.71 Electoral Law No.26/2010). This last criterion was also applied by the Transitory Electoral

---

dex.php?_url=/nacional/TCP-constitucional-Estatuto-Autonomico-Pando_0_2030796986.html; Luis Mealla, "TCP aprueba Estatuto Autonómico paceño", 09.09.2014, *La Razón*, at http://www.la-razon.com/index.php?_url=/nacional/Documento-TCP-aprueba-Estatuto_Autonomico-paceno_0_2122587771.html; ANA Noticias/Potosí "El Estatuto Autonómico de Potosí es 100 por ciento constitucional", 31.10.2014, at http://www.ananoticias.com/autonomia-departamental/item/1390-el-estatuto-autonomico-de-potosi-es-100-por-ciento-constitucional. For the latest developments, see the official website of "Autonomic News" at http://www.ananoticias.com [Last access to all 15.12.2014].

1420 As mentioned, all the legislation adopted the lettering of "peasant native indigenous peoples or nations", but in this case they are spelled out separately.

Law No.4021/2009 for the 2010 elections (art.71), which were held in the nine departments and in 337 municipalities (on the number of municipalities and the issues of territorial limitations see below section 5.4).

The Departmental, regional and municipal elections of 2015 were regulated by Resolutions Nos.0623/2014 and 145/2015 of the Supreme Electoral Court (*Tribunal Supremo Electoral*).[1421] This regulation foresaw the following distribution of seats to indigenous peoples: Beni, 2 reserved seats in total out of 28 for indigenous peoples among the listed ones (Tacana, Pacahuara, Itonama, Joaquiniano, Maropa, Guarasugwe, Mojeño, Sirionó, Baure, Tsimane, Movima, Cayubaba, Moré, Cavineño, Chacobo, Canichana, Mosetén, and Yuracaré), and another two for peasants (arts.71-72);[1422] Tarija, 3 reserved seats out of 30 (all titular, and no substitutes), one for each of the three listed indigenous peoples (Guaraní, Weenhayek and Tapiete; arts.67-68), according to own laws and procedures but under the supervision of the Departmental Electoral Court; Pando, 3 reserved seats out of 21 (plus another 3 as substitutes) for indigenous peoples among the listed ones (Cavineño, Yaminahua, Esse Ejja, Machinerí, Tacana, and the-yet-uncontacted-people of Pacahuara, in case of contact) to be elected according to own laws and procedures but under the supervision of the Departmental Electoral Court (arts.73-74); Santa Cruz 5 reserved seats out of 28 (all titular, and no substitutes), one for each of the listed indigenous peoples (Chiquitano, Guaraní, Guarayo, Ayoreo and Yuracaré-Mojeño; arts.69-70), to be elected according to own laws and procedures but under the supervision of the Departmental Electoral Court; Chuquisaca 2 reserved seats (plus another 2 as substitutes) out of 21 for the indigenous people Guaraní (arts.57-58) to be elected according to own laws and procedures but under the supervision of the Departmental Electoral Court; La Paz 5 reserved seats out of 45, one for each of the listed indigenous peoples (Afroboliviano, Mosetén, Leco, Kallawaya y Tacana, and Araona; arts.59-60), to be elected according to own laws and procedures but under the supervision of the Departmental Electoral Court; Cochabamba 2 reserved seats (plus another 2 as substitutes) out of 34 the two listed indigenous peoples (Yuki and Yuracaré; arts.61-62), to be elected

1421 Regulation for the Election of Departmental, Regional and Municipal Elections of 2015, *Reglamento para la Elección de Autoridades Políticas Departamentales, Regionales y Municipales Elecciones Subnacionales 2015, aprobado mediante Resolución TSE-RSP Nº 0623/2014, modificada por Resolución TSE-RSP Nº 145/2015.*

1422 In this case, the two reserved seats for peasants are spelled literally as such (*campesinos*).

according to own laws and procedures but under the supervision of the Departmental Electoral Court; Oruro, 1 reserved seat (plus another one as substitute) for either one of the two listed indigenous peoples (Chipaya and Murato) out of 33 (arts.63-64), to be elected according to own laws and procedures but under the supervision of the Departmental Electoral Court; and none in Potosí (out of 32 parliamentary members; arts.65-66), as also previously foreseen.

As to the results of local elections, in the 2010 administrative elections of departmental and municipal authorities the President Morales' party (MAS) lost some votes in comparison to 2009, but won in six out of nine departments and in the majority of the municipalities. Among others, notably, in 2010 MAS lost the mayor's offices of La Paz and Oruro (which were won by the *Movimiento Sin Miedo* (MSM), a former ally of the MAS).[1423] The Supreme Electoral Court (*Tribunal Supremo Electoral*) scheduled the local elections for 29 March 2015[1424] and the second ballot for the runoff voting of governors for 3 May 2015.[1425] Prior to the elections, the vice-president of the MAS party Concepción Ortiz declared it will be Morales himself who was going to approve the candidates of the MAS for the posts of governors and mayors.[1426] Eventually, the MAS-IPSP won in seven departments (Cochabamba, Oruro, Potosí and Pando at the first electoral round, and Chuquisaca and Beni at the runoff voting) and in the majority of the municipalities, but lost key departments (La Paz and Santa Cruz). Moreover, the opposition parties Ipsos–Soberanía y Libertad (Sol.bo), Movimiento Demócrata Social (Demócratas) and Unidad

---

1423 Corte Nacional Electoral del Estado Plurinacional de Bolivia, "Acta de Cómputo Nacional Elecciones Departamentales, Municipales y Regional 2010", La Paz, 2010 (as to the municipalities of La Paz and Oruro, see p.87 and p.126, respectively), at http://politicadebolivia.blogspot.it/2010/09/resultados-oficiales-de-las-elecciones.html [Last access 22.08.2014]; Deheza, "Bolivia 2011: Gobernando con el Conflicto", pp.39-42 and 46. Also Georgetown University has an online database with some of the results of the 2009 and 2010 elections, see http://pdba.georgetown.edu/Elecdata/Bolivia/bolivia.html [Last access 07.12.2014].

1424 Supreme Electoral Court/Tribunal Supremo Electoral, "Calendario Electoral. Elección de Autoridades Políticas Departamentales, Regionales y Municipales 2015", La Paz, 2014, p.6, at http://www.oep.org.bo [Last access 01.12.2014].

1425 Supreme Electoral Court/Tribunal Supremo Electoral, "Calendario Electoral Segunda Vuelta. Elección de Gobernadoras y Gobernadores 2015", La Paz, 2014, p.2, at http://www.oep.org.bo [Last access 01.12.2014].

1426 Página Siete, "Evo definirá los candidatos a gobernaciones y Municipios", *Página Siete*, 27.10.2014, at http://www.paginasiete.bo/nacional/2014/10/27/definira-candidatos-gobernaciones-municipios-36441.html [Last access 15.12.2014].

Departamental Autonomista won crucial cities such as El Alto and Cochabamba.[1427] For the departments of Beni, Tarija and Chuquisaca the runoff voting of governors was held, as scheduled, on 3 May 2015.[1428] In Beni, the MAS-IPSP eventually won with a very narrow percentage of votes (50.23% versus 49.77%, i.e., for 800 votes) and in a highly contested atmosphere.[1429] The MAS-IPSP also won in Chuquisaca. The opposition party *Unidad Departamental Autonomista* (UD-A) won in Tarija against the MAS-IPSP with 62.1% of votes in favor.[1430]

Regarding the participation of indigenous peoples in other state organs, it is remarkable that the 2009 Constitution foresees that at least two out of the seven members of the Supreme Electoral Court, which is one body of the Electoral Organ, must be of (peasant native) indigenous origins (art.206.2).[1431] This requirement is confirmed in art.12 of the Law on the Plurinational Electoral Organ No.18/2010. Furthermore, the Law on the Plurinational Constitutional Court No.27/2010 establishes that two out of seven judges of this Court shall be (peasant native) indigenous as per self-identification (art.13.2).[1432] The judges are to be voted by the population according to art.20 of this law. The pre-selection of candidates is to be made by the Parliament (art.19.3 and art.158.1.5 of the Constitution). The present judges, as well as those of the Farm-Environmental Court (*Tribunal Agroambiental*), Council of Magistrates (*Consejo de la Magistratura*) and

1427 Página Siete/La Paz, "El MAS sufre revés electoral", *Página Siete*, 30.03.2015, http://www.paginasiete.bo/decision2015/2015/3/30/sufre-reves-electoral-51790.html [Last access 14.04.2015].

1428 Santiago Masetti, "Habrá segunda vuelta en tres departamentos", *Portal del Sur – Agencia Latinoamericana de Noticias*, 06.04.2015, at http://portaldelsur.info/2015/04/habra-segunda-vuelta-en-tres-departamentos [Last access 15.06.2015].

1429 The party at the opposition (*NACER*) denounced that they contested and prepared three formal requests for revisions and none was accepted. Página Siete/La Paz, "Ferrier gana las elecciones con 789 votos a Dellien en el Beni", *Página Siete*, 08.05.2015, at http://www.paginasiete.bo/nacional/2015/5/8/ferrier-gana-elecciones-votos-dellien-beni-55970.html [Last access 15.06.2015].

1430 Eabolivia.Com Diario Digital - Noticias de Bolivia, "Resultados de elecciones (segunda vuelta) en Beni y Tarija 2015", 03.05.2015, at http://www.eabolivia.com/politica/22445-resultados-de-elecciones-segunda-vuelta-en-beni-y-tarija-2015.html [Last access 15.06.2015].

1431 Six of these members are voted by the Parliament and one by the President (art.206.3-5). See the current composition of the Plurinational Electoral Organ at http://www.oep.org.bo/index.php/vocales-tse [Last access 22.08.2014].

1432 The Constitution only states that candidates to stand for election as judges of the Plurinational Constitutional Court may be proposed by indigenous organizations (art.199.2).

the Supreme Court of Justice (*Tribunal Supremo de la Justicia*),[1433] were elected on 16 October 2011 in a tense political atmosphere.[1434] For the posts of judges within these High Courts, the Parliament received 350 applications, 125 of which were selected. However, the opposition parties claimed that some candidates were chosen only because they were affiliated to the MAS party,[1435] and asked their electorates to invalidate their votes.[1436] Indeed, the majority of votes were spoiled or left blank (44.03% and 13.87%, respectively), particularly in the cities.[1437] The elections were nevertheless considered valid.[1438]

5.3.2 Consultation and FPIC of indigenous peoples in Bolivia

5.3.2.1 Legislative framework

Bolivia ratified the ILO Convention 169 in 1991 (Law No.1257/1991) as well as the UNDRIP (Law 3720/2007), despite the fact that the latter is not a treaty in *stricto sensu* (see section 5.2.1).

Moreover, the Constitution provides indigenous peoples with the right to consultation through appropriate procedures and, in particular, through their representatives whenever an administrative or legislative measure is likely to affect them. In this framework, their right to prior and mandatory consultation, to be realized by the State in good faith and agreement, shall be respected and guaranteed in cases of the exploitation of non-renewable natural resources in the territories inhabited by them (art.30.2, no.15).[1439] Moreover, art.403.1 of the Constitution, which deals with the TIOC,

1433 Notably, it is rather unusual to call the population to vote for the judges of High Courts in Latin America. Deheza, "Bolivia 2011: Gobernando con el Conflicto", p.38.

1434 Deheza, "Bolivia 2011: Gobernando con el Conflicto", pp.38-39.

1435 *Ibid.*, p.38.

1436 *Ibid.*, p.39.

1437 *Ibid.*, pp.39-40.

1438 *Ibid.*, p.39. See the current composition of the Plurinational Constitutional Court is at http://www.tcpbolivia.bo/tcp/content/magdo-efrain-choque-capuma and in the left menu [Last access 22.08.2014].

1439 My translation. The original text reads as follows: "A ser consultados mediante procedimientos apropiados, y en particular a través de sus instituciones, cada vez que se prevean medidas legislativas o administrativas susceptibles de afectarles. En este marco, se respetará y garantizará el derecho a la consulta previa obligatoria, realizada por el Estado, de buena fe y concertada, respecto a la explotación de los recursos naturales no renovables en el territorio que habitan."

recognizes the right of indigenous peoples to prior and informed consultation and to participate in the benefit-sharing of the exploitation of non-renewable natural resources that are situated on their territories.

Before the adoption of the Constitution, arts.114-118 of the Hydrocarbons Law No.3058/2005 (*Ley de Hidrocarburos*),[1440] of which a revision was announced but not yet adopted,[1441] regulated the right to consultation of indigenous peoples whenever a hydrocarbon activity was planned. This is due to the insistent lobby mainly made by the organization Assembly of Guaraní People (*Asemblea del Pueblo Guaraní* – APG).[1442] This law provides for an extensive and far-reaching regulation of this right, recalling and even enhancing many of the standards set forth in the ILO Convention 169 (in good faith; with transparency; with appropriate procedures and according to the circumstances and characteristics of each indigenous people; with an evaluation of how each indigenous people will be affected; and with the aim of reaching an agreement or their consent; art.115). In particular, this provision states that "prior consultation" is mandatory (art.114) and that the decisions resulting from the consultation shall be respected (art.115). The consultation shall be conducted both prior to the tender, authorization, contracting, call, and approval of the hydrocarbon measures, works or projects, and prior to the approval of the Environmental Impact Assessment, which should be more detailed in the case of hydrocarbon projects that would affect indigenous communities or

---

1440 According to art.5 of this law, Bolivian natural resources were nationalized after the Gas War and the 2004 Referendum mentioned above (section 5.1.2).

1441 A new law on hydrocarbons is not under discussion at either the Lower Chamber or the Upper Chamber. See http://www.diputados.bo/index.php/leyes/leyes-en-tra tamiento and http://www.senado.bo/pro yectos_de_ley/camara_de_origen [Last access 07.12.2014]. The last available and reliable news states that the Government and the national(ized) company *Yacimientos Petrolíferos Fiscales Bolivianos* (YPFB) started working on a new draft law of hydrocarbons in April 2014. EFE/ Página Siete, "Bolivia prepara leyes sobre hidrocarburos y de incentivos", *Página Siete*, 11.04.2014, at http://www.paginasiete.bo/economia/2014/4/11/bolivia-pre para-leyes-sobre-hidrocarburos-incentivos-18620.html [Last access 07.12.2014]. The work on this draft, as in the case of the draft law on consultation, may have been postponed due to the then-upcoming general elections of October 2014. However, the texts of the latest Supreme Decrees touching upon the right to consultation of indigenous peoples of late November 2014 and first half of 2015 (see *infra*) consider this law still in force.

1442 Mirna Cuentas, "El derecho a la consulta previa en Bolivia", 14 *Revista de la Fundación para el Debido Proceso Legal Aportes DPLF* 2010, pp.17-20, p.18. The Assembly of Guaraní People (*Asemblea del Pueblo Guaraní* – APG) is one of the regional organizations of CIDOB created in 1987. See the organization's website at http://www.cidob-bo.org/regionales/apg.htm [Last access 22.08.2014].

territories with high levels of biodiversity (art.115, letters a-b). In the case of the negative outcome of a consultation, the State retains the right to start a reconciliation process (art.116). The State bodies charged with organizing the consultations are the Ministries of Hydrocarbons, Sustainable Development and (then abrogated) of Indigenous and Native Peoples Affairs-MAIPO, with financial aid from the government (art.117). Finally, the consultations shall be held with indigenous representatives, irrespective of their organization, but following their uses and customs. Any singular or sectorial consultation will be null and void (art.118). This law thus secured indigenous peoples' right to consultation and, to some extent, also to FPIC.

However, soon after its adoption, Deputy Luis Eduardo Siles Pérez, who was later spokesman of the MNR, brought an appeal of unconstitutionality of the mentioned arts.114, 115, and 116 before the Constitutional Court. He claimed that the consultation could not have a binding character.[1443] The Court eventually declared art.114 to be in line with the (then, 1994) Constitution, but found that arts.115-116 were partially unconstitutional. In particular, the aim of reaching an agreement with indigenous peoples regarding their consent over art.115 and the reconciliation process in case of the negative outcome of a consultation of art.116 were considered to be beyond the scope of the indigenous rights recognized in the 1994 Constitution, since they essentially gave indigenous peoples a veto right.[1444] This has been overruled by Constitutional Decision No. 2003/2010-R of 2010 (see below section 5.3.2.3).

Notwithstanding this decision, the requirements of consultation according to the Hydrocarbon Law were further regulated by Supreme Decree No.29033 adopted in February 2007 (also as a result of the new Constitution), [1445] although it has recently been further modified by Supreme Decree/*Decreto Supremo* No.2298, adopted on 18 March 2015.

Art.4 of the Decree No.29033 incorporated the core international principles of consultation seen in chapter 3 (section 3.3.2), such as the provision and distribution of detailed information, the use of indigenous languages, and good faith. Most importantly, the outcomes of the consultation shall be respected and considered as fundamental criteria for

1443 (Plurinational) Constitutional Court, Decision (*Sentencia Constitucional*) No.0045/2006, File No.2005-12440-25-RDI, 2 June 2006, "I. Antecedentes con Relevancia Jurídica", para.I.1, No.14.

1444 Sentencia Constitucional 0045/2006, 02.06.2006, File No.2005-12440-25-RDI, "Conclusiones", No.3.

1445 *Decreto Supremo* No.29033, 16.02.2007, *Reglamento de Consulta y Participación para Actividades Hidrocarburíferas.*

the execution of any hydrocarbon activity, work, or project (art.8). The consultation procedure was also detailed.

It has to be organized by the Ministry of Hydrocarbons and Energy (*Ministerio de Hidrocarburos y Energía*) in coordination with the Vice-Minister of Biodiversity, Forest Resources, and the Environment (*Viceministerio de Biodiversidad, Recursos Forestales y Medio Ambiente*) and the Vice-Minister of Lands (*Viceministerio de Tierras*; art.5). The costs of the consultation are charged onto the hydrocarbon project budget and therefore borne by the State (art.8.1).

The consultation procedure is composed of four phases: Coordination and information; organization and planning; execution; and agreement (art.9). Each of these steps was further detailed in arts.10-13. In particular, before the modifications introduced by Supreme Decree No.2298/2015, the first phase notably required an announcement and a preliminary meeting, during which detailed, adequate (linguistically and according to the indigenous culture), and complete information on the project and its impact should be distributed to the concerned community (art.10). Second, ten days after this meeting and in the timespan of a further 7 days, another meeting should have been organized to share a written proposal that specifies the consultation timetable and methodology and to reach a provisional agreement (*acta de entendimiento*; art.11) with the community. Third, and it still valid, the consultation is carried out according to the timetable contained in this provisional agreement which, if necessary, may be extended a further 3 months (art.12). Fourth, the consultation shall be concluded by both parties (the State represented by the Ministries and the concerned indigenous peoples) adopting a "validated agreement" (*validación de acuerdos*; art.13). Finally, the outcomes of the consultation should be included in the Environmental Impact Assessment (art.15). If it is information is not included, the concerned indigenous community may request the authority running the consultation to contest the study (art.16).

As mentioned, the following Supreme Decree No.2298/2015, however, modified the consultation procedure. In particular, art.2 of this later Decree amended letter a) of art.10 detailing further the ways to call the preliminary meeting up to a maximum of three times, after which, if no written reply would be provided by indigenous peoples (or the peasant communities) to the competent authority, this would be free to decide the methodology and the timeline for the consultation. Moreover, Supreme Decree No.2298/2015 changed also art.11, which now foresees that during the first session not only the first information will be provided, but will be also circulated the methodology, the timeline and the budget of the consultation which will be reported in a specific act. If an agreement with indigenous peoples on such (fundamental) aspects will not be reached at the first meeting, within 5 days another meeting will be called. If neither during this second meeting an agreement is reached, in another 5 days the competent authority will decide (unilaterally) the three above-mentioned aspects. In addition, the execution of the consultation cannot now last more than 45 days. Finally, art.3 of Supreme Decree No.2298/2015 adds two extra articles to the previous one (Supreme Decree No.29033/2007): The new art.19 now states that any type of presence during the meetings will certify the continuation of the process of consultation; and art.20 states that, any time that it is not possible to carry out the consultation (without specific such cases), the competent authority will be free to adopt an act (*Resolución Administrativa*) that essentially substitute the consultation.

Hence, the previous legislation (Supreme Decree No.29033/2007) had guaranteed the completion of a number of consultations, as will be discussed below (section 5.3.2.3). Many problems had anyways arisen during the carrying out of the consultations, which in practice did not follow this safeguarding procedure. The amendments introduced by Supreme Decree No.2298/2015, however, are more serious: They do legitimize a narrower scope and a lowering of the standards of the right to consultation of indigenous peoples.

The Electoral Law No.26/2010 foresaw prior consultation as an instrument of direct democracy recognized to all Bolivian citizens (art.2.d, and 4.i). The consultation must be conducted prior to any project, work, or activity of natural resource exploitation likely to affect them (art.39). In the case of indigenous peoples, the consultation shall be regulated by their customary rules and procedures (art.39, para.2). The outcomes of the consultations are not binding, but shall be taken into due consideration by the authorities (art.39, para.3).

Finally, the above-mentioned draft law on consultation (*Anteproyecto de Ley de consulta previa, libre e informada*) was presented by the Ministry of the Government and "submitted" to President Morales last May 2014. There was a limited and dubious participation of indigenous leaders from APG in the lowlands and CONAMAQ in the highlands; apparently the main proposals put forward by these organizations –such as the insertion of FPIC and a clear reference to the prior nature of consultations– have been ignored.[1446] Another problematic aspect concerns art.11 of this draft law that allows exceptions to the application of the right to consultation in the

1446 Tamburini, "Bolivia (2014)", pp.171-172.

poorly defined cases of "State or citizen security" or when the consultation cannot be implemented due to its "nature".[1447]

Regarding the mining sector, the new Law on Mining and Metallurgy (Law No.535/14) adopted in May 2014 contains the right to consultation of the indigenous peoples as according to arts.30.15 and 403 of the CPE, but it applies it neither to prospective and exploration mining projects, nor to all those mining projects already approved before the enactment of this law (i.e, May 2014; see art.207 of this law). Furthermore, where applicable, the consultation should be carried out within a maximum of three meetings (art.211.2). This clearly undermines a fair application of the right to consultation of indigenous peoples in the mining sector.

Finally, between November 2014 and May 2015, in addition to Supreme Decree No.2298/2015, President Morales adopted another two Supreme Decrees that indirectly or directly affect the right to consultation of indigenous peoples.[1448] The first, the Supreme Decree No.2195/2014, regulates the monetary compensation based on percentages between 0.3 and 1.5% for those socio-environmental impacts caused by hydrocarbon activities that are taking place onto indigenous territories (TIOC) and were identified during the consultation (art.3), if any. Hence, for those indigenous peoples that would not insist on these aspects, such monetary compensation could be denied. The second is Supreme Decree No.2366/2015 that allows to develop hydrocarbon activities on the whole Bolivian territory, including protected areas.

In sum, the legislative framework vis-à-vis the right to consultation of indigenous peoples was incisive, although with many antinomies (e.g., the standards of the Supreme Decree 29033/2007 and those of the Electoral Law). The adoption of last above-mentioned Supreme Decrees, however, cast a shadow on the future safeguard of the right to consultation of indigenous peoples in this country. Moreover, their constitutionality is doubtful: Indeed, the Bolivian Ombudsman (*La Defensoría del Pueblo del Estado Plurinacional de Bolivia*) organization filed a suit against these

---

1447 The original text is the following: "Artículo 11. (Excepciones A La Consulta Previa Libre E Informada). Las únicas excepciones admitidas a la implementación de los procesos de consulta son aquellas expresamente prohibidas en la Constitución Política del Estado, o que por su naturaleza no admitan la aplicación de este procedimiento o por seguridad del Estado o seguridad ciudadana." See the official text at http://www.gobernabilidad.org.bo/images/documentos/LEY.pdf [Last access 04.12.2014].

1448 Supreme Decree/*Decreto Supremo* No.2195 of 26 November 2014 (no title), and Supreme Decree/*Decreto Supremo* No.2366 of 20 May 2015 (no title).

Decrees after the mobilization of the Guaraní people.[1449] The FPIC is recognized neither in the Constitution nor in other domestic laws. The indigenous organizations repeatedly called for its insertion in the Magna Charta during the Constituent Assembly but the MAS members favored the adoption of a weaker formula.[1450]

Nevertheless, the standards regarding rights enshrined in both the ILO Convention 169 and, most importantly, the UNDRIP are legally binding. Additionally, as will be discussed in section 5.3.2.2, the Constitutional Court of Bolivia adopted one relevant decision in 2010 further safeguarding these rights. However, the consultations held in Bolivia have been carried out without taking into account the aforementioned standards, thus proving to be rather ineffective (particularly those related to the TIPNIS) and thus fuelling further malcontent.

5.3.2.2 Decision No.2003/2010-R of the Constitutional Court

After decision No.0045/2006 mentioned above, the Bolivian Constitutional Court adopted a landmark decision vis-à-vis the rights to consultation of indigenous peoples, i.e., the decision No.2003/2010-R adopted on 25 October 2010.[1451] This case concerned an appeal against the decision of an Amparo that came before the Technical Judge of the Court of O'Connor Province of the Superior Court of Tarija (*Jueza Técnica del Tribunal de Sentencia de la provincia O'Connor de la Corte Superior del Distrito Judicial de Tarija*; hereinafter, Court of O'Connor)[1452] and that was ruled in favor of the Departmental Service of Tarija (*Servicio Departamental de Caminos* – SEDECA). SEDECA had claimed that the Assembly of Guaraní

1449 La Defensoría del Pueblo del Estado Plurinacional de Bolivia, "BOLIVIA: La Defensoría del Pueblo sobre los Decretos Supremos 2195, 2298 Y 2366 y los derechos de los Pueblos Indígenas", 16.06.2015, at http://pradpi.org/bolivia-la-defensoria-del-pueblo-sobre-los-decretos-supremos-2195-2298-y-2366-y-los-derechos-de-los-pueblos-indigenas [Last access 18.06.2015].

1450 Almut Schilling-Vacaflor, "Democratizing Resource Governance through Prior Consultations? Lessons from Bolivia's Hydrocarbon Sector", 184 *GIGA Working Papers* 2012, pp.1-27, p.10, at http://www.giga-hamburg.de/de/system/files/publications/wp184_schilling.pdf [Last access 22.08.2014].

1451 (Plurinational) Constitutional Court, Decision (*Sentencia Constitucional*) No.2003/2010-R, File No.2008-17547-36-RAC, 25 October 2010.

1452 Court of O'Connor (Bolivia)/*Jueza Técnica del Tribunal de Sentencia de la provincia O'Connor de la Corte Superior del Distrito Judicial de Tarija*, Resolution No.1/08 of 29.02.2008, paras. 268-271.

People (*Asemblea del Pueblo Guaraní* – APG) had violated their constitutional labor rights to meet the representatives of PETROSUR SRL, with which SEDECA had signed an agreement but without any consultation of indigenous peoples in accordance with Laws 1257/1991 and 3760/2007 (which ratified the ILO Convention 169 and the UNDRIP, respectively). The Court of O'Connor found that the labor constitutional rights of SEDECA's director were violated by the acts of resistance carried out by the Assembly of Guaraní People.

The Constitutional Court eventually overturned the previous decision by recalling the international standards of the ILO Convention 169, the UNDRIP, and the decision of the Inter-American Court of Human Rights in relation to the case of the *Saramaka People v Surinam* (2007; see chapter 3, section 3.3.3).[1453] Notably, it stated that prior consultation is a duty of the State at all levels and, therefore, must be carried out through representative institutions of indigenous peoples. Additionally, the consultation must be performed in good faith and in appropriate ways in the following cases: before applying laws and measures that may directly affect indigenous peoples; prior to the approval of any project affecting their lands or territories and other resources; before undertaking any exploration or exploitation project of natural resources on indigenous lands; and before using the lands or territories of indigenous peoples for military activities.[1454] The Court finally urged the competent public authorities not only to carry out a due consultation but also to finalize the demarcation process of the indigenous land.[1455]

5.3.2.3 Implementation of indigenous peoples' right to consultation and the controversial case of TIPNIS

In this section, a few examples of consultations realized between 2007 and 2010 will be briefly presented, while the most controversial one, relating to the TIPNIS case, will be analyzed in more detail. Since the adoption of the aforementioned Supreme Decree No.29033/2007, the Ministry of Hydrocarbons and Energy organized and filed the consultation processes

1453 (Plurinational) Constitutional Court, Decision (*Sentencia Constitucional*) No.2003/2010-R, "Por tanto" (conclusions) No.1.

1454 (Plurinational) Constitutional Court, Decision (*Sentencia Constitucional*) No.2003/2010-R, para. III.4.2 "El derecho a la tierra y al territorio".

1455 (Plurinational) Constitutional Court, Decision (*Sentencia Constitucional*) No.2003/2010-R, "Por tanto" (conclusions) No.2.

that were carried out. According to official data, 21 consultation processes were realized between 2007 and 2010,[1456] 4 in 2012, 7 in 2013,[1457] and apparently none in 2011.[1458] According to the Ministry of Hydrocarbons and Energy, in July 2014 they carried out, *inter alia*, one of the consultations originally planned for 2011 on oil exploration in Pando.[1459]

Beyond official documents, which obviously report successful outcomes and underline how the consultations with indigenous peoples guarantee further incomes since they "allow" the exploitation of natural resources[1460], indigenous organizations themselves have contested many consultation processes.

For instance, the planned gas and oil exploration projects run by the French company Total E&P in the Ipati-Aquio block (Santa Cruz and Chuquisaca), where a number of Guaraní communities live, received

1456 Ministerio Hidrocarburos y Energía, "Procesos de Consulta y Participación en el sector hidrocarburos en Bolivia", 2011, at http://www.hidrocarburos.gob.bo/sitio/index.php?option=com_content [Last access 29.11.2011 and on file with author]. Also Schilling-Vacaflor reports such data. Schilling-Vacaflor, "Democratizing Resource Governance through Prior Consultations? …", p.12.

1457 For both 2012 and 2013, see Ministerio Hidrocarburos y Energía, "Ministerio de Hidrocarburos y Energía concluyó siete procesos de Consulta y Participación el 2013", 03.10.2013, at http://www2.hidrocarburos.gob.bo/index.php/prensa/noticias/658-ministerio-de-hidrocarburos-y-energ%C3%ADa-concluy%C3%B3-siete-procesos-de-consulta-y-participaci%C3%B3n-el-2013.html [Last access 22.08.2014].

1458 Although 6 processes were planned during 2011, two of them ("Sísmica 2D Margarita" and "Sísmica 3D Huacaya) were actually completed in 2013 (Ministerio Hidrocarburos y Energía 2013) and another one ("Sísmica Bloque Río Beni") in July 2014 (see below note 204 on Adquisición Sísmica 2D Cuenca Madre de Dios en Pando), but there is no further mention of the other three ("Líneas de recolección pozos de producción Campo El Dorado", "Sísmica Bloque Itacaray", and "Sísmica Bloque Cupesito") that consequently will not have been completed yet.

1459 Ministerio Hidrocarburos y Energía, "Concluye Proceso de Consulta y Participación del proyecto 'Adquisición Sísmica 2D Cuenca Madre de Dios' en Pando", 02.07.2014, at http://www2.hidrocarburos.gob.bo/index.php/prensa/noticias/847-concluye-proceso-de-consulta-y-participaci%C3%B3n-del-proyecto-%E2%80%9Cadquisici%C3%B3n-s%C3%ADsmica-2d-cuenca-madre-de-dios%E2%80%9D-en-pando.html [Last access 23.08.2014].

1460 A recent document of the Ministry of Hydrocarbons and Energy reports that so far the consultations have permitted investments in the sector of up to 950 million dollars. Ministerio Hidrocarburos y Energía , "Consultas a indígenas viabilizaron inversión de 950 millones de dólares en hidrocarburos", 05.06.2013, at http://www2.hidrocarburos.gob.bo/index.php/prensa/noticias/525-consultas-a-indígenas-viabilizaron-inversión-de-950-millones-de-dólares-en-hidrocarburos.html [Last access 23.08.2014].

authorization to start working after 5 months of consultation between June and October 2007. The areas concerned are rich in hydrocarbons and the communities are quite used to dealing with companies and the authorities of the Ministry of Hydrocarbons and Energy. 241 indigenous people and 149 indigenous representatives of the Guaraní people participated in the consultation meetings. Out of the 21 objections to the project, 5 were considered by the company. The "validated agreement" (*validación de acuerdos*) was finally signed by the Ministry of Hydrocarbons and Energy and the communities as prescribed by Supreme Decree 29033/2007 (art.13).[1461] Nevertheless, an onsite investigation revealed that: not all of the communities were involved; improper information was distributed among the participants; many representatives were corrupted by money or the promise of work; and different compensation was agreed upon by the company and the different communities, thus also creating internal conflicts.[1462] However, the government reacted in quite a harsh way, complaining that the consultation delayed extraction and that enormous amounts of money were being extorted. The president of the Assembly of Guaraní People Celso Padilla replies by asking President Morales to show the evidence of the alleged extortion, which was never provided.[1463]

Another interesting case of consultation was held in 2008 in a non-traditional hydrocarbon area north of La Paz (Lliquimuni block). The Government had a strategic interest in the area, where the Bolivian-Venezuelan consortium "YPFB Petroandina Sam" were to operate. The projects were likely to affect the indigenous Mosetén and Leco peoples as well as other communities that had settled in the area more recently. These communities already had past internal conflicts over control of land and natural resources. Eventually, the authorities of the Ministry of Hydrocarbons and Energy carried out a consultation solely with the settler communities, who later signed the "validated agreement" (*validación de*

1461 Schilling-Vacaflor, "Democratizing Resource Governance through Prior Consultations? …", pp.12-13.

1462 Jannette Giné L. and Fruc Villaroel F., *Total E&P Bolivie y sus Impactos en los Derechos Humanos del Pueblo Guaraní de la Capitanía de Muyupampa. El caso del Proyecto de Prospección Sismica del Bloque Ipati-Aquio*, Centro de Estudios Aplicados a los Derechos Económicos, Sociales y Culturales - CEADESC, Santa Cruz, 2011, pp.46-48 and p.53-58, at http://www.ceadesc.org/wp-content/up loads/2011/08/Total_EP_-EIDH.pdf [Last access 23.08.2014].

1463 Ricardo Herrera, "Bolivia. Dilemas y conflictos de la consulta previa", *Noticias Aliadas (NA) Informe Especial* "Consulta Previa: Derecho Fundamental de los Pueblos Indígenas", June 2011, pp.21-22, p.22, at http://www.noticiasaliada s.org/objetos/informe/14PE_consulta_na.pdf [Last access 23.08.2014].

acuerdos) in mid-October. Additionally, individual negotiations were carried out. The organization of the Mosetén and Leco peoples (*Central de Pueblos Indígenas de La Paz* – CPILAP) was excluded from the consultation process, although they explicitly requested to be consulted. Finally, internal conflicts within the organization were also fuelled by contradictory declarations made by the president of CPILAP José Ortiz.[1464]

Finally, the recent and thorny case of the *Territorio Indígena y Parque Nacional Isiboro-Secure* (TIPNIS) further elucidates the reluctance by the Bolivian authorities to carry out proper consultations.

In 2006, the construction of a highway was officially planned to link Cochabamba with the Amazonian department of Beni, which lacks roads and communication routes.[1465] However, the plan was to cross the park and indigenous territory of the TIPNIS along the middle, thus connecting the Cochabamba tropics which house many coca fields. The TIPNIS is home to approximately 60-70 indigenous communities, with a total of 4,000 indigenous inhabitants. The larger communities are of the Mojeño, Yuracaré and Chimane peoples.[1466] This territory was declared a National Park in 1965 and, after the 1990 March for Territory and Dignity, it was recognized as a TCO. In 2005, territorial demarcation was finally secured.[1467] However, financing from the Brazilian bank (*Banco Nacional de Desenvolvimento Economico y Social – BaNDES*) was authorized by Law No.5/2010[1468] and thus secured the realization of this project, which was then conceded to the Brazilian construction company OAS *Empreendimentos*.[1469] The involvement of Brazil is due to the highway

1464 Schilling-Vacaflor, "Democratizing Resource Governance through Prior Consultations? …", pp.13-14; Patricia Costas Monje, "La pluriterritorialidad en el Norte de La Paz. Dos estudios de caso sobre la defensa del territorio", in Juan Chumacero (ed.), *Reconfigurando territorios. Informe 2009. Reforma agraria, control territorial y gobiernos indígenas en Bolivia*, Fundación Tierra, La Paz, 2010, pp.145-172, pp.163-165, at http://www.bivica.org/upload/territorios.pdf [Last access 23.08.2014].

1465 José Aylwin, "Bolivia: Desarrollo o Buen Vivir. El Caso del TIPNIS", in Salvador Martí i Puig, Claire Wright, José Aylwin and Nancy Yáñez, (eds.), *Entre el desarrollo y el buen vivir. Recursos naturales y conflictos en los territorios indígenas*, Libros de la Catarata, Madrid, 2013, pp.168-200, p.187.

1466 Aylwin, "Bolivia: Desarrollo o Buen Vivir. El Caso del TIPNIS", p.184.

1467 *Ibid.*, p.185.

1468 *Ley de Aprobación del Protocolo entre el Estado Plurinacional de Bolivia y la República Federativa del Brasil, sobre el Financiamiento del Proyecto de la Carretera "Villa Tunari-San Ignacio de Moxos"*, No.5, 7 April 2010.

1469 Leonardo Tamburini, "Bolivia (2012)", in International Work Group for Indigenous Affairs (IWGIA), *The Indigenous World 2012*, IWGIA, Copenhagen,

being a part of the umbrella project connecting this country with the Pacific Ocean (*Infrastructura Regional Sur Americana* – IRSA).[1470] Construction began in June 2011 under President Morales.[1471]

The consent of the indigenous peoples that live within this territory was not obtained, nor were they even consulted.[1472] This pushed the Amazonian peoples to their eighth and ninth march in 2011 and 2012, respectively. The former *(VIII Marcha en defensa del TIPNIS, por la Vida, la Dignidad, y lo Derechos de los Pueblos Indígenas*) started in August 2011,[1473] headed by the CIDOB and the TIPNIS organizations, and supported by the highland indigenous organization CONAMAQ. The core claims regarded the interruption of the highway's works and the safeguarding of the Park. An alternative trajectory was proposed.[1474]

The Government reacted in a controversial way: First, it allegedly claimed that the march was sustained by the US cooperation program (US-Aid); second, it sent the Foreign Minister David Choquehuanca, of Aymara origins, to further negotiate with the protesters. In late September 2011, he was sent to the site of the blockade set up in Yucumo on the road from La Trinidad to La Paz and organized by the Settler Federation (*Federación de Colonizadores*). This organization also requested further negotiations but were generally in favor of the highway's construction. All the protesters were in a critical condition, the weather was not in their favor and access to clean water was severely restricted. Minister Choquehuanca criticized the indigenous lowland protesters as acting against the country. Fuelled by frustration, a group of women broke through the blockade, although without harming the Minister. However, to discredit the march, the Government depicted this act as a kind of kidnapping, which was then denied by Choquehuanca himself.[1475] During this same timeframe, police were sent to

---

2012, pp.166-174, p.166; Aylwin, "Bolivia: Desarrollo o Buen Vivir. El Caso del TIPNIS", p.187.

1470 Aylwin, "Bolivia: Desarrollo o Buen Vivir. El Caso del TIPNIS", p.187.

1471 Leonardo Tamburini, "Bolivia (2012)", p.166.

1472 Aylwin, "Bolivia: Desarrollo o Buen Vivir. El Caso del TIPNIS", p.188.

1473 *Ibid.*; Tamburini, "Bolivia (2012)", p.167. The Bolivian NGO Fundación Tierra followed and documented in detail the phases of this march, http://marcha.ftierra.org [Last access 24.08.2014].

1474 Tamburini, "Bolivia (2012)", p.167; Sarela Paz Patiño, "El Conflicto del Territorio Indígena Parque Nacional Isiboror Sécure (TIPNIS) y sus Consecuencias para el Estado Plurinacional de Bolivia", UNDP Bolivia, Proyecto e Fortalecimiento Democrático, Fundación Boliviana para la Democracia Multipartidaria, 2011, at http://www.fbdm.org.bo/fbdm/documento/1290176707/1320853790/2-1320853790.pdf [Last access 24.08.2014], pp.4-5.

1475 Tamburini, "Bolivia (2012)", p.168.

disperse protesters with tear gas and rubber bullets and some leaders were arrested.[1476] The chaos and solidarity generated by these clashes pushed the village of San Borja to obstruct the police officers attempting to pass with a convoy of prisoners.[1477]

The march finally reached La Paz on 19 October 2011.[1478] Morales stepped back and a few days after adopted the so-called Short Law (*Ley Corta*, Law No.180/2011),[1479] which recognized the "intangibility" of the park TIPNIS (art.1.3) and stated that no highways would cross the park including that of Villa Tunari (art.3). It also provided that any act likely to alter the intangibility of the park should be reversed (art.4). This, however, would adversely affect the communities, whose subsistence means were based on the use of some of the park's natural resources.[1480] This was then clarified by art.3 of Supreme Decree 1146/2012 adopted on 24 February 2012.[1481]

However, on 10 February 2012, a law regarding the consultation on the TIPNIS case (Law No.222) was adopted.[1482] According to this law, the Mojeño-Trinitarias, Chimanes, and Yuracarés indigenous communities

1476 *Ibid.*, p.169; Aylwin, "Bolivia: Desarrollo o Buen Vivir. El Caso del TIPNIS", p.188; Paz Patiño 2011, p.6.

1477 Tamburini, "Bolivia (2012)", p.169. The trial against the policemen, as well as the former Government Minister Marcos Farfán, the former police chief Alberto Zapata, and other police authorities began only recently. Página Siete/Agencia de Noticias Fides (ANF), "Fiscalía amplía imputación a 14 policías en caso Chaparina", 07.11.2014, at http://www.paginasiete.bo/sociedad/2014/11/7/fiscalia-amplia-imputacion-policias-caso-chaparina-37530.html. However, the more than 70 indigenous people injured by the September 2011 clashes were excluded from the court audiences. See Página Siete, "Excluyen a Villegas y 2 exjefes policiales del caso Chaparina", 12.11.2014, at http://www.paginasiete.bo/sociedad/2014/11/12/excluyen-villegas-exjefes-policiales-caso-chaparina-38062.html, and Página Siete, "Indígenas del TIPNIS anuncian marcha de Trinidad a Chaparina", 06.08.2014, at http://www.paginasiete.bo/nacional/2014/8/6/indigenas-tipnis-anuncian-marcha-trinidad-chaparina-28672.html [Last access to all 12.12.2014].

1478 Tamburini, "Bolivia (2012)", p.170.

1479 *Ley de Protección del Territorio Indígena y Parque Nacional Isiboro Sécure* TIPNIS, Law No.180 of 24 October 2011. This Law was called "short" because it is composed of 5 articles only.

1480 Tamburini, "Bolivia (2012)", p.170.

1481 Decreto Supremo No.1146 of 24 February 2012. Art.3 ensures that the TIPNIS indigenous peoples can make use of renewable natural resources.

1482 *Ley de Consulta a los Pueblos Indígenas del Territorio Indígena y Parque Nacional Isiboro Sécure* – TIPNIS, Law No.222 of 10 February 2012.

living in the park were to be consulted (art.3) in order to decide whether the Park should be definitively considered intangible (art.4).

The adoption of this law was highly contested by indigenous organizations: It appeared to be the government's last resort to continue constructing the highway.[1483] In fact, the project regarded the completion of three stretches, the second of which was to be through the TIPNIS Park. The Bolivian Minister of Public Works (Vladimir Sánchez) and the Minister to the Presidency (Juan Ramón Quintana) ensured that the work on the other two parts had continued during early 2012, but not for the second contested one in accordance with Law No.180. [1484] However, complications arising from clauses in the contract with the Brazilian construction company OAS *Empreendimentos* and the Brazilian bank (*Banco Nacional de Desenvolvimento Economico y Social – BaNDES*) that provided the loan necessary for the construction bound the government to also construct this second stretch.[1485]

In March 2012, some deputies from both the MAS and the MSM went before the Constitutional Court to claim the unconstitutionality of a number of articles of both Laws Nos.180 and 222 and, in particular, of the "intangibility" of TIPNIS Park (art.1, Law No.180).[1486]

In the meantime, it was announced that the consultation would take place between 10 May and 10 June 2012.[1487] A ninth march, therefore, caused by this disputed consultation was organized by CIDOB[1488] and departed from

1483 El Día, "La Cidob exige anular Ley 222", *El Día*, 22/03/2012, http://eldia.com.bo/index.php?cat=1&pla=3&id_articulo=87586 [Last access 23.08.2014].

1484 Pagína Siete/Noticias Bolivia, "El Gobierno insiste en que no hay contrato para el tramo II", *Pagína Siete/Noticias Bolivia*, 02/04/2012, at http://www.fmbolivia.tv/el-gobierno-insiste-en-que-no-hay-contrato-para-el-tramo-ii [Last access 23.08.2014].

1485 Miguel A. Melendres, "Gobierno boliviano teme ser enjuiciado si brasileña OAS no construye el tramo II", *Pagína Siete/Eju*, 04/04/2012, at http://eju.tv/2012/04/gobierno-boliviano-teme-ser-enjuiciado-si-brasilea-oas-no-c onstruye-el-tramo-ii [Last access 23.08.2014].

1486 (Plurinational) Constitutional Court, Decision (*Sentencia Constitucional*) No.0300/2012 (TIPNIS), 18.06.2012, Files Nos.00157-2012-01-AIA and 00188-2012-01-AIA (merged cases).

1487 Correo del Sur, "La Consulta ya Tiene Fecha y Presupuesto", 21/03/2012, *Correo del Sur*, http://www.correodelsur.com/2012/0321/31.php [Last access 23.08.2014].

1488 El Día, "La Cidob exige anular Ley 222", *El Día*, 22/03/2012, http://eldia.com.bo/index.php?cat=1&pla=3&id_articulo=87586 [Last access 23.08.2014].

the city of La Trinidad on 27 April 2012.[1489] Intense negotiations followed and a few ministers were sent to speak with the protesters,[1490] some of them reaching ambiguous agreements with doubtful leaders.[1491] During the same period, police officers began a strike to demand a salary increase. This protest spread from La Paz to nearly all the other Bolivian cities.[1492] At the doors of La Paz, at the end of June,[1493] the ninth indigenous march stopped to await the resolution of this strike.[1494] However, the government negotiated with the police sector and reached an agreement on the same day in which the march finally entered La Paz.[1495] Despite the public support,[1496] the march was thus suppressed by the police and could not reach the central square (Plaza Murillo, where the government palace is situated). After a week of vain attempts, the protesters decided to return to their villages and organize a "resistance".[1497] Road and river blocks were set up to prevent the entrance of the consultation teams of the Ministry of Hydrocarbons and Energy.[1498]

In mid-June 2012, the Constitutional Court ruled on the abovementioned claims of unconstitutionality filed by MAS and MSM. The court eventually found both norms constitutional, although it declared the conditional constitutionality of the second phrase of art.1 of the Law No.222 regarding the criteria to operate the consultation[1499] and added that a prior agreement (*proceso de concertación*) on the consultation's priorities should be discussed among the parties.[1500]

1489 Leonardo Tamburini, "Bolivia (2013)", in International Work Group for Indigenous Affairs (IWGIA), *The Indigenous World 2013*, IWGIA, Copenhagen, 2013, pp.150-159, p.152; Martín Mendoza-Botelho, "Bolivia 2012: Entre Buenas y Malas Noticas", 33(1) *Revista de Ciencia Política (Santiago SciELO)* 2013, pp.35-54, p.41.

1490 Tamburini, "Bolivia (2013)", p.152.

1491 *Ibid.*, p.155.

1492 *Ibid.*, p.153.

1493 Mendoza-Botelho, "Bolivia 2012: Entre Buenas y Malas Noticas", p.41.

1494 Tamburini, "Bolivia (2013)", p.154.

1495 *Ibid.*, p.154.

1496 Mendoza-Botelho, "Bolivia 2012: Entre Buenas y Malas Noticas", p.41.

1497 Tamburini, "Bolivia (2013)", p.154.

1498 *Ibid.*, p.155.

1499 (Plurinational) Constitutional Court, Decision (*Sentencia Constitucional*) No.0300/2012, "Por tanto" (conclusions) No.2.

1500 *Ibid.*, "Por tanto" (conclusions) No.5.

Notwithstanding this ruling, the Government proceeded with the planned consultation, which was thus delayed and started in late July.[1501]

The frustration of the indigenous peoples brought one of the leaders of TIPNIS Park (Fernando Vargas) to file an Amparo proceeding against the Government before the Chuiquisaca Court, for violation of their constitutional rights by both Laws No.180 and 222.[1502] The Chuiquisaca Court declined its territorial competence on the case and submitted it to the Court of La Paz.[1503] The Court of La Paz did not take the case further by contesting the legitimacy of the leader to present an Amparo proceeding and adding that another proceeding (*Acción de Libertad*),[1504] which is also a kind of Amparo proceeding but regarding the right to freedom included in arts.125-127 of the Constitution, was necessary.[1505]

Thus, the consultation teams (*brigadas de consulta*) of the Government started entering into the TIPNIS Park and meeting with a few communities. The consultation was then declared concluded on 7 December 2012, albeit it among heavy criticism.[1506] The official data declared that 58 out of 69 communities living in the TIPNIS Park were consulted, 11 refused to be consulted, and that 94.8% of the votes (i.e., 55 out of 58) resulted in favor

1501 Plurinational Electoral Body/Órgano Electoral Plurinacional-Supreme Electoral Court/Tribunal Supremo Electoral, Servicio Intercultural De Fortalecimiento Democrático (SIFDE), "Dossier: Consulta Del Tipnis Y Rol Del OEP/TSE Consulta del TIPNIS en cifras", March 2012, p.1.

1502 Agencia de Noticias Fides (ANF), "Presentan Amparo Constitucional contra continuidad de consulta en TIPNIS", 25.07.2012, at http://www.noticiasfides.com/g/sociedad/presentan-amparo-constitucional-contra-continuidad-de-consulta-en-tipnis-3588 [Last access 24.08.2014].

1503 El Deber, "Tribunal rechaza pronunciarse sobre amparo de indígenas del Tipnis", *El Deber.com.bo*, 26.07.2012, at http://www.eldeber.com.bo/tribunal-rechaza-pronunciarse-sobre-amparo-de-indigenas-del-tipnis/120726185014 [Last access 24.08.2014].

1504 Paulo Cuiza, "Justicia paceña rechaza amparo para frenar consulta en el TIPNIS", *La Razón*, 04.08.2012, at http://www.la-razon.com/nacional/Justicia-rechaza-amparo-consulta-TIPNIS_0_1663033744.html [Last access 24.08.2014].

1505 This proceeding was eventually denied by the Beni Departmental Court in July 2013 for lack of competence. La Razón/Agencia de Noticias Fides, "Tribunal de Justicia niega acción de libertad a dirigentes indígenas del TIPNIS", 17.07.2013, *La Razón*, at http://www.la-razon.com/nacional/Tribunal-Justicia-dirigentes-indigenas-TIPNIS_0_1871212938.html [Last access 24.08.2014].

1506 Iván Paredes, "Consulta cierra con la promesa de fondos para la 'vía ecológica'", *La Razón*, 08.12.2012, at http://www.la-razon.com/nacional/Consulta-cierra-promesa-fondos-ecologica_0_1738626180.html [Last access 23.08.2014].

of the construction.[1507] In late July, the CIDOB offices were occupied by an unidentified group of indigenous people removing the President form his mandate given the failure of the ninth march, thus blocking any operations of the organization.[1508]

In this climate of social unrest, CIDOB and other Mojeño leaders tried to invite the Special Rapporteur on the Rights of Indigenous Peoples, who was denied a visa. The leaders thus called upon human rights organizations to investigate the consultation. [1509] Eventually, an Inter-Institutional Commission composed of a representative from the Catholic Church, the Bolivian Permanent Human Rights Assembly (*Asamblea Permanente de los Derechos Humanos de Bolivia* – APDHB) and the famous NGO International Human Rights Federation (*Federación International de Derechos Humanos* – FIDH) was set up and visited 35 of the 58 communities that were consulted between 29 November and 14 December 2012.[1510] Out of these 35 communities, 19 had also been reached by the government's consultation teams but 16 had refused to meet them and one provided contradictory information. [1511] These numbers were in clear contrast with the official data.

After their visit, these organizations declared that some communities had not received any information on the construction and its impact while the information received by other communities was contradictory, particularly vis-à-vis the use of renewable natural resources mentioned above or the type of highway to be constructed.[1512] Moreover, indigenous uses and customs or meeting places were not taken into consideration during the consultations

1507 Ministry of Public Works, Services and Housing and Ministry of Environmnet and Waters, "Informe Final del proceso de Consulta Previa, Libre e Informada a los pueblos Moxeño-Trinitario, Yuracaré y Chimane del Territorio Indígena y Parque Nacional Isiboro Sécure (TIPNIS) 2012", La Paz, 2012, pp.268 and 300-307, at http://www.oopp.gob.bo/uploads/INFORME%20FINAL%20OK1.pdf [Last access 23.08.2014].

1508 Tamburini, "Bolivia (2013)", p.155.

1509 *Ibid.*, p.156.

1510 *Ibid.*, p.157; Asamblea Permanente de los Derechos Humanos de Bolivia (APDHB) and Federación Internacional de los Derechos Humanos (FIDH), "Resumen. Verificación de la consulta en el TIPNIS", April 2013, p.4.

1511 Asamblea Permanente de los Derechos Humanos de Bolivia (APDHB) and Federación Internacional de los Derechos Humanos (FIDH), "Resumen. Verificación de la consulta en el TIPNIS", p.6.

1512 I.e., the communities were told that the highway would have been an "ecological" project. Asamblea Permanente de los Derechos Humanos de Bolivia (APDHB) and Federación Internacional de los Derechos Humanos (FIDH), "Resumen. Verificación de la consulta en el TIPNIS", p.8.

and there were attempts by the ministry's consultation teams to corrupt or threaten many indigenous people.

In sum, there was no good faith and obviously no climate of mutual trust.[1513] Finally, only 3 communities out of the 36 visited by the organizations confirmed their vote in favor of the construction of the highway, while 30 were against and another 3 asked for additional studies and for a revision of the project's trajectory.[1514]

The construction of the Villa Tunari highway appears currently to be blocked, although the works in the first stretch continue and should be finalized by September 2015.[1515] The elections of October 2014 have likely influenced and silenced the whole debate vis-à-vis the TIPNIS. Vice-President Garcia Linera declared in mid-2014 that there was need for further social negotiations about the TIPNIS,[1516] while President Morales has stated that the indigenous peoples' opposition also affects the construction of other highways in Beni,[1517] in a probable attempt to discredit the TIPNIS indigenous peoples. The previous governor of Beni, Carmelo Lens –who supports TIPNIS' indigenous peoples and opposes the highway project– was elected in January 2013 beating the MAS candidate Yessica Jordan, whose electoral campaign was backed personally by Morales and was more inclined to support the highway's completion.[1518] Some alternative

1513 Asamblea Permanente de los Derechos Humanos de Bolivia (APDHB) and Federación Internacional de los Derechos Humanos (FIDH), "Resumen. Verificación de la consulta en el TIPNIS", pp.7-10.

1514 *Ibid.*, p.9. See also the Organizations Press Release of 17 December 2012, Asamblea Permanente de los Derechos Humanos de Bolivia (APDHB) and Federación Internacional de los Derechos Humanos (FIDH), "Resumen de Informe Visita a las Comunidades del TIPNIS", at http://servindi.org/pdf/Comunicado_Publico_APDHB_IGLESIA.pdf [Last access 23.08.2014].

1515 Página Siete, "El Vicepresidente descarta carretera por el TIPNIS", 04.01.2014, *Página Siete*, at http://www.paginasiete.bo/nacional/2014/1/4/vicepresidente-descarta-carretera-tipnis-10441.html [Last access 23.08.2014].

1516 Agencia de Noticias Fides, "Vicepresidente: Construcción de carretera por el TIPNIS debe ser debatida por la sociedad", 24.07.2014, at http://www.noticiasfides.com/g/politica/vicepresidente-construccion-de-carretera-por-el-tipnis-debe-ser-debatida-por-la-sociedad-26318 [Last access 23.08.2014].

1517 El Día, "Evo dice que marcha del TIPNIS afectó la construcción de dos carreteras", 21.03.2014, *El Día*, at http://www.eldia.com.bo/index.php?cat=148&pla=3&id_articulo=141241 [Last access 23.08.2014].

1518 Martín Mendoza-Botelho, "Bolivia 2013: Al Calor Preelectoral",34(1) *Revista de Ciencia Política (Santiago SciELO)* 2014, pp.37-57, p.50; Tamburini, "Bolivia (2014)", p.168.

proposals to the highway, such as the construction of a railroad along the park's border, thus without crossing it, have also been advanced.[1519]

Nevertheless, the construction of the highway continues and it is widely supported by the ruling political party MAS.[1520] In August 2014, some communities in the TIPNIS denounced the renewed use of tear gas by the police in their territories.[1521] Vice President Linera, reelected in the last elections of October 2014, traveled recently to the indigenous communities of Chimanes in the Moxos province of the department of Beni and argued that the highway is necessary to reach the local people, bring them medicines, and provide them other facilities. The Vice President accused "some NGOs" and the American funds to be the supporters of a TIPNIS boycott and asked these communities to support the construction of the highway. During the same visit, the staff of the Vice President distributed food, medicines, and other school materials.[1522] These supplies, however, undermine the credibility of his good faith.

In late 2014, the indigenous authorities of the TIPNIS have announced that they are exploring the possibility of becoming a municipality-based AIOC, [1523] most probably to try to stop the works on the highway. Nevertheless, at the last departmental elections, as mentioned above (section 5.3.1), the MAS-IPSP candidate won in Beni at the runoff voting in early May 2015 with a very narrow percentage of votes and in a highly contested atmosphere. This new governor, Álex Ferrier, by a supposed coincidence, supports the highway project as well as the new governor of Cochabamba, who also belongs to the MAS-IPSP party. Moreover, President Morales himself announced in his political agenda for the November 2014 elections to continue the construction of the highway in the

1519 Página Siete, "Vargas plantea una vía férrea en lugar de camino por el TIPNIS", 27.08.2014, *Página Siete*, at http://www.paginasiete.bo/sociedad/2014/8/27/vargas-plantea-ferrea-lugar-camino-tipnis-30569.html [Last access 12.12.2014].

1520 Beatriz Layme, "El MAS persiste en construir una carretera por el TIPNIS", *Página Siete*, 01.09.2014, at http://www.paginasiete.bo/nacional/2014/9/1/persiste-construir-carretera-tipnis-30977.html [Last access 12.12.2014].

1521 Página Siete/Erbol, "Denuncian que la Policía gasifica a los indígenas del Sécure", 23.08.2014, *Página Siete*, at http://www.paginasiete.bo/sociedad/2014/8/23/denuncian-policia-gasifica-indigenas-secure-30211.html [Last access 23.08.2014].

1522 Página Siete/Agencia de Noticias Fides, "Vice pide apoyo para construir vía por el TIPNIS", 29.10.2014, *Página Siete*, at http://www.paginasiete.bo/nacional/2014/10/29/vice-pide-apoyo-para-construir-tipnis-36667.html [Last access 12.12.2014].

1523 Página Siete/Erbol, "El Tipnis pide municipio autónomo indígena", 10.12.2014, *Página Siete*, at http://www.paginasiete.bo/sociedad/2014/12/10/tipnis-pide-municipio-autonomo-indigena-40786.html [Last access 12.12.2014].

period 2015-2020.[1524] Finally, as mentioned, the recent Supreme Decree No.2366/2015 allows to develop hydrocarbon activities on the whole Bolivian territory, including protected areas, including the TIPNIS.

In sum, the TIPNIS case resulted in the clearest misapplication of the right to consultation of indigenous peoples in one of the countries that was used to have the best legal framework protecting these specific and other rights. Additionally, the TIPNIS marches and resistance have likely ended the alliance between indigenous peoples and President Morales.[1525] In fact, Fernando Vargas, President of the TIPNIS' coordination body and leader of the two marches against the construction of the highway, stood as a Presidential candidate in the November 2014 elections with the green party (*Partido Verde de Bolivia-Instrumento de la Ecología Política*, PVB-IEP). However, he himself admitted to the press that he had little hopes of winning.[1526] Indeed, the party did not reach the necessary threshold to win a single seat in the Parliament. The TIPNIS communities also tried to ally with the more influential party *Unidad Democratica*-UD,[1527] which was the second most voted party, gaining 32 seats in the Lower Chamber and 8 in the Upper one. Nevertheless, there is no guarantee that the UD party will defend the TIPNIS cause and, in any case, the UD will remain in a position of political minority in comparison to the overwhelming majority of seats (121) won by the MAS-IPSP party (see above section 5.3.1).

1524 Página Siete/ANF, "Carretera por el TIPNIS, en la mira del oficialismo", 12.05.2015, *Página Siete*, at http://www.paginasiete.bo/nacional/2015/5/12/carretera-tipnis-mira-oficialismo-56312.html [Last access 01.06.2015].

1525 Mendoza-Botelho, "Bolivia 2012: Entre Buenas y Malas Noticas", p.40; Ruy D'Alencar, "Pueblos originarios pasan a segundo plano", *Noticias Aliadas*, 07.06.2013, at http://www.noticiasaliadas.org/articles.asp?art=6837 [Last access 23.08.2014].

1526 Página Siete/Erbol, "Fernando Vargas admite que no ganará los comicios en el TIPNIS", 06.10.2014, *Página Siete*, at http://www.paginasiete.bo/nacional/2014/10/6/fernando-vargas-admite-ganara-comicios-tipnis-34303.html [Last access 15.12.2014].

1527 Nancy Vacaflor, "Indígenas del TIPNIS sellan alianza con Doria Medina", *Página Siete*, 30.09.2014, at http://www.paginasiete.bo/nacional/2014/9/30/indigenas-tipnis-sellan-alianza-doria-medina-33704.html [Last access 15.12.2014].

5.4 *Participation through autonomy/self-government arrangements and the preservation of indigenous institutions*

The second element regarding the implementation of the *composite right* to political participation of indigenous peoples in Bolivia is addressed here. This aspect, as discussed in chapter 3, section 3.4, regards indigenous peoples' autonomy/self-government arrangements as well as the preservation of indigenous institutions and is of particular interest in the case of Bolivia. In fact, indigenous autonomy in Bolivia finally received formal recognition in the 2009 Constitution, which established a new (formal) system of (Peasant Farmer Native) indigenous autonomies (*Autonomía Indígena Originaria Campesina*, henceforth AIOC or indigenous autonomy). This has been introduced as the fourth type of autonomy in the new complex Bolivian system. In December 2009, 11 municipalities succeeded in becoming AIOCs by referendum and the comprehensive Autonomy Law (*Ley Marco de Autonomías y Descentralización* No. 031) was enacted in July 2010. Hence, this section addresses and analyses the complex legal framework of the AIOCs with its latest progress and shortcomings. The legal assessment was completed with literature, media sources (mainly, newspapers), and field-based interviews conducted in Bolivia in November 2010 with NGO practitioners, journalists, and representatives of the Bolivian State. The author expresses her gratitude once again for their priceless availability and the information provided by all of the interviewees.

5.4.1 The indigenous autonomy proposed by indigenous peoples in Bolivia

As well as the conceptualization of indigenous autonomy discussed in chapter 3 (section 3.3.3), the reflections in this section will also be made taking into account the concept of "indigenous autonomy" proposed by a number of large Bolivian indigenous organizations in 2006.[1528] In essence, they asserted that autonomy is the (pre)condition to guarantee indigenous peoples' freedom, decolonization, and self-determination. In such general terms, they probably referred to the sociological concept of governing one's own affairs. They add, however, a number of characteristics which the

1528 Confederación Sindical Única de Trabajadores Campesinos de Bolivia et al., "Propuesta para la Nueva Constitución Política del Estado ...", pp.11-13.

Bolivian indigenous autonomy should contain. Based on a defined territory, the indigenous autonomy would have a culturally-diverse population and should be administered by indigenous (as well as peasant and native) customary self-government, rules, and justice. It should control and collectively manage the territory, the land, and (especially) the natural resources. On this last issue, they also specified that, prior to allowing extraction projects regarding natural resource exploitation, the indigenous peoples residing in or close to the territory should not only be consulted but also have the right to veto it. Furthermore, indigenous peoples should also receive shared benefits for this extraction.

5.4.2 Looking for a Bolivian history of autonomy

A few weeks before the adoption of the Autonomy Law, the Bolivian Ministry of Autonomies declared in its periodical bulletin, *Bolivia Autonómica* No. 11, that the autonomy process was not new to the country. The document claimed, rather, that the process began more than a hundred years before.[1529] The Autonomy Law is, in fact, entitled to Andrés Ibáñez, who claimed "equality for all" during the national election campaign in 1874 in Santa Cruz and was the founder of Santa Cruz' first autonomous/federal experience.[1530] Similar to the autonomy process, the AIOC's historical trajectory is also outlined in the bulletin, declaring that the indigenous autonomy is "millenary".[1531] For example, one of the claimed autonomy milestones was the forementioned 1921 popular insurrection in the actual AIOC Jesús de Machaca and the 1973 Tiahuanacu Aymara manifesto or, more recently, the 1990 march for Territory and Dignity.

For the purposes of this study, it can be said that it is certainly true that members of communities whom nowadays we call indigenous experienced (different) forms of autonomy and participation throughout Bolivian history

1529 Ministerio de Autonomía, "Bolivia Autonómica No.11", La Paz, 2010, p.3.

1530 This self-government lasted five months (from Christmas 1876 until 1 May 1877) before being repressed by the central government and the shooting of Ibáñez. Emilio Durán Ribera and Guillermo Pinckert Justiniano, *La revolución igualitariade Andrés Ibáñez*, Editorial Universitaria, Santa Cruz de la Sierra, 1988, pp.8-9 and 36-37. A province within the Santa Cruz department has also been dedicated to his memory. The decision to name this law after the "hero" of the Bolivian half-moon may have been made to please the *Oriente*.

1531 Ministerio de Autonomía, "Bolivia Autonómica No. 11", p.3.

and this should be neither forgotten nor exploited. That being said, there is strong scepticism pertaining to the declarations of the Bolivian authorities that the autonomy project has a centuries-old trajectory. It is more than arduous to trace back in history, through five long and dense centuries, a continuum of what may be today conceived as indigenous autonomy. Hence, the role played by indigenous peoples throughout Bolivian history is undeniable and this should be neither forgotten, nor, most importantly, exploited for other purposes.

5.4.3 The complex Bolivian (autonomous) administrative and territorial system

The Bolivian autonomy system does not fall under the scope of this study *per se*. However, to fully understand the complex legal framework in which AIOCs are inserted, this section aims to give an overview of this new decentralization process.

Since the adoption of the new Constitution (hereinafter 2009 Constitution or CPE) and the contested referenda on autonomy between 2006 and 2009 mentioned above (section 5.1.2), the construction of a decentralized system has been a central issue in Bolivia. The legal sources are both the 2009 CPE and the complex *Ley Marco de Autonomías y Descentralización* (Law No.031/2010, hereafter, Autonomy Law) enacted in July 2010. Prior its adoption, approximately forty unofficial drafts of the Autonomy Law were prepared.[1532] In addition, the core claim of the Seventh indigenous march in June 2010 was to amend these draft laws (see section 5.1.2).

The very first article of the CPE clarifies the form of State that Bolivia takes, which is that of a unitary social State based on plurinational 'communitarian' law and that is is free, independent, sovereign, democratic, decentralized and with autonomies. Within art.6.2, Nos.2-3 of the Autonomy Law, the "decentralized and with autonomies" aspects are clarified. "Administrative decentralization"' is explained as the "transfer of competences (or powers)[1533] from a public body to another which is hierarchically inferior".[1534] Autonomy, instead, is defined as a

1532 Tamburini, "Bolivia (2011)", p.176.

1533 In this section 5.4, the term "competences" is used as a synonym of the "powers" of an administrative unit.

1534 The original text is as follows: "Descentralización Administrativa. Es la transferencia de competencias de un órgano público a una institución de la misma administración sobre la que ejerza tuición", art.6.2, No.2 of the Autonomy Law.

"governmental qualification" which implies hierarchal equality of all the autonomous layers (see further below), the direct election of members of the governing bodies, the administration of its own economic sources, and the exercise of its legislative (including the regulation of norms/decrees), fiscal, and executive powers.[1535]

As mentioned, art.269 of the CPE states that in Bolivia there are *five* types of administrative-territorial units: departments, [1536] provinces, municipalities, the Peasant Farmer Native Territory (*Territorio Indígena Campesino Originario*, henceforth TIOC) and regions –insofar as the terms and the conditions established by law are respected (see further below). The first three units are pre-defined by law. The number of municipalities increased to more than 300 after the adoption of the 1994 Popular Participation Law and was revised further with the 1999 Municipalities Law. Presently, there are 337 municipalities (as per the 2010 elections).[1537] Prior to this law, only 20 municipalities effectively existed.[1538] A region is not a pre-defined territory but may be constituted by unifying provinces and municipalities provided that they share some cultural and historical continuity. However, a region may not be constituted beyond the borders of one of the nine departments. Additionally, a "metropolitan region" may be formed wherever the population of the suburban areas (*conurbaciones*) are

1535 The original text is as follows: "3. Autonomía. Es la cualidad gubernativa que adquiere una entidad territorial de acuerdo a las condiciones y procedimientos establecidos en la Constitución Política del Estado y la presente Ley, que implica la igualdad jerárquica o de rango constitucional entre entidades territoriales autónomas, la elección directa de sus autoridades por las ciudadanas y los ciudadanos, la administración de sus recursos económicos y el ejercicio de facultades legislativa, reglamentaria, fiscalizadora y ejecutiva por sus órganos de gobierno autónomo, en el ámbito de su jurisdicción territorial y de las competencias y atribuciones establecidas por la Constitución Política del Estado y la ley. La autonomía regional no goza de la facultad legislativa", art.6.2, No.3 of the Autonomy Law.

1536 The departments were also the object of a previous law to devolve power, in 1995. The Administrative Decentralization Law (*Ley de Descentralización Admini strativa*, Law No.1654/1995) aimed to transfer part of the competences and financial sources from the central level to the departmental one and thus improve the general political participation of the whole population. However, the lack of efficient management, coordination with the other administrations, and of political responsibility by the prefectures caused the system to fail. Del Campo, "Participación Política y Democracia Local en Bolivia", pp.17-18.

1537 Corte Nacional Electoral del Estado Plurinacional de Bolivia, "Acta de Cómputo Nacional Elecciones Departamentales, Municipales y Regional 2010", pp.78 and ff.

1538 Assies, "Pueblos Indigenas y Reforma del Estado en America Latina", p.35

more than five hundred thousand (art.280.1 CPE). According to art.281 of the CPE, a region may enjoy some administrative-normative powers. In particular, art.301 of the CPE and art.41.2 of the Autonomy Law specify that a region may exercise those competences conferred upon it by both the State and the territorial units forming it. In other words, a region has no original legislative powers (art.6.2, No.3 Autonomy Law). In the 2010 elections, the members of three regional assemblies were elected (Gran Chaco-Yacuiba, Gran Chaco-Caraparí, and Gran Chaco-Villamontes).[1539] Lately, the metropolitan region of "Takana" has been established by (national) Law No.553 of 27 May 2014.[1540] It groups together the seven municipalities of Cochabamba with the surrounding municipalities of Sacaba, Tiquipaya, Colcapirhua, Quillacollo, Vinto and Sipe Sipe and started its monthly meetings last July 2014.[1541] Given its blurred definition both in the Constitution and within the Autonomy Law, the creation of other regions appears uncertain.

Autonomous status is granted to departments (art.277 CPE), regions (art.280 CPE), municipalities (art.283 CPE), and the (Peasant Farmer Native) indigenous autonomies AIOC (art.289 CPE).Therefore, on the one hand, the nine departments and all of the 337 municipalities of Bolivia are to be considered autonomous as in the terms identified by the Autonomy Law mentioned above. Thus, they enjoy hierarchical equality before each other and they are provided with legislative (including the regulation of norms/decrees), fiscal, and executive powers. They are also in charge of the administration of their own economic resources and are formed by governing bodies whose members are elected. Despite the fact that they are an official administrative-territorial unit, provinces cannot be autonomous. On the other hand, two more types of administrative-territorial units subject to conversion processes may become autonomous, i.e., regions and the AIOCs. The former, as mentioned above, may be created by unifying provinces and municipalities. The latter may be created over a TCO/TIOC, a municipality, or a region itself (see further below).

1539 Corte Nacional Electoral del Estado Plurinacional de Bolivia, "Acta de Cómputo Nacional Elecciones Departamentales, Municipales y Regional 2010", pp.77-78.

1540 *Ley de creación de la Región Metropolitana "KANATA" del Departamento de Cochabamba*, Regional Cochabamba Law No.533 of 27 May 2014.

1541 ANA Noticias/Cochabamba, "Sesiona por primera vez el Consejo de la Región Metropolitana 'Kanata'", *Agencia de Noticias Autonómicas ANA*, 14.07.2014, at http://www.ananoticias.com/autonomia-regional/item/1229-sesiona-por-prime ra-vez-el-concejo-de-la-region-metropolitana-kanata [Last access 15.12.2014].

Legally speaking, the choice of giving autonomous status to some administrative-territorial units rather than others is surprising and it is still very unclear what this would imply in practice. For instance, one may wonder what the role of the provinces would be. The Autonomy Law is silent on this. Moreover, the hierarchal equality of the autonomous units would imply that the decisions made by a department should not infringe on the autonomy and the powers of each single municipality situated within their borders and vice versa. This may lead to many potential conflicts regarding competences and practical problems of application of departmental laws or decrees in contradiction with municipal ones. The division of competences drawn by the CPE in arts.299-304 is not (totally) helpful either, as some powers overlap.[1542] For instance, both the departments and the municipalities have the same exclusive power in enhancing labor conditions in the framework of the corresponding national policies.[1543] In other words, in this case, both departments and municipalities enjoy the very same exclusive competence, which is a contradiction in itself: How can an exclusive power belong to more than one body? The answer appears uncertain but may be related to coordination among the autonomous layers. Thus, a few more details vis-à-vis the coordination between the central level and the peripheries are briefly analyzed below.

The Autonomy Law established three bodies that are in charge of different aspects of the autonomies' coordination: the National Autonomy Council (*Consejo Nacional de Autonomías*), the State Autonomy Office (*Servicio Estatal de Autonomías* – SEA), and the State Integral Planning System (*Sistema de Planificación Integral del Estado*) (Autonomy Law art.121). The first body is chaired by the Bolivian President and composed

1542 Art.297 of the CPE specifies that there are four types of powers. The subjects which are the total monopoly of the State - i.e., their legislation, regulation, and execution remain in the hands of the State - are called *competencias privativas*. Subsequently, there are competences whose legislation is exclusively adopted by the State, which, however, may transfer its regulation and execution to other autonomous units (*competencias exclusivas*). Finally, the *competencias concurrentes* and *compartidas* are those powers that the autonomous units share with the State. The former covers those subjects on which the other autonomous units may apply or execute State acts. The latter includes those matters on which the other autonomous units may enact further regulation to implement a State framework law.

1543 Both Nos.4 of arts.300 and 302 have the same wording: "[Son competencias exclusivas de los gobiernos departamentales/municipales autónomos, en su jurisdicción: [...] [la p]romoción del empleo y mejora de las condiciones laborales en el marco de las políticas nacionales".

of three ministers (the ones to the Presidency, Development Planning, and Autonomy), the governors of the nine Bolivian departments, and another eleven stakeholders five of which shall come from the Federation of Municipality Associations, five from the AIOCs, and one from the regional autonomies (Autonomy Law art.123). The National Autonomy Council has a solely political function. The State Autonomy Office-SEA is an operative body led by an executive director and formed by operative units (Autonomy Law art.127). The aim of the State Autonomy Office-SEA is to give technical and administrative support to the autonomous administrations during the decentralization process (Autonomy Law art.126). Indeed, *inter alia*, the State Autonomy Office-SEA is in charge of the resolution of potentially competing roles between the central level and the peripheries as well as among the different autonomous structures (Autonomy Law art.129.1, No.1). In addition, this body shall establish the criteria to transfer or delegate competences/powers to other levels (Autonomy Law art.129.1, No.2). The third body is the State Integral Planning System, which should bring together representatives from all the public administrations of all the territorial units in a forum and thus debate and propose participatory and bottom-up strategies (Autonomy Law art.130.1). Lastly, a number of Sectorial Coordination Councils (*Consejos de Coordinación Sectorial*) should be established and led by the appropriate Minister *ratione materiae* (Autonomy Law art.132). The aim is to coordinate the central and the peripheral governments on specific subjects, e.g., labor policies, etc. In a personal interview with Mr. Justino Avendaño Redeno (one of the main consultants and drafter of the Autonomy Law), held on November, 26 in 2010, it was affirmed that approximately 20 councils were to be appointed by law or decree. This process took longer than was expected but, by late 2013, four Sectorial Coordination Councils were established: Tourism, Productive Development (*Desarrollo Productivo*), Citizen Security (*Seguridad Ciudadana*) and Health.[1544]

In sum, one may see that the coordination system of the four autonomy layers is also complex. It remains unclear whether a coordination system comprised of so many bodies will be able to work effectively. The key body is clearly the State Autonomy Office-SEA, which is the logistic and

1544 Ministerio de Autonomía, "Bolivia Autonómica No.34", La Paz, 2013, p.11. See also Ministerio de Autonomía, "En cumplimiento a la Ley Marco de Autonomías: Cuatro consejos sectoriales han sido conformados", 2013, at http://www.autonomia.gob.bo/portal3/index.php/historico-de-noticias/244-en-cumplimiento-a-la-ley-marco-de-autonomias-cuatro-consejos-sectoriales-han-sido-conformados-.html [Last access 24.08.2014].

operative organ. It will settle conflicts regarding the division of competences not only between the State (central level) and the autonomies (departments, municipalities, and regions-if created), but also between these last levels of government. Furthermore, this is the body that decides the criteria for transferring or delegating further powers. As stated by the above-mentioned Mr Avendaño Redeno, "If the SEA works, the autonomy process will work in an organized way" ("Si el Servicio funcionará, funcionará el proceso autonómico de forma ordenada").[1545] On 23 February 2011, Supreme Decree No.802 was adopted thanks to which, inter alia, the executive director of the SEA was appointed on 8 September 2011 (art.8 of this decree). The operations of this body were thus launched on the very same date.[1546]

5.4.4 The AIOCs

5.4.4.1 Overall introduction to the AIOC and its legal framework

As mentioned above, one of the autonomous layers in Bolivia is the Peasant Farmer Native Indigenous Autonomy (*Autonomía Indígena Originaria Campesina*) or simply AIOC. However, the AIOC (like the "regions") differs from the other two layers (departments and municipalities) since it does not represent a pre-defined territory or entity. Rather, it is the result of a conversion process which may be initiated by selected territorial units. The territorial units that may opt to convert to an AIOC are the following (art.44 Autonomy Law):

- Municipalities;
- TCO/TIOC; or
- Regions (if created).

Currently, the only existing AIOCs are the eleven municipalities which voted for their conversion via referendum in 2009 and two TCO/TIOCs which are at different stages.

1545 Interview with Justino Avendaño Redeno, drafter of the Autonomy Law in Bolivia, on 26 November 2010 [on file with author].

1546 *Servicio Estatal de Autonomías*–SEA, "Presentación oficial del Servicio Estatal de Autonomías", 8 September 2011, at http://www.sea-autonomias.gob.bo/index.php?option=com_content&view=article&id=18:noticia2&catid=17:noticias-del-home [Last access 24.08.2014].

The following introduction and explanation of the legal framework concern both the existing AIOCs as well as possible new AIOCs. They are subject to the same conversion process but to (partially) different pre-requisites. Firstly, it should be specified that, as for the other autonomies (departments, municipalities, and regions), the legal sources of the AIOC are also both the Constitution (CPE) and the Autonomy Law. As mentioned, the indigenous right to autonomy and to self-government is constitutionally guaranteed by art.2of the CPE, which guarantees the right to self-determination of indigenous peoples in such terms. However, more details on the AIOCs' legal framework are to be found in the seventh chapter in arts.289-296 and 303-304 of the CPE. The AIOC is thus conceived as a form of self-government in exercising their (right to) self-determination (art.289 CPE), in a very similar wording to art.4 of the UNDRIP, which, as repeatedly flagged, has binding effects in Bolivia as per Law No.3760/2007.

5.4.4.2 The existing AIOCs: Process of creation and rules

The first eleven municipality-based AIOCs started their conversion process on 6 December 2009 as per Supreme Decree (*Decreto Supremo*) No.0231/2009 and the prioritized procedure consistent with Transitory Disposition 3 of Transitory Electoral Law No.4021/2009. The presidential election and the referendum for autonomy in those departments that had voted against it in 2006 (Chiquisaca, Cochabamba, La Paz, Oruro, Potosí) –prior to the 2007 contestations by the *Oriente* forces and the tragic accidents in Pando in 2008– were also held on the same occasion.

The national referendum approving the new Constitution on 25 January 2009 catalyzed the work on indigenous autonomy in Bolivia.[1547] The Transitory Electoral Law No 4021/2009 allowed the organization of provisional elections in April 2010. Prior to these elections, the following converting AIOC (Jesús de Machaca, La Paz) proclaimed its Peasant Farmer Native Indigenous Autonomic Council (*Consejo Autonómico Indígena Originario*) during a visit from the Ministry of Autonomy.[1548]

1547 As known, the Constitution was approved with 61.43 per cent of votes in favour. Bolpress, "Evo promulga el sábado la primera Constitución aprobada en referéndum popular", 02.02.2009, *Bolpress*, at http://www.bolpress.com/art.php?Cod=2009020206 [Last access 24.08.2014].

1548 Wilfredo Plata, "De Municipio a Autonomía Indígena: Los once municipios que transitan a la Autonomía Indígena Originaria Campesina" in VV.AA, *Bolivia Post-*

This occurrence intensified the debate in other rural municipalities, especially in the highlands. Following these events, Supreme Decree No.0231 was adopted. On the date of its signature (2 August), an informal event was organized by the Ministry of Autonomy and indigenous organizations. It was chaired by President Morales and held in the town of Camiri (Santa Cruz). This date, which was previously celebrated as "Agrarian Reform Day" and "Indio Day", was thus relabelled "Indigenous Day".[1549] Subsequent seminars and workshops were held by the Ministry of Autonomy and other NGOs in October and November.[1550]

On 6 December, 19 municipalities voted to convert to municipality-based AIOCs. According to art.6 of Supreme Decree No.231, some criteria had to be met in order to organize the conversion process (art.290 of the CPE). These were (1) a certificate provided by the Autonomy Ministry; and (2) a decree adopted by the municipality's council with a qualified two-thirds majority of votes in favor. The first criteria (the certificate by the Autonomy Ministry) required three conditions: (1a) The municipal territory had to correspond to the ancestral land inhabited by the indigenous peoples currently living in it; (1b) the claiming indigenous peoples had to exist prior to Bolivia's colonization; and (1c) the claiming indigenous peoples had to share specific common features, i.e., the same cultural identity, language, historical tradition, territoriality, worldview (*cosmovisión*), and their juridical, political, social, and economic organization or institutions had to be demonstrated (art.6.1 of Supreme Decree No. 231). Needless to say, these prerequisites were extremely difficult to prove, especially the correspondence between the ancestral land and the one currently inhabited by an indigenous community. In addition, the territoriality aspect is still a very delicate issue as only 30 out of 337 municipalities in Bolivia (9%) enjoy settled territorial boundaries.[1551]

Therefore, the National Electoral Court (*Corte Nacional Electoral*) did not admit seven municipalities' requests (Corque, Santiago de Andamarca Santiago de Huari, and Turco in the department of Oruro; Gutiérrez and

---

Constituyente: Tierra, territorio y autonomías indígenas. Memoria del Seminario Internacional 2009, Fundación Tierra, La Paz, 2009, pp.247-272, p.254.

1549 Plata, "De Municipio a Autonomía Indígena... ", p.255.

1550 *Ibid.*, pp.255-257.

1551 Agencia de Noticias Autonómicas ANA, "De los 339 municipios del país, sólo 30 tienen sus límites definidos por ley", 28.01.2013, at http://www.ananoticias.com/limites/item/588-de-los-339-municipios-del-pa%C3%ADs-s%C3%B3lo-30-tienen-sus-l%C3%ADmites-definidos-por-ley [Last access 24.08.2014].

Lagunillas in Santa Cruz; and Inquisivi in La Paz) due to unfilled requirements (e.g., the municipality's decree adopted with fewer than two-thirds of 'yes' votes; delays in submitting the full documentation needed).[1552]

Thus, only 12 municipalities voted. In one of them (Carahuara de Carangas, Oruro) the 'no' vote won. The reasons behind this failure likely lie in the fear of changing a (rather successful) participatory system under the former Popular Participation Law, which had already taken (too) much time before its realization. Three other AIOCs were unlikely to get the green light (i.e., Huacaya and Charagua in Chaco and Jesús de Machaca in La Paz) where the 'yes' votes were slightly over the 50% mark.[1553]

In sum, after this referendum, eleven municipalities started the procedure to become full AIOCs. These are: Jesús de Machaca and Charazani (La Paz); Mojocoya, Huacaya and Tarabuco (Chiquisaca); Salinas Garci de Mendoza, Chipaya, Pampa Aullagas and Totora (Oruro); Chayanta (Potosí); and Charagua (Santa Cruz).

Thus, there are seven AIOCs in the Highlands and only two in the Lowlands.[1554] In addition, only 4 out of the 36 constitutionally recognized indigenous peoples (art.5 CPE) are actually pioneering the indigenous autonomies. Indeed, five AIOCs have self-identified as Aymara (Jesús de Machaca, Carangas, Salinas de Garci Mendoza, Pampa Aullagas, and Totora); four as Quechua (Charazani, Mojocoya, Tarabuco, and Chayanta); two as Guaraní (Charagua and Huacaya); and, finally, one as Uru-chipaya (Chipaya). Thus, the Guaranies are the sole indigenous people from the Lowlands taking part in this process.[1555]

Despite the conversion referendum and initial fervour, the procedure to fully convert these eleven municipalities into outright AIOCs remained pending until the adoption of the Autonomy Law in July 2010. Neither the elaboration nor the adoption of this law was as fast or smooth as originally anticipated. The core claim of the seventh indigenous march held in June 2010 was to amend the Autonomy draft law with special regard to a requisite (the numerical quota of the population, *Base Poblacional*), which will be applicable to new and/or future AIOCs.[1556] I also believe that frustration and confusion were driving forces of this march. For instance, at

1552 Ministerio de Autonomía, "Bolivia Autonómica No.7", La Paz, 2009, pp.4-5; Plata, "De Municipio a Autonomía Indígena... ", p.250.

1553 Tamburini, "Bolivia (2010)", p.201.

1554 Plata, "De Municipio a Autonomía Indígena... ", p.254.

1555 *Ibid.*

1556 Tamburini, "Bolivia (2011)", p.177.

the Great Assembly of the Amazonian Indigenous Peoples of Bolivia (*Gran Asamblea de Pueblos* Indígenas-GANPI) held in Santa Cruz in late November 2010 –and which I attended– many indigenous leaders had no clear idea about the conversion process or the prerequisites. These first eleven municipality-based AIOCs were supposed to adopt their statutes within 360 days of the provisional elections held in April 2010 with a potential extension of a further 360 days in accordance with Transitory Disposition 14 of the Autonomy Law, i.e., until approximately March 2012. At the GANPI, some indigenous leaders were convinced that they had to hurry to create a new AIOC. This feeling was actually shared across the country, until the Autonomy Minister (at that time, still Carlos Romero), clarified that there was no deadline for either the statutes or the creation of new AIOCs.[1557] Nevertheless, the first eleven municipality-based AIOCs started their procedure to fully convert into outright AIOCs (see below section 5.4.4.4).

Finally, it needs to be mentioned that since July 2010 a Coordination body of the AIOCs (*Coordinadora Nacional de Autonomías Indígena Originario Campesina* – CONAIOC) was created to enhance the AIOC procedure.[1558]

5.4.4.3 The regulation of new/future AIOCs

The prerequisites to form new AIOCs differ slightly from the ones already required by the eleven existing municipality-based AIOCs in 2009. Art.290 of the CPE outlines three preconditions for the conversion of a municipality, a TCO/TIOC, or a region (when created) into an AIOC: (1) A territory which may be claimed to be the ancestral land of the indigenous peoples requesting an AIOC; (2) the willingness to create it shown by the community (via referendum or consultation, see below); and (3) the application of customary norms and institutions. As to the second aspect, the Autonomy Law specifies that a converting referendum or –in the case of the TIOC– a consultation with the population of each territorial entity should be held (art.293.1; art.294.2; art.295.3 of the CPE, and art.50 Autonomy Law).

1557 Erbol, "Ministro Romero asegura que no hay plazos para implementar las autonomías indígenas", *Erbol Comunicaciones Periódico Digital*, 25 February 2011, at http://cedla.org/content/21519 [Last access 24.08.2014].

1558 Fundación Tierra, "La CONAIOC es un espacio de coordinación y representación", 9 *Monthly Bulletin Nuestra Tierra* September 2012, at http://www.ftierra.org/nuestraTIERRA/9/nt5m.html [Last access 24.08.2014].

Besides these three constitutional requirements, arts.56 and 58 of the Autonomy Law add further prerequisites which differ in the case of each entity (municipality, TCO/TIOC, region) and may be listed as follows:
a) Evidence that the territory inhabited is 'ancestral';
b) Territorial continuity;
c) Governmental trusteeship (Viabilidad Gubernativa);
d) Population's "quota" (Base Poblacional).
a) The first of the criteria (evidence that the territory inhabited is "ancestral") is relevant for the municipalities. Thus, evidence that the lands occupied by the claiming indigenous peoples have been inhabited by them since times immemorial, or a similar interpretation, should be provided by any municipality which would opt for a conversion process, prior to organizing a referendum (art.56.2 Autonomy Law). This is what art.290 of the CPE also prescribes.

a & b) Along with this "ancestral-territory" evidence, territorial continuity is required by the (potential) applicant regions (art.56.3 Autonomy Law).

a, b, c & d) In the case of the TCOs/TIOCs, two more conditions apply, i.e., governmental trusteeship (*Viabilidad Gubernativa*, art.57 Autonomy Law), and the population's quota (*Base Poblacional*, art.58 Autonomy Law). The former (the governmental trusteeship) should be a ministerial decree, resolution, or certificate which would be released if two further prerequisites are met. These are: evidence of the "existence, representation, and effective implementation of an organizational structure" and a territorial plan including institutional and financial strategies. The latter (the population's quota) is a numerical condition which should be fulfilled. These quotas are 10,000 people for the highlands –reducible to 4,000 in exceptional cases– and 1,000 for the lowlands. Thus, not only is it difficult to prove territorial continuity –especially in the lowlands, where, as seen, 58.2% of the TCOs/TIOCs in the Amazonian region are affected by territorial discontinuity–[1559] but two more quite arbitrary preconditions are required. This profoundly undermines the possibility for indigenous peoples, particularly those in the lowlands, to create their own autonomous TCO/TIOC.

d with a question mark) This last condition seems to also be applicable to the municipalities. The Autonomy Law is silent on this, but in practice such quotas have been the threat which the seventh march of indigenous

1559 Colque and Chumacero, *Informe 2010: Territorios Indígena Originario Campesinos en Bolivia*, p.108.

peoples was protesting against in June 2010. Moreover, it has also been discussed within municipalities and indicated as a requirement in NGOs' material addressing the direct stakeholders.[1560]

5.4.4.4 Common conversion procedure and other norms

To conclude the overview on the legal framework of the AIOC, a few more common regulations provided by both the CPE and the Autonomy Law should be mentioned here.

First and foremost, the conversion procedure from a (standard) municipality, TCO/TIOC, or a region is the same and applies both to the eleven existing municipality-based AIOCs and to possible new/future ones. It consists of an initial step plus four further steps.[1561] A pre-requisite is the referendum or consultation (in the case of TCO/TIOC) on the conversion into an AIOC (art.293.1; art.294.2; art.295.2 of the CPE, and art.50 Autonomy Law). If the yes vote wins, four other steps follow. (1) The indigenous peoples of the municipality have to establish a deliberative council (art.53 Autonomy Law), which is charged with (2) drafting and approving the statute via a qualified two-thirds majority vote. Once adopted, (3) the statute shall be subject to a constitutional check. Lastly, if approved, (4) another referendum will be held among the local population (art.275 CPE). If consistent with the CPE, the AIOC will come into effect after the establishment of its governing bodies (art.55 Autonomy Law). It goes without saying that the AIOC shall be constituted, formed, and ruled in a way that is consistent with the CPE and the Autonomy Law (art.296 CPE). As far as step 2 (statute's drafting) is concerned, the CPE prescribes that indigenous peoples' own rules and procedures should apply during the elaboration process (art.292 CPE). This same indigenous customary law should also rule over the functioning of the AIOC governing body (art.296 CPE) once it is established and working.

1560 Fundación Tierra, "Los requisitos y procedimientos traban la autonomía indígena", 9 *Monthly Bulletin Nuestra Tierra* September 2012, at http://www.ftierra.org/nuestraTIERRA/9/nt5c.html [Last access 24.08.2014].

1561 For the sake of clarity, it should be specified that this procedure has to be followed by any autonomous territorial unit, i.e., also the departments and the other municipalities, in accordance with art.275 of the CPE. Indeed, this article establishes that each AIOC shall adopt its statute, which then has to pass through a constitutional check and a referendum within the municipality before entering into force (art.275 CPE).

Another sensitive issue is the division of powers between the state and the AIOC, which is regulated by the CPE. First, since the AIOC is or would be a converted municipality, TCO/TIOC or region,[1562] it should absorb the competences of a converted entity (art.303 CPE). Second, art.304 of the CPE establishes a number of exclusive powers left to the AIOC, which are 23 in total. Third, AIOCs have further powers that are shared with the state, i.e., four *competencias concurrentes* and ten *competencias compartidas*. Leaving aside the complete list, for the purpose of this study two aspects should be noted. On the one hand, some exclusive powers retained by the AIOCs, such as the definition and management of their own development projects according to the own indigenous culture (art.304.2), may be considered significant in terms of ensuring the exercise of self-ruling powers by the indigenous autonomy. On the other hand, the AIOCs only have implementation powers (*competencias concurrentes* and *competencias compartidas*) vis-à-vis key competences such as health, education, environmental, and (non-renewable) natural resource policies, which are left to the State. This denies AIOCs control over these (crucial) aspects and therefore substantially limits their overall power, as will be discussed below (section 5.4.4.6).

5.4.4.5 The current status of the AIOCs

Since their creation, the AIOCs are constantly developing and changing, following both positive and negative trends. To understand these shifts, they have been monitored by conducting both field and desk research (via NGOs bulletins, newspapers and official documents) since May 2011. This date is relevant since it was one year after the provisional elections for the municipality's council members in charge of leading the conversion process. Thus, the main progresses and shortcomings (until December 2014) are displayed in the following graph (figure 5.1), capturing the overall trend. The period monitored covers approximately three years, highlighting five periods (May 2011, August-September 2012, December 2013, July 2014 and December 2014). The measurement's scale ranges from 1 to 5 to represent the stages of the conversion procedure mentioned above. Additionally, intermediate values have been specified to better indicate the

1562 In this last case, the AIOC would be entitled solely to those regional powers that would be expressly transferred to it by the provinces and municipalities forming it, which do not cease to exist (art.303.2).

developments of each AIOC. Therefore, stage 0.5 means that the AIOC is working to establish the deliberative council; stage 1 is the establishment of the deliberative council; stage 1.5 is the drafting of the Statute; stage 2 is the adoption of the statute by two-thirds of the deliberate council; stage 3 is the statute's submission to the Plurinational Constitutional Court for its constitutional check; stage 3.25 means that the AIOC is working on the revisions required by the Constitutional Court; stage 3.5 is the approval by the Constitutional Court; stage 3.75 refers to the organization of the second referendum; stage 4 is the realization of the second referendum for statute approval within the community; finally, stage 5 is when the AIOC is fully established properly functioning.

Figure 5.1: Status of AIOCs (December 2014)

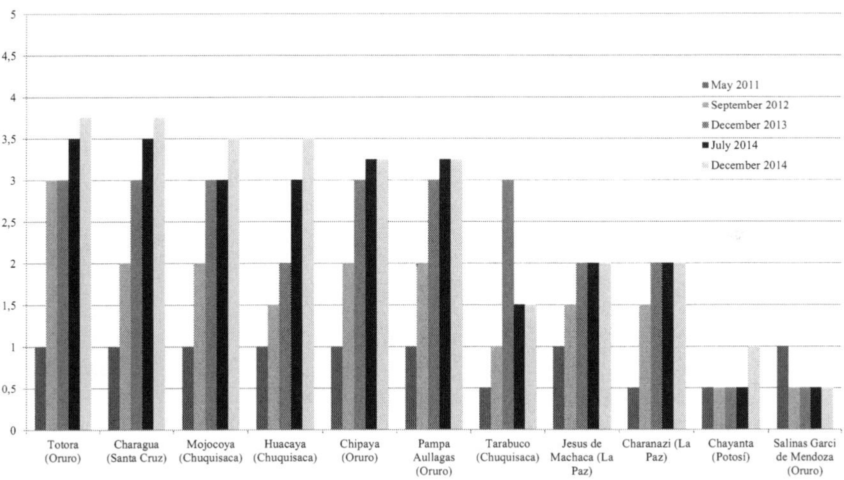

Source: Own elaboration

Legend of Figure 5.1: Current status of AIOCs conversion process

0.5	Working to establish the Deliberative Council
1	Establishment of Deliberative Council
1.5	Drafting the Statute
2	Statute vote
3	Statute under constitutional check
3.25	Working on first revisions required by Constitutional Court
3.5	Statute approved

3.75 Organization of the second referendum
4 2nd referendum for Statute approval
5 AIOC starts working

For the aims of this study, it is sufficient to focus on the last two years,[1563] during which time seven AIOC Statutes were submitted to the Plurinational Constitutional Court[1564] and four were approved (during 2014). The AIOC of Totora (Oruro) was the first to receive the constitutionality declaration in February 2014.[1565] Mojocoya (Chuquisaca), Charagua (Santa Cruz) and Pampa Aullagas (Oruro) submitted their Statutes in October 2012: The former on 12 October 2012 and the latter two on 31 October 2012.[1566] Shortly after, Chipaya (Oruro) followed on 23 October 2012.[1567] Of these four, Pampa Aullagas and Chipaya received a preliminary constitutional approval subject to further revisions in mid-June 2014;[1568] on this same day, Charagua received the final constitutional approval;[1569] and the Statute of

1563 For details on the previous periods, see Alexandra Tomaselli, "(Peasant Farmer Native) Indigenous Autonomies in Bolivia: Developments and Shortcomings (2009-2012)", in Marc Becker (ed.), *Cases of Exclusion and Mobilization of Race and Ethnicities in Latin America*, Cambridge Scholars Publishing, Newcastle upon Tyne, 2013, pp.130-173.

1564 Fundación Tierra, "Piensan una ley para elegir autoridades en municipios que tramitan autonomía indígena", 13.12.2013, at http://www.ftierra.org/index.php/pueblos-y-autonomias-indigenas/40-piensan-una-ley-para-elegir-autoridades-en-municipios-que-tramitan-autonomia-indigena [Last access 24.08.2014].

1565 Fundación Tierra, "Totora: Tribunal Constitucional declara constitucional el primer estatuto indígena", 06.02.2014, at http://www.ftierra.org/index.php/pueblos-y-autonomias-indigenas/55-totora-tribunal-constitucional-declara-constitucional-el-primer-estatuto-indigena [Last access 24.08.2014].

1566 Ministerio de Autonomías & Servicio Estatal de Autonomías, *Estado de situación de las autonomías en Bolivia: Una mirada a tres años*, La Paz, 2013, pp.31-32.

1567 *Ibid.*; Fundación Tierra, "La CONAIOC es un espacio de coordinación y representación", p.3.

1568 ANA Noticias, "Otros 3 estatutos tienen observaciones: TCP declara constitucional Estatuto de Charagua", *Agencia de Noticias Autonómicas ANA*, 12.06.2014 at http://www.ananoticias.com/autonomia-indigena/item/1169-otros-3-estatutos-tienen-observaciones-tcp-declara-constitucional-estatuto-de-charagua [Last access 15.12.2014].

1569 ANA Noticias/Santa Cruz, "TCP declara constitucional el Estatuto Autonómico de Charagua", *Agencia de Noticias Autonómicas ANA*, 12.06.2014 at http://www.ananoticias.com/autonomia-indigena/item/1170-tcp-declara-constitucional-el-estatuto-autonomico-de-charagua; Lorenzo Soliz Tito, "A cinco años de la norma, ninguna autonomía indígena", *Página Siete*, 05.08.2014, at http://www.paginasiete.bo/opinion/2014/8/5/cinco-anos-norma-ninguna-autonomia-indigena-28536.html [Last access to both 15.12.2014].

Mojocoya was approved in mid-November 2014.[1570] Therefore, both Totora and Charagua are now organizing the second referendum on the final approval of their statutes.[1571] Moreover, the formulation of the question of this second referendum in the case of Charagua was already endorsed by the Constitutional Court in late October 2014.[1572] Huacaya and Tarabuco (Chuquisaca) submitted their Statute in June 2013[1573] and Tarabuco in late 2013. The Statute of the former was approved last 30 October 2014.[1574] In the case of the latter, the Statute needed to be amended as per the decision of the Plurinational Constitutional Court in June 2014. The amendments were not done in time, and therefore the deliberate council must restart the Statute drafting procedure:[1575] This is why there is a fall to stage 1.5 in the graph above. The AIOCs Jesús de Machaca and Charazani (La Paz) adopted

1570 ANA Noticias/Chuquisaca, "Mojocoya celebra la compatibilidad de su Estatuto Indígena con la CPE", *Agencia de Noticias Autonómicas ANA*, 12.11.2014, at http://www.ananoticias.com/autonomia-indigena/item/1416-mojocoya-celebra-la-compatibilidad-de-su-estatuto-indigena-con-la-cpe [Last access 15.12.2014].

1571 Nancy Vacaflor, "Norma viabiliza referendos para las autonomías indígenas", *Página Siete*, 31.10.2014, at http://www.paginasiete.bo/nacional/2014/10/31/norma-viabiliza-referendos-para-autonomias-indigenas-36904.html [Last access 15.12.2014].

1572 The question will be the following: "Do you agree with the Native Autonomous Statute of Charagua and its entering into force?" (in the original: ¿Usted está de acuerdo con el Estatuto Autonómico Originario de Charagua y su puesta en vigencia?"). ANA Noticias/Chuquisaca, "TCP declara constitucional la pregunta para el referéndum aprobatorio del Estatuto de Charagua", *Agencia de Noticias Autonómicas ANA*, 30.10.2014, at http://www.ananoticias.com/autonomia-indigena/item/1378-tcp-declara-constitucional-la-pregunta-para-el-referendum-aprobatorio-del-estatuto-de-charagua [Last access 15.12.2014]; see also Vacaflor, "Norma viabiliza referendos para las autonomías indígenas".

1573 Ministerio de Autonomías & Servicio Estatal de Autonomías, *Estado de situación de las autonomías en Bolivia: Una mirada a tres años*, pp.31-32.

1574 ANA Noticias/Chuquisaca, "TCP emite declaración constitucional sobre el estatuto indígena de Huacaya", *Agencia de Noticias Autonómicas ANA*, 31.10.2014, at http://www.ananoticias.com/autonomia-indigena/item/1389-tcp-emite-declaracion-constitucional-sobre-el-estatuto-indigena-de-huacaya [Last access 15.12.2014].

1575 Erbol, "Estatuto indígena de Tarabuco vuelve a foja cero", 02.07.2014, *Erbol Comunicaciones Periódico Digital*, at http://www.erbol.com.bo/noticia/indigenas/02072014/estatuto_indigena_de_tarabuco_vuelve_foja_cero; ANA Noticas Chuquisaca, "Tarabuco recompone su Asamblea Autonómica para viabilizar las observaciones al estatuto", *Agencia de Noticias Autonómicas ANA*, 21.07.2014, at http://www.ananoticias.com/autonomia-indigena/item/1237-tarabuco-recompone-su-asamblea-autonomica-para-viabilizar-las-observaciones-al-estatuto [Last access to both 15.12.2014].

their Statute internally but have not yet submitted it.[1576] Finally, in Salinas de Garci Mendoza and in Chayanta (Oruro), the work on their Statutes have still yet to be started,[1577] but in the latter case the deliberative council was set up in October 2014.[1578]

As for the formation of new municipality-based AIOCs, it was quite worrying that no municipality had organized a conversion referendum for a long period of time.[1579] In November 2012, Milton Chacay, Secretary of Autonomies of the Guaraní People Assembly, announced that six Guaraní groups (*capitanías*) aspire to create municipality-based AIOCs in both Gutiérrez and Lagunillas (Santa Cruz) and Macharetí (Chuquisaca).[1580] Out of these, the conversion referendum was announced to take place in Gutiérrez in April 2015.[1581] The Ministry of Autonomies was also evaluating the conversion proposal of the municipality of San Miguel de Velasco (Santa Cruz).[1582] Interestingly, in July 2014 the municipality of

---

1576 Ministerio de Autonomías & Servicio Estatal de Autonomías, *Estado de situación de las autonomías en Bolivia: Una mirada a tres años*, pp.31-32; Fundación Tierra, "Piensan una ley para elegir autoridades en municipios que tramitan autonomía indígena". The overall process in Jesús de Machaca has been particularly complex and contested due to internal conflicts. For a recent analysis, see Gonzalo Colque and Wilfredo Plata, *El Proceso Autonómico de Jesús de Machaca 2004-2010*, Fundación Tierra, La Paz, 2014.

1577 Ministerio de Autonomías & Servicio Estatal de Autonomías, *Estado de situación de las autonomías en Bolivia: Una mirada a tres años*, pp.31-32; Fundación Tierra, "Piensan una ley para elegir autoridades en municipios que tramitan autonomía indígena".

1578 ANA Noticias/Potosí, "Órgano Deliberativo de Chayanta perfila su conformación", *Agencia de Noticias Autonómicas ANA*, 31.10.2014, at http://www.ananoticias.com/autonomia-indigena/item/1388-organo-deliberativo-de-chayanta-perfila-su-conformacion [Last access 15.12.2014].

1579 Anf-Agencia, "De los 337 municipios, sólo 11 asumieron autonomía indígena originario campesina", *Los Tiempos*, 30.06.2011, at http://www.lostiempos.com/diario/actualidad/nacional/20110630/de-los-337-municipios-solo-11-asumieron-autonomia-indigena-originario_131924_267282.html [Last access 24.08.2014].

1580 Fundación Tierra, "Hay municipios que buscarán la autonomía indígena a pesar de las dificultades del trámite." 20.11.2012, at http://www.ftierra.org/ftierra2012/index.php?option=com_content&view=article &id=12803:rair&catid=177:autonomias-indigenas&Itemid=243 [Last access 24.08.2014].

1581 Erbol, "Anuncian referendo para conversión de Gutiérrez", 09.02.2015, *Erbol Comunicaciones Periódico Digital*, at http://www.erbol.com.bo/noticia/indigenas/09022015/anuncian_referendo_para_conversion_de_gutierrez [Last access 26.02.2015].

1582 Ministerio de Autonomías & Servicio Estatal de Autonomías, *Estado de situación de las autonomías en Bolivia: Una mirada a tres años*, p.34.

Curva (La Paz) received the certificate of "ancestral territory", i.e., evidence that the territory inhabited is 'ancestral' (requisite letter a), section 5.4.4.4). They started the procedure in 2011[1583] and it thus took three years just to receive this certificate. The next step will be the organization of the first referendum. Finally, other sources reported recently that a further 14 municipalities are considering converting to AIOC, but no other details have been specified.[1584]

Regarding the TCOs/TIOCs, the requirements of ancestral territoriality, governmental trusteeship, and population quota were regulated between 2012 and 2013. The former was by Ministerial Resolution of the Ministry of Autonomies (*Resolución Ministerial*) No.091/2012 and the latter two by Ministerial Resolution 032/2013. This also sped up the procedure for the TCOs/TIOCs that increased from the initial 2 (Raqaypampa and Lomerio) to 6 between 2013 and 2014 (in addition to the two that have already been mentioned, Monte Verde, Marka Camata, Consejo Indígena Yuracaré, and Territorio Indígena Cavineño).[1585] Of all these TCOs/TIOCs, Raqaypampa approved the statute at the end of 2012[1586] and submitted it to the Constitutional Court on 20 November 2013,[1587] but it still waiting for its approval.[1588] The Consejo Indígena Yuracaré started preparing the required documents in 2013.[1589] Monte Verde and Marka Camata received the certificate of territorial ancestrally in May 2013.[1590] Lomerio and Territorio

1583 ANA Noticias, "Curva recibe certificado de ancestralidad", *Agencia de Noticias Autonómicas ANA*, 17.07.2014, at http://www.ananoticias.com/autonomia-indigena/item/1233-curva-recibe-certificado-de-ancestralidad [Last access 15.12.2014].

1584 Soliz Tito, "A cinco años de la norma, ninguna autonomía indígena".

1585 Ministerio de Autonomías & Servicio Estatal de Autonomías, *Estado de situación de las autonomías en Bolivia: Una mirada a tres años*, p.34.

1586 Estatuto de la Autonomía Indígena Originaria de Raqaypampa, 31/10/2012, http://www.cedib.org/leyes/estatuto-de-la-autonomia-indigena-originaria-de-raqaypampa [Last access 24.08.2014].

1587 Fundación Tierra, "Piensan una ley para elegir autoridades en municipios que tramitan autonomía indígena".

1588 The last available source is the following: ANA Noticias, "Raqaypampa espera su Estatuto mientras ejerce la autonomía indígena", *Agencia de Noticias Autonómicas ANA*, 08.04.2014, at http://www.ananoticias.com/autonomia-indigena/item/849-raqaypampa-espera-su-estatuto-mientras-ejerce-la-autonomia-indigena [Last access 15.12.2014]. No other information was found as of mid-2015.

1589 Ministerio de Autonomías & Servicio Estatal de Autonomías, *Estado de situación de las autonomías en Bolivia: Una mirada a tres años*, p.34.

1590 *Ibid.*

Indígena Cavineño received such certificate in December 2013 and in August 2014, respectively.[1591]

5.4.4.6 Final remarks on the AIOCs

The evaluation of the AIOCs' lastest achievements and failures in this concluding paragraph is twofold. On one hand, whether the AIOC arrangement fulfils some of the (basic) features that might represent an indigenous autonomy as delineated in chapter 3, section 3.3.3 has to be assessed. On the other, assuming that the AIOC system could work as it stands now on paper, much is yet to be done on the ground.
As to the former aspect, the AIOC system may formally fulfil many of the aspects identified above to realize an indigenous autonomy. The AIOC is territorially based; it has many exclusive powers, including those of self-definition and the management of economic, social, political, and cultural development plans (art.304.1, No.2 CPE); it respects and applies traditional/own rules, even in the formation of the statutes (art.304.1, Nos.1 and 8 CPE); it gives space for traditional/own authorities and institutions (art.304.1, No.23 CPE); it has, in principle, fiscal powers (art.304.1, Nos.12, 13 and 14 CPE); and it has a budget provided by the state (art.304.4 CPE). However, when it comes to indigenous education, health, and the extraction of non-renewable natural resources, in which Bolivia is very rich, the AIOC, as mentioned, enjoys executive powers only (*competencias concurrentes*; art.303.3 CPE).

Moreover, the legal procedure to fully establish an AIOC is extremely complex. On one hand, it aims to safeguard broad participation and to guarantee the AIOC's legitimacy thanks to a number of democratic mechanisms, e.g., the double referenda and the statute adoption via a two-thirds majority of the deliberative council. On the other hand, however, it was designed assuming a homogenous sociocultural environment and did not consider mechanisms to overcome potential internal conflicts. This is

---

1591 On Lomerio, see Erbol, "Entregan certificado de ancestralidad a los Monkóxi", 13.01.2014, *Erbol Comunicaciones Periódico Digital*, at http://www.erbol.com.bo/noticia/indigenas/13012014/entregan_certificado_de_ancestralidad_los_monkoxi; on the Territorio Indígena Cavineño, see Erbol, "Indígenas cavineños logran certificación de ancestralidad", 29.08.2014, *Erbol Comunicaciones Periódico Digital*, at http://www.erbol.com.bo/noticia/indi genas/29082014/indigenas_cavinenos_logran_certificacion_de_ancestralidad [Last access to both 26.02.2015].

particularly evident in the current 11 working AIOCs. As has been recently argued with regard to minorities in Europe, adopting a rather pragmatic approach, autonomy could work better when "ethnically neutral",[1592] "de-ethnicised" and "de-politicised",[1593] i.e., aimed at the development and management of the territory as a whole, prioritizing good governance guarantees.[1594] This concept could probably also help in the case of Bolivia. However, when dealing with a deeply divided society like that of Bolivia, in which large groups that have suffered and continue to suffer marginalization and acute discrimination[1595] have recently gained a stronger voice within society, it is virtually impossible to deny indigenous peoples' aspiration to (finally) hold the balance of power. Moreover, it is extremely difficult to set aside political implications (and ambitions), especially during times of profound change as is the case of Bolivia. In any case, it is undeniable that the AIOC conversion process and, in particular, the statutes' adoption, have been over-delayed. In order to speed up matters, a time limit was initially provided (up to two years, i.e., by March 2012; Transitory Disposition 14 of the Autonomy Law), which, as seen, frightened –rather than encouraged– indigenous communities away from opting for this solution.

As to the creation of territorial AIOCs (in form of TCOs/TIOCs), which could be an option for indigenous peoples in the lowlands, the prerequisites required (governmental trusteeship – *Viabilidad Gubernativa* and population quota – *Base Poblacional*, arts.57 and 58 of the Autonomy Law, respectively) are much too demanding (e.g., the quantity of documentation required from communities without any administrative support), unrealistic (e.g., in the case of the numerically very small peoples), and subject to arbitrariness with regard to the evaluation of the governmental trusteeship.

1592 See Francesco Palermo, "Autonomia territoriale e tutela delle minoranze: Una riflessione critica", in Antonio Reposo, Lucio Pegoraro, Roberto Scarciglia, Maurillo Gobbo, Sergio Gerotto (eds.), 5-6 *Il diritto della regione, special edition on Federalismo, decentramento e revisione costituzionale negli ordinamenti policentrici* 2009, pp.181-196, p.196.

1593 Francesco Palermo, "When the Lund Recommendations are Ignored. Effective Participation of National Minorities through Territorial Arrangements", 16(4) *International Journal on Minority and Group Rights* 2009, pp.653-663, p.662.

1594 *Ibid.*, pp.660-661.

1595 See the case of slavery of *Guaraní* communities in the department of Chaco reported by the Inter-American Commission of Human Rights, "Comunidades Cautivas: Situación del Pueblo Indígena Guaraní y Formas Contemporáneas de Esclavitud en el Chaco de Bolivia", Organization of American States, Doc. No. OEA/Ser.L/V/II (58), 24 December 2009, at http://www.cidh.org/country rep/ComunidadesCautivas/cautivasindice.sp.htm [Last access 24.08.2014].

Even if recently regulated, these aspects remain controversial. For instance, the territorial ancestrality certificate, which in itself may also be extremely difficult to obtain and released arbitrarily, must first be released by the Ministry of Autonomy and then submitted together with a number of other documents in order to request governmental trusteeship.[1596] This generates fear among indigenous peoples and suggests a general lack of political will to enhance indigenous autonomy. As seen, only one of the municipalities aspiring to convert to AIOC (Curca, La Paz) has obtained it. As to the population quota, the Araona people (La Paz) were considering forming an indigenous region with other indigenous peoples since they have only 200 members dispersed in six communities.[1597]

Therefore, as for the legal aspects, the Autonomy Law has apparently complicated the already blurred AIOC constitutional form even further. Moreover, (dangerous) legal uncertainties together with other social, economic, and political challenges need to be faced. First, much fear and confusion is shared by indigenous peoples due to the aforementioned requirements, especially in the lowlands. Indeed, only 3 municipalities' requests out of the 19 admitted for the December 2009 AIOC referendum came from the *Oriente* departments; in particular, from the department of Santa Cruz. No formal request was fulfilled by any municipality in Beni or Pando for that referendum.[1598] In these departments many indigenous communities are dispersed in large territorial areas and/or are numerically inferior,[1599] which would explain the probable lack of information on the AIOCs and its procedures. In addition, in the lowlands, further obstacles are caused by land disputes between indigenous peoples and non-indigenous colonizers, competing economic interests in non-renewable natural resources,[1600] demarcation issues of municipalities and departments, and

1596 *Reglamento para la Emisión de Certificación de Viabilidad Gubernativa y Verificación de Base Poblacional via TIOC*, art.3 (*Solicitud*).

1597 Alvaro Luksic, "Los araonas quieren unirse a otro pueblo para alcanzar la autonomía Indígena", *El País Online*, 11 April 2011, at http://www.elpaisonline.com/index.php/2013-01-15-14-16-26/local/item/45395-los-araonas-quieren-unirse-a-otro-pueblo-para-alcanzar-la-autonomia-indigena [Last access 24.08.2014].

1598 Plata, "De Municipio a Autonomía Indígena... ", p.252.

1599 Plata, "De Municipio a Autonomía Indígena... ", p.253.

1600 Iván Bustillos Zamorano, "Autonomías territoriales bajo 'fuego cruzado'", *La Razón*, 12.06.2011, at http://www.ftierra.org/ftierra2012/index.php?option=com_content&view=article&id=6368:autonomias-territoriales-bajo-fuego-cruzado-&catid=177:autonomias-indigenas&Itemid=243 [Last access 24.08.2014].

territorial discontinuity issues that affect 58.2% of the TCOs/TIOCs in the Amazonian region.

In addition, 17 territorial borders are contested both in the highlands and the lowlands.[1601] The Law on Territorial Units No.339/2013 (*Ley de Unidades Territoriales*) was adopted on 31 January 2013 and pertains to the settlement and altering of borders. The indigenous organizations, however, have contested it. Notably, the law does not follow the principle of equal hierarchy among the autonomous territorial units (art.276 CPE; art.6.2, No.3 Autonomy Law) nor were indigenous peoples consulted on this law, although it affects them.[1602] Other conflicts may arise among competences of the different autonomous layers and, thus, autonomies' organizational bodies (see section 5.4.3) would have a heavy burden of work.

Another relevant aspect concerns the finances of municipalities and other public and territorial entities. Many mayors complained about the Taxes Law No.154/2011. Indeed, art.6 of this law reduces the municipalities' powers to establish new taxes, despite the increasing demand for public services by the population.[1603]

Finally, another fear among indigenous peoples is what will occur with AIOCs at the upcoming administrative elections of 2015. Since late 2013, the Coordination body of the AIOC has requested that in the municipality-based AIOCs the authorities should be voted for according to traditional

1601 Luis Mealla, "17 conflictos por límites no se resuelven por falta de una ley", *Página Siete/Eju.tv*, 21.08.2011, at http://eju.tv/2011/08/17-conflictos-por-lmites-no-se-resuelven-por-falta-de-una-ley [Last access 24.08.2014].

1602 Agencia Intercultural de Noticias Indígenas de Bolivia (AINI), "CIDOB rechaza el anteproyecto de Ley de Unidades Territoriales", *Agencia Intercultural de Noticias Indígenas de Bolivia*, 27 April 2011, at http://www.aininoticias.org/2011/04/cidob-rechaza-el-anteproyecto-de-ley-de-unidades-territoriales [Last access 24.08.2014].

1603 Iván Bustillos Zamorano, "Ley de Clasificación de Impuestos, jaque a las autonomías Municipales: La Asamblea Legislativa debate otra polémica norma", *La Razón*, 19.06.2011, at http://www.ftierra.org/ftierra2012/index.php?option=com_content&view=article&id=6462:rair&catid=177:autonomias-indigenas&Itemid=243 [Last access 24.08.2014].

customary rules and procedures,[1604] but it is unlikely that this request will be met.[1605]

In conclusion, Bolivia is running the risk of paying lip service to indigenous autonomy, unless some fundamental steps are taken soon to implement it successfully. Other scholars working on the AIOCs have expressed their scepticism.[1606] The dynamic Bolivian scenario may indeed take us by surprise in the coming years as it has in the past. The institutional reform experienced by the Andean state is recent and still very much a work in progress. Positive news, for instance, regards the government's submission to the Parliament of a Draft Law (No.411 of 2014, currently under discussion in the Lower Chamber) that regulates funding for the upcoming second referendum for the final endorsement of the statutes of those AIOCs that received the constitutional approval (i.e., Totora and Charagua) by the local population.[1607]

1604 Fundación Tierra, "Piensan una ley para elegir autoridades en municipios que tramitan autonomía indígena"; Nancy Vacaflor,"Indígenas en vigilia amenazan con ejercer su 'autogobierno'", *Página Siete*, 23.09.2014, at http://www.pagina siete.bo/nacional/2014/9/23/indigenas-vigilia-amenazan-ejercer-autogobierno-33 045.html [Last access 15.12.2014].

1605 Página Siete, "Descartan la aprobación de ley corta para autonomías", *Página Siete*, 12.08.2014, at http://www.paginasiete.bo/nacional/2014/8/12/descartan-aprobacion-corta-para-autonomias-29128.html [Last access 15.12.2014].

1606 Jason Tockman and John Cameron, "Indigenous Autonomy and the Contradictions of Plurinationalism in Bolivia", 56(3) *Latin American Politics and Society* 2014, pp.46-69, p.64.

1607 Draft Law/*Proyecto de Ley No 411/2014-2015: Transferencia de recursos económicos de los Gobiernos Autónomos Municipales en conversión a Autonomías Indígena Originario Campesinas*. To date (15.12.2014), the draft law may be found at http://www.diputados.bo/images/Docs/PL/INF14-15/INF14_41 1.pdf, and is under discussion (*Tramitación*) at the Lower Chamber (Cámara de Diputados): http://www.diputados.bo/index.php/leyes/leyes-en-tratamiento. See also Vacaflor, "Indígenas en vigilia amenazan con ejercer su 'autogobierno'"; ANA Noticias, "Senado sanciona ley de transferencia de recursos para referendos de los estatutos indígenas", *Agencia de Noticias Autonómicas*, 30.10.2014, at http://www.ananoticias.com/autonomia-indigena/item/1383-senado-sanciona-le y-d e-transferencia-de-recursos-para-referendos-de-los-estatutos-indigenas [Last access to all 15.12.2014].

5.5 Concluding remarks on the Bolivian case

This chapter addressed the recognition and application of the *composite right to political participation of indigenous peoples* proposed in chapter 3 at domestic level in the case of Bolivia. This *composite right* follows a two-fold approach. First, it refers to the combination of *ad hoc* political rights, thus (1) (a) indigenous peoples' representation in State bodies or in other public posts, including in decision-making processes and in the judiciary, both at the national and the local level, as well as their rights to (b) consultation and (c) free, prior and informed consent (FPIC). Second, to indigenous autonomy/self-government arrangements, including the preservation of indigenous traditional institutions (chapter 3, section 3.4). This proposal focuses on the rights of indigenous peoples to "have a say" in the national and local political arenas and in all matters likely to affect them, which implies much more than their participation in elections.

This concluding section explores whether this composite right may also become one of the effective applications of the right to self-determination of indigenous peoples in Bolivia and thus enhance their protection and offer a compromise solution for the State. As discussed in chapter 2, sections 2.2.5 and 2.2.6, the recognition of the right to self-determination of indigenous peoples should no longer be an issue. The conceptualization of this right of indigenous peoples has undergone substantial developments both in international law practice and in academia. Starting from the concepts of autonomy and political rights, which remain essential parts of indigenous peoples' right to self-determination, other facets such as: The indigenous peoples rights' to land, natural resources, and thus to consultation and FPIC; identity and cultures; and socio-economic development. This has also been clarified by both the HRC and the CESCR (chapter 2, section 2.2.2.2). The majority of indigenous peoples do not aspire to Statehood but rather to have the instruments to somehow self-determine their future. Therefore, at the international level the core problem concerns *which expressions of the right to self-determination* indigenous peoples may effectively exercise as right-holders. Thus, this chapter analyses whether *one* of these expressions, i.e., the above-mentioned proposed *composite right to political participation of indigenous peoples*, is both recognized and applied in the case of Bolivia.

Bolivia recognizes the right to self-determination of indigenous peoples in three constitutional provisions, namely arts.2, 30.4 and 289 (as well as in the preamble). According to these, indigenous peoples' right to self-determination consists of their right to autonomy, self-government, own culture, the recognition of their own institutions, and the consolidation of their territorial entities within the broader Bolivian legal framework. However, the Bolivian legal framework also provides indigenous peoples with rights to participation within State organs (parliaments, judiciary, etc.) both at national and local level, to consultation, and (partially) to FPIC. Most importantly, Bolivia has ratified both ILO Convention 169 and the UNDRIP, which is properly binding in this country. Finally, the 2009 Bolivian Constitution introduced a new system of autonomies, which also foresees the establishment of (territorial) "indigenous native peasant farmer" autonomies, i.e., the *Autonomía Indígena Campesino Originaria* (art.289). In sum, Bolivia provides indigenous peoples a thorough recognition of the proposed *composite right to political participation*. Nevertheless, and regrettably, the implementation of this right is rather poor. It seems that indigenous issues in Bolivia are no longer a priority in President Morales' mandates.[1611]

The following tables aim to display whether and how the international standards regarding the *composite right* are implemented in the Bolivian case on the base of the findings of this chapter. The purpose is to assess how this *composite right* is applied at the Bolivian domestic level and whether it may also become one of the effective applications of the right to self-determination of indigenous peoples in this country. Table 1 regards indigenous peoples' representation in State and local bodies and their participation in domestic decision-making processes (chapter 3, section 3.3.1.3); table 2, the right to consultation (chapter 3, section 3.3.2.2.1) in the three consultation cases discussed above; table 3, the right to FPIC (chapter 3, section 3.3.2.2.2); and, table 4, the standards concerning indigenous autonomy (chapter 3, section 3.3.3.4). Whenever a standard is fully applied, the symbol (√) is used; if the standard is applied only partially, another marker (~) is inserted; if the standard is not implemented at all, the letters NN are written; finally, if one standard is considered not applicable, the letters NA will be found. Also, see the legends and the explanations for each table.

1611 As well as the thorny issue TIPNIS, see the recent investigation of Derrick Hindery, *From Enron to Evo. Pipeline politics Global Environmentalism, and Indigenous Rights in Bolivia*, University of Arizona Press, Tucson, 2013, and, in particular, pp.216-231 in which the author illustrates the contradictions of Morales' governments in relation to environmental issues.

Table 5.1: Standards of indigenous peoples' representation applied in Bolivia

1. Reservation of seats or "quotas" in national and local parliaments, judiciary, other governmental bodies, such as ministries, as well as other public offices	√
2. Recognition of the right for indigenous peoples to form their own political parties	√
3. Lower thresholds for indigenous parties	NA
4. Possibility for indigenous peoples to engage in other political parties to bring forward their agenda	~
5. A proportional electoral system	√
6. Ad hoc parliamentary/local assemblies' procedures, including (various degrees of) the right to veto or, at least, a reinforced enactment procedure	NN
7. Use of indigenous languages in States' acts	√
8. Educational measures on indigenous peoples' cultures for other parliamentary or public staff	NA
9. Creation of specialized governmental bodies with the direct participation of members of indigenous peoples or consultative bodies composed of indigenous representatives with negotiating powers on the decisions likely to affect indigenous peoples	~

Legend
√ = standard applied;
~ = standard applied only partially;
NN = no implementation;
NA = not applicable.

Explanations
Bolivia has implemented points 1, 2, 5 and 7. Points 4 and 9 are only partially applied. The former is due to the still scarce participation of indigenous peoples in other parties. The latter regards the abolition of the Ministry on Indigenous Affairs (MAIPO) and a rather partial and conflicting relation with indigenous movements. Concerns mainly regard point 6, since no special procedure is foreseen when a measure is likely to affect indigenous peoples. In Bolivia, indigenous peoples have resorted to marches. Finally, points 3 and 8 are considered not applicable because the general threshold is low in Bolivia (3%) and educational measures on indigenous peoples' cultures are probably no longer necessary.

Table 5.2: Standards of consultation applied in Bolivia

	Hydrocarbons' exploration in the Ipati-Aquio block (2007)	Hydrocarbons' exploration in the Lliquimuni block (2008)	The Villa Tunari's highway in the Territorio Indígena y Parque Nacional Isiboro-Secure – TIPNIS (2012)
Prior	√	√	NN
Not mere information	~	~	NN
In good faith and at a level of mutual trust	~	NN	NN
Adequate - Completed through indigenous representative institutions	~	~	NN
Adequate - Held within a proper allocation of time	√	NN	NN
Adequate - in a language understandable to indigenous peoples	√	√	~
Systematic and transparent	~	NN	NN
Agreement or consent	~	~	NN

Legend
√ = standard applied;
~ = standard applied only partially.
NN = no implementation;
NA = not applicable.

Explanations
In the first consultation analyzed regarding hydrocarbons' explorations in the Ipati-Aquio block, the standards regarding the right to consultation have been partially applied. Notably, the consultation was conducted prior to the execution of the project and held within a proper allocation of time (5 months). However, indigenous peoples complained of a lack of thorough information, bilateral agreements with some representatives, differences in compensation to the diverse communities, and thus a rather contested final agreement. The case of the Lliquimuni block was worse: Only a few representatives of the settlers' communities were involved; an agreement was reached with them, but ignoring the other concerned indigenous peoples. Finally, the TIPNIS case is the most emblematic. No standards have been respected. This remains one of the thorniest issues in present-day Bolivia.

Table 5.3: Standards of indigenous peoples' FPIC applied in Bolivia

	Hydro-carbons' exploration in the Ipati-Aquio block (2007)	*Hydro-carbons' exploration in the Lliquimuni block (2008)*	*The Villa Tunari highway in the Territorio Indígena y Parque Nacional Isiboro-Secure – TIPNIS (2012)*
No coercion, intimidation or manipulation is directed towards indigenous peoples	NN	NN	NN
Consent is sought sufficiently in advance; this also implies that the FPIC should be sought in phases of assessment, planning, implementation, monitoring, evaluation and closure of a project	~	~	NN
Full information is provided (e.g., nature, size, pace, reversibility and scope of any proposed project or activity; reason(s) or purpose(s) of the project and/or activity; duration; locality of affected areas; preliminary assessment of the likely economic, social, cultural and environmental impact)	NN	NN	NN
Fair and equitable benefit-sharing in a context that respects the precautionary principle	NN	NN	NN

Legend
√ = standard applied;
~ = standard applied only partially;
NN = no implementation;
NA = not applicable.

Explanations
As for the standards of FPIC, no standards have been respected in any of these cases, apart from the timing of it being sought in the two cases of Ipati-Aquio and Lliquimuni, where the consultation was held at the beginning of the explorations.

Table 5.4: Standards of Indigenous Autonomy applied in the case of AIOCs in Bolivia

	Municipality-based AIOCs	*Territorial based (TCOs/TIOCs) AIOCs*
Territory	√	~
Rights over the land and renewable/ non-renewable natural resources	~	~
Customary law and own institutions	√	√
Financial aspects	~	~
Education and culture	~	~

Legend
√ = standard applied;
~ = standard applied only partially;
NN = no recognition, thus no implementation;
NA = not applicable.

Explanations

Although the official recognition and start of the process to implement AIOCs in Bolivia may be considered milestones, these indigenous autonomies face a variety of difficulties in their process of conversion. Additionally, the standards discussed in chapter 3 (section 3.3.3) regarding how an indigenous autonomy should be best organized, are barely met. The most problematic issues regard the non-recognition of their rights over non-renewable natural resources. These are particularly important not only for financial purposes, but also to safeguard their own lands from potentially devastating natural resource exploitation. This is particularly relevant in the case of the deficient application of the rights to consultation and FPIC.

In conclusion, the *composite right to political participation* is broadly recognized in Bolivia –apart from the increasingly undermined right to consultation– but is poorly applied. Although it does embody an expression of the right to self-determination of indigenous peoples, it is neither respected nor implemented in this country. The legal framework extensively guarantees this right, but to ensure its implementation, indigenous peoples have to resort to the strategy of marches. This seems to be the only way to properly negotiate, even with the "indigenous" President Morales. Indigenous peoples have repeatedly requested a meaningful voice in the Bolivian political arena. The implementation of the proposed *composite right to political participation* may thus potentially reduce social tensions and improve the relations between the State and the indigenous peoples. However, this appears to be a distant reality, even in the promising case of Bolivia.

6. The Chilean case

This chapter explores the recognition and application at domestic level of the *composite right to political participation of indigenous peoples* proposed in chapter 3 in the case of Chile. As mentioned in the Introduction and chapter 4, Chile has not yet granted constitutional recognition to the indigenous peoples that live within its borders. Thus, indigenous peoples in Chile enjoy the rights recognized in domestic legislation and more specifically in the so-called Indigenous Law No.19.253 of 1993 (*Ley sobre Protección, Fomento y Desarrollo de los Indígenas*, but mainly known as *Ley Indígena*). However, in 2008 Chile ratified the ILO Convention 169, "Convention concerning Indigenous and Tribal Peoples in Independent Countries" (hereinafter, ILO Convention 169). This prompted a new debate on indigenous rights and a wave of initiatives aimed at further protecting indigenous peoples, with particular regard for their rights to consultation and participation within State bodies. Therefore, after introducing the Chilean context and the latest developments particularly vis-à-vis a number of socio-environmental conflicts and the student protests of 2011 (section 6.1), the legal protection granted to indigenous peoples in Chile is assessed (section 6.2). As in the previous chapter on Bolivia, this analysis then focuses on the rights that enable indigenous peoples to exercise the proposed twofold *composite right to political participation.* Thus, first, initiatives to enhance indigenous peoples' representation in State bodies, including decision-making processes at (mainly) national level, and their rights to consultation and free, prior and informed consent (FPIC) are analysed from 2006 onwards, i.e., from the first mandate of President Bachelet (section 6.3). It needs to be already specified here that indigenous peoples have essentially no chance of participating in State bodies at local level. The few exceptions are the newly created Mapuche Wallmapuwen party and the appointment of half of the board of the National Corporation of Indigenous Development CONADI (*Corporación Nacional de Desarrollo Indígena*; see further in section 6.3.1). Finally, the attempts of indigenous peoples to establish a form of autonomous indigenous territory with two communities in the

South of Chile –as well as the State's opposition to it are tackled (section 6.4).[1612]

6.1 The Chilean context

6.1.1 Data on indigenous peoples in Chile

According to the last 2012 census, Chile has 15,429,749 inhabitants, of which more than 10% self-identified as belonging to one of the nine indigenous peoples recognized in the Indigenous Law (*Ley sobre Protección, Fomento y Desarrollo de los Indígenas*, but mainly known as *Ley Indígena*), Law No.19.253 enacted on 5 October 1993 (see below section 6.2.2). This law recognizes "indigenous ethnicities" or "ethnic groups", namely -according to the ordering inserted in the law– the Mapuche, Aymara and Rapa Nui or *Pascuenses*; the indigenous communities of Atacameñas, Quechuas, Collas and Diaguitas in northern Chile;[1613] and the communities of Kawashkar or Alacalufe and Yámana or Yagán of the austral are (art.1, para.2). In relation to the three first cited indigenous peoples, the Mapuche live predominately in the South in the regions of lakes and volcanos; the Aymara live in the North; and the Rapa Nui on Easter Island, which is situated 3,800 km away from the Chilean coast and geographically forms part of Polynesia.[1614]

In the previous censuses, the percentages were much lower. In 1992, citizens could only choose from three indigenous groups (Mapuche, Aymara or Rapanui).[1615] Despite the narrower range of choice, in comparison to the

1612 Parts of sections 6.1.2.1, 6.1.2.2, 6.1.2.3 and 6.2.2.2 are based on the author's article: Alexandra Tomaselli, "Natural resources" claims, land conflicts and self-empowerment of indigenous movements in the *Cono Sur*. The case of the Mapuche People in Chile", 19(2) *International Journal of Minority and Group Rights (BRILL)* 2012, pp.153-174.

1613 However, the Diaguitas were only recognized as an indigenous group later on, by means of Law No.20,117 of 8 August 2006 that modified para.2 of art.1. *Ley* 20,117, *Reconoce la Existencia y Atributos de la Etnia Diaguita y la Calidad de Indígena Diaguita.*

1614 Pedro Marimán Quemenado, "Chile (2011)", in International Work Group for Indigenous Affairs (IWGIA), *The Indigenous World 2011*, IWGIA, Copenhagen, 2011, pp.211-219, pp.211 and 215.

1615 Chilean National Institute of Statistics/Instituto Nacional de Estadísticas Chile, Comisión Nacional del XVII Censo de Población y de Vivienda, "Síntesis de Resultados", p.23. The question in 1992 was "If you're a Chilean national, do you

following 2002 census, 998,385 on 13,348,401 Chileans at that time, or 7.47% of the total population self-declared as indigenous and belonging to one of the three groups.[1616]

In 2002, Chile registered 15,116,435 inhabitants,[1617] out of which 692,192 persons older than 15 years (i.e., 4.6% of the total population) declared that they belonged to either one of the eight (recognized at that time) indigenous mentioned groups. The question and the options were: "Do you belong to one of the following ethnicities/ethnic groups? Alacalufe or Kawashkar; Atacameño; Aymara; Colla; Mapuche; Quechua; Rapa Nui; Yámana or Yagán".[1618] The change of options in the 2002 census was due to the entering into force of the Indigenous Law. This census was thus the first one to include a wider range of possibilities vis-à-vis the self-recognition and self-identification of indigenous peoples, albeit with many limits.

---

belong to one of these cultures? 1. Mapuche, 2. Aymara, 3. Rapa Nui 4. None of them" (In Spanish "Si usted es chileno ¿se considera perteneciente a alguna de las siguientes culturas? 1. Mapuche, 2. Aymara, 3. Rapa Nui, 4. Ninguna de las Anteriores). Jorge Sanderson Espinoza, "El censo y encuestas territoriales", paper presented at the conference "Pueblos Indigenas y Afrodescendientes de América Latina y el Caribe: Relevancia y pertinencia de la información sociodemográfica para políticas y programas", Economic Commission for Latin America and the Caribbean (ECLAC)/Comisión Económica para América Latina y el Caribe (CEPAL), UN Regional Commission, Santiago de Chile, 27-29 April 2005, p.2, at http://www.ecl ac.org/celade/noticias/paginas/7/21237/JSanderson.pdf [Last access 01.09.2014].

1616 See the table of Mapuche, Aymara and Rapa Nui population in 1992 by Chilean National Institute of Statistics/Instituto Nacional de Estadísticas Chile, "Población Mapuche, Aymara y Rapanui. Censo 1992", 1992, at http://www.in e.cl/canales/chile_estadistico/estadisticas_sociales_culturales/etnias/xls/etnias1992.xls [Last access 01.09.2014].

1617 Chilean National Institute of Statistics/Instituto Nacional de Estadísticas Chile, Comisión Nacional del XVII Censo de Población y de Vivienda, "Síntesis de Resultados", Santiago de Chile, March 2003, p.9, at http://www.ine.cl/cd2002/sin tesiscensal.pdf [Last access 01.09.2014].

1618 The original version in Spanish was "¿Pertenece usted a alguno de los siguientes pueblos originarios o indígenas? 1. Alacalufe (Kawashkar); 2. Atacameño; 3. Aimara; 4. Colla; 5. Mapuche; 6. Quechua; 7. Rapa Nui; 8. Yámana (Yagán); 9. Ninguno de los anteriores". Chilean National Institute of Statistics/Instituto Nacional de Estadísticas Chile, Comisión Nacional del XVII Censo de Población y de Vivienda, "Síntesis de Resultados", pp.23-24. See also Chilean National Institute of Statistics/Instituto Nacional de Estadísticas Chile, Departamento de Atención al Usuario y Difusión Subdepartamento Centro de Documentación, "Manual Censal", [no date], p.8, at http://www.ine.cl/canales/chile_estadisti co/censos_poblacion_vivienda/censo2002/manual_censal/pdf/manualcensal.pdf [Last access 01.09.2014].

For instance, the "Diaguita" group was not included as an option, since it was not recognized until 2006 by Law No.20,117.[1619] Furthermore, the reference to belonging to an ethnicity/ethnic group was considered as belonging to a "different culture" under the topic of "cultural property/belonging" (*Propiedades culturales*).[1620] This may have created confusion and may explain the lower results compared to 1992. The self-identification methodology is widely accepted at international level as seen in chapter 1. Nevertheless, as mentioned in chapter 4, the recognition of indigenous peoples is an extremely delicate issue, as is defining *a priori* who may be indigenous or not, or what indigenous may mean or may have meant along the history. In the case of Chile, many descendants of indigenous peoples may not have self-identified or self-declared indigenous for a number of reasons, including the persistent discrimination they have suffered (see below section 6.1.2).[1621] However, the 2002 data registered the Mapuche as the larger group, i.e., representing 87.31% (or 604,349 people) of the total self-identified indigenous individuals. They were followed by the Aymara at 7.01% (48,501 people) and the Atacameños with 3.04% (21,015 people). The other indigenous peoples were grouped in the remaining 2.64%, as follows: 6,175 Quechuas (0.89%); 4,647 Rapa Nui (0.67%); 3,198 Collas (0.46%); 2,622 Alacalufes or Kawashkar (0.38%); 1,685 Yámanas o Yagánes (0.24%).[1622] According to the data, indigenous peoples are spread throughout Chile.[1623] High percentages of some groups, however, inhabit a determined territory, e.g., 83.9% of the Aymara live in the 1st Region (Tarapacá); 65.9% of the Atacameños in the II Region (Antofagasta); and 33.6% and 30.3% of the Mapuche live, respectively, in the 9th (La Araucanía) and the Metropolitan

---

1619 See note 2 on Law No.20,117.

1620 Chilean National Institute of Statistics/Instituto Nacional de Estadísticas Chile, Departamento de Atención al Usuario y Difusión Subdepartamento Centro de Documentación, "Manual Censal", p.8.

1621 Sanderson Espinoza, "El censo y encuestas territoriales", p.5.

1622 Chilean National Institute of Statistics/Instituto Nacional de Estadísticas Chile, Comisión Nacional del XVII Censo de Población y de Vivienda, "Síntesis de Resultados", p.24.

1623 See the table of the Chilean population belonging to an indigenous people by Chilean National Institute of Statistics/Instituto Nacional de Estadísticas Chile, "Población por sexo, según pertenencia a pueblos originarios o indígenas, Censo 2002", at http://www.ine.cl/canales/chile_estadistico/estadisticas_sociales_culturales/etnias/xls/etnia2002.xls [Last access 01.09.2014].

Regions (Santiago Metropolitan – RM).[1624] Compared to non-indigenous citizens, indigenous peoples are more likely to inhabit rural areas, [1625] are younger and have a lower life expectancy,[1626] have a higher level of analphabetism,[1627] and have a lower level of (standard, i.e., non-indigenous) education.[1628] Nevertheless, indigenous peoples in Chile are more economically active, since out of the 50.4% economically active indigenous peoples (i.e., employed or actively seeking employment), 84.6% of them are employed, 2% more than the non-indigenous population.[1629] The indigenous group with the highest employment rate is the Alacalufe or Kawashkar in the North (61.8% on the total population self-declared as such). The highest unemployment rate is found, instead, among the Mapuche (49.8%).[1630] As

1624 Chilean National Institute of Statistics/Instituto Nacional de Estadísticas Chile, Comisión Nacional del XVII Censo de Población y de Vivienda, "Síntesis de Resultados", p.24.

1625 Chilean National Institute of Statistics/Instituto Nacional de Estadísticas Chile, "Hojas Informativas. Estadísticas Sociales Pueblos Indígenas en Chile. Censo 2002", p.1, at http://www.ine.cl/canales/chile_estadistico/estadisticas_sociales_culturales/etnias/pdf/info_etniascenso2002.pdf [Last access 01.09.2014]. However, the majority of indigenous peoples are concentrated in urban contexts. Chilean National Institute of Statistics/Instituto Nacional de Estadísticas Chile, "Hojas Informativas. Estadísticas Sociales Pueblos Indígenas en Chile. Censo 2002", p.2.

1626 The majority of indigenous peoples are between 10 and 40 years old. Chilean National Institute of Statistics/Instituto Nacional de Estadísticas Chile, "Hojas Informativas. Estadísticas Sociales Pueblos Indígenas en Chile. Censo 2002", p.2.

1627 The percentage of analphabetism among indigenous peoples of over 10 years of age in 2002 was 8.2%. Chilean National Institute of Statistics/Instituto Nacional de Estadísticas Chile, "Hojas Informativas. Estadísticas Sociales Pueblos Indígenas en Chile. Censo 2002", p.4.

1628 29.8%, of indigenous peoples have a high school diploma and 7.9% have a University degree, Chilean National Institute of Statistics/Instituto Nacional de Estadísticas Chile, "Hojas Informativas. Estadísticas Sociales Pueblos Indígenas en Chile. Censo 2002", p.5.

1629 Chilean National Institute of Statistics/Instituto Nacional de Estadísticas Chile, "Hojas Informativas. Estadísticas Sociales Pueblos Indígenas en Chile. Censo 2002", p.5. See also Ninoska Damianovic Camacho, *Estadísticas Sociales de los pueblos indígenas en Chile. Censo 2002*, Chilean National Institute of Statistics/Instituto Nacional de Estadísticas Chile, Santiago de Chile, 2005, p.98, at http://www.ine.cl/canales/chile_estadistico/estadisticas_sociales_culturales/etnias/pdf/estadisticas_indigenas_2002_11_09_09.pdf [Last access 01.09.2014].

1630 Chilean National Institute of Statistics/Instituto Nacional de Estadísticas Chile, "Hojas Informativas. Estadísticas Sociales Pueblos Indígenas en Chile. Censo 2002", p.5; Damianovic Camacho, *Estadísticas Sociales de los pueblos indígenas*

for the economic activities, 20.2% of indigenous peoples work in the agriculture, cattle, hunting, forestry, and fishing sectors,[1631] another 16% in commercial activities[1632] and 11.2%, mainly women, in domestic service (e.g., housecleaning, child care, gardening, etc.).[1633]

In the last 2012 census, the data have changed substantially. The total number of self-identified indigenous peoples, this time over 5 years of age, has risen to 11.11%, i.e., 1,714,677 people out the total Chilean population, which amounts to 15,429,759.[1634] The overall increase in numbers may be due to the inclusion of children between 5-14 years, but most probably to the progress made over the last years vis-à-vis indigenous rights. The question of whether someone belongs to an indigenous people or not contemplated more possible answers this time, thus including the Diaguita people or "other".[1635] This may also be due to the consultations that the organizing census committee carried out with selected stakeholders, included certain indigenous communities.[1636] The higher percentage regards the Mapuche people (84.11%; 1,442,215 people), followed by the Aymara (6.25%; 107,167 people), Other (4.63%; 79,389 people), Diaguita (2.53%; 43,381 people), Quechua (0.76%; 13,032), Colla (0.75%; 12,860 people), Rapa Nui (0.46%; 7,887 people), Likan Antai (called "Atacameños" in 2002; 0.33%; 5,658 people), Yagán o Yámana (0.07%; 1,200 people), and another 0.10%

---

en Chile. Censo 2002, p.99. The larger composition of the Mapuche group compared to the Alacalufe or Kawashkar, which included, as mentioned, just 2,622 self-identified people, is worth noting.

1631 Damianovic Camacho, *Estadísticas Sociales de los pueblos indígenas en Chile. Censo 2002*, p.109.

1632 *Ibid.*

1633 *Ibid.*, p.110. For other data, see the table in Damianovic Camacho, *Estadísticas Sociales de los pueblos indígenas en Chile. Censo 2002*, p.109.

1634 Chilean National Institute of Statistics/Instituto Nacional de Estadísticas Chile, "Síntesis de Resultados. Censo 2012", 2013, p.11, at http://www.iab.cl/wp-content/themes/IAB/download.php?archivo=11803%7Cresumencenso_2012.pdf [Last access 01.09.2014].

1635 Chilean National Institute of Statistics/Instituto Nacional de Estadísticas Chile, "Síntesis de Resultados. Censo 2012", p.11. The other novelty of this census was the question regarding religion with answers including indigenous religions (*Espiritualidad Indígena*), although the numbers were quite low (14,570 persons). Chilean National Institute of Statistics/Instituto Nacional de Estadísticas Chile, "Síntesis de Resultados. Censo 2012", p.15.

1636 David Bravo et al., "Informe final. Comisión Externa Revisora del CENSO 2012", 2013, pp.11-12, para.21, at http://www.censo.cl/documentos/informe_final-comision-nacional.pdf [Last access 01.09.2014].

that did not specify anything ("Ignored", 17,147 people).[1637] Therefore, in comparison to 2002, although some indigenous peoples, such as the Mapuche or the Aymara, have slightly decreased in percentage, their absolute number have more than doubled (e.g., the Mapuche increased from 604,349 to 1,442,215 persons and the Aymara from 48,501 to 107,167 persons). The Quechua and the Rapa Nui have also roughly doubled in number, while the Collas have quadrupled. Solely the Yagán o Yámana have substantially decreased in number by more than 400 persons, while the drastic decrease in the number of Likan Antai/Atacameños is most probably due to the change in the use of their name. This would also explain why there are so many replies stating "Other" as well as the 0.10% that did not specify any particular people. These figures may also refer to indigenous peoples migrating from neighboring countries that may have settled in Chile over the last ten years. Indeed, the multiple choices to the question erroneously included nationalities (e.g., Bolivian, German, etc.) or other references such as to the Afro-descendants. This may have created further confusion.[1638] Nevertheless, even detracting the approximately 100,000 persons of the "Other" and "Ignored" categories, the number of indigenous peoples remain extremely high (i.e., approx. 1,600,500). Lastly, similarly to 2002, the concentration of indigenous peoples is greater in the (new) northern 15th Arica y Parinacota region (28.87%)[1639] and in the southern 9th La Araucanía region (31.58%). However, the neighboring regions to the 9th, i.e., the (new) 14th region Los Ríos and the 10th region Los Lagos also register a high percentage of indigenous peoples (23.10% and 22.75%, respectively).[1640] These are the regions traditionally inhabited by the Mapuche people. In the North, the 3rd region (Atacama) also sees a substantial presence of indigenous peoples (13.53%). In the very south, the 12th (Aysén del General Carlos Ibáñez del Campo) and 13th (Magallanes y de la Antártica Chilena) regions also record

---

1637 Chilean National Institute of Statistics/Instituto Nacional de Estadísticas Chile, "Síntesis de Resultados. Censo 2012", p.11.

1638 David Bravo et al., "Informe final. Comisión Externa Revisora del CENSO 2012", p.36, para.106.

1639 There were 13 regions of Chile, according to art.1 of the Law Decree No.575 of 13 July 1974 (*Regionalización del País*). The new 14th region of "Los Ríos" in the South (including the city of Valdivia) and the 15th region of "Arica y Parinacota" in the very North of Chile were created solely in 2007 by Laws No.20.174/2007 and No.20.175/2007, respectively. This is why they did not appear in the 2002 census.

1640 Chilean National Institute of Statistics/Instituto Nacional de Estadísticas Chile, "Síntesis de Resultados. Censo 2012", p.11.

relevant numbers of indigenous peoples, i.e., 23.85% and 18.74%, respectively. The other regions register percentages below 10%, including the Metropolitan region of the capital Santiago with 9.29%.[1641] As to poverty rates, the Chilean survey on the socio-economic situation of the country "CASEN" (*Encuesta de Caracterización Socioeconómica Nacional*) of 2011 registered a general decrease in poverty among the Chilean population over the last 15 years. However, the poverty rates of indigenous peoples remains high (20%, i.e., one in every five) and 5% higher than other sectors of Chilean society.[1642] Finally, the illiteracy rates regarding indigenous peoples are also worrying. As seen, the majority of indigenous peoples live in rural areas, where the average years of education is just 8 (thus, up to 14 years of age), in comparison to 11 in the urban areas.[1643] Other sources affirm that the illiteracy rates result double in comparison with the rest of the population.[1644]

6.1.2 The "other" history of Chile, indigenous peoples' land dispossession and recent social unrest

This section aims to give an overview of the "other" (i.e., from the indigenous perspective) history of Chile, by highlighting the dispossession of the lands that indigenous peoples have suffered since the *Conquista*, as well as both before and after Pinochet's dictatorship. Many historical events are only briefly mentioned here. In particular, since they do not fall under the scope of this study, Pinochet's dictatorship and the Chilean democratic transition are briefly tackled solely in connection to indigenous issues.[1645] Fi-

---

1641 *Ibid.*

1642 Chilean Ministry of Social Development/Ministerio de Desarrollo Social, "CASEN 2011. Encuesta de Caracterización Socioeconómica Nacional. Indicadores de Pobreza", 2011, p.14, at http://observatorio.ministeriodesarrolloso cial.gob.cl/layout/doc/casen/pobreza_casen_2011.pdf [Last access 11.08.2014].

1643 Chilean survey Chilean Ministry of Social Development/Ministerio de Desarrollo Social, "Encuesta CASEN 2011. Módulo Educación", 2011, p.2, at http://observatorio.ministeriodesarrollosocial.gob.cl/layout/doc/casen/2013_04_01_Educacion_CASEN_2011.pdf [Last access 11.08.2014].

1644 Pedro Marimán Quemenado, "Chile (2012)", in International Work Group for Indigenous Affairs (IWGIA), *The Indigenous World 2012*, IWGIA, Copenhagen, 2012, pp.204-213, p.204.

1645 For an overview of Pinochet's dictatorship and Chile's democratic transition see, *inter alia*, Mark Ensalaco, *Chile Under Pinochet: Recovering the Truth*, University

nally, this section also addresses the recent social unrest that has characterized the country particularly from 2010 onwards. In particular, the current developments in Chile, also vis-à-vis indigenous peoples, cannot be understood without taking into account the social change that the Chilean society has experienced since the outburst of the students' mobilization, which is analyzed in section 6.1.2.4.

6.1.2.1 Introduction

Since the Spaniards and the Chilean non-indigenous colonizers took control over the territory that today forms Chile, indigenous peoples' access to land and natural resources was drastically reduced. Chile still fails to find a fair balance, despite the adoption of the Indigenous Law in 1993 and the procedure of land acquisitions for indigenous peoples. As seen in chapter 3, land rights imply many aspects, in particular: Land ownership and/or use; the right to natural resources, especially the right to water; and the right to environmental protection and conservation. These aspects are particularly relevant in a country where the few recognized indigenous territories are constantly faced with a high density of hydro-electric plants,[1646] mainly in the

of Pennsylvania Press, Philadelphia, 2000, and Paul W. Drake and Ivan Jaksic (eds.), *The Struggle for Democracy in Chile*, University of Nebraska Press, revised edition, Lincoln NE, 1995.

1646 James Anaya, "Informe del Relator Especial sobre la situación de los derechos humanos y las libertades fundamentales de los indígenas", Human Rights Council, UN Doc. A/HRC/12/34/Add.6, p.13, 5 October 2009, para. 35; Marzia Rosti, "Reparations for Indigenous Peoples in Two Selected Latin American Countries", in Federico Lenzerini, *Reparations for Indigenous Peoples: International and Comparative Perspectives*, Oxford University Press, 2008, pp.345-362, pp.359-360.

South,[1647] and mines,[1648] particularly in the North,[1649] a disproportionate forest exploitation due to pine and eucalyptus plantations and logging exploitation,[1650] artificial salmon farming,[1651] and an increasing tourist industry.[1652]

The problematic aspect of land ownership and use of natural resources was highlighted in both reports of the Special Rapporteur's visits to Chile. In 2004, Rodolfo Stavenhagen underlined the slow and underfunded procedure for land re-distribution; the lack of the right to return to former communal land; the over-exploitation of lands granted to indigenous peoples; and the controversial recognition of water rights.[1653]

1647 José Aylwin and Hernando Silva, "Chile", in International Work Group for Indigenous Affairs (IWGIA), *The Indigenous World 2014*, IWGIA, Copenhagen, 2014, pp.203-213, p.208.

1648 Victor Toledo Llancaqueo, "Tierra Mapuche y Concesiones Mineras. El case de Rucañanco, Lago Lleu Lleu", *Centro de Políticas Públicas y Derechos Indígenas*, 2006, at www.politicaspublicas.net/panel/mineria/372-tierras-mapuches-y-concesiones-mineras.html [Last access 01.09.2014]; Hernando Silva Neriz, "Chile", in International Work Group for Indigenous Affairs (IWGIA), *The Indigenous World 2013*, IWGIA, Copenhagen, 2013, pp.188-196, p.193; Aylwin and Silva, "Chile", p.208; Rosti, "Reparations for Indigenous Peoples in Two Selected Latin American Countries", pp.359-360.

1649 Marimán Quemenado, "Chile (2011)", p.217; Rosti, "Reparations for Indigenous Peoples in Two Selected Latin American Countries", pp.359-360.

1650 Both species are not native and have damaged the soil by tree resin and erosion. José Aylwin, "The Ralco Dam and the Pehuenche People in Chile: Lessons from an Ethno-Environmental Conflict", Paper presented at the Conference "Towards Adaptive Conflict Resolution: Lessons From Canada and Chile", Centre for the Study of Global Issues, University of British Columbia, Vancouver, Canada, 25-27 September 2002, p. 4. See also Rodolfo Stavenhagen, "Report of the Special Rapporteur on the situation of human rights and fundamental freedoms of indigenous people, submitted in accordance with Commission resolution 2003/56. Addendum, Mission to Chile", Commission of Human Rights, Sixtieth session, 17 November 2003, UN Doc. E/CN.4/2004/80/Add.3, p.9, para. 19a; and Silva Neriz, "Chile", p.191.

1651 Aylwin and Silva, "Chile", p.208; John Soluri, "Chile's Blue Revolution, Commodity Diseases, and the Problem of Sustainability", 46 *Latin America Research Review* (LARR) 2011, pp.55-81, p.75; Paolo Moiola, "Ecosistema marino depredado", 18.06.2014, *Noticias Aliadas*, at http://www.noticias aliadas.org/articles.asp?art=7030 [Last Access 06.09.2014].

1652 This is particularly evident in the case of Easter Island, but it is also the case of Mapuche communities living close to the Andes in the south, e.g., the well-known winter resort of Pucón, in the Araucanía region.

1653 Rodolfo Stavenhagen, "Report of the Special Rapporteur on the situation of human rights and fundamental freedoms of indigenous people, submitted in accordance

In 2009, James Anaya underlined the problematic construction of hydroelectric plants and other environmentally hazardous projects on indigenous peoples' lands (see section 6.1.2 below);[1654] the absent water rights;[1655] and, in a specific section, the issue of Mapuche land occupations followed by police repression.[1656] Furthermore, he stressed the need to adopt a procedure for the recognition of traditionally occupied land,[1657] an aspect also emphasized during the fifth human rights periodic review of Chile[1658] and formally guaranteed by the Indigenous Law (art.12.2). In fact, it is now estimated that, until 2009, 657,520ha had been bought and distributed to indigenous peoples by the National Corporation of Indigenous Development CONADI (*Corporación Nacional de Desarrollo Indígena*; see further in section 6.3.1).[1659] However, the procedure to apply to the fund for land acquisition was confusing and the land prices increased speculatively, which caused a delay in the restitution process.[1660] For instance, in 1998, 15,000ha

with Commission resolution 2003/56. Addendum, Mission to Chile", p. 2, and paras. 19-27.

1654 Anaya, "Informe del Relator Especial sobre la situación de los derechos humanos y las libertades fundamentales de los indígenas", paras. 33-35.

1655 *Ibid.*, paras. 36-37.

1656 *Ibid.*, paras. 40-47. The delays and the incompliance with Indigenous Law, art.63 on land rights' recognition of the northern indigenous peoples (Aimara, Atacameñas, Quechuas, Collas y Diaguita) (para.30) was mentioned; the ignored Chiloe Island's claim over their land according to the 1826 Tratado de Tantauco (para.31) was also mentioned.

1657 Anaya, "Informe del Relator Especial sobre la situación de los derechos humanos y las libertades fundamentales de los indígenas", para. 25.

1658 HRC, "Concluding observations of the Human Rights Committee: Chile", UN Doc. CCPR/C/CHL/CO/5, 18 May 2007, para. 19.

1659 Anaya, "Informe del Relator Especial sobre la situación de los derechos humanos y las libertades fundamentales de los indígenas", para. 24. However, apparently, not all the returned land was profitable. More than 40 per cent of the lands bought between 2000 and 2005 and given to indigenous peoples were barely fertile. In addition, the property over part of these lands was contested or, sometimes, even claimed as belonging to other indigenous communities. Victor Toledo Llancaqueo, "Presupuesto del Sector Público y Políticas Indígenas. Chile 1994- 2008", *Documentos de Politicas Públicas y Derechos Indígenas – Informe N° 36*, Santiago de Chile, 28 October 2007, p. 4. Please note that, *e.g.*, the Arauco-Angelini and CMPC-Grupo Matte forest companies own about 1.000.000ha and 700.000ha, respectively. Mapuexpress, "Chile: El Doble discurso Presidencial en Materia Indígena", 30.06.2010, at http://www.mapuexpress.net/content/news/print.php?id=5734 [Last access 01.09.2014].

1660 Rodolfo Stavenhagen, "Report of the Special Rapporteur on the situation of human rights and fundamental freedoms of indigenous people, submitted in accordance with Commission resolution 2003/56. Addendum, Mission to Chile", para. 20.

were under dispute among 473 families.[1661] Furthermore, the CONADI still applies a restrictive interpretation of the Indigenous Law provisions on indigenous land protection and re-distribution (arts.12-22), considering only those requests based on pre-dictatorship property titles.[1662] However, as will be mentioned below, many of these titles were in fact revoked under the dictatorship. Lastly, the CONADI tends to not make proper use of the available funds. During the 2010 administration, of 158 million dollars of Land Funds, approximately 100 million were returned to the Treasury due to a lack of implementation of the planned actions, mostly due to incomplete land purchases.[1663] This negative trend continued and in 2011 the budget for land acquisitions was reduced by 16%.[1664] It was never increased afterwards.[1665] Conversely, the proportion of lands in the hands of private owners and companies is extremely high.[1666] The historical land dispossession suffered by indigenous peoples in Chile and the failed attempts to provide indigenous peoples with a coherent legal protection has fuelled a number of internal socio-environmental conflicts particularly in recent years. Protests and land occupations, particularly by Mapuche people, increasingly gave way to violent repression by the police.[1667] The most recent and symbolic episodes are reported in section 6.1.2.3.

1661 David Carruthers and Patricia Rodriguez, "Mapuche Protest, Environmental Conflict and Social Movement Linkage in Chile", 30(4) *Third World Quarterly* 2009, pp.743-760, p.749.

1662 Aylwin and Silva, "Chile", p.207.

1663 Marimán Quemenado, "Chile (2011)", p.212.

1664 Marimán Quemenado, "Chile (2012)", p.207.

1665 Aylwin and Silva, "Chile", p.207.

1666 See supra note 48 on the quality of returned land.

1667 In 2008 and 2009, two Mapuche youngsters were shot by *Carabineros* during these occupations, namely Matías Valentín Catrileo Quezada and Jaime Facundo Mendoza Collio. See, inter alia, El Ciudadano, "Muerte de Matías Catrileo Quezada: Estado policial en zona Mapuche", 3 March 2008, at www.elciudadano.cl/2008/03/11/muerte-de-matias-catrileo-quezada-estado-policial-en-zona-mapuche; Elías Paillan, "Jaime Facundo Mendoza Collio, de 24 años, es mapuche asesinado por carabineros", 12 August 2009, *El Ciudadano*, at http://www.elciudadano.cl/2009/08/12/10262/mapuche-asesinado-por-carabineros-seria-jaime-facundo-mendoza-collio-de-24-anos. The police agent who shot Matías Valentín Catrileo Quezada was not sentenced to prison, but only to probation. El Mostrador, "Corte Marcial lo condenó a tres años y un día pero con el beneficio de la libertad vigilada. Carabinero que asesinó a Matías Catrileo no irá a la cárcel", 19 August 2010, at www.elmostrador.cl/noticias/pais/2010/08/19/cara binero-que-asesino-a-matias-catrileo-no-ira-a-la-carcel [Last access to all websites 01.09.2014].

6.1.2.2 Indigenous peoples' historical land dispossession

The current territory which composes Chile has been occupied and colonized by Spaniards at different times. Although the foundation of Chile is dated at 1810, not all the territories were then controlled by the (new) Chileans (see below). For instance, the current Aymara and Atacameños peoples living in the northern territories of Arica, Iquique, Antofagasta, Calama, and Pozo Almonte were annexed to Chile after the Pacific Wars of 1879-1884, after which Bolivia lost access to the sea.[1668]

The Mapuche and the Rapa Nui "other" (i.e., from their perspective) histories are particularly enlightening on the colonizers' repression and land dispossessions vis-à-vis indigenous peoples in Chile. In the native language *Mapudungun*, the word Mapuche means "people of the land" (Mapu=land; Che=people),[1669] while Rapa Nui indicates inhabitants of the on the Eastern Island or *Te Pito o Te Henua* in their language, which signifies "the centre of the world".[1670]

As for colonization, only in 1540 was the Spaniard condottiere Pedro de Valdivia able to cross the Atacama Desert with a few solders and (indigenous) slaves.[1671] The capital city of Santiago was thus founded by Valdivia

---

1668 Hans Gudermann, "Las poblaciones indígenas andinas de Chile y la experiencia de la ciudadanía", in Hans Gudermann, Rolf Foester and Jorge Iván Vergara (eds.), *Mapuches y Aymaras. El debate entorno al Reconocimiento y los Derechos Colectivos*, RIL Editores, Santiago de Chile, Buenos Aires, 2003, pp.19-104, pp.43-44. Bolivia has recently made a claim against Chile before the International Court of Justice to regain access to the Pacific coast. The case (*Obligation to Negotiate Access to the Pacific Ocean (Bolivia v. Chile)*) is still pending. Last 16 July 2014, Chile raised a preliminary objection to the jurisdiction of the Court, to which Bolivia can reply until 14 November 2014. See the developments of the case at http://www.icj-cij.org/docket/index.php?p1=3&p2=1&case=153 [Last access 02.09.2014].

1669 Lorenzo Nesti, "The Mapuche-Pehuenche and the Ralco Dam on the Bíobío River: the Challenge of Protecting Indigenous Land Rights', 9 *International Journal on Minority and Group Rights* 2002, pp. 1-40, p.2

1670 Marimán Quemenado, "Chile (2011)", p.215.

1671 Osvaldo Silva G., *Atlas de Historia de Chile*, Editorial Universitaria, Santiago de Chile, 1983, p.34. Previously, the attempt of Diego de Almagro between 1535 and 1537 had failed mainly because of the harsh traveling and environmental conditions. After having reached Copiapó by passing the Andean mountains, Almagro returned to Cuzco in 1537 to capture the Pizarro brothers with the aim of being entitled the new Governor of New Toledo, but he was eventually defeated and put to death. Silva G., *Atlas de Historia de Chile*, p.32.

and his soldiers in 1541 after clashes with (indigenous) Diaguita.[1672] The historical border with the Inca Empire was the Maule River.[1673] In this area there were Mapuches-Picunches (or people of the North) who were subject to the Inca empire, but they decreased in number drastically after the *Conquista*.[1674] The first clash with the peoples, whom nowadays we also call Mapuche, followed in 1546.[1675] In particular, many happenings are bound to the historical and legendary figure of Lautaro, a Mapuche child that grew up as slave under the Spaniards and then escaped. He learned the Spaniards' strategies and, in particular, the horse riding: The indigenous peoples of the south had never seen them before the *Conquista* and were thus afraid of them. *Inter alia*, Lautaro leaded thousands of warriors against the Spaniards in 1553 and defeated Valdivia.[1676] The Mapuche continued to fiercely resist the occupation until 1641, when a peace treaty was signed between the Spaniards and the Mapuche after the meeting known as *Parlamento de Quilín* or *Quillín*. In particular, in exchange for the respect of the border of the Bío-Bío River and their freedom, the Mapuche were formally nominated "subjects" of the Spanish Crown and missionaries were allowed to enter

1672 Silva G., *Atlas de Historia de Chile*, p.34. In particular, among Pedro de Valdivia's retinue, there was a lady, Inés Suárez, who apparently decapitated seven indigenous prisoners in an attempt to defend Santiago from an attack in September 1541, on one occasion when Valdivia was absent. This eventually helped in keeping the control over Santiago. Silva G., *Atlas de Historia de Chile*, p.34.

1673 Nesti, "The Mapuche-Pehuenche and the Ralco Dam on the Bíobío River …", p.4.

1674 José Bengoa, *Historia del Pueblo Mapuche Siglo XIX y XX*, LOM Ediciones, Santiago de Chile, 2000, p.20.

1675 *Ibid.*, p.34. The Mapuche living in the current provinces of Valdivia, Osorno and Llanquihue were known as Huilliche and apparently particularly warrior-like. Bengoa, *Historia del Pueblo Mapuche Siglo XIX y XX*, p.21. In fact, before colonization, the Toltén river was roughly the border of two indigenous groups, namely the Mapuches and the Huilliches. Further south, the Maullín river defined the southern border of the Huilliche territory, who were known as Juncos. Maria Ximena Urbina Carrasco, *La Frontera de Arriba en Chile Colonial, Interacción hispano-indígena en el territorio entre Valdivia y Chiloé e imaginario de sus bordes geográficos, 1600-1800*, Pontificia Universidad Católica de Valparaíso, Valparaíso, Snatiago de Chile, 2009, p.23. Thus, in colonial times there were the above-mentioned Picunches living in the area of Maule, the Mapuche between the Bío-Bío and Toltén rivers, the Huilliches sourthern than the Toltén river till Maullín River. Further, they were subdivided into other peoples, as follows: Puelche in the east; Lafquenche in the western Pacific coast; Pehuenche in the area of Bío-Bío river; Waidefche, in the Andes; and Ranquilche in the centre. Nesti, "The Mapuche-Pehuenche and the Ralco Dam on the Bíobío River ...", p.4.

1676 Silva G., *Atlas de Historia de Chile*, p.40.

their territory to "Christianize" them.[1677] The following Parliaments of Negrete (1726) and Tepihue (1738) confirmed the border and the independence of the Mapuche people.[1678] However, colonizers who were descendants of Europeans or new settlers in Chile spontaneously started to occupy lands that were south of the Bío-Bío River.[1679] For instance, by 1850, at the coast of the present-day 9th region, there were 14,000 Spanish descendants or people living and cropping the land. This was an immense number in comparison to the estimated 1,600 indigenous peoples living at that time in the same (vast) territory.[1680] Thus, the State started to enact a series of acts trying to regulate both the "colonization" and the non-indigenous presence over such territories.[1681] Nevertheless, de facto, the territories south of the Bío-Bío watercourse were administered mainly according to the abovementioned treaties until the civil war of 1859.[1682] Afterwards, violent fights between the Chilean militias and the Mapuche inhabitants concluded with the military occupancy of Araucanía in 1881,[1683] sealed in 1883 with the artificial Peace of Araucanía of Villarrica (*Pacificación de la Araucanía*).[1684] Between 1884 and 1919, about 80,000 Mapuche people were confined in roughly 3,000 reserves (*Reducciones*), corresponding to circa

---

1677 See Laura Giraudo, *La questione indigena in America Latina*, p. 23; Bengoa, *Historia del Pueblo Mapuche Siglo XIX y XX*, p. 38. See also C. Contreras Panemal, "Los Parlamentos", in C. Contreras Panemal (ed.), *Actas del Primer Congreso Internacional de Historia Mapuche. Congreso Internacional de Historia Mapuche*, Eigenverlag, Siegen, 2003, pp.59-61, and note 26, in which the author cites Tomás Guevara, *Chile Prehispanico*, Universidad de Chile, Ediciones Balcells, Santiago de Chile, 1925, p. 373.

1678 Bengoa, *Historia del Pueblo Mapuche Siglo XIX y XX*, pp.39-40. Other "Parliaments" were held in 1651, 1683, 1693-94, 1712, 1726, 1738, 1746, 1756, 1760, 1764, 1771, 1774, 1784, 1787, 1793, 1803 and 1816. Alamiro de Avila Martel, "Régimen jurídico de la guerra de Arauco", III Congreso del Instituto Internacional de Historia del Derecho Indiano, Instituto Internacional de Estudios Jurídicos, Madrid, 1973 as cited by José Aylwin, *Tierra y territorio mapuche: un análisis desde una mirada històrico jurídica*, Proyecto Mapu Territorialidad, Instituto de Estudios Indígenas, Universidad de la Frontera, Temuco, 2002, p. 3, note 4, at http://200.10.23.169/trabajados/tierra_jose_aylwin.pdf [Last access 02.09.2014].

1679 José Aylwin, *Estudio sobre Tierras Indígenas de la Araucanía: Antecedentes Históricos Legislativos (1850-1920)*, Instituto de Estudios Indígenas, Universidad de la Frontera, Temuco, 1995, p.4.

1680 *Ibid.*, p.6.

1681 *Ibid.*, p.10.

1682 Bengoa, *Historia del Pueblo Mapuche Siglo XIX y XX*, p.153.

1683 *Ibid.*, pp.207-323.

1684 *Ibid.*, pp.325-326.

475,000ha,[1685] i.e., about 5% of the territory that they originally occupied.[1686] A further 40,000 Mapuche people were not re-accommodated in the *Reducciones* and had to find other lodgings.[1687] This confinement was facilitated by the Mapuche's unawareness of the concept of individual property rights, which was then unknown in their culture.[1688] This process caused a rupture within the Mapuche society, especially with regard to their traditional hierarchies and solidarity, since they were relocated arbitrarily.[1689] Furthermore, the State supported a number of "colonizations" of lands in the Araucanía, e.g., by granting land in concession to small enterprises thanks to other legislation enacted in 1874[1690] or later by "importing" foreign settlers "in good health" and able to crop the land for at least 6 years into this area (Supreme Decree of 10 October 1882).[1691] Despite the opposition of the Mapuche deputies and other leaders belonging to the "Sociedad Caopolicán Defensora de la Araucanía",[1692] founded in Temuco in 1911, Decree No.266 of 1931 explicitly stated that land partition was necessary to finally include indigenous peoples in "civilization".[1693] Before the agrarian reform of the 1960s, a further 25% of Mapuche land was absorbed by a number of colonizers, who entered unlawfully the land assigned to them

1685 *Ibid*., p.355. The Bío-Bío River roughly divides Chile into two equal parts, each of them amounting to approximately 35 million hectares. Thus, the Mapuche, who previously controlled at least 10 million hectares (down to Puerto Montt), were confined to just half a million hectares .

1686 Marzia Rosti, "Reparations for Indigenous Peoples in Two Selected Latin American Countries", p.357.

1687 Bengoa, *Historia del Pueblo Mapuche Siglo XIX y XX*, p. 356.

1688 Nesti, "The Mapuche-Pehuenche and the Ralco Dam on the Bíobío River ...", p. 4.

1689 Bengoa, *Historia del Pueblo Mapuche Siglo XIX y XX*, pp. 361–362.

1690 Aylwin, *Estudio sobre Tierras Indígenas de la Araucanía*, p.49. For instance, 50,000ha in the area of Lumaco were given to the "Nueva Italia" firm, but they created a de facto village (Capitán Pastene which still exists), and in 1908 obtained the definitive property title over 7,537ha. Aylwin, *Estudio sobre Tierras Indígenas de la Araucanía*, p.50. Other methods to "colonize" Araucanía were by promoting "national" non-indigenous colonization, military officials, creating new villages, and creating ad hoc legislation legitimizing their property titles. Aylwin, *Estudio sobre Tierras Indígenas de la Araucanía*, p. 51-54 and p.62 ff.

1691 Aylwin, *Estudio sobre Tierras Indígenas de la Araucanía*, p.46. By 1890, 7,120 foreigners settled in the traditional areas of Mapuche people in the present-day IX region. Aylwin, *Estudio sobre Tierras Indígenas de la Araucanía*, p.47.

1692 Bengoa, *Historia del Pueblo Mapuche Siglo XIX y XX*, pp.384-386. On the Mapuche deputies see section 6.3.1.

1693 Rosti, "Reparations for Indigenous Peoples in Two Selected Latin American Countries", p.357.

and enlarged their properties bit by bit, then seeking the legitimization of their occupations in early 1900.[1694]

With regard to the Rapa Nui, the original inhabitants of the Eastern Island are descendants of peoples that occupied the island probably around 30 AD, most probably coming from the Marquesas Islands of the French Polynesia.[1695] The island takes the name from the first (documented) European visit of the Dutch navigator Jacob Roggeween, who disembarked on the island on Easter Day of 1722.[1696] During the 18th century only three more European vessels visited the island,[1697] but their frequency increased dramatically during the 19th century. The saddest events regard the "slave expeditions" to the island after the 1823 ban on the transportation of slaves from Africa. Between 1864 and the 1877, the Rapa Nui decreased from 2,000 to 111 people.[1698] Meanwhile, missionaries arrived on the islands and in 1868 the French merchant Jean Baptiste Onésime Dutroux-Bornier (also known as "Pitopito") "bought" a considerable area of land from the indigenous peoples by doubtful means (e.g., making contracts with children, etc.). Moreover, the Rapa Nui did not realize that they were giving away their lands "forever", as a traditional system of shared land utilisation was in use.[1699] The island was then declared annexed to Chile in 1888 by the signature of the Agreement of Wills between the navy captain Policarpo Toro, who represented the State of Chile and the Rapa Nui king Atamu Tekena.[1700] According to this treaty, the Rapa Nui were guaranteed ownership of their ancestral land.[1701] However, since then, the lands were controlled and given in concession by the Chilean State without considering any claims of the Rapa Nui people.[1702] The whole island was registered as part of the Chilean State at the Valparaiso Recorder of Deeds in 1933 as vacant lands (*terra nullius*) according to the then art.590 of the Civil

1694 Bengoa, *Historia del Pueblo Mapuche Siglo XIX y XX*, p. 374.

1695 Susana Rochna Ramirez, *La Propriedad de la Tierra en la Isla de Pascua*, CONADI, AECID, Santiago de Chile, 1996, p.16.

1696 Rochna Ramirez 1996, p.18.

1697 *Ibid.*, p.19.

1698 *Ibid.*, pp.20-21.

1699 *Ibid.*, pp.22-25. The titles of land properties also gave rise to a number of inheritance cases before courts in France and Tahiti, with little respect for the Rapa Nui claims. Rochna Ramirez, *La Propriedad de la Tierra en la Isla de Pascua*, p.25.

1700 Clem Chartier, Alberto Chirif and Nin Tomas, *The Human Rights of the Rapa Nui People on Easter Island*, Observatorio Ciudadano and International Work Group for Indigenous Affairs (IWGIA), Report No.15, Santago, 2011, p.7.

1701 Marimán Quemenado, "Chile (2011)", p.216.

1702 Rochna Ramirez, *La Propriedad de la Tierra en la Isla de Pascua*, p.31 and ff.

Code.[1703] This registration was filed in 2012 before the Supreme Court by a Rapa Nui family with regard to a property transfer that occurred in the 1980s. However the Court eventually validated the registration and the property titles enacted thereof.[1704] The Rapa Nui were kept in semi-slavery until late 1960s, when the Eastern Law (*Ley Pascua*) No.16.441 was adopted in 1967.[1705] A National Park (*Hanga Roa*) was created in the 1980s,[1706] but it is administered by the State through the National Forestry Corporation (*Corporación Nacional Forestal* – CONAF),[1707] with no indigenous participation.[1708] The other part of the State's ownership is managed by a private commercial company (*Sociedad Agricola y Servicios Isla de Pascua Limitada* – SASIPA).[1709] Nowadays, 13% of the island's lands are property of the Rapa Nui people, 70% is in the hands of the State (including, the Park), and the remaining part (17%) belongs to private owners.[1710] However, as the story of the French merchant illustrates, many of these lands may have been passed to the hands of private owners via questionable agreements. Some Rapa Nui are still convinced that they retain collective property based on the Agreement of Wills and their customs and laws.[1711] This also led to protests that exploded in 2010 (see below section 6.1.2.3).

Meanwhile, some positive steps were taken during the 1960s and 1970s, most probably due to the influence of the integrationist *indigenista* movement mentioned in chapter 4.[1712] Decree No. 60 of the Ministry of Lands and Colonization, promulgated in early 1964, established a Directorate of Indian Affairs.[1713] Law No. 17.729 enacted in 1972 contained a provision

---

1703 Marimán Quemenado, "Chile (2011)", p.216; Chartier et al. 2011, p.7.

1704 Silva Neriz, "Chile", p.194.

1705 Chartier et al., *The Human Rights of the Rapa Nui People on Easter Island*, p.7.

1706 Rochna Ramirez, *La Propriedad de la Tierra en la Isla de Pascua*, p.41.

1707 Marimán Quemenado, "Chile (2012)", p.210.

1708 Aylwin and Silva, "Chile", p.213, note 5. See also Leslie Cloud, "La patrimonialización de Te Pito O Te Henua: historia del Parque Nacional Rapa Nui – Chile", *Revista de Estudios Sociales Comparativos*, Vol. 7, issue No.1, 2013, pp.18-31, pp.21-25.

1709 Aylwin and Silva, "Chile", p.213, note 5.

1710 Marimán Quemenado, "Chile (2012)", p.210.

1711 *Ibid.*, p.211.

1712 Also the following Law No. 17,729 of 1972 contained a reference on the duty to "integrate" indigenous peoples within the state (art.68).

1713 Decree No. 60/1964 of the Ministry of Lands and Colonization, *Ministerio de Tierras y Colonizacion Aprueba el Reglamento Organico de la Direccion de Asuntos Indigenas*, at www.leychile.cl/Navegar?idNorma=8444 [Last access 02.09.2014].

on land restitutions (art.17) and created an Institute for Indigenous Development (arts.34 and ff.).[1714] Nonetheless, after the 1973 military *golpe*, Law Decree No.2.568 adopted by the Ministry of Agriculture in 1979 modified the previous Law No. 17.729 deleting any reference to indigenous cultures (art.1) and establishing a more arbitrary distribution of lands (arts.9-26).[1715] In fact, Pinochet's motto was "no indigenous peoples exist, we are all Chileans".[1716] Pinochet's governments also subsidised between 75 and 100% of the timber plantations on Mapuches' former lands by means of Decree No.701 of 1974.[1717] By early 1980, due to the dictatorship's systems of "normalization" (mainly, revocation of expropriations) and "allocation" (re-selling of lands), those lands that had been distributed thanks to the Agrarian reform were privatized but via doubtful transactions (e.g., by contracts taking advantage of barely literate people, including many indigenous peoples).[1718] Finally, the Water Code of 1981 (Decree No.1,122)[1719] initiated the privatization and appropriation of watercourses by private actors and consequently deprived indigenous peoples of them.[1720] This also affected the acquisition of lands from indigenous peoples at very low prices. In fact, the practice has shown that dry lands were sold for low amounts but

1714 Law No. 17.729/1972, Establece Normas Sobre Indigenas Y Tierras De Indigenas. Transforma La Direccion De Asuntos Indigenas En Instituto De Desarrollo Indigena. Establece Disposiciones Judiciales, Administrativas Y De Desarrollo Educacional En La Materia Y Modifica O Deroga Los Textos Legales Que Señala, at www.leychile.cl/Navegar?idNorma=29250 [Last access 02.09.2014].

1715 Law Decree No. 2.568/1979, Modifica Ley N° 17.729, Sobre Proteccion De Indigenas, Y Radica Funciones Del Instituto De Desarrollo Indigena En El Instituto De Desarrollo Agropecuario, Decreto Ley 2568 Ministerio De Agricultura, at www.leychile.cl/Navegar?idNorma=6957 [Last access 02.09.2014]. See also Nesti, "The Mapuche-Pehuenche and the Ralco Dam on the Bíobío River ...", p. 4.

1716 Rosti, "Reparations for Indigenous Peoples in Two Selected Latin American Countries", p.357.

1717 Decreto Ley No.701 of 28 October 1974, *Fija Régimen Legal de los Terrenos Forestales o Preferentemente Aptos para la Forestación, y Establece Normas de Fomento sobre la Materia*. Carruthers and Rodriguez, "Mapuche Protest, Environmental Conflict and Social Movement Linkage in Chile", p.748.

1718 Victor Toledo Llancaqueo, *Pueblo Mapuche. Derechos Colectivos y Territorios: Desafíos para la Sustentabilidad Democratica*, Programa Chile Sustentable, LOM Ediciones, Santiago de Chile 2006, p.56.

1719 Chilean Ministry of Justice/*Ministerio de Justicia*, *Código de Aguas. Decreto con Fuerza de Ley N° 1.122*, Decree No.1,122 of 29 October 1981.

1720 Rosti, "Reparations for Indigenous Peoples in Two Selected Latin American Countries", p.357.

together with "water rights". After private investments in irrigation, these lands became highly profitable.[1721]

6.1.2.3 The developments after the restoration of democracy

After the restoration of democracy, prior to becoming the first democratically-elected President, Patricio Aylwin signed an agreement with some indigenous representatives in 1989. This is known as the (first) Agreement of Nueva Imperial. In exchange for support for his future government, Aylwin had promised, *inter alia*, the constitutional recognition of indigenous peoples and their economic, social, and cultural rights.[1722] While the former promise is still pending today, the former came to fruition during Aylwin's mandate in the adoption of Indigenous Law (*Ley Indígena*) Law No.19.253 in 1993 (see further below in section 6.2). Moreover, Environmental Law No. 19.300 entered into force in 1994,[1723] creating the National Commission of the Environment CONAMA (*Comisión Regional del Medio Ambiente*), in charge, *inter alia*, of evaluating the environmental impact of considerable works such as power plants, etc. (arts.8-10).

However, the Indigenous Law was poorly implemented in the following years, thus indigenous peoples started to organize a few protests. Despite supposedly indigenous-friendly governments, as of the late 1990s the State replied to these manifestations by applying the so called "Antiterrorism Law" to the protesters. This norm (Law No.18.314) was enacted in 1984 during Pinochet's regime as foreseen in art.9 of the (Pinochet) Constitution.[1724] According to this law, crimes such as murder or even arson (art.2) are judged under military law when there is an intention to threaten the population or a part of it (art.1). Evidence of this intention is provided either by the means for and effects produced by such crimes, or by a premeditated criminal plan against a determined group of the population (art.1). The application is, consequently, rather arbitrary. Additionally, this law permits

1721 Romualdo Hernández, "Reforma agraria y evolución del marco jurídico del agua en Chile", 59 *FAO Legislative Study/Estudio Legislativo* 2006, pp.1-18, p.14.

1722 See the (first) Agreement of Nueva Imperial at http://www.politicaspublicas.net/panel/biblioteca/doc_details/21-acuerdo-de-nueva-imperial-1989.html [Last access 02.09.2014].

1723 Law No. 19.300/1994, *Aprueba Ley Sobre Bases Generales Del Medio Ambiente*, at www.leychile.cl/Navegar?idNorma=30667 [Last access 02.09.2014].

1724 Law No.18,314/1984, *Determina Conductas Terroristas y fija su Penalidad*, at www.leychile.cl/Navegar?idNorma=29731 [Last access 02.09.2014].

the use of unidentified witnesses (arts.15-18), known as "faceless" (*sin rostro*), and implies tougher punishments. Although it was reformed in 2010 and 2011,[1725] and another reform is currently (July 2015) under discussion,[1726] the definition of 'terrorist acts' is still very discretionary.[1727] Thus, not only is this law still in force, including the use of unidentified witnesses, but often continues to be applied to indigenous protesters nowadays (see infra).

Additionally, economic interests still prevail over indigenous claims and the fair respect of their rights. The most glaring example is the controversial story of the construction of six hydroelectric plants on the Bío-Bío River by the National Electric Enterprise ENDESA. In 1989 the Pangue-Ralco project was granted authorization thanks to Pinochet's Electrical Services Law, Decree Law No. 1/1982 of the Ministry of Mines.[1728] In 1989, a 500ha area of land occupied by the Mapuche people was flooded and 75 people were

1725 Law No.20,467 of 8 October 2010, adopted after the dramatic hunger strike, amended Law No.18.314/1984 insofar as it admitted the defense against the declaration of "faceless"/unidentified witnesses (art.18 of Law No.20,467/2010; the defense against such declarations had not been admitted before. Later, art.1 of Law No.20,519 (of 21 June 2011) modified art.1 of Law 18,314/1984 by completely banning the application of this procedure to minors.

1726 This is also per effect of the recent decision of the Inter-American Court of Human Rights, Case of *Norín Catrimán y Otros (Dirigentes, Miembros y Activista del Pueblo Indígena Mapuche) v. Chile*, Serie C. No.279, Judgment of 29 May 2014 (see further section 6.2.1). According to the last proposal of reform, the acts of terrorism would finally refer only to organized groups, fall under (standard) criminal law, and be erased from the Constitution. Paula Correa, "Ley Antiterrorista: Gobierno compromete plazo para modificaciones", *Diario Universidad de Chile*, 15.10.2014, at http://radio.uchile.cl/2014/10/15/ley-antiterrorista-gobierno-compromete-plazo-para-modificaciones. The draft law was extensively discussed, to avoid its application to indigenous peoples and Mapuche people in particular, and is currently under discussion in the Senate. Draft Law "Determina conductas terroristas y su penalidad y modifica los Códigos Penal y Procesal Penal", Bulletin/Boletín No. 9692-07. The text may be found at http://www.senado.cl/appsenado/templates/tramitacion/index.php by inserting the bulletin number in the search box "Boletín" [Last access to both 03.02.2015].

1727 Chilean Deputies' Chamber/*Cámara de Diputados*, "Expertos cuestionan reforma a Ley Antiterrorista en Comisión de Constitución", 21 September 2010, at www.camara.cl/prensa/noticias_detalle.aspx?prmid=39679 [Last access 04.09.2014].

1728 Decree Law No. 1/1982, *Aprueba Modificaciones Al D.F.L. N° 4, De 1959, Ley General De Servicios Eléctricos, En Materia De Energía Eléctrica*, at www.cne.cl/archivos_bajar/DFL_N1.pdf [Last access 02.09.2014].

relocated during the building of the "Pangue" dam.[1729] Moreover, the alteration of the normal flow of the river seriously affected the water quality, the fish, and, consequently, the fishing villages.[1730] Meanwhile, the International Finance Corporation (IFC), belonging to the World Bank Group, signed an investment agreement with ENDESA. Other funds were provided by European banks, the Swedish Board for Industrial and Technical Cooperation, and the Norwegian Agency for Development Cooperation.[1731] IFC created a foundation (*Fundación Pehuen*) to mediate with the Mapuche people, who started protesting with the support of environmental organizations.[1732] The Mapuche people living in the zone were only offered reallocation packages, without any further option and /or information, as documented by the anthropologist hired by the same IFC to evaluate the work of the foundation in 1995.[1733] Moreover, during the same year, IFC was taken to court by a local environmental organization, *Grupo de Acción por el Bíobío*, which denounced the violation, *inter alia*, of the World Bank's Operational Directive 4.20 on Indigenous Peoples and 4.01 on Environmental Assessment. In addition, an (illegal) re-allocation of IFC funds to another ENDESA hydro-electric plant in construction (Ralco) was alleged.[1734] In May 1996, the aforementioned Ralco project –the biggest power plant of the six planned by ENDESAwas found by the CONADI to violate Indigenous Law.[1735] A month later, CONAMA found ENDESA's environmental impact assessment unsatisfactory. In 1997, however, the Director of CONADI was replaced by order of the Chilean President Eduardo Frei Ruiz-Tagle[1736] and CONAMA approved the project subject to some conditions,

1729 Nesti, "The Mapuche-Pehuenche and the Ralco Dam on the Bíobío River ...", p. 7. See also Carruthers and Rodriguez, "Mapuche Protest, Environmental Conflict and Social Movement Linkage in Chile", pp.747-748.

1730 For an in-depth analysis see Nesti, "The Mapuche-Pehuenche and the Ralco Dam on the Bíobío River ...", and Aylwin, *Tierra y territorio mapuche*.

1731 Nesti, "The Mapuche-Pehuenche and the Ralco Dam on the Bíobío River ...", p. 8; Lila Barrera-Hernández, "Indigenous Peoples, Human Rights and Natural Resource Development: Chile"s Mapuche Peoples and the Right to Water", 11(1) *Annual Survey of International and Comparative Law* 2005, pp. 1-28, p. 13.

1732 Nesti, "The Mapuche-Pehuenche and the Ralco Dam on the Bíobío River ...", p. 8.

1733 *Ibid.*, p. 9.

1734 *Ibid.*

1735 *Ibid.*, p. 11.

1736 *Ibid.*; Carruthers and Rodriguez, "Mapuche Protest, Environmental Conflict and Social Movement Linkage in Chile", p.748.

such as a resettlement site and reduced power-generation.[1737] ENDESA and CONAMA were then taken to court by some Mapuche representatives both in a *Recurso de Protección* (Protection Proceeding) according to Article 20 of the Chilean Constitution and in trial on over procedural irregularities, which remained pending until 2003, when the Ralco plant was basically concluded.[1738] The former case was dismissed by the Santiago Court of Appeal, which, however, declared that CONADI's project approval was mandatory.[1739] This endorsement eventually occurred when the director appointed by Frei, Domingo Namoncura, was lso replaced. The new director, Rodrigo Gonzales López, of non-indigenous origins, started the approval procedures in 1998.[1740]

The case also reached the Inter-American Commission of Human Rights (IACommHR) in 2002.[1741] The complaint, filed by some Mapuche women, was never considered by the IACommHR regarding the merits.[1742] On 31 July 2003, however, the Commission granted a precautionary measure submitted by the petitioners, requesting Chile to "[r]efrain from taking any

---

1737 CONAMA Resolution No. 010/97 (*Resolución Exenta* N°010/97), 6 June 1997; Nesti, "The Mapuche-Pehuenche and the Ralco Dam on the Bíobío River ...", p. 12; Barrera-Hernández, "Indigenous Peoples, Human Rights and Natural Resource Development ...", p. 16.

1738 Recurso de Protección a favor de Pehuenches de Ralco Lepoy y Quepuca Ralco, Court of Appeal of Santiago/Corte de Apelaciones de Santiago, 19 June 1997, No.002499–97; Nicolasa Quintremán y Otras contra CONAMA, ENDESA S.A., Acción de Nulidad de Derecho Público, at www.xs4all.nl/~rehue/ral co/ral028b.html [Last access 02.09.2014]; Barrera-Hernández, "Indigenous Peoples, Human Rights and Natural Resource Development ...", p. 17.

1739 Barrera-Hernández, "Indigenous Peoples, Human Rights and Natural Resource Development ...", p. 17

1740 Aylwin, *Tierra y territorio mapuche*, p. 15; Centro Documentazione Conflitti Ambientali, "Centrale Idroelettrica Endesa-Ralco sul fiume Biò-Biò", at www.cdca.it/spip.php?article123 [Last access 02.09.2014].

1741 Inter-American Commission of Human Rights, *Mercedes Julia Huenteao Beroiza Et Al. V. Chile*, Petition 4617/02, 10 December 2002; Inter-American Commission of Human Rights, Friendly Settlement of *Mercedes Julia Huenteao Beroiza Et Al. V. Chile*, Report No.30/04, 11 March 2004, at www.cidh.org/annualrep/2004 eng/chile.4617.02eng.htm [Last access 02.09.2014].

1742 Barrera-Hernández, "Indigenous Peoples, Human Rights and Natural Resource Development ...", p. 18; as the author mentions, the IACommHR would have had to interpret the reservation of Chile to the convention on the right to property. See also the reservation at www.oas.org/juridico/english/sigs/b-32.html [Last access 02.09.2014].

steps that might alter the status quo in the matter".[1743] Later that year, the government signed a compensation agreement with ENDESA and the Mapuche people, known as the 16th September Agreement. [1744] The IACommHR finally opted for a Friendly Settlement which was adopted on 11 March 2004. The Friendly Settlement included, *inter alia*, the obligation for Chile to ratify the ILO Convention No. 169 and to resolve the pending legal proceedings linked to the Ralco case.[1745] It is difficult to evaluate whether the agreement was really satisfactory for both parties, since, when the Ralco plant was inaugurated on 27 September 2004, 91 families, i.e., approx. 500 people, were relocated, and many traditional cemeteries and other sacred territories were flooded without letting the Mapuche people recover the human remains of their ancestors. In addition, the environmental damage to flora, fauna, and water quality remain inestimable.[1746] As per today (July 2015), however, the compensation agreed was never provided to indigenous peoples. Moreover, in December 2013, one of the Mapuche women that had lead the protest, Nicolasa Quitreman, drowned in the waters of the dam. This tragic happening brought national attention back to the Ralco plant, which is very profitable, although the Alto Bío Bío municipality remains one of the poorest in the country.[1747]

Things seemed to change after the victory of Michelle Bachelet at the 2006 elections. Similarly to the former President Aylwin, President Bachelet also signed an agreement titled the (second) Agreement of Nueva Imperial (*Acuerdo de Nueva Imperial II*). This document also contained a "Commitment to Indigenous Peoples" (*Compromiso por los Pueblos Indígenas*)[1748] to develop a full and effective indigenous participation in

---

1743 Inter-American Commission of Human Rights, Friendly Settlement of *Mercedes Julia Huenteao Beroiza Et Al. V. Chile*, para. 15.

1744 Barrera-Hernández, "Indigenous Peoples, Human Rights and Natural Resource Development ...", pp. 18-19.

1745 *Ibid.*, pp. 18-19.

1746 José Aylwin, "Se inauguró la central hidroeléctrica Ralco en el Alto Bío Bío", 2004, at www.mapuche-nation.org/espanol/html/medioambiente/ma-ntcs-05.htm [Last access 02.09.2014]; see also Nesti, "The Mapuche-Pehuenche and the Ralco Dam on the Bíobío River ...", p. 11.

1747 Aylwin and Silva, "Chile", pp.209-210. See also Eva Vergara, "Mapuche leader found dead in reservoir she opposed in Chile", 26.12.2013, at http://www.denverpost.com/nationworld/ci_24793772/mapuche-leader-found-dead-reservoir-she-opposed-chile [Last access 02.09.2014].

1748 *Compromiso por los Pueblos Indígenas* (2006), at www.mideplan.cl/index.php?option=com_rubberdoc&view=doc&id=359&format=raw&Itemid=91 [Last access 02.09.2014].

public affairs, including in the decision-making processes, and a general increase of indigenous representatives in both governmental and regional bodies. Later, the "New Foci of Indigenous Policy" (*Nuevos Ejes de la Política Indígena*) were launched.[1749] These included five main points: (1) enhancing political participation of indigenous peoples through consultation; (2) recognizing indigenous peoples by reforming the constitution; (3) ratifying ILO Convention 169; (3) improving the policies vis-à-vis the urbanized indigenous people, and (4) of indigenous women; (5) promoting cultural diversity in the education field, including the teaching of indigenous languages in primary schools in those regions with a high percentage of indigenous population. Notwithstanding the (declared) priority given to the implementation of these policies, only one was finally achieved, i.e., the ratification of the ILO Convention 169. This certainly represents a milestone in indigenous affairs in Chile.[1750] As per the ratification and entry into force of the Convention on 15 September 2009, a number of consultations were carried out between 2009 and 2010, albeit with many limits and confusion (see further section 6.3.2)

In 2008, President Bachelet launched a (partially, revised) policy titled "Re-Conocer. Pacto Social por la Multiculturalidad",[1751] which included a number of activities that had already been carried out and some other to be carried out with regard to the same five aforementioned themes. Constitutional recognition and a number of other initiatives regarding indigenous participation in State organs were also put forward before the end of Bachelet's first mandate (see further section 6.3.1.1). However, none of these initiatives were discussed any further.

In his inaugural speech on 21 May 2010, President Sebastian Piñera promised a new indigenous land policy, the reform of the National Corporation of Indigenous Development CONADI, and the due constitutional recognition of indigenous peoples.[1752] The draft constitutional amendment,

1749 Sala de Prensa del MIDEPLAN, "Presidenta Bachelet anuncia nueva política indígena", 30 April 2007 [on file with author].

1750 The debate surrounding and the indigenous demand to ratify the ILO 169 began after the adoption of this treaty in 1989 which coincided with the democratization process of the country after Pinochet's dictatorship.

1751 This may be literally translated as "Re-Cognition. Social Pact for Multiculturalism". However, the original Spanish wording refers to a double meaning, i.e., *Re-Conocer* means both recognition and re-knowing (or getting to meet/know again each other).

1752 Sebastian Piñera Echenique, "Del Chile del Bicentenario al País de las Oportunidades", Mensaje a la Nación, de S.E. el Presidente de la República 2010,

which had been promoted by the former President Bachelet since 2007 (see further section 6.2.2.1), was then blocked for discussion in the Senate.[1753] After, the same 2007 draft, very contested by indigenous peoples and other commentators (see further section 6.2.2.1), was object of a large (online) consultation which was launched in April-May 2011[1754] but was ultimately left unconcluded. A similar consultation had already been realized in 2009 under Bachelet's government, although the results had not been made public (see further section 6.3.2).[1755]

Afterwards, Chile has gone through hectic, if not turbulent, years. In 2010, the South American country was at the centre of international attention because of the 33 miners that became trapped in the mine in the desert of Atacama in August and who were, all (luckily) rescued later in October. These events, however, indirectly contributed to 'hide' the exceptional 80 day-hunger strike of 34 Mapuche 'political prisoners' between the same burning July and October 2010.[1756] These prisoners, self-defined 'political' due to their convictions under the Antiterrorism Law, started this hunger strike to protest against the application of military justice to their cases. The majority of the detainees were convicted of terrorist acts all connected to land recuperations and other protests regarding access to natural resources

---

21.05.2010, pp.33-34, at www.gobiernodechile.cl/media/2010/05/Mensaje-presidencial-21-de-mayo.pdf [Last access 02.09.2014].

1753 *Proyecto de reforma constitucional que reconoce el aporte de los pueblos originarios a la conformación de la nación chilena*, Bulletin/*Boletín* No.5324-07, at http://www.senado.cl/appsenado/templates/tramitacion/index.php by inserting the bulletin number in the search box "Boletín" [Last Access 05.02.2015].

1754 CONADI, "Minuta Explicativa sobre Reconocimiento Constitucional de los Pueblos Indigenas", at http://www.conadi.gob.cl/images/doc-consulta/rec/Minu ta%20reconocimiento%20constitucional%20final%20_14-04-091_.pdf [Last access 02.09.2014]; Consultaindigena.cl, "Ministro Kast anuncia realización de gran Consulta de Institucionalidad Indígena", 8 May 2011, at http://www.con sultaindigenamds.gob.cl/Consulta-2010-2014/articulo080311_1.html [Last access to all 02.09.2014];.

1755 CONADI, "Proceso de Consulta sobre Reconocimiento Constitucional de los Pueblos Indígenas", at www.conadi.gob.cl/index.php/component/content/arti cle?layout=edit&id=353 [Last access 02.09.2014].

1756 Eighteen Mapuche prisoners in Temuco's and Concepción's jails started their hunger strike on 12 July 2010; another one joined them from the prison of Valdivia on 19 July, and another ten from Angol's jail between 19 and 26 July; finally another five started their hunger strike between the end of July and beginning of September 2010. Observatorio Ciudadano, "61 días, 34 presos políticos mapuche en huelga de hambre, últimos comunicados", 06.09.2010 [on file with author].

and environmental exploitation.[1757] Some of them were involved in the LLeu LLeu Lake dispute. In 2005, the Chilean media had documented a "Mapuche attack" on a public delegation visiting the rivers of the LLeu LLeu Lake in the 8th Region of Chile, Province of Arauco.[1758] The protesters were demonstrating against a "mine"' shouting "¡A la minera! ¡A la minera!". In previous months, many technical visits and surveys had been realized, confirming the rumours of an imminent mining exploration among the population.[1759] In fact, on the 4 August 2004, the mining exploration concession was granted by the Civil Court of Cañete,[1760] according to the Mining Code (arts.55-58).[1761] The mining project was to be carried out on a Mapuche territory, where 17 indigenous families lived.[1762] The Mapuche communities of the villages of Rucañanco and Lleu Lleu were already demonstrating against controversial forest exploitation.[1763] The mining project was, thus, the latest in a series of violations of their land rights. Both the Indigenous Law (art.13, on the inalienability of indigenous land) and the Mining Code (art.17, on additional permits to be granted in case of mining projects in natural parks or places declared of historical interest) would have offered the relevant legal background to contrast this project. The risks were indeed very high. As well as the land dispossession, the planned iron mine would have implied serious consequences for the surrounding environment, e.g., perforations and chemical treatments to improve the iron's quality, the mine's waste disposal, the high concentration of fine particles and, thus, water and air pollution.[1764] The frustration of the local Mapuche people soon exploded. Information and leaflets on the controversial project

---

1757 Some of them continued until 9 October. El Mostrador/Efe, "Mapuches presos en la cárcel de Angol ceden y ponen fin a huelga de hambre", *El Mostrador*, 09.10.2010, at www.elmostrador.cl/noticias/pais/2010/10/09/mapuches-presos-en-la-carcel-de-angol-ceden-y-ponen-fin-a-la-huelga-de-hambre [Last access 02.09.2014].

1758 Toledo Llancaqueo, "Tierra Mapuche y Concesiones Mineras. El case de Rucañanco, Lago Lleu Lleu", p. 1.

1759 *Ibid.*, pp. 1-2.

1760 *Ibid.*, p. 3.

1761 *Codigo de Minería*, adopted on 26 September 1983, at http://www.minmineria.cl/574/articles-5761_recurso_1.pdf [Last access 02.09.2014].

1762 Toledo Llancaqueo, "Tierra Mapuche y Concesiones Mineras. El case de Rucañanco, Lago Lleu Lleu", p. 3.

1763 *Ibid.*, p. 5.

1764 Edgar Muñoz, "Minera Explorará El Fierro En Lleu-Lleu", La Nalhue Noticias, 04.062007, in *Observatorio Latinoamericano de conflictos ambientales*, at http://www.olca.cl/oca/chile/region08/mineras011.htm [Last access 02.09.2014].

had circulated since 2007.[1765] On 15 October 2008, the Chilean special public prosecutor for Mapuche affairs denounced that the Lleu Lleu Mapuche protesters had made attempts on his life. The public prosecutor in charge of investigations grouped this case with other 'terrorist acts', e.g., 'terrorist association', 'terrorist arson', et al. Nineteen Mapuches were charged under the above-mentioned Antiterrorism Law. An exceptional number of unidentified witnesses (243) were called to testimony during the trial. Moreover, it seemed that other Mapuche prisoners in a bordering conflict zone (Pascual Coña) were offered immediate release in exchange for their testimony.[1766] One unidentified witness, after the judgment, declared that he had been threatened and mistreated by the police, who forced him to give a false testimony.[1767] The Criminal Court of Cañete's judgement, officially announced on 22 March 2011, sentenced 4 of the 17 defendants to 20 or 25 years of jail.[1768] A contested appeal to the Supreme Court, which reduced the punishment to 8-14 years of prison, followed, accompanied by another dramatic hunger strike.[1769] Afterwards, the Mapuches who had been convicted declared that they would have brought the case before the Inter-

---

1765 See, e.g., Mapuche.info, "Proyecto Minero en el Lago Lleu Lleu", 2007, at www.mapuche.info/mapu/no_minera070920.pdf [Last access 02.09.2014].

1766 For this reconstruction, see Francisco Marín Castro, "Estado antimapuche en el año del bicentenario", *El Ciudadano*, 01.09.2010, at www.elciudadano.cl/2010/09/01/estado-antimapuche-en-el-ano-del-bicentenario [Last access 02.09.2014].

1767 País Mapuche, "Cañete: "Testigos protegidos" rompen el miedo y denuncian las torturas por parte de la Fiscalía", 17.01.2011, at http://paismapuche.org/?p=2920 [Last access 02.09.2014].

1768 Many human rights organizations and journalists underlined the injustices behind this judgment. See, e.g., Corporación de Promoción y Defensa de los Derechos del Pueblo, Observatorio Ciudadano, Federación Internacional de Derechos Humanos, "Vulneración del debido proceso en el juicio de Cañete: solicitamos a la Corte Suprema de Justicia resolver recurso de nulidad", 26.04.2011, at www.fidh.org/Vulneracion-del-debido-proceso-en [Last access 02.09.2014].

1769 See the Supreme Court Sentence/*Rol* No.2921-2011, 3 June 2011; Cooperativa.cl, "Corte Suprema anuló parcialmente fallo contra comuneros mapuche", 03.06.2011, at http://www.cooperativa.cl/corte-suprema-anulo-parcialmente-fallo-contra-comuneros-mapuche/prontus_nots/2011-06-03/130030.html; La Tercera Editorial, "Sentencia de la Corte Suprema en caso mapuches", 10.06.2011, *La Tercera*, at http://latercera.com/noticia/opinion/editorial/2011/06/894-371993-9-sentencia-de-la-corte-suprema-en-caso-mapuches.shtml. The second hunger strike lasted another 80 days, and for one of the condemned persons, Pamela Pezoa, up to 86 day. SoyTemuco.cl, "Esta mañana trasladaron a los reos mapuche en huelga de hambre al Hospital de Victoria", 26.05.2011, at www.soychile.cl/Temuco/Sociedad/2011/05/26/17350/Esta-manana-trasladaron-a-los-reos-mapuche-en-huelga-de-hambre-al-Hospital-de-Victoria.aspx; El Mostrador, "Mapuches ceden y bajan

American Court of Human Rights.[1770] However, this Court decided a similar case last May 2014 condemning Chile for the use of the Antiterrorism Law (see further section 6.2.1). At the end of 2013, four cases involving 16 indigenous defendants under the Antiterrorism Law remained open.[1771] Thus, the situation of all the prisoners judged under this law may soon be revised by the announced reforms of the Antiterrorism Law. The three above-mentioned convicted Mapuches announced in mid-2014 that, if no action is taken, they would be ready to start another hunger strike,[1772] which they eventually declared to have restarted in March 2015.[1773]

In 2011, the student marches demanding educational reform sent shockwaves throughout the whole region (see further section 6.1.2.4). Between 2012 and 2013, the wider public opinion was again divided over the thorny case of the wildfires that killed several people. Apparently, some of these fires were started by groups of indigenous peoples who sought to claim back ancestral land. Although human rights lawyers defended them, Rodrigo Hinzpeter from the then Ministry of Internal Affairs declared the Mapuche responsible for the wildfires.[1774] In the case of two elderly people who died

huelga de hambre al crearse comisión que promete velar por sus derechos", 09.06.2011, *El Mostrador*, at www.elmostrador.cl/noticias/pais/2011/06/09/se-acaba-la-huelga-de-hambre-mapuche-luego-de-86-dias; The Associated Press (AP), "Mapuches chilenos cumplen 80 días en huelga de Hambre", 02.06.2012, at http://noticias.terra.com.co/internacional/latinoamerica/mapuches-chilenos-cumplen-80-dias-en-huelgade-hambre,a15aea95ad050310VgnVCM4000009bf154d0RCRD.html [Last access to all 02.09.2014].

1770 Paula Correa, "Mapuches condenados en Cañete recurrirán a Corte Interamericana de Derechos Humanos", *Radio Universidad De Chile*, 09.11.2011, at http://radio.uchile.cl/noticias/129677 [Last access 02.09.2014].

1771 Aylwin and Silva, "Chile", p.211.

1772 Paula Correa, "Héctor Llaitul: Presos mapuche no descartan nueva huelga de hambre", *Radio Universidad De Chile*, 06.08.2014, at http://radio.uchile.cl/2014/08/06/hector-llaitul-presos-mapuche-no-descartan-nuevas-huelgas-de-hambre [Last access 02.09.2014].

1773 Comisión de Comunicaciones Meli Wixan Mapu, "Comunicado público presos mapuche cárcel de Angol. Inicio Nueva Huelga de Hambre a partir de hoy, 23 de marzo", 24.03.2015, at http://meli.mapu ches.org/spip.php?article3335 [Last access 25.03.2015].

1774 See EFE, "Incendios remiten en Chile y el Gobierno tiende mano a mapuches tras polémica", *ABC Noticias*, 07.01.2012, at www.abc.es/agencias/noticia.asp?no ticia=1059266; Pedro Cayuqueo, "Bomberos de Carahue desmiente hipótesis del gobierno y apunta a faenas ilegales de carbón", 06.01.2012, at www.theclinic.cl/2012/01/06/bomberos-de-carahue-desmiente-hipotesis-del-go bierno-y-

in the wildfire on their property in January 2013, the Mapuche Celestino Córdova was eventually condemned to 18 years of prison by the Court of Temuco, then confirmed by the Supreme Court last May 2014.[1775]

There are also many pending and controversial projects regarding natural resource exploitation, especially mining, currently in the planning stages or in process in other parts of the country.[1776] In 2013, a Mapuche ceremonial place was "temporarily" flooded to allow the construction of the contested Neltume hydroelectric plant of ENDESA-Enel in the municipality of Panguipulli.[1777] In the north, the Aymara people have continually demonstrated against hazardous mining projects since 2010.[1778] Mining companies control 30% of the watercourses.[1779] Moreover, during 2009, as per Law No.19,657/2000 on Geothermal Energy Concession (*Ley de Concesiones de Energía Geotérmica – Sernageomin*), 20 thermal water sites

---

apunta-a-faenas-ilegales-de-carbon; see also the CNN Chile interview with the human rights lawyer Jorge Contesse, at www.youtube.com/watch?gl=US&v=hKt4l9EJnvw; [Last access to all 02.09.2014].

1775 See Karen Soto Galindo, "Celestino Córdova es condenado a 18 años de cárcel por la muerte del matrimonio Luchsinger-Mackay", *La Tercera*, 28.02.2014, at http://www.latercera.com/noticia/nacional/2014/02/680-567408-9-celestino-cordova-es-condenado-a-18-anos-de-carcel-por-la-muerte-del-matrimonio.shtml; CNN Chile, "Corte Suprema confirmó condena de 18 años para machi Celestino Córdova", *CNN Chile*, 12.05.2014, at http://www.cnnchile.com/noticia/2014/05/12/corte-suprema-confirmo-condena-de-18-anos-para-machi-celestino-cordova; [Last access to all 02.09.2014].

1776 See e.g. Diana Porras, "Indígenas de Arica y Parinacota rechazan anuncio de Piñera sobre explotación minera en Parque Nacional", *Radio Universidad De Chile*, 11.06.2010, at http://radio.uchile.cl/noticias/70812; El Mostrador, "ONGs de Chile y el extranjero se oponen a instalación de minas decarbón a tajo abierto en Isla Riesco", *El Mostrador*, 01.07.2010, at www.elmostrador.cl/noticias/pais/2010/07/01/ongs-de-chile-y-el-extranjero-se-oponen-a-instalacion-de-minas-decarbon-a-tajo-abierto-en-isla-riesco; [Last access to all 02.09.2014].

1777 Aylwin and Silva, "Chile", p.208.

1778 Comunicaciones Observatorio Ciudadano, "Antonio Mamani, dirigente aymara: "La lucha de las comunidades aymara contra las mineras, es una pelea desequilibrada"", *Mapuexpress*, 27.10.2010, at http://www.mapuexpress.net/content/news/print.php?id=6189 [Last access 02.09.2014].

1779 Marimán Quemenado, "Chile (2011)", p.217.

were granted to private companies without consulting the communities concerned.[1780] The El Morro and Pascua Lama large-scale mining projects affected the Diaguitas' agricultural activities, which led to the displacement of many Diaguita farmers during 2012.[1781]

In addition, the Rapa Nui indigenous people were victims of violent police repression for claiming secession from Chile after a contentious land occupation during 2010.[1782] A group of families had peacefully occupied private and public buildings around mid-2010. The aim was to pressurize the government to recognize their (denied) land rights and claim a fair application of the ILO Convention 169. However, the police forcibly evicted the occupants on different dates later in December 2010. Many were injured by these clashes. At the same time, the Easter Island Criminal Court eventually charged several Rapa Nui with alleged crimes of violating private residences.[1783] In January 2012, the Special Rapporteur on the Rights of Indigenous Peoples urged a dialogue among the parties and a limited use of police repression.[1784] Later in February that year, the Inter-American Commission on Human Rights issued a precautionary measure in favour of the Rapa Nui people. The IACommHR ordered Chile to cease and refrain from

1780 *Ibid.*, p.218.

1781 Silva Neriz, "Chile", p.194. See also the analysis of Cynthia Vel, "Respecting the "Guardians of Nature: Chile's violations of the Diaguita indigenous peoples' environmental and human rights and the need to enforce obligations to obtain Free, Prior, and Informed Consent", 2(2) *American Indian Law Journal* 2014, pp.641-680.

1782 See Radio New Zealand International, "Rapa Nui Parliament wants to secede from Chile", 16.08.2010, at www.rnzi.com/pages/news.php?op=read&id=55321; Radio Bío-Bío, "Parlamento Rapa Nui rechaza propuestas del Gobierno para solucionar conflicto territorial", 23.10.2010, *Radio Bío-Bío*, at http://www.biobiochile.cl/2010/10/23/parlamento-rapa-nui-rechaza-propuestas-del-gobierno-para-solucionar-conflicto-territorial.shtml; Radio Bío-Bío, "Consejo de Ancianos de Rapa Nui marcha exigiendo la restitución del estado de derecho en la isla", 29 October 2010, *Radio Bío-Bío*, at http://www.biobiochile.cl/2010/10/29/consejo-de-ancianos-de-rapa-nui-marcha-exigiendo-la-restitucion-del-estado-de-derecho-en-la-isla.shtml; [Last access to all 02.09.2014].

1783 Marimán Quemenado, "Chile (2011)", p.216.

1784 James Anaya, "Chile/Isla de Pascua: declaración del Relator Especial de la ONU sobre los derechos de los pueblos indígenas, James Anaya, ante los desalojos de indígenas Rapanuis", 12.01.2012, at http://unsr.jamesanaya.org/statements/chile-isla-de-pascua-declaracion-del-relator-especial-de-la-onu-sobre-los-derechos-de-los-pueblos-indigenas-james-anaya-ante-los-desalojos-de-indigenas-rapanuis or at http://www.ohchr.org/SP/NewsEvents/Pages/DisplayNews.aspx?NewsID=10627&LangID=S [Last access 02.09.2014].

to the use of armed violence against Rapa Nui.[1785] An international mission was also sent to the island in August 2012.[1786] The team reported that Rapa Nui leaders, as well as government officials and other residents, erroneously believed the entire island to be ancestral land of the former,[1787] which is not the case as seen above in section 6.1.2.2. Eventually, the IACommHR lifted the precautionary measure and archived the case on 31 October 2012.[1788]

In 2014, the State officially apologized to the Mapuche people for "depriving them of their lands" ("por el despojo de sus tierras").[1789] Indeed, in the latest Presidential Message of 21 May 2015, President Bachelet declared that 466 million square meters (i.e., 46,600 hectares) of land was given back to indigenous individuals and communities in 2014. Moreover, the budget for the restitution of waters and lands to indigenous peoples in the North increased to 76%.[1790] Hopefully, this positive trend will continue in upcoming years.

6.1.2.4 The 2011 students' mobilization, the 2014 elections and the hope for a change of Chilean institutions

After the earthquake and the rescue of the trapped miners, President Piñera had to face the massive students' mobilization that erupted in May 2011. After a controversial declaration to privatize the *Universidad Tecnologica Metropolitana*, on 30 June, 400,000 students lead by the Chilean Students Confederation (*Confederación de Estudiantes de Chile* – CONFECH) started to protest. The movement used different forms of mobilization, from

1785 During the demonstrations and the evictions, the police had committed acts of violence and intimidation against the Rapa Nui. Inter-American Commission on Human Rights, "Annual Report of the Inter-American Commission on Human Rights 2011, Chapter III C. Petitions and cases before the Inter-American Commission on Human Rights", Precautionary measure (PM) No. 321/10, Rapa Nui Indigenous People, Chile, p.78, para.35.

1786 Marimán Quemenado, "Chile (2012)", p.210.

1787 *Ibid.*, p.211.

1788 Inter-American Commission on Human Rights, "Annual Report of the Inter-American Commission on Human Rights 2011 …", p.78, para.35.

1789 La Mañana de Cordoba, "Estado chileno pide perdón a los Mapuche", 14.03.2014, *La Mañana de Cordoba*, at http://www.lmcordoba.com.ar/nota/158717_estado-chileno-pide-perdon-a-los-mapuche [Last access 21.03.2014].

1790 Michelle Bachelet, "Mensaje Presidencial 21 de Mayo de 2015", 21.05.2015, p.25, at http://www.go b.cl/cuenta-publica/2015/2015_mensaje_presidencial.pdf [Last access 14.06.2015].

marches to occupation of school and university buildings (some were occupied up to 6 months).[1791] The main national media controlled by right-wing party at the government initially showed violent acts on the part of the students. However, the social media (Facebook, Twitter, etc.) demonstrated later that the violent acts on their part were isolated and rather the police had violently repressed the manifestations.[1792] After a number of intermediate meetings, the negotiation that took place on 3 September 2011 failed.[1793] In October, almost 1.5 million people participated in the referendum for free education, 90.7% of which voted in favor of the proposals to abolish the lucrative private system and improve the education system. Although it had no legal validity, is was highly symbolic.[1794] However, by the end of the year the movement had lost some intensity. Moreover, a number students were urged to get back to school to finish the school year. The government thus promised to solve the issue during 2012.[1795] Although the students mobilized throughout 2012 and 2013,[1796] the upcoming presidential elections of 2013 and the negotiations between Bachelet and one of the most charismatic leaders of the movement, Camila Vallejo, reduced the social tension. As mentioned in chapter 4, Vallejo was elected to Congress at the 2013 November elections within the coalition between her party (*Partido Comunista de Chile*) and Bachelet's party "New Majority" (Nueva

1791 Carolina Segovia and Ricardo Gamboa, "Chile: El Año en que Salimos a la Calle", 32(1) *Revista de Ciencia Política (Santiago SciELO)* 2012, pp.65-85, p.69.

1792 Juan Carlos Ramírez Figueroa, "Crónica sobre la Movilización Popular Chilena", *Pagina 12*, 08.09.2011, at http://www.pagina12.com.ar/diario/suplementos/no/12-5601-2011-09-08.html [Last Access 03.09.2014]. By the end of 2011, there were, among police staff and protesters, 4.045 prisoners, 235 wounded and one adolescent shot by the police. Juan Fernández Labbé, "Movimiento Estudiantil en Chile (2011): Repertorios de Acción, Marcos de Acción Colectiva, Impactos y Desafíos para la Política Pública", 31 *Circunstancia* 2013, at http://www.ortegaygasset.edu/fog/ver/1534/circunstancia/ano-xi---n--31---mayo-%202013/articulos/mo vimiento-estudiantil-en-chile--2011---repertorios-de-accion--marcos-de-accion-c olectiva--impactos-y-desafios-para-la-politica-publica [Last access 03.09.2014].

1793 Ramírez Figueroa, "Crónica sobre la Movilización Popular Chilena".

1794 Fernández Labbé, "Movimiento Estudiantil en Chile (2011) …".

1795 Segovia and Gamboa, "Chile: El Año en que Salimos a la Calle", p.70.

1796 E.g., on 11 July 2013 around 200,000 gathered for a big national protest. Other important social actors of the protests after 2011, have been the National Coordination of Secondary (education) Pupils (Coordinadora Nacional de Estudiantes Secundarios – CONES) and the union Unitary Central of Workers (Central Unitaria de Trabajadores (CUT). Rocío Alorda, "Movimiento estudiantil continúa movilizado", 31.07.2013, *Noticias Aliadas*, at http://www.noticias aliadas.org/articles.asp?item=1&art=6856 [Last access 03.09.2013].

Mayoría). A further three student leaders were elected with a remarkable majority, although with different parties, namely Giorgio Jackson (*Revolución Democratica*), Gabriel Boric (Independent), and Karol Cariola (*Juventudes Comunistas*).[1797]

This was not the first protest against Chile's privatized and expensive education system. In 2006, under Bachelet's first mandate, around 700,000 "penguins" (i.e., students in their uniforms) had marched against the government asking better school facilities and scholarships for the poorest pupils. After a peaceful demonstration in June that year, in August another 2,000 marched again to demand the acceleration of the promised reforms. Eventually, 200 people were arrested and dozens injured.[1798]

In general, as mentioned, recent years have seen intense social unrest. In Santiago alone, 134 public marches were authorized in 2010, but in 2011 they rose to 240, i.e. 20 marches per month.[1799] Other protests were organized against, e.g., the HidroAysén controversial project,[1800] which has recently been blocked until an undefined date.[1801] However, the student mobilization has undoubtedly represented the most relevant social movement

---

1797 See Redacción BBC Mundo, "Los exlíderes estudiantiles que arrasaron en las elecciones en Chile", 18.11.2013, *BBC*, at http://www.bbc.co.uk/mundo/noticias/2013/11/131118_chile_elecciones_exlideres_estudiantiles_arrasan_para_diiputados_ch.shtml [Last access 19.08.2014]; Redacción Semana, "Camila Vallejo: de líder estudiantil a diputada", 18.11.2013, *Semana*, at http://www.semana.com/mundo/articulo/lider-estudiantil-camila-vallejo-diputada-en-chile/365018-3 [Last access 19.08.2014].

1798 Ramírez Figueroa, "Crónica sobre la Movilización Popular Chilena"; and BBC, "Chile student rally turns violent", 23.08.2006, at http://news.bbc.co.uk/2/h i/americas/5277190.stm [Last access 03.09.2014]

1799 Segovia and Gamboa, "Chile: El Año en que Salimos a la Calle", p.67.

1800 This project, announced in 2007, foresaw the construction of five hydroelectric plants by ENDESA-Enel on the Baker and Pascua rivers in the (uncpolluted) region of Aysén to generate and transport electric energy by land from the very south to Santiago. Apart from the huge environmental impact, the 2010 February earthquake provoked even stronger public opinion against this project. During 2011, except in the region of Aysén, protests against this project were held in the majority of Chilean cities and towns. In June 2014, the environmental permits were finally withdrawn. BBC News, "Chile rejects huge hydro-electric project in Patagonia", 10.06.2014, at http://www.bbc.com/news/world-latin-america-27788286[Last access 04.09.2014]

1801 In August (2014), the Hydroaysen consortium announced that it will appeal against the revocation of the environmental permits. Arnaldo Pérez Guerra, "HidroAysén impugnó revocación de permiso ambiental", 28.08.2014, Noticias Aliadas, at http://www.noticiasaliadas.org/articles.asp?art=7063. Now, the decision to block

since the restoration of democracy,[1802] counting on broad public support,[1803] and it has been characterized by a high level of organization and incisiveness of its leaders.[1804] The motto of the movement is still "public, free, and high-quality education" (*educación pública, gratuita y de calidad*).[1805]

Since 2009, the Chilean education system has established six years of mandatory basic schooling (*Educación Básica*) plus a further six years of secondary education (*Educación Media*) before going to (optional) University (*Ley General de Educación* – Education General Law No.20,370/2009, arts.4, 17-21, and 25). This Law abrogated, albeit partially, the previous legislation enacted by the Military Junta and promulgated by Pinochet on 10 March 1990 (*Ley Orgánica Constitutional de Enseñanza*, Law No.18,962/1990). This previous law foresaw mandatory education only for the (then) first eight years of basic education. However, Law No.19,876 of 2003 reformed art.19.10 of the (1980) Constitution and stated the obligatory and free nature of secondary education as well. Notwithstanding the educational reforms of 2003 and 2009, the third (apart from it para.2) and fourth titles of Law No.18.962/1990 regarding secondary education are still in force in accordance with art.70 of Law No.20370/2009. Thus, while public schools can only be created by law (art.30, para.1), art.30 (para.2) of Law No.18.962/1990 allows the creation of private (secondary) schools by any natural or legal person and according to private (civil) law. Additionally, private universities may be established by either public or private deed in accordance with art.44. This led to an impressive number of private schools and universities from 1990 onwards. Both public and private schools are subsidized by the State.[1806] Since 1988, there has been a system to measure

---

the project has been taken by the constructor ENDESA due to losses in their investments. El Mostrador Mercados, "Endesa anuncia a sus inversionistas la paralización indefinida de HidroAysén y Punta Alcalde", *El Mostrador Mercados*, 29.01.2015, at http://www.elmostrador.cl/pais/2015/01/29/suspension-de-hidroaysen-y-punta-alcade-genera-perdidas-en-us-143-millones-para-endesa [Last access 03.02.2015].

1802 Segovia and Gamboa, "Chile: El Año en que Salimos a la Calle", p.69; Fernández Labbé, "Movimiento Estudiantil en Chile (2011) …".

1803 The Economist, "Progress and its discontents", *The Economist*, 12.04.2012, at http://www.economist.com/node/21552566 [Last access 03.09.2014].

1804 Fernández Labbé, "Movimiento Estudiantil en Chile (2011) …".

1805 *Ibid.*

1806 The latter are subsided in accordance with the Educational Subsidies Law (*Ley de Subvenciones Educacionales*), Decree No.3476/1980 re-approved by Decree No.2 of Education of 21 February 1990. See UNESCO, International Bureau of Education (IBE), "World Data on Education. VII Ed. 2010/2011", "Chile", July 2010,

educational quality (*Sistema de Medición de la Calidad de la Educación* – SIMCE).[1807] According to the SIMCE, public schools tend to produce worse results in comparison to private schools.[1808] Thus, before 2003, those Chileans who wanted to study the (then) four years of secondary education preferred to go to private schools. This empowered these schools and the fees for the best schools increased. After 2003, although a number of public (free) secondary schools were established, the best were still the private ones. The same situation happened with universities. Therefore, parents were (and are) often pushed to request loans to be able to send their children to the best (private) schools. In sum, in Chile it is the families who finance education (or students' loans): Families pay up to the 85.4% of the total education expenses, while the sole remaining 15.6% is covered by the State.[1809]

This vicious circle also has another effect, which is to create further disparities among different socio-economic sectors of society. In fact, Chile is one of the countries in the world with the highest socio-economic discrepancy.[1810] Another worrying issue is the drop-out rate from universities, which are more common among the poorest students who, however, remain indebted for years.[1811]

Thus, in the student movement of 2011, the social tension vis-à-vis such disparities merged in the symbolic request of a "public, free, and high-quality education".[1812] In fact, whereas the policy of neoliberalism found a first and solid start under the Pinochet dictatorship, after the restoration of democracy and due the economic crisis left by Pinochet, social policy un-

---

UNESCO Doc. IBE/2010/CP/WDE/cl, p.3, at http://www.ibe.une sco.org/fileadmin/user_upload/Publications/WDE/2010/pdf-versions/Chile.pdf [Last access 03.09.2014].

1807 UNESCO, International Bureau of Education (IBE), "World Data on Education. VII Ed. 2010/2011", "Chile", p.40.

1808 E.g., in the 2013 ranking of the second year of basic education, only 9 schools are among the top 100. Emol, "Ranking: Los 100 colegios con mejor puntaje en SIMCE de 2° básico", *Emol Chile*, 20.06.2013, at http://www.emol.com/noti cias/nacional/2013/06/20/604715/ranking-los-100-colegios-con-mejores-puntajes-en-el-simce-de-2-basico.html [Last access 03.09.2014].

1809 Ramírez Figueroa, "Crónica sobre la Movilización Popular Chilena".

1810 Fernández Labbé, "Movimiento Estudiantil en Chile (2011) …"; The Economist 2012.

1811 Ramírez Figueroa, "Crónica sobre la Movilización Popular Chilena"; The Economist 2012.

1812 Fernández Labbé, "Movimiento Estudiantil en Chile (2011) …".

doubtedly received more attention and investment, but within the macroeconomic limits of neoliberalism to avoid the risk of a pursuant inflationary disequilibrium.[1813] Despite the attempts of several administrations, neoliberalism is extremely difficult to revert in Chile without risking huge, negative consequences in the short- to mid-term.[1814]

Furthermore, the student movement also had the effect, first, of showing the Chilean government's incapacity to promptly meet society's demands. Two ministers stood down during the 2011 protests and Piñera's popularity decreased dramatically. Second, to include within the political arena another powerful actor who (at that time) refused to work with any party.[1815] Finally, in May 2014, it prompted another reform of the educational system, which was under discussion in the Chilean Congress during 2015,[1816] and will be applied progressively until 2023.[1817]

In conclusion, the eruption of the student movement may be due to: Progress in the country's socio-economic development; Chile's neoliberal crisis; or a general political crisis within the country. Additionally, it has represented a new political opportunity for the country's democratization process.[1818] This remains to be seen under the second, currently promising, mandate of President Bachelet (2014-2018).

1813 Rafael Guerrero Rodríguez, "Neoliberal transition in Latin America: examining the gap between theory and practice. The cases of Chile and Mexico", Revista Espacialidades, Vol.4, No.2, July-December 2014, pp. 66-88, pp.75-76.

1814 Guerrero Rodríguez, "Neoliberal transition in Latin America …", p.83.

1815 Segovia and Gamboa, "Chile: El Año en que Salimos a la Calle", p.70.

1816 Draft Law "Regula la admisión de los y las estudiantes, elimina el financiamiento compartido y prohíbe el lucro en establecimientos educacionales que reciben aportes del Estado", Bulletin/Boletín No. 9366-04. The text may be found at http://www.senado.cl/appsenado/templates/tramitacion/index.php by inserting the bulletin number in the search box "Boletín". See also the official website of the government dedicated to the educational reform at http://reformaeducacional.gob.cl. [Last Access to both 03.02.2015]

1817 Rodrigo Rojas, "Senado despacha el proyecto de fin al lucro, la selección y el copago", *Diario Universidad de Chile*, 22.01.2015, at http://radio.uchile.cl/2015/01/22/senado-despacha-el-proyecto-de-fin-al-lucro-la-seleccion-y-el-copago [Last access 03.02.2015].

1818 Fernández Labbé, "Movimiento Estudiantil en Chile (2011) …".

6.2. *The legal protection of indigenous peoples in Chile*

6.2.1 International human rights law applicable to indigenous peoples in Chile

Chile ratified the nine binding, core human rights treaties also seen in the case of Bolivia in chapter 5 (ICERD, ICCPR, ICESCR, CEDAW, CAT, CRC, ICRMW, CPED, and CRPD).[1819] Moreover, Chile was among the founders and the first signing countries of the United Nations Charter.[1820] In addition, as per the application of GA Resolution no. 60/251 on 15 March 2006, Chile is subject to Universal Periodic Review (UPR).[1821]

Chile signed the Convention on the Elimination of All Forms of Racial Discrimination (ICERD) on 3 October 1966, i.e., a few months after its adoption and ratified it on 20 October 1971. However, Chile did not accept the competence of the treaty's monitoring body (the Committee on the Elimination of Racial Discrimination, CERD) to receive and consider communications from individuals or groups of individuals[1822] until 18 May 1994, after the restoration of democracy, when it made the required declaration according to art.14.1.[1823] Moreover, it did not sign the Amendment

---

1819 See Office of the United Nations High Commissioner for Human Rights, International Law, at http://www.ohchr.org/EN/ProfessionalInterest/Pages/Core Instruments.aspx [Last access 04.09.2014].

1820 See the United Nations membership at http://www.un.org/en/members/growth.shtml and http://www.un.org/en/members. For Chile it corresponds to the entry into force of the UN Charter on 24 October 1945.

1821 The first UPR conducted on Chile was during the 5th session (4-15 May 2009) on 8 May 2009, see at http://www.ohchr.org/EN/HRBodies/UPR/Pages/Mee tingsHighlightsSession5.aspx. The next one was scheduled during the 18th session to take place in October 2013, see at http://www2.ohchr.org/SPdocs/UPR/UPR-FullCycleCalendar_2nd.doc, but was eventually realized last 28 January 2014, see at http://www.ohchr.org/EN/HRBodies/UPR/Pages/CLSession18.aspx [Last access to all 04.09.2014].

1822 Art.14.1 ICERD states "A State Party may at any time declare that it recognizes the competence of the Committee to receive and consider communications from individuals or groups of individuals within its jurisdiction claiming to be victims of a violation by that State Party of any of the rights set forth in this Convention. No communication shall be received by the Committee if it concerns a State Party which has not made such a declaration".

1823 See the United Nations Treaty Collection, Status of Treaties, ICERD, at http://treaties.un.org/Pages/ViewDetails.aspx?src=TREATY&mtdsg_no=IV-2&chapter=4&lang=en. See Chile's declaration accepting CERD"s competence by clicking on "Chile" [Last access 04.09.2014].

to article 8 of the ICERD on the financing of the CERD, which is not yet in force.[1824] As for the ICCPR and ICESCR, Chile's signature arrived three years after their adoption in the GA, on 16 September 1969, and their ratification on 10 February 1972.[1825] The declaration to recognize the competence of the Human Rights Committee to consider inter-state complaints (ICCPR art.41)[1826] was made by Chile on 7 September 1990, but limited its application to actions initiated after 11 March 1990 alone.[1827] This was probably due to concerns about receiving communications related to crimes committed under the Pinochet dictatorship. Indeed, Chile accessed the 1966 ICCPR-OP1 on 27 May 1992, stating clearly in its declaration that individuals' communications would refer to acts committed by the State after the protocol's entry into force or, in any case, after 11 March 1990.[1828] ICCPR-OP2 was signed by Chile on 15 November 2001, with the explicit reservation allowed by art.2.1 of applying the death penalty in time of war, in accordance with the 1980 Chilean constitution, drawn up before the restora-

1824 UN Doc. CERD/SP/45. See the United Nations Treaty Collection, Status of Treaties, Amendment to article 8 of the ICERD, at http://treaties.un.org/Pages/ViewDetails.aspx?src=TREATY&mtdsg_no=IV-2-a&chapter=4&lang=en [Last access 04.02.2015].

1825 See the United Nations Treaty Collection, Status of Treaties, ICCPR and ICESCR, respectively, at http://treaties.un.org/Pages/ViewDetails.aspx?src=TREATY&mtdsg_no=IV-4&chapter=4&lang=en, and http://treaties.un.org/Pages/ViewDetails.aspx?src=TREATY&mtdsg_no=IV-3&chapter=4&lang=en [Last access to all 04.09.2014].

1826 Art.41 of the ICCPR states "A State Party to the present Covenant may at any time declare under this article that it recognizes the competence of the Committee to receive and consider communications to the effect that a State Party claims that another State Party is not fulfilling its obligations under the present Covenant. Communications under this article may be received and considered only if submitted by a State Party which has made a declaration recognizing in regard to itself the competence of the Committee. No communication shall be received by the Committee if it concerns a State Party which has not made such a declaration. [...]".

1827 See the United Nations Treaty Collection, Status of Treaties, ICCPR at http://treaties.un.org/Pages/ViewDetails.aspx?src=TREATY&mtdsg_no=IV-4&chapter=4&lang=en, by clicking on "Chile" [Last access 04.09.2014].

1828 See the United Nations Treaty Collection, Status of Treaties, Optional Protocol to the ICCPR, at http://treaties.un.org/Pages/ViewDetails.aspx?src=TREATY&mtdsg_no=IV-4&chapter=4&lang=en, and http://treaties.un.org/Pages/ViewDetails.aspx?src=TREATY&mtdsg_no=IV-5&chapter=4&lang=en#EndDec or by clicking on "Chile" [Last access to all 04.09.2014].

tion of democracy in 1989. The protocol was finally ratified on 26 September 2008.[1829] As for the 2008 ICESCR-OP, to enable the CESCR to receive and consider communications for individual complaints, it entered into force in May 2013. While Chile signed it on 24 September 2009, it has not yet ratified it.[1830]

The 1979 Convention on the Elimination of All Forms of Discrimination against Women (CEDAW) was signed by Chile quite early –on 17 July 1980– still under the dictatorship. Upon its signature, Chile declared that "some of the provisions of the Convention are not entirely compatible with current Chilean legislation", but that a reform of the civil code was due and that changes to the legislation would be made to implement the CEDAW fully.[1831] The ratification of the CEDAW, indeed, came only on 7 December 1989.[1832] Almost immediately thereafter, Chile signed the OP-CEDAW regarding the possibility of the Committee on the Elimination of Discrimination against Women receiving communications by individuals or a group of individuals, but it has not yet ratified it.[1833]

With regard to the 1984 Convention against Torture and Other Cruel, Inhuman or Degrading Treatment or Punishment (CAT), signed by Chile on 23 September 1987, i.e., three years after its adoption, and ratified on 30 September 1988,[1834] initially Chile did not recognize the competence of the

1829 See the United Nations Treaty Collection, Status of Treaties, ICCPR-OP2, at http://treaties.un.org/Pages/ViewDetails.aspx?src=TREATY&mtdsg_no=IV-12&chapter=4&lang=en, and http://treaties.un.org/Pages/ViewDetails.aspx?src=TREATY&mtdsg_no=IV-12&chapter=4&lang=en#EndDec or by clicking on "Chile" [Last access to all 04.09.2014].

1830 See the United Nations Treaty Collection, Status of Treaties, ICESCR-OP, at http://treaties.un.org/Pages/ViewDetails.aspx?src=TREATY&mtdsg_no=IV-3-a&chapter=4&lang=en [Last access 04.02.2015].

1831 See the United Nations Treaty Collection, Status of Treaties, CEDAW *Declarations and Reservations*, Chile, at http://treaties.un.org/Pages/View Details.aspx?src=TREATY&mtdsg_no=IV-8&chapter=4&lang=en#EndDec, or at http://treaties.un.org/Pages/ViewDetails.aspx?src=TREATY&mtdsg_no=IV-8&chapter=4&lang=en by clicking on "Chile" [Last access to all 04.09.2014].

1832 See the United Nations Treaty Collection, Status of Treaties, CEDAW, at http://treaties.un.org/Pages/ViewDetails.aspx?src=TREATY&mtdsg_no=IV-8&chapter=4&lang=en [Last access 04.09.2014].

1833 See the United Nations Treaty Collection, Status of Treaties, OP-CEDAW, at http://treaties.un.org/Pages/ViewDetails.aspx?src=TREATY&mtdsg_no=IV-8-b&chapter=4&lang=en [Last access 04.09.2014].

1834 See the United Nations Treaty Collection, Status of Treaties, CAT, at http://treaties.un.org/Pages/ViewDetails.aspx?src=TREATY&mtdsg_no=IV-9&chapter=4&lang=en [Last access 04.02.2015].

Committee against Torture by virtue of article 28.1, but withdrew its position with a communication registered on 7 September 1990. It finally (15 March 2004) recognized the competence of the Committee against Torture to receive and consider communications by other state parties and from –or on behalf of– individuals in accordance with arts.21 and 22 of the CAT.[1835]

Chile promptly signed and ratified the 1989 Convention on the Rights of the Child (CRC) on 26 January 1990 and 13 August 1990, respectively, [1836] and likewise the 1995 amendment to article 43.2 of the CRC regarding the increasing number of experts in the Committee from ten to eighteen,[1837] the 2000 Optional Protocol to the Convention on the Rights of the Child on the Involvement of Children in armed conflict (CRC-OP1),[1838] and the 2000 Optional Protocol to the Convention on the Rights of the Child on the Sale of Children, Child Prostitution and Child Pornography (CRC-OP2).[1839]

The signature and ratification of the 2006 Convention on the Rights of Persons with Disabilities (CRPD) and its Optional Protocol (OP-CRPD) to allow the Committee on the Rights of Persons with Disabilities to receive and consider communications from –or on behalf of– individuals or groups of individuals, were promptly carried out by Chile, on 30 March 2007 and 29 July 2008, respectively.[1840]

1835 See the United Nations Treaty Collection, Status of Treaties, CAT *Declarations and Reservation*, Chile, and CAT *Declarations made under articles 21 and 22*, Chile, at http://treaties.un.org/Pages/ViewDetails.aspx?src=TREATY&mtdsg_no=IV-9&chapter=4&lang=en#EndDec, and CAT note 17, at http://treaties.un.org/Pages/ViewDetails.aspx?src=TREATY&mtdsg_no=IV-9&chapter=4&lang=en#17 [Last access to all 04.09.2014].

1836 See the United Nations Treaty Collection, Status of Treaties, CRC, at http://treaties.un.org/Pages/ViewDetails.aspx?src=TREATY&mtdsg_no=IV-11&chapter=4&lang=en [Last access 04.09.2014].

1837 See the United Nations Treaty Collection, Status of Treaties, Amendment to article 43.2 of the CRC, at http://treaties.un.org/Pages/ViewDetails.aspx?src=TREATY&mtdsg_no=IV-11-a&chapter=4&lang=en [Last access 04.09.2014].

1838 See the United Nations Treaty Collection, Status of Treaties, OP-CRC-AC, at http://treaties.un.org/Pages/ViewDetails.aspx?src=TREATY&mtdsg_no=IV-11-b&chapter=4&lang=en [Last access 04.09.2014].

1839 See the United Nations Treaty Collection, Status of Treaties, OP-CRC-SC, at http://treaties.un.org/Pages/ViewDetails.aspx?src=TREATY&mtdsg_no=IV-11-c&chapter=4&lang=en [Last access 04.09.2014].

1840 See the United Nations Treaty Collection, Status of Treaties, CRPD, at http://treaties.un.org/Pages/ViewDetails.aspx?src=TREATY&mtdsg_no=IV-15&chapter=4&lang=en, and OP-CRPD, at http://treaties.un.org/Pages/View Details.aspx?src=TREATY&mtdsg_no=IV-15-a&chapter=4&lang=en.

Finally, the 1990 International Convention on the Protection of the Rights of All Migrant Workers and Members of their Families (ICRMW) and the 2006 Convention for the Protection of All Persons from Enforced Disappearance (CPED) were both signed by Chile quite promptly after their adoption.[1841] The former was ratified by Chile only recently, in 2005, with a reservation on art.22.5 regarding the compensation and re-entry in the state in the case of annulment of an already executed expulsion.[1842] The latter was ratified on 8 December 2009, accompanied by the required declaration to recognize the competence of the Committee to receive and consider communications from –or on behalf of– individuals under arts.31-32 of CPED.[1843]

During the 2009 and 2014 UPRs, the recommendations to Chile concerning indigenous peoples were to adopt measures and legislation to ensure full respect for their rights, particularly those contained in the ILO Convention 169 and the UNDRIP,[1844] and to remove the obstacles that prevent the application of such rights, with particular regard to indigenous women's rights.[1845] Chile was then recommended to recognize indigenous peoples constitutionally;[1846] to reduce discrimination and xenophobia against them, particularly against women;[1847] to fight impunity and violations of (human

1841 See the United Nations Treaty Collection, Status of Treaties, ICRMW, at http://treaties.un.org/Pages/ViewDetails.aspx?src=TREATY&mtdsg_no=IV-13 &chapter=4&lang=en, and CPED, at http://treaties.un.org/Pages/View Details.aspx?src=TREATY&mtdsg_no=IV-16&chapter=4&lang=en [Last access to all 04.09.2014].

1842 See the United Nations Treaty Collection, Status of Treaties, ICRMW, at http://treaties.un.org/Pages/ViewDetails.aspx?src=TREATY&mtdsg_no=IV-13 &chapter=4&lang=en by clicking on "Chile" [Last access 04.09.2014].

1843 See the United Nations Treaty Collection, Status of Treaties, CPED, at http://treaties.un.org/Pages/ViewDetails.aspx?src=TREATY&mtdsg_no=IV-16 &chapter=4&lang=en by clicking on "Chile" [Last access 04.09.2014].

1844 Report of the Working Group on the Universal Periodic Review, Chile, Human Rights Council, twelfth session, Universal Periodic Review, 4 June 2009, UN Doc. A/HRC/12/10, para.96, no.66; Report of the Working Group on the Universal Periodic Review, Chile, Human Rights Council, Twenty–sixth session, Universal Periodic Review, 2 April 2014, UN Doc. A/HRC/26/5, paras.121.170 and 121.171.

1845 Report UPR Chile 2009, para.96, nos.16, 18, 19, 59, 64, 65 and 68; Report UPR Chile 2014, paras.121.160, 121.161, 121.162, 121.164, 121.169 and 121.178.

1846 Report UPR Chile 2009, para.96, nos.57 and 58; Report UPR Chile 2014, paras.121.163 and 121.164.

1847 Report UPR Chile 2009, para.96, nos.19, 61 and 64; Report UPR Chile 2014, paras.121.56, 121.65, 121.66, 121.67 and 121.68.

and) indigenous rights;[1848] to avoid the use of the Antiterrorism Law and ensure that it does not undermine indigenous peoples' rights;[1849] to investigate violent acts allegedly committed by police forces against indigenous peoples;[1850] to reduce socio-economic discrepancy between the indigenous and non-indigenous population;[1851] to alleviate poverty, especially among indigenous peoples;[1852] to ensure access to education and to reduce illiteracy of indigenous peoples (particularly of women) and to pursue bilingual education;[1853] to combat forms of child labor and discrimination against indigenous children;[1854] to enhance employment, health-care, and social welfare of vulnerable groups, including indigenous peoples;[1855] to continue transferring land to indigenous peoples and demarcating their lands;[1856] to promote initiatives to build dialogue between indigenous peoples and the State and to enhance indigenous participation (particularly of women) in decision-making processes, in particular in those addressing land rights;[1857] to properly consult indigenous peoples before granting concession for natural resource exploitation;[1858] and to minimize the effect of economic activities affecting indigenous peoples.[1859]

As for other international organizations, Chile is currently the second Latin American country to adhere to the Organisation for Economic Co-operation and Development (OECD).[1860]

1848 Report UPR Chile 2009, para.96, no.40.

1849 Report UPR Chile 2009, para.96, nos.68, 69 and 70; Report UPR Chile 2014, paras.121.167, 121.168 and 121.169.

1850 Report UPR Chile 2014, para.121.81.

1851 Report UPR Chile 2009, para.96, no.60.

1852 Report UPR Chile 2009, para.96, nos.54, 56 and 61; Report UPR Chile 2014, para.121.165.

1853 Report UPR Chile 2009, para.96, nos.55 and 56; Report UPR Chile 2014, paras.121.40 and 121.154, 121.155 and 121.165.

1854 Report UPR Chile 2009, para.96, no.53.

1855 Report UPR Chile 2014, para.121.40 and 121.176

1856 Report UPR Chile 2009, para.96, nos.66 and 67.

1857 Report UPR Chile 2009, para.96, nos.62, 63, 64, 65 and 66; Report UPR Chile 2014, paras.121.38, 121.166, 121.168, 121.169, 121.172, 121.174 and 121.175.

1858 Report UPR Chile 2009, para.96, no.67; Report UPR Chile 2014, paras.121.38, 121.172, 121.173 and 121.174.

1859 Report UPR Chile 2014, para.121.177.

1860 The first was Mexico in 1994. Organisation for Economic Co-operation and Development, "Members and partners (Current membership)", at http://www.oecd.org/about/membersandpartners [Last access 04.09.2014].

At the Inter-American level, Chile signed the OAS Charter upon its adoption in Bogotá in 1948 and ratified it on 5 May 1953.[1861] With regard to the ACHR, Chile was among the first signatories upon its adoption on 22 November 1969. However, similarly to the ICCPR-OP1, it only ratified the convention on 10 August 1990, which was registered on the 21 August, after which Chile recognized the competence of the Inter-American Commission on Human Rights in accordance with art.45 of the ACHR and, most importantly, the jurisdiction of the Inter-American Court of Human Rights.[1862] In the accompanying declaration, Chile stated that, once again, only the events subsequent to the date of its deposit or in any case not prior to 11 March 1990 could fall under the jurisdiction of the Commission.[1863] Furthermore, Chile declared that the two bodies, when applying art.21.2 of the ACHR, "may not make statements concerning the reasons of public utility or social interest taken into account in depriving a person of his property".[1864] This may have played a role in the Ralco case before the Inter-American Commission in 2002 which ended, as mentioned, with a Friendly Settlement.

As for the other OAS Conventions, Chile ratified, in chronological order, the Inter-American Convention to Prevent and Punish Torture in 1988;[1865]

1861 See the Charter of the Organization of American States, Signatories and Ratifications, at http://www.oas.org/dil/treaties_A-41_Charter_of_the_Organi zation_of_American_States_sign.htm [Last access 04.09.2014].

1862 See the American Convention on Human Rights, Signatories and Ratifications, at http://www.cidh.oas.org/basicos/english/Basic4.Amer.Conv.Ratif.htm [Last access 04.09.2014].

1863 See the American Convention on Human Rights, Signatories and Ratifications, Declarations / Reservations / Denunciations / Withdrawals, Chile, at http://www.cidh.oas.org/basicos/english/Basic4.Amer.Conv.Ratif.htm#5 [Last access 04.09.2014].

1864 See the American Convention on Human Rights, Signatories and Ratifications, Declarations / Reservations / Denunciations / Withdrawals, Chile, at http://www.ci dh.oas.org/basicos/english/Basic4.Amer.Conv.Ratif.htm#5 [Last access 04.09. 2014]. Art.21 of the ACHR concern the right to property and, as well-known, was the key norm of the notorious case *The Mayagna (Sumo) Awas Tingni Community v. Nicaragua*, Serie C No. 79 Judgment of 31 August 31 2001. Art.21.2 reads as follows: "No one shall be deprived of his property except upon payment of just compensation, for reasons of public utility or social interest, and in the cases and according to the forms established by law."

1865 See Signatures and Current Status of Ratifications of the Inter-American Convention to Prevent and Punish Torture, at http://www.oa s.org/juridico/english/sigs/a-51.html [Last access 21.08.2014].

the Inter-American Convention on the Prevention, Punishment and Eradication of Violence against Women "Convention of Belem do Pará" in 1996;[1866] the Inter-American Convention on the Elimination of All Forms of Discrimination against Persons with Disabilities in 2002;[1867] the Inter-American Convention on Forced Disappearance of Persons in 2010;[1868] and the Protocol to the American Convention on Human Rights to Abolish the Death Penalty in 2008. However, this last protocol has been blocked since 1990 and is not yet in force.[1869] Chile signed the Additional Protocol to the American Convention on Human Rights in the Area of Economic Social and Cultural Rights – "Protocol of San Salvador" in 2001, but has not yet ratified it.[1870] Likewise, Chile has signed neither the Inter-American Convention Against All Forms of Discrimination and Intolerance, nor the Inter-American Convention Against Racism, Racial Discrimination, and Related Forms of Intolerance adopted by OAS in June 2013.[1871] Finally, the Inter-American Democratic Charter was the sole OAS treaty that explicitly mentioned indigenous peoples prior to the adoption of the 2013 Inter-American Convention Against Racism, Racial Discrimination, and Related Forms of Intolerance. Chile, along with the majority of the American states, supported and voted in favour of the Charter's adoption on 11 September

1866 See Signatures and Current Status of the Inter-American Convention on the Prevention, Punishment and Eradication of Violence against Women "Convention of Belem do Pará", at http://www.oas.org/juridico/english/sigs/a-61.html [Last access 21.08.2014].

1867 See Signatures and Current Status of the Inter-American Convention on the Elimination of All Forms of Discrimination against Person with Disabilities, at http://www.oas.org/juridico/english/sigs/a-65.html [Last access 21.08.2014].

1868 See Signatures and Current Status of the Inter-American Convention on Forced Disappearance of Persons, at http://www.oas.org/juridico/english/sigs/a-60.html [Last access 21.08.2014].

1869 See Signatures and Current Status of Ratifications of the Protocol to the American Convention on Human Rights to Abolish the Death Penalty, at http://www.oas.org/juridico/english/sigs/a-53.html [Last access 04.02.2015].

1870 See Signatures and Current Status of Ratifications of the Additional Protocol to the American Convention on Human Rights in the Area of Economic Social and Cultural Rights "Protocol of San Salvador", at http://www.oas.org/juri dico/english/sigs/a-52.html [Last access 04.02.2015].

1871 See Signatures and Current Status of Ratifications of the Inter-American Convention Against All Forms of Discrimination and Intolerance and of the Inter-American Convention Against Racism, Racial Discrimination, and Related Forms of Intolerance at http://www.oas.org/en/sla/dil/inter_american_treaties_A-69_di scrimination_intolerance_signatories.asp and http://www.oas.org/en/sla/dil/inte r_american_treaties_A-68_racism_signatories.asp, respectively [Last access 04.02.2015].

2001,[1872] the day of the attack on the twin towers in the US and the anniversary of the *golpe* in Chile in 1973.

As seen in chapter 4 (section 4.2), a draft of the American Declaration on the Rights of Indigenous Peoples was approved in 1997. During the meeting of the Working Group to Prepare the Draft American Declaration on the Rights of Indigenous Peoples of November 2009, a classification on the provisions that could facilitate consensus over the Declaration text was adopted.[1873] The "difficult texts" included the provision on "Traditional forms of property and cultural survival – Right to land, territory, and Resources", which would conform art.24 of a later text. In relation to the first paragraph of this provision,[1874] Chile declared that it would reserve the right to review the term "territories" used in this clause.[1875] Nevertheless, the adoption of the Draft American Declaration is still pending[1876] and Chile might consider revising this declaration.

With regard to the Inter-American system of human rights –apart from the above-mentioned case of the Ralco hydroelectric plant that was brought before the Inter-American Commission on Human Rights and solved with a Friendly Settlement adopted on 11 March 2004– last May 2014 the Inter-American Court of Human Rights adopted a landmark decision vis-à-vis indigenous (Mapuche) rights, namely *Norín Catrimán and Other v.*

1872 See the Inter-American Democratic Charter "Actas de las sesiones", at http://scm.oas.org/doc_public/SPANISH/HIST_01/AC00535T06.doc [Last access 04.09.2014].

1873 Organization of American States, Committee on Juridical and Political Affairs, Working Group to Prepare the Draft American Declaration on the Rights of Indigenous Peoples, "Classification of provisions that could facilitate consensus – Updated upon the conclusion of the Eleventh Meeting of Negotiations", OAS Doc. No.OEA/Ser.K/XVI, GT/DADIN/doc.329/08 rev. 3, 19 November 2009, at http://www.oas.org/dil/GT-DADIN-doc_329-08_rev3_eng.pdf [Last access 04.09.2014].

1874 The first paragraph of art.24 of the debated text reads as follows: "Indigenous peoples have the right to maintain and strengthen their distinctive spiritual, cultural, and material relationship to their lands, territories, and resources and the [duty] to assume their responsibilities to preserve them for themselves and for future generations".

1875 Organization of American States, Committee on Juridical and Political Affairs, Working Group to Prepare the Draft American Declaration on the Rights of Indigenous Peoples 2009, p.16, note 32.

1876 See the website of the Working Group (*Grupo de Trabajo Encargado de Elaborar el Proyecto de Declaración Americana sobre los Derechos de los Pueblos Indígenas*) at http://www.oas.org/consejo/sp/CAJP/Indigenas.asp [Last access 04.02.2015].

Chile.[1877] This case concerned eight Mapuche people, some of them traditional authorities (*Lonkos*) or spokespersons (*Werken*), condemned to between five and ten years of prison for crimes of threats of (terrorist) arson, wildfires, and arson of a private company's truck committed between 2000 and 2001 and judged under military justice by application of the abovementioned Antiterrorism Law (see section 6.1.2.3). The Court eventually found that all the Mapuche claimants suffered violations of the following principles and rights: The principle of legality and the right of presumption of innocence (arts.9 and 8.2 of the American Convention on Human Rights – ACHR);[1878] the principle of equality and non-discrimination and the right to equal protection before the law (arts.24 in relation with art.1.1 ACHR);[1879] the right of personal freedom (arts. 7.1, 7.3, 7.5 and 8.2 ACHR);[1880] and the right to appeal (art.8.2.h in relation with art.1.1 ACHR).[1881] Additionally, for two claimants the right of the defence to reply to witnesses' declarations (arts.24, 8.1, 8.2.f and 8.2.h in relation with art.1.1 ACHR) was also violated.[1882] Finally, the right to freedom of thought and expressions of three claimants (arts.13 and 23 ACHR)[1883] and the political rights of the other five plaintiffs (arts.23 in relation with art.1.1 ACHR)[1884] were also infringed. Therefore, the Court affirmed that the State of Chile must promptly comply with the following obligations: to adopt within 6 months all the necessary legislative and administrative measures to render null and void the criminal decisions against the eight Mapuche claimants, to halt their punishments, and to release them;[1885] to grant free and immediate medical and psychological or psychiatric assistance to all the detainees;[1886] to disseminate the outcomes of this decision in the media (radio, TV and publications);[1887] to give scholarships to the children of the

---

1877 Inter-American Court of Human Rights, Case of *Norín Catrimán y Otros (Dirigentes, Miembros y Activista del Pueblo Indígena Mapuche) v Chile*, Serie C No.279, Judgment of 29 May 2014.
1878 *Ibid.*, para.174.
1879 *Ibid.*, para.230.
1880 *Ibid.*, paras.327, 343, 355 and 358.
1881 *Ibid.*, para.291.
1882 *Ibid.*, paras.252 and 260.
1883 *Ibid.*, para.366.
1884 *Ibid.*, para.386.
1885 *Ibid.*, paras.422 and 478.1.
1886 *Ibid.*, paras.425-426 and 478.2.
1887 *Ibid.*, paras.428-429 and 478.3.

detainees;[1888] and, apart from covering the case expenses,[1889] to compensate each of the claimants with 50.000 US dollars for both material and non-material damages.[1890] Most importantly, the Court stated that Chile must regulate with clarity and legal certainty the procedure of using unidentified witnesses and ensure that this would be an exceptional measure subject to judicial control based on the principles of necessity and proportionality. Additionally, such measures cannot be used in the upper instance (i.e., after which there is no other possibility to appeal) and counterbalancing measures must be regulated.[1891] Finally, the Court affirmed that the presumption of a “terrorist intention” of the Antiterrorism Law, which is quite arbitrary, as seen above, violates the principle of legality and presumption of innocence in accordance with arts.9 and 8.2 of the ACHR. This decision is certainly a milestone in indigenous rights in Chile, but much remains to be seen with regard to the Chilean State’s reply the and the recently announced reform of the Antiterrorism Law (see section 6.1.2.3). In her recent visit to Chile in late 2014, the Rapporteur on the Rights of Indigenous Peoples of the Organization of American States also stressed the need to halt the application of this law to indigenous peoples and promptly reform it.[1892]

More specifically on indigenous rights, Chile voted for the adoption of the UNDRIP in 2007[1893] and ratified the ILO Convention 169 in 2008,[1894] which entered into force on 15 September 2009 in accordance with art.38 of the Convention. The adoption of the ILO Convention 169 experienced continuous setbacks following the restoration of democracy. During the debates on whether to ratify the Convention in the late 1990s, the Chilean

---

1888 *Ibid.*, paras.432 and 478.4.

1889 *Ibid.*, paras. 452, 453, 470, 471, 475, 478.7 and 478.8.

1890 *Ibid.*, paras.446, 471, 475 and 478.6.

1891 *Ibid.*, paras.242-247, 436 and 478.5.

1892 Francisca Rivas, “Autoridad de Comisión Interamericana de DDHH se reunió con dirigentes mapuche en Temuco”, *Radio Bío-Bío*, 27.11.2014, at http://www.biobiochile.cl/2014/nov/27/autoridad-de-comision-interamericana-d e-ddhh-se-reunio-con-dirigentes-mapuche-en-temuco.shtml [Last access 05.02. 2015]. On the Rapporteur on the Rights of Indigenous Peoples of the Organization of American States see chapter 4, section 4.2.

1893 See webpage of United Nations Human Rights, “Declaration on the rights of indigenous peoples”, at http://www.ohchr.org/en/Issues/IPeoples/Pages/De claration.aspx [Last access 18.07.2014].

1894 Decree of the Ministry of External Affairs (*Ministerio de Relaciones Exteriores*) No.236 of 2 October 2008, at http://www.leychile.cl/Navegar/?id Norma=279441&idVersion=2009-09-15&idParte [Last access 04.09.2014].

Constitutional Court (*Tribunal Constitucional de Chile*) was called to decide on an alleged constitutional incompatibility of the ILO Convention 169 raised by a number of deputies.[1895] The Court eventually declared that: The Convention was constitutional; arts.6.1 (right to consultation) and 7.1 (right to participation in plans and projects) of the ILO Convention 169 were self-executing, thus not in need of any further legislation to enter into force; these norms were to be considered of constitutional level;[1896] and that the aim of the consultation is to reach an agreement or consent in good faith.[1897] In 2008, the alleged unconstitutionality of the ILO Convention 169 was brought again before the Constitutional Court.[1898] The Court reiterated the constitutionality of the ILO Convention 169, but adopted a more cautious approach in comparison to its decision of 2000. In particular, it concluded that the outcome of the consultation as referred to in art.6.2 (the reaching of an agreement or the consent) is neither binding nor a mandatory negotiation, but just "a collection of opinions.[1899] This is in stark contrast to its previous jurisprudence and international standards.[1900] Nevertheless, this decision has not been considered so much as the previous one by the Court of Appeals in the Amparo proceedings regarding the right to consultation (see section 6.3.2.3).

After the ratification of the ILO Convention 169, according to arts.32.15 and 54.1 of the Chilean Constitution (*Constitución Política de la República de Chile* – CPR) all the necessary reforms required by the ratification of an international treaty should be adopted by the Congress and the President. However, during the first years, the ILO Convention 169 has essentially been applied solely by the Courts of Appeal in the cases of Amparo proceedings (in Chile called *Recurso de Protección* according to art.19 of the Constitution), as will be discussed below (section 6.3.2.3).

1895 Chilean Constitutional Court/*Tribunal Constitucional de Chile*, Decision/*Sentencia Rol* 309 of 4 August 2000 on "Requerimiento formulado por diversos Diputados para que el Tribunal resuelva la Constitucionalidad del Convenio N° 169, sobre Pueblos Indígenas y Tribales en Países Independientes, adoptado por la Organización Internacional del Trabajo, el 27 de junio de 1989, de acuerdo al artículo 82, N° 2, de la Constitución Política de la República".

1896 *Ibid.*, 6th, 7th ans 8th *Considerando* (Considering), para.5.

1897 *Ibid.*, 7th *Considerando* (Considering), para.5.

1898 Chilean Constitutional Court, Decision Rol 1.050, 3 April 2008.

1899 *Ibid.*, 14th *Considerando* (Considering).

1900 Jorge Contesse and Domingo Lovera, "Pueblos Indígenas y Participación Política en la Óptica del Tribunal Constitucional", in Javier Couso (ed.), *Anuario de Derecho Público 2010*, Ediciones Universidad Diego Portales, Santiago de Chile, 2010, pp.21-37, p.16.

The first review of the application of the ILO Convention No. 169 in accordance with art.22 of the ILO Constitution occurred under Piñera's presidency in late 2010.[1901] The ILO Committee of Experts on the Application of Conventions and Recommendations (CEACR) first recommended the government to reply to the issues of a lack of implementation raised by two trade unions representing Mapuche organizations,[1902] because of the great contrast between the reports of the government and those of indigenous organization.[1903] Secondly, the CEACR raised other relevant points, thus addressing a direct request to the government according to art.25 of the ILO Constitution.[1904] The Committee, in particular, requested the Chilean

1901 See the official review prepared by CONADI for Chile's government, "Memoria Presentada por el Gobierno de Chile en conformidad con las disposiciones del artículo 22 de la Constitución de la Organización Internacional del Trabajo correspondiente al periodo 15 de septiembre de 2009 al 15 de septiembre de 2010 acerca de las medidas adoptadas para dar efectividad a las disposiciones del Convenio sobre Pueblos Indígenas y Tribales, 1989 (NÚM. 169), ratificado por Chile el 15 de septiembre de 2008", 10 August 2010, at www.dere choshumanos.udp.cl/wp-content/uploads/2010/10/memoria-oficial-convenio-16 9-oit-1c2b0-septiembre-2010.pdf [Last access 04.09.2014]. Art.22 of the ILO Constitution states: "Each of the Members agrees to make an annual report to the International Labour Office on the measures which it has taken to give effect to the provisions of Conventions to which it is a party. These reports shall be made in such form and shall contain such particulars as the Governing Body may request."

1902 The *Confederación Nacional de Pescadores Artesanales de Chile* (CONAPACH), and the *Central Unitaria de Trabajadores de Chile* (CUT) represented the *Coordinación de Organizaciones y Comunidades Mapuches, Región de la Araucanía* and the *Centro de Cultura Pueblos Nación Mapuche Pelón Xaru*.

1903 Confederación Nacional de Pescadores Artesanales de Chile (CONAPACH), "Informe Alternativo 2010 respecto del cumplimiento del Convenio 169 sobre Pueblos Indígenas y Tribales de la OIT, al cumplirse un año de su entrada en vigencia en Chile", 01.09.2010, at www.derechoshumanos.udp.cl/wp-content/uploads/20 10/10/memoria-alternativa-convenio-169-oit-chile-2010-1.pdf; Victor Toledo Llancaqueo, "Chile deberá repetir examen ante OIT en 2011 por Convenio 169. El imperativo del diálogo", 16.02.2011, at www.politicaspublicas.net/panel/c169noticias/728-chile-convenio169-chile-repite-examen-2011.html [Last access to both 04.09.2014].

1904 See International Labour Conference, "Report III (1A). Report of the Committee of Experts on the Application of Conventions and Recommendations", ILO Doc. No. ILC.100/III/1A, 2011, p.790, at http://www.ilo.org/wcmsp5/groups/publi c/---ed_norm/---relconf/documents/meetingdocument/wcms_151556.pdf; and Committee of Experts on the Application of Conventions and Recommendations, "Direct Request (CEACR) - adopted 2010, published 100th ILC session (2011)" to Chile, 2011, at http://www.ilo.org/dyn/normlex/en/f?p=1000:13100:0::N O:13100:P13100_COMMENT_ID:2334939 [Last access 04.09.2014]. Art.25 of the ILO Constitution states: "If no statement is received within a reasonable time

government to amend the domestic legislation on natural resources, in order to be consistent with art.15 of the ILO Convention No. 169. According to the CEACR, a proper consultation with indigenous peoples shall be carried out whenever a large environmental project may affect directly indigenous peoples, who shall also have a share in the benefits.[1905] A reply by the Chilean government was sent on 16 May 2011.[1906] On the aforementioned issue, after having provided some evidence on the consultations carried out between 2009 and 2010, the government replied that a new "Broad Consultation" was launched in 2011.[1907] As will be discussed below, the results of the consultations were not made public and the consultation was finally suspended (see section 6.3.2.2). In 2013, the CEACR sent another direct request[1908] and reiterated the need to provide further information on the implementation of the ILO Convention 169 by 2015, with regard to land, participation, and consultation rights (art.6, 7, and 13-16 of the Convention). In particular, in its Observation of 2013, the CEASCR noted a "persistence of a situation that is not in compliance with the Convention" vis-à-vis land rights (art.13-14 of the Convention).[1909]

from the government in question, or if the statement when received is not deemed to be satisfactory by the Governing Body, the latter shall have the right to publish the representation and the statement, if any, made in reply to it."

1905 Committee of Experts on the Application of Conventions and Recommendations, "Direct Request (CEACR) - adopted 2010, published 100th ILC session (2011)".

1906 See Chilean Government, "Respuesta a la Solicitud Directa 2010/81 y a la Observación 2010/81 de la OIT", 16.05.2011, at www.observatorio.cl/sites/default/files/biblioteca/observacion-2010-81-oit-01-09-11_.pdf [Last access 04.09.2014].

1907 Chilean Government, "Respuesta a la Solicitud Directa 2010/81 y a la Observación 2010/81 de la OIT", pp.74-75.

1908 Committee of Experts on the Application of Conventions and Recommendations, "Direct Request (CEACR) - adopted 2013, published 103rd ILC session (2014)", 2014, at http://www.ilo.org/dyn/normlex/en/f?p=1000:13100:0::NO:13100:P13100_COMMENT_ID:3140784:NO [Last access 04.09.2014].

1909 Committee of Experts on the Application of Conventions and Recommendations, "Observation (CEACR) – adopted 2013, published 103rd ILC session (2014)", 2014 at http://www.ilo.org/dyn/normlex/en/f?p=1000:13100:0::NO:13100:P13100_COMMENT_ID:3140788:NO [Last access 04.09.2014].

6.2.2 Domestic protection of indigenous peoples' rights

6.2.2.1 The lack of constitutional recognition

As mentioned in chapter 4, Chile is one of the six Latin American countries which have not yet constitutionally recognized the indigenous peoples living within their national borders.[1910] The Constitution is still the text adopted under Pinochet in 1980, although it has been consistently revised since the restoration of democracy in 1989.[1911] Moreover, the student protests and the inclusion of their leaders in the current ruling party New Majority (*Nueva Mayoría*) of Michelle Bachelet, as discussed above (section 6.1.2.4), prompted a new debate on establishing a Constituent Assembly.[1912]

1910 The others are Cuba, Costa Rica, Dominican Republic, El Salvador, Puerto Rico, and Uruguay. Two of these states at least recognize the duty of the state to protect (Costa Rica) and also to teach indigenous languages (El Salvador). See chapter 4.

1911 See all the reforms at http://www.leychile.cl/Navegar?idNorma=242302 under "Versiones" [Last access 04.09.2014].

1912 In 2010, thanks to the support of some senators (in Chile, the popular legislative initiative does not exist), some organizations had put forward a proposal called "Fourth Ballot Box" (*Cuarta Urna*) to consult the population on a potential Constituent Assembly during the elections. Since 2013, and also during the presidential electoral campaign, a number of organizations are again pursuing the establishment of a Constituent Assembly.
These organizations include: Mark your vote (*Marca Tu Voto*), Constituent Convergence (*Convergencia Constituyente*), Constituent Process (*Proceso Constituyente*), and the radio ad hoc programme Constitutent Hour (*Hora Constituyente*). Paulina Acevedo, "Asamblea Constituyente: Una demanda que crece", *Observatorio Ciudadano*, 22.10.2014, at http://observatorio.cl/2014/asamblea-constituyente-una-demanda-que-crece. See also the above-mentioned organizations' websites at, respectively: www.marcatuvoto.cl; www.convergenciaconstituyente.cl; www.procesoconstitu yente.cl; www.horaconstituyente.cl. In October 2014, a number of indigenous organizations and indigenous-friendly political parties signed a petition addressed to President Bachelet to support the demand of a Constituent Assembly. Moreover, some Mapuche leaders organized a traditional meeting (*Trawun*) of chiefs (*Lonko* or *Longko*) to support, *inter alia*, the call for a Constituent Assembly. Elías Paillan, "Organizaciones de La Araucanía solicitan a Bachelet una nueva constitución por medio de una Asamblea Constituyente: A medio día entregaron carta en la Intendencia", *Observatorio Ciudadano*, 03.10.2014, at http://observatorio.cl/no de/12244; Asemblea Constituyente, "Histórico Trawún Mapuche acuerda avanzar hacia la Asamblea Constituyente", at http://constituyentechile.cl/noticias/tra wun.mapuche-acuerda-asamblea-constituyente.html [Last Access to both 05.02.2015].

This initiative gained considerable political[1913] and popular[1914] support during 2014, and was announced to start in late 2015 according to the annual Presidential Message on 21 May 2015.[1915]

Debates on a constitutional recognition of indigenous peoples have been going on since 1991, when the first draft was submitted to the senate by President Patricio Aylwin Azócar, elected in 1990 after Pinochet's dictatorship. The reform was blocked by the Senate (or High Chamber) in 2012[1916] and continues to be so today (July 2015). It is worth reporting here the main steps from 1991 onwards.

A presidential message of 8 October 1991 (Bulletin No.513-07) contained the first proposal of the constitutional recognition of indigenous peoples. This first proposal mentioned indigenous peoples insofar as they were "integrated" into the Chilean nation, but nothing else.[1917] In July 1992, the State's duty to ensure indigenous peoples' development and legal protection was added. The Chamber of Deputies (or Low Chamber) approved this text, but it was then archived due to the approval of the Indigenous Law. Eight years later, in 2000, a slightly more comprehensive version was rejected during the first discussions in the Low Chamber.[1918]

1913 Gonzalo Castillo, "Nueva Constitución: La batalla que se viene", *Diario Universidad de Chile*, 28.01.2015, at http://radio.uchile.cl/2015/01/28/nueva-constitucion-la-batalla-que-se-viene [Last access 05.02.2015].

1914 Pro-Constituent Assembly marches took place throughout Chile on 23 November 2014. They were planned by the above-mentioned organizations, but large sectors of the population eventually participated. Apart from Santiago, the larger marches were held in Arica, Antofagasta, Valparaíso and Concepción. Andrés Ojeda, "Asamblea Constituyente recibe apoyo transversal en marchas a lo largo del país", *Diario Universidad de Chile*, 23.11.2014, at http://radio.uchile.cl/2014/11/23/asamblea-constituyente-recibe-apoyo-transversal-en-mrchas-a-lo-largo-del-pais [Last access 05.02.2015].

1915 Michelle Bachelet, "Mensaje Presidencial 21 de Mayo de 2015", 21.05.2015, p.10.

1916 See *Proyecto de reforma constitucional que reconoce el aporte de los pueblos originarios a la conformación de la nación chilena*, Bulletin/Boletín No.5324-07. All the draft laws hereinafter cited may be found at http://www.senado.cl/app senado/templates/tramitacion/index.php by inserting the bulletin number in the search box "Boletín" [Last access 05.02.2015].

1917 See *Reforma Constitucional relativa a los pueblos indígenas*, Bulletin/*Boletín* No.513-07.

1918 Victor Toledo Llancaqueo "Trayectoria de una Negación. La transición chilena y el compromiso de reconocimiento de los Derechos de los Pueblos Indígenas. 1989-2006", *Politicas Publicas*, 2006, p.12, at http://www.politicaspublicas.net/panel/component/content/article/290-trayectoria-de-una-negacion-los-proyectos-de-qreconocimiento-constitucional-indigenaq-de-la-transicion-chilena-1990-2006.html?blogid=1&month=6&year=2012&d=n&p=m [Last access 04.09.2014].

In 1999 a motion of the deputies Huenchumilla, Elgueta, René García, Tuma, Hernandéz, Ojeda, Luksic, Juan Bustos, Ceroni, and Juan Pablo Latelier contained new, significant, and specific proposals to safeguard indigenous peoples, and especially their right to political participation (Bulletin No.2360-07). They proposed to reserve ten seats in the Low Chamber and three in the High Chamber for indigenous representatives; to create an indigenous Congress; and to add indigenous councilors in municipalities with more than 5% indigenous population. This project was not taken forward.[1919]

In a subsequent motion by the senators Bitar, Hamilton, Silva, and Viera-Gallo in 2000, in the framework of a project of broader constitutional reform (Bulletin No.2534-07), the recognition of indigenous peoples disappeared, who were considered an "integrating" part of the Chilean nation. The promoters suggested the insertion of a general State duty to enhance the respect for and development of indigenous cultures and their social participation. In 2001, this motion was amended by a proposal to add a paragraph to art.1 of the Constitution that the Chilean nation is "indivisible" and that cultural diversity is recognized, without the literal recognition of indigenous peoples. This motion was passed by the Senate in January 2002, but subsequent versions, containing the idea that the Chilean nation is "one and indivisible" and other limiting provisions on indigenous peoples' rights, were finally rejected in 2005.[1920]

In 2006, another proposal was presented by the deputies Ascendio Diaz, Ojeda, Tuma, Meza, Navarro, Saffirio, and Soto (Bulletin No. 4069-07), that recommended (again) adding a paragraph to art.1 stating that the Chilean nation is "one and indivisible" and inserting a generic reference to a law (presumably, the Indigenous Law already in force) to secure indigenous peoples' rights as part of the Chilean nation. Only the amendment to art.1

1919 See *Reforma constitucional que reconoce la existencia de los pueblos indígenas y les otorga participación política en el Estado*, Bulletin/*Boletín* No.2360-07; and Toledo Llancaqueo "Trayectoria de una Negación …", pp.13-14.

1920 See *Reforma constitucional sobre elecciones de Diputados y Senadores, composición del Senado, integración y atribuciones del Tribunal Constitucional, Fuerzas Armadas, Consejo de Seguridad Nacional, Plebiscito y otras materias que indica*, Bulletin/*Boletín* No.2534-07; and Toledo Llancaqueo "Trayectoria de una Negación …", pp.15-18.

was approved on 10 January 2006 by the Chamber of Deputies, but the project was archived in April 2009.[1921]

Finally, on 6 September 2007, the senators Allmand, Cantero, Thorn, Garcia, and Romero filed another motion (Bulletin No.5324-07),[1922] which was then merged with the draft constitutional initiated by the Presidential Message No.1101-355 of 23 November 2007 (Bulletin No. 5522-07), which absorbed the previous Presidential Message No.178-355 of the 4 October 2007 and the proceedings in the Chamber of Deputies for the same constitutional reform (Bulletin No. 5427-07).

Initially, President Bachelet's proposal regarded the possibility of adding to art.3 of the Chilean Constitution a fourth paragraph stating that Chile is multicultural; the State recognizes the existence of indigenous peoples on its territory and the right of these peoples and communities to preserve, develop, and strengthen their identity, languages, institutions, and social and cultural traditions. Moreover, Bachelet proposed adding a paragraph to art.19.24 (at the tenth position) that specifies that the law will protect indigenous peoples' lands and right to waters.[1923]

Afterwards, the Commission of Constitution, Legislation, Justice and Ruling (*Comisión de Constitución, Legislación, Justicia y Reglamento*) prepared a report on the proposed reform that was submitted to the Senate on 23 January 2009.[1924] The phobia over the recognition of the word "people"

1921 See *Establece una reforma constitucional sobre pueblos indígenas*, Bulletin/*Boletín* No.4069-07; and Toledo Llancaqueo "Trayectoria de una Negación ...", pp.19-20.

1922 *Proyecto de reforma constitucional que reconoce el aporte de los pueblos originarios a la conformación de la nación chilena*, Bulletin/Boletín No.5324-07.

1923 My translation. The Spanish original text stated: "1) Agregase el siguiente inciso cuarto al Art. 3º: i. 'La nación chilena es multicultural. ii. El Estado reconoce la existencia de los pueblos indígenas que habitan su territorio y el derecho de los pueblos, comunidades y personas indígenas a conservar, desarrollar y fortalecer su identidad, idiomas, instituciones y tradiciones sociales y culturales'. 2) Agrégase el siguiente nuevo inciso 10º al artículo 19 Nº 24, pasando el actual a ser 11º en el siguiente sentido: i. 'Con todo, la ley deberá proteger las tierras y derechos de aguas de las personas y comunidades indígenas.'", *Reconoce a los pueblos indígenas de Chile*, Presidential Message No.1101-355 of 23 November 2007, Bulletin/*Boletín* No. 5522-07, pp.6-7.

1924 Chilean Commission of Constitution, Legislation, Justice and Ruling/*Comisión de Constitución, Legislación, Justicia y Reglamento*, "Primer informe de Comisión de Constitución, Legislación, Justicia y Reglamento", 23 January 2009, at http://www.senado.cl/appsenado/templates/tramitacion/index.php by inserting the bulletin number 5324-07in the search box "Boletín", and clicking on "Informe Comparado".

is clearly visible in the Commission's discussion. However, the Commission concludes that the word "people" in combination with "communities" clarifies (and limits) the subjects of the constitutional reform.[1925] The right to water was also extensively debated. The main issues relate to the special protection of the waters of the Aymara and Atacama communities in the Indigenous Law (art.64). The protection provided by this norm is, however, subject to the signing of an agreement, and there cannot be any exceptions to the Water Code in the part that establishes the procedures for establishing the rights to use water (Water Code art.117).[1926]

Nevertheless, the fundamental problem is that there are no "water rights" left in Chile.[1927] Art.24 of the Constitution, in fact, recognizes a right to property for those individuals or firms that inscribed a right to use a spring in the national register. In other words, in Chile, according to art.24 of the Constitution, the right to use a spring equated to the right to permanently own it. It is an absurd inheritance of the Pinochet dictatorship which overprotects the private exploitation of water. This has led to a massive privatization of watercourses and the registration of "water rights", which have already been secured by private companies. The concern over the recognition of water rights to indigenous peoples is still very pressing. During the sessions of this Commission, Senator Larrain argued that there are undoubtedly no ancestral rights of indigenous communities over water, because although indigenous peoples certainly occupied the territory before the arrival of the Spaniards but they never channeled watercourses for irrigating fields or other purposes. The waterworks began in the central valley in the nineteenth century. Therefore, according to Larrain, it cannot be argued that there are indigenous water use rights of ancestral character and thus this cannot be established in the Constitution.[1928] It goes without saying that this claim appears to be a desperate attempt to deny water rights to indigenous peoples, since it cannot be argued that there has been ancestral use of land without using water. Such ancestral uses may create the legal basis for the recognition and enjoyment of both rights. In addition, arts.20, 21, and 22 of the Indigenous Law regulate the Fund for Indigenous Land and Water, under which CONADI can finance the institution, regularization, or purchase of water rights, finance works aimed at obtaining this resource (art.20, letter c), and receive water rights by the State (art.21.3). Therefore, indigenous

1925 *Ibid.*, p.21.
1926 *Ibid.*, pp.19-20
1927 *Ibid.*, p.16, statement by Senator Espina.
1928 *Ibid.*, p.19.

peoples' water rights are already recognized, not only in the Indigenous Law but also, as affirmed in the *Chusmiza* case, in the ILO Convention 169 (see section 6.3.2.3). Recently, the further desertification of the northern areas of Chile and the above-mentioned problems caused by the indefinite appropriation of water rights have prompted civil society organizations to insistently demand a reform of the Water Code.[1929] In 2011, the Lower Chamber's Commission of Natural Resources, National Goods and Environment (*Comisión de Recursos Naturales, Bienes Nacionales y Medio Ambiente*) started working to reform the Water Code.[1930] Since May 2013, the Lower Chamber's Commission of Hydric Resources and Desertification (*Comisión de Recursos Hídricos y Desertificación*) has been working on a draft law to reform the Water Code with regard to subterranean watercourses[1931] and, since December 2014, on another draft law to modify the Law of General Health Services to improve the provision of drinking water.[1932] The main achievements so far (July 2015) concern the reform of the Water Code (Bulletin 8960-33) and are the following: The recognition of the right to water as a human right and its interconnection with land rights in the case of indigenous peoples;[1933] and the introduction of a 30-year limit for water concessions, thus eliminating permanent water rights.[1934]

Eventually, the draft reform that was approved by the Commission (still) foresees substituting art.4 of the Constitution with the following text: "The Chilean Nation is one, indivisible and multicultural. The State recognizes the existence of indigenous peoples living on its territory and the right of their communities, organizations and members to maintain, strengthen and develop their identity, culture, language, traditions and institutions and to

---

1929 Sara Larrain, "Reforma al Código de Aguas: Insuficiente", *Chile Sustentable*, 27.10.2014, at http://www.chilesustentable.net/reforma-al-codigo-de-aguas-4 [Last access 05.02.2015].

1930 *Reforma el Código de Aguas*, Bulletin/Boletín No.8960-33.

1931 *Modifica Código de Aguas y otros cuerpos legales, respecto al uso de las aguas subterráneas*, Bulletin/Boletín No.8960-33.

1932 Modifica la ley General de Servicios Sanitarios, en el sentido de privilegiar la disposición de aguas servidas tratadas, para usos en actividades agrícolas y mineras, Bulletin/Boletín No.9779-33.

1933 Patricio Segura, "Histórico avance en Comisión de Recursos Hídricos de la Cámara", *Observatorio Ciudadano*, 10.01.2015, at http://observatorio.cl/20 15/historico-avance-en-comision-de-recursos-hidricos-de-la-camara [Last access 05.02.2015].

1934 Misle Sepúlveda, "Nueva Mayoría aprueba fin a perpetuidad de derechos de agua", *Chile Sustentable*, 23.01.2015, at http://www.chilesustentable.net/nueva-mayoria-aprueba-fin-a-perpetuidad-de-derechos-de-agua [Last access 05.02.2015].

participate in economic, social, political and cultural development according to the national legal order. Indigenous peoples may organize their lives according to their customs, provided that they do not contravene the Constitution and laws".[1935] Moreover, they agreed to add a last paragraph to art.19.24 of the Constitution stating that the law protects the indigenous peoples' property over land and their rights to water use in accordance with the Constitution and the other laws.[1936]

In sum, the last draft constitutional reform had two main limits. On the one hand, only a generic "existence" of indigenous peoples is inserted. On the other hand, more importantly, the right to a water supply should be subjected to the law creating the conditions for a conflict between the Indigenous Law (art.64 on right to water of the northern indigenous peoples) and the Water Code or, even worse, with the right to property of water contained in art.24 of the Constitution, as mentioned above. Finally, if the constitutional reform were taken forward and approved with this current text, any law providing indigenous peoples with rights to water would be formally subject to this limiting constitutional provision.

Nevertheless, as mentioned, the reform is still blocked in the Senate. The debate gained momentum in 2009 thanks to the visit of the UN Special Rapporteur on the situation of human rights and fundamental freedoms of indigenous people (hereinafter, Special Rapporteur).[1937] A consultation on the text was launched during that same year, but the outcomes were never pub-

---

1935 My translation. The Spanish original text states: "Reemplázase el artículo 4° por el siguiente: 'Artículo 4°.- La Nación chilena es una, indivisible y multicultural. El Estado reconoce la existencia de los pueblos indígenas que habitan su territorio y el derecho de sus comunidades, organizaciones e integrantes a conservar, fortalecer y desarrollar su identidad, cultura, idiomas, instituciones y tradiciones y a participar en la vida económica, social, política y cultural del país en la forma que establece el orden jurídico nacional. Los pueblos indígenas podrán organizar su vida de acuerdo a sus costumbres, siempre que ello no contravenga la Constitución y las leyes.'" *Proyecto de reforma constitucional que reconoce el aporte de los pueblos originarios a la conformación de la nación chilena*, Bulletin/Boletín No.5324-07.

1936 My translation. The Spanish original text affirms: "La ley protege la propiedad sobre las tierras de las personas y comunidades indígenas y sus derechos de aprovechamiento de aguas conforme lo establecido en la Constitución y las leyes." *Proyecto de reforma constitucional que reconoce el aporte de los pueblos originarios a la conformación de la nación chilena*, Bulletin/Boletín No.5324-07.

1937 James Anaya, "Principios Internacionales aplicables a la Consulta en relación con la reforma constitucional en Chile", 2009, at www.politicaspublicas.net/panel/re/docs/393-ppios-consulta.html [Last Access 05.09.2014].

lished. Later, this very same text was subject to the following "Broad Consultation" (*Gran Consulta*) promoted by Piñera's administration, which was then suspended (see further below section 6.3.2.2). The recent plans for a Constituent Assembly in late 2015 will probably also include the debate on the constitutional recognition of indigenous peoples.[1938] Indeed, as argued recently by Gajardo Falcón, the Chilean Constitution is far from the Latin American constitutionalism in terms of recognition of cultural diversity but there is the sufficient ideological consensus on the need for such a reform.[1939]

6.2.2.2 The Indigenous Law and other norms

As mentioned, the Indigenous Law[1940] provides indigenous peoples with the protection of (some of) their rights. It was enacted on 5 October 1993 under Aylwin's presidency, after a couple of years of discussion and a number of drafts.[1941] The main features of this Law may be summarized as follows:

- The recognition of the existence of the above-mentioned 9 indigenous "ethnicities" (art.1);
- The creation of Indigenous Communities (arts.9-10);
- The recognition of land rights according to Acts of the 19th century (arts.12-19);
- The constitution of a fund for indigenous land and water for land (re)distribution (arts.20-22), and of another fund to finance ad hoc programmes for indigenous economic development (arts.23-27);
- The recognition of cultural rights (arts.28-31);

1938 Michelle Bachelet, "Mensaje Presidencial 21 de Mayo de 2015", 21.05.2015, p.10.

1939 Jaime Gajardo Falcón, "Multiculturalismo y el debate constitucional chileno", 6 *Revista de Derecho – Escuela de Posgrado* 2014, pp.205-236, pp.233-234.

1940 *Ley sobre Protección, Fomento y Desarrollo de los Indígenas*, but mainly known as *Ley Indígena*, Law No. 19.253 of 5 October 1993.

1941 Instituto de Estudios Indígenas, Universidad de la Frontera, *Los derechos de los pueblos indígenas en Chile. Informe del Programa de Derechos Indígenas*, LOM Ediciones, Santiago de Chile, 2003, p.15. See also Sara Mabel Villalba, "Protestas y Reconocimiento Indígenas en el Cono Sur", in Sara Mabel Villalba and Salvador Marí i Puig (eds.), *Protestas necesarias para derechos imprescindibles. Acción colectiva y legislación favorable a los pueblos indígenas en América* Latina, Dictus Publishing, Saabrücken, 2014, pp.66-91, pp.72-76.

- The introduction of indigenous intercultural and bilingual education (arts.32-33);
- The recognition of "participation" rights (arts.34-35);
- The creation of CONADI, a public agency with legal status, regional agencies and a budget, in charge, inter alia, of promoting the indigenous policy of the state and implementing the Indigenous Law (arts.38-40);
- The establishment of the CONADI National Council, the steering body of CONADI, formed by 17 members, 8 of which are to be elected by indigenous communities (arts.41-44).

In short, the limits of this Law regard: The recognition of "ethnicities" rather than "peoples"; the artificial creation of indigenous communities by registration at the CONADI, which resulted in further subdivisions of communities and internal conflicts;[1942] the limits on the use of land distribution, as discussed above (section 6.1.2.2); an excessive concentration of powers in the hands of CONADI, which has proved to be easy to manipulate, as seen in the Ralco case mentioned earlier; the rural focus of the law, which does not foresee potential applications in urban contexts;[1943] and the "participation" rights, which are extremely limiting, as will be discussed below. Additionally, there is no guarantee against forced relocations of indigenous peoples and no rights to natural resources were recognized.[1944] However, the main shortcoming regards the lack of implementation of the Indigenous Law as a whole.[1945] This is particularly evident in the problematic management of land funds and in the lack of intercultural and bilingual education. Present-day education in Chile tends to remain monolingual and mono-cultural.[1946]

1942 Instituto de Estudios Indígenas, Universidad de la Frontera, *Los derechos de los pueblos indígenas en Chile*, p.17.

1943 Jorge Iván Vergara, Hans Gundermann and Rolf Foerster, "Legalidad y legitimidad: ley indígena, Estado chileno y pueblos originarios (1989-2004)", 24(71) *Estudios Sociológicos* 2006, pp.331-361, pp.356-357.

1944 Instituto de Estudios Indígenas, Universidad de la Frontera, *Los derechos de los pueblos indígenas en Chile*, p.17.

1945 Instituto Nacional de Derechos Humanos, *Situación de los Derechos Humanos en Chile. Informe 2013*, Instituto Nacional de Derechos Humanos, Santiago de Chile, 2013, p.269.

1946 Andrew Webb and Sarah Radcliff, "Mapuche Demands during Educational Reform, the Penguin Revolution and the Chilean Winter of Discontent", *Studies in Ethnicity and Nationalism*, Vol. 13, No. 3, 2013, pp.319-341, pp.330-332.

During Bachelet's first mandate, in early 2008, Law No.20,249 was adopted.[1947] It establishes the creation of coastal marine space(s) for indigenous peoples. The regulation to this Law was adopted the following August 2008 by Supreme Decree No.134.[1948] This Law is also known as "Ley Lafkenche", i.e, to refer to the Mapuche peoples of the coast and, as mentioned, aims to create (or, as others would say, to restitute) marine costal spaces for indigenous peoples, as well as to preserve the customary use of such territories, the traditions, and the use of natural resources by those indigenous peoples leaving at the coast (art.3, Law No.20,249). In other words, this law allows the creation of marine spaces for those indigenous peoples that have exercised a customary use over them. Although it was eventually adopted under Bachelet's first mandate, the process to adopt this law lasted for two and a half years. It was part of President Ricardo Lagos' policies of "New Treatment" (*Política del Nuevo Trato*), adopted in 2005 after the Ralco accidents.[1949] The previous Fishing and Aquaculture Law No.18,892 of 1989 (*Ley General de Pesca y Acuicultura*) allowed the creation of marine reserves for traditional fishing, although it is very limited and subject to industrial exploitation (art.29 Law No.18,892/1989). Thus, the Mapuches Lafkenches campaigned for a more incisive safeguard of their costal territories,[1950] which, as seen above, were also the first to be "occupied" by new settlers since the mid-1800. The adoption of this Law, thus, represented an important achievement in indigenous rights in the country[1951] but, regrettably, it is also poorly implemented.[1952] The main problems relate to: The procedure and delays in establishing the spaces and releasing the permits; the extension of these spaces; the confusion regarding "internal" waters, i.e., salt water that forms lakes near to the coast;[1953] and the different cartography system used by the indigenous communities requesting such spaces and the system used officially by the Sub-Secretariat

1947 *Ley* 20,490, adopted on 31 January 2008 (published on 16 February 2008), *Crea el Espacio Costero Marino de los Pueblos Originarios*.

1948 *Decreto Supremo* No.134, *Aprueba Reglamento de la Ley 20,249 que Crea el Espacio Costero Marino de los Pueblos Originarios*, 29 August 2008.

1949 Ingrid Kaempfe and Guillermo Ready, "Comentarios a la Ley N° 20.249, que crea los ECMPO y su Relación con el Convenio N° 169 de la OIT", 1(9) *Ideas para Chile* 2011, pp.1-33, p.1.

1950 *Ibid.*, p.2.

1951 *Ibid.*, p.1.

1952 *Ibid.*, p.7; Aylwin and Silva, "Chile", p.203.

1953 Kaempfe and Ready, "Comentarios a la Ley N° 20.249 …", p.7.

of Fishing (*Subsecretaría de Pesca*). Therefore, the indigenous communities came into conflict with private companies regarding fishing permits.[1954] In fact, there are very pressing and competing economic interests vis-à-vis fishing rights in Chile. 1,016 different species live in its Pacific waters, thanks to the low temperatures, the Antarctic currents and thus the purity of the water. Fish exports have always represented a high income for Chile. According to 2012 data, Chile is the sixth exporter of fish in the world. In 2011, it contributed to 4% of the total fishing exportations gaining 3,797 million of US dollars with an increase of 30% in comparison to 2010.[1955] One of the most pressing issues regards salmon farming and fishing, which is rather unsustainable and polluting (see also below section 6.3.2.3).[1956]

Leaving aside the legislation on indigenous peoples consultation, which will be addressed below in section 6.3.2, the Antidiscrimination Law No.20,609 of 2012 needs to be briefly mentioned here.[1957] This law establishes a judicial mechanism to remedy "arbitrary" discrimination (art.1). This type of discrimination is envisaged when acts carried out by civil servants aim –without any reasonable justification– to exclude or restrict the rights of the citizens, or to limit, disturb or threaten the legitimate exercise of the fundamental rights contained in the Constitution and in the international treaties ratified by Chile. Discrimination will be envisaged particularly if such actions are driven by reasons based on race or ethnicity, nationality, socio-economic situation, language, political ideology or opinion, religion or beliefs, association to trade unions, sex, sexual orientation, gender identity, civil status, age, filiation, appearance, disease, or disability (art.2, 1st paragraph).[1958] The complaints can be brought before the Judge of

1954 *Ibid.*, p.8.

1955 World Trade Center Santiago, "Estudio de mercado. La exportación mundial de pescado chileno", 2012, at http://www.wtcs.cl/sites/default/files/EXPORTA CIONES%20DE%20PESCADO%20AGOSTO%202012.pdf [Last Access 05.09.2014].

1956 Soluri, "Chile's Blue Revolution, Commodity Diseases, and the Problem of Sustainability", p.75; Moiola, "Ecosistema marino depredado"; Aylwin and Silva, "Chile", p.208.

1957 *Ley* 20609, entered into force on 12 July 2012, *Establece Medidas contra la Discriminación*.

1958 My translation. The original text is the following: "Artículo 2°.- Definición de discriminación arbitraria. Para los efectos de esta ley, se entiende por discriminación arbitraria toda distinción, exclusión o restricción que carezca de justificación razonable, efectuada por agentes del Estado o particulares, y que cause privación, perturbación o amenaza en el ejercicio legítimo de los derechos fundamentales esta-

First Instance (*Juzgado de Letras*),[1959] or the administration that committed the discriminatory act. Broadly speaking, this law is considered a major achievement in Chile, particularly because of its symbolic value and for introducing the categories of discrimination based on socio-economic situation, sexual orientation, and gender identity, which characterize many discriminatory acts in Chile. Nevertheless, this law is insufficient to really combat discrimination in Chile; indeed, a full reform would be needed. In particular, a case of "justified" discrimination is foreseen but it should not be contemplated due to the arbitrary nature of this qualification. Moreover, a differentiation of the types of discrimination (direct vs. indirect, etc.), the prevision of precautionary measures, and a general harmonization with international standards are also needed.[1960] Finally, indigenous peoples are not directly mentioned in the law: There is just a generic reference to "ethnicity". Thus, it is difficult to ascertain whether this law also covers discriminatory acts against indigenous peoples or not. Furthermore, in the former case, they should then file their complaints before the Judge of First Instance. If so, one may presume that this would be a way to prevent the increasing use of the Amparo proceedings by indigenous peoples. These proceedings, that protect the Constitutional fundamental rights, are quite incisive, there are no relevant delays either in the adoption of the decision by the Court of Appeal or by the following instance (the Supreme Court);

---

blecidos en la Constitución Política de la República o en los tratados internacionales sobre derechos humanos ratificados por Chile y que se encuentren vigentes, en particular cuando se funden en motivos tales como la raza o etnia, la nacionalidad, la situación socioeconómica, el idioma, la ideología u opinión política, la religión o creencia, la sindicación o participación en organizaciones gremiales o la falta de ellas, el sexo, la orientación sexual, la identidad de género, el estado civil, la edad, la filiación, la apariencia personal y la enfermedad o discapacidad".

1959 The *Juzgado de Letras* is a one or two-person tribunal sitting in each municipality that essentially acts as Court of First Instance mainly in civil/private law matters. Arts.27, 27-bis, 27-ter and 27 quarter of then Chilean Courts Code (*Código Orgánico de Tribunales*), Law No.7421 of 1943 (*Ley que aprueba el Código Orgánico de Tribunales*).

1960 Alberto Coddou, Judith Schönsteiner and Tomás Vial, "La Ley Antidiscriminación: avances e insuficiencias en la protección de la igualdad y la no discriminación en Chile", in Tomás Vial (ed.), *Informe Anual sobre Derechos Humanos en Chile 2013*, Ediciones Universidad Diego Portales, Santiago de Chile, 2013, pp.285-309, p.308. at http://www.derechoshumanos.udp.cl/wp/wp-content/uploads/2013/10/Informe-Anual-2013-completo.pdf [Last access 05.09.2014].

consequently indigenous peoples make a great use of them (see further below section 6.3.2.3). However, the application of this law remains to be seen.

Finally, three draft laws on indigenous linguistic rights have been presented in May and July 2014 and are all still (July 2015) under discussion in the respective chambers. These drafts are the following: Draft Law "Sobre derechos lingüísticos de los pueblos indígenas de Chile", Bulletin/Boletín No.9363-04 of 20 May 2014; Draft Law, "Establece Ley General de Derechos Lingüísticos de los Pueblos Originarios de Chile", Bulletin/Boletín No.9424-17 of 1 July 2014; and Draft Law, "Sobre reconocimiento, fomento y amparo de los derechos lingüísticos de los pueblos indígenas de Chile", Bulletin/Boletín No.9412-04 of 27 July 2014.[1961] The most interesting features of the drafts, which partially overlap with and repeat each other, are the recognition of the Chilean society as pluri-cultural and pluri-lingual ("pluricultural y plurilingüe"); the recognition of the listed indigenous languages (Aymara, Quechua, Mapuche, Rapa nui, Likan Antay, Kaweskar, Selknam, Yagan, Diaguita and Colla) as national and official languages in the regions in which they are spoken; the collective dimension of the indigenous linguistic rights; the public use of indigenous languages, hence, in principle, also before the public administration and during the consultations; and the creation of an Institute of Linguistic Rights (*Instituto de los Derechos Lingüísticos*). However, it remains to be seen which draft law will eventually be adopted and with which potential modifications.

6.3 Indigenous peoples' participation in decision-making processes

In this section, the first component of the implementation of the *composite right* to political participation of indigenous peoples will be analyzed in the case of Chile. The first aspect, as seen in chapter 3 and, particularly, in section 3.4, regards indigenous peoples.' representation in State bodies or in other public posts, including decision-making processes and the judiciary,

1961 Draft Law "Sobre derechos lingüísticos de los pueblos indígenas de Chile", Bulletin/Boletín No. 9363-04 of 20 May 2014; Draft Law, "Establece Ley General de Derechos Lingüísticos de los Pueblos Originarios de Chile", Bulletin/Boletín No.9424-17 of 1 July 2014; and Draft Law, "Sobre reconocimiento, fomento y amparo de los derechos lingüísticos de los pueblos indígenas de Chile", Bulletin/Boletín No. 9412-04 of 27 July 2014. The texts of all the three draft laws may be found at http://www.senado.cl/appsenado/templates/tramitacion/in dex.php by inserting the bulletin number in the search box "Boletín" [Last access 31.07.2015].

both at national and local level, as well as their rights to consultation and free, prior and informed consent (FPIC). Thus, the (attempted) participation of indigenous peoples in the national Parliament (Congress) and in other public posts –such as in the CONADI– as well as the recent creation of the indigenous (Mapuche) party *Wallmapuwen* will be addressed first (section 6.3.1). The implementation of their right to consultation, but not of their FPIC, will be then explored (section 6.3.2). The analysis of the legal frameworks vis-à-vis these two aspects will be conducted separately in each case and will be completed by an assessment of their application.

6.3.1 Indigenous peoples' representation at national and local level

The Chilean electoral system –inherited from the Pinochet dictatorship, reformed only recently[1962] and in force until the last general elections of 2013– was extremely restrictive and unrepresentative, as will be discussed below. In particular, it rendered the representation of non-mainstream parties almost unachievable and, thus, of those non-dominant sectors of society, such as the indigenous peoples. Currently, indigenous peoples' participation in public posts is guaranteed only in the CONADI, albeit with recent negative trends (section 6.3.1.1).

However, indigenous representatives have always run for elections, both at national and local level. Before the dictatorship, seven Mapuche deputies were elected: in 1924, Francisco Meliwilu (or Milivilu) with the Democrat Party (*Partido Demócrata*), later re-elected twice in 1926 and 1930; in 1926, Manuel Manquilef with the Liberal Democratic Party (*Partido Liberal Democratico*), re-elected also in 1930; in 1932, Arturo Huenchullan (or Wenchiwan) with the Democrat Party (*Partido Democrata*) with the Mapuche organization "Federación Araucana"; in 1945, Venancio Coñopepán with the United Conservative Party (*Partido Conservador Unido*), re-elected twice in 1949 and 1965; in 1953, Esteban Romero and José Cayupí with the National Christian Party (*Partido Nacional Cristiano*;

1962 Electoral reform was among the first initiatives of the second mandate of President Bachelet. The draft law was discussed between May 2014 and 22 January 2015 and, before the Chilean summer break, was submitted to the Constitutional Court for its evaluation. The draft law is Boletín/Bulletin No.9326-07 (*Sustituye el sistema electoral binominal por uno de carácter proporcional inclusivo y fortalece la representatividad del Congreso Nacional*) that will amend the Constitutional Organic Law on Popular Elections and Vote Counting No.18,700 of 1988 (*Ley Orgánica Constitucional sobre Votaciones populares y Escrutinio*), see below.

Cayupí and other Mapuche candidates has also run unsuccessfully for 1938 elections); in 1965, Manuel Rodríguez Wenumañ with the Christian Democrat Party (*Partido Demócrata Cristiano*). Venancio Coñopepán was also nominated Ministry of Land and Colonization in the 1950s. After the coup, Rosendo Huenamán was elected only once with the Communist party (*Partido Comunista*) in 1973.[1963] Moreover, some Mapuche people have been involved in local municipal affairs during the 20th century.[1964] Later, in 1990, 1994 and 1998, Francisco Huenchumilla was elected with the Christian Democrat Party (*Partido Demócrata Cristiano*).[1965]

More recently, Bachelet's administrations proposed a few draft laws aimed at enhancing indigenous peoples' participation both in late 2009 – before the end of her (first) mandate– and in June 2014 (section 6.3.1.2). Congress, in fact, did not consider Bachelet's first proposals under Piñera's presidential mandate. Several of them were just considered within the "Broad Consultation" organized in 2011 (see section 6.3.2.2). The recent electoral reform does not foresee reserved seats for indigenous representatives, as also recently suggested by the newly established Advisory Presidential Commission on Decentralization and Regional Development (see further in section 6.4). Nevertheless, the new proportional system and the changes to requirements for the registration of political parties give hope to enhancing indigenous representation in both chambers.. In this framework, the recent creation of the indigenous (Mapuche) party *Wallmapuwen* may also enhance indigenous peoples' participation (see section 6.3.1.3).

6.3.1.1 The restrictive Chilean electoral system and the obstacles to indigenous peoples' participation

The Chilean Congress is bicameral, i.e., composed by the Chamber of Deputies (or Lower Chamber) and the Senate (or Upper Chamber) according to

---

1963 Interview with Pedro Marimán, one of the founding members of the recently created Mapuche Party *Wallmapuwen*, on 9 December 2010 [on file with author]; Bengoa, *Historia del Pueblo Mapuche Siglo XIX y XX*, pp.385-386; Víctor Tricot, "Chile: Pasando de la Galería a la Cancha. Partido Político Mapuche Wallmapuwen: Un Instrumento Descolonizador hacia la Autodeterminación", in Salvador Martí i Puig, Claire Wright, José Aylwin and Nancy Yáñez, (eds.), *Entre el desarrollo y el buen vivir. Recursos naturales y conflictos en los territorios indígenas*, Libros de la Catarata, Madrid, 2013, pp.293-321, pp.304-305.

1964 Interview with Pedro Marimán on 9 December 2010.

1965 Tricot, "Chile: Pasando de la Galería a la Cancha …", p.305.

art.46 of the 1980 Chilean Constitution (and following reforms). The former is composed of 120 deputies (art.47 Const.) and the latter of a number of senators according to the electoral districts set forth in the regions (art.49 Const.), which is 38, i.e., two for each of the 19 electoral districts.[1966] The Chilean electoral system has been strictly binominal until the adoption of the recent reform.

The binominal system was a feat of electoral engineering inherited from the Pinochet dictatorship. Prior to the constitutional reforms of 1989, the number of deputies was identical (120, former art.43 of 1980 Const.), but according to art.45 of the Constitution 26 senators –i.e., two for each of the (then) 13 regions– would be elected by odd-numbered and even-numbered regions in alternating periods of four years each. However, no further electoral law was enacted until the late 1980s. In 1986, Law No. 18,556 regulated enrollment in the electoral registers.[1967] In 1988, the Constitutional Organic Law on Popular Elections and Vote Counting was finally adopted (Law No.18,700).[1968] Nevertheless, this norm did not regulate the elections of either deputies or senators. The legislation containing the formula to elect the Congress' members was adopted only after Pinochet's defeat at the 1988 plebiscite.[1969] Law No.18,799 was adopted by the Military Junta in May 1989 just before the elections and art.109-bis introduced in Law 18,700.[1970] This provision established the rule of two-member districts for the elections of both Chambers. In other words, in each electoral district the citizens could vote for two members of each Chamber. Moreover, an intricate system of subdivision of the two seats according to the votes' number was introduced. Thus, the party or the coalition that would win the majority of votes would gain one seat, but the second seat would be reserved for the second winning party or coalition. Both seats could be captured by the first winning party/coalition only if it received more than the double number of

---

1966 Art.181 of the *Ley Orgánica Constitucional sobre Votaciones populares y Escrutinio*, Law No.18,700 of 1988.

1967 *Ley Orgánica Constitucional sobre Sistema de Inscripciones Electorales y Servicio Electoral*, Law No.18,556 of 1 October 1986.

1968 *Ley Orgánica Constitucional sobre Votaciones populares y Escrutinio*, Law No.18,700 of 6 May 1988.

1969 At the plebiscite on the renovation for eight more years in 1988 as according to Transitory Dispositions No.27-29 of the original text of the 1980 Constitution. Pinochet received the 43% of votes against the 55% that voted against him. Daniel Pastor, "Origins of the Chilean Binominal Election System", *Revista de Ciencia Política (Santiago SciELO)*, Vol.24, No.1, 2004, pp.38-57, p.45.

1970 *Modifica Leyes Orgánicas Constitucionales N°s. 18.603 y 18.700*, Law No.18,799 of 26 May 1989; Pastor 2004, p.44.

votes of the second winning party/coalition. This means that in an electoral district where only two parties/coalitions competed, 33.4% of votes was sufficient to win one seat, while to win both seats each party/coalition needed 66.7% of votes. In general, after 1989, a third competing party/coalition won 10% of votes. Thus, the thresholds to win the two seats were lower.[1971] In practice, this intricate system has made it possible to allocate half of the representatives to each of the mainstream parties. At the 2013 elections, as seen, two of the student leaders were voted outside these parties.[1972]

This system was created *ad hoc* to allow the right-wing party of Pinochet to remain in power after the plebiscite of 1988.[1973] As Pastor, Rojas, and Navia have demonstrated, the minimum percentages needed to win at least one seat were designed according to Pinochet's support (around 30%) and the electoral districts were also gerrymandered to guarantee the presence of the right-wing party,[1974] particularly in the Chamber of Deputies.[1975] In fact, by calculating the potential votes of the right-wing party in support of Pinochet –votes that were higher in rural than in urban areas– the drafters of Law 18,799 allocated 40 seats of the Lower Chamber to be elected by the 20 least-inhabited (rural) districts; a further 6 seats by 3 –somehow– balanced districts; but the last 14 seats by the 7 most-populated urban districts, which however had the same population as the 20 rural districts, thus being considerably underrepresented.[1976] It goes without saying that indigenous

1971 Pastor, "Origins of the Chilean Binominal Election System", p.45.

1972 As mentioned above, Camila Vallejo (*Partido Comunista de Chile*) and Karol Cariola (*Juventudes Comunistas*) were elected within the coalition between their parties and Bachelet's "New Majority" party (Nueva Mayoría), but another two student leaders were either elected by their own party (Giorgio Jackson for *Revolución Democratica*, a party founded by the students themselves, see at www.revoluciondemocratica.cl) or stood as an independent candidate (Gabriel Boric).

1973 Pastor, "Origins of the Chilean Binominal Election System", p.45.

1974 *Ibid.*

1975 Priscilla Rojas and Patricio Navia, "Representación y tamaño de los distritos electorales en Chile, 1988-2002", *Revista de Ciencia Política (Santiago SciELO)*, Vol.25, No.2, 2005, pp.91-116, pp.111-112.

1976 Pastor, "Origins of the Chilean Binominal Election System", p.45; Rojas and Navia, "Representación y tamaño de los distritos electorales en Chile, 1988-2002", pp.95-97. It has been argued that indigenous peoples widely support Pinochet notwithstanding his repressive policies. Although this may be true in the North, Morales Quiroga and González G. have recently statistically demonstrated that in the South there is no relation among Mapuches' votes and those received by the right-

peoples could barely be voted within one of these mainstream parties. In the 9th region, where approximately 30% of the (total) Mapuche live two out of 35 candidates that stood for the Lower Chamber elections in 2005 were Mapuches; that figure increased to seven in 2009. None of them were eventually elected[1977] and currently, no indigenous people have representatives in Congress.[1978]

This strictly binominal system has affected not only the first administration, but also all the attempts of the following ones to modify the Constitution, for which a qualified majority of two-thirds was needed according to art.118 of the (original) 1980 text of the Constitution.[1979] In essence, from 1989 until 2013, the votes at the elections were divided into two major coalitions: the right wing on one hand and the left-wing *Concertación*[1980] on the other.[1981]

A reform of the electoral system towards a proportional system has been adopted in 2015. This reform contains a new proportional system thanks to the increase of the number of senators and deputies (to 50 and 155, respectively) and the redesign of the electoral districts. These changes should guarantee a proportional representation of the population for both chambers, although with the limit on the number of candidates for each district to avoid overrepresentation. Thus, the reform eliminates the requisite of a fixed number of deputies or senators irrespective of the population, which had thus far caused underrepresentation of some regions. Regarding political parties, they may now also be formed at regional level (and not national

---

wing party. Mauricio Morales Quiroga and Jaime A. González G., "Electoral tendencies of indigenous groups in Chile", 37(4) *Revista Eure - Revista de Estudios Urbano Regionales* 2011, pp.133-157.

1977 Andrés Jouannet V., "Participación Política Indígena en Chile: el caso Mapuche", in Víctor Hugo Cárdenas et al. (eds.), *Participación Política Indígena y Políticas Públicas para Pueblos Indígenas en América Latina*, Konrad Adenauer Stiftung, La Paz, 2011, pp.93-139, p.125.

1978 Aylwin and Silva, "Chile", p.210.

1979 Currently, art.127 of the (reformed) Constitution foresee the qualified majority of three-fifths to amend the Constitution.

1980 *Concertación de Partidos por la Democracia* (Coalition of Parties for Democracy), often called simply *Concertación*. All the Presidents after Pinochet, except Piñera, belonged to this coalition.

1981 Also for this reason, it has been argued that the Chilean process of democratization did not end with the restoration of democracy in the late 1980s. Felipe Agüero, "Chile. Unfinished Transition and Increased Political Competition", in Jorge I. Domínguez and Micheal Schifter, *Constructing Democratic Governance in Latin America*, The Johns Hopkins University Press, Baltimore and London, 2003, pp.292-320, p.293.

only) and with half of the previously required signatures; moreover, they are allowed to negotiate more pacts among themselves (i.e., political parties are no longer restricted to one coalition only). Finally, in both chambers there will be a gender quota, according to which there must be a gender balance between 40 and 60 per cent for the candidates of each political party. [1982]

At regional level, the members of the Regional Councils were voted directly for the first time by the population in concomitance with presidential and legislative elections held in November 2013.[1983] However, despite the efforts of the new indigenous (Mapuche) party *Wallmapuwen* (see below section 6.3.2.3), indigenous peoples have no representatives in these councils.[1984] Furthermore, the regional and provincial governors are still appointed by the Government.[1985] At provincial level, the Governor appoints the members of his Advisory Committee and no member is directly elected by the population.[1986]

The Organic Constitutional Law of Municipalities (*Ley Organica Constitucional de Municipalidades*) No.18,695 of 1988 (and the several following amendments)[1987] regulate the local election of communities in Chile.

1982 See Presidential Message No.076-362 of 22 April 2014 (*Mensaje de S.E. la Presidenta de la República con el que inicia un proyecto de ley que sustituye el sistema electoral binominal por un sistema electoral proporcional inclusivo y fortalece la representatividad del congreso nacional*) at http://www.senado.cl/app senado/templates/tramitacion/index.php by inserting the bulletin number in the search box "Boletín" and then "Mensaje/Moción" [Last access 05.02.2015]. For an overview, see also Mauricio Morales Quiroga, Kevin Díaz and Alexis Marambio, "Reforma al Sistema Electoral Binominal. Análisis, Simulaciones y Actores", 1 *Documento de Trabajo ICSO* 2014, Universidad Diego Portales, at http://www.icso.cl/wp-content/uploads/2014/05/ICSO_DT1_2014_Morales.pdf [Last access 05.09.2014].

1983 Law No.20,678 of 19 June 2013 (*Establece la Elección Directa de los Consejeros Regionales*). See the official results of these elections by the Chilean Electoral Service/*Servicio Electoral de Chile*, "Elección de Consejeros Regionales CORE 2013", at http://www.servel.cl/ss/site/eleccion_core_2013.html [last access 05.09.2014].

1984 Aylwin and Silva, "Chile", p.210. Before 2013, the regional councilors were appointed among provincial and municipal representatives in accordance with the previous art.7 of Law Decree (*Decreto Ley*) No.575 of 13 July 1974 (*Regionalización del País*).

1985 Arts.1 and 25 (still in force) of Law Decree No.575 of 1974.

1986 Art.27 (still in force) of Law Decree No.575 of 1974.

1987 The last significant amendment that unified the text has been adopted by Law Decree (Decreto con Fuerza de Ley) No.1 of 26 July 2006, *Fija el Texto Refundido,*

The mayor is voted by simple majority (art.57 of Law No.18,695) and the members of the assemblies according to a proportional system (art.71 of Law No.18,695). Thus, in principle the electoral system of municipalities allows a wider participation and, in the case of indigenous peoples, the concrete possibility of being elected as either mayor or councilor. According to the studies by Gundermann (2007) and Jouannet (2011), between 1992 and 2000, the electoral results of Aymara, Atacameños, Quechua, and Rapa Nui were rather good;[1988] in 2004, 12% of all candidates at municipal elections were indigenous and 10% of them were then elected; and in 2008, the percentage of indigenous candidates at the same elections increased to 13%, of which again 10% were elected.[1989] The last municipal elections were held in the 345 Chilean municipalities in October 2012.[1990] The number of members of the municipal assemblies increased thanks to the automatic enrollment of citizens in the electoral register established by Law No.20,568 of

---

Coordinado y Sistematizado de la Ley Nº 18.695, Organica Constitucional De Municipalidades. See also the recent reform onthe internal organization and finances of municipalities, Law No.20,742 of 1 April 2014, *Perfecciona el Rol Fiscalizador del Concejo; Fortalece la Transparencia y Probidad en las Municipalidades; Crea Cargos y Modifica Normas sobre Personal y Finanzas Municipales*.

1988 According to the analysis of Gundermann, all these peoples obtained between 55% and 80% of the Councils' seats. Hans Gundermann, "Municipios y pueblos indígenas en Chile", in Willem Assies and Hand Gundermann (eds.), *Movimientos Indígenas y Gobiernos Locales en América Latina*, Universidad Católica del Norte, Línea Editorial IIAM, Antofagasta, 2007, pp.161-198, p.183.

1989 Jouannet V., "Participación Política Indígena en Chile: el caso Mapuche", p.119-121.

1990 See the official results published by the Chilean Electoral Service (*Servicio Electoral de Chile*), "Elección Municipal 2012", at http://www.servel.cl/ss/si te/resultados_eleccion_municipal_2012.html [last access 05.09.2014]. There are no official data regarding the origins of the various elected representatives. Generally, the competent offices may cross-check the registers of CONADI, where the indigenous peoples, to be considered as such, must enroll according to Indigenous Law art.2. In principle, this calculation cannot be made by researchers for privacy reasons. However, thanks to the fieldwork carried out in Chile, it is possible to recognize Mapuche surnames. Therefore, for instance, the new mayor of the Community of Alto Bio-Bio is Nivaldo Piñaleo Llaulen, who has two typical Mapuche surnames. This may lead to the assumption that this mayor is Mapuche and thus may represent the interests of his community. Needless to say, this cannot be counterproved. See the list of all elected mayors published by the Chilean Electoral Service/*Servicio Electoral de Chile*, "Elección de Alcades 2012", at http://www.servel.cl/ss/site/documento/res_ter_alcaldes_oficial2012.xlsx or at http://www.servel.cl/ss/site/resultados_eleccion_municipal_2012.html [Last access 05.09.2014].

2012.[1991] Notwithstanding this, the participation was rather low (41%).[1992] The *Concertación* won in the cities of Santiago, Providencia and Concepción, obtaining 49.5% of the vote,[1993] thus announcing the potential victory of Bachelet the following year.

Finally, as for public posts, as mentioned, the CONADI National Council, which is the steering body of CONADI, is formed by 17 members, 8 of which are to be elected by indigenous communities (arts.41-44 of Indigenous Law). However, as seen in the Ralco case, this body's incisiveness in protecting indigenous rights cannot always be guaranteed. Furthermore, since 2011 and under Piñera's administration, only the Director of CONADI is in charge of purchasing the land plots to be redistributed to indigenous families by virtue of Regulation No.61,011 of the Office of the National Controller-General. Thus, neither the CONADI National Council, nor other indigenous advisors are involved anymore.[1994] Indeed, the reform of CONADI has been considered for consultation by indigenous peoples since 2009 (see section 6.3.2.2). For their part, indigenous leaders consider it rather obsolete.[1995] Hence, this cannot be considered a proper space for indigenous peoples' participation within State bodies.

6.3.1.2 Initiatives to include indigenous peoples in decision-making processes

During and shortly before the end of her first mandate in October 2009, President Bachelet and a number of deputies promoted the adoption of measures to enhance indigenous peoples' participation in decision-making processes. In June 2008, a Ministerial Council for Indigenous Affairs was

---

1991 Ley No.20,568, published on 31 January 2012, *Regula la Inscripción Automática, Modifica el Servicio Electoral y Moderniza el Sistema de Votaciones*.

1992 In 2008, 58% of (then) enrolled citizens had voted. Robert L. Funk, "Chile en 2012: la campaña permanente", 33(1) *Revista de Ciencia Política (Santiago SciELO)* 2013, pp.83-99, p.87.

1993 Funk, "Chile en 2012: la campaña permanente", p.87.

1994 Marimán Quemenado, "Chile (2012)", p.207.

1995 Rocío Alorda, "Chile: Enorme desconfianza de pueblos indígenas hacia gobierno", *Noticias Aliadas Informe Especial*, "Por una institucionalidad pública con participación efectiva de pueblos indígenas", July 2013, pp.17-18, p.18, at http://www.noticiasaliadas.org/objetos/informe/19PE_instituc-ind-na.pdf [Last access 05.09.2014].

created to put into action the aforementioned initiatives, regrettably without any indigenous representative or consultation.[1996]

As mentioned, the first review of the application of the ILO Convention No. 169 occurred under President Piñera's presidency in late 2010. Curiously, the (new?) legislative measures adopted by the government *vis-à-vis* indigenous issues included the (re)creation of the Ministerial Council on Indigenous Issues (by Decree No. 101/2010).[1997] Nevertheless, upon closer inspection, Piñera's decree is exactly the same as Bachelet's Decree No.70/2008. In other words, Bachelet's decree was abrogated (decree No.100/2010) and re-adopted immediately by Piñera's decree after with very, very few modifications.[1998] This Decree is still in force and recently Bachelet started to chair the Ministerial Council.[1999]

The other initial proposals of President Bachelet and her government regarded the creation of four bodies dealing with indigenous issues: (1) A permanent Commission of Indigenous Affairs within the Deputies' chamber in Congress; (2) a Ministry of Indigenous Affairs; (3) an Indigenous

---

1996 Decree No.70 in the Official Gazette (*Diario Oficial de Chile*), 24 June 2008 (No. 39095).

1997 CONADI for Chile's government, "Memoria Presentada por el Gobierno de Chile en conformidad con las disposiciones del artículo 22 de la Constitución de la Organización Internacional del Trabajo .....", p.138.

1998 The few changes between the two decrees regard the ministries that are members of the Council. In particular, the Ministries for Health, Public Works, Urbanism and Social Housing, and Environment were substituted by the Ministry for Culture; the Ministries of the Presidential Secretary and those for Planning, Internal Affairs, External Relations, Agriculture, Economy-Promotion and Reconstruction were confirmed as members of the Council (Article 1 of Decree 101/2010). In addition, the task of the Council to formulate recommendations to overcome the difficulties in applying the ILO Convention 169 was cancelled (art.2). See Decree No. 70, 24 June 2008, and Decree No. 100, 14 July 2010. I would like to underline that according to the "*Considerando*" No. 6 of the Decree No. 101 the revocation of the former (Bachelet's) Council was deemed to be necessary in order to guarantee a due renovation of the Council. However, reading both texts of Bachelet's and Piñera's decrees (respectively, Decree Nos. 70 and 101), as mentioned, there are basically no changes. The revocation of Decree No. 70 rather seems a political choice, i.e., to show that the Council was created by Piñera and not by Bachelet.

1999 Chilean Ministry of Social Development/*Ministerio de Desarrollo Social*, "Presidenta Bachelet encabezó Consejo de Ministros de Asuntos Indígenas", 04.08.2014, at http://www.consultaindigenamds.gob.cl/articulos/articulo0508 14_1.html [Last access 05.09.2014].

Development Agency, to substitute CONADI; and (4) a Council of Indigenous Peoples.[2000] However, none of these drafts were discussed further or approved. In the 2010 presidential message of Piñera, only the reform of CONADI was mentioned.[2001] The texts of the draft laws on the Indigenous Development Agency and the Council of Indigenous Peoples were only slightly changed under Piñera and left to "Broad Consultation" (see below section 6.3.2.2).

(1) The first proposal (Bulletin/*Boletín* No.6720-16), a motion by some Deputies, concerned the creation of a Standing Committee in the Lower Chamber to deal with legislation on indigenous affairs, thus modifying the rules of the Chamber. The direct participation of indigenous peoples in this Committee was neither mentioned nor denied *a priori*. However, the project was discussed but remained locked in the Lower Chamber.

The other drafts were more substantial and both were urged by Presidential initiatives through Messages addressed to the Chamber of Deputies.

(2) The Ministry of Indigenous Affairs and (3) the Indigenous Development Agency (Bulletin/*Boletín* No.6726-06), in the draft laws presented by Bachelet, were conceived as bodies with essentially legislative and executive powers, respectively. Moreover, they would have substituted CONADI. This draft law was very ambitious, particularly taking into account the few resources that, according to the same text, these bodies would have been granted. Most of the contributions would have depended on the Financial Law (*Ley de Presupuestos*) which, for instance, devoted solely 0.3% to indigenous policies for the year 2011, including the Fund for Lands and Waters.[2002] However, the direct participation of indigenous peoples in both bodies was neither mentioned nor denied *a priori*. Finally, President Piñera abandoned the proposal of creating the Ministry of Indigenous Affairs.

2000 *Creación de una Comisión de Asuntos Indígenas* (Bulletin/*Boletín* No. 6720-16); *Creación de un Ministerio de Asuntos Indígenas y una Agencia de Desarrollo Indígena* (Bulletin/*Boletín* No.6726-06); *Consejo de Pueblos Indígenas* (Bulletin/*Boletín* No.6743-06). These procedure to adopt these initiatives was blocked between 2009 and 2010. Nevertheless, the original texts are still at http://www.senado.cl/appsenado/templates/tramitacion/index.php by inserting the bulletin number in the search box "Boletín" [Last Access 06.02.2015].

2001 See Sebastian Piñera Echenique, "Del Chile del Bicentenario al País de las Oportunidades", pp. 33-34.

2002 Centro de Políticas Públicas y Derechos Indígenas, "Proyecto de Presupuesto Público 2011 y políticas indígenas. ¿Acorde con las obligaciones del estado y la realidad indígena?", 23.07.2010, at http://www.politicaspublicas.net/panel/gob/g presupuesto/664-presupuesto-2011.html [Last access 05.09.2014].

(4) The Council of Indigenous Peoples (Bulletin/*Boletín* No.6743-06) was designed to be a representative body of indigenous peoples before the State administration, the Congress, the judiciary, and the other public bodies. This bill was quite detailed in some points, especially on the powers of the Council or the requirements for the candidates (arts.1 and 4). The number of councilors seemed adequate, i.e., 43 members subdivided proportionally per (recognized) indigenous people, with a majority of Mapuches (25 seats out of 43; art.2). Both the (indigenous) candidates and voters should have enrolled in a "Special Indigenous Register" and demonstrated their "indigeneity" by having obtained or seeking a certificate in accordance with art.3 of the Indigenous Law (art.8 of the first draft). However, the draft was rather superficial on other issues, such as the process of election (arts.14-16), which was delegated to the Indigenous Development Agency. In particular, several issues were not specified, including: the location of the polling stations; whether they should fall under the responsibility of this Agency or other bodies; and how the elections should take place, whether at the regional or community level. Also, an alarming detail was the requisite of every candidate to be supported by 0.2% of the indigenous people inscribed in the "Special Indigenous Register" of his/her village or region (art.4), but in all cases by not less than 100 people, which is quite a high figure. This would have potentially decreased the number of candidates or brought about the participation of just a few candidates. Most importantly, art.23 of the draft spoke of "agreements" of the Council and not of "decisions". Also, by analyzing the Council's powers, these "agreements" would have not been binding for the State organs to which they are addressed. Finally, a competence sounded particularly controversial: The Council would have been represented in national-level processes of consultation initiated by the organisms of the State (art.1, letter h of the draft law of the Bachelet, letter g of the draft law of President Piñera). This, however, would have denied the right to consultation to the directly affected indigenous peoples.

All these four initiatives were submitted for a first consultation in 2009, although the results were not made public and were then blocked. Those regarding the Indigenous Development Agency and the Council of Indigenous Peoples formed (again) part of President Piñera's "Broad Consultation" of 2011, which was heavily criticized and finally suspended, although it was followed by a controversial adoption of another regulation of the right to consultation (see below sections 6.3.2.1 and 6.3.2.2).

Nevertheless, during President Bachelet's current second mandate (2014-2018), similar proposals regarding the creation of the Ministry of Indigenous Affairs and the Council(s) of Indigenous Peoples have been re-presented and re-formulated. On 24 June 2014, the National Indigenous Day, which corresponds to the beginning of the year according to Mapuche culture (on winter solstice), a new process of consultation on the creation of these two bodies was announced[2003] and it has been carried out between September 2014 and January 2015 according to Resolutions Nos.275 and 276 of 24 June 2014 (see also below section 6.3.2.2).[2004]

With regard to these new proposals, the powers and composition of the potential Ministry of Indigenous Affairs did not differ substantially from those contained in the previous draft law mentioned above, apart from the fact that the establishment of an Indigenous Development Agency is no longer mentioned and thus all the powers of CONADI and additional legislative initiatives regarding indigenous rights may be absorbed by this Ministry (this option was left open in the consultation).[2005] There is no reference to this body having indigenous representatives, but neither is this excluded *a priori*, particularly with regard to the regional seats of the Ministry (*Secretarías Regionales Ministeriales*; para.III of the proposal). The participation of indigenous peoples in the sessions of the Ministry is then foreseen in three cases, albeit with a generic reference ("with the participation of…"): (1) In the elaboration of the regulation of the Register of Traditional Authorities and Organization (*Registro de Autoridades y Organizaciones Tradicionales Indígenas*) together with the "Sub-secretary of Indigenous Peoples" (*Subsecretario/a de Pueblos Indígenas*)–the direct collaborator of the Ministry (para.III, power No.v); (2) in the elaboration, application, and evaluation of the Indigenous National Policy (*Política Nacional Indígena*;

2003 Chilean Ministry of Social Development/Ministerio de Desarrollo Social, "Presidenta Bachelet: "Estamos en el momento para ampliar y reconocer los derechos de los Pueblos Indígenas en Chile", 24.06.2014, at http://www.consultaindigena-mds.gob.cl/articulos/articulo240614_1.html [Last access 05.02.2015].

2004 *Resolución número 275 exenta.- Inicia procedimiento administrativo y convoca a proceso de consulta que indica; Resolución número 276 exenta.- Inicia procedimiento administrativo y convoca a proceso de consulta que indica*, Official Gazette (Diario Oficial) of Chile of 24 June 2014, No. 40.890, also at http://www.consultaindigena.gob.cl/docs/DO-2014-06-24.pdf [Last access 05.02.2015].

2005 Chilean Ministry of Social Development/*Ministerio de Desarrollo Social*, "Medida Legislativa Ministerio de Pueblos Indígenas", at http://www.con sultaindigenamds.gob.cl/doc/MEDIDALEGISLATIVADEMINISTERIODEPUEBLOSINDIGENAS.pdf [Last access 05.02.2015].

para.IV); and (3) in the establishment of territorially-based indigenous "areas" aimed at enhancing the economic development of indigenous peoples (*Áreas de Desarrollo Indígena*; para.VI). However, the creation of an Inter-Ministerial Committee, composed by a number of Ministries and in charge of coordinating initiatives affecting indigenous peoples, does not require any direct indigenous participation. Finally, the designation of potential representatives both at central and regional level is not specified, but maybe governed later by ad hoc regulations. Recently, the Rapa Nui people complained that they have been excluded from the nomination process of their four representatives at the Ministry. These four candidates were designated urgently in a last-minute meeting organized by the Regional Ministerial Secretary of Development (*Secretaría Regional Ministerial – SEREMI de Desarrollo*).[2006]

The proposal concerning the Council of Indigenous Peoples has, instead, changed substantially. First, nine Councils, one for each indigenous people (Aymara, Quechua, Atacameño, Diaguita, Colla, Rapa Nui, Kawésqar, Yagan and Mapuche), should be created. These Councils should be autonomous, representative, participative, and organs of consultation and should have "essentially" powers to represent the interests, necessities, and collective rights of each indigenous people before all the State bodies as well as private entities. Finally, it should embody the "instance of participation and consultation" in all subjects of public politics.[2007] This statement sounds limiting: The powers of this Council regard only the formulation of proposals, observations, and recommendations.[2008] Indeed, this has been one critical point discussed during the last consultation of 2014-2015: The proposal put forward and included in the final report of the consultation contains a binding effect of the decisions to be taken by the Councils.[2009] An

---

2006 LOGIN Noticias, "Pueblo Rapa Nui denuncia fraudulenta designación de delegados al Ministerio de Asuntos Indígenas", *LOGIN Noticias*, at http://www.login.cl/regional/492-pueblo-rapa-nui-denuncia-fraudulenta-designa cion-de-delegados-al-ministerio-de-asuntos-indigenas [Last access 05.02.2015].

2007 Chilean Ministry of Social Development/Ministerio de Desarrollo Social, "Medida Legislativa del Consejo o Consejos de Pueblos Indígenas", p.2, at http://www.consultaindigenamds.gob.cl/doc/MEDIDALEGISLATIVADELCONSEJOOCONSEJOSDEPINDIGENAS.pdf [Last access 06.09.2014].

2008 Chilean Ministry of Social Development/Ministerio de Desarrollo Social, "Medida Legislativa del Consejo o Consejos de Pueblos Indígenas", pp.3-6.

2009 Chilean Ministry of Social Development/Ministerio de Desarrollo Social, "Sistematización Proceso de Consulta Previa Indígena, Ministerio de Desarrollo Social. Informe Final", 2015, p.24, at http://www.ministeriodesarrollosocial.gob.cl/pdf/up

alternative was left for the consultation to decide whether the councilors should be voted according to traditional customs and rules or whether an ad hoc legislation should be enacted. The outcome of the consultation of 2014-2015 was to opt for an electoral roll to be managed by the above-mentioned the "Sub-secretary of Indigenous Peoples" (*Subsecretario/a de Pueblos Indígenas*).[2010] As to the composition, again, the consultation of 2014-2015 proposed to increase the number of councilors in the cases of the Mapuche, Aymara and Diaguita peoples. For the others, the initial proposals remained the same, while with regard to the number of representatives for the Quechua and the Colla peoples no agreement could be reached.[2011] Finally, each Council should adopt an internal regulation.[2012]

Second, a National Council of Indigenous Peoples should be established. Likewise, this Council should be autonomous, representative, participative, and an organ of consultation; it should represent all indigenous peoples; and it should have strong relations with the President of Chile and the Ministry of Indigenous Affairs.[2013] It should be composed of nine indigenous representatives, one coming from each Council of Indigenous Peoples,[2014] and it should also adopt an internal regulation.[2015] The number should now increase to 15 as according to the outcomes of the consultation of 2014-2015. Therefore, the Council shall have five Mapuche representatives, two for each Diaguita and Aymara, while the others would keep only one representative.[2016] The powers of this body appear more incisive, e.g., to promote measures to ensure the respect of indigenous peoples' rights and solve the issues regarding indigenous peoples' collective rights raised by one or more of the single (nine) Councils of Indigenous Peoples.[2017] However, the previous provision to adopt "agreements" and formulate recommendations to State organs regarding indigenous peoples' protection was still present in

load/Informe%20Nacional%20CONSULTA%20PREVIA%20INDIGENA.pdf [Last access 15.07.2015].

2010 *Ibid.*, p.26.

2011 *Ibid.*

2012 Chilean Ministry of Social Development/Ministerio de Desarrollo Social, "Medida Legislativa del Consejo o Consejos de Pueblos Indígenas", pp.3-6.

2013 *Ibid.*, p.8.

2014 *Ibid.*, p.10.

2015 *Ibid.*, p.11.

2016 Chilean Ministry of Social Development/Ministerio de Desarrollo Social, "Sistematización Proceso de Consulta Previa Indígena, Ministerio de Desarrollo Social. Informe Final", p.27.

2017 Chilean Ministry of Social Development/Ministerio de Desarrollo Social, "Medida Legislativa del Consejo o Consejos de Pueblos Indígenas", p.8, letters a and b.

the draft.[2018] As mentioned, also in this case, the outcomes of the consultation of 2014-2015 proposed to give binding effect of the decisions to be taken by the Council.[2019]

In sum, under President Bachelet's current mandate, concrete developments vis-à-vis a major inclusion of indigenous peoples in States' bodies may be appreciated. In the Presidential Message of 21 May 2015, President Bachelet promised to submit the revised draft laws during the last trimester of 2015.[2020] Also the Advisory Presidential Commission on Decentralization and Regional Development (*Comisión Asesora Presidencial para la Descentralización y el Desarrollo Regional*) presented other interesting proposals (see further section 6.4). However, much remains to be seen in relation to the real establishment of these organs in the coming years.

6.3.1.3 The Mapuche Wallmapuwen party

As mentioned previously (section 6.3.1), at the beginning of the 20th century, Mapuche started to organize their first associations, e.g.: the "Sociedad Caopolicán Defensora de la Araucanía" in 1911; the "Sociedad Mapuche de Protección Mutua" in 1913 (which will be referred to as "Federación Araucana"); the "Defensora de la Araucanía" and the "Moderna Araucanía" in 1918; and the "Unión Araucana" in 1926.[2021] In 1938, the "Sociedad Caopolicán Defensora de la Araucanía" merged with the "Federación Araucana" and created the "Corporación Araucana".[2022] One of these associations ("Federación Araucana") was also able to support a candidate in the 1932 elections (Arturo Huenchullan or Wenchiwan), elected with the Democrat Party (*Partido Democrata*).[2023] A further eight Mapuche deputies were elected during the 20th century.

Since the restoration of democracy, and prompted by the adoption of the Indigenous Law, a group of Mapuche leaders started thinking about creating a Mapuche Party in 1997. From the outset, the overall aim was to pursue

2018 *Ibid.*, p.9, letter h.

2019 Chilean Ministry of Social Development/Ministerio de Desarrollo Social, "Sistematización Proceso de Consulta Previa Indígena, Ministerio de Desarrollo Social. Informe Final", p.24.

2020 Michelle Bachelet, "Mensaje Presidencial 21 de Mayo de 2015", 21.05.2015, p.25.

2021 Interview with Pedro Marimán on 9 December 2010; Bengoa, *Historia del Pueblo Mapuche Siglo XIX y XX*, p.385; Tricot 2013 pp.302-303 and p.318, endnote 7.

2022 Tricot, "Chile: Pasando de la Galería a la Cancha …", p.303.

2023 *Ibid.*, p.304.

the granting of autonomy or self-government as well as to secure land rights for the Mapuche people of the extensive area south of the Bío-Bío River and embracing the current 9th, 10th and 14th regions of Araucanía, Los Lagos, and Los Ríos. However, during the first meetings, two main issues were raised and the subject of heated discussions: whether to use a "western" instrument such as the political party that does not traditionally belong to the Mapuche culture; and whether the creation of a political party was the correct instrument to invoke the proper application of indigenous rights. From then onwards, some of the members radicalized and formed other groups (e.g, the *Coordinadora Arauco-Malleco*), which, *inter alia*, occupied lands that had been expropriated during the dictatorship. The following events, such as the increasing use of the Antiterrorist Law and the unfavorable legal framework, delayed the creation of a party further.[2024]

The Mapuche Wallmapuwen party was thus founded in 2005.[2025] The party collected members from NGOs, Mapuche bloggers, and other militants. [2026] They were, however, criticized for being influenced by the "Chilean system" by other activists.[2027]

The political project of the Wallmapuwen party currently focuses on: the demand of autonomy as a form of self-determination;[2028] a broader decentralization within a constitutional reform; a greater popular and indigenous peoples' participation in decision-making processes; the revitalization of the Mapuche identity, their language and the recovery of historical memory; a better land redistribution policy; more sustainable economic policies and the definitive abandonment of neoliberalism; implementation of labor rights; better health, housing and education conditions; and the amendment of the Mining and Water Codes.[2029] These demands have also been put forward by other social movements in Chile. Notably, the Steering Body of the party (*Mesa Directiva*) is composed of 6 people, including non-indigenous individuals. The headquarters are located in Temuco, the capital city of the

2024 Interview with Pedro Marimán on 9 December 2010.

2025 *Ibid.*; see also the website of the party at http://www.wallmapuwen.cl, and the recent work of Anna Maria Kowalczyk, "Indigenous Peoples and Modernity: Mapuche Mobilizations in Chile", 40 *Latin American Perspectives* 2013, pp.121-135, p.128.

2026 Interview with Pedro Marimán on 9 December 2010; see also Tricot, "Chile: Pasando de la Galería a la Cancha …", p.309.

2027 Interview with Pedro Marimán on 9 December 2010.

2028 *Ibid.*.

2029 *Ibid.*, and Kowalczyk, "Indigenous Peoples and Modernity: Mapuche Mobilizations in Chile", p.129.

9th region (*Araucanía*) and regional committees were also created in Padre Las Casa and Puerto Saavedra (other towns in the 9th region).[2030]

The party, however, has faced a number of problems in gaining accreditation by the Electoral Service (*Servicio Electoral de Chile*, SERVEL) as a "political party" according to the 1987 Law No.18,603 of Political Parties [2031] and the 1988 Constitutional Organic Law on Popular Elections and Vote Counting Law No.18,700, also mentioned above.[2032] As well as collecting the sufficient number of signatures since 2007 onwards, the Statute of the party had to be amended many times: they had to delete the concepts of self-determination, territory, self-identification as a "people", and all the references to traditional authorities and their own language.[2033] Notwithstanding the high number of signatures collected and all the changes to the Statute, their enrollment as a party is still pending.[2034] They supported 16 candidates at the 2012 municipal elections.[2035] However, they had to seek the alliance with another party, i.e., the Progressive Party (*Partido Progresista*) in order to do so.[2036] Of these 16 candidates, 14 eventually stood for the municipal elections within the Progressive Party,[2037] or as independent candidates,[2038] and two were finally elected as councilors.[2039] They also attempted to support a number of candidates for the 2013 elections to Regional Councilors, but the Electoral Service (SERVEL) eventually denied

---

2030 Tricot, "Chile: Pasando de la Galería a la Cancha ...", p.310.

2031 *Ley Organica Constitucional de los Partidos Politicos*, Law No.18,603 of 23 March 1987.

2032 Interview with Pedro Marimán on 9 December 2010; see also Kowalczyk, "Indigenous Peoples and Modernity: Mapuche Mobilizations in Chile", p.129 and Tricot, "Chile: Pasando de la Galería a la Cancha ...", p.309.

2033 Interview with Pedro Marimán on 9 December 2010.

2034 Wallmapuwen, "Inchiñ-Quienes Somos", at http://www.wallmapuwen.cl/#!about/c10fk [Last access 05.02.2015].

2035 Wallmapuwen, "Politiku Kuzaw-Elecciones", at http://www.wallmapuwen.cl/#!politiku-kuzaw/c2sv [Last access 06.09.2014].

2036 Tricot, "Chile: Pasando de la Galería a la Cancha ...", p.311.

2037 *Ibid.*, p.311.

2038 See, for instance, in the case of Gustavo Quilaqueo in the municipality of Teodoro Schmidth, according to the official results published by the Chilean Electoral Service/*Servicio Electoral de Chile*, "Elección de Consejales 2012", at http://www.servel.cl/ss/site/resultados_eleccion_municipal_2012.html or at http://www.servel.cl/ss/site/documento/concejales_oficial2012.xlsx [last access 05.09.2014]. [last access 05.09.2014].

2039 Roberto Cayul in Lonquimay and José Millalen in Galvarino as according to the official results published by the Chilean Electoral Service/*Servicio Electoral de Chile*, "Elección de Consejales 2012".

their enrollment.[2040] The members of the party filed an Amparo proceeding before the Temuco Court of Appeal on 4 October 2013,[2041] but their request was eventually rejected.[2042]

The recent electoral reform has however created new opportunities for parties such as the Wallmapuwen, which may finally be registered thanks to the above-mentioned changes in requirements for the enrollment of political parties. After the final vote on the reformed text, the Wallmapuwen declared its appreciation for this reform as well as another proposal for decentralization,[2043] which will be discussed below (section 6.4). Indeed, the Wallmapuwen party has eventually been able to start the official procedure to register as a political party in June 2015 and should officially become the first (official) Mapuche party in the region of Araucanía by early 2016.[2044]

6.3.2 Consultation and FPIC of indigenous peoples in Chile

6.3.2.1 Legislative framework

As mentioned, Chile ratified the ILO Convention 169 in 2008 and it entered into force on 15 September 2009. According to the mainstream Chilean human rights literature, the ratification of an international treaty would be sufficient to bind the State organs to apply it, in accordance with art.5 of the Constitution.[2045] Thus, in principle, the ILO Convention 169 standards regarding the right to consultation are binding. This has been confirmed by

---

2040 Aylwin and Silva, "Chile", p.210.

2041 Court of Appeal of Temuco, Decision/*Sentencia Rol.* No.13,878 of 4 October 2013.

2042 Aylwin and Silva, "Chile", p.211.

2043 Wallmapuwen, "Wallmapuwen ante la reforma al sistema electoral binominal", 28.01.2015, at http://www.mapuexpress.org/2015/01/28/wallmapuwen-ante-la-reforma-al-sistema-electoral-binominal [Last access 05.02.2015].

2044 Mapuexpress, "Wallmapuwen inicia proceso de legalización como partido político en Wallmapu", 01.06.2015, at http://www.mapuexpress.org/?p=1966 [Last access 14.08.2015].

2045 Matías Meza-Lopehandía G., "VI. El Convenio N° 169 de la OIT en el sistema normativo chileno", in Matías Meza-Lopehandía G. (ed.), *Las implicancias de la ratificación del Convenio N° 169 de la OIT en Chile*, Programa de Derechos de los Pueblos Indígenas del Observatorio Ciudadano, Temuco, 2010, 2nd edition, pp.103-160, p.106, note 201. Art. 5 of the Constitution states that it's a duty of

later jurisprudence (see section 6.3.2.3). Moreover, as mentioned, the Constitutional Court in its decision Rol 309 of 4 August 2000, had declared art.6.1, letter a, and art.7.1, self-executing and equal to constitutional norms.

However, approaching the end of President Bachelet's first mandate, the debate about constitutional recognition, criticism over, and the need to manage the fervent demand for a full realization of the right to consultation prompted the adoption of a decree regulating this right. Thus, on September 4 2009, Decree No.124 of the Ministry for Planning was adopted in order to regulate (in principle, only temporarily) art.34 of the Indigenous Law, which contains a kind of right to consultation. However, the right is framed here in a rather confused and narrow text compared to art.6 of ILO Convention 169: It states that the public administrations and territorial organizations "will have to hear and consider the opinion" of indigenous peoples when dealing with indigenous issues. [2046] Curiously, this decree was adopted and published during the same period in which the ILO Convention 169 entered into force.[2047] This Decree was eventually derogated by the –recent– Decree No.66 of 2014 (see infra).

The most striking aspect of the previous Decree No.124 is that it regulated, in principle, the consultation and participation of indigenous peoples but was adopted without consulting them, although other consultations had been already carried out during 2009 (see below) . The *mala fides* of this act was raised by Bartolomé Clavero, (then) member of the Permanent UN Forum on Indigenous Issues. He argued that the Government of Chile attempted to neutralize its obligations under the ILO Convention 169 before it came into force, thus proving that Chile had no good faith in assuming its

---

each State bodies to respect and promote human rights as according to the Constitution and the Treaties in force and ratified by Chile. My translation of the following original text: "[...] Es deber de los órganos del Estado respetar y promover tales derechos, garantizados por esta Constitución, así como por los tratados internacionales ratificados por Chile y que se encuentren vigentes".

2046 My translation. The original text of art.34 of the Indigenous Law is the following: "Los servicios de la administración del Estado y las organizaciones de carácter territorial, cuando traten materias que tengan injerencia o relación con cuestiones indígenas, deberán escuchar y considerar la opinión de las organizaciones indígenas que reconoce esta ley."

2047 As mentioned above, the ILO Convention 169 entered into force on 15 September 2009; Decree No.124 was enacted on 4 and published (and thus, entered into force) on 25 September 2009. See the text of the Decree 124/2009 at http://www.leychile.cl/Navegar?idNorma=1006486&tipoVersion=0 [Last access 05.09.2014].

international commitments.[2048] In addition, the decree appeared to refer to art.34 of the Indigenous Law only, but stated in the preamble that the obligation to "listen" also embodied art.6 of the ILO Convention 169. The decree essentially aimed to bind consultation to a pure expression of opinion (art.2 of Decree 124). There were many critical aspects, some of which were more alarming than others. For example, art.16 tasked the state administration with evaluating whether a consultation was necessary without clarifying the criteria or mentioning the obligation to consult indigenous peoples whenever the adoption of acts are likely to affect them, in accordance with art.6 of the ILO Convention 169. This norm also left open the possibility of rejecting a consultation. Finally, art.12 narrowed down the scope of reaching an agreement or consent by affirming that only reasonable, possible, necessary, and pertinent modifications could have been made to the consulted legislative measure and that the adoption of the latter could have not be impeded by the consultation. In other words, this last provision left it to the administrative bodies to decide what was reasonable, possible, etc. in relation to the consultation and whether and how to amend the draft legislation. This implied that the consultation, essentially, had no effect.

After the hail of criticism and allegations made by indigenous organizations in relation to the Decree No.124 that regulated the "Broad Consultation",[2049] in September 2011 the Government tasked a "Consultation Commission" within the CONADI with preparing another draft regulation of the consultation.[2050] Almost one year later, on 8 August 2012, the Government presented a proposal of a "New Regulation of Consultation" (hereinafter, the Proposal)[2051] to the Council of CONADI, in order to pursue a consultation on the draft.

2048 Bartolomé Clavero, "Puesta en Práctica de Convenio o Puesta en Evidencia de Chile (Por los Informes del Relator Anaya)", 18 September 2009, at http://www.politicaspublicas.net/panel/c169/consultacl/391-reglamento-c169-inconsulto.html [Last access 05.09.2014].

2049 James Anaya, "Comentarios del Relator Especial sobre los derechos de los pueblos indígenas en relación al documento titulado 'Propuesta de gobierno para una nueva normativa de consulta y participación indígena de conformidad a los artículos 6° y 7° del Convenio 169 de la organización Internacional del Trabajo', Chile", November 2012, p.6, at http://www.ohchr.org/Documents/Issues/IPeoples/SR/In forme-ConsultaChile.pdf [last access 05.09.2014].

2050 Silva Neriz, "Chile", p.190.

2051 Chilean Government, "Propuesta de gobierno para una nueva normativa de consulta y participación indígena de conformidad a los artículos 6° y 7° del Convenio 169 de la organización Internacional del Trabajo" (Government's proposal for a new regulation for consultation and indigenous participation in accordance with

Inter alia, the following problematic aspects were highlighted by the (then) Special Rapporteur on Indigenous Rights James Anaya:[2052]

- The Proposal made no mention of a right to consultation but rather of a process of dialogue and reaching agreements of mutual benefit (art.2 of the Proposal). These were important aspects but the consultation is a right for indigenous peoples and a duty for the State in accordance with arts. 6-7 of the ILO Convention 169;
- Arts.1 and 4 of the Proposal did not clearly indicate that consultation is a duty for all administrative organs;
- The administrative measures to be consulted in accordance with art.18 of the Proposal were those decrees or resolutions of "general effects". Additionally, art.9 of the Proposal stated that the consultations should be carried out only if a situation is likely to "involve" or have a "significant impact" on indigenous peoples. Both provisions would have not respected the international standards, which imply a duty to consult indigenous peoples on any administrative act likely to affect indigenous peoples' rights and interests;
- Finally, art.20 of the Proposal presented one of the doubtful issues of Decree No.124, i.e., the power of the state administration to evaluate whether a consultation was necessary or not without clarifying the criteria.

In early 2013, some indigenous organizations submitted to the government a counterproposal on the regulation of the consultation,[2053] which was eventually denied. Thus, the draft was not brought to consultation and was finally partially reworked and merged into the Supreme Decree No.66 of 15 November 2013,[2054] which derogated the previous Decree No.124. However, this Decree is not in keeping with the standards enshrined in the ILO

articles 6 and 7 of the Convention 169 of the International Labour Organization), at http://unsr.jamesanaya.org/docs/data/2012-08-08-propuesta-de-normativa-de-consulta-gobierno-chile.pdf [Last access 05.09.2014].

2052 Anaya, "Comentarios del Relator Especial sobre los derechos de los pueblos indígenas en relación al documento titulado 'Propuesta de gobierno para una nueva normativa de consulta …", pp.10-19.

2053 Noticias Senado, "Pueblos originarios entregarán contra propuesta al proyecto del gobierno sobre mecanismo de consulta permanente", 12.03.2013, at http://www.senado.cl/pueblos-originarios-entregaran-contra-propuesta-al-proyecto-del-gobierno-sobre-mecanismo-de-consulta-permanente/prontus_senado/2013-03-12/112447.html [Last access 05.09.2014].

2054 Decree/*Decreto* No.66 of the Ministry of Social Development of 15 November 2013, published on 14 March 2014, *Aprueba Reglamento que Regula el Procedi-*

Convention 169, particularly art.6.2. The most problematic aspects regard art.7 that, similarly to art.9 of the Proposal discussed above, provides that the consultation should be required only when a legislative and administrative measure cause a "significant and specific impact" on indigenous peoples; art.3 affirms that the duty to consult of an administrative body will be considered fulfilled if this organ has made all the possible efforts to reach an agreement or obtain the consent of the concerned indigenous peoples also in those cases when neither of them have been achieved; finally, art.4 abstains public companies, armed forces and local administrative bodies, such as the municipalities, from the duty to consult indigenous peoples. This is extremely worrying, since many projects likely to affect indigenous peoples are approved by these organs, especially by the municipalities: This provision essentially denies the indigenous peoples' right to consultation.[2055]

Additionally, in May 2012, a draft regulation of the system of Environmental Impact Assessment was approved by the Council of Ministers for sustainability.[2056] This draft aimed to regulate the Environmental Impact Assessment of all investment projects, thus also those likely to affect indigenous peoples of Chile.[2057] The bill was eventually published as Supreme Decree No.40 of 2013.[2058] Also in this case, the Decree fails to meet the standards regarding the right to consultation enshrined in the ILO Convention 169, although some of them are inserted in art.85 (e.g., in good faith and with appropriate socio-cultural mechanisms). In particular, a few aspects are extremely problematic and essentially deny the right to consultation of indigenous peoples. The most pressing issues regard a limited duty

---

miento de Consulta Indígena en virtud del artículo 6 N° 1 Letra A) y N° 2 del Convenio N° 169 de la Organización Internacional del Trabajo y deroga normativa que indica.

2055 Aylwin and Silva, "Chile", p.204.

2056 Anaya, "Comentarios del Relator Especial sobre los derechos de los pueblos indígenas en relación al documento titulado 'Propuesta de gobierno para una nueva normativa de consulta ...", p.7; Ministerio del Medio Ambiente, Consejo de Ministros para la Sustentabilidad, "Acuerdo N° 8/2012: Se pronuncia sobre nuevo Reglamento del Sistema de Evaluación de Impacto Ambiental", Santiago de Chile, 2012.

2057 Anaya, "Comentarios del Relator Especial sobre los derechos de los pueblos indígenas en relación al documento titulado 'Propuesta de gobierno para una nueva normativa de consulta ...", pp.7 and 19-21.

2058 Decree/*Decreto* No.40 of the Ministry of Environment of 12 August 2013, published on 30 October 2013, *Aprueba Reglamento del Sistema de Evaluación de Impacto Ambiental.*

to consult indigenous peoples only for those projects likely to have a "high impact" on them, which are the relocation or a "significant alteration" of their lifestyle and customs (art.83 in relation to art.7), whereas for projects of "low impact" some informative meetings should be held (art.86). The qualification of "significant alteration" of indigenous peoples' lifestyle and customs may be subject to arbitrary interpretation, as no further criteria are clarified by this Decree. Additionally, the duty to consult indigenous peoples will be considered fulfilled even if their consent is not obtained (art. 85, para.2).

In sum, the right to consultation of indigenous peoples in Chile since the ratification of the ILO Convention 169 has been subject to contradictory legislation that still fails to meet the international standards. Notwithstanding this situation, a number of consultations, albeit limited, were held during the first mandate of Bachelet, and another one has recently been carried out (September 2014-January 2015). Most interestingly, since 2009 onwards, the Courts of Appeal have adopted several decisions safeguarding the right to consultation of indigenous peoples by recalling the ILO Convention 169, as discussed below.

6.3.2.2 Application of the indigenous peoples' right to consultation in Chile

After the debate on the ILO Convention 169 became more intense and following the visit of the Special Rapporteur on Indigenous Rights, as of 2009 a number of consultations were organized through the CONADI regional offices on behalf of the above-mentioned policy *Re-Conocer* of President Bachelet. In this section, five of these consultations are analyzed. The first three consultations were conducted under the first mandate of President Bachelet; the fourth one under the administration of President Piñera; and the last one under the current second mandate of President Bachelet. They addressed indigenous participation in Congress and the creation of the Council of Indigenous Peoples (2009); constitutional recognition (2009); constitutional reform in immigration matters of Easter Island/Rapa Nui regarding art.126bis of the Constitution (2009); the so called "Broad Consultation" (*Gran Consulta*; 2011); and the creation of the Ministry of Indigenous Affairs and the Council(s) of Indigenous Peoples (2014-2015). The latter, as already mentioned, regarded (again) the constitutional recognition of indigenous peoples, the transformation of the CONADI into a new Indigenous Development Agency, and the Council of Indigenous Peoples already consulted under the Bachelet administration in 2009. Curiously, two consultations were held even before the ILO Convention 169 entered into force. As mentioned, Chile had ratified it on 15 September 2008 but it entered into force in September 2009. Finally, the last consultation on the creation of the Ministry of Indigenous Affairs and the Council(s) of Indigenous Peoples carried out between September 2014 and January 2015 will be briefly presented, since the results are not available yet and it is too early to assess its impact.

These consultations have been selected for analysis here because from a legal point of view they should have the greatest impact. It should be recalled that there have been at least 11 consultations.[2059] In addition to those mentioned above, the others regarded a variety of matters, with very diverse degrees of importance: The tender to grant fiscal lands for the development of a wind farm in Lasaña-Conchi Viejo, Atacama Region; the project for establishing the National Park Salar de Huasco; the temporary expatriation of a Moai from Rapa Nui/Easter Island; the repatriation of indigenous remains found in Zurich; the general procedure of consultation and participation; the Araucanía regional development strategy; and the requests for the creation of the marine coastal spaces of Punta Capitanes and of Punta San Luis. These two latter consultations were made within the framework of the Law 20,249 on Marine Coastal Spaces mentioned above (section 6.2.2.2). However, many other required consultations were not held, such as in the case of the El Morro mine, which adversely affects the Diaguita people (see below section 6.3.2.3).[2060]

1) The very first consultation was entitled "Consultation on indigenous participation in the Congress and creation of the Council of indigenous peoples" and dealt with proposals for the creation of a Secretariat for Indigenous Affairs, a Committee of Ministers for Indigenous Affairs in every Ministry, a Unit of Indigenous Affairs in the regional Governor's offices, and a Council of Indigenous Peoples (*Proceso de Consulta sobre Participación Indígena en el Parlamento y Creación del Consejo de Pueblos Indígena*). The consultation was organized via letters and "participatory dialogues" between 7 January and 3 March 2009, i.e., in the midst of Chilean

2059 See the documents on almost all the consultations at CONADI, "Consultas", http://www.conadi.gob.cl/index.php/component/content/article?layout=edit&id=353 [Last access 06.09.2014].

2060 See the analysis of Vel, "Respecting the "Guardians of Nature: Chile's violations of the Diaguita indigenous peoples' …".

summertime. The CONADI central office sent a letter with instructions to the 4,599 indigenous organizations listed in the register of CONADI according to art.12 of the Indigenous Law without considering how many people represent each organization. According to the final report of this consultation, only 410 replies were received from 409 organizations and 1 from an individual. This means that less than 10% of the supposedly contacted organizations replied. As for the "participatory dialogues", the data affirm that 789 people took part.[2061] This means, again, about 11% of the population that self-identified as indigenous according to the 2002 census (and much less in comparison to the 2012 census data). Thus, the main problematic aspects regarding this consultation were the following: the timeframe very short; it was held in a period during which normally many indigenous persons are far from their communities due to seasonal jobs; and the mailing of letters to the indigenous organizations was not a fortunate decision. Instead of sending letters, a more transparent process could have been organized at municipal level or by the offices of CONADI with posters and infodesks. It is probable that many letters were lost in the mailing process, also considering the high level of isolation of many communities or indigenous organizations in Chile.

2) The second consultation under analysis here was carried out between 13 April and 5 June 2009 and regarded the constitutional recognition of indigenous peoples (*Proceso de Consulta sobre Reconocimiento Constitucional de los Pueblos Indígenas*). According to the Official Notes (*Minutas*) of this consultation,[2062] five different phases were foreseen, as follows: a) the mailing of instructions and guidelines for the consultation to indigenous organizations, communities, and associations via letter or email (from 13 April until 1 June); b) the dissemination in the local media of instructions and guidelines for the consultation (from 13 April until 1 June); c) the training of civil servants who work closely with indigenous communities or organizations (Tuesday 21 April 2009); d) workshops on the consultation at

2061 CONADI, "Informe final del proceso de consulta sobre participación política de los pueblos indígenas en la Cámara de Diputados, en los Consejos Regionales y la creación del Consejo De Pueblos Indígenas", Santiago de Chile, June 2009, at http://www.conadi.gob.cl/images/doc-consulta/doc_informe-final/Informe%20final%20Consulta%20Participacion%20Politica%20%288-07-09%29.pdf [Last access 06.09.2014].

2062 CONADI, "Minuta para la Consulta sobre Reconocimiento Constitucional de los Pueblos Indígenas", 2009, at http://www.conadi.gob.cl/images/doc-consulta/rec/Minuta%20reconocimiento%20constitucional%20final%20_14-04-091_.pdf [Last acces 06.09.2014].

provincial or municipal level (from 24 until 31 April); and e) a cycle of local meetings on demand to the local CONADI office (from 22 April until 5 June). The results and the observations of this consultation have never been published. There is only a mention in the document sent to the ILO CEACR in which it is declared that they received 428 replies that were sent to the national Congress for its consideration.[2063] Apart from this, other limits of this consultation were: the short timeframe; the scarce participation; the organization of only one training day for the civil servants; and the realization of the workshops in just one week. Finally, the considerations made above with regard to the formula of mailing letters, instead of other means, also applies in this case. However, the use of media to disseminate the call for consultation was remarkable.

3) The third consultation analyzed here refers to the draft constitutional reform regulating migration flows to Easter Island/Rapa Nui (*Proceso de Consulta sobre Proyecto de Reforma Constitucional en Materia Migratoria que modifica el artículo 126 bis sobre Territorios Especiales de Isla de Pascua y Archipiélago de Juan Fernández*). This consultation was carried out with the aim of achieving an agreement with the members of the Rapa Nui community to regulate the increasing migration of the continental Chilean population to the island. This was requested by the Rapa Nui people to reduce the potential risk of turning into a numerical minority in the island. Therefore, the proposal consisted in inserting an additional paragraph to art.126-bis of the Constitution, which recognizes the Special Territory of Easter Island and the surrounding archipelago of Juan Fernández (*Territorios Especiales de Isla de Pascua y Archipiélago de Juan Fernández*).[2064] The new second paragraph would specify that the migratory flow could be limited by law in order to protect the environment and sustainable development.[2065] The consultation was realized between 11 and 24 October 2009

2063 CONADI for Chile's government, "Memoria Presentada por el Gobierno de Chile en conformidad con las disposiciones del artículo 22 de la Constitución de la Organización Internacional del Trabajo …", p.38

2064 Art.126-bis, para.1, recognizes such territories and states that these shall be governed by special Statutes: "Art. 126 bis. Son territorios especiales los correspondientes a Isla de Pascua y al Archipiélago Juan Fernández. El Gobierno y Administración de estos territorios se regirá por los estatutos especiales que establezcan las leyes orgánicas constitucionales respectivas".

2065 The text that was thus under consultation was the following: "Podrá suspenderse o restringirse en dichos territorios especiales el ejercicio de los derechos de permanencia o de residencia, en la forma que establezca la ley orgánica constitucional respectiva, con el fin de proteger el medio ambiente y propender a su desarrollo

with limited success. Regrettably, the constitutional reform was eventually driven by President Piñera's government, which adopted another text in March 2012.[2066] Led by frustration regarding this missed reform, the Rapa Nui occupied the National Park in March 2015 of the island to try to trigger national and international attention on their case.[2067] Moreover, this reform nullified the effects of this consultation, which was among the few that mostly respected the international standards. In fact, as to the process of consultation, in comparison with the others, apart from the extremely short timeframe, it consultation was also widely disseminated in the local radio (Radio *Manukena*) and TV station (Canal 13 *Mata o te Rapa Nui*), and posters and brochures were distributed in the town of Hanga Roa. Additionally, five consultation desks were organized in a number of schools that served as polling stations. Then, all of the Rapa Nui aged 18 years or above included in the CONADI register (approximately 1,300 people) were invited to vote, of which 706 eventually did so. Other Rapa Nui individuals could also vote by presenting themselves and registering at the polling stations. The result of the vote was in favor of the reform, although the same report

---

sustentable". However, this text was then changed in the Lower Chamber as follows: "En dichos territorios, y con el fin de proteger el medio ambiente y propender a su desarrollo sustentable, podrá restringirse el ejercicio de los derechos de permanencia o residencia, como asimismo el de libre circulación hacia ellos, en los casos y en la forma que establezca la ley orgánica constitucional respectiva." Natalia Piergentili Domenech, María Josefina Pérez Cruz, Darío Cabezas Astorga and Álvaro Villanueva Rojas, "Informe Final del Proceso de Consulta sobre el Proyecto de Reforma Constitucional en Materia Migratoria que modifica el artículo 126 bis sobre Territorios Especiales de Isla de Pascua y Archipiélago de Juan Fernández", December 2009, p.7.

2066 The final text inserted in the Constitution by virtue of Law 20,573 of 6 March 2012 (*Reforma Constitucional sobre Territorios Especiales de Isla de Pascua y Archipiélago Juan Fernández*) states that the rights and freedoms of circulation and residence (reside, stay and move) guaranteed by the Constitution in these territories should be exercised according to special laws adopted with a qualified majority ("Los derechos a residir, permanecer y trasladarse hacia y desde cualquier lugar de la República, garantizados en el numeral 7° del artículo 19, se ejercerán en dichos territorios en la forma que determinen las leyes especiales que regulen su ejercicio, las que deberán ser de quórum calificado"). Therefore, the references to the safeguarding of the environment and sustainable development were deleted. Silva G. 2013, p.195.

2067 Cristián Moreno Pakarati, "El Caso Rapa Nui", 13.04.2015, Cátedra Indígena de la Universidad de Chile, at http://www.uchileindigena.cl/el-caso-rapa-nui [Last access 22.04.2015].

affirms that not all indigenous voters were aware of what they were voting for.[2068]

4) The "Broad Consultation" (*Gran Consulta*) launched by President Piñera was to be carried out via internet between April and September 2011. It dealt with various issues: the constitutional recognition of indigenous peoples; the establishment of the Indigenous Development Agency and of the Council of Indigenous Peoples; and the consultation procedure itself.[2069] indigenous peoples may express their vote via internet and/or at CONADI's offices. Consequently, the few of them that had internet access could therefore vote at home, but also in the offices of the CONADI. According to the official documents, a number of workshops were held between June and July 2011.[2070] However, there are no minutes or lists of participants of these meetings, which casts doubt on their realization. Due to the hails of criticism mentioned in section 6.3.2.2, this consultation was eventually suspended in September 2011. The vote via internet or at CONADI's office was potentially a sound method, but it would have guaranteed the participation of only those indigenous peoples with access to internet at home, which is rather rare, or of those living in the main towns, thus potentially excluding a large number of indigenous peoples who live in rural areas. This consultation's outcome could potentially have been biased. Notwithstanding these elements, the most striking aspect was that indigenous peoples would have been consulted on issues on which they had been already consulted in early 2009 (consultations nos.1-2), as seen above. Undoubtedly, the repeated consultations on the very same themes and with slight differences in the texts may have provoked much confusion.

2068 Piergentili Domenech, Pérez Cruz, Cabezas Astorga and Villanueva Rojas, "Informe Final del Proceso de Consulta sobre el Proyecto de Reforma Constitucional en Materia Migratoria que modifica el artículo 126 bis sobre Territorios Especiales de Isla de Pascua y Archipiélago de Juan Fernández", pp.9-19.

2069 Gobierno de Chile, "¿Qué es la Consulta?", and "Minuta Explicativa sobre el Procedimiento para Llevar a Cabo los Procesos de Consulta y Participación", 2011. Both these documents were available on the former institutional website of consultation in Chile (http://www.consultaindigena.cl), which now redirects to the new website (http://www.consultaindigena.gob.cl). All the documents related to the 2011 consultations were lastly consulted and downloaded by the author on 25.11.2011 and are on file with author. On the 2011 consultation, see also Marimán Quemenado, "Chile (2012)", pp.204-206.

2070 Gobierno de Chile, "Difusión e Inscripción", and "Etapas del Proceso de Consulta", 2011. Both were at http://www.consultaindigena.cl/proc-01difu sioneinscripcion.html [until 25.11.2011], on file with author.

5) This last criticism may also regard the last consultation on the creation of the Ministry of Indigenous Affairs and the Council(s) of Indigenous Peoples carried out recently (September 2014-January 2015).[2071] In essence, this is the third time that indigenous peoples have been consulted on the reform of CONADI and the establishment of these bodies. Later on, indigenous peoples will also be called to be consulted on the creation of the Ministry of Culture and Heritage to be carried out by the National Council of Culture and Arts.[2072] All these consultations are and will be governed by the above-mentioned Decree No.66 of 2014. Therefore, only the indigenous communities recorded in the CONADI register may participate (art.5 Decree No.66). A five-step procedure was hence followed: Plan of the process; distribution of the informative material; deliberation within the communities; "dialogue"; "systematization" and communication of results; and conclusion (art.16 of Decree No.66).[2073] Both international bodies and one of the best universities in social studies in Chile (Universidad Diego Portales) agreed to observe the consultation process.[2074] However, some aspects remained obscure. The distribution of informative material took place in a period of just two weeks. Most importantly, there was no guarantee on what the "dialogue" consists of and thus whether the outcome of indigenous peoples' consultation will be ever considered. Finally, according to art.3 of Decree No.66, the workshops were interpreted as the "best efforts" to consult the indigenous peoples and thus consider this duty fulfilled. The end of the consultation was proclaimed on 30 January 2015. The official press release

2071 Resolutions No.575 and 576 of 24 June 2014; Chilean Ministry of Social Development/*Ministerio de Desarrollo Social*, "Medida Legislativa del Consejo o Consejos de Pueblos Indígenas", and Chilean Ministry of Social Development/*Ministerio de Desarrollo Social*, "Presidenta Bachelet: "Estamos en el momento para ampliar y reconocer los derechos de los Pueblos Indígenas en Chile".

2072 Chilean Ministry of Social Development/*Ministerio de Desarrollo Social*, "Presidenta Bachelet: "Estamos en el momento para ampliar y reconocer los derechos de los Pueblos Indígenas en Chile".

2073 See also the webpage "Stages" (*Etapas*) of this last consultation at http://www.consultaindigenamds.gob.cl/etapas.html [Last access 05.02.2015].

2074 Chilean Ministry of Social Development/*Ministerio de Desarrollo Social*, "Organismos Internacionales respaldan proceso de Consulta a los Pueblos Indígenas", 13.08.2014, at http://www.consultaindigenamds.gob.cl/articulos/articulo130814_2.html [Last access 07.09.2014]; Chilean Ministry of Social Development/*Ministerio de Desarrollo Social*, "Ministerio de Desarrollo Social suscribe convenio de colaboración con Universidad Diego Portales para observación de Consulta Indígena", 04.09.2014, at http://www.consulta indigenamds.gob.cl/articulos/articulo040914_2.html [Last access 07.09.2014].

claimed a great success,[2075] while the indigenous and other civil society organizations denounced many irregularities.[2076] From the start, many indigenous organizations have voiced their discontent regarding this consultation, but essentially because it was regulated by the –limiting– Decrees No.40 and 66.[2077] After the end of the consultation, the complaints now regard a worrying lack of transparency and manipulation: Apparently, some indigenous leaders called to be consulted were not legitimized by their communities; some communities could not designate their representatives to participate in the consultation; and, in some cases, the consultation was held in remote places.[2078] The Ministry for Social Development María Fernanda Villegas declared that, this time, the process was highly participative, and was held in 122 localities.[2079] This data is confirmed by the final report of this consultation, according to which 6,833 indigenous representatives or leaders of indigenous organizations actively participated in the consultation.[2080] However, indigenous marches against the consultation were held throughout January both in the South by Mapuche and Kawsqar, and in Santiago by Aymara, Mapuche and Quechua.[2081]Additionally, some indig-

2075 Chilean Ministry of Social Development/*Ministerio de Desarrollo Social*, "Los nueve pueblos aprueban la creación del Ministerio y los Consejos de Pueblos Indígenas", 30.01.2015, at http://www.consultaindigenamds.gob.cl/articulo.php?id=13849 [Last access 06.02.2015].

2076 Andrés Ojeda, "Pueblos originarios acusan vicios en Consulta Indígena", Diario Universidad de Chile, 02.02.2015, at http://radio.uchile.cl/2015/02/02/pueblos-originarios-acusan-vicios-en-consulta-indigena [Last access 06.02.2015].

2077 Many indigenous organizations released a number of declarations against the consultation published on the websites of the NGOs *Observatorio Ciudadano* or *Mapuexpress*: "Declaración en rechazo a Consulta Indígena de las Autoridades Ancestrales y Dirigentes de los Pueblos Indígenas Autoconvocados", August 2014, at http://observatorio.cl/node/12019; "Asamblea indígena de Iquique y Pozo Almonte rechazan 'consulta' y exigen derogación Decretos 66 y 40", 03.09.2014, at http://www.mapuexpress.org/2014/09/05/asamblea-indigena-de-iquique-y-pozo-almonte-rechazan-consulta-y-exigen-derogacion; "Declaración de Pueblos Indígenas de la Cuenca de Tarapacá que rechaza consulta indígena", 04.09.2014, at http://observatorio.cl/node/12041 [Last access to all 06.02.2015].

2078 Reports of Prof. Salvador Millaleo, Director of the Indigenous Rights Programme of the (well-established and known) University of Chile, interviewed by Ojeda, "Pueblos originarios acusan vicios en Consulta Indígena".

2079 Ojeda, "Pueblos originarios acusan vicios en Consulta Indígena".

2080 Chilean Ministry of Social Development/Ministerio de Desarrollo Social, "Sistematización Proceso de Consulta Previa Indígena, Ministerio de Desarrollo Social. Informe Final", p.23.

2081 Ojeda, "Pueblos originarios acusan vicios en Consulta Indígena".

enous organizations sued local and national authorities in Amparo proceedings before the competent Courts of Appeal accusing them, *inter alia*, of false declarations, omission of documents, and a lack of proper information regarding the realization of the consultation. One of these claims has been rejected by the Court of Appeal of Temuco (Decision/*Rol* No.4081-2014 of 30 January 2015).[2082] Nevertheless, the main results of this consultation consists of: Having confirmed the creation of both the Ministry of Indigenous Affairs and the Council(s) of Indigenous Peoples; the former shall safeguard (*resguardar*) instead of only supervise (*velar*) the proper application of indigenous rights; a body in charge of the consultation process should be established within the Ministry; the Ministry shall keep a register of the Traditional Authorities (with an exception clause for the Rapa Nui people); the CONADI shall be reformed and the funds so far managed by it shall then be administered by the Ministry; the Council(s) of Indigenous Peoples may also have binding powers; and an increase of the numbers of representatives in the Councils.[2083] As mentioned above, now it remains to be seen whether these proposals will be seriously inserted in the draft laws and if these latter ones will be adopted by the end of 2015 as promised by President Bachelet in her Presidential Message of 21 May 2015.[2084]

In conclusion, it is remarkable that a number of consultations were organized both before and after the ILO Convention 169 entered into force and for the first time ever in Chile. However, two main issues remain worryingly pending. First, the reiteration of consultations on the very same issues and subjects has certainly created confusion among those in charge of organizing them and, most importantly, the indigenous peoples consulted. Second, many consultations that would be required according to the ILO Convention 169 (and the UNDRIP) in practice are not carried out. This lack of consultation has been denounced by indigenous peoples themselves, whom brought their cases before the Court of Appeals in Amparo proceedings, as will be discussed below (section 6.3.2.3). This may suggest that the big announcements of broad consultations such as those carried out in 2011

2082 *Ibid.* and Observatorio Ciudadano, "El proceso de consulta indígena del Ministerio de Desarrollo Social y la ausencia de un clima de confianza", *Observatorio Ciudadano*, 05.02.2015, at http://observatorio.cl/2015/el-proceso-de-consulta-in digena-del-ministerio-de-desarrollo-social-y-la-ausencia-de-un-clima [Last access 06.02.2015].

2083 Chilean Ministry of Social Development/Ministerio de Desarrollo Social, "Sistematización Proceso de Consulta Previa Indígena, Ministerio de Desarrollo Social. Informe Final", pp.24-26.

2084 Michelle Bachelet, "Mensaje Presidencial 21 de Mayo de 2015", 21.05.2015, p.25.

and 2014-2015 aim to distract the public indigenous (and non-indigenous) opinion from those most pressing cases of natural resources exploitations that adversely affect indigenous peoples.

6.3.2.3 The recent Amparo proceedings vis-à-vis the right to consultation

Since 2009, thanks to the mobilization of indigenous peoples and other organizations that supported them, the Court of Appeals has played the most important role in the application of the ILO Convention 169 and, in particular, of the right to consultation of indigenous peoples in Chile. The Courts that often ruled in favor of indigenous peoples are located in those regions where a high percentage of the population is indigenous, both in the North (Arica-Parinacota, Iquique y Antofagasta) and in the South (Bío-Bío, Araucanía, Los Ríos y Los Lagos). The judges of these Courts may have had a greater sensitiveness vis-à-vis indigenous issues.

Notably, by the end of 2012, at least 16 cases were brought before and decided by such Courts or by the Supreme Court,[2085] which often upheld the verdicts of the Court of Appeals.[2086] All the cases were filed as Amparo

---

2085 In the *Recurso de Protección*, the Supreme Court is the competent court to handle appeals filed against the decisions of the Court of Appeal.

2086 The cases are the following, in chronological order: 1) Case *Concesión de Exploración de Energía Sollipulli*: a) Court of Appeal of Santiago. Decision of 28 September 2009. Rol No. 8.304/2009; b) Supreme Court. Decision of 7 December 2009. Rol No. 8.155-2009; 2) Case *Chusmiza* (*Comunidad Indígena Aimara Chusmiza y Usmagama con la sociedad Agua Mineral Chusmiza S.A.I.C.*): a) Court of Iquique Rol No. 817/2006 of 9 April 2008; b) Supreme Court. Decision of 25 November 2009. File/*Recurso* 2840/2008; Resolution/*Resolución* 41242; 3) Case *Machi Francisca Linconao contra Sociedad Palermo Limitada*: a) Court of Appeal of Temuco. Decision of 16 September 2009. Autos 1773/2008; b) Supreme Court. Decision of 30 November 2009. File/*Recurso* 7287/2009; 4) Case *Empresa Constructora JCB S.A. contra Luci Loncón Veloso y otros*: a) Court of Appeal of Temuco. Decision of January 2010. Rol No. 1485-2009; b) Supreme Court. Decision de 25 March 2010. Rol No. 570-2010; 5) Case *Proyecto Piscicultura Palguin*: a) Court of Appeal of Temuco. Decision of 21 January 2010; b) Supreme Court. Decision of 17 May 2010; 6) Case *Proyecto Minero Catanave*: Court of Appeal of Arica. Decision of 19 February 2010. File/*Recurso* Rol No.16/2010; 7) Case *Empresa Pesquera Los Fiordos Ltda.*: a) Court of Appeal of Puerto Montt. Decision of 27 July 2010. Causa Rol No. 36/2010; b) Supreme Court. Decision of 15 September 2010. Causa Rol No. 5.757/2010; 8) Case *Cerro Colo Colo*: Court of Appeal of Concepción. Decision of 10 August 2010. Causa Rol No. 289/2010; 9) Case *Ducto Celco*: a) Court of Appeal of Valdivia. Decision of 26 May 2010. Causa Rol No. 148/2010; b) Supreme Court. Decision of 14 October 2010. Causa Rol No.

proceedings, apart from the *Chusmiza* case. In Chile, the Amparo proceeding is called *Recurso de Protección* and, as in other Latin American countries, it is a judicial guarantee against the violations of the citizenry's fundamental rights in accordance with arts.19-20 of the Chilean Constitution. A large part of this jurisprudence regarded the "right to live in an unpolluted environment" (art.19.8 of the Constitution). The indigenous claimants also invoked the application of the ILO Convention 169, mostly on the violation of the duty to consult indigenous peoples (arts.6-7). The judges often recalled these norms in their reasoning and eventually obliged a number of public administrations to apply them. In one case, a Court also used a standard enshrined in the UNDRIP. The extensive jurisprudence on this subject is thus evolving and currently settling its fundamental principles. Thus, first, this section presents the two pioneer cases in which the ILO Convention 169 was applied. Second, it discusses five relevant lawsuits brought to Court and decided by the Court of Appeals and the Supreme Court between 2009 and 2015, in which the main claim was the right to consultation. In the majority of e cases, this right was then judicially recognized to indigenous peoples.

In the *Chusmiza* case, the Aymara indigenous community *Chusmiza y Usmagama* claimed first before the (first instance) Court (*Juzgado*) of Pozo Almonte and then appealed at the Court of Appeal of Iquique (Rol No. 817/2006 of 9 April 2008) over the use of water by the Chusmiza spring. Both Courts denied this use. However, in late 2009 the Supreme Court eventually rejected the proceeding of cassation filed by the mineral water society *Agua Mineral Chusmiza S.A.I.C.* and recognized the "ancestral water

---

4078/2010; 10) Case *Mini Central Cayucupil*: Court of Appeal of Concepción. Decision of 1 December 2010. Causa Rol No. 401/2010; 11) Case *Estación de transferencia de residuos sólidos Lanco-Panguipulli*: a) Court of Appeal of Valdivia. Decision of 4 August 2010. Causa Rol No. 243/2010; b) Supreme Court. Decision of 4 January 2011. Causa Rol No. 6062; 12) Case *Aeropuerto Quepe*: a) Court of Appeal of Santiago. Decision of 31 January 2011. Causa Rol No .1794/2010; b) Supreme Court. Decision of 6 May 2011. Causa rol No. 1608/2011; 13) Case *Comerciantes Ambulantes Mapuches*: a) Court of Appeal of Temuco. Decision of 30 May 2011. Causa Rol No.166/2011; b) Supreme Court. Decision of 1 July 2011. Causa Rol No. 5159/2011; 14) Case *Plano Regulador San Pedro Atacama*: Supreme Court. Decision of 13 July 2011. Causa Rol No. 258/2011; 15) Case *Parque Eólico Chiloé*: a) Court of Appeal of Puerto Montt. Decision of 11 October 2011. Causa Rol No. 239/2011; b) Supreme Court. Decision of 22 March 2012. Rol No. 10.090-2011; 16) Case *El Morro*: a) Court of Appeal de Antofagasta. Decision of 17 February 2012. Causa Rol No. 618/2011; b) Supreme Court. Decision of 27 April 2012. Causa Rol 2211-2012.

rights" of the community six times.[2087] Additionally, the Court stated that the lack of a registration of "customary" water rights does not imply their inexistence, rather it is an omission of formalization, since this right does exist as and is recognized by (the Indigenous) law.[2088] In its argument, for the first time ever, the Court affirms that art.15.1 of the ILO Convention 169 on natural resources and art.13.2 on the concept of land as habitat, which also includes the watercourses, are necessary to interpret correctly art.64 of the Indigenous Law (on water rights of Atacameños and Aymara peoples of the North).[2089]

The case of *Machi Francisca Linconao Huircapan con Sociedad Palermo Itda* regarded logging exploitation close to Mapuche land. The case was brought before the Temuco Court of Appeal that admitted the Amparo proceeding of the *Machi* and affirming that the State had to comply with the duties contained in arts.13 and 14 of the ILO Convention 169 that had just entered into force at that time (September 2009).[2090] The Court found that the logging activities of the *Palermo* company had damaged sacred Mapuche sites (*menocos*) close to the *Cerro Rahue* hill in the Araucanía region, and thus adversely affected the collection of herbs and the practice of traditional medicine. The Supreme Court upheld this decision on 30 November 2009.[2091]

These two decisions prompted a wave of lawsuits also in relation to the right to consultation of indigenous peoples. One of these cases, the so called *Palguín case*, concerned water pollution caused by a fishery to be constructed close to Mapuche territories.[2092] Two Mapuche peasants, a *Longko*

2087 Considerings/*Considerandos* Nos.5, 6, 7 and 8, Supreme Court, Decision/*Rol* No.2840/2008.

2088 Supreme Court, Decision/*Rol* No.2840/2008, Considering/*Considerando* No.4, which originally states: "La eventual ausencia de inscripción de los derechos de aguas consuetudinarios no acarrea su inexistencia, sino sólo la falta de su formalización registral y así, precisamente porque el derecho existe, se le reconoce por la ley".

2089 Supreme Court, Decision/*Rol* No.2840/2008, Considering/*Considerando* No.7, fifth paragraph. For further details on this case, see Rodrigo Cespedes, "Environmental Justice for Indigenous People in the Post-Pinochet Chile", in Karen Druffel (ed.), *Looking Within: Finding an Environmental Justice and Global Citizenship Lens*, Inter-Disciplinary Press, Oxford, 2013, pp.93-102, p.97.

2090 Court of Appeal of Temuco, Decision/*Rol* No. 1773-2008, 16 September 2009.

2091 Supreme Court, Decision/*Rol* No.7287/2009, 30 November 2009.

2092 Court of Appeal of Temuco, *Mariano Puelman Ñanco and Manuel del Carmen Rivera v. Sociedad Agrícola Terratur Limitada*, Decision/*Rol* No.1705-2009, 21 January 2010.

(chief) and a president of two communities, had filed the Regional Environmental Commission (*Comisión Regional del Medio Ambiente* – COREMA) with an Amparo proceeding before the Temuco Court of Appeal to declare void Resolution No.242 of 9 October 2009 of this Commission. In this resolution, on the basis of a controversial Environmental Impact Assessment, COREMA had granted the permit to the company *Sociedad Agricola Terratur Limitada* to establish a farm fishing called "Palguín" located very close (720 meters) to the Mapuche communities of the claimants. The Court admitted the Amparo proceeding and declared null and void the Resolution since the communities had not been consulted on such project according to the legislation on the right to consultation of indigenous peoples. In particular, the Court recalled the abovementioned Decision/*Rol* No.309 of 2000 of the Constitutional Court and reminded that art.6.1, letter a, and art.7.1 are self-executing, thus it is an imperative duty of the State to consult the indigenous peoples affected by projects of this kind.[2093] In addition, the Court stated that Decree No.124, which was also adopted in that period, ruled the consultation according to the Indigenous Law, but that it could not regulate the ILO Convention 169, that provides indigenous peoples with a far more incisive protection.[2094] Finally, in case of similar projects, the norm should always be interpreted in favor of the most vulnerable group, i.e., the indigenous peoples, according to the constitutional fundamental rights and the value of human dignity.[2095] Regrettably, the Supreme Court eventually overruled this decision, by stating that the environmental "citizen participation" according to the environmental law was sufficient to declare viable the farm fishing project.[2096] The reasons behind such a strict approach remains unknown.

The following case regards pollution of Mapuche land by a salmon farming.[2097] The Court of Appeal of Puerto Montt admitted in July 2010 the Amparo proceeding of the Mapuche indigenous community Huilliche

2093 *Ibid.*, Considerings/*Considerandos* Nos.5-6.

2094 *Ibid.*, Considering/*Considerando* No.7.

2095 *Ibid.*, Considering/*Considerando* No.8.

2096 Supreme Court, Decision/*Rol* No.1525-2010, 18 May 2010. On the "citizenry participation" according to environmental law see arts.74, 90, 91, 93, 94, 96 and 102 of the Supreme Decree No.95 of 2001 on the regulation of the Environmental Impact Assessment (*Reglamento del Sistema de Evaluación de Impacto Ambienta*l), and arts.7, 7-bis, 7-ter, 7-quáter, 18 and 29 of the (previous) Environmental Law (*Ley de medioambiente, Aprueba Ley sobre Bases Generales del Medio Ambiente*) No.19,300 of 9 March 1994.

2097 Court of Appeal of Puerto Montt, Decision/*Rol* No.36-2010, 27 July 2010.

Pepiukelen against the salmon farming company *Los Fiordos S.A.* The Court found the defendant guilty of illegal occupation of neighbouring indigenous lands and of environmental damage for having contaminated a natural lake located on this territory. Despite the outcome of the decision, four points raised by the Court are worth mentioning. First, the concept of land needs to be considered as the whole habitat, in accordance with art.13.2 of the ILO Convention 169.[2098] Second, that the State has an absolute and binding duty to consult indigenous peoples. Third, the right to consultation of indigenous peoples is different from and far more incisive than "citizen participation" under the environmental law, thus in contrast with the decision of the Supreme Court in the *Palguín* case. Finally, this Court also flagged the self-executing value of arts.6.1.a and 7.1 of the ILO Convention 169.[2099] This case was upheld by the Supreme Court the following September 2010.[2100]

In August 2010, the Court of Appeal of Valdivia admitted another Amparo proceeding by the Lanco-Panguipulli Mapuche communities against a resolution of the National Environmental Commission (*Comisión Nacional del Medio Ambiente* – CONAMA) regarding the allocation of waste in the area contiguous to the communities' lands and the consequent destruction of Mapuche ceremonial area without having consulted the affected indigenous peoples.[2101] This case is particularly relevant since the Court also mentions art.25 of the UNDRIP,[2102] besides arts.6-7 of the ILO Convention 169. The Supreme Court upheld this case the following January 2011.[2103]

The *Plano Regulador San Pedro Atacama* case decided by the Supreme Court on 13 July 2011 is worth being mentioned next.[2104] In this case, the indigenous association of Atacameños Peoples' Council (*Asociación Indígena Consejo de Pueblos Atacameños*) and the Indigenous Atacameño Community (*Comunidad Atacameña Toconao*) sued the Regional Environmental Commission (*Comisión Regional del Medio Ambiente* – COREMA)

2098 *Ibid.*, Considering/*Considerando* No.10.

2099 *Ibid.*, Considering/*Considerando* No.9.

2100 Supreme Court, Decision Rol No.5,757-2010 of 15 September 2010.

2101 Court of Appeal of Valdivia, Decision/*Rol* No. 243-2010, 4 August 2010.

2102 Art.25 of the UNDRIP states: "Indigenous peoples have the right to maintain and strengthen their distinctive spiritual relationship with their traditionally owned or otherwise occupied and used lands, territories, waters and coastal seas and other resources and to uphold their responsibilities to future generations in this regard".

2103 Supreme Court, Decision/*Rol* No. 6062/2011, 4 January 2011.

2104 Supreme Court, Decision/*Rol* No. 258/2011, 13 July 2011.

of Antofagasta, similarly to the cited *Palguín* case. The indigenous plaintiffs complained that the COREMA had approved –with resolution (*resolución exenta*) No.275 of 2010– the updating of the Zoning Plan (*Plan Regulador*) of the region without conducting the due Environmental Impact Assessment according to (then) Environmental Law No.19,300 and, most importantly, without consulting the indigenous peoples living on the different territories and who were thus (more than) likely to be affected.[2105] Interestingly, the Supreme Court specified that "giving information" cannot be framed as a proper consultation and that the affected indigenous peoples must participate in the elaboration of these plans: In the approved plan no analysis was made of its potential effects on the indigenous Atacameño culture, identity, customs, traditions, and institutions. This is considered by the Court to be another aspect of this resolution's illegality.[2106] Finally, according to the Court, the lack of consultation in this case was equivalent to a violation of the right to equality.[2107] In conclusion, the Supreme Court declared null and void the above-mentioned resolution and obliged the COREMA to elaborate an Environmental Impact Assessment and carry out a due consultation.[2108]

More recently, in the (first) *El Morro* case, the Diaguita of Huascoaltinos Peasant Community (*Comunidad Agrícola Diaguita de Los Huascoaltinos*) filed before the Court of Appeal of Antofagasta the Environmental Evaluation Commission of the 3rd region of Atacama.[2109] This Commission approved the study of Environmental Impact Assessment of the mine *El Morro* favourably with resolution No.049 in 2011. This mining project, belonging to two Canadian companies, Goldcorp (70%) and Newgold (30%), consisted of the construction of an open-pit mine of gold and copper on 2,463 hectares of land in the 3rd region, including a considerable part of the indigenous Diaguita *Huascoaltinos* territories.[2110] Thus, the Court found that the resolution failed to mention that the project would have affected

---

2105 *Ibid.*, Considering/*Considerando* Nos.2-4 and 7.
2106 *Ibid.*, Considering/*Considerando* No.8.
2107 *Ibid.*, Considering/*Considerando* No.9.
2108 *Ibid.*, Considering/*Considerando* No.10.
2109 Court of Appeal of Antofagasta, Decision/*Rol* No.618/2011, 17 February 2012.
2110 For further information on this project, see also Elías Paillan, "Corte Suprema revoca calificación ambiental de proyecto minero El Morro: Fallo es calificado como 'hito histórico'", 08.10.2014, *Observatorio Ciudadano*, at http://observatorio.cl/node/12275 [Last access 07.02.2015]

recognized indigenous lands (the *Estancia de Los Huasco Altinos*),[2111] caused the displacement of huascoaltino breeders, and affected their land and water rights as well as their customs and way of life.[2112] Additionally, the Court recognized that no proper consultation was carried out. Indeed, according to the Court, the mining project was proposed unilaterally; other Diaguita communities participated in a round-table dialogue (*mesa de dialogo*) but those affected were not invited, which implies *mala fide* on the part of the companies; and this round-table in any case could not be framed as a proper consultation since it was established after the Environmental Impact Assessment was issued and thus no indigenous peoples could have potentially intervened in it.[2113] Additionally, the Court (re)affirmed the self-executing nature of art.6.2 of the ILO Convention 169 as recognized by the Constitutional Court (Rol No.309/2000) and the ILO CEACR. This qualification requires that the consultation must be carried out in accordance with art.6.2 of the ILO Convention 169, not a "similar mechanism" foreseen in the Chilean legislation.[2114] In conclusion, the Court of Appeal of Antofagasta declared null and void the resolution of the defendant[2115] and recognized that the plaintiff Peasant Community Diaguita of Huascoaltinos are indigenous Diaguita and, as such –as well as the neighbouring indigenous communities– have a number of rights recognized in Chilean law. These are the rights to equality (art.19.2 of the Constitution), property (art.19.24 of the Constitution), "territory" (arts.1-2 of the Indigenous Law), and to participation in keeping with arts.6, 7 and 15 of the ILO Convention 169 and arts.26-27 of the ICCPR.[2116] The Supreme Court upheld this decision shortly after and ordered an amendment of the environmental resolution and the study of Environmental Impact Assessment by taking into consideration the concerns raised by the Court of Appeal of Antofagasta vis-à-vis the Diaguita indigenous peoples.[2117] However, this case did not end here. Following the Supreme Court's decision, on 22 June 2012, the Environmental Evaluation Commission of the 3rd region of Atacama requested that companies should submit an additional report by 5 July, but this was eventually postponed –first– to the following March and –then– to December 2013.

2111 Court of Appeal of Antofagasta, Decision/*Rol* No.618/2011, 17 February 2012, Considering/*Considerando* No.1.1.
2112 *Ibid.*, Considering/*Considerando* No.1.2.
2113 *Ibid.*, Considering/*Considerando* No.1.3.
2114 *Ibid.*
2115 *Ibid.*, Considering/*Considerando* No.12.
2116 *Ibid.*, Considering/*Considerando* No.10.
2117 Supreme Court, Decision/*Rol* No. 2211/2012, 27 April 2012.

Since that March, a consultation was organized, but without following international standards. Thus, the Diaguita people brought their case before (this time, due to territorial competence) the Court of Appeal of Copiapó, which suspended the consultation in May 2013.[2118] However, on 3 October 2013, the Environmental Evaluation Commission approved the mining project again with resolution No.221, according to a report of the companies that have complied with the consultation. However, the Environmental Evaluation Commission simply organized a one-day debate on 31 July and then sent letters to the Diaguita people in late September with the minutes of the meeting and a proposal to accept the "consultation". The Diaguita community had just one week to reply and send observations, and consequently asked the Environmental Evaluation Commission to extend the deadline. The Environmental Evaluation Commission did not reply to this request and, on 8 October 2013, it reported that the community had not collaborated on the consultation.[2119] On the following 22 October, the Environmental Evaluation Commission approved the study of Environmental Impact Assessment with resolution No.232. The regional office of CONADI also did the same with acts No.00 and 564 of 2013. The Diaguita people sued the relevant institutions over these acts before the Court of Appeal of Copiapó, which however found that no violation had occurred. Thus, the Diaguita people appealed to the Supreme Court, which finally found a violation of their right to consultation for lack of *bona fide*, declared null and void the mentioned acts, and ordered the CONADI to fully comply with a due consultation process with the affected Diaguita peoples.[2120]

In conclusion, both the Court of Appeals and the Supreme Court started to produce an extremely evolving and interesting jurisprudence since 2009. These decisions may thus be considered the most advanced and effective application of the right to consultation of indigenous peoples in Chile.

2118 Paulina Acevedo, "Corte de Apelaciones de Copiapó suspende proceso de consulta sobre proyecto minero El Morro: Por no cumplir con estándares internacionales", 02.05.2013, *Observatorio Ciudadano*, at http://www.observatorio.cl/2013/corte-de-apelaciones-de-copiapo-suspende-proceso-de-consulta-sobre-proyecto-minero-el-morro-por [Last access 07.02.2015].

2119 Paulina Acevedo, "Comunidad diaguita Huascoaltinos rechaza aprobación de proyecto minero El Morro y denuncia mala fe de la autoridad frente a derecho a consulta", 28.10.2013, *Observatorio Ciudadano*, at http://www.observatorio.cl/node/10205 [Last access 07.02.2015].

2120 Supreme Court, Decision/*Rol* No. 11,299/2014, 7 October 2014, Considering /*Considerando* No.33.

6.4 Participation through autonomy/self-government arrangements and the preservation of indigenous institutions – indigenous autonomy claims in Chile

The second component of the implementation of the *composite right* to political participation of indigenous peoples in Chile is addressed here. This aspect, as seen in chapter 3, section 3.4, regards the indigenous peoples' claim to autonomy/self-government arrangements and, thus, also to preserve their indigenous institutions.

As mentioned, Chile is subdivided into 15 regions and 345 municipalities. The members of the Regional Councils were previously appointed among provincial and municipal councilors and were directly voted for the first time only last November 2013. Additionally, the regional and provincial governors, who chair and lead the corresponding councils, are still appointed by the Government (see section 6.3.1.1). The regions and the provinces enjoy a rather reduced set of powers, which are managed by the respective Governors. The former are supported by regional ministerial secretariats[2121] However, all these bodies essentially act as purely administrative offices.[2122] During the debates on decentralization in early 1990 (see infra), there was a discussion on granting autonomy to the regions, but this proposal was eventually rejected.[2123]

At local level, the participation of indigenous peoples in the municipal offices of mayor and councilor is not guaranteed a priori but, thanks to the proportional system, it is potentially achievable, particularly in those communities where a high percentage of the population is indigenous. After the restoration of the democracy, a number of decentralization reforms were pursued by the *Concertación*'s governments to reinforce the role of regions and municipalities, particularly to abolish the dictatorship's system of Councils of Municipal Development (*Consejos de Desarrollo Comunales* – CODECOs), according to which all mayors were designated by Pinochet (except 15, who were nominated by the President, thus Pinochet himself until 1988).[2124] After reaching pre-agreements with the right-wing party on

2121 *Secretarías Regionales Ministeriales*, arts14 and ff. of the Law Decree No.575 of 13 July 1974.

2122 See the limited powers in (still in force) art.5 of the Law Decree No.575 of 13 July 1974.

2123 Rodrigo Mardones Z., "Descentralización y Transición en Chile", 26(1) *Revista de Ciencia Política (Santiago SciELO)* 2006, pp.3-24, p.8.

2124 Mardones Z., "Descentralización y Transición en Chile", p.5.

the reforms –due to the impasse caused by the binominal system– in 1996 the main reforms regarding the election of mayors and councils were adopted and in 2005 those reforms relating to the increase of municipalities' finances were likewise adopted.[2125]

Since then, despite many financial limitations,[2126] municipalities have become potential spaces for participation and enjoy a number of powers within their territory, e.g., local development plans and the town plan (art.3 of Law No.18,695 of 1988 and following amendments). Other public services, such as health care and education, may be organized by the municipalities following the directives of the competent State bodies (art.4 of Law No.18,695). As mentioned, according to the Indigenous Law (arts.9-11), indigenous peoples may register indigenous communities within the municipal territory. Therefore, within a municipality, more indigenous communities may exist.

During her current, second mandate, in April 2014 President Bachelet established an Advisory Presidential Commission on Decentralization and Regional Development (*Comisión Asesora Presidencial para la Descentralización y el Desarrollo Regional*, hereinafter, the Commission). The primary goal of this commission was to elaborate a plan to decentralize powers from the central to the regional level.[2127] This Commission presented its final report on 7 October 2014.[2128] Very interestingly, the Commission proposed to declare the 9th region of Chile (*La Araucanía*) "plurinational and

2125 Law No.19,452 of 16 April 1996 (*Modifica Disposiciones que Indica de la Ley N° 18.695, Orgánica Constitucional de Municipalidades*), and Law No.20,033 of 2 July 2005 (*Modifica La Ley N° 17.235, Sobre Impuesto Territorial; el Decreto Ley N° 3.063, Sobre Rentas Municipales; la Ley N° 18.695, Orgánica Constitucional De Municipalidades, y Faculta a las Municipalidades para Otorgar Condonaciones que Indica*), also known as the 2nd Municipalities' Finances Law (*Ley de Rentas Muncisipales II*). See also Mardones Z., "Descentralización y Transición en Chile", pp.7, 10 and 17. As mentioned, the last reform regarding municipalities was adopted in 2014, by Law 20,742.

2126 Mardones Z., "Descentralización y Transición en Chile", pp.17-18.

2127 Comisión Asesora Presidencial para la Descentralización y el Desarrollo Regional, "Qué Hacemos", [no date], at http://descentralizacion.cl/?page_id=482 [Last Access 07.02.2015].

2128 Comisión Asesora Presidencial para la Descentralización y el Desarrollo Regional, "Informe final. Propuesta de Política de Estado y Agenda para la Descentralización y el Desarrollo Territorial de Chile. Hacia un país desarrollado y justo", 07.10.2014, at http://descentralizacion.cl/?wpfb_dl=78 [Last Access 07.02.2015].

multicultural" by amending art.126-bis of the Chilean Constitution.[2129] Approximatively a third of the Mapuche people live in this region, as seen in section 6.1.1. The Commission further suggested that this region shall adopt its own statute, which should: Mention the origins of the indigenous peoples living there and the regional symbols; regulate the use of (two) official languages; recognize and guarantee "multiculturalism" and indigenous rights; and establish the forms of indigenous participation and organization in the regional political institutions, including a percentage of reserved seats for indigenous citizens in the elections of municipal and regional councilors (for a period of 20 years), as well as deputies and senators, and the creation of indigenous municipalities.[2130] In fact, the Commission proposed the creation of more categories of municipalities given the high cultural and socio-economic differences among them. These categories also including the establishment of "autonomous indigenous municipalities" (*municipio autónomo indígena*), which would correspond to those municipalities inhabited by a majority of indigenous peoples. These municipalities should be governed by indigenous forms of organization; have powers over communitarian rules, communal lands and the use of natural resources; and negotiate financial sources for their administration. Notably, the Commission stated that examples of such municipalities may be Temucuicui in Ercilla (see below) or the Aymara communities in the northern Chilean highlands.[2131] Furthermore, the Commission advised the adoption of a Law on Regional Incomes to secure the effective execution of the decentralized powers to the regions. In this framework, it foresees extra budget from the energy projects, which must be authorized only if in due compliance with the rights to participation and consultation of indigenous peoples.[2132] Finally, the Commission also suggested the participation of indigenous peoples in the Regulation Councils to guarantee the correct use of their languages in the application of a new law on toponymy.[2133] It also recommended the participation of indigenous peoples in an Assembly of Regional Civil Society's Organizations (*Asamblea de Organizaciones dela Sociedad Civil Regional*) for those regions with an indigenous population that is higher than 5%.[2134] Finally, the Commission suggested empowering civic,

2129 *Ibid.*,, p.35.
2130 *Ibid.*
2131 *Ibid.*, p.54.
2132 *Ibid.*, p.60, para.1.2, letter d.
2133 *Ibid.*, p.67.
2134 *Ibid.*, p.101.

democratic education by enhancing e bilingual education, to be designed by an indigenous consultative body.[2135]

Nevertheless, it remains to be seen whether the Commission's proposal will be put into practice. So far (July 2015), there is no provision in Chile regarding the exercise of autonomy or self-government of indigenous peoples. This, however, has not prevented indigenous demands for autonomy. In particular, since 1990 Mapuche autonomy has been demanded by the organization Aukiñ Wallmapu Ngulam, which, two years later, called for self-determination and introduced the flag of the "Mapuche Nation".[2136] Additionally, as seen above, since the first meetings in late 1990s prior to the creation of the Mapuche Party Wallmapuwen, the demand for autonomy has been their main claim. Also the Rapa Nui people recently reiterated their demand for territorial autonomy.[2137]

For the aims of this study, however, one particular case is worth analysing. In the municipality of Ercilla, in the province of Malleco (9th region of Aracanía), two indigenous communities –namely the *Comunidad Autónoma de Temucuicui* and the *Comunidad Cacique José Guiñon*– self-declared their autonomous status with an official letter that they sent to President Bachelet on 29 January 2010 despite the missing legal ground for such a claim. They announced the creation of their own, self-governing Assembly (*Parlamento*). By this, they essentially aimed to control their own territories and preserve their traditional lifestyle, authorities, language, and education. [2138] In general, indigenous peoples that refer to "autonomy" in Chile mean the possibility to adopt their own decisions (i.e., in decision-making processes) aimed at social development and taking control over their own natural resources and territories.[2139]

2135 *Ibid.*, p.104.

2136 Kowalczyk, "Indigenous Peoples and Modernity: Mapuche Mobilizations in Chile", p.127.

2137 Tania González, "Pueblo Rapanui reclama autonomía de la Isla de Pascua", 13.09.2014, Diario Universidad de Chile, at http://radio.uchile.cl/2014/09/13/pueblo-rapanui-reclama-autonomia-de-la-isla-de-pascua [Last access 07.02.2015].

2138 Pablo Ruiz Espinoza, "Comunidades de Malleco crean Parlamento", 06.02.2010, at http://revista-amauta.org/2010/02/chile-comunidades-mapuches-de-malleco-crean-parlamento; see also the community blog at http://comunidadtemucuicui.blogspot.it [Last access 06.09.2014].

2139 Pablo Alberto Maremán Quemenado, "La autonomía en el Cono Sur. El caso Mapuche de la Araucanía (Chile) y el Newken (Argentina), in Felipe Gómez Isa and Susana Ardanaz Iriarte (eds.), *La plasmación política de la diversidad. Autonomía y participación política indígena en América Latina*, Universidad de Deusto, Bilbao, 2011, pp.59-88, p.76.

Both communities are located a few kilometres away from the centre of Ercilla and are inhabited by about 1,000 people each. The traditional authorities of the "Machi" (a woman that, among different roles, also acts as the community healer), "Longko" (chief of the community, normally a man) and "Werken" (spokesperson, also generally a man) are preserved and exercised in both communities. The majority of the inhabitants live of subsistence means, such as farming and cattle breeding of a few animals.[2140] The two communities were victims of the expropriation policy perpetrated by Pinochet. In particular, in the case of Temucuicui, during the Agrarian Reform, the indigenous community collectively cropped the land, but in 1974 this land was expropriated and "returned" to private owners.[2141] Since the adoption of the Indigenous Law, in 1993, the communities have started to claim back their territories. However, as seen, the process of land restitution has been rather unsuccessful, which fuelled their frustration.[2142] Moreover, the expropriated lands in 1974 later became property of the logging company *Forestal MININCO S.A.* of the giant Arauco-Angelini group.[2143] In late 1999, indigenous peoples started the pacific occupation of these lands to claim them back, but the reaction on the part of the police (*Carabineros*) called by the official owner has always been extremely violent. For instance, in 1999, a 22-year boy was shot 8 times in his legs.[2144] From then onwards, the police brutal repressions have been innumerable. Many indigenous persons, including women and children, of this community have also been arrested and judged under the Antiterrorism Law, and participated in the 2010 dramatic hunger strike mentioned above (section

---

2140 Sergio Rodríguez, "Temucuicui, la comunidad que vive en alerta", *La Tercera*, 08.12.2013, at http://www.latercera.com/noticia/nacional/2013/12/680-555290-9-temucuicui-la-comunidad-que-vive-en-alerta.shtml [Last access 06.09.2014]; Rosa Sepúlveda Navarro and Adelmo Millaqueo Millapán, "Informe Diagnóstico y de Intervención Comunidad Cacique José Guiñón Ercilla", Programa Salud Mapuche, Servicio Salud Araucanía Norte, 2004, p.10.

2141 Eduardo Mella Seguel and Matías Meza-Lopehandía Glaesser, *Temucuicui: Paradigma de la vulneración de los derechos fundamentales de los pueblos indígenas en Chile*, Observatorio de Derechos de los Pueblos Indígenas (Observatorio Ciudadano), Temuco, 2006, p.6.

2142 Mella Seguel and Meza-Lopehandía Glaesser, *Temucuicui: Paradigma de la vulneración de los derechos fundamentales de los pueblos indígenas en Chile*, p.9.

2143 As mentioned, the Arauco-Angelini group owns approximately 1.000.000ha of land.

2144 Mella Seguel and Meza-Lopehandía Glaesser, *Temucuicui: Paradigma de la vulneración de los derechos fundamentales de los pueblos indígenas en Chile*, p.10.

6.1.2.3).[2145] During late 2011, the continued attacks on this community by policemen were condemned by the Temuco Court of Appeal, which prohibited the use of tear gas and acts of violence vis-à-vis indigenous women and children when the police 'enter' into indigenous communities.[2146] In 2012, the same Court blamed the police for having arrested without any mandate some indigenous people who were simply walking nearby the community of Temucuicui.[2147] In the same days, again, the Court of Appeal of Temuco denounced a state of "permanent militarization" of the area surrounding Temucuicui.[2148]

Notwithstanding these Court decisions, violent acts persist nowadays[2149] and are finally being reported by the national media such as *La Tercera*.[2150] One may wonder how and why these two tiny communities may threaten State authorities to the point that they constantly send policemen to repress them. Moreover, on-site visits have proved that they are mainly inhabited by elderly women and children.[2151] A number of national NGOs visited and supported the Temucuicui cause,[2152] although no further action followed on the part of the State, except for the recent proposals of the Advisory Presidential Commission on Decentralization and Regional Development. No

2145 AP/Emol, "Tercer mapuche en huelga de hambre debió ser trasladado a un hospital", Emol.cl, 01.09.2010, at http://www.emol.com/noticias/nacional/2010/09/01/433813/tercer-mapuche-en-huelga-de-hambre-debio-ser-trasladado-a-un-hospital.html; Comunidad Autónoma Temucuicui, "Otro prisionero Politico Mapuche, sacado de urgencia al hospital y toman muestra de sangre", 01.09.2010, at http://comunidadtemucuicui.blogspot.it/2010/09/otro-prisionero-politico-mapuche-sacado.html [last access to all 06.09.2014].

2146 Court of Appeal of Temuco, Decision/*Rol* No.342-2011 of 16 December 2011.

2147 Court of Appeal of Temuco, Decision/*Rol* No.1026-2012 of 28 December 2012, *Considerando* (Considering) No.2.

2148 Court of Appeal of Temuco, Decision/*Rol* No.838-2012 of 20 December 2012.

2149 Comunidad Mapuche Autónoma Temucuicui, "Fuerzas especiales de carabinero irrumpe a comunidades de Temucuicui", 02.02.2015, Comunidad Autonoma Temucuicui blog, at http://comunidadtemucuicui.blogspot.it/2015/02/fuerzas-especiales-de-carabinero.html [last access 07.02.2015].

2150 Rodríguez, "Temucuicui, la comunidad que vive en alerta".

2151 Alberto Coddou, Nicolas Godoy and Adrian Vergara, "Fuerza Estatal y Conflicto Mapuche", in Tomás Vial (ed.), *Informe Anual sobre Derechos Humanos en Chile 2013*, Ediciones Universidad Diego Portales, Santiago de Chile, 2013, pp.223-252, p.233.

2152 See the intervention of the co-director of Observatorio Ciudadano at Radio Nuevo Mundo, Nancy Yáñez, Presan Nuevo Mundo, "Nancy Yáñez acusa violencia del Gobierno a mapuches", 10 October 2013, at http://www.radionuevomundo.cl/nancy-yanez-el-allamiento-a-temucuicui-fue-para-defender-los-intereses-de-pinera [last access 06.09.2014].

conciliation process has ever been initiated. The impunity of policemen with regard to violent acts obviously disappointed indigenous peoples.[2153] However, on 16 January 2013, at the "First Summit of Mapuche Peoples" held in the Ñielol hill in Temuco, those indigenous peoples that were present demanded a dialogue with the State and an end to the violent repression of indigenous peoples in Chile.[2154]

Hopefully, President Bachelet will address this request and during her new mandate the request of autonomy by these communities will be effectively addressed by implementing the recent proposals of the Advisory Presidential Commission on Decentralization and Regional Development, also in compliance of arts.3 and 4 of the UNDRIP, which has been signed by Chile.

6.5 Concluding remarks on the Chilean case

This chapter addressed the recognition and application at domestic level of the *composite right to political participation of indigenous peoples* proposed in chapter 3 in the case of Chile. This *composite right* follows a twofold approach. First, it refers to the combination of *ad hoc* political rights, thus (a) indigenous peoples' representation in State bodies or in other public posts, including in decision-making processes and in the judiciary, both at national and local level, as well as their rights to (b) consultation and (c) free, prior and informed consent (FPIC). Second, to indigenous autonomy/self-government arrangements, including the preservation of traditional indigenous institutions (chapter 3, section 3.4). This proposal focuses on the rights of indigenous peoples to "have a say" in the national and local political arenas and in all matters likely to affect them, which implies much more than the individual participation in elections available to every citizen.

This concluding section explores whether this composite right may also become one of the effective applications of the right to self-determination of indigenous peoples in Chile, and thus enhance their protection and offer a compromise solution for the State. As seen in chapter 2, sections 2.2.5 and

2153 E.g., the police agent who shot Matías Valentín Catrileo Quezada was not sentenced to prison. On an overall analysis of the use of the force by the State agains the Mapuche and the so called "Mapuche conflict", see Coddou, Godoy and Vergara, "Fuerza Estatal y Conflicto Mapuche".

2154 Instituto Nacional de Derechos Humanos, *Situación de los Derechos Humanos en Chile. Informe 2013*, Santiago de Chile, 2013, p.19.

2.2.6, the recognition of the right to self-determination of indigenous peoples should no longer be an issue. The conceptualization of this right of indigenous peoples has developed substantially both in international legal practice and academia. Starting from the concepts of autonomy and political rights, which remain essential parts of indigenous peoples' right to self-determination, other facets of these rights are the indigenous peoples' rights to land, natural resources, and thus to consultation and FPIC, identity and cultures, and socio-economic development. This has also been clarified by both the HRC and the CESCR (chapter 2, section 2.2.2.2). The majority of indigenous peoples do not aspire to Statehood, but rather to have the instruments to somehow self-determine their destinies. Therefore, at international level the core problem concerns *which expressions of the right to self-determination* indigenous peoples may effectively exercise as right-holders. Thus, this chapter analysed whether *one* of these expressions, i.e., the above-mentioned proposed *composite right to political participation of indigenous peoples,* is both recognized and applied in the case of Chile.

Chile has ratified nearly all of the international and Inter-American human rights treaties. It signed the UNDRIP in 2007 and ratified the ILO Convention 169 one year later, which entered into force in September 2009. However, Chile does not constitutionally recognize indigenous peoples and a draft reform that has been discussed since 1991 might be finally achieved if a Constituent Assembly is truly set up, as recently announced by President Bachelet in her Presidential Message of 21 May 2015.[2155] Thus, the domestic protection of indigenous peoples is guaranteed by the Indigenous Law No.19,253 adopted in 1993. Additionally, Law No.20,249 would allow the creation of indigenous peoples' marine coastal spaces. Recently, Decree No.66 of 2014 and Decree No.40 of 2103 regulated indigenous peoples' right to consultation, but not of FPIC, albeit with many limits as discussed above (section 6.3.2.1). The Chilean legal framework will guarantee the rights to participation and consultation as framed in the ILO Convention 169. However, the controversial, recent regulation of the latter right casts a shadow over its application. indigenous peoples and other human rights organizations brought a number of Amparo proceeding cases before the Court of Appeals or the Supreme Court, most of which safeguarded indigenous peoples rights or condemned the defendants to apply the standards of the ILO Convention 169, and also of UNDRIP, particularly vis-à-vis the right to consultation. Under President Bachelet's current, second mandate, the

---

2155 Michelle Bachelet, "Mensaje Presidencial 21 de Mayo de 2015", 21.05.2015, p.10.

proposals to create a Ministry of Indigenous Affairs and ten Councils of Indigenous Peoples (one for each indigenous people and one at national level) may be appreciated as new developments vis-à-vis a major inclusion of indigenous peoples in State bodies. However, much remains to be seen regarding the real establishment of such organs in the coming years. Finally, there is no provision regarding the right to autonomy/self-government of indigenous peoples, but the recent proposals of the Presidential Advisory Commission on Decentralization and Regional Development to declare the 9th region of Chile (*La Araucanía*) "plurinational and multicultural" and to create "autonomous indigenous municipalities" are quite promising.

Therefore, to finally assess how this *composite right* is applied at the Chilean domestic level and whether it may also become one of the effective applications of the right to self-determination of indigenous peoples in the case of Chile, in the following tables the potential implementations of the international standards regarding the composite right drawn in chapter 3 are applied to the Chilean case on the basis of the findings of this chapter, as follows. Table 1 regards indigenous peoples' representation in State and local bodies and participation in domestic decision-making processes (chapter 3, section 3.3.1.3); table 2, the right to consultation (chapter 3, section 3.3.2.2.1) in three consultation cases seen above; table 3, the right to FPIC (chapter 3, section 3.3.2.2.2); and, table 4, the standards of indigenous autonomy (chapter 3, section 3.3.3.4). Whenever a standard is fully applied, the symbol (√) is used; if the standard is applied only partially, this other marker (~) is inserted; if the standard is not implemented at all, the letters NN are written; finally, if a standard is considered to not be applicable, the letters NA will be found. See also the legends and the explanations for each table.

Table 6.1: Standards of indigenous peoples' representation applied in Chile

1. Reservation of seats or "quotas" in national and local parliaments, judiciary, other governmental bodies, such as ministries, as well as other public offices	NN / Future?
2. Recognition of the right for Indigenous peoples to form their own political parties	~
3. Lower thresholds for indigenous parties	~
4. Possibility for Indigenous peoples to engage in other political parties to bring forward their agenda	~
5. A proportional electoral system	√
6. Ad hoc parliamentary/local assemblies' procedures, including (various degrees of) the right to veto or, at least, a reinforced enactment procedure	NN
7. Use of indigenous languages in States' acts	NN
8. Educational measures on Indigenous peoples' cultures for other parliamentary or public staff	NN
9. Creation of specialized governmental bodies with the direct participation of members of Indigenous peoples or consultative bodies composed of indigenous representatives with negotiating powers on the decisions likely to affect Indigenous peoples	~

Legend
√ = standard applied;
~ = standard applied only partially;
NN = no implementation;
NA = not applicable.

Explanations
Thanks to the recent reform of the Congress' elections, Chile now fulfills point 5, but does so only partially for points 2-4. As to these three latter points, the creation of parties by indigenous peoples was not denied explicitly *a priori*, but in practice the Mapuche Wallmapuwen party faced many difficulties in both registering and supporting candidates for national or local elections. Now, the electoral reform allows a lower requisite of signatures to register a party and the possibility to form alliances with more parties. In the last 2012 municipal elections, the Wallmapuwen party could not propose its own candidates, but an alliance with the Progressive Party (*Partido Progresista*) ultimately served to vote for and also elect indigenous candidates. Moreover, the election of deputies and senators are no longer

bound to the restrictive binominal system, which had prevented the participation of minor parties for almost 25 years. This reform, as well as the recent proposal of the Presidential Advisory Commission on Decentralization and Regional Development to reserve seats for indigenous representatives in both chambers and at local and regional level (point 1), gives hope to enhancing indigenous representation in both chambers. At municipal level, thanks to the reforms of the 1990s and 2000s, the election of the mayor is direct and by simple majority, and the councilors are elected with a proportional system. In principle, this allows a high participation of indigenous peoples in these offices, as appears to have happened since 1992, particularly in the North. At regional level, the councilors have been voted for the first time last November 2013 with a proportional system, but indigenous peoples were not able to position their candidates. As to point 9, as seen, the creation of the Ministry of Indigenous Affairs and, most interestingly, of nine Councils of Indigenous Peoples and another National Council of Indigenous Peoples have been under consultation to indigenous peoples from September 2014 until January 2015. If these bodies were established, they would certainly represent a milestone in the legal protection of indigenous rights in Chile and of their participatory rights in particular. Nevertheless, the limited participation of indigenous peoples in the activities of the Ministry and the constrained functions of these Councils (the prevision of reaching "agreements", in particular) cast a shadow over the real negotiating powers of indigenous peoples.

Table 6.2: Standards of Consultation applied in Chile

	1) Indigenous participation in the Congress and creation of the Council of indigenous peoples (2009)	*2) Constitutional recognition of indigenous peoples (2009)*	*3) Draft constitutional reform regulating the migration flows to the Eastern Island/Rapa Nui, art.126bis Constitution (2009)*	*4) Broad Consultation/Gran Consulta (2011)*	*5) The last consultation on the creation of the Ministry of Indigenous Affairs and the Council(s) of Indigenous Peoples (2014-2015)*
Prior	√	√	√	√	√

Not mere information	NN	NN	~	NN	~
In good faith and at a level of mutual trust	NN	NN	√	NN	NN
Adequate - Completed through indigenous representative institutions	~	~	~	~	~
Adequate - Held within a proper allocation of time	NN	NN	~	√	√
Adequate - in a language understandable to indigenous peoples	√	√	√	√	√
Systematic and transparent	NN	NN	√	NN	√
Agreement or consent	NN	NN	√ but not respected	NA	~

Legend
√ = standard applied;
~ = standard applied only partially;
NN = no implementation;
NA = not applicable.

Explanations

All the consultations analyzed were carried out prior to taking the indicated measure. However, apart from the consultation held in the Eastern Island/Rapa Nui, in the other consultations only generic information were distributed. Consultation No.3 in the Eastern Island/Rapa Nui also reached a good level of genuine dialogue, although some Rapa Nui went to the polling stations without knowing what the vote was about.

It is difficult to say whether these consultations were carried out in good faith and in a climate of mutual trust, but apparently they were not. Again, with regard to Consultation No.3, the reports are much more detailed and included both positive and negative aspects of the consultation. In addition, information about the consultation was more widely disseminated, through different media (incl., local radio and television), which may imply more commitment and good faith on the part of governmental bodies. Finally, the modality of the vote may be appreciated. Regarding Consultation No.5, which came to an end on 30 January 2015, the official press release stated that it had been a great success, but the indigenous and other civil society organizations denounced many irregularities, including the invitation of indigenous leaders not legitimized by their communities and the denial by some communities to designate their representatives for the consultation.

Then, in order to assess whether a consultation was adequate, three perspectives need to be analyzed: representativeness, language, and timeframe. On the first point, the indigenous organizations recorded in the CONADI register were considered representative of the indigenous peoples, also for the last Consultation No.5 in accordance with art.5 Decree No.66. However, these registers tend not to be updated, as the scarce number of replies to the letters prove. As for the linguistic dimension, all the consultations were conducted in Spanish, a language spoken and understood by most, if not all, indigenous peoples in Chile. For these reasons, the five consultations can be considered adequate from a linguistic point of view. Surely, material in the native languages would have been appreciated. Finally, as to the timeframe, as already seen, it is clear that only the last two of these consultations may be considered adequate: A timeframe of 5-6 months may be considered sufficient. In the case of Consultation No.3, despite the short timeframe, the participation of indigenous peoples at the consultation was high.

As for the last aspects, no consultation was systematic or transparent, especially when publishing the results, except, once again, Consultation No.3 but also Consultation No.5, since the results were duly published and are currently (July 2015) of public domain.[2156] However, in general terms, Consultation No.3 may be considered the worst process: Its outcome was unilaterally and arbitrarily overturned by the Government, which eventually proposed a different text to the Congress, and which was later inserted in the Constitution as discussed above. The results of Consultations Nos.1 and 2 remained unknown, thus no agreement or consent was achieved, and additionally indigenous peoples were consulted again on these same subjects in Consultation No.5. In the case of Consultation No.4, this aspect is considered not applicable since the consultation was suspended before being concluded.

As to the reaching of an agreement or the consent, it is remarkable that the final report of Consultation No.5 clearly states what has been agreed or remained pending for further decisions. However, it remains to be seen whether all the proposals contained in the outcomes of this consultation will be duly inserted in the draft laws that, as promised by President Bachelet, should be discussed in the last trimester of 2015; and which procedure will be followed in those cases in which there dissent (e.g., in the number of representatives of the Quechua and Colla peoples in the Council(s) of Indigenous Peoples; see above sections 6.3.1.2 and 6.3.2.2).

Finally, it needs to be stressed here that none of these consultations regarded projects of natural resource exploitation likely to affect indigenous peoples. This type of consultations are either not implemented, as in the case of the Diaguita people and the El Morro mine, or should be subject to the new regulation of Decree No.40 which, as seen, fails to meet the standards regarding the right to consultation enshrined in ILO Convention 169. In particular, only a limited duty to consult indigenous peoples for those projects likely to have a "high impact" on them is foreseen. The "high impact" is conceived as relocation or a "significant alteration" of their lifestyle and customs (art.83 in relation to art.7). For projects of "low impact", only informative meetings should be held (art.86). However, the "significant alteration" of indigenous peoples' lifestyle and customs may be subject to arbitrary interpretation, as no further criteria are clarified by this Decree. This may potentially deny the right to consultation of indigenous peoples in projects of natural resource exploitation that are likely to affect them.

2156 Chilean Ministry of Social Development/Ministerio de Desarrollo Social, "Actas proceso Consulta Indígena", 2015, at http://www.consultaindigenamds.gob.cl/Documentos.html [Last access 15.07.2015].

Table 6.3.1: Standards of indigenous peoples' FPIC applied in Chile

	1) Indigenous participation in the Congress and creation of the Council of indigenous peoples (2009)	*2) Constitutional recognition of indigenous peoples (2009)*	*3) Draft constitutional reform regulating the migration flows to the Eastern Island/Rapa Nui, art.126bis Constitution (2009)*
No coercion, intimidation or manipulation is exercised upon indigenous peoples	~	~	~
The consent is sought sufficiently in advance; this implies also that the FPIC should be sought in phases of assessment, planning, implementation, monitoring, evaluation and closure of a project	~	~	~
Full information is provided (e.g., nature, size, pace, reversibility and scope of any proposed project or activity; reason(s) or purpose(s) of the project and/or activity; duration; locality of affected areas; preliminary assessment of the likely economic, social, cultural and environmental impact	NN	NN	~
Fair and equitable benefit-sharing in a context that respects the precautionary principle	NA	NA	NA

Table 6.3.2: Standards of indigenous peoples' FPIC applied in Chile

	4) Broad Consultation/Gran Consulta (2011)	*5) The last consultation on the creation of the Ministry of Indigenous Affairs and the Council(s) of Indigenous Peoples (2014-2015)*
No coercion, intimidation or manipulation is exercised upon indigenous peoples	~	~
The consent is sought sufficiently in advance; this implies also that the FPIC should be sought in phases of assessment, planning, implementation, monitoring, evaluation and closure of a project	~	√
Full information is provided (e.g., nature, size, pace, reversibility and scope of any proposed project or activity; reason(s) or purpose(s) of the project and/or activity; duration; locality of affected areas; preliminary assessment of the likely economic, social, cultural and environmental impact	NN	~
Fair and equitable benefit-sharing in a context that respects the precautionary principle	NA	NA

Legend
√ = standard applied;
~ = standard applied only partially;
NN = no implementation;
NA = not applicable.

Explanations
With regard to the standards of FPIC, there has been no coercion, intimidation or manipulation in these consultations. However, in Chile there has undoubtedly been a climate of rejection and repression of indigenous peoples' claims, at least until very recently. The consent of indigenous peoples was

certainly sought in advance, but in some cases the results remained unknown, and in the case of the reform of art.126-bis of the Constitution, the outcome was reversed unilaterally by the Government as discussed above. As mentioned, none of these consultations concerned natural resource exploitations likely to affect indigenous peoples. This is why the category of benefit-sharing is not applicable here. The consultations on projects likely to affect indigenous peoples, if any, will be regulated by Decree No.40, which foresees the exemption from obtaining indigenous peoples' consent in certain circumstances (art. 85). This suggests that FPIC in Chile is essentially denied to indigenous peoples.

Table 6.4: Standards of Indigenous Autonomy applied in the case of Chile

	Comunidad Autónoma de Temucuicui and Comunidad Cacique José Guiñon
Territory	NN / Future?
Rights over land and renewable and non-renewable natural resources	NN / Future?
Customary law and own institutions	~ / Future?
Financial aspects	NN / Future?
Education and culture	NN

Legend
√ = standard applied;
~ = standard applied only partially;
NN = no recognition, thus no implementation;
NA = not applicable.

Explanations
The Indigenous Law allows the preservation of indigenous peoples' own institutions and authorities, whom in both communities are maintained. Chile signed the UNDRIP but, so far (July 2015), there is no recognition of indigenous autonomy in Chile. A few attempts have been and are violently repressed. The only development worth mentioning is the proposal of the Presidential Advisory Commission on Decentralization and Regional Development to create "autonomous indigenous municipalities" (*municipio*

autónomo indígena), which would correspond to those in which a majority of indigenous peoples live. These municipalities should be governed by indigenous peoples' own forms of organization; have powers over communitarian rules, communal lands and use of natural resources; and negotiate financial sources for their administration.

In conclusion, the *composite right to political participation* is poorly recognized and applied in Chile, and does not represent currently an effective application of the right to self-determination of indigenous peoples in this country. Under the first and the current mandates of President Bachelet, interesting proposals to enhance indigenous peoples' participation the decision-making processes have been put forward, but their implementation remains to be seen. The autonomy claims and indigenous peoples' mobilization in bringing their cases before the Courts of Appeal to safeguard their right to consultation suggest that indigenous peoples are strongly fighting to have a say in the Chilean political arena. Moreover, the indigenous protests extended beyond the national borders.[2157] This international mobilization shows a high level of organization of the indigenous movements. As in the case of Bolivia, the implementation of the proposed *composite right to political participation* may thus potentially reduce social tensions and meliorate State-IPs relations. Consequently, the second mandate of President Bachelet (2014-2018) will be crucial in that sense.

2157 For instance, President Piñera's official visit to Europe in late October 2010 was interrupted by Mapuche people's supporters during his public speeches in all the three capitals visited, i.e., London, Paris and Berlin See Jonathan López, "Chile president's London visit sparks protests from Chilean community", 21.10.2010, at www.thefirstpint.co.uk/2010/10/21/chile-presidents-london-visit-sparks-protests-from-chilean-community; El Clarín, "Activistas por la causa mapuche protestan en París ante Piñera", 21.10.2010, *El Clarin*, at www.elclarin.cl/index.php?option=com_content&task=view&id=22720&Itemid=44; Efe, "Activistas pro mapuche convocan a una protesta durante actividad de Piñera en Berlín", 21.10.2010, *El Mercurio online*, at www.emol.com/noticias/nacional/detalle/detallenoticias.asp?idnoticia=442769 [Last access to all 02.09.2014].

Conclusions

This study proposed a *composite right to political participation of indigenous peoples*, identified its recognition in international human and indigenous rights law, and explored its application in two apparently divergent – but substantially more similar than expected– case studies in Latin America, namely Bolivia and Chile.

As explained in the Introduction, this study thus addressed the following research questions:

1. May a (composite) right to political participation (including, participation in decision-making bodies, consultation, FPIC and autonomy/self-government2158) of indigenous peoples descend from their right to self-determination?
2. How is it recognized in international human and indigenous rights law?
3. May this right represent one of the expressions, or better, effective applications of the right to self-determination of indigenous peoples?
4. How is this right recognized and applied at domestic level in Latin America and, more specifically, in the cases of Bolivia and Chile?
5. What considerations may be drawn from its application?

The aim of this concluding section is therefore to address the research questions and provide an answer to each of them based on the findings of this study.

The first question required an analysis of the meaning and the implications of the right to self-determination of indigenous peoples. However, a set of problems arise when tackling this right. This is mainly due to its persistent understanding at international level as equal (solely or mainly) to secession, independence or annexation. In other words, States still perceive it as a threat to their territorial integrity and barely consider any alternatives.

The best-known legal classification of self-determination is the one that distinguishes between its external and internal dimensions. This dichotomy has deep roots and has provoked a complex debate on its different meanings both in international law and in academia.[2159] Indeed, the consensus over this dichotomy is widely accepted, but not codified.[2160] This distinction has

2158 In this study, these two terms are considered interchangeable. For details, see chapter 3, sections 3.2.2.2.

2159 See further chapter 2, section 2.1.4.

2160 Quane, "The UN Declaration on the Rights of Indigenous Peoples ...", p.260.

been authoritatively and extensively argued by Cassese, but can already be found in the works of Wengler in 1957.[2161] Hence, in line with the "Declaration on Principles of International Law Friendly Relations and Co-operation among States in Accordance with the Charter of the United Nations" of 1970, external self-determination refers to the right to freely determine an international status, i.e., to form a new State or integrate or associate with another,[2162] not only in the case of colonial peoples but also other peoples subject to foreign domination or occupation.[2163] Internal self-determination, for its part, represents "the right to authentic self-government, that is, the right for a people really and freely to choose its own political and economic regime […]".[2164] Notwithstanding its usefulness, this dichotomy presents a set of problems linked to the symbolic values of each of the two internal and external dimensions, and especially by the view of the latter as solely equal to Statehood and thus a threat to territorial integrity. Other authors have proposed different conceptualizations. In sum, the understandings of self-determination may be summarized in the minimalist and the maximalist approaches identified by Xanthaki.[2165] The former tends to limit self-determination to a principle and not a right, equating it to secession; or to divide it merely into independence on the one hand and democratic government on the other hand[2166] (which is essentially the internal-external dichotomy). The latter envisages self-determination with a wider significance, e.g., following more closely the formulation of both arts.1 of ICCPR and ICESCR with regard to economic, cultural and social development.[2167]

Indeed, the focus needs to detach from the (increasingly misleading) external and internal dichotomy, and to move toward an approach of *multiple expressions of self-determination*, which differ from a right-holder to another, as in the case of indigenous peoples. As stated by Kingsbury, "[s]elf-determination is about the relation between state and community".[2168] Thus, a reorientation "from an end-state approach to a relational approach of self-determination" is needed.[2169] This may also be more in line with the principle of territorial integrity, as the threat of or the actual use of force is not

2161 Cassese, *Self-Determination of Peoples*, p.70, note 6.
2162 *Ibid.*, p.90, and Quane, "The UN Declaration on the Rights of Indigenous Peoples …", p.260.
2163 Cassese, *Self-Determination of Peoples*, p.90.
2164 *Ibid.*, p.101.
2165 Xanthaki, "The Right to Self-Determination: Meaning and Scope", p.20.
2166 *Ibid.*
2167 *Ibid.*p.27.
2168 Kingsbury, "Reconstructing Self-Determination: A Relational Approach", p.26.
2169 *Ibid.*, p.22.

necessary to guarantee some of the current and future expressions of self-determination.

Additionally, there are relatively new exceptions to the principles of non-interference and territorial integrity, such as the "Responsibility to Protect (R2P)" and "Remedial Secession".[2170] The former undoubtedly envisages an exception to the prohibition of interference/non-intervention and is likely to become fully-fledged customary law soon. The latter is not clearly enshrined in current international law, but an entitlement to it may emerge in the near future. This further suggests that both theories already exert or in the future will exert significant influence over the right to self-determination.

The international customary law nature of self-determination as well as its post-colonial applicability then seem broadly accepted.[2171] Moreover, the interconnections between democracy and self-determination suggest that the right to self-determination is *a continuing right*.[2172] Finally, the people individuated by both arts.1 of ICCPR and ICESCR cannot be equated to the entire population of existing States, otherwise this right would make no sense. In fact, as asserted by Thornberry, "the meaning of 'people' for purposes of international law is not fixed in stone".[2173] The same goes for international law, which is "no monolith, but is more like a network of interlinked, evolving and eminently challengeable assumptions".[2174]

In this framework, the situations of Scotland, Catalonia, and New Caledonia are worth mentioning since these are the latest cases in which the population will be or has been called to vote in (very different) referenda to decide upon their "self-determination". These three cases share the existence of powerful independentist movements but are extremely different from each other in terms of status and the referenda's timeframe and modalities. Scotland and Catalonia are regions of two established States (UK and Spain, respectively) and enjoy diverse degrees of autonomy/ self-government, New Caledonia is a former French colony and currently an overseas territory. Again, in the former two cases, the referenda were carried out in extremely different modalities in September (Scotland) and November

2170 See further in chapter 2, section 2.1.7.
2171 On these and the following assumptions, see detailed arguments in Chapter 2, section 2.1.5.
2172 Cassese, *Self-Determination of Peoples*, pp.52 and 54, and Crawford, "The Right to Self-Determination in International Law", pp.25-26.
2173 Thornberry, "The Democratic or Internal Aspect of Self-Determination ...", p.47.
2174 Thornberry, *Indigenous Peoples and Human Rights*, p.87.

(Catalonia) 2014, while in the latter the referendum will be probably held before or during 2018. However, in Scotland and New Caledonia the referenda were and are negotiated with their central governments and regulated by different Acts. In Catalonia, the plebiscite has been repeatedly denied by the Spanish authorities. Finally, in both Catalonia and Scotland, the secessionist movements apparently also channeled other causes of popular frustration, particularly vis-à-vis the economic crisis in connection with the potential loss of autonomy/ self-government (Catalonia) or a missed opportunity to further enhance it (Scotland). Indeed, the results of the referendum in Scotland may suggest popular support for a wider and more effective devolution of powers than the current one. This same assumption may also apply to Catalonia: The increase in secessionist supporters may be read as dissatisfaction in relation to the current –and potentially reduced– autonomy arrangement. Hence, in essence, while the case of New Caledonia remains to be seen, the other two cases may suggest that effective autonomy arrangements and further devolution of powers may meet popular requests and needs within the self-determination discourse without opting for an extreme solution such as secession.[2175]

In conclusion, the right to self-determination is (necessarily) evolving.[2176] There is a considerable necessity to understand self-determination as a flexible principle that underlines the whole international order,[2177] "re-thinking the concept [...] and suggesting possible avenues for the future development of the law in this area".[2178] In this context, indigenous peoples' right to self-determination represents one of these further developments.

The recognition of the right to self-determination of indigenous peoples, and more importantly, *which implication and application* of the right to self-determination, is however still a thorny issue. Indigenous peoples are among those groups that do not necessarily ask for their own State, at least not all of them.[2179] Only in case of persistent repressive acts by governments, the theory of Remedial Secession may find an application (also) in the case of indigenous peoples.[2180] It would probably be reductive to state

2175 See further chapter 2, section 2.1.7.

2176 Cassese, *Self-Determination of Peoples*, p.52 and 55; Crawford, "The Right to Self-Determination in International Law", p.25 and 26; Alfredsson, "Different Forms of and Claims to the Right of Self-Determination", p.79; Hannum, "Self-Determination in the Post-Colonial Era", pp.26 and 37.

2177 Thürer and Burri, "Self-Determination", para.26.

2178 Cassese, *Self-Determination of Peoples*, p.341.

2179 See further in chapter 2, section 2.2.

2180 Barelli, "Shaping Indigenous Self-Determination ...", p. 426.

that no indigenous people across the world aspire to Statehood. The majority of statements made by indigenous spokespersons over the last thirty years nevertheless suggest that Statehood would be a desired option for very few indigenous peoples.[2181] Rather, there is a pressing necessity to rethink the right of self-determination of indigenous peoples since the adoption of the Draft Declaration on the Rights of Indigenous Peoples of 1993.[2182] Nowadays, after the adoption of the new formula contained in the United Nations Declaration on the Rights of Indigenous Peoples of 2007 (UNDRIP), other forms of expressions of this right need to be taken seriously into account.

The right to self-determination of indigenous peoples has been extensively debated both by UN bodies and in academia. The scholarly works may be grouped into two main conceptualizations.[2183] The first envisages self-determination as mainly expressions of autonomy/ self-government and, in some cases, political rights and Free, Prior and Informed Consent (FPIC). In particular, the formulation of art.4 of the UN Declaration on the Rights of Indigenous Peoples (UNDRIP) re-launched the debate on the right to autonomy/self-government as (one of the) expression(s) of their right to self-determination. A proposal regarding the recognition of an indigenous right to autonomy was included since the Declaration of Principles on the Rights of Indigenous Peoples approved by a number of NGOs in Geneva on 26 July 1985 and submitted to the Working Group on Indigenous Populations (WGIP).[2184] During their first continental meeting held in Quito in 1990, indigenous peoples strongly claimed autonomy in terms of self-government and control over territory. At international level, the debate on indigenous autonomies was then (re-)launched in 1991, when a group of experts met in Greenland under the auspices of the United Nations Human Rights Commission. In particular, they emphasized the potential of autonomy/self-government for indigenous peoples as a means of realizing their right to self-determination and to foster national unity and thus securing, rather than threatening, territorial integrity.

The right to autonomy/self-government and its interconnections with the right to self-determination of indigenous peoples was also a crucial theme

2181 Thornberry, "The Democratic or Internal Aspect of Self-Determination …", p.63 and Daes, "The Right of Indigenous Peoples to 'Self-Determination' in the Contemporary World Order", p.54.

2182 Scott, "Indigenous Self-Determination and Decolonization …", p.819.

2183 For references, see chapter 2, section 2.2.4.

2184 See chapter 3, section 3.3.3.2.

for the Working Group on Indigenous Populations (WGIP) and the following Working Group on the Draft Declaration (WGDD).[2185] This right was spelled out as a part, form, evolution or exercise of the right to self-determination first in the Draft Declaration (art.31) and then in the aforementioned UNDRIP (art.4). However, it needs to be stressed here that art.4 affirms that the right to autonomy/self-government exists for indigenous peoples as *one of the expressions* of their (wider) right to self-determination. In other words, the UNDRIP serves as a starting point for the codification of a right to autonomy/self-government for indigenous peoples in international law within their right to self-determination, but does not reduce the scope of the latter (self-determination) to the former (autonomy/self-government).[2186]

A second conceptualization frames the right to self-determination of indigenous peoples as including, in addition to autonomy/self-government and political rights, other interlinked aspects such as mutual respect, a remedy to past discrimination and injustices, cultural integrity and identity, land rights, rights to subsistence and natural resources, and to the right to (self-determined) development. The UN Declaration on the Right to Development and the Concluding Observations of both the UN Human Rights Committee (HRC) and the Committee on Economic, Social and Cultural Rights (CESCR) of the last years also support this wider conceptualization.[2187] Even the Cobo-Martinez Study outlined the multifaceted nature of the right to self-determination of indigenous peoples. According to this study, the right to self-determination of indigenous peoples implies: Economic, social, cultural, and political aspects; land rights and political participation in public and State affairs as well as respect for internal organizations; and, finally, autonomy/self-government. Moreover, self-determination is the basic "precondition" for the enjoyment of all indigenous peoples' rights.[2188]

In sum, starting from the concepts of autonomy/self-government and political rights, other facets such as indigenous peoples' rights to land, natural resources –and thus to consultation and FPIC– identity and cultures, and socio-economic development are also included in indigenous peoples' right to self-determination, which can only be defined as a *multifaceted right*. Furthermore, all of these facets are interdependent. Indigenous autonomy arrangements tend to be established in relation to specific territories, which

2185 See chapter 2, sections 2.2.2.3 and 2.2.2.4.
2186 See further chapter 2, section 2.2.2.5.
2187 See such Concluding Observations in chapter 2, section 2.2.2.2.
2188 See chapter 2, section 2.2.2.1.

thus suggests that, within the framework of the right to (economic) self-determination, control over and the use of lands and natural resources should be recognized. This may also lead to the socio-economic development of indigenous peoples and the potential preservation of indigenous cultures and languages. These last three aspects may be part of the competences of the autonomy/self-government. Additionally, to guarantee all this, political rights may make it possible for indigenous peoples to have a say in both the national political arena and local governments, together with the rights to consultation and FPIC, which play a key role in guaranteeing indigenous peoples a fair use of lands and natural resources.

Therefore, a *composite right of political participation of indigenous peoples* that refers to the combination of (1) (a) *ad hoc* political rights (indigenous peoples' representation in State bodies or in other public posts, including in decision-making processes and in the judiciary, both at national and local level) and their (b) rights to consultation and (c) free, prior and informed consent (FPIC) on the one hand, and (2) autonomy/ self-government arrangements (including the preservation of indigenous traditional institutions) on the other, may be seen as one expression of the multi-faceted right to self-determination of indigenous peoples.

This replies the first research question mentioned above. This "language" of self-determination, furthermore, reassures to States that the risk of secession is limited. Secession could thus become a viable option solely in those cases of a potential application of Remedial Secession, that is to say, when a State is brutally repressing the human rights of their citizens or of a part of them. Additionally, the proposed *composite right* embodies a collective right. This is clear regarding the case of the rights to consultation and FPIC on one hand and the rights to autonomy/self-government and the preservation of indigenous institutions on the other. Also the *ad hoc* indigenous political rights (such as participation in decision-making processes or in State bodies) are considered here as a collective expression of indigenous peoples.[2189] The individual rights of members of indigenous peoples to participate in public life are considered as parallel to but not part of this proposed *composite right to political participation of indigenous peoples*. It is then important to stress that the author of this study is conscious that the proposed *composite right* proposed here certainly belongs to a Western liberal

2189 On the collective nature of the rights to participation, consultation and FPIC see Yrigoyen Fajardo, "El Derecho a la Libre Determinación del Desarrollo ...", p.103.

human rights matrix. Nevertheless, where some of the political rights proposed here have been applied, the level of social exclusion of indigenous peoples has decreased, at least in the Latin American context.[2190] Therefore, this *composite right* is proposed with the twofold aim of enhancing the application of indigenous rights through the promotion of their political participation, as well as finding a solution of compromise with States.

The second research question regarded the recognition of this *composite right of political participation of indigenous peoples* in international law. As seen, this proposed *composite right* descends from the right to self-determination but this does not limit its scope. It refers to a combination of the aforementioned rights that, upon close inspection, are fully recognized not only in international human rights law but also in minority protection and, more specifically, in indigenous international instruments such as the UNDRIP and the ILO "Convention concerning Indigenous and Tribal Peoples in Independent Countries", Convention No.169 of 1989.[2191] Furthermore, the recent jurisprudence of the Inter-American Court of Human Rights (*YATAMA v. Nicaragua* (2005), *Saramaka People v. Suriname* (2007), *Sarayaku v. Ecuador* (2012))[2192] have contributed to hardening the three components of (a) their participation in decision-making in decisions likely to affect them, with particular attention to access to elections of indigenous peoples and formation of indigenous political parties, and thus their representation; (b) their right to consultation; and to (c) their FPIC. Likewise, both the CESCR in its General Comment No.21 of 2009 and the HRC in the case of *Ángela Poma Poma v. Peru* (2009)[2193] have flagged their importance by requiring (a) the participation of indigenous peoples in the design and implementation of laws and policies likely to affect them, (b) that participation of indigenous peoples in the decision-making process must be effective, and (c) that not mere consultation is carried out, but (d) the FPIC of all members of the community is finally obtained. In particular, the reasoning by both the Inter-American Court of Human Rights and the HRC in the abovementioned decisions demonstrated the interdependence of these rights. Finally, despite the debates on whether the outcome of the consultation is binding –which would be a contradiction in terms–[2194] the practice of providing consultation *and* FPIC in megaprojects affecting in-

2190 Ströbele-Gregor, "Autoridad, poder y liderazgo …", p.86.
2191 For further details, see chapter 3, section 3.3.1.
2192 For details, see chapter 3, sections 3.3.1.4 and 3.3.2.3.
2193 For further details, see chapter 2, section 2.2.2.2 and chapter 3, section 3.3.2.1.
2194 For details, see chapter 3, section 3.3.2.2.3.

digenous peoples is increasingly required by both UN bodies and multinational companies worldwide. Similarly, both the right to consultation and FPIC have been sufficiently defined by UN and ILO bodies, as well as the Inter-American Court of Human Rights, as requiring full and not merely superficial information, including a preliminary assessment of all potential risks; a proper allocation of time; a language understandable to indigenous peoples; and taking into account the cultural and social patterns of the indigenous peoples concerned. Lastly, both the right to consultation and FPIC must be: systematic and transparent and exercised prior to the commencement of and during any project likely to affect indigenous community; in good faith and at a level of mutual trust; realized through indigenous representative institutions; with no use of coercion, intimidation or manipulation; and aimed at reaching an agreement or a consent, including the right "to say no".[2195]

A number of mechanisms may be applied to ensure that the first aspect of the composite right is effectively applied. These range from those designed to ensure indigenous peoples' representation, e.g., by the allocation of reserved seats in parliamentary assemblies to *ad hoc* parliamentary/local assemblies' procedures, including (various degree of) the right to veto or, at least, a reinforced enactment procedure.[2196] In addition, fair and transparent consultations and the requirement of FPIC, as described above, enhance the chances of indigenous peoples of having a say on projects likely to affect them.

Regarding the second aspect of the composite right proposed here, the right to autonomy/self-government has been gradually recognized and may become an international standard, at least for indigenous peoples (and minorities), as the extensive State practice in different parts of the world clearly illustrates.[2197] The peculiarity of indigenous autonomies is moreover the combination of preserving and applying both national/constitutional arrangements together with traditional institutions and customary law. Finally, (territorially-based) indigenous autonomies and the preservation of indigenous institutions epitomize indigenous peoples' local spaces for control and management over their lands and natural resources, their socio-cultural and economic development, and, thus, of their lives. Also, considering the indigenous peoples' (generally) strong connection with the land, a ter-

2195 For details, see chapter 3, section 3.3.2.2.
2196 For details, see chapter 3, section 3.3.1.3.
2197 For details, see chapter 3, section 3.3.3.

ritorial autonomy seems preferable to non-territorial arrangements. Nevertheless, non-territorial autonomies (e.g., an indigenous education board) shall not be excluded a priori, especially either for those territories inhabited by indigenous and non-indigenous populations or where the members of indigenous peoples are dispersed within the country.

Hence, the proposed *composite right of political participation of indigenous peoples* does indeed represent one of the expressions of the right to self-determination of indigenous peoples (research question No.3). However, the effective application of *this expression* requires empirical analysis of case studies, which leads to research question No.4.

As of the 1960s, and particularly after the 1990s, indigenous movements have become influential actors in Latin American political arenas. Similarly, the participation of indigenous peoples in electoral processes has progressed. The evolving and groundbreaking jurisprudence of the Inter-American Court of Human Rights shows a growing recognition and protection of indigenous peoples in the region. These factors suggest that the Latin American context is an excellent case to "test" how the *composite right to political participation* of indigenous peoples is recognized and applied (research question No.4). Additionally, as specified in the Introduction, the two cases of Bolivia and Chile were selected not with the aim of comparing the two legal systems vis-à-vis the protection of indigenous rights, but rather as a contrast. Bolivia is currently the most advanced State in Latin America in terms of recognition of indigenous rights. Chile provides indigenous peoples with very limited protection, although it has recently shown very interesting developments.

First, I have explored whether this composite right may become one of the effective applications of the right to self-determination of indigenous peoples in the case of Bolivia and thus enhance their protection and offer a compromise solution for the State. Bolivia recognizes the right to self-determination of indigenous peoples in three constitutional provisions, namely arts.2, 30.4 and 289 (as well as in the Preamble). According to these provisions, indigenous peoples' right to self-determination consists of their right to autonomy, self-government, own culture, the recognition of their own institutions, and the consolidation of their territorial entities within the broader Bolivian legal framework. Moreover, Bolivia also provides indigenous peoples with rights to participation within State organs (parliaments, judiciary, etc.) both at national and local level, to consultation, and (partially) to FPIC. It has ratified both ILO Convention 169 and the UNDRIP, which is properly binding in this country.[2198] Finally, the 2009 Bolivian Constitution introduced a new system of autonomies, which also foresees the establishment of (territorial) "indigenous native peasant farmer" autonomies, i.e., the *Autonomía Indígena Campesino Originaria* (art.289).[2199] In sum, Bolivia provides indigenous peoples a thorough recognition of the proposed *composite right to political participation*. Nevertheless, the implementation of this right is rather poor. For instance, a (reduced) number of seats are reserved for indigenous peoples in national and local parliaments, judiciary, other governmental bodies, such as ministries, as well as other public offices. However, no procedures in parliaments or local assemblies, including the right to veto or, at least, a reinforced enactment procedure is foreseen. Hence, indigenous representatives are easily outvoted. The FPIC would be required by the (in the case of Bolivia, binding) UNDRIP, but de facto their international standards have not been met in a number of consultations. Lastly, the emblematic consultation on the construction of a highway in the indigenous territory *Territorio Indígena y Parque Nacional Isiboro-Secure* (TIPNIS) suggests that indigenous issues in Bolivia are no longer a priority in President Morales' mandates.[2200]

For its part, Chile has ratified almost all the international and Inter-American human rights treaties. It signed the UNDRIP in 2007 and ratified the ILO Convention 169 one year later, which entered into force in September 2009. However, Chile does not constitutionally recognize indigenous peoples and a draft reform discussed since 1991 might finally be achieved if a Constituent Assembly is set up, as recently demanded by civil society organizations. Thus, the domestic protection of Indigenous peoples is guaranteed by the Indigenous Law No.19,253 adopted in 1993. Additionally, Law No.20,249 would allow the creation of marine coastal spaces of indigenous peoples. Recently, Decree No.66 of 2014 and Decree No.40 of 2103 regulated the right to consultation but not of FPIC, of indigenous peoples, albeit with many limits.[2201] The Chilean legal framework shall guarantee the rights to participation and consultation as framed in the ILO Convention 169. However, the controversial recent regulation of the latter right cast a

2198 See further in chapter 5, section 5.3.

2199 See further in chapter 5, section 5.4.

2200 The assessment of the implementation of the *composite right* in both cases is also schematically displayed in tables in which there is an evaluation of whether and how the individuated international standards are respected. See further in chapter 5, section 5.5, and chapter 6, section 6.5.

2201 See further in chapter 6, section 6.3.2.1.

shadow over its application.[2202] Indigenous peoples and other human rights organizations brought a number of Amparo proceeding cases before the Court of Appeals or the Supreme Court, most of which safeguarded indigenous rights or condemned the defendants to apply the standards of the ILO Convention 169, and also of UNDRIP, particularly vis-à-vis the right to consultation.[2203] Under the current second mandate of President Bachelet, the proposals to create a Ministry of Indigenous Affairs and ten Council of Indigenous Peoples (nine for each indigenous people recognized in Chile and one at national level) may be appreciated as new developments vis-à-vis a meaningful inclusion of Indigenous peoples in States' bodies. However, the real establishment of such organs remains to be seen in the coming years. Finally, there is no provision regarding the right to autonomy/self-government of indigenous peoples, although the recent proposals of the Advisory Presidential Commission on Decentralization and Regional Development to declare the 9th region of Chile (*La Araucanía*) "plurinational and multicultural" and to create "indigenous autonomous municipalities" are quite promising.[2204]

The analyses of these case studies suggest a number of considerations (research question No.5).

First and foremost, as (painfully) expected, neither international nor domestic recognition of the *composite right to political participation of indigenous peoples*, although extremely advanced, can guarantee a fair application of its provisions.

A second interlinked consideration is that the legal recognition of this *composite right* does matter but de facto the implementation does not vary substantially even in two countries with opposite legal frameworks. Bolivia does have a more advanced legal framework of this *composite right* but in essence participation is very limited both at State level and in terms of autonomy/self-government. In particular, the implementation of the right to consultation of indigenous peoples does not vary significantly in the two countries. Indeed, the *Amparo* proceedings brought before Courts by indigenous peoples in Chile have proved to be a useful tool to safeguard their rights. This leads to a third consideration, namely that the application of international law and the appeal to international indigenous rights' standards may be more incisive where domestic protection is rather weak (Chile).

2202 See further in chapter 6, section 6.3.2.2.
2203 See further in chapter 6, section 6.3.2.3.
2204 See further in chapter 6, section 6.4.

In Bolivia, the *composite right to political participation of indigenous peoples* does embody an expression of their right to self-determination, but it is neither respected nor implemented. Indigenous peoples have repeatedly requested a meaningful voice in the Bolivian political arena. However, having no guarantee of the implementation of their rights, indigenous peoples have to resort to the strategy of marches. This seems to be the only way to properly negotiate, even with the "indigenous" President Morales. In the case of Chile, the *composite right to political participation of indigenous peoples* is poorly recognized and applied and it currently does not represent an effective application of their right to self-determination. The interesting proposals advanced under Bachelet's mandates regarding indigenous peoples' participation in the decision-making processes, the autonomy/self-government claims, and indigenous peoples' mobilization in bringing their *Amparo* cases before the Courts of Appeal to safeguard their right to consultation show that indigenous peoples are putting up a fight to have a say in the Chilean political arena as well. Moreover, the indigenous protests have extended beyond the national borders. This international mobilization shows a high level of organization of the indigenous movements. In sum, in both cases, the implementation of the proposed *composite right to political participation* has been vociferously demanded by indigenous peoples. Confronted with the missed opportunity to implement of their rights, indigenous peoples resorted to mobilization. Hence, a fourth consideration is that the (partial) application of the *composite right to political participation of indigenous peoples* in both case studies has been achieved not only thanks to the international recognition of these rights but also as a result of indigenous mobilization.

Finally, the fifth and last consideration is that an effective application of this *composite right* may potentially reduce social tensions and improve relations between the State and indigenous peoples. The *composite right of political participation of indigenous peoples* presented in this study was indeed proposed as a tool to answer indigenous peoples' claims and to embody one of the expressions, or better, effective applications, of the multifaceted right to self-determination of indigenous peoples. However, considering the growing international and national interest in the subject and the empowerment of indigenous peoples' movements, particularly in Latin America, this *composite right* may also become a solution of compromise acceptable for States to promote peaceful relations and mutual understandings between indigenous peoples and other sectors of the society. This, in principle, should also enhance stability and social cohesion, and avoid conflict.

Selected bibliography

Books, articles and media

Agüero Felipe, "Chile. Unfinished Transition and Increased Political Competition", in Jorge I. Domínguez and Micheal Schifter, *Constructing Democratic Governance in Latin America*, The Johns Hopkins University Press, Baltimore and London, 2003, pp.292-320.

Aguilar Gonzalo, LaFosse Sandra, Rojas Hugo and Steward Rebecca, "The Constitutional Recognition of Indigenous Peoples in Latin America", *Pace International Law Review Online Companion*, 2010, pp.44-104.

Akermark Sia Spiliopoulou, "The World Bank and Indigenous Peoples", in Nazila Ghanea and Alexandra Xanthaki (eds.), *Minorities, Peoples and Self-Determination,* Brill, Leiden, 2005, pp.93-112.

Albó Xavier, "Bolivia: Avances y tropezones hacia un nuevo país plurinacional e Intercultural", in Salvador Martí i Puig (ed*.), Pueblos Indígenas y Política en América Latina: El reconocimiento de sus derechos y el impacto de sus demandas a inicios del siglo XXI,* Fundació CIDOB, Barcelona, 2007, pp.335-359.

Albó Xavier, "Bolivia: From Indian and Campesino Leaders to Councillors and Parliamentary Deputies", in Rachel Sieder (ed.), *Multiculturalism in Latin America. Indigenous Rights, Diversity and Democracy*, Palgrave Macmillan, New York, 2002, pp.74-102.

Albó Xavier, "Making the Leap From Local Mobilization to National Politics", 29(5) *NACLA Report in the Americas* 1996, pp.15-22.

Alfredsson Gudmundur, "Different Forms of and Claims to the Right of Self-Determination", in Donald Clark and Robert Williamson, *Self-Determination. International Perspectives*, MacMillan Press, HoundsMill, Basingstoke and London, 1996 and St. Martin's Press, New York, 1996, pp.58-85.

Alfredsson Gudmundur, "Minorities, Indigenous and Tribal Peoples, and Peoples: Definitions of Terms as a Matter of International Law", in Nazila Ghanea and Alexandra Xanthaki (eds.), *Minorities, Peoples and Self-Determination,* Brill, Leiden, 2005, pp.163-172.

Alfredsson Gudmundur, "The Right of Self-Determination and Indigenous Peoples", in Christian Tomuschat (ed.), *Modern Law of Self-Determination*, Martinus Nijhoff Publishers, Dordrecht, Boston, London, 1993, pp.41-54.

Altmann Philipp, *Die Indigenenbewegung in Ecuador. Diskurs und Dekolonialität*, Reihe Global Studies, Transcript Verlag, Bielefeld, 2013.

Alva Arévalo Amelia Isabel, "Algunas reflexiones sobre los alcances del derecho a la consulta previa post movilización social indígena en la selva peruana", 10(2) *Revista de Investigaciones Políticas y Sociológicas* 2011, pp. 97-116.

Alva Arévalo Amelia Isabel, *El Derecho a la Consulta previa de los Pueblos Indígenas en Derecho Internacional*, Cuadernos Deusto de Derechos Humanos, No.76, Universidad de Deusto, Bilbao, 2014.

Álvarez Molinero Natalia, "El Sujeto Indígena y el Derecho de Autodeterminación en la Declaración de Naciones Unidas sobre Derechos de los Pueblos Indígenas: ¿Tienen los Pueblos Indígenas Personalidad Jurídica Internacional?", in Natalia Álvarez Molinero, J. Daniel Oliva Martínez, Nieves Zúñiga García-Falces (eds.), *Declaración sobre los Derechos de los Pueblos Indígenas. Hacia un Mundo Intercultural y Sostenible*, Catarata, Madrid, 2009, pp.233-265.

Anaya James and Grossman Claudio, "The Case of Awas Tingni v. Nicaragua: A New Step in the International Law of Indigenous Peoples", 19(1) *Arizona Journal of International and Comparative Law* 2002, pp.1-15.

Anaya James, "Self-Determination as a Collective Human Rights under Contemporary International Law", in Pekka Aikio and Martin Scheinin (eds.), *Operationalizing the Rights of Indigenous Peoples to Self-Determination*, Institute for Human Rights, Åbo Akademi University, Saarijärvi, 2000.

Anaya James, "The Right of Indigenous Peoples to Self-Determination in the Post-Declaration Era", in Claire Charters and Rodolfo Stavenhagen (eds.), *Making the Declaration Work. The United Nations Declaration on the Rights of Indigenous Peoples*, International Work Group for Indigenous Affairs (IWGIA), Doc. No.127, Copenhagen, 2009, pp.184-198.

Anaya James, *Indigenous Peoples in International Law*, Oxford University Press, New York, Oxford, 1996.

Anaya James, *Indigenous Peoples in International Law*, Oxford, New York, Oxford University Press, 2nd edition, 2004.

Aparicio Wilhelmi Marco, "Los derechos políticos de los pueblos indígenas en la Declaración de Naciones Unidas", in Mikel Berraondo (ed.), *La Declaración sobre los Derechos de los Pueblos Indígenas. Punto y seguido*, AlterNativa, Barcelona, 2008.

Aparicio-Wilhelmi Marco, "El Derecho de los Pueblos Indígenas a la Libre Determinación", in Mikel Berraondo (ed.), *Pueblos Indígenas y Derechos Humanos*, Serie Derechos Humanos, Vol.14, Universidad de Deusto, Bilbao, 2006, pp.399-421.

Argelaguet Jordi, "From Autonomism to Independentism: The Growth of Secessionism in Catalonia (2010-2013)", in Jaime Lluch (ed.), *Constitutionalism and the Politics of Accommodation in Multinational Democracies*, Palgrave Macmillan, 2014, Palgrave e-book available at http://www.palgraveconnect.com/pc/doifinder/10.1057/9781137288998.0001 [Last access 29.01.2015].

Asbjørn Eide and Daes Irene-Erica, "Working Paper on the Relationship & Distinction between the Rights of Persons Belonging to Minorities & Those of Indigenous Peoples'", UN Doc. E/CN.4/Sub.2/2000/10, 2000.

Asbjørn Eide, "Peaceful Group Accommodation as an Alternative to Secession in Sovereign States", in Donald Clark and Robert Williamson, *Self-Determination. International Perspectives*, MacMillan Press, HoundsMill, Basingstoke and London, 1996 and St. Martin's Press, New York, 1996, pp.87-109.

Asian Indigenous and Tribal Peoples Network (AITPN), "Implementation of CHT Peace Accord: Will they, Won't they?", 4(1-2) *Indigenous Rights Quarterly* 2009.

Assies Willem, "Pueblos Indígenas y Reforma del Estado en América Latina", in Willem Assies, Gemma van der Haar and André Hoekema (eds.), *El reto de la diversidad: Pueblos indígenas y reforma del Estado en América Latina*, El Colegio de Michoacán, Zamora-Michoacán, 1999, pp.21-55.

Aylwin José and Silva Hernando, "Chile", in International Work Group for Indigenous Affairs (IWGIA), *The Indigenous World 2014*, IWGIA, Copenhagen, 2014, pp.203-213.

Aylwin José, "Bolivia: Desarrollo o Buen Vivir. El Caso del TIPNIS", in Salvador Martí i Puig, Claire Wright, José Aylwin and Nancy Yáñez, (eds.), *Entre el desarrollo y el buen vivir. Recursos naturales y conflictos en los territorios indígenas*, Libros de la Catarata, Madrid, 2013, pp.168-200.

Aylwin José, "The Ralco Dam and the Pehuenche People in Chile: Lessons from an Ethno-Environmental Conflict", Paper presented at the Conference "Towards Adaptive Conflict Resolution: Lessons From Canada and Chile", Centre for the Study of Global Issues, University of British Columbia, Vancouver, Canada, 25-27 September 2002.

Aylwin José, *Estudio sobre Tierras Indígenas de la Araucanía: Antecedentes Históricos Legislativos (1850-1920)*, Instituto de Estudios Indígenas, Universidad de la Frontera, Temuco, 1995.

Aylwin José, *Tierra y territorio mapuche: un análisis desde una mirada històrico jurídica*, Proyecto Mapu Territorialidad, Instituto de Estudios Indígenas, Universidad de la Frontera, Temuco, 2002.

Baracco Luciano (ed.), *National Integration and Contested Autonomy: The Caribbean Coast of Nicaragua*, Algora Publications, New York, 2011.

Bárcena Alicia, "Distribuir la Riqueza. La pobreza y la desigualdad han disminuido en América Latina en los últimos años, pero aún queda mucho por hacer", *Finanzas & Desarrollo*, March 2011, pp.20-21.

Bárcenas Francisco López, "Autonomías indígenas en América: de la demanda de reconocimiento a su construcción", in Mikel Berraondo (ed.), *Pueblos Indígenas y Derechos Humanos*, Universidad de Deusto, Bilbao, 2006, pp.423-450.

Barelli Mauro, "Shaping Indigenous Self-Determination: Promising or Unsatisfactory Solutions?", 13(3) *International Community Law Review* 2011, pp.413-436.

Barrera Anna, Nolte Detlef and Schilling-Vacaflor Almut, *New Constitutionalism in Latin America from a Comparative Perspective: A Step Towards Good Governance?*, Hamburg, 2011, Proceedings of the homonymous conference organized by the German Institute of Global and Area Studies (GIGA) of Hamburg (Germany), 25-26 November 2010.

Bello Álvaro, *Etnicidad y ciudadanía en América Latina. La acción colectiva de los pueblos indígenas*, United Nations, Santiago de Chile, 2004.

Bengoa José, *Historia del Pueblo Mapuche Siglo XIX y XX*, LOM Ediciones, Snatiago de Chile, 2000.

Bengoa José, *La emergencia indígena en América Latina*, Mexico City, Fondo de Cultura Economica, 2nd edition, 2007.

Blázquez Martín Diego, "Algunas Reflexiones Acerca de los Derechos de Representación Política de los Pueblos Indígenas al Hilo de la Declaración", in Natalia Álvarez Molinero, J. Daniel Oliva Martínez, Nieves Zúñiga García-Falces (eds.), *Declaración sobre los Derechos de los Pueblos Indígenas. Hacia un Mundo Intercultural y Sostenible*, Catarata, Madrid, 2009 pp.267-282.

Bollen Kenneth A., "Political Rights and Political Liberties in Nations: An Evaluation of Human Rights Measures, 1950 to 1984", 567(8) *Human Rights Quarterly* 1986, pp.567-591.

Brems Eva, "Methods in Legal Human Rights Research", in Fons Coomans, Fred Grünfeld and Menno T. Kamminga (eds.), *Methods of Human Rights Research*, Intersetia, Antwerp, Oxford, Portland, 2009, pp.77-90.

Brewer-Carías Allan R., *Constitutional Protection of Human Rights in Latin America. A Comparative Study of Amparo Proceedings*, Cambridge University Press, Cambridge, 2009.

Brysk Alison, *From Tribal Village to Global Village: Indian Rights and International Relations in Latin America*, Stanford University Press, Stanford (CA, USA), 2000.

Burguete Cal y Mayor Araceli (ed.), *Indigenous Autonomy in Mexico,* IWGIA Document No. 94, IWGIA, Copenhagen, 2000.

Callahan Michael D., *Mandates and Empire: The League of Nations and Africa, 1914-1931*, Sussex Academic Press, Eastbourne, 2008.

Cárdenas Víctor Hugo, "Participación Política Indígena y Políticas Públicas para Pueblos Indígenas en Bolivia", in Víctor Hugo Cárdenas et al. (eds.), *Participación Política Indígena y Políticas Públicas para Pueblos Indígenas en América Latina*, Konrad Adenauer Stiftung, LA Paz, 2011, pp.17-64.

Carmen Andrea, "The Right to Free, Prior and Informed Consent. A Framework for Harmonious Relations and New Processes of Redress", in Jackie Hartley, Paul Joffe and Jennifer Preston (eds.), *Realizing the UN Declaration on the Rights of Indigenous Peoples: Triumph, Hope and Action*, Purich Publishing, Saskatoon, 2010, pp.120-134.

Carruthers David and Rodriguez Patricia, "Mapuche Protest, Environmental Conflict and Social Movement Linkage in Chile", 30(4) *Third World Quarterly* 2009, pp.743-760.

Caspersen Nina, "The South Caucasus after Kosovo: Renewed Independence Hopes?", 65(5) *Europe-Asia Studies* 2013, pp.929-945.

Cassese Antonio, *International Law*, Oxford University Press, Oxford, New York, 2nd edition, 2005.

Cassese Antonio, *Self-determination of Peoples. A Legal Reappraisal*, Cambridge University Press, Cambridge, New York, 1995.

Castellino Joshua, "Conceptual Difficulties and the Right to Indigenous Self-Determination", in Nazila Ghanea and Alexandra Xanthaki (eds.), *Minorities, Peoples and Self-Determination*, Brill, Leiden, 2005 pp.55-74.

Castellino Joshua, "Indigenous Rights and the Right to Development: Emerging Synergies or Collusion?", in Stephen Allen and Alexandra Xanthaki (eds.), *Reflections on the Un Declaration on the Rights of Indigenous Peoples*, Hart Publishing, Oxford, Portland, 2011, pp.367-386.

Castellino Joshua, "Territorial Integrity and the 'Right' to Self-Determination: An examination of the Conceptual Tools", 33(2) *Brooklyn Journal of International Law* 2008, pp.503-568.

Castellino Joshua, *International Law and Self-determination*, Martinus Nijhoff Publishers, Leiden, Boston, 2000.

Cayuqueo Nilo, "1977 and the Participation of Indigenous peoples in the United Nations and the International Arena", in Roxanne Dunbar-Ortiz et al. (eds.), *Indigenous Peoples' Rights in International Law: Emergence and application. Book in Honor of Asbjørn Eide at Eighty*, Gáldu and IWGIA, Kautokeino, Copenhagen, Gáldu Čála serie No.2/2015, 2015, pp.38-41.

Cespedes Rodrigo, "Environmental Justice for Indigenous People in the Post-Pinochet Chile", in Karen Druffel (ed.), *Looking Within: Finding an Environmental Justice and Global Citizenship Lens*, Inter-Disciplinary Press, Oxford, 2013, pp.93-102.

Chairmane White Face Zumila Wobaga, *Indigenous Nations' Rights in the Balance. An analysis of The Declaration on the Rights of Indigenous Peoples*, Living Justice Press, Saint Paul (MN, USA), 2013.

Charters Claire "A Self-Determination Approach to Justifying Indigenous Peoples' Participation in International Law and Policy Making", 17(2) *International Journal on Minority and Group Rights* 2010, pp.215-240.

Charters Claire and Stavenhagen Rodolfo, "The UN Declaration on the Rights of Indigenous Peoples: how it came to be and what it heralds", in Claire Charters and Rodolfo Stavenhagen (eds.), *Making the Declaration Work. The United Nations Declaration on the Rights of Indigenous Peoples*, International Work Group for Indigenous Affairs (IWGIA), Doc. No.127, Copenhagen, 2009, pp.10-14.

Chartier Clem, Chirif Alberto and Tomas Nin, *The Human Rights of the Rapa Nui People on Easter Island*, Observatorio Ciudadano and International Work Group for Indigenous Affairs (IWGIA), Report No.15, Santiago de Chile, 2011.

Chávez León Marxa Nadia, "'Autonomías indígenas' y 'Estado Plurinacional'. Proyectos políticos de los movimientos indígenas y campesinos en Bolivia", 24 *Revista OSAL* 2008, pp.51-71.

Chávez Luis Enrique, "The Declaration on the Rights of Indigenous Peoples. Breaking the *Impasse*: the Middle Ground", in Claire Charters and Rodolfo Stavenhagen (eds.), *Making the Declaration Work. The United Nations Declaration on the Rights of Indigenous Peoples*, International Work Group for Indigenous Affairs (IWGIA), Doc. No.127, Copenhagen, 2009, pp.96-106.

Christian Walter, "Postscript: Self-Determination, Secession, and the Crimean Crisis 2014", in Christian Walter, Antje von Ungern-Sternberg, and Kavus Abushov (eds.), *Self-Determination and Secession in International Law*, Oxford University Press, Oxford, New York, 2014, pp.293-311.

Chuvirú, Marcela, "Bolivia", in Málaga Montoya (ed.), *Seminario Regional Andino. Pueblos indígenas y democracia intercultural: un debate desde los países andinos; Bolivia, Ecuador, Colombia, Venezuela, Chile, Perú*, Centro de Estudios Regionales Bartolomé de las Casas, Cuzco, 2008, pp.51-54.

Clavero Bartolomé, "Derechos Indigenas y Constituciones Latinoamericanas", in Mikel Berraondo (ed.), *Pueblos Indígenas y Derechos Humanos*, Universidad de Deusto, Bilbao, 2006, pp.313-338.

Clavero Bartolomé, "Nota sobre el alcance del mandato contenido en el artículo 42 de la Declaración sobre los derechos de los pueblos indígenas y el mejor modo de satisfacerlo por parte del Foro Permanente para las Cuestiones Indígenas, presented by

Bartolomé Clavero, Member of the Permanent Forum on Indigenous Issues", UN Doc. E/C.19/2008/CRP.6, 26 March 2008.

Cleary Edward L., *Mobilizing for Human Rights in Latin America*, Kumarian Press, Sterling (VA, USA), 2007, pp.59-60.

Clech Lâm Maivân, *At the Edge of the State: Indigenous Peoples and Self-Determination*, Transnational Publishers, Ardsley, New York, 2000.

Cloud Leslie, "La patrimonialización de Te Pito O Te Henua: historia del Parque Nacional Rapa Nui – Chile", 7(1) *Revista de Estudios Sociales Comparativos* 2013, pp.18-31.

Coddou Alberto, Godoy Nicolas and Vergara Adrian, "Fuerza Estatal y Conflicto Mapuche", in Tomás Vial (ed.), *Informe Anual sobre Derechos Humanos en Chile 2013*, Ediciones Universidad Diego Portales, Santiago de Chile, 2013, pp.223-252.

Coddou Alberto, Schönsteiner Judith and Vial Tomás, "La Ley Antidiscriminación: avances e insuficiencias en la protección de la igualdad y la no discriminación en Chile", in Tomás Vial (ed.), *Informe Anual sobre Derechos Humanos en Chile 2013*, Ediciones Universidad Diego Portales, Santiago de Chile, 2013, pp.285-309.

Colque Gonzalo and Chumacero Juan Pablo, *Informe 2010: Territorios Indígena Originario Campesinos en Bolivia Entre la Loma Santa y la Pachamama*, Fundación Tierra, La Paz, 2011.

Colque Gonzalo and Plata Wilfredo, *El Proceso Autonómico de Jesús de Machaca 2004-2010*, Fundación Tierra, La Paz, 2014.

Colque Gonzalo and Sotomayor Carlos, *Nuestros Derechos en la Constitución*, Fundación Tierra, La Paz, 2010.

Confederación Sindical Única de Trabajadores Campesinos de Bolivia–CSUTCB; Confederación de Pueblos Indígenas de Bolivia–CIDOB; Confederación Sindical de Colonizadores de Bolivia–CSCB; Federación Nacional de Mujeres Campesinas de Bolivia, 'Bartolina Sisa'–FNMCB-BS; Consejo Nacional de Ayllus y Markas del Qullasuyu–CONAMAQ; Coordinadora de Pueblos Étnicos de Santa Cruz–CPESC; Movimiento Sin Tierra de Bolivia–MST; Asamblea del Pueblo Guaraní–APG; Confederación de Pueblos Étnicos Moxeños de Beni–CPEMB. Asamblea Nacional de Organizaciones Indígenas, Originarias, Campesinas y de Colonizadores de Bolivia, "Propuesta para la Nueva Constitución Política del Estado: Por un Estado plurinacional y la autodeterminación de los pueblos y naciones indígenas, originarias y campesinas", Sucre, 5 August 2006, 22(166) *Revista OSAL - Observatorio Social de América Latina* 2007.

Contesse Jorge and Lovera Domingo, "Pueblos Indígenas y Participación Política en la Óptica del Tribunal Constitucional", in Javier Couso (ed.), *Anuario de Derecho Público 2010*, Ediciones Universidad Diego Portales, Santiago de Chile, 2010, pp.21-37.

Contreras Panemal C., "Los Parlamentos", in C. Contreras Panemal (ed.), *Actas del Primer Congreso Internacional de Historia Mapuche. Congreso Internacional de Historia Mapuche*, Eigenverlag, Siegen, 2003.

Craig Scott, "Indigenous Self-Determination and Decolonization of the International Imagination: A Plea", 18 *Human Rights Quarterly* 1996, pp.814-820.

Crawford James, "The Right to Self-Determination in International Law", in Philipp Alston, *Peoples' Rights*, Oxford University Press, 2001, pp.7-67.

Crawford James, *The Creation of States in International Law*, Clarendon Press, Oxford, 1979.

Cuentas Mirna, "El derecho a la consulta previa en Bolivia", 14 *Revista de la Fundación para el Debido Proceso Legal Aportes DPLF* 2010, pp.17-20.

Cunningham Kain Myrna, "La participación política de los pueblos indígenas. Escenarios, estrategias, modalidades y resultados", in Felipe Gomez Isa and Mikel Berraondo (eds.), *Los derechos indígenas tras la Declaración. El desafío de la implementación*, Universidad de Deusto, Bilbao, 2013, pp.247-285.

Daes Erica-Irene, "The Right of Indigenous Peoples to 'Self-Determination' in the Contemporary World Order", in Donald Clark and Robert Williamson, *Self-Determination. International Perspectives*, MacMillan Press, HoundsMill, Basingstoke and London, 1996 and St. Martin's Press, New York, 1996, pp.47-57.

Daes Erica-Irene, "The Spirit and Letter of the Right to Self-Determination of Indigenous Peoples: Reflections on the Making of the United Nations Draft Declaration", in Pekka Aikio and Martin Scheinin (eds.), *Operationalizing the Rights of Indigenous Peoples to Self-Determination*, Institute for Human Rights, Åbo Akademi University, Saarijärvi, 2000, pp.67-84.

Daes Erica-Irene, "The UN Declaration on the Rights of Indigenous Peoples: Background and Appraisal", in Stephen Allen and Alexandra Xanthaki (eds.), *Reflections on the Un Declaration on the Rights of Indigenous Peoples*, Hart Publishing, Oxford, Portland, 2011, pp.11-40.

Dahl Jens, *IWGIA. A History*, International Work Group for Indigenous Affairs (IWGIA), Document No.125, Copenhagen, 2009, p.40.

Damianovic Camacho Ninoska, *Estadísticas Sociales de los pueblos indígenas en Chile. Censo 2002*, Chilean National Institute of Statistics/Instituto Nacional de Estadísticas Chile, Santiago de Chile, 2005.

Danspeckgruber Wolfgang (ed.), *The Self-Determination of Peoples. Community, Nation and State in an Interdependent World*, Lynne Rienner Publishers in association with the Liechtenstein Institute on Self-Determination, Princeton University, Boulder, London, 2002.

Danspeckgruber Wolfgang, "Introduction", in Wolfgang Danspeckgruber (ed.), *The Self-Determination of Peoples. Community, Nation and State in an Interdependent World*, Lynne Rienner Publishers, Boulder, London, in association with the Liechtenstein Institute on Self-Determination, Princeton University, 2002, pp.1-9.

De Avila Martel Alamiro, "Régimen jurídico de la guerra de Arauco", paper presented at the conference "III Congreso del Instituto Internacional de Historia del Derecho Indiano", Instituto Internacional de Estudios Jurídicos, Madrid, 1973.

De la Fuente Rosa, *La autonomía indígena en Chiapas: Un nuevo imaginario socio-espacial,* Catarata, Madrid, 2008.

Deheza Grace I., "Bolivia 2011: Gobernando con el Conflicto", 32(1) *Revista de Ciencia Política (Santiago SciELO)* 2012, pp.31-48.

Del Campo Esther, "Participación Política y Democracia Local en Bolivia", in Esther Del Campo (ed.), *Democratización y Descentralización en Bolivia*, Catarata, Madrid, 2007, pp.15-42.

Del Mar Katherine, "The Myth of Remedial Secession", in Duncan French (ed.), *Statehood and Self-Determination. Reconciling Tradition and Modernity in International Law*, Cambridge University Press, Cambridge, New York, 2013, pp.79-108.

Del Popolo Fabiana, Oyarce Ana María, Schkolnik Susana and Velasco Fernanda of *Comisión Económica para América Latina*, "Censos 2010 y la inclusión del enfoque étnico: hacia una construcción participativa con pueblos indígenas y afrodescendientes de América Latina", Santiago de Chile, 2010.

Departament de la Presidència (ed.), *Bolivia: la refundación de un país/Bolívia: la refundació d'un país*, Casa América Catalunya, Barcelona, 2006.

Díaz-Polanco Héctor, *Autonomía regional. La autodeterminación de los pueblos indios*, D.F. Mexico, Siglo Veintiuno Editores, 1991.

Dinstein Yoram, "Autonomy (International Guarantees of Autonomy)", in Zelin A. Skurbaty (ed.), *Beyond a One-Dimensional State: An Emerging Right to Autonomy?*, Martinus Nijhoff Publishers, Leiden, Boston, 2005, pp.243-254.

Dominguez-Redondo Elvira, "The Universal Periodic Review. Is there life beyond naming and shaming in human rights implementation?", 4 *New Zealand Law Review*, 2012, pp.673-706.

Doyle Cathal and Cariño Jill, *Making Free, Prior & Informed Consent a Reality. Indigenous Peoples and the Extractive Sector*, Indigenous Peoples Links (PIPLinks), Middlesex University School of Law, The Ecumenical Council for Corporate Responsibility, London, 2013.

Doyle Cathal and Gilbert Jerémié, "Indigenous Peoples and Globalisation: From 'Development Agression' to 'Self-Determinted Development'", 8 *European Yearbook of Minority Issues (EYMI)* 2009, 2011, pp.219-267.

Drake Paul W. and Jaksic Ivan (eds.), *The Struggle for Democracy in Chile*, University of Nebraska Press, revised edition, Lincoln (NE, USA), 1995.

Drzewicki Krzysztof, "The Lund Recommendations on the Effective Participation of National Minorities in Public Life – Five Years After and More Years Ahead", 12 *International Journal on Minority and Group Rights* 2005, pp.123-131.

Durán Ribera Emilio and Pinckert Justiniano Guillermo, *La revolución igualitariade Andrés Ibáñez*, Editorial Universitaria, Santa Cruz de la Sierra, 1988.

Duthu Bruce, *American Indians and the Law*, Viking-Penguin, New York, 2008.

Eide Asbjørn, "Rights of Indigenous Peoples – Achievements in International Law during the Last Quarter of a Century", 26 *Netherlands Yearbook of International Law* 2006, pp.155-212.

Ensalaco Mark, *Chile Under Pinochet: Recovering the Truth*, University of Pennsylvania Press, Philadelphia, 2000.

Errico Stefania, "The UN Declaration on the Rights of Indigenous Peoples is Adopted: An Overview", 7(4) *Human Rights Law Review* 2007, pp.756-759.

Fitzmaurice Andrew, "The genealogy of Terra Nullius", 38(129) *Australian Historical Studies* 2007, pp.1-15.

Fontana Lorenza, "The 'indigenous native peasant' trinity: imagining a plurinational community in Evo Morales' Bolivia", 32(3) *Environment and Planning D: Society and Space* 2014, pp.518-534.

Forsythe David P., "Human Rights Studies: On the Dangers of Legalistic Assumptions", in Fons Coomans, Fred Grünfeld and Menno T. Kamminga (eds.), *Methods of Human Rights Research*, Intersetia, Antwerp, Oxford, Portland, 2009, pp.59-75.

Foster Carolina E., "Articulating Self-determination in the Draft Declaration on the Rights of Indigenous Peoples", 12(1) *European Journal of International Law* 2001, pp.141-157.

Fundación Konrad Adenauer Stiftung (KAS), *Participación Política Indígena. Mitos y Realidades*, Fundación Konrad Adenauer Stiftung, La Paz, 2006.

Funk Robert L., "Chile en 2012: la campaña permanente", 33(1) *Revista de Ciencia Política (Santiago SciELO)* 2013, pp.83-99.

García-Falces Nieves Zúñiga, "'Emergencia del Movimiento indígena en América Latina: de 'objeto' a 'sujeto'", in Salvador Martí i Puig and Josep Maria Sanahuja (eds.), *Etnicidad, autonomía y gobernabilidad en América Latina*, Universidad de Salamanca, Salamanca, 2004, pp.35-52.

Gay Oonagh, "The Scotland Bill: Devolution and Scotland's Parliament", 98(1) *House of Commons Library Research Paper* 1998, pp.1-87.

Geisler Charles, "New *Terra Nullius* Narratives and the Gentrification of Africa's 'Empty Lands'", 28(1) *Journal of World Systems Research* 2012, pp. 15-29.

Genugten Willem van, Meijknecht Anna and Rombouts Bas, "Stateless Indigenous People(s). The Right to a Nationality, Including Their Own", 19 *Tilburg Law Review* 2014, pp.98-107.

Ghai Yash, *Public Participation of Minorities*, Minority Rights Group International, London, 2003.

Gilbert Jerémié, *Indigenous Peoples' Land Rights under International Law. From Victims to Actors*, Transnational Publisher, Ardesley NY, 2006.

Gilbert Jeremie, Tugendhat Helen, Couillard Valérie and Doyle Cathal, "Business, Human Rights and Indigenous Peoples: The Right to Free, Prior and Informed Consent", Forest Peoples Programme, Working Paper Series, April 2009.

Giraudo Laura and Sánchez Juan Martín, "Neoindigenismo y movimientos indígenas en América Latina", in Carlos Malamud, Paul Isbell and Concha Tejedor (eds.), *Anuario Iberoamericano* 2008, Ediciones Pirámide, Madrid, 2008, pp.63-76.

Giraudo Laura, "El Instituto Indigenista Interamericano y la participación indígena (1940-1998)", 62(2) *América Indígena* 2006, pp.6-34.

Giraudo Laura, *La questione indigena in America Latina*, Carocci, Roma, 2009.

Glanville Luke, "The Responsibility to Protect", 12(1) *Human Rights Law Review* 2012, pp.1-32.

Göcke Katja, "The Case of *Ángela Poma Poma v. Peru* before the Human Rights Committee. The Concept of Free, Prior ad Informed Consent and the Application of the International Covenant on Civil and Political Rights to the Protection and the Promotion of Indigenous Peoples' Rights", in A. von Bogdandy and R. Wolfrum (eds.), 14 *Max Planck Yearbook of United Nations Law* 2010, pp.337-370.

Gomez Isa Felipe (ed.), *El caso Awas Tigni. Derechos Humanos entre lo local y global*, Universidad de Deusto, Bilbao, 2013.

Gómez Isa Felipe, "El derecho al desarrollo de los Pueblos Indígenas", in Felipe Gómez Isa and Mikel Berraondo (eds.), *Los derechos indígenas tras la Declaración. El desafío de la implementación*, Universidad de Deusto, Bilbao, 2013, pp.175-190.

Goméz Sanchéz Julio, "El Brasil portugués", in Juan Bosco Amores Carredano (coord.), *Historia de América*, Editorial Ariel, Barcelona, 2006, pp.877-960.

Graham Lorie M., "Resolving Indigenous Claims to Self-Determination", 10 *ILSA Journal of International and Comparative Law* 2003-2004, pp.385-420.

Gudermann Hans, "Las poblaciones indígenas andinas de Chile y la experiencia de la ciudadanía", in Hans Gudermann, Rolf Foester and Jorge Iván Vergara (eds.), *Mapuches y Aymaras. El debate entorno al Reconocimiento y los Derechos Colectivos*, RIL Editores, Santiago de Chile, Buenos Aires, 2003, pp.19-104.

Gudmundur Alfredsson, "Different Forms of and Claims to the Right of Self-Determination", in Clark Donald and Williamson Robert, *Self-Determination. International Perspectives*, MacMillan Press, HoundsMill, Basingstoke and London, 1996 and St. Martin's Press, New York, 1996, pp.58-85.

Gudmundur Alfredsson, "The Right of Self-Determination and Indigenous Peoples", in Christian Tomuschat (ed.), *Modern Law of Self-Determination*, Martinus Nijhoff Publishers, Dordrecht, Boston, London, 1993, pp.41-54.

Guerrero Rodríguez Rafael, "Neoliberal transition in Latin America: examining the gap between theory and practice. The cases of Chile and Mexico", 4(2) *Revista Espacialidades* 2014, pp.66-88.

Guevara Tomás, *Chile Prehispanico*, Universidad de Chile, Ediciones Balcells, Santiago de Chile, 1925.

Gundermann Hans, "Municipios y pueblos indígenas en Chile", in Willem Assies and Hand Gundermann (eds.), *Movimientos Indígenas y Gobiernos Locales en América Latina*, Universidad Católica del Norte, Línea Editorial IIAM, Antofagasta, 2007, pp.161-198.

Guthrie Jason, "The International Labour Organization, Community Development, and the Roots of the International Technocratic Class, 1944-1966", paper presented at the conference "Transnational Social Policies. Reformist networks and the International Labour Organization (1900-2000)", University of Paris X, 7-9 May 2009.

Hagopian Frances and Mainwaring Scott P. (eds.), *The Third Wave of Democratization in Latin America. Advances and Setbacks*, Cambridge University Press, Cambridge, New York, 2005.

Hannikainen Lauri, "Self-Determination and Autonomy in International Law", in Markku Suksi (ed.), *Autonomy: Applications and Implications*, Kluwer Law International, The Hague, Cambridge MA, Dordrecht, 1998, pp.79-95.

Hannum Hurst and Lillich Richard B., "The Concept of Autonomy in International Law", in Yoram Dinstein (ed.), *Models of Autonomy*, Transaction Books, Rutgers, New Brunswick, 1981, pp.215-254.

Hannum Hurst and Lillich Richard B., "The Concept of Autonomy in International Law", 74(4) *The American Journal of International Law* 1980, pp.858-889.

Hannum Hurst, "Rethinking Self-Determination", 34(1) *Virginia Journal of International Law* 993-1994, pp.1-69.

Hannum Hurst, "Self-Determination in the Post-Colonial Era", in D. Clark and R. Williamson (eds.), *Self-Determination: International Perspectives*, MacMillan Press, Houndmills, 1996, pp.12-40.

Hannum Hurst, "The Road to Autonomy in Aceh", in Panel "State Sovereignty and Regional Autonomy: The Asian Experience", 102 *Proceedings of the Annual Meeting of the American Society of International Law* 2008, pp.116-118.

Hannum Hurst, *Autonomy, Sovereignty, and Self-Determination: The Accommodation of Conflicting Rights*, University of Pennsylvania Press, 1996.

Harhoff Frederick, "Institutions of Autonomy", 55 *Nordic Journal of International Law* 1986, pp.31-40.

Harris Richard H., "Dependency, Underdevelopment, and Neoliberalism", in Richard H. Harris and Jorge Nef (eds.), *Capital, Power, and Inequality in Latin America and the Caribbean*, Rowman & Littlefield Publishers, Lanham (MD, USA), 2008, pp.49-95.

Harten Sven, *The Rise of Evo Morales and the MAS*, Zed Books, London, New York, 2011.

Heidbüchel Esther, *The West Papua Conflict in Indonesia: Actors, Issues and Approaches*, Johannes Herrmann J&J-Verlag, Wettenberg, 2007.

Heintze Hans Joachim, "On the Legal Understanding of Autonomy", in Markku Suksi (ed.), *Autonomy: Applications and Implications*, Kluwer Law International, The Hague, Cambridge (MA, USA), Dordrecht, 1998, pp.7-32.

Henrard Kristin, "'Participation', 'Representation' and 'Autonomy' in the Lund Recommendations and their Reflections in the Supervision of the FCNM and Several Human Rights Conventions", 12 *International Journal on Minority and Group Rights* 2005, pp.133-168.

Henrard Kristin, *Devising an Adequate System of Minority Protection. Individual Human Rights, Minority Rights and the Right to Self-Determination*, Martinus Nijhoff Publishers, The Hague, 2000.

Henriksen John B., "Sami Self-Determination. Autonomy and Self-Government: Education, Research and Culture", 2 *Gáldu Čála Journal of Indigenous Peoples Rights* 2009, pp.7-40.

Henriksen John B., "The Right of Self-Determination: Indigenous Peoples versus States", in Pekka Aikio and Martin Scheinin (eds.), *Operationalizing the Rights of Indigenous Peoples to Self-Determination*, Institute for Human Rights, Åbo Akademi University, Saarijärvi, 2000, pp.131-142.

Hernandez Artinelio, Martínez Atilio, Castillo Bernal and Limnio Irik, "Informe Nacional de Panama", LATAUTONOMY Project Report, 2003.

Hernández Romualdo, "Reforma agraria y evolución del marco jurídico del agua en Chile", 59 *FAO Legislative Study/Estudio Legislativo* 2006, pp.1-18.

Hidalgo Blandón Josefina et al., "Informe Nacional: Regiones Autónomas del Atlántico de Nicaragua", LATAUTONOMY Project report, 2004.

Hindery Derrick, *From Enron to Evo. Pipeline politics Global Environmentalism, and Indigenous Rights in Bolivia*, University of Arizona Press, Tucson, 2013.

Hirschman Albert O., "Exit, Voice, and the State", 31(1) *World Politics* 1978, pp.90-107.

Hirschman Albert O., *Exit, Voice and Loyalty. Responses to Decline in Firms, Organizations and States*, Harvard University Press, Cambridge (MA, USA) and London, 1970.

Hofmann Rainer and Alistair Gauthier Juri, "Indigenous Peoples and the Right to Development", in A. Eide, J. Möller, I. Ziemele (eds.), *Making Peoples Heard. Essays on Human Rights in Honour of Gudmundur Alfredsson*, Martinus Nijhoff Publishers, Leiden, 2011, pp. 439-461.

Hofmann Rainer, "Political Participation of Minorities", 6 *European Yearbook of Minority Issues (EYMI)* 2006/7, 2008, pp.5-17.

Hofmann Rainer, "The Use of Force and the Responsibility to Protect", comment prepared for the roundtable discussion on UN reform "Building a New Role for the United Nations: the Responsibility to Protect", Madrid, 12 *FRIDE Working Paper* 2005, pp.1-4.

Howe James, "The Kuna of Panama: Continuing Threats to Land and Autonomy", in David Maybury-Lewis (ed.), *The Politics of Ethnicity: Indigenous Peoples in Latin American States*, Harvard University Press, Cambridge (MA, USA), 2002.

Huntington Samuel P., *The Third Wave: Democratization in the Late Twentieth Century*, University of Oklahoma Press, 1991.

Instituto de Estudios Indígenas, Universidad de la Frontera, *Los derechos de los pueblos indígenas en Chile. Informe del Programa de Derechos Indígenas*, LOM Ediciones, Santiago de Chile, 2003.

Instituto Nacional de Derechos Humanos, *Situación de los Derechos Humanos en Chile. Informe 2013*, Instituto Nacional de Derechos Humanos, Santiago de Chile, 2013.

International Work Group for Indigenous Affairs, *The Indigenous World 2007*, IWGIA, Copenhagen 2009.

Iorns Catherine, "Dedicated Parliamentary Seats for Indigenous Peoples: Political Representation as an Element of Indigenous Self-Determination", 10(4) *Murdoch University Electronic Journal of Law* 2003, at http://www.murdoch.edu.au/elaw/issues/v10n4/iorns104nf.html [Last access 05.02.2015].

Irurozqui Victoriano Marta, "Conversos a la patria boliviana: Identidad y participación política indígenas en las revoluciones de 1870 y 1899", in VV.AA., *Relaciones sociales e identidades en América: IX Encuentro-Debate América latina ayer y hoy*, Barcelona, 2004, pp.385–400.

Irurozqui Victoriano Marta, "Los hombre Chacales en armas: Militarización y criminalización indígenas en la revolución federal boliviana de 1899", in Marta Irurozqui Victoriano (ed.), *La mirada esquiva: Reflexiones históricas sobre la interacción del Estado y la ciudadanía en los Andes, (Bolivia, Ecuador y Perú), siglo XIX*, Consejo Superior de Investigaciones Científicas, Madrid, 2005, pp.285-320.

Irurozqui Victoriano Marta, "The Sound of the *Pututos*. Politicisation and Indigenous Rebellions in Bolivia, 1826-1921", 32(1) *Journal of Latin American Studies* 2000, pp.85-114.

Jaime Gajardo Falcón, "Multiculturalismo y el debate constitucional chileno", 6 *Revista de Derecho – Escuela de Posgrado* 2014, pp.205-236.

Jellinek Georg, *Allgemeine Staatslehre,* H. Gentner, Bad Hamburg vor der Höhe, 3rd edition, 1960.

Jilamita Murillo Luis Jesús and Gastón Soto Quiroz Veimar, *Los ayllus en el actual departamento de Potosí: Una aproximación a la comprensión de su historia y situación contemporánea* (Soluciones Prácticas, Potosí, 2005), pp.17-19.

Josefsen Eva, "The Saami and the National Parliaments – Channels for Political Influence", 2 *Gáldu Čála Journal of Indigenous Peoples Rights* 2007, at http://www.galdu.org/govat/doc/national_parlaments.pdf.

Joseph Sarah, "Resolving conflicting claims of territorial sovereignty and external self-determination, part 1: A proposed formula", *The International Journal of Human Rights*, Volume 3, Issue 1, 1999, pp. 40-61.

Joseph Sarah, Schultz Jenny and Castan Melissa, *The International Covenant on Civil and Political Rights: Cases, Materials, and Commentary*, Oxford University Press, Oxford, New York, 2000.

Jouannet V.Andrés, "Participación Política Indígena en Chile: el caso Mapuche", in Víctor Hugo Cárdenas et al. (eds.), *Participación Política Indígena y Políticas Públicas para Pueblos Indígenas en América Latina*, Konrad Adenauer Stiftung, La Paz, 2011, pp.93-139.

Kadelbach Stefan, "*Jus Cogens*, *Obligations Erga Omnes* and other Rules – The Identification of Fundamental Norms", in Christian Tomuschat and Jean-Marc Thouvenin (eds.), *The Fundamental Rules of the International Legal Order. Jus Cogens and Obligations Erga Omnes*, Martinus Nijhoff Publishers, Leiden, Boston, 2006, pp.21-40.

Kaempfe Ingrid and Ready Guillermo, "Comentarios a la Ley N° 20.249, que crea los ECMPO y su Relación con el Convenio N° 169 de la OIT", 1(9) *Ideas para Chile* 2011, pp.1-33.

Karakras Ampam, "¿Quién habla por quién? Reflexiones sobre la representatividad y legitimidad de organizaciones y la institucionalidad indígena, estatal y de la cooperación internacional", in Sabine Speiser (ed.), *¿Quién habla por quién? Representatividad y legitimidad de organizaciones y representantes indígenas. Un debate abierto*, Unidad Coordinadora de Pueblos Indígenas en América Latina y el Caribe (KIVLAK) and Deutsche Gesellschaft für Internationale Zusammenarbeiten (GIZ), Quito, 2013, pp.19-38.

Kearney Michael and Varese Stefano, "Indigenous Peoples: Changing Identities and Forms of Resistance", in Richard H. Harris and Jorge Nef (eds.), *Capital, Power, and Inequality in Latin America and the Caribbean*, Rowman & Littlefield Publishers, Lanham (MD, USA), 2008, pp.196-224.

Khakeea Anna, "The MINURSO Mandate, Human Rights and the Autonomy Solution for Western Sahara", 19(3) *Mediterranean Politics* 2014, pp.456-462.

Kingsbury Benedict, "Reconstructing Self-Determination: A Relational Approach", in Pekka Aikio and Martin Scheinin (eds.), *Operationalizing the Rights of Indigenous Peoples to Self-Determination*, Institute for Human Rights, Åbo Akademi University, Saarijärvi, 2000, pp.19-38.

Kohl Benjamin, "Democratizing Decentralization in Bolivia: The Law of Popular Participation", 23 *Journal of Planning Education and Research* 2003, pp.153-164.

Koivurova Timo, "From High Hopes to Disillusionment: Indigenous Peoples' Struggle to (re)Gain Their Right to Self-determination", 15(1) *International Journal on Minority and Group Rights* 2008, pp.1-26.

Koskenniemi Martti, “National Self-Determination Today: Problems of Legal Theory and Practice”, 43 *International and Comparative Law Quarterly*, 1994, pp.241-269.

Kowalczyk Anna Maria, “Indigenous Peoples and Modernity: Mapuche Mobilizations in Chile”, 40 *Latin American Perspectives* 2013, pp.121-135.

Kymlicka Will, “Beyond the Indigenous/Minority Dichotomy?”, in Stephen Allen and Alexandra Xanthaki (eds.), *Reflections on the Un Declaration on the Rights of Indigenous Peoples*, Hart Publishing, Oxford, Portland, 2011, pp.183-208.

Kymlicka Will, *Multicultural Citizenship: A Liberal Theory of Minority Rights*, Oxford University Press, Oxford, New York, 1995.

Langer Erick D., “Introduction”, in Eric D Langer and Elena Munoz, “Contemporary Indigenous Movements in Latina America”, Scholarly Resources Inc., Wilmington (DE, USA), 2003, pp.xi-xxix.

Lantschner Emma, Constantin Sergiu and Marko Joseph (eds.), *Practice of Minority Protection in Central Europe*, Nomos, Baden-Baden, 2012.

Lapidoth Ruth, *Autonomy: Flexible Solutions to Ethnic Conflicts,* United States Institute of Peace Press, Washington, 1997.

Légaré André, “Canada’s Experiment with Aboriginal Self-Determination in Nunavut: From Vision to Illusion”, 15(2-3) *International Journal on Minority and Group Rights* 2008, pp.335-367.

Lenzerini Federico (ed.), *Reparations for Indigenous Peoples. International and Comparative Perspectives*, Oxford University Press, Oxford, New York, 2008.

Lenzerini Federico, “Sovereignty Revisited: International Law and Parallel Sovereignty of Indigenous Peoples”, 42 *Texas International Law Journal* 2006, pp.155-189.

Lenzerini Federico, “The Trail of Broken Dreams: The Status of Indigenous Peoples in International Law”, in Federico Lenzerini (ed.), *Reparations for Indigenous Peoples. International and Comparative Perspectives*, Oxford University Press, Oxford, New York, 2008, pp.73-116.

Libermann Kitula and Godínez Armando (eds.), *Territorio y dignidad: Pueblos indígenas y medio ambiente en Bolivia*, Nueva Sociedad, Caracas, 1992.

Lijphart Arend, “Constitutional Design for Divided Societies”, 15(2) *Journal of Democracy* 2004, pp.96-109.

Lila Barrera-Hernández, “Indigenous Peoples, Human Rights and Natural Resource Development: Chile”s Mapuche Peoples and the Right to Water”, 11(1) *Annual Survey of International and Comparative Law* 2005, pp. 1-28.

Littlechild Wilton, “Comment on agenda items at the Oslo Conference on Indigenous Peoples’ Rights”, in Roxanne Dunbar-Ortiz et al. (eds.), *Indigenous Peoples’ Rights in International Law: Emergence and application. Book in Honor of Asbjørn Eide at Eighty*, Gáldu and IWGIA, Kautokeino, Copenhagen, Gáldu Čála serie No.2/2015, 2015, pp.18-23.

López Fuentes José Luis, *El derecho a la libre determinación de los pueblos indígenas en Bolivia*, Centro de Ecología y Pueblos Andinos (CEPA), Latinas Editores, Oruro, 2007.

Loukacheva Natalia, “On Autonomy and Law”, *Globalization and Autonomy Online Compendium Research Articles* 2005, at http://globalautonomy.ca/global1/article.jsp?index=RA_Loukacheva_AutonomyLaw.xml [Last access 05.08.2014].

Loukacheva Natalia, *The Arctic Promise: Legal and Political Autonomy of Greenland and Nunavut,* University of Toronto Press, Toronto, Buffalo, London, 2007.

Lyck Lise, "Greenland: Ten Years of Home Rule", 155(25) *Polar Record* 1989, pp.343-346.

Mabel Villalba Sara, "Protestas y Reconocimiento Indígenas en el Cono Sur", in Sara Mabel Villalba and Salvador Marí i Puig (eds.), *Protestas necesarias para derechos imprescindibles. Acción colectiva y legislación favorable a los pueblos indígenas en América Latina*, Dictus Publishing, Saabrücken, 2014, pp.66-91.

MacKay Fergus, "The Draft World Bank Operational Policy 4.10 on Indigenous Peoples: Progress or More of the Same?", 22(1) *Arizona Journal of International & Comparative Law* 2005, pp.65-98.

MacKay Fergus, *Guía para los derechos de los pueblos indígenas en el sistema interamericano*, International Work Group for Indigenous Affairs (IWGIA), Copenhagen, 2002.

Malezer Les, "Permanent Forum on Indigenous Issues: 'Welcome to the Family of the UN'", in Joshua Castellino and Niamh Walsh (eds.)*, Indigenous peoples and International Law,* Martinus Nijhoff Publishers and Raoul Wallenberg Institute Human Rights Library, Leiden, Boston, 2005, pp.67-85.

Malgosia Fitzmaurice, "The question of indigenous peoples' rights: a time for reappraisal?", in Duncan French (ed.), *Statehood and Self-Determination. Reconciling Tradition and Modernity in International Law*, Cambridge University Press, Cambridge, New York, 2013, pp.349-376.

Mallol Vicente Cabedo, *Constitucionalismo y Derecho Indígena en América Latina*, Universidad Politécnica de Valencia, Amadis, 2004.

Manus Peter, "Sovereignty, Self-Determination and Environment-Based Cultures: The Emerging Voice of Indigenous Peoples in International Law", 23 *Wisconsin International Law Journal* 2005, pp.553-642.

Marc Weller, "Introduction", in Marc Weller and Katherine Nobbs (eds.), *Asymmetric Autonomy and the Settlement of Ethnic Conflicts*, University of Pennsylvania Press, Philadelphia, 2010, pp.1-13.

Mardones Z.Rodrigo, "Descentralización y Transición en Chile", 26(1) *Revista de Ciencia Política (Santiago SciELO)* 2006, pp.3-24.

Maremán Quemenado Pablo Alberto, "La autonomía en el Cono Sur. El caso Mapuche de la Araucanía (Chile) y el Newken (Argentina), in Felipe Gómez Isa and Susana Ardanaz Iriarte (eds.), *La plasmación política de la diversidad. Autonomía y participación política indígena en América Latina*, Universidad de Deusto, Bilbao, 2011, pp.59-88.

Marimán Quemenado Pedro, "Chile", in International Work Group for Indigenous Affairs (IWGIA), *The Indigenous World 2011*, IWGIA, Copenhagen, 2011, pp.211-219.

Marimán Quemenado Pedro, "Chile", in International Work Group for Indigenous Affairs (IWGIA), *The Indigenous World 2012*, IWGIA, Copenhagen, 2012, pp.204-213.

Marko Josef, "The Law and Politics of Diversity Management: A Neo-institutional Approach", 6 *European Yearbook of Minority Issues (EYMI)* 2006/7, 2008, pp.251-279.

Martí i Puig Salvador (ed.), *Pueblos Indígenas y Política en América Latina. El Reconocimiento de sus Derechos y el Impacto de sus Demandas a inicio del Siglo XXI*, Fundació CIDOB, Barcelona, 2007.

Martí i Puig Salvador, "Después de la 'década de los pueblos indígenas', ¿Qué?", 227 *Nueva Sociedad* 2010, pp.68-82.

Mayorga Fernando, "Referéndum y Asamblea Constituyente: Autonomías Departamentales en Bolivia", 37 *Reforma y Democracia-Revista del CLAD* 2007.

McCorquodale Robert, "Self-Determination: A Human Rights Approach", 43 *International and Comparative Law Quarterly* 1994, 857-885.

Mella Seguel Eduardo and Meza-Lopehandía Glaesser Matías, *Temucuicui: Paradigma de la vulneración de los derechos fundamentales de los pueblos indígenas en Chile*, Observatorio de Derechos de los Pueblos Indígenas (Observatorio Ciudadano), Temuco, 2006.

Mendoza-Botelho Martín, "Bolivia 2012: Entre Buenas y Malas Noticas", 33(1) *Revista de Ciencia Política (Santiago SciELO)* 2013, pp.35-54.

Mendoza-Botelho Martín, "Bolivia 2013: Al Calor Preelectoral", 34(1) *Revista de Ciencia Política (Santiago SciELO)* 2014, pp.37-57.

Meza-Lopehandía G.Matías, "VI. El Convenio N° 169 de la OIT en el sistema normativo chileno", in Matías Meza-Lopehandía G. (ed.), *Las implicancias de la ratificación del Convenio N° 169 de la OIT en Chile*, Programa de Derechos de los Pueblos Indígenas del Observatorio Ciudadano, Temuco, 2010, 2nd edition, pp.103-160.

Ministerio de Autonomías & Servicio Estatal de Autonomías, *Estado de situación de las autonomías en Bolivia: Una mirada a tres años*, La Paz, 2013.

Mires Fernando, *La rebelión permanente: las revoluciones sociales en América Latina*, Siglo XXI, Mexico, 1988, pp.59-79.

Molina Barrios Figueroa Ramiro, Milenka and Quisbert Isabel, "Los pueblos indígenas de Bolivia: diagnóstico sociodemográfico a partir del censo del 2001", Comisión Económica para América Latina y el Caribe (CEPAL), Santiago de Chile, 2005.

Molina Martínez Miguel, "La organización administrativa de las Indias", in Juan Bosco Amores Carredano (coord.), *Historia de América*, Editorial Ariel, Barcelona, 2006, pp. pp. 217-285.

Morales Quiroga Mauricio and González G.Jaime A., "Electoral tendencies of indigenous groups in Chile", 37(4) *Revista Eure - Revista de Estudios Urbano Regionales* 2011, pp.133-157.

Morales Quiroga Mauricio, Díaz Kevin and Marambio Alexis, "Reforma al Sistema Electoral Binominal. Análisis, Simulaciones y Actores", 1 *Documento de Trabajo ICSO* 2014, Universidad Diego Portales, at http://www.icso.cl/wp-content/uploads/2014/05/ICSO_DT1_2014_Morales.pdf [Last access 05.09.2014].

Morton Gregory and Carniero da Cunha Manuela, "Indigenous Rights and Brazilian democracy: An Interview Manuela Carneiro da Cunha", *Cultural Anthropology*, Serie "Protesting Democracy in Brazil", available at http://www.culanth.org/fieldsights/460-indigenous-rights-and-brazilian-democracy-an-interview-manuela-carneiro-da-cunha [Last access 12.08.2014].

Musafiri Prosper Nobirabo, "Right to Self-Determination in International Law: Towards Theorization of the Concept of Indigenous Peoples/National Minority?", 19(4) *International Journal of Minority and Group Rights* 2012, pp.481-532.

Musgrave Thomas D., *Self-Determination and National Minorities*, Oxford University Press, Oxford, New York, 2002.

Mutz Diana C. Mutz, *Hearing the Other Side. Deliberative versus Participatory Democracy*, Cambridge University Press, Cambridge, New York, 2006.

Myntti Kristian, "The Right to Self-Determination and Effective Participation", in Pekka Aikio and Martin Scheinin (eds.), *Operationalizing the Rights of Indigenous Peoples to Self-Determination*, Institute for Human Rights, Åbo Akademi University, Saarijärvi, 2000, pp.85-130.

Nesti Lorenzo, "The Mapuche-Pehuenche and the Ralco Dam on the Bíobío River: the Challenge of Protecting Indigenous Land Rights', 9 *International Journal on Minority and Group Rights* 2002, pp.1-40.

Newman Dwight G., "Theorizing Collective Indigenous Rights", 31(2) *American Indian Law Review* 2006-2007, pp.273-289.

Novak Manfred, "The International Covenant on Civil and Political Rights", in Raija Hanski and Marku Sukksi (eds.), *An Introduction to the International protection of Human Rights. A Textbook*, Abo Academy University of Turku, Abo, 1997, pp.79-98.

Nowak Manfred, *U.N. Covenant on Civil and Political Rights: CCPR Commentary*, N.P. Engel Publishers, Kehl am Rhein, 1993.

Nuchera Patricio Hidalgo, "Expansión, gobierno y defensa de las Indias", in Juan Bosco Amores Carredano (ed.), *Historía de América*, Editorial Ariel, Barcelona, 2006, pp.287-325.

O'Phelan Godoy Scarlett, "Algunas reflexiones sobre las Reformas Borbonicas y las rebeliones del siglo XVIII", in Charles F. Walker (ed.), *Entre la retórica y la insurgencia: las ideas y los movimientos sociales en los Andes, siglo XVIII*, Centro de Estudios Regionales Andinos "Bartolomé de las Casas", Cusco, 1995, pp.309-317.

Oklopcic Zoran (guest editor), "The Crisis in Ukraine", Special Issue, 16(3) *German Law Journal* 2015, pp.350-712, at https://www.germanlawjournal.com/pdfs/FullIssues/PDF_Vol_16_No_3_full%20issu.pdf.

Ordoñez Ganoza Silvia, "La Relación entre los Pueblos Indígenas de la Amazonía con el Estado Peruano desde la Perspectiva de los Indígenas Awajún de Huampami", 43 *Iberoamericana. Nordic Journal of Latin American and Caribbean Studies* 2013, pp.67-90.

Orellana Halkyer René, "Municipalización de Pueblos Indígenas en Bolivia: Impactos y perspectivas", in Willem Assies, Gemma van der Haar, and André Hoekema (eds.), *El reto de la diversidad: Pueblos indígenas y reforma del Estado en América Latina*, El Colegio de Michoacán, Zamora-Michoacán, 1999, pp.315-340.

Orellana Marcos A., "Saramaka People v. Suriname. Judgement (Preliminary Objections, Merits, Reparations, and Costs), Serie C, No.172. Inter-American Court of Human Rights, November 28, 2007", 102 *American Journal of International Law* 2008, pp.841-847.

Ortega Hegg Manuel, "La Autonomia Regional en Nicaragua", LATAUTONOMY Project Report, 2003.

Ortiz-T. Pablo, "Ecuador", in International Work Group for Indigenous Affairs, *The Indigenous World 2009*, IWGIA, Copenhagen, 2009, pp.148-160.

Ospina Peralta Pablo, "Estado plurinacional y autogobierno territorial: Demandas indígenas en Ecuador", in Miguel González, Araceli Burguete Cal y Mayor and Pablo Ortiz-T. (eds.), *La autonomía a debate: Autogobierno indígena y Estado plurinacional en América Latina*, FLACSO, GTZ, Ministerio Federal de Cooperación Económica y Desarrollo, IWGIA, CIESAS, Universidad Intercultural de Chiapas, Quito, 2010, pp.201-218.

Packer John, "The Origin and Nature of the Lund Recommendations on the Effective Participation of National Minorities in Public Life", 11(4) *Helsinki Monitor*, 2000, pp.29-61.

Palermo Francesco, "Autonomia territoriale e tutela delle minoranze: Una riflessione critica", in Antonio Reposo, Lucio Pegoraro, Roberto Scarciglia, Maurillo Gobbo, Sergio Gerotto (eds.), 5-6 *Il diritto della regione* 2009, pp.181-196.

Palermo Francesco, "Bridges in Self-Determination Disputes? External Relations of Sub-national Entities and Minority Groups", in Marc Weller and Barbara Metzger (eds.), *Settling Self-Determination Disputes. Complex Power-Sharing in Theory and in Practice*, Martinus Nijhoff, Leiden, Boston, 2008, pp.667-688.

Palermo Francesco, "When the Lund Recommendations are Ignored. Effective Participation of National Minorities through Territorial Arrangements", 16(4) *International Journal on Minority and Group Rights* 2009, pp.653-663.

Palermo Francesco, Woelk Jens, *Diritto Costituzionale Comparato dei Gruppi e delle Minoranze*, CEDAM, Padova, 2008.

Park Jungwon, "Integration of Peoples and Minorities: An Approach to the Conceptual Problem of Peoples and Minorities with Reference Self-determination under International Law", 13 *International Journal of Minority and Group Rights* 2006, pp.69-93.

Pastor Daniel, "Origins of the Chilean Binominal Election System", 24(1) *Revista de Ciencia Política (Santiago SciELO)* 2004, pp.38-57.

Paul J. Magnarella, "The Evolving Right of Self-Determination of Indigenous Peoples", 14 *Saint Thomas Law Review* 2001-2002, pp.452-447.

Paz Patiño Sarela, *El Conflicto del Territorio Indígena Parque Nacional Isiboror Sécure (TIPNIS) y sus Consecuencias para el Estado Plurinacional de Bolivia*, UNDP Bolivia, Proyecto e Fortalecimiento Democrático, Fundación Boliviana para la Democracia Multipartidaria, 2011.

Pérez-Bustillo Camilo, "The Counter-Hegemonic Origins and Potential of Human Rights: the Rights of Indigenous Peoples and the World Bank as a Case Study", in Roxanne Dunbar-Ortiz et al. (eds.), *Indigenous Peoples' Rights in International Law: Emergence and application. Book in Honor of Asbjørn Eide at Eighty*, Gáldu and IWGIA, Kautokeino, Copenhagen, Gáldu Čála serie No.2/2015, 2015, pp.470-486.

Piñero-Royo Rodríguez Luis, "Political Participation Systems Applicable to Indigenous Peoples", in Marc Weller and Katharine Nobbs (eds.), *Political Participation of Minorities: A Commentary on International Standards and* Practice, Oxford University Press, Oxford, 2010, pp.308-342.

Plata Wilfredo, "De Municipio a Autonomía Indígena: Los once municipios que transitan a la Autonomía Indígena Originaria Campesina" in VV.AA, *Bolivia Post-Constituyente: Tierra, territorio y autonomías indígenas. Memoria del Seminario Internacional 2009*, Fundación Tierra, La Paz, 2009, pp.247-272.

Postero Nancy Grey, *Now We Are Citizens*, Stanford University Press, Stanford, 2007.

Protsyk Oleh, "The representation of minorities and indigenous peoples in parliament", IPU and UNDP, Mexico, 2010.

Quane Helen, "A Further Dimension to the Interdependence and Indivisibility of Human Rights?: Recent Developments concerning the Rights of Indigenous Peoples", 25 *Harvard Human Rights Journal* 2012, pp.49-83.

Quane Helen, "The UN Declaration on the Rights of Indigenous Peoples: New Directions for Self-Determination and Participatory Rights?", in Stephen Allen and Alexandra Xanthaki (eds.), *Reflections on the UN Declaration on the Rights of Indigenous Peoples*, Hart Publishing, Oxford, Portland, 2011, pp.259-287.

Roach Steven C., *Cultural Autonomy, Minority Rights, and Globalization*, Ashgate, Aldershot, Hampshire, Burlington (VT, USA), 2006.

Rochna Ramirez Susana, *La Propriedad de la Tierra en la Isla de Pascua*, CONADI, AECID, Santiago de Chile, 1996.

Rodríguez Piñero-Royo Luis, "'Where Appropriate': Monitoring/Implementing of Indigenous Peoples' Rights Under the Declaration", in Claire Charters and Rodolfo Stavenhagen (eds.), *Making the Declaration Work. The United Nations Declaration on the Rights of Indigenous Peoples*, International Work Group for Indigenous Affairs (IWGIA), Doc. No.127, Copenhagen, 2009, pp.314-343.

Rodríguez Piñero-Royo Luis, "El sistema interamericano de los derechos humanos y los pueblos indígenas", in Mikel Berraondo (ed.), *Pueblos Indígenas y Derechos Humanos*, Universidad de Deusto, Bilbao, 2006, pp.153-203.

Rodríguez Piñero-Royo Luis, "Political Participation Systems Applicable to Indigenous Peoples", in Marc Weller and Katharine Nobbs (eds.), *Political Participation of Minorities: A Commentary on International Standards and Practice,* Oxford University Press, Oxford, 2010, pp.308-342.

Rodríguez Piñero-Royo Luis, *Indigenous peoples, Postcolonialism, and International Law. The ILO Regime (191-1989)*, Oxford University Press, Oxford, New York, 2005, reprinted in 2010.

Rojas Priscilla and Navia Patricio, "Representación y tamaño de los distritos electorales en Chile, 1988-2002", 25(2) *Revista de Ciencia Política (Santiago SciELO)* 2005, pp.91-116.

Romero Bonifaz Carlos, *El Proceso constituyente boliviano: el hito de la cuarta marcha de tierras bajas*, Centro de Estudios Jurídicos e Investigación Social-CEJIS, Santa Cruz de la Sierra, 2005.

Ronen Dov, *The Quest for Self-Determination*, Yale University Press, New Haven and London, 1979, pp.25-26.

Rossells Beatriz, "Los cementerios, los héroes y la memoria patriótica en Bolivia", 7(13) *Revista Domínios Da Imagem* 2013, pp.8-23.

Rosti Marzia, "Reparations for Indigenous Peoples in Two Selected Latin American Countries", in Federico Lenzerini, *Reparations for Indigenous Peoples: International and Comparative Perspectives*, Oxford University Press, 2008, pp.345-362.

Rousseau Stéphanie, "Indigenous and Feminist Movements at the Constituent Assembly in Bolivia", 46(2) *Latin American Research Review* (LARR) 2011, pp.5-28.

Sambo Dorough Dalee, "The Revision of International Labour Organization Convention No. 107: A Subjective Assessment", in Roxanne Dunbar-Ortiz et al. (eds.), *Indigenous Peoples' Rights in International Law: Emergence and application. Book in Honor of Asbjørn Eide at Eighty*, Gáldu and IWGIA, Kautokeino, Copenhagen, Gáldu Čála serie No.2/2015, 2015, pp.250-277.

Samson Colin, "The Rule of *Terra Nullius* and the Impotence of International Human Rights for Indigenous Peoples", 5(1) *Essex Human Rights Review* 2008, pp.1-12.

Sanders Douglas, "Is Autonomy a Principle of International Law?", 55 *Nordic Journal of International Law* 1986, 17-21, in Hans Joachim Heintze, "On the Legal Understanding of Autonomy", in Markku Suksi (ed.), *Autonomy: Applications and Implications*, Kluwer Law International, The Hague, Cambridge MA, Dordrecht, 1998, pp.7-32.

Sanders Douglas, "Self-Determination and Indigenous Peoples", in Christian Tomuschat (ed.), *Modern Law of Self-Determination*, Martinus Nijhoff Publishers, Dordrecht, Boston, London, 1993, pp.55-81.

Sanderson Espinoza Jorge, "El censo y encuestas territoriales", paper presented at the conference "Pueblos Indigenas y Afrodescendientes de América Latina y el Caribe: Relevancia y pertinencia de la información sociodemográfica para políticas y programas", Economic Commission for Latin America and the Caribbean (ECLAC)/Comisión Económica para América Latina y el Caribe (CEPAL), UN Regional Commission, Santiago de Chile, 27-29 April 2005.

Saul Ben, Kinley David, and Mowbray Jacqueline, *The International Covenant on Economic, Social and Cultural Rights. Commentary, Cases, and Materials*, Oxford University Press, Oxford, 2014.

Saul Matthew, "The Normative Status of Self-Determination in International Law: A Formula for Uncertainty in the Scope and Content of the Right?",11(4) Human Rights Law Review 2011, pp. 609-644.

Scheinin Martin, "The Right to Self-Determination under the Covenant on Civil and Political Rights", in Pekka Aikio and Martin Scheinin (eds.), *Operationalizing the Rights of Indigenous Peoples to Self-Determination*, Institute for Human Rights, Åbo Akademi University, Saarijärvi, 2000, pp.179-198.

Scheinin Martin, "What are indigenous peoples?", in Nazila Ghanea and Alexandra Xanthaki (eds.), *Minorities, Peoples and Self-Determination,* Brill, Leiden, 2005, pp. 3-13.

Schilling-Vacaflor Almut, "Democratizing Resource Governance through Prior Consultations? Lessons from Bolivia's Hydrocarbon Sector", 184 *GIGA Working Papers* 2012, pp.1-27.

Schilling-Vacaflor Almut, "Identidades indígenas y demandas político-jurídicas de la CSUTCB y el CONAMAQ en la Constituyente boliviana", 23-24 *T'inkazos - Revista de Ciencias Sociales* 2008, pp.149-166.

Schkolink Susana and del Popolo Fabiana, "Los censos y los pueblos indígenas en América Latina: Una metodología Regional", paper presented at the conference "Pueblos Indígenas y afrodescendientes de América Latina y Caribe: relevancia y pertinencia de la información sociodemográfica para políticas y programas", *Comisión Económica para América Latina* – CEPAL, Santiago de Chile, 27-29 April 2005.

Scott James C., *Weapons of the Weak: Everyday Forms of Peasant Resistance*, Yale University Press, New Haven (CT, USA), 1985.

Segovia Carolina and Gamboa Ricardo, "Chile: El Año en que Salimos a la Calle", 32(1) *Revista de Ciencia Política (Santiago SciELO)* 2012, pp.65-85.

Sepúlveda Navarro Rosa and Millaqueo Millapán Adelmo, "Informe Diagnóstico y de Intervención Comunidad Cacique José Guiñón Ercilla", Programa Salud Mapuche, Servicio Salud Araucanía Norte, 2004.

Silva G.Osvaldo, *Atlas de Historia de Chile*, Editorial Universitaria, Santiago de Chile, 1983.

Silva Neriz Hernando, "Chile", in International Work Group for Indigenous Affairs (IWGIA), *The Indigenous World 2013*, IWGIA, Copenhagen, 2013, pp.188-196.

Silvel Elías, "Guatemala", in International Work Group for Indigenous Affairs, *The Indigenous World 2014*, IWGIA, Copenhagen 2014, pp.76-84.

Skurbaty Zelin A., "Introduction", in Zelin A. Skurbaty (ed.), *Beyond a One-Dimensional State: An Emerging Right to Autonomy?,* Martinus Nijhoff Publishers, Leiden, Boston, 2005, pp.xxxi–lviii.

Soluri John, "Chile's Blue Revolution, Commodity Diseases, and the Problem of Sustainability", 46 *Latin America Research Review* 2011, pp.55-81.

Spiry Emmanuel, "From 'Self-Determination' to a Right to 'Self-Development' for Indigenous Groups", 38 *German Yearbook of International Law*, 1995, pp.129-286.

Stavenhagen Rodolfo, "Indigenous Peoples and the State in Latin America: An Ongoing Debate", in Rachel Sieder (ed.), *Multiculturalism in Latin America. Indigenous Rights, Diversity and Democracy*, Palgrave Macmillan, New York, 2002, pp.24-43.

Ströbele-Gregor Juliana, "Autoridad, poder y liderazgo: Observaciones conceptuales acerca de la práctica de representación de los pueblos indígenas", in Sabine Speiser (ed.), *¿Quién habla por quién? Representatividad y legitimidad de organizaciones y representantes indígenas. Un debate abierto*, Unidad Coordinadora de Pueblos Indígenas en América Latina y el Caribe (KIVLAK) and Deutsche Gesellschaft für Internationale Zusammenarbeiten (GIZ), Quito, 2013, pp.73-89.

Suksi Markku, *Sub-State Governance through Territorial Autonomy*, Springer, Heidelberg, Dordrecht, 2011.

Summers James, "The Internal and external aspects of self-determination reconsidered", in Duncan French (ed.), *Statehood and Self-Determination. Reconciling Tradition and Modernity in International Law*, Cambridge University Press, Cambridge, New York, 2013, pp.229-249.

Summers James, "The Right of Self-Determination and Nationalism in International Law", 12 *International Journal on Minority and Group Rights* 2005, pp.325-354.

Swepston Lee, "Development of the ILO Conventions", in Roxanne Dunbar-Ortiz et al. (eds.), *Indigenous Peoples' Rights in International Law: Emergence and application. Book in Honor of Asbjørn Eide at Eighty*, Gáldu and IWGIA, Kautokeino, Copenhagen, Gáldu Čála serie No.2/2015, 2015, pp.226-249.

Taiaiake Alfred, "From Sovereignty to Freedom: Towards An Indigenous Political Discourse", 3 *Indigenous Affairs* 2001, pp.22-34.

Tamburini Leonardo, "Bolivia (2009)", in International Work Group for Indigenous Affairs (IWGIA), *The Indigenous World 2009*, IWGIA, Copenhagen, 2009, pp.174-183.

Tamburini Leonardo, "Bolivia (2010)", in International Work Group for Indigenous Affairs, *The Indigenous World 2010*, IWGIA, Copenhagen, 2010, 195–206.

Tamburini Leonardo, "Bolivia (2011)", in International Work Group for Indigenous Affairs, *El mundo indígena 2011*, IWGIA, Copenhagen, 2011, pp.174-182.

Tamburini Leonardo, "Bolivia (2012)", in International Work Group for Indigenous Affairs (IWGIA), *The Indigenous World 2012*, IWGIA, Copenhagen, 2012, pp.166-174.

Tamburini Leonardo, "Bolivia (2013)", in International Work Group for Indigenous Affairs (IWGIA), *The Indigenous World 2013*, IWGIA, Copenhagen, 2013, pp.150-159.

Tamburini Leonardo, "Bolivia (2014)", in International Work Group for Indigenous Affairs (IWGIA), *The Indigenous World 2014*, IWGIA, Copenhagen, 2014, pp.167-175.

Tedesco Laura and Diamint Rut, "Latin America Democracy. What to do with the Leaders?", 33(1) *Bulletin of Latin American Research* 2014, pp.31-45.

Thomas Franck, "Postmodern Tribalism and the Right to Secession," in Christine Brölmann, R. Lefeber, and Marjoleine Zieck (eds.), *Peoples and Minorities in International Law*, Dordrecht: Martinus Nijhoff, 1993, pp.3-27.

Thornberry Patrick, "Images of Autonomy and Individual and Collective Rights in International Instruments on the Rights of Minorities", in Markko Suksi (ed.), *Autonomy: Applications and Implications*, The Hague, Cambridge, Dordrecht, Martinus Nijhoff Publishers, 1998, pp.97-124.

Thornberry Patrick, "Self-Determination and Indigenous Peoples: Objections and Responses", in Pekka Aikio and Martin Scheinin (eds.), *Operationalizing the Rights of Indigenous Peoples to Self-Determination*, Institute for Human Rights, Åbo Akademi University, Saarijärvi, 2000, pp.39-64.

Thornberry Patrick, "The Democratic or Internal Aspect of Self-Determination with some remarks on federalism", in Christian Tomuschat (ed.), *Modern Law of Self-Determination*, Dordrecht, Nijhoff, 1993, pp.101-138.

Thornberry Patrick, *Indigenous Peoples and Human Rights*, Manchester University Press, Manchester 2002.

Thürer Daniel and Burri Thomas, "Self-Determination", in *Max Planck Encyclopedia of Public International Law*, 2008, Oxford Public International Law, at http://opil.ouplaw.com/home/epil.

Toledo Llancaqueo Victor, "Presupuesto del Sector Público y Políticas Indígenas. Chile 1994- 2008", *Documentos de Politicas Públicas y Derechos Indígenas – Informe N° 36*, Santiago de Chile, 28 October 2007.

Toledo Llancaqueo Victor, *Pueblo Mapuche. Derechos Colectivos y Territorios: Desafíos para la Sustentabilidad Democratica*, Programa Chile Sustentable, LOM Ediciones, Santiago de Chile, 2006.

Tomaselli Alexandra and Granholm Petra, "The Frustrations of the Right to Political Participation of Minorities: Practical Limitations in the Case of the Nordic Sámi and the Roma", 8 *European Yearbook of Minority Issues* 2009, 2011, pp.149-185.

Tomaselli Alexandra, "(Peasant Farmer Native) Indigenous Autonomies in Bolivia: Developments and Shortcomings (2009-2012)", in Marc Becker (ed.), *Cases of Exclusion and Mobilization of Race and Ethnicities in Latin America*, Cambridge Scholars Publishing, Newcastle upon Tyne, 2013, pp.130-173.

Tomaselli Alexandra, "*Autonomía Indígena Originaria Campesina* in Bolivia: Realizing the indigenous autonomy?", 1 *European Diversity and Autonomy Papers* (EDAP) 2012, at http://www.eurac.edu/edap.

Tomaselli Alexandra, "II.5 Indigenous peoples. Should they be defined?", in VV.AA., "Material for specialized media", report of the EURASIA-Net project, EURAC, Bolzano/Bozen, 2008.

Tomaselli Alexandra, "Indios, Indigenous, Native People: not just a question of terminology", Special topic online Indigenous peoples in the Americas, EURAC website, Bolzano/Bozen, 31 January 2008.

Tomaselli Alexandra, "Natural resources" claims, land conflicts and self-empowerment of indigenous movements in the *Cono Sur*. The case of the Mapuche People in Chile", 19(2) *International Journal of Minority and Group Rights* 2012, pp.153-174.

Tomuschat Christian, "Self-Determination in a Post-Colonial World", in Christian Tomuschat (ed.), *Modern Law of Self-Determination*, Dordrecht, Nijhoff, 1993, pp.1-20.

Tomuschat Christian, *Human Rights. Between Idealism and Realism*, Oxford University Press, Oxford, New York, 2003.

Tramontana Enzamaria, "The Contribution of the Inter-American Human Rights Bodies to Evolving International Law on Indigenous Rights over Land and Natural Resourses", 17 *International Journal on Minority and Group Rights* 2010, pp.241-263.

Tricot Víctor, "Chile: Pasando de la Galería a la Cancha. Partido Político Mapuche Wallmapuwen: Un Instrumento Descolonizador hacia la Autodeterminación", in Salvador Martí i Puig, Claire Wright, José Aylwin and Nancy Yáñez, (eds.), *Entre el desarrollo y el buen vivir. Recursos naturales y conflictos en los territorios indígenas*, Libros de la Catarata, Madrid, 2013, pp.293-321.

Trifunovska Snežana, "One Theme in Two Variations – Self Determination for Minorities And Indigenous Peoples", 5 *International Journal on Minority and Group Rights*, 1997, pp.175-197.

Trifunovska Snežana, "The Impact of the 'Kosovo Precedent' on Self-Determination Struggles", in James Summers (ed.), *Kosovo: A Precedent?* , Martinus Nijhoff, Leiden, Boston, 2011, pp. 375-393.

Ulloa Astrid, "Colombia: Autonomías indígenas en ejercicio. Los retos de su consolidación", in Miguel González, Araceli Burguete Cal y Mayor and Pablo Ortiz-T. (eds.), *La autonomía a debate: Autogobierno indígena y Estado plurinacional en América Latina*, FLACSO, GTZ, Ministerio Federal de Cooperación Económica y Desarrollo, IWGIA, CIESAS, Universidad Intercultural de Chiapas, Quito, 2010, pp.149-176.

Urbina Carrasco Juncos. Maria Ximena, *La Frontera de Arriba en Chile Colonial, Interacción hispano-indígena en el territorio entre Valdivia y Chiloé e imaginario de sus bordes geográficos, 1600-1800*, Pontificia Universidad Católica de Valparaíso, Valparaíso, Santiago de Chile, 2009.

Uscátegui Gómez Luis Gonzalo (ed.) *El derecho a la consulta previa en América Latina. Del reconocimiento formal a la exigibilidad de los derechos de los pueblos indígenas*, ILSA-Instituto Latinoamericano de Servicios Legales Alternativos, Bogotà, 2009.

Vadillo Alcides, "Constitución Política del Estado y pueblos indígenas: Bolivia, país de mayoría indígena", in Magdalena Gomez (ed.), *Derecho Indígena. Seminario Internacional*, Instituto Nacional Indigenista, Mexico City, 1997, pp.331-355.

Van den Driest Simone, *Remedial Secession. A Right to External Self-Determination as a Remedy to Serious Injustices?*, Intersentia, Cambridge, Mortsel, 2013.

Van Lee Cott Donna, "De los movimientos a los partidos: retos para los movimientos de los pueblos indígenas", in Salvador Martí i Puig (ed.), *Pueblos Indígenas y Política en América Latina: El reconocimiento de sus derechos y el impacto de sus demandas a inicios del siglo XXI*, Fundació CIDOB, Barcelona, 2007, pp.103-125.

Van Lee Cott Donna, *From Movements to Parties in Latin America. The Evolution of Ethnic Politics*, Cambridge University Press, Cambridge, New York, 2005.

Van Lee Cott Donna, *The Friendly Liquidation of the Past: the politics of diversity in Latin America*, University of Pittsburgh Press, Pittsburgh, 2000.

Vel Cynthia, "Respecting the "Guardians of Nature: Chile's violations of the Diaguita indigenous peoples' environmental and human rights and the need to enforce obligations to obtain Free, Prior, and Informed Consent", 2(2) *American Indian Law Journal* 2014, pp.641-680.

Vellinga Menno, "Globalization and Neoliberalism: Economy and Society in Latin America", 32(2) *Iberoamericana. Nordic Journal of Latin American and Carrebean Studies* 2002, pp.25-43.

Vergara Jorge Iván, Gundermann Hans and Foerster Rolf, "Legalidad y legitimidad: ley indígena, Estado chileno y pueblos originarios (1989-2004)", 24(71) *Estudios Sociológicos* 2006, pp.331-361.

Verstichel Annelie, *Participation, Representation and Identity*, Intersetia, Antwerp, Oxford, Portland, 2009.

Verstichel Annelies, "Recent Developments in the UN Human Rights Committee's approach to Minorities, with a Focus on Effective Participation", 12 *International Journal on Minority and Group Rights* 2005, pp.25-41.

Vidmar Jure, "Remedial Secession in International Law: Theory and (Lack of) Practice," 6(1) *St Antony's International Review* 2010, pp. 37-56.

Vidmar Jure, "The Right of Self-Determination and Multiparty Democracy: Two Sides of the Same Coin?", 10 *Human Rights Law Review* 2010, pp.239-268.

Villarroel Sandoval Carlos, "La Aplicación en Bolivia del Convenio 169 sobre los Pueblos Indígenas y Tribales en Países Independientes de la OIT", in José Emilio Rolando Ordóñez Cifuentes (ed.), *Análisis Interdisciplinario del Convenio 169 de la OIT. IX Jornadas Lascasianas*, Mexico City, 2000, pp.189-207.

Vinopal Kelly, *Researching Public International Law*, American Society of International Law, 2013.

Walker Charles F., *The Tupac Amaru Rebellion*, Harvard University Press, Cambridge (MA, USA), London, 2014.

Walsh Niamh, "Minority Self-Government in Hungary: Legislation and Practice", 2 *Journal on Ethnopolitics and Minority Issues in Europe* 2000, pp.1-73.

Walter Christian, Von Ungern-Sternberg Antje, and Abushov Kavus (eds.), *Self-Determination and Secession in International Law*, Oxford University Press, Oxford, New York, 2014.

Warren Kay B. and Jackson Jean E., *Indigenous Movements, Self-Representation and the State in Latin America*, University of Texas Press, Austin (TX, USA), 2002.

Watson Irene and Venne Sharon, "Talking up Indigenous Peoples' original intent in a space dominated by state interventions", in Elvira Pulitano (ed.), *Indigenous Rights in the Age of the UN Declaration*, Cambridge University Press, Cambridge, 2012, pp.87-109.

Watts Sir Arthur, "Appendix B. The Liechtenstein Draft Convention on Self-Determination Through Self-Administration", in Wolfgang Danspeckgruber (ed.), *The Self-Determination of Peoples. Community, Nation and State in an Interdependent World*, Lynne Rienner Publishers in association with the Liechtenstein Institute on Self-Determination, Princeton University, Boulder, London, 2002, pp.365-392.

Webb Andrew and Radcliff Sarah, "Mapuche Demands during Educational Reform, the Penguin Revolution and the Chilean Winter of Discontent", 13(3) *Studies in Ethnicity and Nationalism* 2013, pp.319-341.

Welhengama Gnanapala, *Minorities' Claims: From Autonomy to Secession. International Law and State Practice*, Aldershot, Burlington, 2000.

Weller Marc, "Article 15", in Marc Weller (ed.), *The Rights of Minorities. A Commentary on the European Framework Convention for the protection of National Minorities*, Oxford, New York, Oxford University Press, 2005.

Weller Marc, "The Self-Determination Trap", 4(1) *Ethnopolitics* 2005, pp.3-28.

Weller Marc, "Why the Legal Rules on Self-Determination Do Not Resolve Self-Determination Disputes", in Marc Weller and Barbara Metzger (eds.), *Settling Self-Determination Disputes. Complex Power-Sharing in Theory and in Practice*, Martinus Nijhoff, Leiden, Boston, 2008, pp.17-45.

Weller Marc, "Working paper Towards a General Comment on Self-Determination and Autonomy", UN Doc. E/CN.4/Sub.2/AC.5/2005/WP.5, 25 May 2005.

Weller Marc, *Escaping the Self-Determination Trap*, Martinus Nijhoff Publishers, Leiden, 2008.

Wengler W., "Le droit à la libre disposition des peuples comme principe de droit international", 10 *Revue hellénique de droit international*, 1957.

West Ronald, "The American Companion Report", in Mark D. Dole and Ronald West, *The Right of Self-Determination of Peoples and its Application to Indigenous Peoples in the USA*, Nomos, Baden-Baden, 2000, pp.67-111.

Whelan Anthony, "Wilsonian Self-Determination and the Versailles Settlement", 43 *International and Comparative Law Quarterly* 1994, pp.99-115.

Wiessner Siegfried, "Indigenous Sovereignty: A Reassessment in Light of the UN Declaration on the Rights of Indigenous Peoples", 41 *Vanderbilt Journal of Transnational Law* 2008, pp.1141-1176.

Willemsen-Diaz Augusto, "How Indigenous Peoples' Rights Reached the UN", in Claire Charters and Rodolfo Stavenhagen (eds.), *Making the Declaration Work. The United Nations Declaration on the Rights of Indigenous Peoples*, International Work Group for Indigenous Affairs (IWGIA), Doc. No.127, Copenhagen, 2009, pp.16-31.

Wolff Stefan and Peen Rodt Annemarie, "Self-Determination After Kosovo", 65(5) *Europe-Asia Studies* 2013, pp.799-822.
Wright Claire, "Estado, Justicia y ciudadanía en el constitucionalismo boliviano", 3(2) *Cuestiones Jurídicas* 2009, pp.55-72.
Wright Claire, "Executives and Emergencies: Presidential Decrees of Exception in Bolivia, Ecuador, and Peru", 60 *Documentos de Trabajo Instituto de Estudios Latinoamericanos IELAT* 2014.
Xanthaki Alexandra and O'Sullivan Dominic, "Indigenous Participation in Elective Bodies: The Maori in New Zealand", 16(2) *International Journal on Minority and Group Rights* 2009, pp.181-207.
Xanthaki Alexandra, "The Right to Self-Determination: Meaning and Scope", in Ghanea Nazila and Xanthaki Alexandra (eds.), *Minorities, Peoples and Self-Determination*, Brill, 2005, pp.15-33.
Xanthaki Alexandra, *Indigenous Rights and United Nations Standards. Self-Determination, Culture and Land*, Cambridge University Press, Cambridge, 2007.
Yashar Deborah J., *Contesting Citizenship in Latin America. The Rise of Indigenous Movements and the Postliberal Challenge*, Cambridge University Press, Cambridge, New York, 2005.
Yrigoyen Fajardo Raquel Z., "El Derecho a la Libre Determinación del Desarrollo. Participación, Consulta y Consentimiento", in Marco Aparicio Wilhelmi (ed.), *Los Derechos de los Pueblos Indígenas a los Recursos Naturales y al Territorio. Conflicto y Desafíos en América Latina*, Icaria Editorial, Barcelona, 2011, pp.103-146.
Zarza Rondón Gloria de los Ángeles, "El largo camino hacia la ciudadanía: la población indígena en la Constitución de 1812", in AA.VV., *Actas XIV Encuentro de los Latinoamericanistas de España, Congreso Internacional, 1810-2010: 200 años de Iberoamérica*, Santiago de Compostela 15-18 September 2010, pp.2639-2650.
Žižek Slavoj, "Trouble in Paradise", 35(14) *London Review of Books* 18 July 2013, pp.11-12.
Zunes Stephen and Mundy Jacob, *Western Sahara: War, Nationalism and Conflict Irresolution*, Syracuse University Press, Syracuse, 2010.

Interviews

Interview with Justino Avendaño Redeno, drafter of the Autonomy Law in Bolivia, on 26 November 2010 [on file with author].
Interview with Pedro Marimán, one of the founding members of the recently created Mapuche Party *Wallmapuwen*, on 9 December 2010 [on file with author].

UN Resolutions and Documents

Capotorti Francesco, Special Rapporteur of the Sub-Commission on Prevention of Discrimination and Protection of Minorities, "Study on the Rights of Persons Belonging to Ethnic, Religious, and Linguistic Minorities", UN Doc. E/CN.4/Sub.2/384/Rev.1, New York, 1979.

Commission on Human Rights, "Human rights and indigenous issues", Resolution No.2001/57, UN Doc. E/CN.4/RES/2001/57, 24 April 2001.

Commission on Human Rights, "Human rights and indigenous issues", Resolution No.2004/62, UN Doc. E/CN.4/RES/2004/62, 21 April 2004.

Commission on Human Rights, "Report of the Meeting of Experts to Review the Experience of Countries in the Operation of Schemes of Internal Self-Government for Indigenous Peoples", Nuuk (Greenland), 24-28 September 1991, UN Doc. E/CN.4/1992/42, 25 November 1991.

Commission on Human Rights, "Report of the Working Group established in accordance with Commission on Human Rights resolution 1995/32 of 3 March 1995", UN Doc. E/CN.4/1996/84, 4 January 1996.

Commission on Human Rights, "Report of the working group established in accordance with Commission on Human Rights resolution 1995/32 of 3 March 1995 on its eleventh session", 22 March 2006, UN Doc. E/CN.4/2006/79, Annex I, "Revised Chairman's summary and proposal on the draft Declaration".

Commission on Human Rights, "Report of the Working Group established in accordance with Commission on Human Rights Resolution 1995/32", UN Doc. E/CN.4/2001/85, 6 February 2001,

Commission on Human Rights, "Report of the working group established in accordance with Commission on Human Rights resolution 1995/32", E/CN.4/2001/85, 6 February 2001.

Commission on Human Rights, Sub-Commission on Prevention of Discrimination and Protection of Minorities, Working Group on Indigenous Populations, "Report of the Tribal Summit on the Draft Declaration on the Rights of Indigenous Peoples", UN Doc. E/CN.4/Sub.2/AC.4/1992/3/Add.1, 1992.

Commission on Human Rights, Sub-Commission on Prevention of Discrimination and Protection of Minorities, Working Group on Indigenous Populations, "Report on the Workshop on Indigenous Peoples, Private Sector Natural Resource, Energy and Mining Companies and Human Rights", UN Doc. E/CN.4/Sub.2/AC.4/2002/3, 17 June 2002.

Commission on Human Rights, Sub-Commission on Prevention of Discrimination and Protection of Minorities, Working Group on Indigenous Populations, "Standard-Setting Activities: Evolution of Standards Concerning the Rights of Indigenous Populations. Note by the Secretary-General. Information received from non-governmental organizations. Report of the Tribal Summit on the Draft Declaration on the Rights of Indigenous Peoples, Denver, 16-18 June 1992 organized by the International Organization of Indigenous Resource Development", UN Doc. E/CN.4/Sub.2/AC. 4/1992/3/Add.1, 1 July 1992.

Commission on Human Rights, Sub-Commission on Prevention of Discrimination and Protection of Minorities, "Draft declaration on the rights of indigenous peoples. Revised working paper submitted by the Chairperson-Rapporteur, Ms. Erica-Irene Daes, pursuant to Sub-Commission resolution 1992/33 and Commission on Human Rights resolution", UN Doc. 1993/31E/CN.4/Sub.2/1993/26, 8 June 1993.

Commission on Human Rights, Sub-Commission on Prevention of Discrimination and Protection of Minorities, "Explanatory note concerning the draft declaration on the rights of indigenous peoples", by Erica-Irene A. Daes, UN Doc. E/CN.4/Sub.2/1993/26/Add.1, 19 July 1993.

Commission on Human Rights, Sub-Commission on Prevention of Discrimination and Protection of Minorities, "Conclusions, proposals and recommendations", Chapters XXI-XXII of the "Study of the Problem of Discrimination against Indigenous Populations", UN Doc. E/CN.4 Sub.2/1983/21/Add.8, 30 September 1983.

Commission on Human Rights, Sub-Commission on Prevention of Discrimination and Protection of Minorities, "Study of the Problem of Discrimination against Indigenous Populations", Chapter 18, "Political Rights", UN Doc. E/CN.4 Sub.2 /1983/21/Add.6, 24 May 1984.

Commission on Human Rights, Sub-Commission on Prevention of Discrimination and Protection of Minorities, "Study of the Problem of Discrimination against Indigenous Populations", UN Doc. E/CN.4 Sub.2/1983/21/Add.8, 30 September 1983.

Committee on Economic, Social and Cultural Rights, "Concluding observations of the Committee on Economic, Social and Cultural Rights: Russian Federation", UN Doc. E/C.12/1/Add.94, 12 December 2003.

Committee on Economic, Social and Cultural Rights, "Concluding observations of the Committee on Economic, Social and Cultural Rights: Philippines", UN Doc. E/C.12/PHL/CO/4, 1 December 2008.

Committee on Economic, Social and Cultural Rights, "Concluding observations of the Committee on Economic, Social and Cultural Rights: Sweden", UN Doc. E/C.12/SWE/CO/5, 1 December 2008.

Committee on Economic, Social and Cultural Rights, "Concluding observations of the Committee on Economic, Social and Cultural Rights: Brazil", UN Doc. E/C.12/BRA/CO/2, 12 June 2009.

Committee on Economic, Social and Cultural Rights, "Concluding observations of the Committee on Economic, Social and Cultural Rights: Cambodia", UN Doc. E/C.12/KHM/CO/1, 12 June 2009.

Committee on Economic, Social and Cultural Rights, "Concluding observations of the Committee on Economic, Social and Cultural Rights: Democratic Republic of Congo", UN Doc. E/C.12/COD/CO/4, 16 December 2009.

Committee on Economic, Social and Cultural Rights, "Concluding observations of the Committee on Economic, Social and Cultural Rights: Argentina", UN Doc. E/C.12/ARG/CO/3, 14 December 2011.

Committee on Economic, Social and Cultural Rights, "Concluding observations of the Committee on Economic, Social and Cultural Rights: New Zealand", UN Doc. E/C.12/NZL/CO/3, 31 May 2012.

Committee on Economic, Social and Cultural Rights, General comment No. 21, "Right of everyone to take part in cultural life (art. 15, para. 1 (a), of the International Covenant on Economic, Social and Cultural Rights)", UN Doc. E/C.12/GC/21, 21 December 2009.

Committee on the Elimination of Racial Discrimination (CERD), General Recommendation No.23, "Indigenous Peoples", UN Doc. A/52/18, annex V, 18 August 1997.

Committee on the Elimination of Racial Discrimination, General Recommendation 21, "The right to self-determination", UN Doc. A/51/18, 1996.

Cristescu Aureliu, Special Rapporteur of the Sub-Commission on the Prevention of Discrimination and Protection of Minorities of the Commission on Human Rights, *The Right to Self-Determination. Historical and Current Development in the basis of the United Nations Instruments*, United Nations, New York, 1981.

Daes Erica-Irene, "Standard-Setting Activities: Evolution of Standards Concerning the Rights of Indigenous People - New Developments and General Discussion of Future Action", UN Doc. E/CN.4/Sub.2/AC.4/1995/3, 21 June 1995.

Daes Erica-Irene, "The UN Declaration on the Rights of Indigenous Peoples: Background and Appraisal", p.18, that reports the UN Economic and Social Council, Sub-Commission on Prevention of Discrimination and Protection of Minorities, "Report of the Working Group on Indigenous Populations on its fourth session", 27 August 1985, UN Doc. E/CN.4/Sub.2/1985/22.

De Varennes Fernand, "Towards Effective Political Participation and Representation of Minorities", UN Doc. E/CN.4/Sub.2/AC.5/1998/WP.4, 1 May 1998.

Department of Economic and Social Affairs, *State of the World's Indigenous Peoples*, United Nations, New York, 2009.

Economic and Social Council, "Establishment of a Permanent Forum on Indigenous Issues", Resolution No.2000/22, UN Doc. E/RES/2000/22 (2000), 28 July 2000.

Economic and Social Council, "Establishment of a working group of the Commission on Human Rights to elaborate a draft declaration in accordance with paragraph 5 of General Assembly resolution 49/214", Resolution No. 1995/32, UN Doc. E/RES/1995/32, 25 July 1995.

Economic and Social Council, "Establishment of a Working group of the Commission on Human Rights to elaborate a draft declaration in accordance with paragraph 5 of General Assembly resolution 49/214", Resolution No. 1995/32, UN Doc. E/RES/1995/32, 25 July 1995.

Economic and Social Council, "Establishment of the Working Group on Indigenous Populations", Resolution No.1982/34, UN Doc. E/RES/1982/34, 28th plenary meeting of the UN Economic and Social Council, 7 May 1982.

Economic and Social Council, Appointment of José R. Martínez Cobo Special Rapporteur on the situation of human rights and fundamental freedoms of indigenous peoples to prepare a "Study on the Problem of Discrimination Against Indigenous Populations", Resolution No.1589(L), 21 May 1971.

Economic and Social Council, Sub-Commission on Prevention of Discrimination and Protection of Minorities, "A working paper by Ms. Erica-Irene A. Daes containing a set of draft preambular paragraphs and principles for insertion into a universal declaration of indigenous rights", UN Doc. E/CN.4/Sub.2/1988/25, 21 June 1988.

Economic and Social Council, Sub-Commission on Prevention of Discrimination and Protection of Minorities, "Report of the Working Group on Indigenous Populations on its fourth session", UN Doc. E/CN.4/Sub.2/1985/22, 27 August 1985.

Economic and Social Council, Sub-Commission on Prevention of Discrimination and Protection of Minorities, "Report of the Working Group on Indigenous Populations on its fourth session", UN Doc. E/CN.4/Sub.2/1987/22, 24 August 1987.

Economic and Social Council, Sub-Commission on Prevention of Discrimination and Protection of Minorities, "Report of the Working Group on Indigenous Populations on its ninth session", UN Doc. E/CN.4/Sub.2/1991/40, 15 August 1991.

Economic and Social Council, Sub-Commission on Prevention of Discrimination and Protection of Minorities, "Report of the Working Group on Indigenous Populations on its tenth session", UN Doc. E/CN.4/Sub.2/1992/33, 20 August 1992.

Economic and Social Council, Sub-Commission on Prevention of Discrimination and Protection of Minorities, "Report of the Working Group on Indigenous Populations on its fourth session", UN Doc. E/CN.4/Sub.2/1993/29, 23 August 1993.

European Centre for Minority Issues, "Towards Effective Participation of Minorities", UN Doc. E/CN.4/Sub.2/AC.5/1999/WP.4, 1999.

Expert Mechanism on the Rights of Indigenous Peoples, "Final study on indigenous peoples and the right to participate in decision-making", UN Doc. A/HRC/EMRIP/2011/2, 26 May 2011.

Expert Mechanism on the Rights of Indigenous Peoples, "Progress report on the study on indigenous peoples and the right to participate in decision-making", UN Doc. A/HRC/EMRIP/2010/2, 17 May 2010.

General Assembly and Economic and Social Council, "Progress made in the implementation of the outcome document of the high-level plenary meeting of the General Assembly known as the World Conference on Indigenous Peoples, Report of the Secretary-General", UN Doc. A/70/84–E/2015/76, 15 May 2015.

General Assembly, "Declaration on Principles of International Law Friendly Relations and Co-operation among States in Accordance with the Charter of the United Nations", Resolution No.2625(XXV), 24 October 1970.

General Assembly, "Declaration on the granting of independence to colonial countries", Resolution No.1514(XV), UN Doc. A/RES/25/2625, 14 December 1960.

General Assembly, "Draft Programme of Action for the Second International Decade of the World's Indigenous People", UN Doc. A/60/270, 18 August 2005.

General Assembly, "Draft resolution submitted by the President of General Assembly. Outcome document of the high-level plenary meeting of the General Assembly known as the World Conference on Indigenous Peoples", UN Doc. A/69/L.1, 15 September 2014.

General Assembly, "Importance of the universal realization of the right of peoples to self-determination and of the speedy granting of independence to colonial countries and peoples for the effective guarantee and observance of human rights", UN Doc. A/RES/2787(XXVI), 1971.

General Assembly, "Importance of the universal realization of the right of peoples to self-determination and of the speedy granting of independence to colonial countries and peoples for the effective guarantee and observance of human rights", UN Doc. A/RES/2955(XXVII), 1972.

General Assembly, "Importance of the universal realization of the right of peoples to self-determination and of the speedy granting of independence to colonial countries and peoples for the effective guarantee and observance of human rights", UN Doc. A/RES/3070(XXVIII), 1973.

General Assembly, "Importance of the universal realization of the right of peoples to self-determination and of the speedy granting of independence to colonial countries and peoples for the effective guarantee and observance of human rights", 1974 UN Doc. A/RES/3246(XXIX).

General Assembly, "Importance of the universal realization of the right of peoples to self-determination and of the speedy granting of independence to colonial countries and peoples for the effective guarantee and observance of human rights", UN Doc. A/RES/3382(XXX), 1975.

General Assembly, "Indigenous issues", Resolution No. 65/198, UN Doc. A/RES/65/198, 3 March 2011.

General Assembly, "International Decade of the World's Indigenous People", Resolution No.48/163, UN Doc. A/RES/48/163 (1993), 21 December 1993.

General Assembly, "Letter dated 10 September 2013 from the Permanent Representatives of the Plurinational State of Bolivia, Denmark, Finland, Guatemala, Mexico, New Zealand, Nicaragua, Norway and Peru to the United Nations addressed to the Secretary-General", UN Doc. A/67/994, 13 September 2013.

General Assembly, "Outcome document of the high-level plenary meeting of the General Assembly known as the World Conference on Indigenous Peoples", 22 September 2014, UN Doc. A/RES/69/2 based on the "Draft resolution submitted by the President of General Assembly", UN Doc. A/69/L.1, 15 September 2014.

General Assembly, "Outcome document of the high-level plenary meeting of the General Assembly known as the World Conference on Indigenous Peoples", UN Doc. A/RES/69/2, 22 September 2014.

General Assembly, "Principles which should guide Members in determining whether or not an obligation exists to transmit the information called for under Article 73 of the Charter", Resolution No.1541(XV), 15 December 1960.

General Assembly, "Report of the Third Committee", UN Doc. A/61/448, 6 December 2006.

General Assembly, "Report on Implementing the Responsibility to Protect", UN Doc. A/63/677, 12 January 2009.

General Assembly, "Request for the inclusion of an item in the provisional agenda of the forty-eight session. Effective realization of the Right to Self-Determination through Autonomy", UN Doc. A/48/147/Add.1, 29 September 1993.

General Assembly, "Resolution 61/295. United Nations Declaration on the Rights of Indigenous Peoples", UN Doc. A/RES/61/295, 13 September 2007.

General Assembly, "Resolution adopted by the General Assembly on 16 September 2005. 60/1. 2005 World Summit Outcome", UN Doc. A/RES/60/1, 24 October 2005.

General Assembly, "Right of Peoples to Self-Determination. Letter dated 28 September 1995 from the Permanent Representative of Liechtenstein to the United Nations addressed to the Secretary General", UN Doc. A/50/492, 2 October 1995.

General Assembly, "Rights of indigenous peoples", Resolution No. 68/149, UN Doc. A/RES/68/149, 12 February 2014.

General Assembly, "Second International Decade of the World's Indigenous People", Resolution No.59/174, UN Doc. A/RES/59/174, 20 December 2004.

General Assembly, "The importance of the universal realization of the right of peoples to self-determination and of the speedy granting of independence to colonial countries and peoples for the effective guarantee and observance of human rights", Resolution No.2649, UN Doc. A/RES/2649(XXV) 1970.

General Assembly, "United Nations Voluntary Fund for Indigenous Populations", Resolution No.40/131, UN Doc. A/RES/40/131, 13 December 1985.

General Assembly, Declaration on the Right to Development, 97th plenary meeting, UN Doc. A/RES/41/128, 4 December 1986.

General Assembly, Report of the Human Rights Council, "Working group of the Commission on Human Rights to elaborate a draft declaration in accordance with paragraph 5 of General Assembly resolution 49/214 of 23 December 1994", UN Doc. A/C.3/61/L.18/Rev.1, 20 November 2006.

General Assembly, Second International Decade of the World's Indigenous People, UN Doc. A/RES/59/174, 20 December 2004.

Gros Espiell Héctor, Special Rapporteur of the Sub-Commission on the Prevention of Discrimination and Protection of Minorities of the Commission on Human Rights, *The Right to Self-Determination. Implementation of the UN Resolutions*, United Nations, New York, 1980.

Human Rights Committee, "Concluding observations of the Human Rights Committee: Chile", UN Doc. CCPR/C/CHL/CO/5, 18 May 2007.

Human Rights Committee, "Concluding observations of the Human Rights Committee: Australia", UN Doc. CCPR/CO/69/AUS, 28 July 2000.

Human Rights Committee, "Concluding observations of the Human Rights Committee: Brazil", UN Doc. CCPR/C/BRA/CO/2, 1 December 2005,.

Human Rights Committee, "Concluding observations of the Human Rights Committee: Canada", UN Doc. CCPR/C/79/Add.105, 7 April 1999.

Human Rights Committee, "Concluding observations of the Human Rights Committee: Canada", UN Doc. CCPR/C/CAN/CO/5, 20 April 2006.

Human Rights Committee, "Concluding observations of the Human Rights Committee: Chile", UN Doc. CCPR/C/CHL/CO/5, 18 May 2007.

Human Rights Committee, "Concluding observations of the Human Rights Committee: Mexico", UN Doc. CCPR/C/79/Add.109, 27 July 1999.

Human Rights Committee, "Concluding observations of the Human Rights Committee: Norway", UN Doc. CCPR/C/79/Add.112, 1 November 1999.

Human Rights Committee, "Concluding observations of the Human Rights Committee: Panama", UN Doc. CCPR/C/PAN/CO/3, 17 April 2008.

Human Rights Committee, "Concluding observations of the Human Rights Committee: Peru", UN Doc. CCPR/CO/70/PE, 15 November 2000.

Human Rights Committee, "Concluding observations of the Human Rights Committee: Philippines", UN Doc. CCPR/CO/79/PHL, 1 December 2003.

Human Rights Committee, "Concluding observations of the Human Rights Committee: Sweden", UN Doc. CCPR/CO/74/SWE, 24 April 2002.

Human Rights Committee, "Concluding observations of the Human Rights Committee: United States", UN Doc. CCPR/C/USA/CO/3, 25 September 2006.

Human Rights Committee, "Consideration of Reports submitted by States Parties under article 40 of the Covenant. International Covenant on Civil and Political Rights. Comments of the Human Rights Committee. Mexico", UN Doc. CCPR/C/79/Add.50, 18 April 1994.

Human Rights Committee, "Consideration of Reports submitted by States Parties under article 40 of the Covenant. International Covenant on Civil and Political Rights.

Comments of the Human Rights Committee. United States of America", UN Doc. CCPR/C/79/Add.50, 7 April 1995.

Human Rights Committee, General Comment No. 25 "The right to participate in public affairs, voting rights and the right of equal access to public service (Art. 25)", UN Doc. CCPR/C/21/Rev.1/Add.7, 12 July 1996.

Human Rights Committee, General Comment No.12, "Article 1 (The Right to self-determination of peoples"), UN Doc. HRI/GEN/1/Rev.9 (Vol. I), 13 March 1984.

Human Rights Committee, General Comment No.23, "The rights of minorities (Art. 27)", UN Doc. CCPR/C/21/Rev.1/Add.5, 8 April 1994.

Human Rights Council , "Report of the Working Group on the Universal Periodic Review: Chile", UN Doc. A/HRC/12/10, 4 June 2009.

Human Rights Council, "Expert mechanism on the rights of indigenous peoples", Resolution No.6/36, UN Doc. A/HRC/RES/6/36, 14 December 2007.

Human Rights Council, "Human rights and indigenous peoples: Mandate of the Special Rapporteur on the situation of human rights and fundamental freedoms of indigenous people", Resolution No.6/12, UN Doc. A/HRC/RES/6/12, 28 September 2007.

Human Rights Council, "Human rights and indigenous peoples: Mandate of the Special Rapporteur on the situation of human rights and fundamental freedoms of indigenous people", Resolution No.15/14, UN Doc. A/HRC/RES/15/14, 6 October 2010.

Human Rights Council, "Human rights and indigenous peoples: Mandate of the Special Rapporteur on the situation of human rights and fundamental freedoms of indigenous people", Resolution No.29/4, UN Doc. A/HRC/RES/24/9, 8 October 2013.

Human Rights Council, "Report of the Working Group on the Universal Periodic Review: Chile", UN Doc. A/HRC/26/5, 2 April 2014.

Human Rights Council, Report of the Working Group on the Universal Periodic Review, Bolivia (Plurinational State of), , Universal Periodic Review, UN Doc. A/HRC/14/7, 15 March 2010.

Human Rights Council, Report of the Working Group on the Universal Periodic Review, Bolivia (Plurinational State of), Universal Periodic Review, UN Doc. A/HRC/28/7, 17 December 2014.

Human Rights Council, Resolution No. 2006/2, "Working group of the Commission on Human Rights to elaborate a draft declaration in accordance with paragraph 5 of the General Assembly resolution 49/214 of 23 December 1994", 29 June 2006.

Martínez Miguel Alfonso, "Final Report on the Study on treaties, agreements and other constructive arrangements between States and indigenous populations", UN Doc. E/CN.4/Sub.2/1999/20, 22 June 1999.

Permanent Representative of Liechtenstein to the United Nations, "Draft Convention on Self-Determination Through Self-Administration", New York, 1994.

Report of the United Nations Conference on Environment and Development, Rio de Janeiro, UN Doc. A/CONF.151/26, 3-14 June 1992.

Security Council Resolution 1674, "On protection of civilians in armed conflict", S/RES/1674 (2006), 28 April 2006.

Security Council, Resolution No.1970 (2011), "Peace and security in Africa", adopted by the Security Council at its 6491st meeting, 26 February 2011, UN Doc. S/RES/1970 (2011).

Security Council, Resolution No.1973 (2011), "The situation in Libya", Adopted by the Security Council at its 6498th meeting, 17 March 2011, UN Doc. S/RES/1973 (2011).

Stavenhagen Rodolfo, "Promotion and protection of all human rights, civil, political, economic, social and cultural rights, including the right to development. Report of the Special Rapporteur on the situation of human rights and fundamental freedoms of indigenous people. Mission to Bolivia", Human Rights Council, eleventh session, 18 February 2009, UN Doc.A/HRC/11/11.

Stavenhagen Rodolfo, "Report of the Special Rapporteur on the situation of human rights and fundamental freedoms of indigenous people, submitted in accordance with Commission resolution 2003/56. Addendum, Mission to Chile", UN Doc. E/CN.4/20 04/80/Add.3, 17 November 2003.

Sub-Commission on Prevention of Discrimination and Protection of Minorities "Report of the Sub-Commission on Prevention of Discrimination and Protection of Minorities on its Forty-Sixth Session (Geneva, 1-26 August, 1994)", UN Doc. E/CN.4/Sub.2/1994/56, 28 October 1994.

Sub-Commission on Prevention of Discrimination and Protection of Minorities, "Draft United Nations Declaration on the Rights of Indigenous Peoples", Resolution No.1994/45, 26 August 1994.

Tamang Parshuram, "An Overview of the Principle of Free, Prior and Informed Consent and Indigenous Peoples in International and Domestic Law and Practices", paper presented at the "International Workshop on Methodologies regarding Free, Prior and Informed Consent and Indigenous Peoples" organized by the Secretariat of the UN Permanent Forum on Indigenous Issue, New York, UN Doc. PFII/2004/WS.2/8, 17-19 January 2005.

UN Permanent Forum of Indigenous Issues, "Examination of the situation of indigenous peoples and their participation in democracies and electoral processes in Latin America under the United Nationas Declaration on the Rights of Indigenous Peoples", UN Doc. E/C.19/2014/6, 26 February 2014.

UN Permanent Forum on Indigenous Issues, "Expert group meeting on the theme 'Dialogue on an optional protocol to the United Nations Declaration on the Rights of Indigenous Peoples'", UN Doc. E/C.19/2015/8, 17 February 2015.

UN Permanent Forum on Indigenous Issues, "Item 7 (continued), Ongoing priorities and themes and follow-up: (d) Post-2015 development agenda", UN Doc. E/CN.19/2014/CRP.3, 12-23 May 2014.

UN Permanent Forum on Indigenous Issues, "Report of the International Workshop on Methodologies regarding Free, Prior and Informed Consent and Indigenous Peoples", UN Doc. E/C.19/2005/3, 17 February 2005.

UN Permanent Forum on Indigenous Issues, "Report of the International Workshop on Methodologies regarding Free, Prior and Informed Consent and Indigenous Peoples", UN Doc. E/C.19/2005/3, 17 February 2005.

UN Permanent Forum on Indigenous Issues, "Report on the eleventh session (7-18 May 2012)", Economic and Social Council Official Records, Supplement No. 23, UN Docs. E/2012/43-E/C.19/2012/13, 2012.

UN Permanent Forum on Indigenous Issues, "Report on the fourteenth session (20 April-1 May 2015)", Economic and Social Council Official Records, Supplement No. 23, UN Docs. E/2015/43-E/C.19/2015/10, 2015.

UN Permanent Forum on Indigenous Issues, "Report on the tenth session", Economic and Social Council Official Records, 2011, Supplement No. 23, UN Docs. E/2011/43 and E/C.19/2011/14, 16-27 May 2011.

UN Permanent Forum on Indigenous Issues, "Study on an optional protocol to the United Nations Declaration on the Rights of Indigenous Peoples focusing on a voluntary mechanism", UN Doc. E/C.19/2014/7, 4 March 2014.

United Nations Economic and Social Council (ECOSOC), "Establishing the Committee on Economic, Social and Cultural Rights (CESCR)", Resolution No.1985/17, 28 May 1985.

Victoria Tauli Corpuz, "Report of the Special Rapporteur on the rights of indigenous peoples", UN Doc. A/HRC/27/52, 11 August 2014.

International (soft and hard) Case Law

African Commission on Human and Peoples Rights, *Centre for Minority Rights Development ("CEMIRIDE") (Kenya) and Minority Rights Group International on behalf of Endorois Welfare Council v. Kenya (Endorois case)*, Communication No.276/2003, 4 February 2010.

African Commission on Human and Peoples' Rights, *Katangese Peoples' Congress v. Zaire*, Communication No.75/92 (1995).

European Court of Human Rights, *Chassagnou and others v. France*, Applications Nos.25088/94, 28331/95 and 28443/95, Judgement, 29 April 1999.

Human Rights Committee, *Ángela Poma Poma v. Peru*, Communication No. 1457/2006, UN Doc. CCPR/C/95/D/1457/2006, 27 March 2009.

Human Rights Committee, *Apirana Mahuika et al v. New Zealand,* Communication No. 547/1993, UN Doc. CCPR/C/70/D/547/1993, 20 October 2000.

Human Rights Committee, *Chiiko Bwalya v. Zambia*, Communication No. 314/1988, UN Doc. CCPR/C/48/D/314/1988, 27 July 1993.

Human Rights Committee, *Debreczeny v. The Netherlands*, Communication No. 500/1992, UN Doc. CCPR/C/53/D/500/1992, 4 April 1995.

Human Rights Committee, *E.P. et al v. Colombia,* Communication No. 318/1988, UN Doc. CCPR/C/39/D/318/1988, 25 July 1990.

Human Rights Committee, *Ivan Kitok v. Sweden*, Communication No. 197/1985, UN Doc. CCPR/C/33/D/197/1985, 27 July 1988.

Human Rights Committee, *J.G.A. Diergaardt (late Captain of the Rehoboth Baster Community) et al. v. Namibia*, Communication No. 760/1997, UN Doc. CCPR/C/69/D/760/1997, 6 September 2000.

Human Rights Committee, *Länsman et al. v. Finland*, Communication No. 511/1992, UN Doc. CCPR/C/52/D/511/1992, 8 November 1994.

Human Rights Committee, *Lubicon Lake Band v. Canada*, Communication No. 167/1984, UN Doc. Supp. No. 40 (A/45/40), 26 March 1990.

Human Rights Committee, *Mikmaq v. Canada*, Communication No. 78/1980 (30 September 1980), UN Doc. Supp. No. 40 (A/39/40), 29 July 1984.

Human Rights Committee, *Ms. Marie-Hélène Gillot v. France* case, Communication No. 932/2000, UN Doc. A/57/40, 15 July 2002.

Human Rights Committee, *Sandra Lovelace v. Canada*, Communication No. R.6/24, UN Doc. Supp. No. 40 (A/36/40), 30 July 1981.

Human Rights Committee, *Vid. Marshall et al v. Canada,* Communication No. 205/1986, UN Doc. CCPR/C/43/D/205/l986, 4 November 2006.

Inter-American Commission of Human Rights, Friendly Settlement of *Mercedes Julia Huenteao Beroiza Et Al. V. Chile*, Report No.30/04, 11 March 2004.

Inter-American Commission of Human Rights, *Mercedes Julia Huenteao Beroiza Et Al. V. Chile*, Petition 4617/02, 10 December 2002.

Inter-American Commission on Human Rights, *Case Tribu Aché (Paraguay)*, No.1802, 27 May 1977.

Inter-American Commission on Human Rights, *Fondo Comunidades Indígenas Mayas del Distrito de Toledo Belice*, Report No.40/04, Case No.12,053, 12 October 2004.

Inter-American Commission on Human Rights, *Informe anual de la Comisión Interamericana de Derechos Humanos 1973,* OAS Doc. No.OEA/Ser.L/V/II.32, doc.3 rev.2, 14 February 1974.

Inter-American Commission on Human Rights, *Informe anual de la Comisión Interamericana de Derechos Humanos 1975,* OAS Doc. No.OEA/Ser.L/V/II.37, doc.20 corr.1", 28 June 1976.

Inter-American Commission on Human Rights, *Mary and Carrie Dann v. United States*, Report No.75/02, Case No.11,140, 27 December 2002.

Inter-American Commission on Human Rights/Comisión Interamericana de Derechos Humanos, *Resolución sobre el Procedimiento de Solución Amistosa sobre la Situación de los Derechos Humanos de un Sector de la Población Nicaragüense de Origen Miskito c. Nicaragua* e *Informe sobre la situación de los derechos humanos de un sector de la población nicaragüense de origen miskito*, OAS Doc. No. OEA/Ser.L/V/II.62, 29 November 1983.

Inter-American Court of Human Rights, case of *Comunidad Indígena Xákmok Kásek v. Paraguay*, Serie C No.214, Judgement of 24 August 2010.

Inter-American Court of Human Rights, case of *YATAMA v. Nicaragua*, Series C No.127, Judgment of 23 June 2005.

Inter-American Court of Human Rights, *Comunidad Indígena Sawhoyamaxa v. Paraguay*, Serie C No.146 Judgement of 29 March 2006.

Inter-American Court of Human Rights, *Comunidad Indígena Xákmok Kásek v. Paraguay*, Serie C No.214, Judgement of 24 August 2010.

Inter-American Court of Human Rights, *Comunidad Mayagna (Sumo) Awas Tingni Community v. Nicaragua*, Serie C No.79, Judgment of 31 August 2001.

Inter-American Court of Human Rights, *Comunidad Yakye Axa v.* Paraguay, Serie C No.125, Judgement of 17 June 2005.

Inter-American Court of Human Rights, *Kichwa Ingenous People of Sarayaku v. Ecuador*, Serie C No.245, Judgment of 27 June 2012.

Inter-American Court of Human Rights, *Mayagna (Sumo) Awas Tingni Community v. Nicaragua*, Serie C No. 79, Judgment of 31 August 2001.

Inter-American Court of Human Rights, *Norín Catrimán y Otros (Dirigentes, Miembros y Activista del Pueblo Indígena Mapuche) v Chile*, Serie C No.279, Judgment of 29 May 2014.

Inter-American Court of Human Rights, *Saramaka People v. Suriname*, Serie C No.172, Judgment of 28 November 2007.

Inter-American Court of Human Rights, *Velásquez Rodríguez* v. *Honduras*, Series C, No.4, Judgement of 29 July 1988.

Inter-American Court of Human Rights, *YATAMA v. Nicaragua*, Serie C. No.127, Judgment of 23 June 2005.

International Court of Justice, *Accordance with International Law of the Unilateral Declaration of Independence in Respect of Kosovo,* Advisory Opinion, 22 July 2010, ICJ Reports 2010, p.403.

International Court of Justice, *Advisory Opinion on the Legal Consequences for States of the Continued Presence of South Africa in Namibia (South West Africa) notwithstanding Security Council Resolution 276 (1970)*, Advisory Opinion, 21 June 1971, ICJ Reports of 1971.

International Court of Justice, *Frontier Dispute* (*Burkina Faso v. Mali*), Judgment, 22 October 1986, ICJ Reports 1986, p.554.

International Court of Justice, *Legal Consequences of the Construction of a Wall in the Occupied Palestinian Territory*, Advisory Opinion, 9 July 2004, ICJ Reports 2004, p.136.

International Court of Justice, *Western Sahara*, Advisory Opinion, 16 October 1975, ICJ Reports 1975, p.12.

International Labour Organization/Organización Internacional del Trabajo, *Informe del Comité establecido para examinar la reclamación en la que se alega el incumplimiento por Colombia del Convenio sobre pueblos indígenas y tribales, 1989 (núm. 169), presentada en virtud del artículo 24 de la Constitución de la OIT por la Central Unitaria de Trabadores (CUT)*, ILO Doc. No. GB.276/17/1, GB.282/14/3 (2001).

International Labour Organization/Organización Internacional del Trabajo, *Informe del Comité encargado de examinar la reclamación en la que se alega el incumplimiento por Guatemala del Convenio sobre pueblos indígenas y tribales, 1989 (núm. 169), presentada en virtud del artículo 24 de la Constitución de la OIT por la Federación de Trabajadores del Campo y la Ciudad (FTCC)*, ILO Doc. No. GB.294/17/1, GB.299/6/1 (2007).

International Labour Organization/Organización Internacional del Trabajo, *Informe del Comité encargado de examinar la reclamación en la que se alega el incumplimiento por Brasil del Convenio sobre pueblos indígenas y tribales, 1989 (núm. 169), presentada en virtud del artículo 24 de la Constitución de la OIT por el Sindicato de Ingenieros del Distrito Federal (SENGE/DF)*, ILO Doc. No. GB.295/17, GB.304/14/7 (2009).

International Labour Organization/Organización Internacional del Trabajo, *Informe del Comité encargado de examinar la reclamación en la que se alega el incumplimiento por México del Convenio sobre pueblos indígenas y tribales, 1989 (núm. 169), presentada en virtud del artículo 24 de la Constitución de la OIT por el Frente Auténtico del Trabajo (FAT)*, ILO Doc. No. GB.283/17/1, GB.289/17/3 (2004).